T0220797

Lecture Notes in Computer Science 13640

More information about this series at https://link.springer.com/bookseries/558

Willy Susilo · Xiaofeng Chen ·
Fuchun Guo · Yudi Zhang ·
Rolly Intan (Eds.)

Information Security

25th International Conference, ISC 2022
Bali, Indonesia, December 18–22, 2022
Proceedings

Editors
Willy Susilo
University of Wollongong
Wollongong, NSW, Australia

Fuchun Guo
University of Wollongong
Wollongong, NSW, Australia

Rolly Intan
Petra Christian University
Surabaya, Indonesia

Xiaofeng Chen
Xidian University
Xian, China

Yudi Zhang
University of Wollongong
Wollongong, NSW, Australia

ISSN 0302-9743 ISSN 1611-3349 (electronic)
Lecture Notes in Computer Science
ISBN 978-3-031-22389-1 ISBN 978-3-031-22390-7 (eBook)
https://doi.org/10.1007/978-3-031-22390-7

This Springer imprint is published by the registered company Springer Nature Switzerland AG
The registered company address is: Gewerbestrasse 11, 6330 Cham, Switzerland

Preface

On behalf of the Program Committee, it is our pleasure to present the proceedings of the 25th Information Security Conference (ISC 2022). ISC is an annual international conference covering research in theory and applications of information security. Both academic research with high relevance to real-world problems and developments in industrial and technical frontiers fall within the scope of the conference.

The 25th edition of ISC was organized by the Petra Christian University, Surabaya, Indonesia, and was held as a hybrid conference in Bali, Indonesia during December 18–22, 2022. Rolly Intan (Petra Christian University, Indonesia) and Fuchun Guo (University of Wollongong, Australia) served as the general chairs. The Program Committee comprised 23 members from top institutions around the world. Out of 72 submissions, the Program Committee eventually selected 21 papers for presentation at the conference and publication in the proceedings, resulting in an acceptance rate of 29%. The review process was double blind and it was organized and managed through the EasyChair online reviewing system, with all papers receiving at least three reviews. The final program was quite balanced in terms of topics, containing both theoretical/cryptography papers and more practical/systems security papers.

A successful conference is the result of the joint effort of many people. We would like to express our appreciation to the Program Committee members and external reviewers for the time spent reviewing papers and participating in the online discussion. We deeply thank our invited speakers for their willingness to participate in the conference. Further, we express our appreciation to Yudi Zhang (University of Wollongong, Australia) and Jianfeng Wang (Xidian University), who served as the publication chairs. Finally, we thank Springer for publishing these proceedings as part of their LNCS series, and the ISC Steering Committee for their continuous support and assistance.

ISC 2022 would not have been possible without the authors who submitted their work and presented their contributions, as well as the attendees who joined the conference sessions. We would like to thank them all, and we look forward to their future contributions to ISC.

October 2022

Willy Susilo
Xiaofeng Chen

Organization

Program Chairs

Willy Susilo	University of Wollongong, Australia
Xiaofeng Chen	Xidian University, China

General Chairs

Rolly Intan	Petra Christian University, Indonesia
Fuchun Guo	University of Wollongong, Australia

Publication Chairs

Yudi Zhang	University of Wollongong, Australia
Jianfeng Wang	Xidian University, China

Steering Committee

Zhiqiang Lin	The Ohio State University, USA
Javier Lopez	University of Malaga, Spain
Masahiro Mambo	Kanazawa University, Japan
Eiji Okamoto	University of Tsukuba, Japan
Michalis Polychronakis	Stony Brook University, USA
Jianying Zhou	Singapore University of Technology and Design, Singapore

Program Committee

Mauro Conti	University of Padua, Italy
Josep Domingo-Ferrer	Universitat Rovira i Virgili, Spain
Chunpeng Ge	Nanjing University of Aeronautics and Astronautics, China
Jinguang Han	Southeast University, China
Debiao He	Wuhan University, China
Xinyi Huang	Fujian Normal University, China
Peng Jiang	Beijing Institute of Technology, China
Angelos Keromytis	Georgia Institute of Technology, Georgia
Hiroaki Kikuchi	Meiji University, Japan
Hyoungshick Kim	Sungkyunkwan University, South Korea
Miroslaw Kutylowski	Wroclaw University of Technology, Poland
Jianchang Lai	Southeast University, China
Xueqiao Liu	University of Wollongong, Australia

Mark Manulis	Universität der Bundeswehr München, Germany
Khoa Nguyen	University of Wollongong, Australia
Josef Pieprzyk	CSIRO/Data61, Australia
Partha Sarathi Roy	University of Wollongong, Australia
Atsushi Takayasu	The University of Tokyo, Japan
Qianhong Wu	Beihang University, China
Ge Wu	Southeast University, China
Toshihiro Yamauchi	Okayama University, Japan
Xun Yi	RMIT University, Australia
Zuoxia Yu	The Hong Kong Polytechnic University, Hong Kong
Xingliang Yuan	Monash University, Australia
Fangguo Zhang	Sun Yat-sen University, China
Mingwu Zhang	Hubei University of Technology, China
Jianying Zhou	Singapore University of Technology and Design, Singapore

External Reviewers

Haoyang An
Nhat Quang Cao
Priyanka Dutta
Subir Halder
Mengdie Huang
Gulshan Kumar
Quanrun Li
Chengjun Lin
Khalid Mahmood
Ke Ren
Masaya Sato
Siwei Sun
Yangguang Tian
Yulin Wu
S. J. Yang
Yunru Zhang
Zhen Zhao
Xiaotong Zhou
Zijian Bao
Cong Peng
Shota Fujii
Kai He
Xiaoying Jia
Hiroki Kuzuno
Yannan Li
Chao Lin
Wenze Mao
Rongwei Yu
Gang Shen
Teik Guan Tan
Harsha Vasudev
Shengmin Xu
Terry Yang
Peiheng Zhang
Jun Zhao
Rahman Ziaur
Alessandro Brighente
Sabyasachi Dutta
Amrita Ghosal
Hua Shen
Andrei Kelarev
Yumei Li
Zengpeng Li
Junwei Luo
Russell Paulet
Rahul Saha
Yongcheng Song
Min Tang
Yuzhu Wang
Lei Xu
Zheng Yang
Xiaoyu Zhang
Yifeng Zheng

Keynote and Invited Talks

Efficiently Deployable and Efficiently Searchable Encryption (EDESE) – Applications, Attacks, and Countermeasures

Robert H. Deng

School of Information Systems, Singapore Management University, Singapore
robertdeng@smu.edu.sg

Abstract. The volume of data stored in the public cloud is growing exponentially. With this growth, the risk of data breaches and the challenges of data protection grow just as rapidly. As more organizations opt for using encryption to protect their data in the cloud and in web services, the ability to efficiently search over encrypted data becomes increasingly important.

Though numerous searchable encryption (SE) schemes have appeared in the literature, Efficiently Deployable & Efficiently Searchable Encryption (EDESE) is the most popular SE scheme being deployed in practical applications at the expense of information leakages that were considered acceptable. In this talk, we first look at single user EDESE and multiuser EDESE schemes and their real-world deployments. We then review some of the recent attacks to EDESE that can accurately recover the underlying keywords of query tokens based on partially known documents and the L2 leakage. Finally, we discuss possible means to counter such attacks.

Bio: Robert Deng is AXA Chair Professor of Cybersecurity, Director of the Secure Mobile Centre, and Deputy Dean for Faculty & Research, School of Computing and Information Systems, Singapore Management University (SMU). His research interests are in the areas of data security and privacy, network security, and applied cryptography. He received the Outstanding University Researcher Award from National University of Singapore, Lee Kuan Yew Fellowship for Research Excellence from SMU, and Asia-Pacific Information Security Leadership Achievements Community Service Star from International Information Systems Security Certification Consortium. He serves/served on the editorial boards of ACM Transactions on Privacy and Security, IEEE Security & Privacy, IEEE Transactions on Dependable and Secure Computing, IEEE Transactions on Information Forensics and Security, Journal of Computer Science and Technology, and Steering Committee Chair of the ACM Asia Conference on Computer and Communications Security. He is a Fellow of IEEE and Fellow of Academy of Engineering Singapore.

Software Vulnerability Detection by Fuzzing and Deep Learning

Yang Xiang

Swinburne University of Technology, Australia
yxiang@swin.edu.au

Abstract. In this keynote talk, we introduce the current research and trend in the software vulnerability detection research. Then we present a series of novel approaches to deal with the vulnerability issues, such as the fuzzing, deep learning, and the combined approach to improve the effectiveness of the detection.

Keywords: Cybersecurity · Cyber-attacks · Software · Vulnerability · Deep learning · Fuzzing

Introduction

Cybersecurity has become one of the top priorities in the research and development agenda globally today. New and innovative cybersecurity technologies that can effectively address this pressing danger are critically needed. Data-driven and system approaches to solve cybersecurity problems have been increasingly adopted by the cybesecurity research community. They have two areas of focus: detection and prediction of cyber threats. Recently, there have been significant efforts to detect software vulnerabilities. New methods and tools, consequently, must follow up to adapt to this emerging security paradigm.

Software lifecycles include development, deployment and usage, and maintenance phases. Current practice involves avoiding vulnerabilities during the development phase and removing vulnerabilities via patching during the deployment and usage phase. In fact, due to rampant security breaches in software, detecting vulnerabilities in different stages of software lifecycles has never become an easy job. Existing methods face significant technical challenges caused by code representation, computational resource constraints, and algorithm bottlenecks.

Summary of the Talk

In this talk, we introduce the current research and trend in the software vulnerability detection research. Then we will present a series of novel approaches to deal with the vulnerability issues, such as the fuzzing, deep learning, and the combined approach to improve the effectiveness of the detection. The focus of the fuzzing approach is on automatic black-box fuzzing especially for firmware; and the focus of the deep learning approach is to reduce the training samples and improve the detection rate.

Existing techniques take much time to detect and verify vulnerabilities, which is too slow for massive code detection in the development phase. While a bug is an unintended code state, a vulnerability is a bug that attackers can exploit. The code states are usually vast, and the bug locations are unknown, making it difficult to detect bugs efficiently and effectively. In the maintenance stage, developers must reproduce, test, and fix bugs, which may require specific inputs and complex execution states to trigger them. Both deep learning and fuzzing methods have pros and cons in detecting, verifying vulnerabilities, and performance. Current techniques face key challenges that urgently require practical solutions:

Fast detection of massive codes – From the software developer's perspective, one can use pre-trained model to fast detect the vulnerabilities automatically from time to time during the development process by scanning codes. From the user's perspective, static analysis can fast scan the executable codes. Among the static analysis techniques, machine learning, especially deep learning has been used for software vulnerability detection. Deep learning-based static analysis techniques have been widely accepted given that it can automatically extract high feature representations and interpret complex non-linear structure. Thorough detection – One often wants to check every piece of code when it is unknown that whether a potential bug exists. The power schedule determines the number of mutations assigned to each seed, and a seed is an input that makes process in code coverage. While these improvements have considerably decreased the time required to visit different parts of a target application, it is important to understand that code coverage alone is a necessary but not sufficient condition to discover bugs.

Solutions and future research directions will be discussed following above.

Cybersecurity Policies and Challenges in Indonesia

Rolly Intan and Adriel A. Intan

Petra Christian University, Surabaya, Indonesia
rintan@petra.ac.id

Abstract. In this era of digital, almost all aspects of life are connected to the internet. This causes the role of cybersecurity to ensure the convenience and security of transacting and doing business through cyberspace to be very important. This talk describes the situation and condition of cybersecurity in Indonesia from 2018 to 2021. The number of cyberattacks every year has increased exponentially since 2018. Fluctuations in the number and types of cyberattacks are highly dependent on situations and conditions that are influenced by political and economic interests. The motivation for cyberattacks can be triggered by protests, expressions of disappointment, or just for fun, so they are not always related to cybercrimes driven by political or economic interests. This talk also discusses the challenges and opportunities faced by Indonesia in maintaining and improving cyber security in the IoT era in relation to Industry 4.0 and Society 5.0. Quad helix collaboration among government, educational institutions, industry, and communities is needed to build strong cyber resilience.

Keywords: Cybersecurity · Cyberattacks · Cybercrime

Introduction

As the 10th largest economy in terms of purchasing power parity, the world's fourth most populous country, and the country with the most islands in the world, Indonesia has become the largest spender on Information Technology (IT) in Southeast Asia. To implement cybersecurity effectively and efficiently by utilizing, developing, and consolidating all elements related to cybersecurity, the president of Indonesia established National Cyber and Crypto Agency (Indonesian: Badan Siber dan Sandi Negara, abbreviated as BSSN) on 19 May 2017 under Presidential Decree No. 53/2017 and 133/2017 as the constituting documents. According to Global Cybersecurity Index (GCI) 2020 published by International Telecommunication Union, Indonesia ranks 24th globally and 6th in Asia Pacific region with a score of 94.88. This rank of Indonesia jumped from 41st globally and 9th in the Asia Pacific region in 2018. However, based on the information given by BSSN, the number of cyberattacks increased significantly from 2018 to 2021 as shown in Table 1. The huge number of cyberattacks in 2021 caused a potential economic loss of approximately IDR 14.2 trillion (USD 1 billion). Besides, it is also predicted that 22% of companies have experienced cyberattack incidents at that time. The significant increase in cyberattacks is strongly correlated to the covid-19 pandemic. During the covid-19 pandemic, work from home via cyberspace was widely adopted in private and public offices causing the number of cyberattacks to dramatically increase globally. Dan Lohrmann mentioned "the year the covid-19 crisis brought a cyber pandemic". Therefore, there is no causal relationship between the Global Cybersecurity Index of Indonesia and the number of cyberattacks, especially during the covid-19 pandemic.

Table 1. A user set in the PHR sharing system

Year	The number of cyberattacks
2018	232,447,974
2019	290,381,283
2020	495,337,202
2021	1,637,973,022

Considering that the damages of cyberattacks cannot be avoided, it is necessary to plan and design how to build and strengthen cyber resilience for recovery.

First, this talk observes the current situation and condition of cybersecurity in Indonesia, including cyberattacks, cybercrime, and cyber policies in the past three years starting from 2018. Next, the challenges and opportunities of cybersecurity in Indonesia are discussed in the relation to social welfare and disruptive innovation and technology in the era of Society 5.0 and Industry 4.0. Finally, we summarize the observation and discussion and give some suggestions.

Blockchain Security: Primitives and Protocols

Yannan Li

Institute of Cybersecurity and Cryptology, School of Computing and Information Technology, University of Wollongong, Wollongong, NSW 2522, Australia
yannan@uow.edu.au

Abstract. It is widely accepted that blockchain is a disruptive technology that reshapes the way of doing business in finance due to its decentralization, transparency and immutability. Blockchain can serve as the backbone technique in various applications with its salient features. However, these blockchain-based systems may still suffer from security concerns. In this talk, we will discuss blockchain security, in terms of its underlying primitives and built-on protocols. To be more specific, we will talk about the privacy and regulation in blockchain-based cryptocurrencies, the security concerns in blockchain-based e-voting and the non-equivocation in blockchain systems. In each scenario, we will discuss the remaining problems of the existing works and present possible solutions.

Introduction

Blockchain is a distributed database that records all the transactions in the system. Blockchain can be used to achieve fully decentralized systems with its consensus, incentive, transparency and immutability. Gartner, a leading research and advisory company, forecasts that the business value generated by blockchain will reach $176 billion by 2025 and $3.1 trillion by 2030, respectively [2]. Blockchain has a spectrum of applications ranging from healthcare, manufacture, transportation to IoT. However, there are still many things to do to improve blockchain security. In this talk, we will introduce several cryptographic primitives and protocols to enhance blockchain security and achieve blockchain-based secure protocols. protocols. This talk is structured into three important scenarios in blockchain and the corresponding security issues and potential solutions

Cryptocurrencies are among the successful applications of blockchain, with growing attention and significant influence. The global crypto market capitalization is $2.05 trillion US dollars (Sep 2022). Compared to the traditional trading model in real life, which leak personal information, Bitcoin uses pseudonyms, which is a random account rather than real-world identities, to conduct transactions in the system so as to

Y. Li—This work is also supported by the Australian Research Council Discovery Early Career Researcher (ARC DECRA DE230100001).

protect users' privacy. However, it is proved that the security level provided only by pseudonyms is far from satisfactory. These pseudonyms can be linked to real-world identities if enough transactions are collected and analyzed [3]. Therefore, anonymous cryptocurrencies were proposed to intensively protect transaction privacy and user anonymity based on various of cryptographic tools, such as Zerocoin [4], Zerocash [5] and Monero [6]. Anonymous cryptocurrencies gain attention due to enhanced privacy guarantee, however, this makes blockchain susceptible to abuse, security concerns, and even cybercrimes. Besides, the governments are politically conservative about blockchain. For example, the decentralized payment company Ripple (https://ripple.com/) was sustained a $700,000 fine by the U.S. Financial Crimes Enforcement Network (FINCEN) because of inadequate regulation on their transactions networks [7]. In Feb 2020, the Australian government released National Blockchain Roadmap, with a special emphasis on blockchain security and regulation [8]. How to deal with the conflict user privacy and proper regulation on malicious users is a tricky problem. In the first part of this talk, we introduce a protocol to balance the anonymity and regulation in privacy-preserving cryptocurrencies Monero [9, 10]. Specifically, we provide two mechanisms to trace the one-time key and long-term key of a malicious user, while still maintaining the privacy of honest users.

Election is one of the most important measures to achieve democracy. However, traditional voting with a central election authority suffers from privacy issues when ballots are tallied. With the salient nature of blockchain, it can effectively remove the central party who controls the system with privacy concerns. Thus we proposed a blockchain-based self-tallying e-voting system [11, 12] with no central authority to tally the votes. The voting results can be calculated and released publicly after all the legitimate votes cast their ballots on blockchain. However, the involvement of blockchain will bring new drawbacks in these self-tallying voting systems, that are the fairness issues - the abortive issues and adaptive issues [13, 14]. In the second part of the talk, we will demonstrate the possible solutions to address the security and privacy concerns in blockchain-based e-voting systems, and achieve a secure self-tallying e-voting system with various implementation results [15].

Equivocation is to convey conflicting statements in a protocol, which is a quite common problem and happens often in distributed systems, such as double-spending in cryptocurrencies and issuing two certificates for one identity [16]. Therefore, non-equivocation is one of the fundamental requirements in distributed systems. Existing literature to solve the equivocation problems is based on trusted hardware or strong assumptions, which is not satisfactory in real life. The public logs provide a breakthrough in addressing the equivocation issues in distributed systems. However, all the existing solutions are to deal with double-spending or double authentication [17, 18]. The solutions to tackle more general type of equivocation are still missing in the literature. The third part of this talk is to provide a contractual solution to handle generalized equivocation, which also supports user-defined policies [19]. We will introduce a new cryptographic primitive, the policy-authentication-preventing signatures, to support our design and then introduce the integration with blockchain systems.

References

1. Nakamoto, S., Bitcoin, A.: A peer-to-peer electronic cash system. Bitcoin, 4, p. 2 (2008). https://bitcoin.org/bitcoin.pdf
2. https://www.gartner.com/en/doc/3855708-digital-disruption-profile-blockchains-radical-promise-spans-business-and-society
3. Reid, F., Harrigan, M.: An analysis of anonymity in the bitcoin system. In: Altshuler, Y., Elovici, Y., Cremers, A., Aharony, N., Pentland, A. (eds.) Security and Privacy in Social Networks, pp. 197–223. Springer, New York (2013). https://doi.org/10.1007/978-1-4614-4139-7_10
4. Miers, I., Garman, C., Green, M., Rubin, A.D.: Zerocoin: anonymous distributed e-cash from bitcoin. In: 2013 IEEE Symposium on Security and Privacy, pp. 397–411. IEEE (2013)
5. Sasson, E.B., et al.: Decentralized anonymous payments from bitcoin. In: 2014 IEEE Symposium on Security and Privacy, pp. 459–474. IEEE (2014)
6. Noether, S.: Ring signature confidential transactions for monero. IACR Cryptol. ePrint Arch. 2015:1098 (2015)
7. https://www.financemagnates.com/cryptocurrency/news/ripple-fined-700k-by-ncen-for-msb-aml-violations/
8. https://www.industry.gov.au/data-and-publications/national-blockchain-roadmap
9. Li, Y., Yang, G., Susilo, W., Yu, Y., Au, M.H., Liu, D.: Traceable monero: anonymous cryptocurrency with enhanced accountability. IEEE Trans. Dependable Secure Comput. **18**(2), 679–691 (2021)
10. Li, Y., et al.: Toward privacy and regulation in blockchain-based cryptocurrencies. IEEE Netw. **33**(5), 111–117 (2019)
11. Hao, F., Zielinski, P.: A two-round anonymous veto protocol. In: Security Protocols Workshop, pp. 202–211 (2006)
12. Kiayias, A., Yung, M.: Self-tallying elections and perfect ballot secrecy. In: Naccache, D., Paillier, P. (eds.) Public Key Cryptography. PKC 2002. LNCS, vol. 2274, pp. 141–158. Springer, Heidelberg. https://doi.org/10.1007/3-540-45664-3_10
13. Liu, J., Jager, T., Kakvi, S.A., Warinschi, B.: How to build time-lock encryption. Des. Codes Crypt. **86**(11), 2549–2586 (2018)
14. Jager, T.: How to build time-lock encryption. Cryptology ePrint Archive, Report 2015/478 (2015). http://eprint.iacr.org/
15. Li, Y., et al.: A blockchain-based self-tallying voting protocol in decentralized IoT. IEEE Trans. Dependable Secure Comput. **19**(1), 119–130 (2022)
16. Ruffing, T., Kate, A., Schröder, D.: Liar, liar, coins on fire! Penalizing equivocation by loss of bitcoins. In: Proceedings of the 22nd ACM SIGSAC Conference on Computer and Communications Security, pp. 219–230 (2015)
17. Poettering, B., Stebila, D.: Double-authentication-preventing signatures. Int. J. Inf. Secur. **16** (1), 1–22 (2017)
18. Derler, D., Ramacher, S., Slamanig, D.: Short double-and n-times-authentication-preventing signatures from ECDSA and more. In: IEEE European Symposium on Security and Privacy, pp. 273–287 (2018)
19. Li, Y., Susilo, W., Yang, G., Yu, Y., Phuong, T.V.X., Liu, D.: Non-equivocation in blockchain: double-authentication-preventing signatures gone contractual. In: Proceedings of the 2021 ACM ASIACCS, pp. 859–871 (2021)

Covert Communication: Past, Present and Future

Peng Jiang

School of Cyberspace Science and Technology, Beijing Institute of Technology, Beijing, China
pengjiang@bit.edu.cn

Abstract. Covert communication is defined as the exchange of information/data via a covert channel. It enables the covert information transmission against communication signal detection, such that no attackers can launch illegal behaviors without detecting the signal. Covert communication has been mandatory for the message transmission in many applications such as underwater acoustic and military communications.

In this talk, I will first review the traditional covert communication including the basic model and mechanisms. A core task in the covert communication is to design and deploy the covert channel which is usually built upon the network protocol. Such network-based covert channels have limitations on concealment, reliability and anti-traceability. Next, I will introduce present solutions for covert communication using blockchain, i.e., blockchain-based covert communication, which hides covert information into transactions and breaks through the above limitations. I will depict its system architecture and potential application scenarios, such as digital evidence preservation. Blockchain's inherent features, like low throughput, flooding propagation, openness and transparency, incur new challenges and impede the construction of blockchain-based covert channels. For the covert channel building, I will present three key technologies: information embedding, transaction filtering, and transaction obfuscation. To better evaluate blockchain-based covert channel, I will present metrics of concealment, bandwidth, transmission delay, robustness and transmission cost. Finally, I will point out the possible privacy issues with perspectives of blockchain users and communicating parties, and provide the potential countermeasures. I will also show technical challenges on the blockchain-based covert communication and offer corresponding research directions in aspects of communication modes, channel building techniques, efficiency, evaluation methods etc.

Contents

Cryptography

Privacy Preserving Computation in Cloud Using Reusable Garbled Oblivious RAMs 3
Yongge Wang and Qutaibah M. Malluhi

Efficient Private Set Intersection Cardinality Protocol in the Reverse Unbalanced Setting 20
Hanyu Li and Ying Gao

Crypto-Steganographic Validity for Additive Manufacturing (3D Printing) Design Files 40
Mark Yampolskiy, Lynne Graves, Jacob Gatlin, J. Todd McDonald, and Moti Yung

Witness Encryption from Smooth Projective Hashing System 53
Yuzhu Wang and Mingwu Zhang

Post-quantum Cryptography

More Efficient Adaptively Secure Lattice-Based IBE with Equality Test in the Standard Model 75
Kyoichi Asano, Keita Emura, and Atsushi Takayasu

QUIC Protocol with Post-quantum Authentication 84
Manohar Raavi, Simeon Wuthier, Pranav Chandramouli, Xiaobo Zhou, and Sang-Yoon Chang

Batched Fully Homomorphic Encryption from TFHE 92
Yuting Jiang and Jianghong Wei

Implicit Rejection in Fujisaki-Okamoto: Framework and a Novel Realization 110
Zhao Chen, Xianhui Lu, Dingding Jia, and Bao Li

Cryptanalysis

Further Cryptanalysis of a Type of RSA Variants 133
Gongyu Shi, Geng Wang, and Dawu Gu

The SAT-Based Automatic Searching and Experimental Verification for Differential Characteristics with Application to Midori64 153
Yingying Li and Qichun Wang

Efficient Scalar Multiplication on Koblitz Curves with Pre-computation. 162
Xiuxiu Li, Wei Yu, and Kunpeng Wang

Blockchain

Efficient ECDSA-Based Adaptor Signature for Batched Atomic Swaps 175
Binbin Tu, Min Zhang, and Chen Yu

Searching for Encrypted Data on Blockchain: An Efficient, Secure and Fair Realization 194
Jianzhang Chen, Haibo Tian, and Fangguo Zhang

GRUZ: Practical Resource Fair Exchange Without Blockchain 214
Yongqing Xu, Kaiyi Zhang, and Yu Yu

Daric: A Storage Efficient Payment Channel with Punishment Mechanism. . . 229
Arash Mirzaei, Amin Sakzad, Jiangshan Yu, and Ron Steinfeld

A Blockchain-Based Mutual Authentication Protocol for Smart Home. 250
Biwen Chen, Bo Tang, Shangwei Guo, Jiyun Yang, and Tao Xiang

Email and Web Security

OblivSend: Secure and Ephemeral File Sharing Services with Oblivious Expiration Control. 269
Yanjun Shen, Bin Yu, Shangqi Lai, Xingliang Yuan, Shi-Feng Sun, Joseph K. Liu, and Surya Nepal

EarlyCrow: Detecting APT Malware Command and Control over HTTP(S) Using Contextual Summaries. 290
Almuthanna Alageel and Sergio Maffeis

Malware

ATLAS: A Practical Attack Detection and Live Malware Analysis System for IoT Threat Intelligence 319
Yan Lin Aung, Martín Ochoa, and Jianying Zhou

Dissecting Applications Uninstallers and Removers: Are They Effective?. . . . 339
Marcus Botacin and André Grégio

Representing LLVM-IR in a Code Property Graph 360
Alexander Küchler and Christian Banse

Why We Need a Theory of Maliciousness: Hardware Performance Counters in Security 381
Marcus Botacin and André Grégio

Anatomist: Enhanced Firmware Vulnerability Discovery Based on Program State Abnormality Determination with Whole-System Replay 390
Runhao Liu, Bo Yu, Baosheng Wang, and Jianbin Ye

AI Security

AspIOC: Aspect-Enhanced Deep Neural Network for Actionable Indicator of Compromise Recognition 411
Shaofeng Wang, Bo Lang, Nan Xiao, and Yikai Chen

HeHe: Balancing the Privacy and Efficiency in Training CNNs over the Semi-honest Cloud 422
Longlong Sun, Hui Li, Shiwen Yu, Xindi Ma, Yanguo Peng, and Jiangtao Cui

Deep Learning Assisted Key Recovery Attack for Round-Reduced Simeck32/64. 443
Lijun Lyu, Yi Tu, and Yingjie Zhang

CFL: Cluster Federated Learning in Large-Scale Peer-to-Peer Networks. 464
Qian Chen, Zilong Wang, Yilin Zhou, Jiawei Chen, Dan Xiao, and Xiaodong Lin

Bilateral Privacy-Preserving Task Assignment with Personalized Participant Selection for Mobile Crowdsensing 473
Shijin Chen, Mingwu Zhang, and Bo Yang

Communication-Efficient and Secure Federated Learning Based on Adaptive One-Bit Compressed Sensing 491
Di Xiao, Xue Tan, and Min Li

Author Index 509

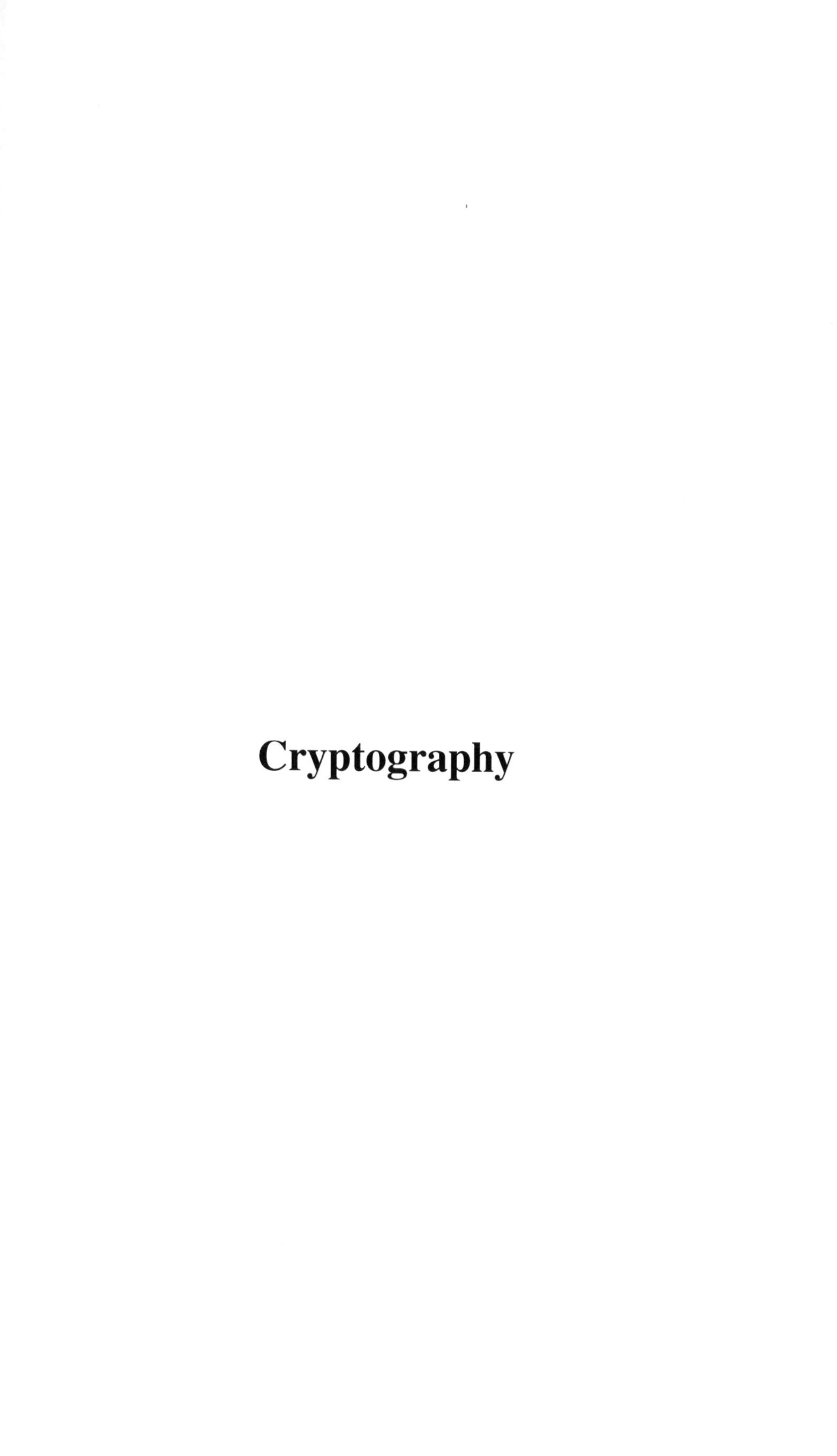

Cryptography

Privacy Preserving Computation in Cloud Using Reusable Garbled Oblivious RAMs

Yongge Wang[1(✉)] and Qutaibah M. Malluhi[2]

[1] UNC Charlotte, 9201 University City Blvd., Charlotte, NC 28223, USA
yonwang@uncc.edu
[2] Qatar University, Doha, Qatar
qmalluhi@qu.edu.qa

Abstract. When users store encrypted data in a cloud environment, it is important for users to ask cloud to carry out some computation on the remote data remotely. ORAM is a good potential approach to carry out this kind of remote operation. In order to use ORAM for this purpose, we still need to have garbled programs to run on ORAM. Goldwasser et al. and Lu-Ostrovsky initiated the study of garbled RAM machines in their 2013 Crypto papers. Goldwasser et al's scheme is based on fully homomorphic encryption schemes and attribute based encryption schemes for general RAM machines. Lu and Ostrovsky's scheme is based on one-time garbled circuits and for each input, one has to design as many one-time garbled circuits as ORAM CPU running steps. That is, for each execution of the program, the data owner needs to upload a new program to the cloud to run on ORAM. Using recent results on indistinguishability obfuscation, this paper designs alternative reusable garbled ORAM programs. The reusable garbled ORAM CPU constructed in this paper is of constant size while the size of the garbled ORAM CPUs by Lu and Ostrovsky depends on the number of ORAM CPU running steps.

1 Introduction

Cloud computing techniques become more and more popular and users begin to store their private encrypted data in cloud services. In order to take full advantage of the cloud computing paradigm, it is important to design efficient techniques to carry out computation over encrypted data in the cloud without downloading the data to a local machine. Though computation over encrypted data helps to protect the privacy of the data, it does not hide the access pattern to data. A natural solution is to use oblivious RAM techniques by Goldreich and Ostrovsky [8] to carry out computation over encrypted data, which provably hides all access patterns.

In order to use ORAM schemes, a trusted CPU is required. Since users may not trust the CPU powers at cloud environments, it has been recommended for the user to run the trusted CPU at client site and to treat the cloud as a large random access memory storage service. The disadvantage of this approach is the heavy communication overhead between the client and the cloud. For example, the most efficient ORAM scheme requires at least $O(\log^2 n)$ memory accesses for each individual memory access, where the cloud database contains n unit blocks of data.

W. Susilo et al. (Eds.): ISC 2022, LNCS 13640, pp. 3–19, 2022.
https://doi.org/10.1007/978-3-031-22390-7_1

Lu and Ostrovsky [17] and Goldwasser et al. [9] initiated an alternative approach to let the cloud run a garbled version of the ORAM CPU. In this approach, the client machine only needs to submit the garbled ORAM CPU to the cloud and the cloud only needs to return the encrypted outputs to the client. Thus the communication overhead could be significantly reduced in case the cloud database size is large. One disadvantage for Lu and Ostrovsky's approach [17] is that their garbled RAM CPU is not succinct and can be used only for one time. For example, if the ORAM CPU runs t-steps for one input x, then the garbled ORAM CPU for the input x is at the size of $O(t)$. Lu and Ostrovsky [17] lists it as a tempting open problem to use Goldwasser et al's [10] reusable garbled circuits to design reusable garbled RAMs. It should be noted that Goldwasser et al. [9] designed reusable garbled RAM machines using fully homomorphic encryption (FHE) and Attribute Based Encryption schemes for RAM machines.

In recent years, several indistinguishability obfuscation schemes have been designed (see, e.g., Jain-Lin-Sahai [13]). By converting the ORAM CPU to an NC^1 circuit and then using obfuscation schemes, this paper designs practical reusable garbled ORAMs for cloud computation over encrypted data. Our scheme is succinct since the garbled ORAM CPU program is of constant size. Furthermore, for commonly used cloud application programs, they are encrypted and stored in the database server together with user data. Thus for each execution of the program over the encrypted database (e.g., a database search query), the user only needs to submit an encrypted keyword to the server, where the encrypted keyword is approximately the same size as the keyword. In a summary, the contributions of this paper are two-folds. First, this paper presents an alternative garbled ORAM program design which is different from Lu-Ostrovsky [17] and Goldwasser et al. [9]. Secondly, the garbled ORAM programs in this paper are reusable while the scheme in [17] is not reusable.

We close this section by introducing some notations. We use κ to denote the security parameter. A function f is said to be negligible in an input parameter κ if there exists κ_0 such that for all $\kappa > \kappa_0$, $f(\kappa) < \kappa^{-n}$ for all $n > 0$. For convenience, we write $f(\kappa) = \text{negl}(\kappa)$. Two ensembles, $X = \{X_\kappa\}_{\kappa\in N}$ and $Y = \{Y_\kappa\}_{\kappa\in N}$, are said to be computationally indistinguishable if for all probabilistic polynomial-time algorithm D, we have $|Pr[D(X_\kappa, 1^\kappa) = 1] - Pr[D(Y_\kappa, 1^\kappa) = 1]| = \text{negl}(\kappa)$.

The structure of this paper is as follows. Section 2 provides a background discussion and reviews necessary techniques required for the construction of garbled ORAMs in this paper. Our main construction of reusable garbled ORAMs is presented in Sect. 3.

2 Cloud Data Storage and Oblivious RAMs

Cloud storage systems may be interpreted as databases stored at the cloud servers, There have been extensive research on public and private databases in the literature. In the public database setting, the database is published and individual users need to retrieve some entries from the database without letting the database server know which entry it has retrieved. A straightforward solution is to let users to download the whole database though it is not practical. To address this challenge, Chor, Goldreich, Kushilevitz, and Sudan [4] introduced the private information retrieval (PIR) concept in an information theoretic setting. PIR protocol makes it possible for users to obtain information from a database without downloading the whole database. At the same time, PIR protocol will not reveal to the database server which entry the user has retrieved. In an extended PIR protocol [4], one could have many copies of the identical database without allowing them to communicate with each other. Chor and Gilboa [3], Ostrovsky and Shoup [19], and others considered the computational PIR, in which the database is restricted to perform polynomial time computations. A single database based PIR was constructed by Kushilevitz and Ostrovsky [16] assuming that certain public-key encryption scheme exists. Since then, several single database PIR schemes with better bounds have been proposed and studied. For a brief survey, it is referred to Ostrovsky and Skeith [20]. Though PIR techniques find important applications in many domains, it is not sufficient to address the challenges in the privacy preserving cloud data distribution systems that we are facing.

In the private database setting, users upload private databases to a remote database server while keeping the database private from the remote database administrators. At a later time, users should be able to search and retrieve entries with certain keyword from the remote database. Based on the physically shielded Central Processing Unit (CPU) technique [15], Goldreich and Ostrovsky [8] proposed a theoretical treatment of software protection by formulating the problem in the setting of learning a program structure by observing its execution. Using this new formulation, they reduced this problem to on-line simulation of any programs on oblivious RAMs (random access machines). A machine is oblivious if its accesses to memory locations are independent of the input values with the same running time. We may apply these schemes in the cloud computing environments (e.g., search over encrypted texts) as follows: the physically shielded CPU is interpreted as the user at the client side and the memory locations are interpreted as the cloud storage. Though the scheme in [7, 8, 18] is asymptotically efficient and nearly optimal, it is inefficient in practice with large hidden constants in the big-O notation and a heavy communication overhead between the client and the server.

In the RAM (random access machine) model, the CPU performs basic arithmetic, logical, control and input/output operations specified by the instructions. The CPU can be considered as a stateful processor where the state Σ is determined by the content in the registers. The registers store program counters, query counters, session information, cryptographic keys, and other information. Among these registers, there is an accumulator where intermediate arithmetic and logic results are stored. Throughout this paper, we will assume that CPU could perform the following operations:

1. Perform arithmetic instructions $+, -, \times, \lfloor x/y \rfloor$. For each arithmetic operation $f(x, y)$, there are two inputs x and y. The value of x should be already in the accumulator and y should be a value in the memory cell to be fetched.
2. Generate a random number and put it in the accumulator.
3. Read data from a memory cell to the accumulator and write the value in the accumulator to a memory cell. Note that this kind of operations will include the user data inputs and outputs if we use some fixed memory cells for user inputs and some other fixed memory cells for user outputs.
4. Control transfer instructions: "GOTO X", "IF $X = 0$ THEN GOTO Y", and "IF $X > 0$ THEN GOTO Y".
5. HALT: terminates the execution of the program.

During the execution of the RAM CPU, each read/write operation to memory cells could be viewed as a query (op, v, x) where op equals to READ or WRITE, v is the data identifier and x is the value. Without loss of generality, we always assume that (op, v, x) is contained in a register that is called an interface register. In the RAM machine model, the actual programs are stored in the memory cells. Thus RAM CPU can be considered as a universal machine that reads programs from the memory cell and executes the instructions step by step. Based on this interpretation, we will not distinguish data and programs throughout this paper.

In order to protect the memory cell access patterns of the RAM CPU, the client holds a secret key for a semantically secure probabilistic encryption scheme. The data and programs uploaded to RAM memory cells are encrypted using the secret key. The clients stores n blocks of data (v_i, x_i) where v_i is the data identifier or location-index and x_i is the data payload. By default, the data block (v_i, x_i) is stored at physical location i in the memory cell. As we have discussed in the previous paragraphs, the RAM CPU interacts with data stored in the memory cells by issuing commands "READ (v_i, x_i)" and "WRITE (v_i, x_i)". By default, the RAM machine does not hide the fact that the CPU has accessed the data stored at the physical position i (by default, it is (v_i, x_i)) even if the data payload (v_i, x_i) itself is encrypted and remains perfectly secure. In order to hide the actual data blocks that the client accessed, the oblivious RAM (ORAM) machine is introduced where the data block (v_i, x_i) is no longer stored at the physical position i. Instead, a random permutation is used to store (v_i, x_i) at a random location. In order to hide the event that one data block is accessed for multiple times, further mechanisms (e.g., a cache) are used. Several commonly used constructions of oblivious RAMs are presented in next sections. The security for ORAMs is expressed in the following definition which is based on [8,11,21].

Definition 1. *Assume that the client store a sequence of data blocks $X = \{(v_1, x_1), \cdots, (v_n, x_n)\}$ at the server. Each data block (v_i, x_i) is located at a physical location $\pi(i)$. The client (or the ORAM CPU) issues a sequence of operations $(op_1, a_1, y_1), \cdots, (op_m, a_m, y_m)$ to the server where each (op_i, a_i, y_i) represents a read or write command. For example, a command $(READ, a_i, y_i)$ asks the server to read the content at the physical location a_i to the variable y_i. The sequence of operations $(op_1, a_1, y_1), \cdots, (op_m, a_m, y_m)$ is called an access pattern $\mathcal{A}(X)$ on client data blocks X. An oblivious RAM machine is* secure *if for any two data blocks X and Y of equal length, the access patterns $\mathcal{A}(X)$ and $\mathcal{A}(X)$ are computationally indistinguishable for any one but the client who holds the secret key.*

The first oblivious RAM simulation was designed by Goldreich [7] using the "square root" construction. For a RAM machine with n memory cells denoted by an array $R[1..n]$, an oblivious RAM with a memory array $OR[1..n + 2\sqrt{n}]$ was designed in [7]. The portion $OR[n + \sqrt{n} + 1..n + 2\sqrt{n}]$ of size $\sqrt{n}$ is used by the ORAM as the cache space (or a shelter). For the first $n + \sqrt{n}$ cells, choose a random permutation

$$\pi : \{1, \cdots, n + \sqrt{n}\} \rightarrow \{1, \cdots, n + \sqrt{n}\}$$

and let $OR[\pi(i)] = R[i] = (v_i, x_i)$, where we assume that $R[i]$ contains a dummy value for $n < i \leq n + \sqrt{n}$. Each time when the ORAM accesses a data block (v_i, x_i) from

$OR[\pi(i)] = R[i]$, it stores this value (v_i, x_i) in the cache $OR[n+\sqrt{n}+1..n+2\sqrt{n}]$. For each new query of a data block (v_j, x_j), ORAM checks all values in $OR[n+\sqrt{n}+1..n+2\sqrt{n}]$ to see whether (v_j, x_j) has been cached there already. If the data block is found, ORAM only needs to make a dummy access to another cell $OR[\pi(n+l)]$ where l is the counter. That is, this is the l-th dummy memory cell access. If the data block is not found, ORAM loads the data block (v_j, x_j) from $OR[\pi(j)]$ directly. After $\sqrt{n}$ memory cell accesses, ORAM needs to re-shuffle data blocks in the memory cells using an oblivious sorting process.

3 Reusable Garbled ORAMs

Lu and Ostrovsky [17] showed how to design one-time non-reusable garbled ORAMs by constructing t pairs of garbled circuits $(\mathcal{O}^i_{ORAM}, \mathcal{O}^i_{CPU})$ for $i = 1, \cdots, t$, where t is the maximum runtime of the ORAM, $\mathcal{O}^i_{ORAM}$ simulates the ith-step memory read-/write command, and $\mathcal{O}^i_{CPU}$ simulates the ith-step shielded CPU operation. Gentry et al. [6] showed that in order to prove the security for the garbled RAM scheme in [17], an additional circularity assumption is required. Gentry et al. [6] then proposed two new constructions to avoid this additional assumption. In this section, we present our construction of practical reusable garbled ORAMs which is based on secure Indistinguishability obfuscation schemes.

3.1 Constrained Peseudo Random Functions

In order to avoid the circularity assumption, Gentry et al. [6] used a concept of revocable PRFs: Let $G : \{0,1\}^s \rightarrow \{0,1\}^{2s}$ be a pseudorandom generator and we can write $G_0(x)$ to denote the left half of the output $G(x)$ and $G_1(x)$ to denote the right half of the output $G(x)$. That is, $G(x) = G_0(x)||G_1(x)$. For any key $k \in \{0,1\}^s$ and input $x \in \{0,1\}^n$, the pseudorandom function is defined as $F_k(x) = G_{x[n-1]}(\cdots(G_{x[0]}(k))\cdots)$.

A constrained (or revocable) pseudorandom function is defined in such a way that given the description of a constrained pseudorandom function, one cannot compute the output of the pseudorandom function for some excluded inputs. This can be easily achieved using GGM-pseudorandom functions. For example, if we want to exclude the input 0^n, instead of giving out the key k, we can give the following description of the pseudorandom function

$$F_k : \{G_1(k), G_0(G_1(k)), \cdots, G_1(G_0(G_0(\cdots(G_0(k))\cdots))))\}$$

.

Goldwasser et al. [9] designed reusable garbled RAMs using fully homomorphic encryption (FHE) schemes and attribute based encryption (ABE) schemes for RAMs. As we have mentioned in previous sections, these schemes are neither efficient nor secure against active adversaries.

3.2 Garbled Circuits (GC)

We first briefly review the formal definition of garbled circuits and related concepts.

Definition 2. *A functional encryption scheme* FE *for a class of functions* $\{\mathcal{F}_n\}_{n\in N}$ *is a tuple of probabilistic polynomial time algorithms* (FE.Setup, FE.KeyGen, FE.Enc, FE.Dec) *with the following properties*

- $(\texttt{fmpk}, \texttt{fmsk}) = \text{FE.Setup}(1^\kappa)$ *outputs a master public key* fmpk *and a master secret key* fmsk *on the security parameter* κ.
- $\texttt{fsk}_f = \text{FE.KeyGen}(\texttt{fmsk}, f)$ *outputs a secret key for a function* f.
- $c = \text{FE.Enc}(\texttt{fmpk}, x)$ *outputs a ciphertext for* x.
- $y = \text{FE.Dec}(\texttt{fsk}_f, c)$ *outputs the value* y *which should equal* $f(x)$.

The functional encryption scheme is correct if $y \neq f(x)$ *with a negligible probability.*

The security of functional encryption scheme requires that an adversary learns nothing about the input x other than the output $f(x)$.

Definition 3 *(FE security). Let* FE *be a functional encryption scheme for a family of functions* $\mathcal{F} = \{\mathcal{F}_n\}_{n\in N}$. *For a pair of probabilistic polynomial time algorithms* $A = (A_0, A_1)$ *and a probabilistic polynomial time simulator* S, *define two experiments:*

$\underline{\text{Exp}^{\texttt{real}}_{\text{FE},A}(1^\kappa):}$	$\underline{\text{Exp}^{\texttt{ideal}}_{\text{FE},A,S}(1^\kappa):}$
$(\texttt{fmpk}, \texttt{fmsk}) \leftarrow \text{FE.Setup}(1^\kappa)$	$(\texttt{fmpk}, \texttt{fmsk}) \leftarrow \text{FE.Setup}(1^\kappa)$
$(f, \texttt{state}_A) \leftarrow A_1(\texttt{fmpk})$	$(f, \texttt{state}_A) \leftarrow A_1(\texttt{fmpk})$
$\texttt{fsk}_f \leftarrow \text{FE.KeyGen}(\texttt{fmsk}, f)$	$\texttt{fsk}_f \leftarrow \text{FE.KeyGen}(\texttt{fmsk}, f)$
$(x, \texttt{state}'_A) \leftarrow A_2(\texttt{state}_A, \texttt{fsk}_f)$	$(x, \texttt{state}'_A) \leftarrow A_2(\texttt{state}_A, \texttt{fsk}_f)$
$c \leftarrow \text{FE.Enc}(\texttt{fmk}, x)$	$\bar{c} \leftarrow S(\texttt{fmpk}, \texttt{fsk}_f, f, f(x), 1^{\lvert x\rvert})$
$\text{output}(\texttt{state}'_A, \texttt{c})$	$\text{output}(\texttt{state}'_A, \bar{\texttt{c}})$

The scheme is said to be (single-key) secure in the full simulation security model if there exists a probabilistic polynomial time simulator S *such that for all pairs of probabilistic polynomial time adversaries* (A_0, A_1), *the outcomes of the two experiments are computationally indistinguishable.*

Definition 4. *Let* $\mathcal{C} = \{\mathcal{C}_n\}_{n\in N}$ *be a family of circuits such that* $\mathcal{C}_n$ *is a set of boolean circuits that take* n*-bit inputs. A garbling scheme for* $\mathcal{C}$ *is a tuple of probabilistic polynomial time algorithms* GC = (GC.Garble, GC.Enc, GC.Eval) *with*

- $(\Gamma, \texttt{sk}) = \text{GC.Garble}(1^\kappa, C)$ *outputs a garbled circuit* Γ *and a secret key* sk.
- $c_x = \text{GC.Enc}(\texttt{sk}, x)$ *outputs an encoding* c_x *for an input* $x \in \{0,1\}^n$.
- $y = \text{GC.Eval}(\Gamma, c_x)$ *outputs* $y = C(x)$.

The garbling scheme GC *is* correct *if the probability that* $\text{GC.Eval}(\Gamma, c_x) \neq C(x)$ *is negligible. The garbling scheme* GC *is* efficient *if the size of* Γ *is bounded by a polynomial and the run-time of* $c = \text{GC.Enc}(\texttt{sk}, x)$ *is also bounded by a polynomial.*

The security of garbling schemes is defined in terms of input and circuit privacy in the literature. The following definition captures the intuition that the adversary learns zero information about the circuit and input given one evaluation of the garbled circuit.

Definition 5 *(Privacy for one-time garbling schemes). A garbling scheme* GC *for a family of circuits $\mathcal{C}$ is said to be* input and circuit private *if there exists a probabilistic polynomial time simulator* $\mathtt{Sim}_{\mathtt{Garble}}$ *such that for all probabilistic polynomial time adversaries A and D and all large κ, we have*

$$\left| Pr[D(\alpha, x, C, \Upsilon, c) = 1 | \mathtt{REAL}] - Pr[D(\alpha, x, C, \tilde{\Upsilon}, \tilde{c}) = 1 | \mathtt{SIM}] \right| = \text{negl}(\kappa)$$

where REAL *and* SIM *are the following events*

$$\mathtt{REAL} : (x, C, \alpha) = A(1^\kappa); (\Upsilon, \mathtt{sk}) = \mathtt{GS.Garble}(1^\kappa, C); c = \mathtt{GS.Enc}(\mathtt{sk}, x)$$
$$\mathtt{SIM} : (x, C, \alpha) = A(1^\kappa); (\tilde{\Upsilon}, \tilde{c}) = \mathtt{Sim}_{\mathtt{Garble}}(1^\kappa, C(x), 1^{|C|}, 1^{|x|}).$$

The reusable garbling schemes for circuits have the same syntax as one-time garbling schemes. In order to differentiate them, we use RGC to denote reusable circuit garbling schemes. The following privacy definition for reusable garbled circuits is adapted from Goldwasser et al. [10].

Definition 6 *(Private reusable garbling circuits). Let* RGC *be a reusable garbling scheme for a family of circuits $\mathcal{C} = \{\mathcal{C}_n\}_{n \in N}$ and $C \in \mathcal{C}_n$ be a circuit with n-bits input. For a pair of probabilistic polynomial time algorithms $A = (A_0, A_1)$ and a probabilistic polynomial time simulator $S = (S_0, S_1)$, define two experiments:*

$\mathtt{Exp}^{\mathtt{real}}_{\mathtt{RGC},A}(1^\kappa)$:	$\mathtt{Exp}^{\mathtt{ideal}}_{\mathtt{RGC},A,S}(1^\kappa)$:
$(C, \mathtt{state}_A) \leftarrow A_0(1^\kappa)$	$(C, \mathtt{state}_A) \leftarrow A_0(1^\kappa)$
$(\mathtt{sk}, \Upsilon) \leftarrow \mathtt{RGC.Garble}(1^\kappa, C)$	$(\tilde{\Upsilon}, \mathtt{state}_S) \leftarrow S_0(1^\kappa, C)$
$\alpha \leftarrow A_1^{\mathtt{RGC.Enc}(\mathtt{sk},\cdot)}(M, \Upsilon, \mathtt{state}_A)$	$\alpha \leftarrow A_1^{O(\cdot,C)[[\mathtt{state}_S]]}(M, \tilde{\Upsilon}, \mathtt{state}_A)$

In the above experiments, $O(\cdot, C)[[\mathtt{state}_S]]$ is an oracle that on input x from A_1, runs S_1 with inputs $1^{|x|}$, $C(x)$, and the latest state of S; it returns the output of S_1 (storing the new simulator state for the next invocation). The garbling scheme RGC *is said to be* private *with reusability if there exists a probabilistic polynomial time simulator S such that for all pairs of probabilistic polynomial time adversaries $A = (A_0, A_1)$, the following two distributions are computationally indistinguishable:*

$$\left\{\mathtt{Exp}^{\mathtt{real}}_{\mathtt{RGC},A}(1^\kappa)\right\}_{\kappa \in N} =_c \left\{\mathtt{Exp}^{\mathtt{ideal}}_{\mathtt{RGC},A,S}(1^\kappa)\right\}_{\kappa \in N} \tag{1}$$

3.3 Indistinguishability Obfuscation and Reusable Garbled Circuits

Jain, Lin, and Sahai [13] proved the following results.

Theorem 1 *(Jain, Lin, and Sahai [13]). Let τ be arbitrary constants greater than 0, and δ, ε in (0, 1). Assume sub-exponential security of the following assumptions, where κ is the security parameter, p is a κ-bit prime, and the parameters l, k, n below are large enough polynomials in κ:*

- *the LWE assumption over Z_p with subexponential modulus-to-noise ratio 2^{k^ε}, where k is the dimension of the LWE secret,*

- *the LPN assumption over* Z_p *with polynomially many LPN samples and error rate* $1/l^{\delta}$*, where* l *is the dimension of the LPN secret,*
- *the existence of a Boolean* PRG *in* NC^0 *with stretch* $n^{1+\tau}$*,*
- *the SXDH assumption on asymmetric bilinear groups of a order* p*.*

Then, (subexponentially secure) indistinguishability obfuscation for all polynomial-size circuits exists.

The functional encryption scheme for circuits $C \in NC^1$ is defined as follows. Choose two standard public-key encryption key pairs $(\mathtt{puk}_1, \mathtt{prk}_1)$ and $(\mathtt{puk}_2, \mathtt{prk}_2)$ in the key generation process of the Functional Encryption scheme. The encryption of an input x consists of two ciphertexts of x under the two public keys $\mathtt{puk}_1$ and $\mathtt{puk}_2$ together with a statistically simulation sound non-interactive zero knowledge (NIZK) proof that both ciphertexts encrypt the same message. The secret key $\mathtt{sk}_C$ for the circuit C is an indistinguishability obfuscation of a program that first checks the NIZK proof and, if the proof is valid, it uses one of the two secret keys $\mathtt{prk}_1$ and $\mathtt{prk}_2$ to decrypt x and then computes and outputs $C(x)$.

A reusable garbled circuit $\overline{C}$ for a circuit $C \in NC^1$ can be constructed using the approach presented in Goldwasser et al. [10]. The owner of circuit C chooses a secret key $\mathtt{sk}$ for an ideal cipher to encrypt the circuit C as $\mathrm{E.Enc}_{\mathtt{sk}}(C)$. Let $U_E(\mathtt{sk}, x) \in NC^1$ be a universal circuit that first uses $\mathtt{sk}$ to decrypt $\mathrm{E.Enc}_{\mathtt{sk}}(C)$ to the circuit C and then runs C on x. Let $\mathtt{sk}_{U_E}$ be the secret key of the functional encryption scheme for U_E. The reusable garbled circuit for C is $\overline{C} = \mathtt{sk}_{U_E}$ and the secret key is $(\mathtt{sk}, \mathtt{puk}_1, \mathtt{puk}_2)$. The input to $\overline{C}$ consists of the two cipher texts of $(\mathtt{sk}, x)$ under the two public keys $\mathtt{puk}_1, \mathtt{puk}_2$ and a NIZK proof that these two cipher texts encrypt the same plain text. In the above arguments, we used the fact that there exists a universal circuit of depth $O(d)$ for all circuits of depth d. By combining the results in Theorem 1, De Caro et al. [5], and Goldwasser et al. [10], we have the following result: Assuming the assumptions of Theorem 1, there exists a reusable garbling scheme RGC for circuits in NC^1 that is secure according to the Definition 6 in the random oracle model.

There exists a functional encryption scheme FE for circuits in NC^1 that is secure according to a standard security definition of functional encryption in the simulation-based security model (see, e.g., Katz et al. [14], Bethencourt et al. [2], Gorbunov et al. [12], and Goldwasser et al. [10]).

3.4 Construction of Reusable Garbled ORAMs

The syntax for reusable garbled ORAMs is the same as that for one-time and reusable garble circuits in Definition 4. The security for ORAMs is defined in Definition 1. The security definition for reusable garbled ORAMs is the same as that for reusable garble circuits in Definition 6. Throughout this paper, we will use $\mathtt{RGO} = (\mathtt{RGO.Garble}, \mathtt{RGO.Enc}, \mathtt{RGO.Eval})$ to denote a reusable garbled ORAM scheme. It is noted that a RAM CPU runs five kinds of operations. For convenience, RAM operations could be further grouped into two categories:

1. interface operation (op, v, x)
2. execute one instruction step to update the CPU state Σ and to produce the next interface operation (op, v, x). CPU state update includes register content update, program pointer update, query counter update, session information update, cryptographic key update, and other information update. The instruction step could be one of the following operations: arithmetic instruction, random sequence generation, control transfer, and halt.

Beame, Cook, and Hoover [1] showed that division could be implemented using a depth $O(\log)$ circuit. Thus the operation of one CPU step could be simulated by a circuit in NC^1.

In the ORAM model, each interface operation (op, v, x) is translated to a sequence of memory cell accesses to hide the actual data-identifier string v. Since we are trying to convert the shielded CPU to a garbled circuit, the evaluator of the garbled CPU can observe how many operations the CPU executes before the next interface command is created. In order to hide this kind of pattern, we assume that the CPU is modified in such a way that each CPU operation is followed by an interface operation. This could be achieved by inserting dummy memory cell accesses or by inserting NOP operations to the CPU instruction sequences.

Let $\mathrm{E} = (\mathtt{E.KeyGen}, \mathtt{E.Enc}, \mathtt{E.Dec})$ be a semantically secure symmetric key cipher and $\mathtt{PKE} = (\mathtt{PKE.KeyGen}, \mathtt{PKE.Enc}, \mathtt{PKE.Dec})$ be a semantically secure public key encryption scheme. Throughout the garbling process of an ORAM, we use a secret key $\mathtt{sk} = \mathtt{E.KeyGen}(1^\kappa)$ and two public key pairs

$$(\mathtt{prk}_1, \mathtt{puk}_1) = \mathtt{PKE.KeyGen}(1^\kappa)$$

and

$$(\mathtt{prk}_2, \mathtt{puk}_2) = \mathtt{PKE.KeyGen}(1^\kappa).$$

The entire memory cells are encrypted inputs to Garg et al's reusable garbled circuits (see Sect. 3.3 for details). That is, each cell value (v, x) is encrypted as a tuple (e_1, e_2, π) where $e_i = \mathtt{PKE.Enc}(\mathtt{puk}_i, \mathtt{sk}||v||x)$ for $i = 1, 2$ and π is a NIZK proof that both e_1 and e_2 encrypt the same message.

An ORAM CPU is modeled as three separate reusable circuits. The graphical description of these circuits and their communication channels are shown in Fig. 1.

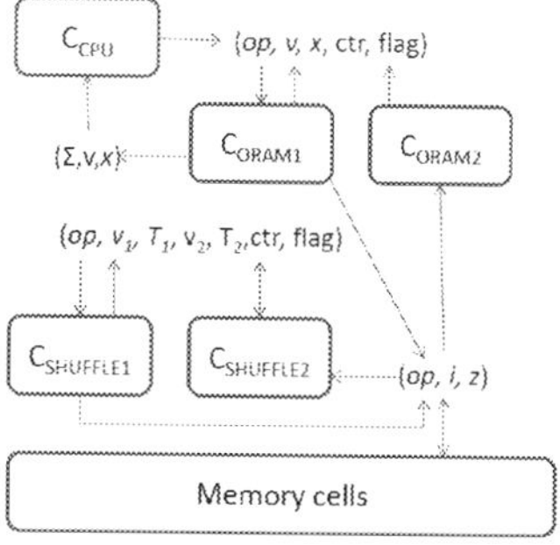

Fig. 1. Garbled ORAM CPU

The first circuit is the reusable CPU circuit $C_{\texttt{CPU}} \in NC^1$ that takes the current CPU state (Σ, v, x) as inputs, checks the consistency of session information contained in the input, runs one CPU step, updates the CPU state Σ and session information, and produces the next encrypted interface command (op, v, x) for the second circuit $C_{\texttt{ORAM}}$ to execute. The details of $C_{\texttt{CPU}}$ are described in Fig. 2.

Inputs: CPU state $\overline{(\Sigma, v, x, \texttt{sctrl}_r)}$ and session control data $(\texttt{session}, \texttt{sctrl}_s)$.
Output: Encoded $\overline{(\Sigma, v, x)}$, $\overline{\texttt{session}}$, and interface command $\overline{\texttt{com}}$

1. if $\texttt{sctrl}_r$ and $\texttt{sctrl}_s$ are inconsistent then exit.
2. simulate ORAM CPU execution for one step with internal state Σ and input (v, x), compute the new state Σ and the next interface command (op, v, x).
3. update session, $\texttt{sctrl}_r$, and $\texttt{sctrl}_s$.
4. encode $\texttt{sk}||(\Sigma, v, x)||\texttt{sctrl}_r$ to obtain $\overline{(\Sigma, v, x)} = (e_1^{\Sigma}, e_2^{\Sigma}, \pi^{\Sigma})$ as an input to a Garg's reusable garbled circuit using public keys $\text{puk}_1, \text{puk}_2$.
5. encode $\texttt{sk}||\texttt{session}||\texttt{sctrl}_s$ to obtain $\overline{\texttt{session}}$ as an input to a Garg's reusable garbled circuit using public keys $\text{puk}_1, \text{puk}_2$.
6. encode $\texttt{sk}||(op, v, x, \texttt{ctr}, \texttt{flag}, \texttt{strl}_c)$ to obtain $\overline{\texttt{com}}$ as an input to a Garg's reusable garbled circuit using public keys $\text{puk}_1, \text{puk}_2$.
7. output $\overline{(\Sigma, v, x)}$, $\overline{\texttt{session}}$, and $\overline{\texttt{com}}$.

Fig. 2. $C_{\texttt{CPU}}$ updates its state and outputs an encoded $\overline{(op, v, x, \texttt{ctr}, \texttt{flag})}$

The interface command (op, v, x) produced by circuit $C_{\texttt{CPU}}$ is in the default format $(op, v, x, \texttt{ctr}, \texttt{flag})$ where $\texttt{ctr} = 0$ and $\texttt{flag} = \texttt{no}$. The second circuit $C_{\texttt{ORAM}}$ translates the command $(op, v, x, \texttt{ctr}, \texttt{flag})$ to a sequence of memory cell access commands to implement the command (op, v, x) obliviously. In order to run (op, v, x) obliviously, the circuit $C_{\texttt{ORAM}}$ needs to keep a record on whether the actual data-identifier string v has been found. This information is kept in the $\texttt{flag}$ field. The counter $\texttt{ctr}$ is used to record the number of memory cells this circuit has accessed for this specific command (op, v, x). In other words, for each (op, v, x) command, the circuit $C_{\texttt{ORAM}}$ is executed t times repeatedly to hide the actual data block it accessed, where t is a constant that is independently of the value (op, v, x).

Specifically, the reusable circuit $C_{\texttt{ORAM}}$ is a pair of circuits $C_{\texttt{ORAM1}}$ and $C_{\texttt{ORAM2}}$. $C_{\texttt{ORAM1}}$ takes the interface command $(op, v, x, \texttt{ctr}, \texttt{flag})$ as the input and produces an interface command (op', i, z) where op' and i are plain texts and $z = \overline{(v, x)}$ is encoded. If $op' =$ READ, the evaluator reads the memory cell at physical location i and loads the encoded content to z. If $op' =$ WRITE, the evaluator writes the encoded value z to the memory cell at physical location i. After the evaluator finishes processing the actual memory cell access, the resulting updated interface command (op', i, z) is given to the circuit $C_{\texttt{ORAM2}}$. $C_{\texttt{ORAM2}}$ decrypts z to a pair (v', x'). If $v = v'$, the actual data block has been found. $C_{\texttt{ORAM2}}$ sets $\texttt{flag} =$ yes and checks whether $op =$ READ. If $op =$ READ, $C_{\texttt{ORAM2}}$ needs to copy the value x' to the field x of $(op, v, x, \texttt{ctr}, \texttt{flag})$. If $v \neq v'$, the actual data block has not been found yet and $C_{\texttt{ORAM2}}$ keeps $\texttt{flag} =$ no. After $C_{\texttt{ORAM2}}$ finishes its job, circuit $C_{\texttt{ORAM1}}$ takes turn again. $C_{\texttt{ORAM1}}$ examines the interface command

$(op, v, x, \texttt{ctr}, \texttt{flag})$ to obtain the values of flag and ctr. Using these values, $C_{\texttt{ORAM1}}$ creates the next memory access instruction according to the oblivious memory access schedule and outputs the corresponding interface command (op', i, z). For each execution of $C_{\texttt{ORAM1}}$, the counter ctr is increased by one. After ctr reaches t, $C_{\texttt{ORAM1}}$ copies the value x from $(op, v, x, \texttt{ctr}, \texttt{flag})$ to the field-x of (Σ, v, x) which is the input to $C_{\texttt{CPU}}$. The evaluator knows the value of t. Thus it lets the circuit $C_{\texttt{CPU}}$ take turn after $C_{\texttt{ORAM1}}$ finishes t steps. The details of circuit $C_{\texttt{ORAM}}$ are described in Fig. 3.

$C_{\texttt{ORAM1}}$:
Inputs: $(\Sigma, v, x, \texttt{sctrl}_r)$, $(op, v, x, \texttt{ctr}, \texttt{flag}, \texttt{sctrl}_\texttt{c})$, $(\texttt{session}, \texttt{sctrl}_s)$
Output: Memory access command (op, i, z)

1. if $\texttt{sctrl}_c$, $\texttt{sctrl}_r$, and $\texttt{sctrl}_s$ are consistent, use session to update $\texttt{sctrl}_c$, $\texttt{sctrl}_r$, and $\texttt{sctrl}_s$ and go to next step 2. Otherwise, exit
2. if $\texttt{ctr} < t$, go to step 5.
3. if $\texttt{ctr} = t$ and $op =$ READ, extract (v, x) from $(op, v, x, \texttt{ctr}, \texttt{flag}, \texttt{sctrl}_\texttt{c})$ and put it in (Σ, v, x).
4. output the encoded $\texttt{sk}||(\Sigma, v, x, \texttt{sctrl}_r)$ in the format of input to an Garg's reusable garbled circuit using public keys $\text{puk}_1, \text{puk}_2$ and exit.
5. use ctr, flag, and oblivious memory access schedule to output the next memory access command (op', i, z), where op' and i are in plain text and $z = \overline{(v, x)}$.

$C_{\texttt{ORAM2}}$:
Inputs: (op', i, z), $(op, v, x, \texttt{ctr}, \texttt{flag}, \texttt{sctrl}_\texttt{c})$, $(\texttt{session}, \texttt{sctrl}_s)$
Output: encoded $\texttt{sk}||(op, v, x, \texttt{ctr}, \texttt{flag}, \texttt{sctrl}_\texttt{c}, z)$ using $\text{puk}_1, \text{puk}_2$

1. if $\texttt{sctrl}_c$ and $\texttt{sctrl}_s$ are inconsistent then exit.
2. use session to update $\texttt{sctrl}_c$ and $\texttt{sctrl}_s$.
3. decode z to $\texttt{sk}||(v', x')$ using the key prk_1.
4. if $v = v'$, then the required data block has been found. Set $\texttt{flag} =$ yes. Furthermore, if $op =$ READ, insert the value of x' to the x-field of $(op, v, x, \texttt{ctr}, \texttt{flag}, \texttt{sctrl}_\texttt{c})$.
5. output encoded $\texttt{sk}||(op, v, x, \texttt{ctr}, \texttt{flag}, \texttt{sctrl}_\texttt{c})$ in the format of input to an Garg's reusable garbled circuit using public keys $\text{puk}_1, \text{puk}_2$.

Fig. 3. $C_{\texttt{ORAM}}$ uses ctr and flag to determine which memory cell to access

The third circuit $C_{\texttt{SHUFFLE}}$ implements the re-shuffling process for ORAM memory cells. $C_{\texttt{SHUFFLE}}$ consists of a pair $(C_{\texttt{SHUFFLE1}}, C_{\texttt{SHUFFLE2}})$ of circuits that implement the randomized data-oblivious Shellsort algorithm for re-shuffling the memory cells. $C_{\texttt{SHUFFLE}}$ is constructed using an oblivious sorting algorithm. Specifically, $C_{\texttt{SHUFFLE1}}$ takes an input with fields $(op, v_1, T_1, v_2, T_2, \texttt{ctr}, \texttt{flag})$ and compare-exchanges the values (v_1, T_1) and (v_2, T_2). After the compare-exchange operation, $C_{\texttt{SHUFFLE1}}$ outputs a next memory cell access command (op, i, z) with plain-text op and i for the evaluator to access the ith memory cell. The updated (op, i, z) is given to $C_{\texttt{SHUFFLE2}}$ that decodes z and inserts it to the corresponding field of $(op, v_1, T_1, v_2, T_2, \texttt{ctr}, \texttt{flag})$ if necessary.

The algorithm for $C_{\texttt{SHUFFLE}}$ is similar to the algorithm for the circuit $C_{\texttt{ORAM}}$ described in Fig. 3. The details are omitted here.

Without loss of generality, we may assume that there exist NC^1 encryption and decryption circuits for the symmetric key cipher E and the public key cipher PKE. Then it is straightforward to show that circuits $C_{\texttt{CPU}}$, $C_{\texttt{ORAM1}}$, $C_{\texttt{ORAM2}}$, $C_{\texttt{SHUFFLE1}}$, and $C_{\texttt{SHUFFLE2}}$ belong to NC^1 also. By Garg et al's results that we discussed in Sect. 3.3, there exist efficient polynomial size reusable garbled circuits $\bar{C}_{\texttt{CPU}}$, $\bar{C}_{\texttt{ORAM1}}$, $\bar{C}_{\texttt{ORAM2}}$, $\bar{C}_{\texttt{SHUFFLE1}}$, and $\bar{C}_{\texttt{SHUFFLE2}}$. Using these constructions, we are ready to give the formal construction of our reusable garbled ORAM machines.

In above paragraphs, we described the construction of a garbled ORAM CPU. In a practical deployment of ORAM programs, the program is generally encoded and stored in the memory cells. In other words, the garbled ORAM CPU could be considered as a garbled universal machine. It reads encoded ORAM programs in memory cells and executes them on inputs. Part of the input is provided by the client and the other part of the input is located in memory cells already. For example, part of memory cells may be considered as an encoded database which is part of the input to the ORAM program. The other part of the input could be an encoded database search query that is submitted by the client. Let $\mathcal{P} = \{\mathcal{P}_n\}_{n\in N}$ be a family of ORAM programs such that P_n is a set of programs that take n-bit inputs. The reusable garbling scheme $\texttt{RGO} = (\texttt{RGO.Garble}, \texttt{RGO.Enc}, \texttt{RGO.Eval})$ for $\mathcal{P}$ is instantiated as follows.

- $(\Gamma, (\texttt{sk}, \texttt{puk}_1, \texttt{puk}_2)) = \texttt{RGO.Garble}(1^\kappa, P)$:
  - $\texttt{sk} = \texttt{E.KeyGen}(1^\kappa)$
  - $(\texttt{prk}_i, \texttt{puk}_i) = \texttt{PKE.KeyGen}(1^\kappa)$ for $i = 1, 2$
  - encode P appropriately and include it as part of the memory cells
  - encode each memory cell content (v, x) to (e_1, e_2, π) which is in the format of input to Garg et al's reusable garbled circuits using $\texttt{sk}, \texttt{puk}_1$, and $\texttt{puk}_2$.
  - use Garg et al's approach to construct reusable garbled circuits for each of the NC^1 circuits $C_{\texttt{CPU}}$, $C_{\texttt{ORAM1}}$, $C_{\texttt{ORAM2}}$, $C_{\texttt{SHUFFLE1}}$, $C_{\texttt{SHUFFLE2}}$ with keys $\texttt{prk}_1$, $\texttt{sk}$, $\texttt{puk}_1$, and $\texttt{puk}_2$.
  - Let $\Gamma = \left(\bar{C}_{\texttt{CPU}}, \bar{C}_{\texttt{ORAM1}}, \bar{C}_{\texttt{ORAM2}}, \bar{C}_{\texttt{SHUFFLE1}}, \bar{C}_{\texttt{SHUFFLE2}}\right)$.
- $c = \texttt{RGO.Enc}((\texttt{sk}, \texttt{puk}_1, \texttt{puk}_2), x)$.
  - Encode $\texttt{sk}||x$ to $c = (e_1, e_2, \pi)$ which is in the format of input to Garg et al's reusable garbled circuits using the two keys $\texttt{puk}_1$, and $\texttt{puk}_2$.
- $y = \texttt{RGO.Eval}(\Gamma, c)$:
  - Run the garbled ORAM CPU

$$\left(\bar{C}_{\texttt{CPU}}, \bar{C}_{\texttt{ORAM1}}, \bar{C}_{\texttt{ORAM2}}, \bar{C}_{\texttt{SHUFFLE1}}, \bar{C}_{\texttt{SHUFFLE2}}\right)$$

    on the memory cells and on c to compute the output $y = P(x)$.

3.5 Proof of Security

We first make a few observations on the garbled ORAM construction in Sect. 3.4. The first observation is that for a given encoded input $c = \texttt{RGO.Enc}(x)$, the running time of $y = \texttt{RGO.Eval}(\Gamma, c)$ is disclosed according to Definition 1. Thus the running time is provided to the simulator in advance. In case that the running time of the execution should be protected also, the ORAM CPU should be revised in such a way that it takes the same time for all inputs of the same length. This could be achieved by adding NOP operations to the ORAM CPU if the calculation ends early than the expected time.

The second observation is that the output $y = \texttt{RGO.Eval}(\Gamma, c)$ is an encoded value (e_1, e_2, π) which is in the format of input to Garg et al's reusable garbled circuits using the keys $\texttt{sk}, \texttt{puk}_1$, and $\texttt{puk}_2$. This is acceptable in practice since generally the garbled ORAM program is executed in the cloud and the cloud does not need to know the actual output. After the computation is finished, the cloud returns the encoded y to the client who can recover the plain text output using either of the secret keys $\texttt{prk}_1$ or $\texttt{prk}_2$.

The third observation is that in our scheme, the garbled ORAM will only run on encoded input provided by the client. The secret key $\texttt{sk}$ of the ideal cipher $\texttt{E}$ and the public keys $\texttt{puk}_1, \texttt{puk}_2$ of the public key scheme $\texttt{PKE}$ are needed to encode the input for the garbled ORAM CPUs. Without correctly encoded inputs with matching session identification, neither garbled CPU circuit $\overline{C}_{\texttt{CPU}}$ nor garbled ORAM circuit $\overline{C}_{\texttt{ORAM}}$ would continue the computation since the session control message validation process would only pass with a negligible probability. Similarly, the adversary could not mix/swap computation states for two inputs since each input contains an input specific session control message. The session control messages in inputs for two sessions (even if the input values are identical) are identical only with a negligible probability.

The fourth observation is that the adversary may play fault-insertion attacks in the memory cells. This kind of attacks have not been discovered or modeled in the traditional simulation-based security model for ORAMs in Definitions 1 and 6. In this section, we prove that our ORAM garbling scheme is secure according to Definition 6.

Theorem 2 *Assuming the existence of a semantically secure symmetric key cipher* $\texttt{E}$*, a semantically secure public key cipher* $\texttt{PKE}$*, and a private reusable garbling scheme for circuits in* NC^1*, there is a private reusable ORAM garbling scheme* $\texttt{RGO}$ *as defined in Definition 6 in the random oracle model.*

Proof. First we observe that the existence of semantically secure ciphers $\texttt{E}$ and $\texttt{PKE}$ implies the existence of cryptographically secure one-way functions. Thus the assumption in Theorem 2 implies the existence of a secure ORAM according to Definitions 1. The correctness of the construction in Sect. 3.4 is straightforward. In order to show that the construction is input and circuit private as defined in Definition 6, we show that there exists a simulator $S = (S_0, S_1)$ simulating the garbled execution given the program output y and the ORAM CPU running time t, so that the equation (1) holds.

Let S_a be the ORAM memory access pattern simulator and $S_{\texttt{PKE}}$ be the simulator for the cipher $\texttt{PKE}$. Let $S_{\texttt{CPU}}, S_{\texttt{ORAM}}$, and $S_{\texttt{SHUFFLE}}$ be the simulators for Garg et al's reusable garble circuits (as described in Sect. 3.3) $\overline{C}_{\texttt{CPU}}, \overline{C}_{\texttt{ORAM}}$, and $\overline{C}_{\texttt{SHUFFLE}}$ respectively.

Assume that an ORAM machine P is selected with the security parameter κ. For the given ORAM CPU running time t and output $y = P(x)$, let $S_a(y, t)$ outputs a sequence of memory access pattern $\eta_1, \cdots, \eta_t$ where η_i $(i \le t)$ is the simulated oblivious memory cell access sequence for the ith memory cell access of the original RAM machine. In other words, each $\eta_i = \{v_{i,1}, \cdots, v_{i,t_i}\}$ is a sequence of memory cells that the simulated ORAM machine accesses to implement the ith memory cell access of the original

RAM machine. $S_a(y,t)$ also outputs a sequence of memory access pattern $\xi_1, \cdots, \xi_{t'}$ where ξ_i ($i \le t'$) is the simulated oblivious memory cell access sequence for the ith re-shuffling process.

Starting from the last memory cell sequence set η_t, for each $\eta_i = \{v_{i,1}, \cdots, v_{i,t_i}\}$, repeat simulators S_{PKE} and $S_{\texttt{ORAM}}$ for t_i times to generate a simulated $\texttt{view}^i_{\texttt{ORAM}}$. Similarly, starting from the last memory cell sequence set $\xi_{t'}$, for each $\xi_i = \{u_{i,1}, \cdots, u_{i,s_i}\}$, repeat simulators S_{PKE} and $S_{\texttt{SHUFFLE}}$ for s_i times to generate a simulated $\texttt{view}^i_{\texttt{SHUFFLE}}$. Lastly, using the views $\{\texttt{view}^i_{\texttt{ORAM}}, \texttt{view}^j_{\texttt{SHUFFLE}} : i \le t \text{and} j \le t'\}$, repeat simulators S_{PKE} and S_{CPU} for $t + t'$ times to generate a simulated $\texttt{view}_{\text{CPU}}$. Without loss of generality, we may assume that the adversaries output their entire views in the above simulation so that any required view could be calculated from these views in a probabilistic polynomial time. In other words, the simulator's view $\left\{\texttt{Exp}^{\texttt{ideal}}_{\texttt{RGO},A,S}(1^\kappa)\right\}_{\kappa \in N}$ in (1) could be calculated in probabilistic polynomial time from S's entire view

$$\{\texttt{view}^i_{\texttt{ORAM}}, \texttt{view}^j_{\texttt{SHUFFLE}}, \texttt{view}_{\text{CPU}} : i \le t \,\text{and}\, j \le t'\}_{\kappa \in N}. \tag{2}$$

In order to show that (1) holds, we consider three experiments.

Experiment 1: The ideal game $\texttt{Exp}^{\texttt{ideal}}_{\texttt{RGO},A,S}(1^\kappa)$ of Definition 6 with the simulator S and the ORAM machine P.

Experiment 2: The same as Experiment 1 except that the ORAM program P is replaced with the reusable garbled ORAM $\overline{P}$: $\overline{C}_{\text{CPU}}, \overline{C}_{\texttt{ORAM}}, \overline{C}_{\texttt{SHUFFLE}}$, and corresponding keys.

Experiment 3: The same as Experiment 2 except that the simulated cipher S_{PKE} is replaced with the actual cipher PKE using keys $\texttt{sk}, \texttt{puk}_1, \texttt{puk}_2, \texttt{prk}_1$.

Since the view of Experiment 1 equals to $\left\{\texttt{Exp}^{\texttt{ideal}}_{\texttt{RGO},A,S}(1^\kappa)\right\}_{\kappa \in N}$ and the view of Experiment 3 equals to $\left\{\texttt{Exp}^{\texttt{real}}_{\texttt{RGO},A}(1^\kappa)\right\}_{\kappa \in N}$, it is sufficient for us to show that the view of Experiment 1 is computationally indistinguishable from the view of Experiment 2 and the view of Experiment 2 is computationally indistinguishable from the view of Experiment 3.

Claim. Assume that $\overline{C}_{\text{CPU}}, \overline{C}_{\texttt{ORAM}}$, and $\overline{C}_{\texttt{SHUFFLE}}$ are private reusable garbled circuits for circuits $C_{\text{CPU}}, C_{\texttt{ORAM}}$, and $C_{\texttt{SHUFFLE}}$. Furthermore, assume that the ORAM access pattern is securely simulated by the simulator S_a. Then the outputs of Experiment 1 and Experiment 2 are computationally indistinguishable.

Proof Outline. Assume that outputs of Experiment 1 and Experiment 2 could be distinguished by a probabilistic polynomial time algorithm D. Then a standard hybrid approach could be used to construct a probabilistic polynomial time algorithm D' to distinguish the view in (2) from the view for the ideal experiments with the ORAM program P. In other words, if S_a securely simulate the ORAM memory cell access pattern, then the view in (2) could be distinguished from the ideal experiments with circuits $C_{\text{CPU}}, C_{\texttt{ORAM}}$, and $C_{\texttt{SHUFFLE}}$. This contradicts the fact that $\overline{C}_{\text{CPU}}, \overline{C}_{\texttt{ORAM}}$, and $\overline{C}_{\texttt{SHUFFLE}}$ are private reusable garbled circuits (see Sect. 3.3). Q.E.D.

Claim. Assume that the cipher PKE be semantically secure. Then the outputs of Experiment 2 and Experiment 3 are computationally indistinguishable.

Proof Outline. Assume that there exist probabilistic polynomial time adversaries $A = (A_1, A_2)$ and a probabilistic polynomial time distinguisher D such that D can distinguish the outputs of Experiment 2 and Experiment 3 with a non-negligible probability. Using the standard hybrid argument, one can construct a probabilistic polynomial time distinguisher D' to distinguish at least one cipher text in Experiment 3 from the corresponding simulated cipher text in Experiment 2 with a non-negligible probability. This contradicts the assumption that PKE is semantically secure. Q.E.D.

Claim 1 and Claim 2 imply that the Eq. (1) holds. This completes the proof of Theorem 2. Q.E.D.

Definition 7 *(Private reusable garbling ORAMs). Let* RGO *be a reusable garbling scheme for ORAM machines. In addition to the attacks that are allowed in Definitions 1 and 6, the adversary is allowed to interfere with the garbled ORAM execution by playing or replaying the garbled ORAM on modified environments (e.g., inserting faults in the memory cells during the execution). The garbling scheme* RGO *is said to be* private with reusability *if there exists a probabilistic polynomial time simulator S such that for all pairs of probabilistic polynomial time adversaries $A = (A_0, A_1)$ as defined above, the two distributions in (1) are computationally indistinguishable.*

Theorem 3. *Assume the existence of a semantically secure symmetric key cipher* E*, a semantically secure public key cipher* PKE*, a secure digital signature scheme* Dsig*, and a private reusable garbling scheme for circuits in NC^1. Then there is a private reusable ORAM garbling scheme* $\mathtt{RGO}_1$ *as defined in Definition 7 in the random oracle model.*

Proof. Let $\mathtt{Dsig} = (\mathtt{Dsig.KeyGen}, \mathtt{Dsig.Sign}, \mathtt{Dsig.Vefy})$ be a secure digital signature scheme and $(\mathtt{SIGsk}, \mathtt{SIGpk}) = \mathtt{Dsig.KeyGen}(1^\kappa)$. Let $\mathcal{P} = \{\mathcal{P}_n\}_{n \in N}$ be a family of square-root ORAM programs such that P_n is a set of functions that take n-bit inputs. The reusable garbling scheme $\mathtt{RGO}_1 = (\mathtt{RGO}_1.\mathtt{Garble}, \mathtt{RGO}_1.\mathtt{Enc}, \mathtt{RGO}_1.\mathtt{Eval})$ for $\mathcal{P}$ is instantiated as in Sect. 3.4 with the following revisions:

- $(\Gamma, (\mathtt{sk}, \mathtt{puk}_1, \mathtt{puk}_2, \mathtt{SIGsk}, \mathtt{SIGpk})) = \mathtt{RGO}_1.\mathtt{Garble}(1^\kappa, P)$: This process is obtained from RGO.Garble in Sect. 3.4 by the following revisions:
  - add a component in circuit $C_{\mathtt{ORAM}}$ to digitally sign the shelter (cache) at the end of the execution of each $C_{\mathtt{CPU}}$ interface command (op, v, x)
  - add a component in circuit $C_{\mathtt{ORAM}}$ to check the validity of the digital signature at the beginning of the execution of each $C_{\mathtt{CPU}}$ interface command (op, v, x).
  - add an component to circuit $C_{\mathtt{SHUFFLE}}$ so that a unique sequence number seq is added to all memory cells. At the same time, the physical location i of the memory cell $OR[i]$ is added to the content of $OR[i]$. In other words, the ith memory cell contains the value $OR[i] = (v, x, \mathtt{seq}, i)$.
  - add a component to circuit $C_{\mathtt{ORAM}}$ to check that the accessed non-shelter memory cells contain the current sequence number and check that the actual physical address of the memory cell is the same as that contained in the content $OR[i] = (v, x, \mathtt{seq}, i)$.

- $c = \texttt{RGO}_1.\texttt{Enc}((\texttt{sk}, \texttt{puk}_1, \texttt{puk}_2), x)$. This is obtained from RGO.Enc by adding a process to digitally sign the entire shelter cells and adding the current sequence number to all non-shelter memory cells if this has not been done yet.
- $y = \texttt{RGO}_1.\texttt{Eval}(\Gamma, c)$: same as $\texttt{RGO.Eval}(\Gamma, c)$.

The remaining part of the proof is similar to the proof of Theorem 2. Q.E.D.

4 Conclusion

In this paper, we designed reusable garbling schemes for ORAMs using alternative techniques. The garbled ORAM design could find a variety of applications in secure cloud computing environments.

References

1. Beame, P.W., Cook, S.A., Hoover, H.J.: Log depth circuits for division and related problems. SIAM J. Comput. **15**(4), 994–1003 (1986)
2. Bethencourt, J., Sahai, A., Waters, B.: Ciphertext-policy attribute-based encryption. In: 2007 IEEE Security and Privacy, pp. 321–334. IEEE (2007)
3. Chor, B., Gilboa, N.: Computationally private information retrieval. In: Proceedings of the 29th STOC, pp. 304–313. ACM (1997)
4. Chor, B., Kushilevitz, E., Goldreich, O., Sudan, M.: Private information retrieval. JACM **45**(6), 965–981 (1998)
5. De Caro, A., Iovino, V., Jain, A., O'Neill, A., Paneth, O., Persiano, G.: On the achievability of simulation-based security for functional encryption. In: Canetti, R., Garay, J.A. (eds.) CRYPTO 2013. LNCS, vol. 8043, pp. 519–535. Springer, Heidelberg (2013). https://doi.org/10.1007/978-3-642-40084-1_29
6. Gentry, C., Halevi, S., Lu, S., Ostrovsky, R., Raykova, M., Wichs, D.: Garbled RAM revisited. In: Nguyen, P.Q., Oswald, E. (eds.) EUROCRYPT 2014. LNCS, vol. 8441, pp. 405–422. Springer, Heidelberg (2014). https://doi.org/10.1007/978-3-642-55220-5_23
7. Goldreich, O.: Towards a theory of software protection and simulation by oblivious RAMs. In: Proceedings of the 19th ACM STOC, pp. 182–194. ACM (1987)
8. Goldreich, O., Ostrovsky, R.: Software protection and simulation on oblivious RAMs. JACM **43**(3), 431–473 (1996)
9. Goldwasser, S., Kalai, Y., Popa, R., Vaikuntanathan, V., Zeldovich, N.: How to run Turing machines on encrypted data. In Proceedings of the CRYPTO, pp. 536–553 (2013)
10. Goldwasser, S., Kalai, Y., Popa, R., Vaikuntanathan, V., Zeldovich, N.: Reusable garbled circuits and succinct functional encryption. In: Proceedings of the 45th STOC, pp. 555–564. ACM (2013)
11. Goodrich, M.T., Mitzenmacher, M.: Privacy-preserving access of outsourced data via oblivious RAM simulation. In: Proceedings of the ICALP, pp. 576–587 (2011)
12. Gorbunov, S., Vaikuntanathan, V., Wee, H.: Functional encryption with bounded collusions via multi-party computation. In: Safavi-Naini, R., Canetti, R. (eds.) CRYPTO 2012. LNCS, vol. 7417, pp. 162–179. Springer, Heidelberg (2012). https://doi.org/10.1007/978-3-642-32009-5_11
13. Jain, A., Lin, H., Sahai, A.: Indistinguishability obfuscation from well-founded assumptions. In: Proceedings of the 53rd Annual ACM STOC, pp. 60–73 (2021)

14. Katz, J., Sahai, A., Waters, B.: Predicate encryption supporting disjunctions, polynomial equations, and inner products. In: Smart, N. (ed.) EUROCRYPT 2008. LNCS, vol. 4965, pp. 146–162. Springer, Heidelberg (2008). https://doi.org/10.1007/978-3-540-78967-3_9
15. Kent, S.T.: Protecting externally supplied software in small computers. Technical report, DTIC Document (1980)
16. Kushilevitz, E., Ostrovsky, R.: Replication is not needed: single database, computationally-private information retrieval. In: FOCS, vol. 97, pp. 364–373 (1997)
17. Lu, S., Ostrovsky, R.: How to garble RAM programs? In: Johansson, T., Nguyen, P.Q. (eds.) EUROCRYPT 2013. LNCS, vol. 7881, pp. 719–734. Springer, Heidelberg (2013). https://doi.org/10.1007/978-3-642-38348-9_42
18. Ostrovsky, R.: Software protection and simulation on oblivious RAMs. Ph.D. thesis (1992)
19. Ostrovsky, R., Shoup, V.: Private information storage. In: Proceedings of the 29th ACM STOC, pp. 294–303. ACM (1997)
20. Ostrovsky, R., Skeith III, W.E.: A survey of single-database private information retrieval: techniques and applications. In: Okamoto, T., Wang, X. (eds.) PKC 2007. LNCS, vol. 4450, pp. 393–411. Springer, Heidelberg (2007). https://doi.org/10.1007/978-3-540-71677-8_26
21. Pinkas, B., Reinman, T.: Oblivious RAM revisited. In: Rabin, T. (ed.) CRYPTO 2010. LNCS, vol. 6223, pp. 502–519. Springer, Heidelberg (2010). https://doi.org/10.1007/978-3-642-14623-7_27

Efficient Private Set Intersection Cardinality Protocol in the Reverse Unbalanced Setting

Hanyu Li[1] and Ying Gao[1,2](✉)

[1] School of Cyber Science and Technology, Beihang University, Beijing 100191, China
gaoying@buaa.edu.cn

[2] Key Laboratory of Aerospace Network Security, Ministry of Industry and Information Technology, Beijing 100191, China

Abstract. Private set intersection cardinality (PSI-CA) is a variant of private set intersection (PSI) that allows two parties, the sender and the receiver, to compute the cardinality of the intersection without leaking anything more to the other party. It's one of the best-studied applications of secure computation, and many PSI-CA protocols in balanced or unbalanced scenarios have been proposed. Generally, unbalanced scenario means that the private set size of the receiver is significantly smaller than that of the sender. This paper mainly focuses on a new scenario in which the receiver's set size (client) is much larger than that of the sender (server) called the reverse unbalanced scenario. We study PSI-CA protocols that are secure against semi-honest adversaries, using the Hash-Prefix filter to effectively reduce the computation and communication overhead. We greatly optimize the previous unbalanced PSI-CA protocol and construct a reverse unbalanced PSI-CA protocol. In addition, we introduce private information retrieval (PIR) to resist the privacy leakage of the Hash-Prefix filter. By implementing all protocols on the same platform, we compare the protocols' performance theoretically and experimentally. Combined with the Cuckoo filter, elliptic curve and multi-threading, the computational and communication efficiency of our protocol is 26.87× and 8.48× higher than the existing unbalanced PSI-CA protocols. By setting sets with significant differences in size, we also prove the feasibility of our protocol in anonymous identity authentication.

Keywords: Private set intersection cardinality · Reverse unbalanced scenario · Hash-prefix filter · Private information retrieval · Cuckoo filter

1 Introduction

PSI was first proposed by Freedman et al. [16], which allows two or more parties to find the intersection of their private sets without disclosing other information.

Supported by: Natural Science Foundation of Beijing Municipality (M21033); National Natural Science Foundation of China (61932011, 61972017).

W. Susilo et al. (Eds.): ISC 2022, LNCS 13640, pp. 20–39, 2022.
https://doi.org/10.1007/978-3-031-22390-7_2

PSI has been used in a wide range of privacy-sensitive scenarios, such as location sharing [29], contact discovery [21,22], measuring the ads conversion rate [32] fully-sequenced genome test [4], as well as collaborative botnet detection [28].

As for scenarios, PSI can be divided into 4 categories: PSI on small sets, PSI on large sets, PSI on unbalanced sets, and private computation on the intersection. PSI-CA belongs to the last one and computes cardinality on the intersection [1,8–11,13,16–20,24,26,35]. It can be mainly used in measuring the conversion rate of ads, for the merchants may need to know how many people have seen ads while buying the corresponding goods. Meanwhile, both parties dislike leaking any personal information.

PSI-CA can also be divided into balanced [1,8–11,16–20,26,35] and unbalanced [13,24] protocols according to the set size relationship. However, in practice, merchants and advertisers often differ a lot on their set size, i.e., the number of ads readers may be much larger than that of buyers. In this scenario, it's possible to combine offline computation and data structures like Bloom filter (BF) to ensure that the online computation and communication complexity is linear to the smaller set size [22]. Recently, there have been many PSI protocols in the unbalanced scenario [21,22]. As for PSI-CA, Lv et al. [24] proposed an efficient PSI-CA in the unbalanced scenario. As for other PSI-CA related works that are mainly designed for balanced scenario [1,8–11,16–20,26,35], they are much less efficient than unbalanced PSI-CA protocol in the unbalanced scenario.

This work focuses on a new variant of the unbalanced scenario: the reverse unbalanced scenario that client (receiver) owns a large set and the server (sender) owns a small set. And the client should directly get the output, while the server gets nothing. The rationality of this scenario is that merchant does not necessarily only find large-scale advertising companies to advertise. Instead, he can also find some small scale companies to widen their sales channels, such as small game companies in the start-up stage and private websites to put advertisements. In this case, the merchant could own a larger set and play the role of the receiver.

As another example, the reverse unbalanced PSI-CA protocol can also apply in the anonymous authentication scenario: Bob wants to authenticate his identity to Alice's system anonymously. Bob needs to prove his identity B is among the set of Alice's valid users, denoted A. Alice should be able to judge that Bob is a legitimate user without learning B. For this, we can directly calculate the PSI-CA between Bob's private data and Alice's user data set. Then the authentication passes when $|A \cap B| = 1$ and fails when $|A \cap B| = 0$. Obviously, Alice should first get the output to authenticate Bob in this scenario. Inspired by this scenario, we can further extend it to multifactor authentication or verification of status (e.g., you are VIP if you have $|A \cap B| > 10$ tokens registered in A).

Indeed, suppose we directly apply unbalanced PSI-CA in the reverse unbalanced scenario. To ensure efficiency, we may let the small set owner send the output to the large set owner. However, this deviates from the original target that only the receiver (the large set owner) can get the result. Moreover, if we allow both parties to get the output, we cannot guarantee the result given by the small set owner is correct and real. However, in the semi-honest model, the adversary must follow the protocol, and the correctness can be satisfied, so maybe a malicious protocol is worthy of further research. But generally, malicious protocol requires introducing techniques such as zero knowledge proof that brings more overhead and communication rounds to support verifiability of the result.

Therefore, this paper tries to solve the above problems without such a strong security guarantee. We trade off the security and efficiency and construct an efficient semi-honest reverse unbalanced PSI-CA protocol to ensure only the large set owner gets the output in the reverse unbalanced scenario.

We describe a new "reverse unbalanced" scenario: "the client owns the larger set, the server owns the smaller set". The innovations and contributions of this paper are listed below.

1. We construct a pre-filtered PSI-CA with leakage resistance protocol in the reverse unbalanced scenario with low computation and communication.
2. Our protocol introduces the Cuckoo filter to resist malicious tampering behavior and the Hash-Prefix filter to reduce the large set size significantly.
3. We found the Hash-Prefix filter has a privacy leakage problem: "party with the large set can query the elements don't belong to the small set" and solve the privacy leakage problem via the idea of PIR. The protocol's security is proved in the semi-honest model under the DDH assumption.
4. We give implementation while introducing multi-threading and ECC to improve efficiency. Compared with the existing most efficient unbalanced PSI-CA protocol, we reduce communication by a factor of 8.48× and computation by a factor of 26.87×.

In addition, the proposed protocol has a significant advantage in efficiency as the gap in set size between the two parties becomes greater.

2 Related Work

The idea of PSI-CA was first proposed by Agrawal et al. [1] based on the DDH assumption and commutative encryption (CE) in the semi-honest model. Currently, PSI-CA can be divided into 4 types: PSI-CA based on oblivious polynomial evaluation(OPE) [15,16], PSI-CA based on BF [3,9–11,13], PSI-CA based on CE [1,8,19,20,24,26] and PSI-CA based on other techniques [11,19,26,27,35].

A. OPE-based PSI-CA. As for PSI-CA based on OPE, Freedman et al. [16] first constructed PSI-CA protocol based on OPE and additive homomorphic encryption. Then Hohenberger et al. [17] extended the protocol of [16] to a two-party PSI-CA protocol that can ensure semi-honest and malicious security without bilinear group, random oracle, or non-interactive zero knowledge proof, and the efficiency is same as [16]. Later, Camenisch et al. [5] constructed a fair two-party PSI-CA protocol for certified sets based on OPE. In 2016, Freedman et al. [15] optimized the protocol [16], which can ensure the security of semi-honest adversaries under the standard model and malicious adversaries under the random oracle model. Combined with cuckoo hashing, the computation cost was optimized to achieve linear complexity. However, for the main computation cost can't be pre-computed offline, the scalability in the unbalanced scenarios is poor.

B. BF-based PSI-CA. PSI-CA based on the Bloom filter was first proposed by Many et al. [25]. This scheme supports multiple participants and combines addition and multiplication in MPC with BF. Participants can estimate PSI-CA through the quantitative properties of BF, but the scheme is not secure because it divulges the private input of other participants. Ashok et al. [3] constructed a more efficient PSI-CA protocol for obtaining approximate output based on the quantitative properties of BF, but lacks simulation-based security proof. Egert et al. [13] pointed out the security problems of [3] and based on the idea of [3], combined with BF and ElGamal encryption, realized a secure PSI-CA against semi-honest adversaries. The advantage of this scheme is that the computational cost is concentrated on one side and can be extended in unbalanced scenarios, but this scheme sacrifices the accuracy of the output. In 2015, Debnath et al. [9] combined BF with Goldwasser-Micali (GM) encryption to construct a semi-honest PSI-CA protocol with linear complexity, the client's set size can be protected, part of the computation overhead can be transferred offline. However, the actual communication overhead in the online stage is linear to the large set, which can't be applied well in unbalanced scenarios. Later, Debnath et al. [10] constructed a malicious secure fair two-party PSI-CA protocol in the standard model based on the DDH assumption, but it's necessary to introduce a semi-honest arbitrator. Davidson et al. [7] combined BF and partially homomorphic encryption to realize PSI-CA protocol secure against semi-honest adversaries, but the online communication overhead is linear to the large set.

As for the implementation, the impact of the BF's length on the efficiency is not trivial, and some efficient schemes usually need to sacrifice the accuracy of outputs. Therefore, although they have somewhat scalability in the unbalanced scenarios, it has no significant advantages over CE-based schemes.

C. CE-based PSI-CA. Since the introduction of CE-based PSI-CA [1], on the one hand, some works research on the variants of PSI-CA, such as multi-party PSI-CA [39] and PSI-CA with the authenticated set. On the other hand, De Cristofaro et al. [8] proposed a new structure based on the CE, which benefits the scheme of Lv et al. [24]. Google [19] presented a variant scheme of PSI-CA based on the Pohlig-Hellman commutative encryption and Paillier homomorphic encryption to get the total money spent by the customers in the intersection. This scheme can compute the cardinality and the sum of the weights attached to the elements in the intersection. Later, Google also considered different constructions based on the DDH assumption, random Oblivious Transfer (ROT), and encrypted BF [19]. Recently, Miao et al. [26] proposed the first PSI-CA protocol secure against malicious adversaries.

In terms of the PSI-CA diversity scenario adaptation, Lv et al. [24] considered PSI-CA protocol in the unbalanced scenario for the first time, introduced BF based on the previous scheme [20] to optimize the communication, and made its communication complexity linear to the smaller set.

D. Other Paradigms. Other construction methods, such as the efficient two-party PSI-CA scheme based on Flajolet-Martin sketches proposed by Dong et al.

[11], achieves logarithmic computation and communication complexity but sacrifices the accuracy of the output. At the same time, the number of communication rounds is high and vulnerable to the network environment. Later, Cheng et al. [27] combined secret sharing and offline pre-computation, gave a semi-honest PSI-CA with efficient computation and constant communication rounds at the cost of result accuracy, and the actual communication overhead is larger than that of the CE based schemes.

Moreover, there have been many delegated PSI-CA protocols in these years [2,12,37,38], which can be used in the context of contact tracing to protect against linkage attacks and benefit by preventing the further spread of COVID-19 without violating individuals' privacy. Most of the protocols rely on the trusted cloud servers and are suitable for the scenario with a large number of parties in the network, so they are not within the scope of our scenario.

In this work, we pay attention to whether the previous schemes can be optimized in the (reverse) unbalanced scenarios. As is shown in Table 1, CE-based PSI-CA is more suitable for extension in the (reverse) unbalanced scenarios.

Table 1. Complexity and unbalanced scalability comparison among prior PSI-CA protocols based on different techniques. x is the server's set size, y is the client's set size, λ is PKE security parameter, k is the number of hash function used in BF, m is the length of BF, $m = 1.44k \cdot x$, d is the output length of hash function.

Based on	Reference	Total Comp.		Total Comm.		Accuracy	Adaptable
		Server	Client	Server	Client		
OPE	[16]	$O(xloglogy)$	$O(x+y)$	$O(x\lambda)$	$O(y\lambda)$	✓	✗
	[15]	$O(x)$	$O(x+y)$	$O(x\lambda)$	$O(y\lambda)$	✓	✗
BF	[13]	$O(2m+2)$	$O(2m)$	$O(1)$	$O((2m+1)\lambda)$	✗	✓
	[9]	$O(kx)$	$O(m+kx)$	$O(kx\lambda)$	$O(m\lambda)$	✓	✗
	[7]	$O(kx)$	$O(m+2x)$	$O(2x\lambda)$	$O(m\lambda)$	✓	✗
CE	[1]	$O(x+y)$	$O(x+y)$	$O(\lambda(x+y))$	$O(y\lambda)$	✓	✓
	[8]	$O(x+y)$	$O(2y)$	$O(xd+y\lambda)$	$O(y\lambda)$	✓	✓
	[24]	$O(x+y)$	$O(2y)$	$O(y\lambda+mx)$	$O(y\lambda)$	✓	✓

3 Preliminaries

3.1 Notations

We denote the parties as server (sender) S and client (receiver) R, and their respective input sets as $X = \{x_1, x_2, ..., x_{n_1}\}$ and $Y = \{y_1, y_2, ..., y_{n_2}\}$ with $|X| = n_1$ and $|Y| = n_2$, where n_2 is much larger than n_1. R receives $|X \cap Y|$ from the protocol, while S receives nothing. We set the symmetric security parameter as $\kappa = 128$, the asymmetric security parameter as $\lambda = 1024$, and elliptic curve size to 256 for SM2 curve. We set the false positive rate of Bloom filters and Cuckoo filters to $10^{-9} \approx 2^{-30}$. We choose SHA-256 as the hash function to implement random oracle and set the hash prefix length to 16 bits.

3.2 Cuckoo Filter

A Cuckoo filter [14] is a data structure similar to the Bloom filter for approximate set membership tests. The Cuckoo filter has practical advantages that:

1. The Cuckoo filter uses less space than the Bloom filter in many scenarios while having the same false positive probability;
2. The Cuckoo filter has better space locality and higher query efficiency;
3. The Cuckoo filter supports the deletion of elements.

Cuckoo filters have been applied in some unbalanced PSI schemes [21,33]. They combine the idea of cuckoo hashing [30] but store fingerprints of elements, which makes them have a lower storage overhead.

As for PSI-CA, Lv et al. [24] mentioned that the sender could maliciously set Bloom filters' bits from 0 to 1 to make the protocol output larger than the actual, which will damage the interests of the receiver in the business cooperation. However, Cuckoo filters can completely resist the malicious behavior. Even if the sender tries to fill the Cuckoo filters maliciously, the successful probability of malicious behavior is equal to the false positive rate of Cuckoo filters.

Indeed, an adversary can create false negatives by deleting some elements, but reducing the intersection cardinality is not conducive to him gaining more benefits in business cooperation or passing the identity authentication. Hence, the Cuckoo filters still have advantages.

3.3 Commutative Encryption

Similar to the definition of Agrawal et al. [1], we introduce the properties based on Pohlig-Hellman encryption. We assume the message and ciphertext space is $\mathcal{F}$, the key space is $\mathcal{K}$, and the commutative encryption f is a polynomial time computable function $f\colon \mathcal{K} \times \mathcal{F} \rightarrow \mathcal{F}$, which is defined on a computable domain satisfying the following properties. In addition $f_e(x) \equiv f(e,x)$ represents message x is encrypted through the key e, and $\in_r$ represents uniform random selection.

1. Commutativity: for all $e, e' \in \mathcal{K}$, $x \in \mathcal{F}$ we have
$$f_e(f_{e'}(x)) = f_{e'}(f_e(x)) \tag{1}$$
2. Each $f_e : \mathcal{F} \rightarrow \mathcal{F}$ is a bijection;
3. f_e^{-1} is computable in polynomial time given e;
4. The distribution of $(x, f_e(x), y, f_e(y))$ is indistinguishable from the distribution of $(x, f_e(x), y, z)$, where $x, y, z \in_r \mathcal{F}$, $e \in_r \mathcal{K}$.

Property 1 says that when we use two different key combinations for encryption, the result is the same regardless of the order. Property 2 says that two different values will never get the same value after encryption. Property 3 says that given a encrypted value $f_e(x)$ and encryption key e, we can get x in polynomial time. Property 4 says that given a value x and its encryption value $f_e(x)$ (but not the key e), for a new value y, we cannot distinguish $f_e(y)$ from random value z in polynomial time, which implies the Decisional Diffie-Hellman (DDH) assumption. This property holds only if x is randomly selected from $\mathcal{F}$. That is, the adversary cannot control the choice of x. Therefore, in the implementation of PSI-CA, we need to randomly map element v to the element $x = h(v)$ on $\mathcal{F}$ through hash function h to ensure that the security can be proved through property 4 [1]. We also need to assume hash function h is a random oracle.

Commutative encryption based on Pohlig-Hellman encryption has been used in PSI-CA schemes [1,8,24]. It is generally implemented on multiplication group G_P, where P is a big prime satisfying $\frac{P-1}{2}$ is also prime. We use ECC (SM2 curve) to improve computation and communication efficiency.

3.4 Hash-Prefix Filter

Hash-Prefix filter is an implementation method of k-anonymity. K-anonymity was first proposed by Samarati et al. [34] in 1998. A release of data is said to have the k-anonymity property if the information for each person contained in the release set K cannot be distinguished from at least $|K|-1$ individuals whose information also appear in the release. Hash-based k-anonymity works by taking a cryptographic hash of one dimensional data and truncating the hash such that there are at least $|K|-1$ hash collisions.

Generally, Hash-Prefix filter can be used as follows:

1. The small set owner calculates the hash values of its set, truncates the hash prefixes to form a prefix set, and sends them to the large set owner;
2. The large set owner calculates the hash prefixes of its elements and queries in the received prefix set through every element's prefix;
3. If the query result is null, the element will be filtered out, and after all elements are queried, a filtered set is generated.

Because the hash-prefix length is short, collisions between different elements happen frequently. For each prefix, we define the anonymity set of possible collisions in the plaintext space as K, and k-anonymity can be satisfied when $|K|$ reaches a certain threshold.

Currently, this technique is mainly used to check for breached password [23,31,36]. The existing compromised credential checking web services, such as HaveIBeenPwned [36], PasswordPing [31], and Google Password Checkup [36], they allow clients to detect whether their username-password pairs are at risk of being compromised. Thomas et al. [36] calculate the SHA-1 or SHA-256 hash function for the pair of username u and password p to obtain $H(u,p)$, and then truncate the t bits prefix $H(u,p)_{[0:t]}$ and send it to the server. Server compares the prefix to its local hash-prefix set $H(S)_{[0:t]} = \{H(u_1,p_1)_{[0:t]}, ..., H(u_n,p_n)_{[0:t]}\}$ can significantly reduce overhead, because a smaller available set S' is obtained and can be used for the subsequent PSI protocol.

However, introducing the Hash-Prefix filter also greatly reduces the complexity of adversaries cracking user passwords. Li et al. [23] pointed out that given the username and the username-password hash-prefix, there is a risk of adversaries damaging the security of clients' passwords. Thomas et al. [36] set the initial threshold to $|K| > 50000$ and combined it with an Inefficient Oracle to ensure the remote adversary cannot efficiently perform guessing attempts. So the choice of $|K|$ actually considers that the adversary can verify the guesses' correctness via login attempts.

Nevertheless, it is different for PSI-CA protocol. Because the output is only the cardinality of the intersection, the adversaries without the intersection content cannot explicitly verify guessing correctness through attempts. Thus the combination of PSI-CA and Hash-Prefix filter is a natural advantage.

The following Theorem 1 states the security definition of the combination of Hash-Prefix filter and commutative encryption in a formal way.

Theorem 1. *Let two elements $x_1, x_2 \in \mathcal{F}, x_1 \neq x_2$, compute their t bits hash-prefixes $H(x_1)_{[0:t]}, H(x_2)_{[0:t]}$, where $H{:}\{0,1\}^* \rightarrow \mathcal{F}$ is a random oracle and $H(x_1)_{[0:t]} = H(x_2)_{[0:t]}$, t is the bit-length of the prefix. We assume there is a common random parameter $s \in_r \mathcal{F}$, a random element $r \in_r \mathcal{F}$ and a private key $a \in_r \mathcal{K}$, satisfies:*

$$D(f_a(H(s, x_1))) \overset{C}{\equiv} D(f_a(H(s, x_2))) \overset{C}{\equiv} D(r) \tag{2}$$

That is, given the hash-prefixes of the two elements are the same, the distributions of $f_a(H(s, x_1))$, $f_a(H(s, x_2))$ and r are computationally indistinguishable in polynomial time to PPT adversary.

Proof. $H(x_1)$,$H(x_2)$ and r are distinguishable and don't meet uniform distribution given the extra information $H(x_1)_{[0:t]} = H(x_2)_{[0:t]}$, which means the adversary controls the choice of elements to some extent, so the Property 4 of CE (Sect. 3.3) can't be met. To fix this, we introduce s and compute $H(s, x_1)$, $H(s, x_2)$, because according to the random oracle assumption, $H(x_1)_{[0:t]}$, $H(x_2)_{[0:t]}$ can't benefit predicting the output of $H(s, x_1)$, $H(s, x_2)$. So $H(s, x_1)$, $H(s, x_2)$ and r are uniform and indistinguishable from each other. And the distribution of $f_a(H(s, x_1))$, $f_a(H(s, x_2))$ and r are computationally indistinguishable in polynomial time to PPT adversary.

The prefix length should be adjusted with the plaintext space size and the smaller set size n_1. Let us discuss how to set these parameters. Let $n_1 = 2^{10}, n_2 = 2^{20}$, assume the plaintext (phone number) space size is 2^{32}, and the prefix length is 16 bits, thus the size of the anonymity set K is $|K| = 2^{32}/2^{16} = 65536$, and larger than 50000 suggested in [36].

In theory, the prefix set of the large set can easily cover all possible prefixes (i.e., $0 \times 0000{\sim}0 \times \mathrm{FFFF}$), because n_2 is much larger than 2^{16}. However, if we suppose the size of the smaller set $n_1 > 2^{16}$ and prefix length is still 16 bits, the expected collision number of each prefix will be larger than 1, which will make the Hash-Prefix filter have no effect in theory (i.e., two sides both have all possible prefixes, so all the elements of the large set owner won't be filtered out). Therefore, we should note that when $n_1 > 2^{prefix-length}$, the prefix length should be increased to at least $log n_1 + 1$ bits to guarantee the effect of the filter.

3.5 The Semi-honest Model

In this model, the adversary controls one of the parties and follows the protocol specification, and tries to learn additional information from the received messages. The following definition is according to [15,24].

Let S and R denote the two parties with inputs X, Y respectively, $F = (F_S, F_R)$ is a two-party function, and let π be a two-party protocol for computing F. The view of S in an execution of π on inputs (X, Y) is

$$View_{\pi,S}(X, Y) = (X, r_S, m_1, ..., m_t), \tag{3}$$

where r_S is the content of the party S's internal random tape and m_i represents the ith message it receives. The output of R can be computed from its view and is denoted $Output_{\pi,R}(X, Y)$.

In the semi-honest model, π is safe if any information computed by the parties can only be obtained from its input and output. The security based on simulation requires that any party's view in protocol execution can be simulated only given its input and output. The definition of the semi-honest model is as follows:

Definition 1. *F and π are defined as above. Protocol π is said to securely compute F in the presence of semi-honest adversaries if there exists probabilistic polynomial time algorithm Sim_S and Sim_R such that*

$$\begin{aligned}&(Sim_S(X, F_S(k, X, Y)), F_R(k, X, Y))_{k\in\mathbb{N},X,Y\in\{0,1\}^*}\\ &\overset{C}{\equiv} \{(View_{\pi,S}(k, X, Y), Output_{\pi,R}(k, X, Y))\}_{k\in\mathbb{N},X,Y\in\{0,1\}^*}\end{aligned} \tag{4}$$

$$\begin{aligned}&(F_S(k, X, Y), Sim_R(Y, F_R(k, X, Y)))_{k\in\mathbb{N},X,Y\in\{0,1\}^*}\\ &\overset{C}{\equiv} \{(Output_{\pi,S}(k, X, Y), View_{\pi,R}(k, X, Y))\}_{k\in\mathbb{N},X,Y\in\{0,1\}^*}\end{aligned} \tag{5}$$

where k is the security parameter.

4 Our Proposal

We combined the technologies mentioned above to optimize the basic protocol [1] to be efficient in the reverse unbalanced scenario, and we get the pre-filter reverse unbalanced protocol with leakage resistance, denoted as π_{CA} protocol. The π_{CA} protocol is divided into online and offline phases and is shown in Fig. 1.

In this paper, we regard the operation that can be precomputed or reused as the offline phase. As shown in Fig. 1, Private Information Retrieval belongs to the offline phase and involves the inputs of both parties. Furthermore, the PIR stage can be reused in the "one-to-many" (one large set owner, many small set owners) scenario. Such as the anonymous identity authentication scenario, the server (receiver) may need to authenticate many users (sender).

Parameters: λ is asymmetric security parameter, H_1:$\{0,1\}^{\sigma+\kappa} \rightarrow \{0,1\}^{256}$ and H_2:$\{0,1\}^{\sigma} \rightarrow \{0,1\}^{256}$ are random oracles, $s \in \{0,1\}^{\kappa}$ is public random parameter, ω is the bit-length of the hash prefix. Y' is the filtered set of Y, and its size is $|Y'| = n'$.
Input: S inputs set $X, |X| = n_1, x_i \in \{0,1\}^{\sigma}(i \in [n_1], \sigma = poly(\kappa))$, R inputs set $Y, |Y| = n_2, y_j \in \{0,1\}^{\sigma}(j \in [n_2])$, n_2 is much larger than n_1.
Output: R outputs $|X \cap Y|$; S outputs $\perp$.

Offline Phase

Pre-computation

1. S and R generate keys $e_S \in_r \mathcal{K}$ and $e_R \in_r \mathcal{K}$, then calculate function H_1 of X and Y to obtain $X_{H_1} = H_1(s, X)$ and $Y_{H_1} = H_1(s, Y)$ respectively.
2. Both parties encrypt the hashed set:

$$X_S = f_{e_S}(X_{H_1}) = f_{e_S}(H_1(s, X))$$

$$Y_R = f_{e_R}(Y_{H_1}) = f_{e_R}(H_1(s, Y))$$

Private Information Retrieval

1. R calculates $H_2(Y)$ and truncates ω bits as prefix to get set $H_2(Y)_{[0:\omega]}$, and generates pair set $Y_{pair} = (Y_{H_2}, Y_R) = (H_2(y_j)_{[0:\omega]}, f_{e_R}(H_1(s, y_j))), j \in [n_2]$. Finally R sends Y_{pair} to S in a shuffled order;
2. S filters the set Y_{pair} according to the first item Y_{H_2} comparing with $H_2(X)_{[0:\omega]}$, then S can pick all the second items Y'_R of the filtered set $Y'_{pair} = (Y'_{H_2}, Y'_R)$, where $Y'_R = f_{e_R}(H_1(s, Y')) = f_{e_R}(H_1(s, y_\phi))(\phi \in [n'], H_2(y_\phi)_{[0:\omega]} \in H_2(X)_{[0:\omega]})$;
3. S encrypts Y'_R and get $[Y'_R]_S = f_{e_S}(Y'_R) = f_{e_S}(f_{e_R}(H_1(s, Y')))$, then maps all ciphertexts into the Cuckoo filter CF_S.

Online Phase

1. S sends X_S to R in a shuffled order;
2. S sends CF_S to R;
3. R encrypts X_S with e_R to get $[X_S]_R = f_{e_R}(f_{e_S}(H_1(s, X)))$, and queries the received CF_S to get $|X \cap Y|$.

Update

1. S prepares update set $Z = \{z_1, ..., z_{n_3}\}$, computes $f_{e_S}(H_1(s, Z)) = \{f_{e_S}(H_1(s, z_1)), ..., f_{e_S}(H_1(s, z_1))\}$ and sends $f_{e_S}(H_1(s, Z))$ with related information $\{update_1, ..., update_{n_3}\}$ to R;
2. R encrypts $f_{e_S}(H_1(s, Z))$ and get $f_{e_R}(f_{e_S}(H_1(s, Z)))$;
3. $\forall i, 1 \leq i \leq n_3$, R execute insertion or deletion upon $f_{e_R}(f_{e_S}(H_1(s, z_i)))$ according to the related information $update_i$. If $update_i == INSERT$, R insert $f_{e_R}(f_{e_S}(H_1(s, z_i)))$ into CF_S. Else if $update_i == DELETE$, R delete $f_{e_R}(f_{e_S}(H_1(s, z_i)))$ from CF_S.

Fig. 1. The pre-filter reverse unbalanced PSI-CA protocol π_{CA}

The π_{CA} protocol is characterized in realizing data compression through the Cuckoo filter and Hash-Prefix filter. Compared with the existing unbalanced PSI-CA protocol [24], it has significant advantages in the reverse unbalanced scenario. In terms of security, it can be seen from Sect. 3.4 that under reasonable parameters, the Hash-Prefix filter meets the k-anonymity privacy. At the same time, it can be seen from Theorem 1 that for the filtered set, when calculating the hashes of elements, it is necessary to introduce the (random and not fixed) public parameter s and calculate $H_1(s, X)$, $H_1(s, Y)$ to ensure that the encrypted ciphertext is computationally indistinguishable from the randomness based on the properties of the commutative encryption.

However, during the construction of the protocol, we notice that if we apply the Hash-Prefix filter in the way suggested in Sect. 3.4, i.e., let the small set owner S generate prefix set and send it to the large set owner R, R will be able to query which elements do not belong to X through the received prefixes. Although this does not directly leak the privacy of X, it still leaks additional information compared with those PSI-CA protocols without Hash-Prefix filter.

Therefore, to protect the privacy of small set owner S, we introduce the idea of PIR. As for the simplest implementation of PIR [6]: the large set owner (server) sends all the encrypted data set to the small set owner (client), then the client can retrieve its selected item locally, which protects the query privacy of the client. Thus corresponding to the reverse unbalanced scenario in Fig. 1, we let the large set owner R send Y_{pair} to S, then S completes the Hash-Prefix filter operation on the received ciphertext set through the hash prefix, and this is the optimal PIR scheme in this scenario. The introduction of PIR resists the leakage of S's privacy, and R's privacy is also protected based on the assumption that the prefix set Y_{H_2} of R can cover all possible prefixes (i.e., $0 \times 0000 \sim 0 \times \text{FFFF}$) with overwhelming possibility. Thus S cannot query which elements don't belong to Y through the hash prefixes. The abstract protocol is shown in Fig. 2.

However, compared with the way that S directly sends the prefix set to R (without PIR), the introduction of PIR solves the privacy leakage at the expense of additional communication (i.e., R needs to send the whole encrypted set and prefix set to S). Nevertheless, in the reverse unbalanced scenario, the protocol [24] also needs R to send the whole encrypted set to S. So compared with [24], PIR doesn't bring much additional communication in the reverse unbalanced scenario, and the Hash-Prefix filter can still perform its efficiency advantage.

Meanwhile, it should be noted that the pair set Y_{pair} of R doesn't need to be regenerated in every setup and can be reused many times, so they have more advantages in scenarios that need to be performed multiple times. For example, in the anonymous authentication scenario, all users can download the server's pair set in advance. Each time they log in, they only need to execute the online phase to complete the authentication. In ads conversion rate computation, a merchant may cooperate with multiple advertisers holding small sets, so there is also a need for multiple executions in practice.

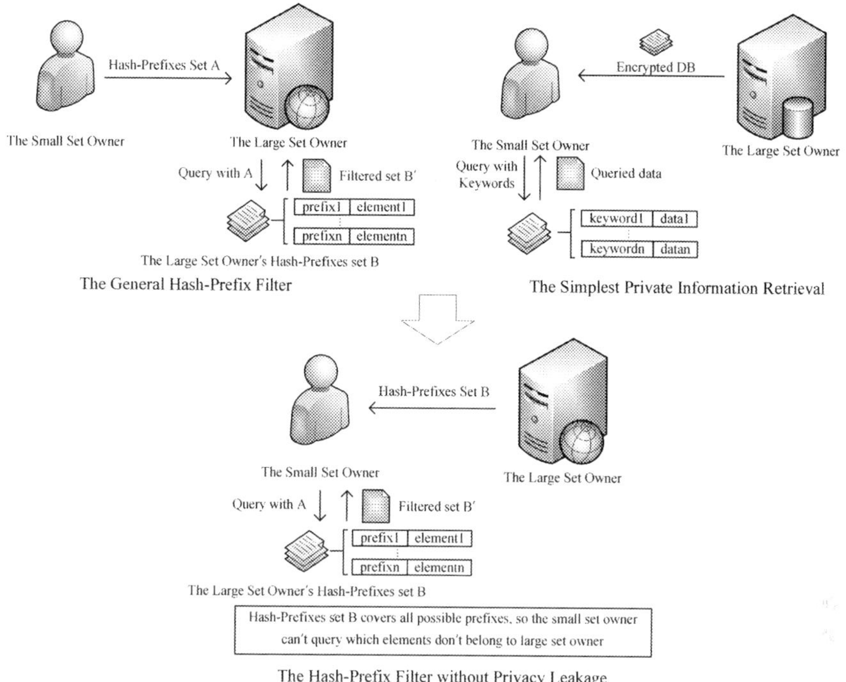

Fig. 2. The combination of Hash-Prefix filter and PIR

5 Security Analysis

This section gives the security proof of the π_{CA} protocol based on the DDH and the RO assumption in Sect. 4 and proves that the π_{CA} protocol is secure in the semi-honest model under the DDH assumption. Similar to the proof of Agrawal et al. [1], we give a simulator, which can ensure that each party's simulated view and real view are computationally indistinguishable given the input of the parties and the cardinality of the intersection.

Theorem 2. *Let X and Y be the sets from input fields, $|X| = n_1, |Y| = n_2$. They are inputs of S and R respectively, where $n_1 << n_2$. The intersection cardinality computation function F is defined as:*

$$F(X, Y) = (F_S(X, Y), F_R(X, Y)) = (\perp, |X \cap Y|) \tag{6}$$

Given the commutative encryption in Sect. 3.3 and the random oracle, π_{CA} protocol (Sect. 4) can securely compute F in the semi-honest model. At the end of the protocol, except for their respective inputs, S only knows $|Y|$ and $H_1(s, Y)_{[0:\omega]}$, and R only knows $|X|$ and $|X \cap Y|$.

Proof. The security proof refers to the standard secure multi-party computation proof method in [1]. If for any X and Y, the distribution of the S's view of the protocol(the information S gets from R) cannot be distinguished from a simulation of this view that uses only V_S and $|V_R|$, then clearly S cannot learn anything from the inputs it gets from R except for Y. Note that the simulation only uses the knowledge S or R is supposed to have at the end of the protocol.

Construct S's simulator Sim_S(simulate the information S gets from R): Sim_S only needs to use $|Y| = n_2$. At step 1 of Private Information Retrieval, the only step where S receives anything, the simulator Sim_S generates n_2 uniform random values $z_i \in_r \mathcal{F}(i \in [n_2])$, and $n_2\omega$ bits random values h_i to form pairs (h_i, z_i), and sends them to S with lexicographical order. According to Theorem 1, in the real view, when prefix $H_2(y_i)_{[0:\omega]}$ is specified, $f_{e_R}(H_1(s, y_i))$ is indistinguishable from the distribution of uniform values, so the distinguisher cannot distinguish $(H_2(y_i)_{[0:\omega]}, z_i)$ and $(H_2(y_i)_{[0:\omega]}, f_{e_R}(H_1(s, y_i)))$. Furthermore, for h_i is uniformly generated, and its distribution is indistinguishable from $H_2(y_i)_{[0:\omega]}$, the distinguisher cannot distinguish (h_i, z_i) and $(H_2(y_i)_{[0:\omega]}, f_{e_R}(H_1(s, y_i)))$. So the simulated view and real view of S are indistinguishable.

In addition, S obtained the prefix set $H_1(s, Y)_{[0:\omega]}$, which somewhat leaks the information of $H_1(s, Y)$ and makes S have a higher probability of learning which elements in the set Y through $H_1(s, X)$. However, even if traversing the whole plaintext space, S can only get an inaccurate set that is large enough to meet the k-anonymity privacy mentioned in Sect. 3.4. Furthermore, based on the characteristics of PSI-CA, the adversary has no chance to verify its guess.

Construct R's simulator Sim_R(simulate the information R gets from S): assume Y' is Y's filtered set, the information Sim_R needs to use include $|X|, Y, |X \cap Y|, H_1, e_R, s$, and it does not know $X - Y'$ and $X \cap Y'$, now assume that:

$$X = \{w_1, ..., w_t, w_{t+1}, ..., w_{n_1}\} \tag{7}$$

$$Y' = \{w_{t+1}, ..., w_{n_1}, w_{n_1+1}, ..., w_\alpha\} \tag{8}$$

where $t = |X - Y'|, n_1 = |X|, \alpha = |X \cup Y'|$. Sim_R generates α random values $v_1, ..., v_\alpha \in_r \mathcal{F}$ to replace $f_{e_S}(H_1(s, w)), w \in X \cup Y'$. At step 1 of online phase, Sim_R selects n_1 values $v_1, ..., v_{n_1}$ to form a set $V_S = \{v_1, ..., v_{n_1}\}$, replaces X_S and sends to R. According to the properties of commutative encryption (Sect. 3.3), without knowing e_S, the distribution of $f_{e_S}(H_1(s, w_j)), j \in [n_1]$ and v_j are indistinguishable. At step 2 of online phase, Sim_R selects set $\{v_{t+1}, ..., v_\alpha\}$ and computes f_{e_R}:

$$V_R = \{f_{e_R}(v_{t+1}), ..., f_{e_R}(v_\alpha)\} \tag{9}$$

Sim_R maps set V_R into Cuckoo filter CF_S, and sends CF_S to R. In the real view, CF_S just stores the fingerprints of $f_{e_S}(f_{e_R}(H_1(s, Y')))$. The mapping location and the stored fingerprints are random mappings and will not leak information other than the stored content itself. According to the properties of commutative encryption, the distribution between $f_{e_S}(f_{e_R}(H_1(s, Y')))$ and $V_R = \{f_{e_R}(v_{t+1}), ..., f_{e_R}(v_\alpha)\}$ are indistinguishable. Thus it can be concluded that the simulated view of R is indistinguishable from the real view.

In summary, the simulated view and the real view of S and R are indistinguishable, so the security of π_{CA} protocol in the semi-honest model is proved.

6 Performance Evaluation

In this section, we compare and analyze the unbalanced PSI-CA protocol [24] and the π_{CA} protocol in Sect. 4 from complexity and overhead. Our implementation is available online[1].

6.1 Complexity Analysis

It can be seen from Table 2 that in the reverse unbalanced scenario, the computation and communication complexity of the π_{CA} protocol is better than the unbalanced PSI-CA [24]. Based on the Hash-Prefix filter technology, the more significant the gap in set size between the two parties, the more efficient π_{CA} is. Based on the ECC, the communication is reduced by factor 4× compared with the protocol based on the Pohlig-Hellman encryption.

Table 2. The sender holds set X, and the receiver holds set Y, $|Y| \gg |X|$, suppose π_{CA} use ECC, λ is public key security parameter; ω is the bit length of the hash prefix, and the value can be referred to Sect. 3.4.

Protocol	Computation		Communication	
	Server	Client	Server	Client
Unbalanced PSI-CA [24]	$O(\|X\| + \|Y\|)$	$O(2\|Y\|)$	$O(\lambda\|Y\|)$	$O(\lambda\|Y\|)$
π_{CA}(ECC)	$O(\|X\| + \frac{\|Y\|}{2^\omega/\|X\|})$	$O(\|X\| + \|Y\|)$	$O(\frac{\lambda}{4}\|X\|)$	$O(\frac{\lambda}{4}\|Y\|)$

We need to explain further how the Server's computation complexity $O(|X|+\frac{|Y|}{2^\omega/|X|})$ is computed: Firstly, through the receiver's set size $|Y|$ and ω bits prefix, we can get the expected number of collisions of each prefix is $\frac{|Y|}{2^\omega}$. Secondly, through the sender's set size $|X|(|X| < 2^\omega)$, we can get the expected number of sender's prefixes is $|X|$, so after the Hash-Prefix filter, the sender will retain $|X|$ groups of elements, i.e., $\frac{|Y|}{2^\omega} \cdot |X| = \frac{|Y|}{2^\omega/|X|}$ for subsequent computation.

Therefore, the Hash-Prefix filter also has the feature that given prefix length and $|Y|$, the smaller $|X|$ is, the better the filtering effect is. Moreover, As for the scenario $|X| = 1$, such as anonymous identity authentication, the effect of the Hash-Prefix filter can reach the best.

[1] https://github.com/liugezi/PSI-CA-Framework.

6.2 Environment and Parameters

In the PC setting, the protocols were implemented in Java, with AMD ryzen 7 4800H with Radeon graphics @ 2.90 GHz CPUs, 16 GB of RAM, we use up to 8 threads. The experimental environment is local network (LAN), and we analyze the performance in the WAN environment via communication overhead. The protocols are implemented in Java. We realize the relevant operation of elliptic curve cryptography based on BouncyCastle library[2], Cuckoo filters using cuckoofilter4j library[3], and Bloom filters using Orestes-Bloomfilter library[4].

6.3 Overhead Analysis

Firstly, we compare the computation and communication efficiency of π_{CA} protocol with the unbalanced PSI-CA protocol [24] in the reverse unbalanced scenario, and details are shown in Table 3.

Table 3. Overhead comparison of π_{CA} and unbalanced PSI-CA

Protocol	$\|X\|$	$\|Y\|$	Running time (seconds)						Communication (KB)		
			$T = 1$		$T = 4$		$T = 8$		Sender	Receiver	Total
			Total	Online	Total	Online	Total	Online			
π_{CA}	2^{10}	2^{16}	23.33	0.25	6.49	0.17	4.02	0.18	78	4,672	4,750
		2^{18}	92.57	0.90	23.94	0.40	13.81	0.38	102	18,688	18,790
		2^{20}	353.78	3.29	95.69	1.32	52.02	0.79	198	74,752	74,950
	2^{15}	2^{16}	40.41	6.53	11.27	2.10	7.42	1.70	2,306	4,672	6,978
		2^{18}	119.56	20.40	32.00	5.56	18.97	3.68	2,680	18,688	21,368
		2^{20}	451.43	80.04	118.16	21.44	64.68	11.34	4,226	74,752	78,978
[24]	2^{10}	2^{16}	88.15	59.20	23.33	15.82	12.30	8.48	19,868	19,861	39,729
		2^{18}	352.93	236.91	92.45	62.85	47.33	33.06	79,402	79,395	158,797
		2^{20}	1397.77	936.23	373.28	253.22	190.95	133.91	317,764	317,757	635,521
	2^{15}	2^{16}	89.06	59.84	24.18	16.20	13.43	8.39	20,035	19,860	39,895
		2^{18}	354.22	238.33	95.25	64.65	48.91	33.42	79,570	79,395	158,965
		2^{20}	1418.82	953.28	382.46	261.42	194.75	135.58	317,904	317,728	635,632

As for the computation overhead, in the reverse unbalanced scenario, the overall running efficiency of π_{CA} protocol is about 2.2–3.95× of [24] protocol. Furthermore, if π_{CA} under 8 threads is compared with the [24] protocol without multi-threading optimization, the efficiency of π_{CA} is improved by factor 21.92–26.87×. For the characteristics of the Hash-Prefix filter technology, the greater difference in set size between the two parties, the optimization efficiency of π_{CA} protocol is higher than that of previous schemes [24]. With the increase in the number of threads, given $|Y| = 2^{20}, |X| = 2^{10}$, the overall efficiency of π_{CA} protocol is optimized from 353.78 to 52.02 s, which is 6.8× higher than that without multi-threading technology. For the online phase, the efficiency of π_{CA} is

[2] https://www.bouncycastle.org/java.html.
[3] https://github.com/MGunlogson/CuckooFilter4J.
[4] https://github.com/Baqend/Orestes-Bloomfilter.

about 4.9–284.7× higher than that of [24], and the efficiency advantage increases with the increase of the difference between the two sets. π_{CA} transfers the Pre-filter and the filtered encryption operation offline to better fit the scenarios that need to execute the protocol multiple times. Therefore, the online phase overhead comparison in Table 3 only represents the comparison results under the online and offline phase division method in this work. But it's not hard to see that even if all the running processes of π_{CA} protocol are regarded as online phase, its efficiency is also obviously better than that of Lv et al. [24].

As for the communication overhead, the overall communication efficiency of π_{CA} is 5.71–8.48× greater than that of the unbalanced PSI-CA; The sender's communication efficiency of π_{CA} is 8.69–1604.87× greater than that of the unbalanced PSI-CA; The receiver's communication efficiency of π_{CA} is 4.25× greater than that of the unbalanced PSI-CA protocol. The optimization degree of the sender's communication efficiency varies greatly because the Hash-Prefix filter's effect determines the overhead. When the set size of the two parties differs significantly, the filter effect will be better. The communication efficiency optimization of the receiver mainly comes from using ECC to reduce the ciphertext length, so the optimization range is relatively stable.

Next, we implement [24] and π_{CA} in the unbalanced and reverse unbalanced scenarios respectively to compare efficiency. We set the same set size and security but different receivers to examine if π_{CA} performs better than [24] in their own scenarios. This means that they can form an efficient semi-honest PSI-CA framework dealing with different scenarios, and details are shown in Table 4.

Table 4. Overhead comparison of π_{CA} and unbalanced PSI-CA in their own scenarios

Protocol	$\|X\|$	$\|Y\|$	Running time (seconds)						Communication (KB)		
			$T = 1$		$T = 4$		$T = 8$		Sender	Receiver	Total
			Total	Online	Total	Online	Total	Online			
[24]	2^{16}	2^{10}	29.89	0.98	7.50	0.32	2.93	0.27	658	311	969
	2^{18}		117.30	0.97	29.97	0.32	13.69	0.19	1,692	311	2,003
	2^{20}		467.96	0.94	119.13	0.27	56.98	0.30	5,834	311	6,145
	2^{16}	2^{15}	59.27	30.06	15.75	8.18	9.08	4.33	10,279	9,932	20,211
	2^{18}		146.11	29.81	37.92	8.27	18.99	4.45	11,309	9,932	21,241
	2^{20}		496.67	30.07	128.92	8.25	62.36	4.53	15,447	9,932	25,379
π_{CA}	2^{10}	2^{16}	23.33	0.25	6.49	0.17	4.02	0.18	78	4,672	4,750
		2^{18}	92.57	0.90	23.94	0.40	13.81	0.38	102	18,688	18,790
		2^{20}	353.78	3.29	95.69	1.32	52.02	0.79	198	74,752	74,950
	2^{15}	2^{16}	40.41	6.53	11.27	2.10	7.42	1.70	2,306	4,672	6,978
		2^{18}	119.56	20.40	32.00	5.56	18.97	3.68	2,680	18,688	21,368
		2^{20}	451.43	80.04	118.16	21.44	64.68	11.34	4,226	74,752	78,978

As for computation, the overall performance of π_{CA} is 1.52 $\sim$ 46.63× better than [24] in their own scenarios. In the online phase, π_{CA} is generally more efficient than [24] after combining multi-threading technology. Therefore, π_{CA}

can serve as the complement in the reverse unbalanced scenario and form an efficient semi-honest PSI-CA framework with [24].

As for communication, compare the communication efficiency of π_{CA} and the unbalanced PSI-CA in their own scenarios, the unbalanced PSI-CA protocol is more efficient in most cases, which is 0.35–12.20× more efficient than π_{CA}. So the communication overhead is the bottleneck of π_{CA}.

However, most communication overhead of π_{CA} is completed offline. If we only consider online communication, the gap between the unbalanced and the reverse unbalanced scenarios is not large. Therefore, from the perspective of practicality, π_{CA} and the unbalanced PSI-CA can form an efficient semi-honest PSI-CA framework dealing with different scenarios.

6.4 Feasibility Analysis of Anonymous Identity Authentication

Anonymous identity authentication is an important application of the reverse unbalanced PSI-CA. The server (receiver) owning a large set should obtain the output of user authentication, while the user (sender) holds a small set with just 1 element. Moreover, in this scenario, a large number of users need to call the reverse unbalanced PSI-CA protocol, so the overhead in the online phase is particularly important. We conducted experiments specifically for anonymous identity authentication. The overhead is shown in Table 5.

Table 5. Anonymous identity authentication overhead analysis table

Protocol	$\|X\|$	$\|Y\|$	Running time(seconds)						Communication(KB)	
			$T = 1$		$T = 4$		$T = 8$		Sender	Receiver
			Total	Online	Total	Online	Total	Online		
π_{CA}	1	2^{18}	88.65	0.069	23.45	0.076	13.43	0.077	4	18,688
		2^{20}	361.10	0.073	92.27	0.073	50.61	0.082	4	74,752
		2^{22}	1456.31	0.092	376.14	0.085	200.61	0.102	4	299,008

As for computation, no matter how the size of the receiver set increases, the running of the online phase is almost constant and efficient, which is only 69–92 ms. The abnormal change in the running time of the online phase with the thread is caused by the normal error of computer performance fluctuation.

Based on the characteristics of the scenario itself, the advantage that "the more significant the gap in set size between the two parties, the more efficient π_{CA} is" (Sect. 6.1) plays an important role. For the size of the small set is only 1, the effect of the Hash-Prefix filter can be very significant. In practice, all users can download the server's "prefix-ciphertext" pair locally in advance and complete the filter and pre-computation. The experiment shows that even for the server with the size of 2^{22}, the offline phase can be completed in only 200.614 s, and the offline phase only needs to be executed once for each user. Later, even if many users need to access the server simultaneously, they just need to execute an efficient online phase to complete authentication.

As for communication, based on the Hash-Prefix filter, the sender's communication overhead is significantly optimized. The sender's communication overhead does not change significantly with the increase of the receiver's set size. Although the receiver's communication overhead increases with $|Y|$, almost all overhead is completed offline. Therefore π_{CA} can also ensure the efficiency in the WAN.

7 Conclusions

We investigate the new "reverse unbalanced" scenario that "the server owns a small set, the client owns a large set" and constructs an efficient reverse unbalanced PSI-CA protocol in the semi-honest model under the DDH assumption, which introduces the Cuckoo filter, Hash-Prefix filter, multi-threading, and ECC. Meanwhile, we solve the privacy leakage problem through PIR, making the Hash-Prefix filter more secure and available in PSI-CA. Finally, we conduct experiments to evaluate the efficiency advantage of our protocol in the reverse unbalanced scenario.

The unbalanced PSI-CA and the reverse unbalanced PSI-CA both have significant advantages in their own scenarios and complement each other. Therefore, they can be further combined to form a scalable PSI-CA framework, which can give efficient implementation according to the practical requirements.

In future work, we plan to solve our protocol's bottleneck in communication (e.g., how to optimize the communication of the whole encrypted set) and consider how to solve the privacy leakage problem at the least cost.

References

1. Agrawal, R., Evfimievski, A., Srikant, R.: Information sharing across private databases. In: Proceedings of the 2003 ACM SIGMOD International Conference on Management of data, pp. 86–97 (2003)
2. Ahmed, N., et al.: A survey of COVID-19 contact tracing apps. IEEE Access **8**, 134577–134601 (2020)
3. Ashok, V.G., Mukkamala, R.: A scalable and efficient privacy preserving global itemset support approximation using bloom filters. In: Atluri, V., Pernul, G. (eds.) DBSec 2014. LNCS, vol. 8566, pp. 382–389. Springer, Heidelberg (2014). https://doi.org/10.1007/978-3-662-43936-4_26
4. Baldi, P., Baronio, R., De Cristofaro, E., Gasti, P., Tsudik, G.: Countering Gattaca: efficient and secure testing of fully-sequenced human genomes. In: Proceedings of the 18th ACM Conference on Computer and Communications Security, pp. 691–702 (2011)
5. Camenisch, J., Zaverucha, G.M.: Private intersection of certified sets. In: Dingledine, R., Golle, P. (eds.) FC 2009. LNCS, vol. 5628, pp. 108–127. Springer, Heidelberg (2009). https://doi.org/10.1007/978-3-642-03549-4_7
6. Chor, B., Goldreich, O., Kushilevitz, E., Sudan, M.: Private information retrieval. In: Proceedings of IEEE 36th Annual Foundations of Computer Science, pp. 41–50. IEEE (1995)

7. Davidson, A., Cid, C.: An efficient toolkit for computing private set operations. In: Pieprzyk, J., Suriadi, S. (eds.) ACISP 2017. LNCS, vol. 10343, pp. 261–278. Springer, Cham (2017). https://doi.org/10.1007/978-3-319-59870-3_15
8. De Cristofaro, E., Gasti, P., Tsudik, G.: Fast and private computation of cardinality of set intersection and union. In: Pieprzyk, J., Sadeghi, A.-R., Manulis, M. (eds.) CANS 2012. LNCS, vol. 7712, pp. 218–231. Springer, Heidelberg (2012). https://doi.org/10.1007/978-3-642-35404-5_17
9. Debnath, S.K., Dutta, R.: Secure and efficient private set intersection cardinality using bloom filter. In: Lopez, J., Mitchell, C.J. (eds.) ISC 2015. LNCS, vol. 9290, pp. 209–226. Springer, Cham (2015). https://doi.org/10.1007/978-3-319-23318-5_12
10. Debnath, S.K., Dutta, R.: Provably secure fair mutual private set intersection cardinality utilizing bloom filter. In: Chen, K., Lin, D., Yung, M. (eds.) Inscrypt 2016. LNCS, vol. 10143, pp. 505–525. Springer, Cham (2017). https://doi.org/10.1007/978-3-319-54705-3_31
11. Dong, C., Loukides, G.: Approximating private set union/intersection cardinality with logarithmic complexity. IEEE Trans. Inf. Forensics Secur. **12**(11), 2792–2806 (2017)
12. Duong, T., Phan, D.H., Trieu, N.: Catalic: delegated PSI cardinality with applications to contact tracing. In: Moriai, S., Wang, H. (eds.) ASIACRYPT 2020. LNCS, vol. 12493, pp. 870–899. Springer, Cham (2020). https://doi.org/10.1007/978-3-030-64840-4_29
13. Egert, R., Fischlin, M., Gens, D., Jacob, S., Senker, M., Tillmanns, J.: Privately computing set-union and set-intersection cardinality via bloom filters. In: Foo, E., Stebila, D. (eds.) ACISP 2015. LNCS, vol. 9144, pp. 413–430. Springer, Cham (2015). https://doi.org/10.1007/978-3-319-19962-7_24
14. Fan, B., Andersen, D.G., Kaminsky, M., Mitzenmacher, M.D.: Cuckoo filter: practically better than bloom. In: Proceedings of the 10th ACM International on Conference on Emerging Networking Experiments and Technologies, pp. 75–88 (2014)
15. Freedman, M.J., Hazay, C., Nissim, K., Pinkas, B.: Efficient set intersection with simulation-based security. J. Cryptol. **29**(1), 115–155 (2016). https://doi.org/10.1007/s00145-014-9190-0
16. Freedman, M.J., Nissim, K., Pinkas, B.: Efficient private matching and set intersection. In: Cachin, C., Camenisch, J.L. (eds.) EUROCRYPT 2004. LNCS, vol. 3027, pp. 1–19. Springer, Heidelberg (2004). https://doi.org/10.1007/978-3-540-24676-3_1
17. Hohenberger, S., Weis, S.A.: Honest-verifier private disjointness testing without random oracles. In: Danezis, G., Golle, P. (eds.) PET 2006. LNCS, vol. 4258, pp. 277–294. Springer, Heidelberg (2006). https://doi.org/10.1007/11957454_16
18. Huberman, B.A., Franklin, M., Hogg, T.: Enhancing privacy and trust in electronic communities. In: Proceedings of the 1st ACM Conference on Electronic Commerce, pp. 78–86 (1999)
19. Ion, M., et al.: On deploying secure computing: private intersection-sum-with-cardinality. In: 2020 IEEE European Symposium on Security and Privacy (EuroS&P), pp. 370–389. IEEE (2020)
20. Ion, M., et al.: Private intersection-sum protocol with applications to attributing aggregate ad conversions. IACR Cryptol. ePrint Arch. **2017**, 738 (2017)
21. Kales, D., Rechberger, C., Schneider, T., Senker, M., Weinert, C.: Mobile private contact discovery at scale. In: 28th {USENIX} Security Symposium ({USENIX} Security 19), pp. 1447–1464 (2019)

22. Kiss, Á., Liu, J., Schneider, T., Asokan, N., Pinkas, B.: Private set intersection for unequal set sizes with mobile applications. Proc. Priv. Enhancing Technol. **2017**(4), 177–197 (2017)
23. Li, L., Pal, B., Ali, J., Sullivan, N., Chatterjee, R., Ristenpart, T.: Protocols for checking compromised credentials. In: Proceedings of the 2019 ACM SIGSAC Conference on Computer and Communications Security, pp. 1387–1403 (2019)
24. Lv, S., et al.: Unbalanced private set intersection cardinality protocol with low communication cost. Futur. Gener. Comput. Syst. **102**, 1054–1061 (2020)
25. Many, D., Burkhart, M., Dimitropoulos, X.: Fast private set operations with sepia. ETZ G93 (2012)
26. Miao, P., Patel, S., Raykova, M., Seth, K., Yung, M.: Two-sided malicious security for private intersection-sum with cardinality. In: Micciancio, D., Ristenpart, T. (eds.) CRYPTO 2020. LNCS, vol. 12172, pp. 3–33. Springer, Cham (2020). https://doi.org/10.1007/978-3-030-56877-1_1
27. Cheng, N., Zhao, Y.-L.: Efficient approach regarding two-party privacy-preserving set union/intersection cardinality. J. Cryptol. Res. **8**(2), 352–364 (2020)
28. Nagaraja, S., Mittal, P., Hong, C.Y., Caesar, M., Borisov, N.: BotGrep: finding P2P bots with structured graph analysis. In: USENIX Security Symposium, vol. 10, pp. 95–110 (2010)
29. Narayanan, A., Thiagarajan, N., Lakhani, M., Hamburg, M., Boneh, D., et al.: Location privacy via private proximity testing. In: NDSS, vol. 11 (2011)
30. Pagh, R., Rodler, F.F.: Cuckoo hashing. J. Algorithms **51**(2), 122–144 (2004)
31. Ping, P.: Block attacks from compromised credentials (2021). https://www.passwordping.com/
32. Pinkas, B., Schneider, T., Segev, G., Zohner, M.: Phasing: private set intersection using permutation-based hashing. In: 24th {USENIX} Security Symposium ({USENIX} Security 15), pp. 515–530 (2015)
33. Resende, A.C.D., Aranha, D.F.: Faster unbalanced private set intersection. In: Meiklejohn, S., Sako, K. (eds.) FC 2018. LNCS, vol. 10957, pp. 203–221. Springer, Heidelberg (2018). https://doi.org/10.1007/978-3-662-58387-6_11
34. Samarati, P., Sweeney, L.: Protecting privacy when disclosing information: k-anonymity and its enforcement through generalization and suppression (1998)
35. Shi, R.H., Mu, Y., Zhong, H., Zhang, S., Cui, J.: Quantum private set intersection cardinality and its application to anonymous authentication. Infor. Sci. **370**, 147–158 (2016)
36. Thomas, K., et al.: Protecting accounts from credential stuffing with password breach alerting. In: 28th {USENIX} Security Symposium ({USENIX} Security 19), pp. 1556–1571 (2019)
37. Trieu, N., Shehata, K., Saxena, P., Shokri, R., Song, D.: Epione: lightweight contact tracing with strong privacy. arXiv preprint arXiv:2004.13293 (2020)
38. Trivedi, A., Zakaria, C., Balan, R., Becker, A., Corey, G., Shenoy, P.: WiFiTrace: network-based contact tracing for infectious diseases using passive WiFi sensing. Proc. ACM Interact. Mobile Wearable Ubiquit. Technol. **5**(1), 1–26 (2021)
39. Vaidya, J., Clifton, C.: Secure set intersection cardinality with application to association rule mining. J. Comput. Secur. **13**(4), 593–622 (2005)

Crypto-Steganographic Validity for Additive Manufacturing (3D Printing) Design Files

Mark Yampolskiy[1(✉)], Lynne Graves[2], Jacob Gatlin[1], J. Todd McDonald[2], and Moti Yung[3,4]

[1] Auburn University, Auburn, USA
mark.yampolskiy@auburn.edu
[2] University of South Alabama, Mobile, USA
[3] Google LLC, Mountain View, USA
[4] Columbia University, New York, USA

Abstract. *Additive Manufacturing* (AM) is an important up and coming manufacturing technology which creates three-dimensional objects based on digital design files. While these digital files simplify outsourcing, it also raises security concerns of *technical data theft* by malicious actors. We propose a novel approach for steganographically embedding validity marks to identify the design owner and outsourced manufacturer in the widely used STL (STereoLithography) file format. It exploits redundancies in STL file encoding and applies basic cryptography to generate a mark that is detectable if illegally modified. While deforming watermarks for 3D-printed objects have been explored, our approach is the first to watermark STL files without affecting the manufactured geometry – a prerequisite for safety-critical functional parts.

Keywords: Applied cryptography · Steganography · Additive manufacturing · Cyber physical systems · Intellectual property protection

1 Introduction

Additive Manufacturing (AM) is a manufacturing technology with which objects are built up incrementally, by depositing and fusing thin layers of source material [8]. Among the key advantages of AM is the production of objects based solely on their digital representation [6]—the universality of digital design make flexible, on-demand outsourcing to AM service providers possible, with over 1500 companies offer such services [1]. Unfortunately, the short-term and low-volume nature [7] of AM outsourcing reduces or eliminates the barriers to malicious activity by a service provider [16]. Of particular concern is the threat of *Technical Data Theft* (TDT).

Initial responses to the threat of TDT in AM [16] considered adapting watermarking approaches from other domains, such as digital 3D models [12,13],

W. Susilo et al. (Eds.): ISC 2022, LNCS 13640, pp. 40–52, 2022.
https://doi.org/10.1007/978-3-031-22390-7_3

but these failed to consider a watermark's impact on physically 3D printed objects [11]. A variety of AM-specific 3D mesh watermarking techniques have been proposed, focusing on integrating watermarks that can be recovered from the printed objects [15,18].

While physically-encoded watermarking is sometimes acceptable, geometric deviations are not tolerated for safety-cricital parts. At a minimum, geometrical modification can violate part certification, but the true danger is degrading the part's physical properties. Failure to meet specifications can cause dangerous and unexpected part failures.

In this paper, we consider an AM outsourcing business model where a design is provided to several AM service providers, one of whom is malicious. This scenario is a version of the Man-at-the-End (MATE) threat model [2]. The adversary has full access to the secured asset, in this case a design file, so we must assume that any technical defenses will eventually be overcome [2].

Under this threat model, a defender would want to integrate into their design file marks to both authenticate the legitimate owner of the IP and identify a malicious service provider. The marks should not interfere with the printing process, and it should be possible to verify their integrity and authenticity. By doing so, bad actors can be identified and legal claims pursued. Functional parts introduce a constraint on the solution: the watermarking method should not affect the manufactured part's geometry [6]).

We propose a solution for the STL (STereoLithography) file format which contains sources of entropy, allowing us to encode arbitrary information. As the modified elements are not specified STL, the resulting watermark should not interfere with the part's geometry. Such a solution will work fully if the file contents are not modified; if they are, it will be possible to detect modifications by invalidating the embedded signature. Furthermore, the mark cannot simply be transferred to another design, as it includes the cryptographic hash of the design file.

2 Background

Steganography is the art of hiding information in plain sight [14]. It has been studied and used extensively since the 1990s in the context of software and digital media protection. Watermarks and fingerprints are two distinct steganographic tools [3]. *Watermarks* identify an owner. Though they cannot prevent illegal copying, they establish a legitimate claim of ownership so long as the mark survives. *Fingerprint* identifies the recipient of the protected digital object. In the xontext of software protection, this allows tracing pirated software back to the original customer. The functional equivalency between the original and watermarked software is known as *semantic preservation*.

In *non-blind* watermark extraction, the mark is identified by comparison between binaries with and without the mark. In the *blind* approach, the marked file is instead compared to a canonical form. The canonical form must be unique, semantically equivalent, and retrievable from marked or unmarked files; this requires a thorough understanding of the STL format.

Structurally, STL files are composed of a series of nested blocks that describe the model. The outermost block is enclosed by the tags *solid* and *endsolid*. Within are a series of *facet* blocks, each of which describes a triangular surface, bounded by the tags *facet* and *endfacet*. The order of facets is not regulated, and can be changed arbitrarily. Each facet is defined by its three vertices and its orientation: orientation is given by a *normal* block which contains the normal vector's x, y, and z coordinates. The normal vector should follow the right hand rule, meaning the vertices are listed in counter-clockwise order when viewed from the normal. The vertices are defined in the innermost block, enclosed by the tags *outer loop* and *endloop*. Each vertex is specified as $vertex\ v_x\ v_y\ v_z$. The three v's are single-precision floating point values representing the x, y, and z coordinates.

Although the STL file describes the object geometry, it cannot be directly printed. First, it is "sliced" by a program known as *slicer* into thin layers. For each layer, a *toolpath* is generated that defines actions for the 3D Printer to execute.

3 Definitions: Watermarking for AM

While the body of steganographic and watermarking literature is substantial, it focuses on digital applications. Working in the AM domain requires adjustments to several definitions.

A **Steganographic Watermarking system** takes an original file and watermarking information and generates a watermarked file, where the watermark is a string with certain properties readable by an agent. A Steganographic Watermarking method is *sound* if, when it has not been modified, (a) the watermark is *verifiable* from the file (i.e., there is a polynomial time algorithm that reads the file and extracts embedded information); and (b) the content is *functional* (i.e., the result of executing the marked file is the same as the original). A Crypto-steganographic Watermarking system is *tamper-evident* if, when the file carrying the mark is modified, a mark verification procedure will detect the modification. A watermarking system is *robust* if, when the file carrying the mark is tampered with, the functionality of the file is lost (i.e., it violates requirement (b) in definition 1) and the modification is detectable. A Crypto-steganographic Watermarking system is *strongly robust* if: (a) it is tamper-evident; and (b) it is robust.

4 Steganographic Channels in STL File Format

Our proposal consists of two parts: (i) a steganographic channel for STL files and (ii) a structure for STL watermarks and fingerprints. The steganographic channel is an expansion of one first discovered and presented in [17].

Throughout this work, we refer to an STL file in which information is encoded as a *carrier*. To distinguish between files in their original state and files with

Table 1. Encoding Capacity (Bits) of Encoding Primitives

Encoding Primitive	Encoding Capacity
Facet Position	$\lfloor \log_2(F_B!) \rfloor \cdot \lfloor F_N/F_B \rfloor$
Vertex Order	
Regarding Right Hand Rule	$\lfloor \log_2(3^{F_N}) \rfloor$ or F_N
Disregarding Right Hand Rule	$\lfloor \log_2(6^{F_N}) \rfloor$ or $2 \cdot F_N$
Normal Vector	F_N
Number Representation	$\log_2(E_N) \cdot 12 \cdot F_N$

F_N – Number of facets in STL file
F_B – Facet number for bit sequence encoding
E_N – Distinct exponents for bit sequence encoding

information encoded, we will use the notations STL and STL^M. We use M to refer the mark.

While encoding or decoding, M is treated as a bit stream. It is encoded as a sequence of transformations applied to the carrier, resulting in a STL^M that incorporates both the original geometry and the mark. It should be possible to retrieve M from the STL^M file by assessing the state of the STL file elements used for encoding. The steganographic channel should support encoding and decoding of an arbitrary length M up to the capacity of the carrier. To support both ASCII and binary STL formats, we restrict ourselves to transformations of structural elements. We also only consider *blind* approaches, i.e., M can be extracted from STL^M without any knowledge of STL.

4.1 STL Transformations for Bit Encoding

We consider a well-formed STL to satisfy the following conditions. First, all facets in the file are unique by their three vertices. Second, all vertices in each facet are distinct. In malformed STL files, facets violating these conditions can be skipped, reducing encoding capacity.

Based on our analysis of the STL file format's structural elements, we identified several transformations that can be used as bit encoding primitives and assessed their encoding capacity (summarized in Table 1):

Facet Position: As the order in which facets are described is not defined, their relative position can be used to encode information. In a STL file with F_N facets, $F_N!$ permutations of these facets are possible. Therefore, facet ordering can be used to represent values up to $\lfloor \log_2(F_N!) \rfloor$ bits long.

In the simplest case, two subsequent facets can be used to represent a single binary value, a bit. For F_B facets, their positions can be used to encode up to $\lfloor \log_2(F_B!) \rfloor$ bits of information. With this scheme, $\lfloor \log_2(F_B!) \rfloor \cdot \lfloor F_N/F_B \rfloor$ bits of information can be encoded in a file with F_N facets. For a binary representation this would result in $\lfloor F_N/2 \rfloor$ bit encoding capacity.

For a blind approach, a canonical form should be introduced, *e.g.*, by defining an order based on the vertices and their coordinates in 3D space. We choose to do this using a less-than ordering for both facets and vertices.

Using this definition, we can associate the bit value 0 with a sequence in which the "smaller" facet is defined first, and 1 otherwise. Applying this definition to the pair of facets, the two facets can be used to define a single bit value.

Vertex Order: As each facet is defined by its three vertices (v_1, v_2, v_3), vertex ordering can be used to encode information. In a well-formed STL file, the order of these vertices should follow the *right hand* rule with respect to the normal vector (see Sect. 2). Based on whether or not the right hand rule is followed during the encoding, we distinguish between the following cases:

Regarding the Right Hand Rule: This case restricts the order in which individual vertices (v_1, v_2, v_3) are listed to their cyclical rotation. Consequently, this permits encoding of up to three values per facet. The actual encoded value can be determined based on the relative $x - y - z$ value of the vertex listed first: whether it is smallest, middle, or largest.

If all three distinct values are used, up to $\lfloor \log_2(3^{F_N}) \rfloor$ bits of information can be encoded. This requires that the bit stream is converted to base 3 for encoding, and back to base 2 upon decoding. Alternatively, a single binary value can be encoded. This eliminates the need for base conversion, but will reduce the encoding capacity to F_N bits.

Disregarding the Right Hand Rule: If the right hand rule is simply ignored, six distinct permutations of the vertices are possible. Such a scheme would allow encoding of up to $\lfloor \log_2(6^{F_N}) \rfloor$ bits of information. However, this would require base conversion from 2 to 6 prior to encoding and back to 2 after decoding. Alternatively, in a base 2 scheme, four of the permutation states could be used to encode two subsequent bits of information with the remaining two states reserved for other purposes like signaling. In this case, up to $2 \cdot F_N$ binary bits of information can be encoded.

Normal Vector: In a well-formed STL file, the normal vector can be derived from the order in which the facet's vertices are defined. This can be exploited to encode bits of information. For example, if the normal still follows the "right hand rule," it can represent bit value 1, and if violates it (e.g., by inverting the normal direction) – bit value 0. With this approach, an encoding capacity of F_N bits can be achieved.

Number Representation: All vertex coordinates can be specified with or without an exponent. In the simplest case, the presence or absence of exponentiation can be used to encode a single bit of information. For the entire STL file, the encoding capacity of this scheme is $12 \cdot F_N$ bits of information. The exponent itself can represent multiple bits of encoded information. With E_N being maximum supported number for an exponent's value, the encoding capacity for the entire STL file will be $\log_2(E_N) \cdot 12 \cdot F_N$.

Numerical problems with single-precision floating point numbers may arise with this method.

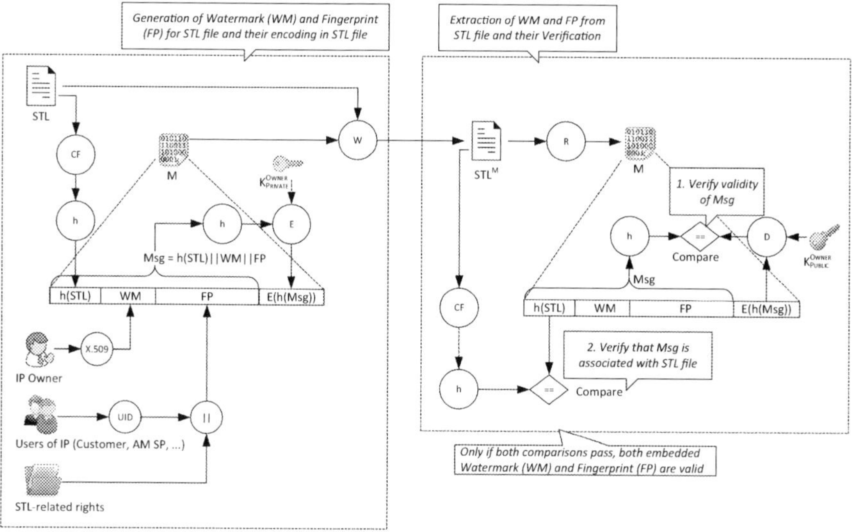

Fig. 1. STL watermarking and fingerprinting: generation and verification

4.2 Steganographic Channels in STL File Format

To define a steganographic channel for STL, we first need to define functions that will write and read individual bits using a specific encoding scheme. Using these functions, we can then define functions for operations on bytes. In the final step, we can define functions for encoding and decoding arbitrary numbers of bytes, as long as the STL file has sufficient encoding capacity.

All functions operate on an object that represents a carrier STL file "opened" for steganographic operations. At present, the object supports only one encoding scheme at a time. This object also keeps track of bit position in the STL file. For read and write operations, this position is translated to a specific STL element, based on the chosen encoding scheme. Upon completion of a read or write, the bit position is advanced.

Defining functions for reading and writing arbitrary byte sequences should take into account that the carrier STL file limits the available bit encoding capacity; furthermore, the bit capacity is not likely to be a multiple of 8 bits. To handle failure modes where the capacity is insufficient, we opted to write as much as possible of the given sequence, and further to "top up" to the end of the carrier STL file if the encoding capacity is not a multiple of 8.

5 Validity: STL Watermarking and Fingerprinting

In this section we propose a method for *watermarking* and *fingerprinting* STL files. The proposal for embedding and validating marks is depicted in Fig. 1. Both watermarks and fingerprints are associated with a particular STL file through the inclusion of a cryptographic hash sum of the file. Prior to hashing the original file, it is converted to a canonical form. This conversion ensures that the hash value is always calculated over the same permutation.

For the watermark, a globally unique identifier for the owner is required; one possible solution is to use the *Serial Number* of an X.509 certificate. For the fingerprint, end user identifying information should be concatenated with terms of use. While the watermark needs to be globally unique to support ownership claims, the fingerprint identifier should be unique enough (at a minimum, unique to the IP owner) to establish traceability.

Additionally, steps need to be undertaken to ensure the integrity and authenticity of the message $Msg = h(STL)||WM||FP$. A common approach is to sign the message Msg [9]. For this, a cryptographic hash sum of the message can be calculated and then signed with the owner's private key, corresponding to the public key in the specified certificate. Both the message, Msg, and its signature, $E(K_{Private}^{Owner}, h(Msg))$, would then be encoded in the STL file, where E is the signing function (see Fig. 1).

To extract and validate the watermark and fingerprint, the message and its signature are decoded from STL^M in a two step process. The signature is validated using K_{Pub}^{Owner} from the owner's X.509 certificate. The hash value is then compared with one calculated over the decoded message Msg. If they are identical, the retrieved message Msg is properly signed by the owner. The second step verifies that the message Msg corresponds to the carrier STL file. To do this, a hash sum calculated over STL^M in its canonical form, $h(CF(STL^M))$ is compared with the hash value stored in the message. If the values match, the watermark and fingerprint fields of M are validated.

To provide a concrete example, if SHA-256 [5] is used, the hash $h(STL)$ will be 32 bytes long. The X.509 certificate is required to support up to 20 byte long serial numbers [4] – we use this for the WM field. The FP field need only be locally unique to the owner of the IP; we assume 4 bytes for UID. For simplicity, we assume no STL-related rights are specified. All this results in a Msg that is 56 bytes long. This Msg must be signed (see Fig. 1 for the method). We assume the use of ECDSA with SHA-256 as a hashing algorithm [10]. ECDSA's output is two field elements of variable length; for this example we specify a reasonable 250 bits resulting in 500 bits total, just under 63 bytes. Summing all fields and rounding up, we come to a capacity requirement of less than 120 bytes to be embedded.

For the test set of models, all but the smallest objects (a simple cube) have available encoding capacity in excess of 1000 bits. This demonstrates the practicality of the approach for protection of models with realistic complexity. For smaller objects MAC will have to replace the signature method.

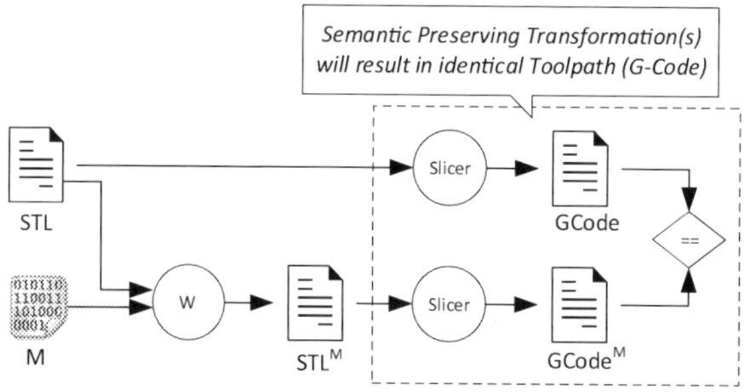

Fig. 2. Approach for verifying toolpath-based semantic preservation

6 Defining and Verifying Semantic Preservation for AM

In this section we define what *semantic preservation* means for AM, then verify whether our encoding schemes satisfy this requirement. We do this by the toolpath representation, as well as the Form, Fit, and Function characterization of a part [6].

Toolpath-Based Semantic Preservation: To manufacture an STL file, slicers convert it to a sequence of toolpath instructions. We can define *Toolpath-based Semantic Preservation* as follows: the information in a carrier STL file is *semantically preserved* if the toolpaths generated from the file with and without an encoded message are functionally identical (see illustration in Fig. 2).

The transition from 3D model to toolpath is dependent on the slicer and its configuration parameters. While a transformation might be semantically preserving with one slicer, it may not be with others.

Form- and Fit-Based Semantic Preservation: Form and Fit are described in the digital design file, through the object's geometry. Therefore, we define that a specific encoding satisfies *Form- and Fit-based Semantic Preservation* if and only if objects 3D printed using STL files with and without an encoded message are identical in their geometry and dimensions.

Function-Based Semantic Preservation: For functional parts, its functional characteristics (e.g., tensile strength or fatigue life) are critical. In AM, these are not solely dependent on the Form and Fit but also on the manufacturing process parameters. Therefore, we define that a specific encoding satisfies *Function-based Semantic Preservation* if and only if objects 3D printed using STL files with and without an encoded message are identical in their functional performance. Evaluating this category may require mechanical testing of the functional characteristics specified in the object's design.

Strict and Bounded Semantic Preservation: Semantic preservation requirements vary for different applications. We propose to distinguish between *strict* and *bounded* semantic preservation. In the toolpath-based definition, semantic preservation is strict if the toolpaths are absolutely identical. For the two other categories, only "bounded" preservation is possible, because of variability in the manufacturing process and error in measurement. Identified bounds can be compared against the tolerances specified for a part.

6.1 Verifying G-Code *Toolpath-Based Semantic Preservation*

We have evaluated toolpath-based semantic preservation using G-Code, a legacy ASCII toolpath format that can be analyzed manually. It is broadly used in desktop 3D printers. To account for the possibility that the choice of slicer could impact the results, we selected two commonly used slicers, *Slic3r* v.1.3.0 and *CuraEngine* v.4.4.0.

We begin with the hypothesis that each encoding approach was semantic preserving. We then sought evidence that the approach does not maintain this property. To that end, we developed a python script that iterated through a set of STL files (ten in total with varying size, geometric complexity, and encoding capacity) and encoded within each a synthetic bit stream[1] using each of our bit encoding primitives (see Sect. 4.1). Next, we sliced the original (STL) and modified (STL^M) files. Then, we compared the generated G-Code toolpath files on the basis of their functional identity. If the toolpath files did not match, we declared the tested encoding primitive as *not* semantic preserving for the associated slicer.

The results, given in Table 2, show differences in the semantic preservation performance of the two slicers. Preservation depends not only on the slicer and transformation, but also on the 3D mesh geometry described in STL file. Only two bit encoding primitives, normal vector and number representation, demonstrated semantic preservation for all test files and only when used in conjunction with the *Cura* slicer. The normal vector's success could be explained if *Cura* ignores the normal field entirely and instead re-calculates the corresponding value. The number representation's success indicates that this particular formulation of the encoding scheme did not cause any numerical problems with *Cura*.

The low results for vertex order encoding while following the right hand rule and adjacent facet position swapping were surprising. A closer analysis of these and other cases violating semantic preservation revealed that the number of differences between the original and marked files varied greatly, ranging from just a few G-Code commands to significant portions of the generated .gcode files. After manual evaluation, the majority of observed differences appeared to be rounding errors on floating point operations, which may bound them.

In conclusion, we found that strict toolpath-based semantic preservation is both slicer- and encoding primitive-dependent. The resulting deviations appear to be bounded, leaving open the question of impacts on Form and Fit.

---

[1] As a synthetic bit stream we used the 256 bytes long ASCII table, cyclically rotated to start with the binary value $10100011b$ ($0xA3$ hex).

Table 2. Semantic preservation test results

ENCODING PRIMITIVE	CURA	SLIC3R
Facet Position		
Entire STL file	✗ (60.0%)	✗ (50.0%)
Adjacent facets	✗ (20.0%)	✗ (50.0%)
Vertex Order		
Regarding Right Hand Rule	✗ (50.0%)	✗ (40.0%)
Violating Right Hand Rule	✗ (10.0%)	✗ (40.0%)
Disregarding Right Hand Rule	✗ (50.0%)	✗ (40.0%)
Normal Vector	✓ (100%)	✗ (30.0%)
Number Representation	✓ (100%)	✗ (40.0%)

6.2 Verification of *Form- And Fit-Based Semantic Preservation*

To validate whether encoding schemes impact Form and Fit, we designed a simple object for which discrepancies can be easily detected in both flat and curved geometry (see Fig. 3). We encoded this test object with the same bit sequence used in the previous experiment. Samples were printed using the Formlabs *Form 3* SLA 3D Printer and the *PreForm* 3.14 Slicer. In addition to the marked STL files, we also printed the original STL twice, to establish possible deviations. We measured the test objects using Mitutoyo 500-196-30 electronic calipers.

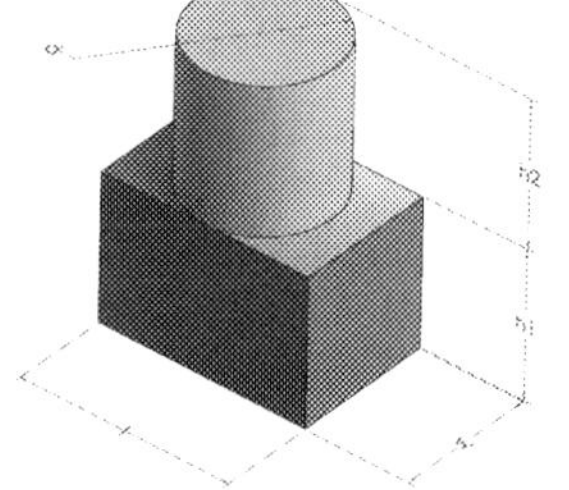

Fig. 3. Experimental test token. Dimensions: l = 30 mm, w = 20 mm, h1 = 20 mm, h2 = 20 mm, d = 20 mm

We identified three quantifiable error sources: (i) the tolerance by the defined STL file (3.00176 μm), (ii) the resolution of the 3D Printer (25 μm in the X and Y directions and 25 to 100 μm in the Z direction), (iii) the measurement error of the calipers (10 μm). Any deviations below 38 μm in X and Y and 113 μm in Z may be attributable to these sources. There is also slight unevenness across the surfaces of the printed parts. While we compensated for this by taking measurements at the same locations, this could have introduced further variance.

Table 3 summarizes the mean-average measurement results for our object dimensions. The results show deviations between our 3D-printed objects and the design for both STL files. Further, while there is deviation between objects printed using the original design and a marked STL, it never exceeded 80 μm. This is small enough to be explained by other error sources, as outlined above. Furthermore, it is significantly smaller than the observed deviations between 3D-

Table 3. Tests of encoding impact on Form and Fit. The last three rows represent the maximum deviation between the (i) original STL and unmarked object, (ii) original STL and marked object, and (iii) unmarked and marked objects.

ENCODING PRIMITIVE	l mm	w mm	$h1$ mm	$h2$ mm	d mm
Using Original STL					
Print 1	30.13	20.06	19.82	20.10	20.07
Print 2	30.08	20.05	19.75	20.07	20.04
Facet Position					
Entire STL file	30.11	20.08	19.78	20.07	20.06
Adjacent facets	30.08	20.11	19.77	20.10	20.06
Vertex Order					
Regarding RHR	30.06	20.05	19.75	20.08	20.04
Violating RHR	30.12	20.07	19.80	20.06	20.06
Disregarding RHR	30.09	20.04	19.74	20.09	20.03
Normal Vector	30.12	20.05	19.78	20.12	20.09
Number Representation	30.11	20.04	19.80	20.11	20.07
MAXIMUM DEVIATION	Δl	Δw	$\Delta h1$	$\Delta h2$	Δd
Using Original STL	0.13	0.06	0.18	0.10	0.07
Using Encoded STLs	0.12	0.11	0.26	0.12	0.09
From Original Object	0.07	0.06	0.08	0.05	0.05

printed objects and the design. We feel this supports that the proposed encoding strategies are bounded for Form and Fit.

7 Conclusion

In Sect. 3 we introduced several definitions to characterise a Steganographic Watermarking System. The requirements on a sound watermarking system, extraction and non-interference, are fulfilled by the proposed approach and were demonstrated during experimental evaluation. Tamper evidence is here achieved by the inclusion of a digital signature. However, the proposed approach is not *robust* nor *strongly robust*. Conforming to our initial requirements, the mark can be added without violating functionality; the same transformations can be applied to remove it without losing functionality.

Attacks on watermarking schemes take many forms. Subtractive attacks are aimed at removing the mark completely. Distortion attacks are aimed at ruining the embedded data, corrupting rightful owner identification or fingerprinting schemes. Additive attacks are intended to introduce an attacker's watermark into an object, allowing the attacker to claim putative ownership of the object and accusing the rightful owner of IP violations. As STL files are not protected against modifications, each of these attacks is possible. A robust version of our watermarking method is an open research question, and the answer may involve either changes in the AM infrastructure (procedural agreement on file hashes, etc.) or the development of more resilient forms of encoding.

To conclude, we proposed a method for watermarks (to assert owner rights) and fingerprints (to identify a data thief) to be directly embedded in STL files. For the four non-deforming categories of STL transformations we identified, we provided our assessment of their bit encoding capacity. We then used these transformations to establish a steganographic channel in STL, to encode data in a file. To characterize these encodings we developed AM-specific definitions of *semantic preservation* and experimentally assessed whether the identified encoding schemes achieve them. The results show that, while the absolute *toolpath-based* semantic preservation could only be achieved for a specific combination of slicer and encoding primitives, bounded *form and fit-based* semantic preservation has been demonstrated in all investigated cases.

References

1. 3D printing business directory (2022). https://www.3dprintingbusiness.directory
2. Collberg, C.: Engineering code obfuscation. In: Invited Talk at EUROCRYPT 2016 (2016)
3. Collberg, C., Nagra, J.: Surreptitious Software: Obfuscation, Watermarking, And Tamperproofing For Software Protection, 1st edn. Addison-Wesley Professional, Boston (2009)
4. Cooper, D., et al.: Internet x. 509 public key infrastructure certificate and certificate revocation list (CRL) profile. RFC 5280, pp. 1–151 (2008)
5. Eastlake, D., Hansen, T.: RFC 6234: US secure hash algorithms (SHA and SHA-based HMAC and HKDF). IETF Std. (2011)
6. Gibson, I., Rosen, D., Stucker, B., Khorasani, M.: Additive Manufacturing Technologies. Springer, Cham (2021). https://doi.org/10.1007/978-3-030-56127-7
7. Graves, L.M., Lubell, J., King, W., Yampolskiy, M.: Characteristic aspects of additive manufacturing security from security awareness perspectives. IEEE Access **7**, 103833–103853 (2019)
8. International, A.: F2792-12a-standard terminology for additive manufacturing technologies. Rapid Manufact. Assoc. **12**, 10–12 (2013)
9. Katz, J., Lindell, Y.: Introduction to Modern Cryptography. CRC Press, USA (2020)
10. Kerry, C.F., Director, C.R.: FIPS PUB 186–4 federal information processing standards publication digital signature standard (DSS) (2013)
11. Macq, B., Alface, P.R., Montanola, M.: Applicability of watermarking for intellectual property rights protection in a 3D printing scenario. In: Proceedings of the 20th International Conference on 3D Web Technology, pp. 89–95. ACM, New York (2015)
12. Ohbuchi, R., Masuda, H., Aono, M.: Watermarking three-dimensional polygonal models. In: ACM Multimedia, vol. 97, pp. 261–272. Citeseer (1997)
13. Ohbuchi, R., Masuda, H., Aono, M.: Watermarking three-dimensional polygonal models through geometric and topological modifications. IEEE J. Sel. Areas Commun. **16**(4), 551–560 (1998)

14. Petitcolas, F.A., Anderson, R.J., Kuhn, M.G.: Information hiding-a survey. Proc. IEEE **87**(7), 1062–1078 (1999)
15. Wang, K., Lavoué, G., Denis, F., Baskurt, A.: A comprehensive survey on three-dimensional mesh watermarking. IEEE Trans. Multimed. **10**(8), 1513–1527 (2008)
16. Yampolskiy, M., Andel, T.R., McDonald, J.T., Glisson, W.B., Yasinsac, A.: Intellectual property protection in additive layer manufacturing: requirements for secure outsourcing. In: Proceedings of the 4th Program Protection and Reverse Engineering Workshop, p. 7. ACM (2014)
17. Yampolskiy, M., Graves, L., Gatlin, J., Skjellum, A., Yung, M.: What did you add to my additive manufacturing data?: steganographic attacks on 3D printing files. In: 24th International Symposium on Research in Attacks, Intrusions and Defenses, pp. 266–281 (2021)
18. Yampolskiy, M., et al.: Security of additive manufacturing: attack taxonomy and survey. Addit. Manuf. **21**, 431–457 (2018)

Witness Encryption from Smooth Projective Hashing System

Yuzhu Wang[1] and Mingwu Zhang[1,2(✉)]

[1] School of Computer Science and Information Security, Guilin University of Electronic Technology, Guilin 541004, China
[2] School of Computer Science, Hubei University of Technology, Wuhan 430068, China
csmwzhang@gmail.com

Abstract. Smooth projective hash functions, also designated as hash proof systems (Eurocrypt '02) and witness encryption (STOC '13), are two powerful cryptographic primitives. The former can produce a hash value corresponding to an NP language instance in two ways, and the latter allows encrypting a message using the description of an instance in an NP language. Mostly, witness encryption is constructed using computationally expensive tools like multilinear maps or obfuscation. In this work, we build a witness encryption scheme using the smooth projection hash function (SPHF), which achieves efficient encryption and decryption. Specifically, we generate a zero-knowledge proof for the witness w of the NP instance x and use this proof as an instance of SPHF to encrypt a message. Next, we instantiate SPHF, the key technique of the WE scheme, supporting the NP-complete circuit SAT problem proved in the NIZK argument. Furthermore, based on our instantiated SPHF, our WE produces a fixed-size ciphertext, and a theoretical comparison with Derler et al. (DCC '18) instantiated SPHF from Gorth-Sahai proofs (GS-proofs) shows that our SPHF instantiation is more efficient than theirs.

Keywords: Witness encryption · Circuit SAT · Smooth projective hashing · NIZK · SNARK

1 Introduction

Witness Encryption. Witness encryption (WE) is a fascinating new concept proposed by Garg, Gentry, Sahai, and Waters [1], which defines for some NP-language $\mathcal{L}$ with a witness relation R so that $\mathcal{L} = \{x \mid \exists\ w : R(x, w) = 1\}$. The encryption algorithm takes as input an instance x along with a message M and produces a ciphertext C. Using a witness w such that $R(x, w) = 1$, the decryptor can recover M from the ciphertext C. Decryption only works if x is actually in

M. Zhang—This work is partially supported by the National Natural Science Foundation of China under grants 62072134 and U2001205, the Key projects of Guangxi Natural Science Foundation under grant 2019JJD170020 and the Innovation Project of GUET Graduate Education 2022YCXS074.

W. Susilo et al. (Eds.): ISC 2022, LNCS 13640, pp. 53–72, 2022.
https://doi.org/10.1007/978-3-031-22390-7_4

the language $\mathcal{L}$ and a ciphertext C hides M if C has been computed with respect to some $x \notin \mathcal{L}$.

The candidate construction of witness encryption for a special NP-complete problem, i.e., an exact cover problem, is designed from generic multilinear maps (MMap) [2], which implies WE for any language $\mathcal{L} \in$ NP via polynomial-time many-one reductions. Subsequently, Garg et al. [3] indicated that indistinguishability obfuscation ($i\mathcal{O}$) [4,5] implies witness encryption, and the only candidate construction of $i\mathcal{O}$ is also based on the MMap [2]. Zhandry [6] gave a constructure of reusable WE using witness pseudorandom functions (witness PRFs) and provided a witness PRFs instantiation from MMap. Most of the existing work in the literatures is based on multilinear mapping (MMap) or obfuscation techniques, thus far from being practical, while these papers address the problems of provable security [7–9], different NP problems [10–13], and new applications of WE, e.g., [1,9,11,12,14].

To achieve a more efficient encryption procedure, Abusalah et al. [15] introduced an interesting variant of WE, i.e., Offline WE (OWE), where the encryption algorithm uses neither multilinear maps nor obfuscation. They achieved efficient encryption by outsourcing the resource-heavy computations to a setup phase that processes necessary tools to produce public parameters for encryption and decryption. Later, several other works [16–18] built upon [6,15] and proposed the selectively secure OWE scheme, or semi-adaptive security OWE scheme for any NP-language. Nonetheless, the setup and decryption stages of the above constructs of OWE still require obfuscation and thus cannot be considered practical. To this end, Derler and Slamanig [19] constructed a practical instantiation of WE that focuses on all aspects, namely encryption and decryption, for efficiency. However, their scheme only supports a restricted class of algebraic languages.

Smooth Projective Hash Functions. Cramer and Shoup [20] introduced at Eurocrypt'02 the concept of smooth projective hash functions, also designated as hash proof systems. They are families of pairs of functions (Hash, ProjHash) defined on some NP-language $\mathcal{L}$ and a hash value can be computed in two ways, useful for producing witness encryption schemes. A common strategy [19,21–23] for constructing WE schemes consists of using an SPHF in the following way: Given an instance x and a message M, an encryptor generates a hashing key hk, a projective key hp, a hash value H_h and hides the message M using H_h. In order to decrypt the ciphertext, the decryptor uses the witness w associated with the instance x along with the projective key hp to compute the projected hash value H_p and retrieve M.

Abdalla et al. in [21], it was first proposed to informally outline the construction of witness encryption from SPHF. Subsequently, Derler et al. [19] gave the first formalized general construction of WE from SPHF. However, their SPHF only supports limited algebraic languages, not all NP languages. Moreover, the computational overhead of instantiating SPHF from the GS proof framework increases with the size of the proof statement. In addition, Faonio et al. [23] construct extractable witness encryption from the Ext-hash proof system (Ext-

HPS). While the extractable WE structure constructed is practical, it supports very basic and restricted languages.

Motivation. Most currently known WE or OWE schemes are constructed from computationally expensive MMap or obfuscations. As a result, these schemes are experiencing inefficiency due to the existing noisy MMap and impracticality of obfuscation. We aim to construct more efficient SPHF and WE for any class of NP languages. Derler et al. [19] proposed a practical witness encryption for restricted algebraic languages that requires SPHF and GS-proofs [24]. We note that they support restricted algebraic languages because SPHF is instantiated based on GS-proofs, which are efficient NIZK proofs for some specific algebraic languages such as paired product equations. Therefore, we consider instantiating our SPHF (and thus WE) using SNARKs for NP-complete problem circuits SAT, to support all classes of NP languages. Furthermore, in order to improve the efficiency of generating hash values when instantiating SPHF from SNARK, we only use part of the public data of zero-knowledge proofs, i.e., a public group element as an instance of SPHF to generate hash values. The two ways of generating the hash value only require exponentiation on 3 and 4 groups, respectively. Therefore, we constructed the WE scheme based on zero-knowledge proof, which needs to realize message encryption and decryption according to the generated zero-knowledge proof as an instance of SPHF, which is similar to the idea of [19] (DCC'18) based on GS-proof. It should be noted that the efficiency of NIZK and SNARK in generating common reference strings (crs) is low, but in our scheme, it is placed in the setup stage and only needs to be run once, which is acceptable.

Our Contribution. The main contributions of this paper are as follows:

- We provide a general framework and construction for witness encryption from SPHF and prove the security of the witness encryption scheme. Different from the existing WE, in our scheme, the encryptor first verifies the witness w of the instance x used by NIZK. After the verification is successful, i.e., $R(x, w) = 1$, and then the generates a zero-knowledge proof as an instance of SPHF to construct a general WE.
- We present practical instantiations of our generic approach witness encryption for circuit SAT. Specifically, we implement the instantiation of SPHF from zk-SNARK for NP complete problem circuit SAT. Besides being practically efficient, our constructions only require standard assumptions (i.e., DLP), which can support most NP languages.
- Our proposed SPHF instantiation (and thus WE) from SNARK is efficient (without MMap or $i\mathcal{O}$), by theoretical analysis and comparison with other WE schemes based on SPHF techniques, our scheme is superior to the existing schemes in terms of encryption and decryption. Furthermore, because ourscheme is constructed by our instantiation of SPHF, the encryption algorithm produces a fixed ciphertext size (a symmetric ciphertext and 3 group elements).

2 Related Work

The approaches in [18,19,25] are similar to how we construct WE. These schemes have similar goals and functionality but differ regarding the formalization and available instantiations.

With puncturable witness pseudorandom function (pWPRF) [18], which can be seen as a variant of (extractable) hash proof systems, Pal et al. aim at building an optimal size ciphertext OWE(or extractable OWE) from pWPRF and providing an instantiation of pWPRF from pPRF and an $i\mathcal{O}(or\ e\mathcal{O})$. Consequently, this only implements the efficient encryption phase, not producing a practical instantiation, where our goal is explicitly to build actual instantiations of WE that encrypt and decrypt efficiently, especially to make them compatible with SNARKs.

The approach to constructing efficient encryption and decryption practical WE from SPHF in [19] is related to our approach, but there are some essential differences. They instantiate an SPHF which is compatible with GS promises. SPHF is instantiated on this NP relation by generating a GS promise π for a message, taking π and the random factor generating the π as an NP relation. In addition, they extend the instantiation of SPHF to the GS-proof framework but only support limited algebraic languages. This differs from our WE goal of building efficient encryption and decryption that supports all NP languages.

Recently, Campanelli et al. [25] proposed that witness encryption over commitments (cWE) is similar to our construction idea. In their cWE, there are two stages: first parties provide a (honestly generated) commitment cm of their private input w. Later, anybody can encrypt to a public input for an NP statement, which also guarantees the correct opening of the commitment. Similar to [19], although it also implements witness encryption based on commitment cm, the specific implementation uses garbled circuits and inadvertent transfer, which is completely different from our idea and cannot be compared.

3 Preliminaries

In this section, we present the techniques used to construct our general WE scheme, mainly including the non-interactive zero knowledge arguments of knowledge, smooth projective hash function, and symmetric key encryption (SKE). The formal definition is as follows.

3.1 Notations and Conventions

We denote our security parameter as $\lambda \in \mathbb{N}$. Let $x \leftarrow S$ denote the process of sampling x uniformly at random from the finite set S. To make our notation more succinct, we will follow the notation in [26] and use $[x]$ for g^x, where $g \in \mathbb{G}$. A function $\mu : \mathbb{N} \rightarrow \mathbb{R}$ is called negligible if $\mu(n) \leq \frac{1}{p(n)}$ holds for every positive polynomial $p(\cdot)$ and all sufficiently large $n \in \mathbb{N}$.

3.2 Non-Interactive Zero-Knowledge Arguments of Knowledge

A key ingredient of our construction is non-interactive zero-knowledge (NIZK) arguments of knowledge. The idea of NIZK is to enable a prover to convince a verifier that a statement is true. In our work, in order to achieve the goal of zero-knowledge verification that the decryptor has a witness w before encrypting, and uses this proof as an instance of SPHF to construct WE. We use NIZK to convince the encryptor that the decryptor has the witness w for instance x, where $R(x, w) = 1$. We require a NIZK that satisfies perfect completeness, perfect zero-knowledge, computational soundness, and computational knowledge soundness. Perfect completeness means that, on input of an instance x and a witness w, the prover outputs a proof π that the verifier accepts. Computational soundness requires that no PPT adversary can produce a proof of a false instance. Perfect zero-knowledge means that a proof does not leak any information besides the truth of the instance.

We first recall the definitions of a non-interactive zero-knowledge (NIZK) arguments of knowledge in [27,28].

Definition 1 (NIZK). *An efficient prover of publicly verifiable non-interactive argument of knowledge for R is defined by the following four PPT algorithms (Setup, prove, Verify, Sim):*

- *Setup(1^λ): On input a security parameter λ, Setup algorithm outputs a common reference string σ and a simulation trapdoor τ.*
- *prove(σ, x, w): On input a common reference string σ and $(x, w) \in R$, prove algorithm outputs a proof π.*
- *Verify(σ, x, π): On input a common reference string σ, an instance x and a proof π, Verify algorithm outputs 1 (accept) or 0 (reject).*
- *Sim(τ, x): On input a simulation trapdoor and an instance x, Sim algorithm outputs a proof π.*

We require the perfect completeness, perfect zero-knowledge, computational soundness, and computational knowledge soundness of NIZK to be defined as follows:

Perfect Completeness. A NIZK scheme is perfect complete, if for all $\lambda \in \mathbb{N}$, $(x, w) \in R$, it holds that

$$\Pr[(\sigma, \tau) \leftarrow \mathsf{Setup}(1^\lambda); \pi \leftarrow \mathsf{prove}(\sigma, x, w) : \mathsf{Verify}(\sigma, x, \pi) = 1] = 1 \tag{1}$$

Perfect Zero-Knowledge. A NIZK scheme is perfect zero-knowledge, if for all $\lambda \in \mathbb{N}$, $(x, w) \in R$ and all adversaries $\mathcal{A}$, it holds that

$$\begin{aligned} &\Pr[(\sigma, \tau) \leftarrow \mathsf{Setup}(1^\lambda); \pi \leftarrow \mathsf{prove}(\sigma, x, w) : \mathcal{A}(\sigma, \tau, \pi) = 1] \\ = &\Pr[(\sigma, \tau) \leftarrow \mathsf{Setup}(1^\lambda); \pi \leftarrow \mathsf{Sim}(\tau, x) : \mathcal{A}(\sigma, \tau, \pi) = 1] \end{aligned} \tag{2}$$

Computational Soundness. A NIZK scheme is computationally soundness, if for all non-uniform polynomial time adversaries $\mathcal{A}$, it holds that

$$\Pr\left[\begin{array}{c}(\sigma,\tau)\leftarrow\mathsf{Setup}\left(1^{\lambda}\right);\\ x\notin\mathcal{L};\ (x,\pi)\leftarrow\mathcal{A}\left(1^{\lambda},\sigma\right)\end{array}:\ \mathsf{Verify}\left(\sigma,x,\pi\right)=1\right]\leq\mu\left(\lambda\right)\tag{3}$$

Computational Knowledge Soundness. A NIZK scheme is computationally knowledge soundness, if for all non-uniform polynomial time adversaries $\mathcal{A}$ there exists a non-uniform polynomial time extractor $\mathcal{X}_{\mathcal{A}}$, it holds that

$$\Pr\left[\begin{array}{c}(\sigma,\tau)\leftarrow\mathsf{Setup}\left(1^{\lambda}\right);\\ (x,w)\notin R;\left(\left(x,\pi\right);w\right)\leftarrow\left(\mathcal{A}\parallel\mathcal{X}_{A}\right)\left(1^{\lambda},\sigma\right)\end{array}:\mathsf{Verify}\left(\sigma,x,\pi\right)=1\right]\leq\mu(\lambda).\tag{4}$$

3.3 Smooth Projective Hashing Functions

One of the critical components of our construction is smooth projective hashing functions (SPHF). SPHF, also known as hash proof systems, are families of pairs of functions (Hash, ProjHash) defined on some NP-language $\mathcal{L}$ and a hash value can be computed in two ways. On an instance $x\in\mathcal{L}$, both functions need to yield the same result, that is, $\mathsf{Hash}(hk,x)=\mathsf{ProjHash}(hp,x,w)$, where the (hk,hp) is a pair of associated keys, evaluation the ProjHash value additionally requires a witness w that $x\in\mathcal{L}$.

In our scheme, SPHFobtains the hash value as the key K in two ways, input instance x and hk in the encryption phase to obtain $\mathsf{Hash}(hk,x)$ as the encryption key K, input an instance x, a witness w and hp in the decryption phase gets decryption key K. We require SPHF that satisfies the correctness and smoothness. Correctness guarantees that the Hash values obtained by the two methods are equal if everyone behaves honestly. Smoothness requires that the hash value looks statistically random for any $x\notin\mathcal{L}$. Formally SPHF are defined as follows (cf. [29]).

Definition 2 (SPHF). *Let us consider a language $\mathcal{L}\in\mathsf{NP}$, and some global parameters for the SPHF, assumed to be in the public parameter pp. The SPHF system over a language $\mathcal{L}$ is defined by the following four PPT algorithms (HashKG, ProjKG, Hash, ProjHash):*

- $\mathsf{HashKG}(pp)$: On input the public parameter pp, HashKG algorithm outputs a hashing key hk.
- $\mathsf{ProjKG}(pp,hk)$: On input the public parameter pp and a hashing key hk, ProjKG algorithm outputs a projective key hp.
- $\mathsf{Hash}(pp,hk,x)$: On input the public parameter pp, a hashing key hk, and an instance x, Hash algorithm outputs a hash value H_h.
- $\mathsf{ProjHash}(hp,x,w)$: On input a projective key hp, an instance x, and a witness w that $R(x,w)=1$, ProjHash algorithm outputs a hash value H_p.

We require the correctness, smoothness, and pseudorandomness of SPHF to be defined as follows:

Correctness. An SPHF for some languages $\mathcal{L} \in \mathsf{NP}$ is correct, if for all $(x, w) \in R$ with w the witness, it holds that

$$\left| \Pr\left[\begin{array}{c} hk \leftarrow \mathsf{HashKG}\,(pp)\,;hp \leftarrow \mathsf{ProjKG}\,(pp, hk) \\ H_h \leftarrow \mathsf{Hash}\,(pp, hk, x) \\ H_p \leftarrow \mathsf{ProjHash}\,(hp, x, w) \end{array} : H_h = H_p \right] - 1 \right| \leqslant \mu(\lambda) \quad (5)$$

Smoothness. An SPHF for some languages $\mathcal{L} \in \mathsf{NP}$ is smooth, if for all $x \notin \mathcal{L}$, the following two distributions are statistically indistinguishable,

$$\mathcal{D}_1 = \{(pp, x, hp, H_h) \,|\, hp \leftarrow \mathsf{ProjKG}\,(pp, hk)\,; H_h \leftarrow \mathsf{Hash}\,(hk, x)\}$$
$$\mathcal{D}_2 = \{(pp, x, hp, H_h) \,|\, hp \leftarrow \mathsf{ProjKG}\,(pp, hk)\,; H_h \leftarrow \Pi\}$$

where $hk \leftarrow \mathsf{HashKG}(crs)$, Π denote the range of the hash function. That is,

$$Adv_{\mathsf{SPHF}}^{Smooth}(\lambda) = \sum\nolimits_{h \in \Pi} |Pr_{\mathcal{D}_1}[H_h = h] - Pr_{\mathcal{D}_2}[H_h = h]| \leqslant \mu(\lambda). \quad (6)$$

3.4 Symmetric Key Encryption

Our general WE scheme adopts the ciphertext indistinguishability secure SKE to achieve efficient encryption and decryption,

Definition 3 (C-IND-SKE). *A symmetric key encryption (SKE) scheme is defined by the following three PPT algorithms (Gen, Enc, Dec):*

- $\mathsf{Gen}(1^\lambda)$: *On input a security parameter 1^λ, Gen algorithm outputs a key K.*
- $\mathsf{Enc}(K, M)$: *On input a key K and a message $M \in \mathcal{M}$, Enc algorithm outputs a ciphertext C.*
- $\mathsf{Dec}(K, C)$: *On input a key K and a ciphertext C, Dec algorithm outputs $M \in \mathcal{M}$, or $\perp$ if it fails.*

We require the correctness and ciphertext indistinguishability (C-IND) of SKE to be defined as follows:

Correctness. A SKE scheme is correct, if for all $\lambda \in \mathbb{N}$, and $M \in \mathcal{M}$ there exists a negligible function $\mu(\cdot)$, it holds that

$$\left|\Pr[K \leftarrow \mathsf{Gen}(1^\lambda); C \leftarrow \mathsf{Enc}(K, M); M' \leftarrow \mathsf{Dec}(K, C) : M = M'] - 1\right| \leqslant \mu(\lambda). \quad (7)$$

C-IND Security. A SKE scheme is ciphertext indistinguishability (C-IND) secure, if for all PPT adversary $\mathcal{A}$ and any pair of equal length messages (M_0, M_1) there exists a negligible function $\mu(\cdot)$, it holds that

$$\left|\Pr[\mathcal{A}(1^\lambda, \mathsf{Enc}(K, M_0)) = 1] - \Pr[\mathcal{A}(1^\lambda, \mathsf{Enc}(K, M_1)) = 1]\right| \leqslant \mu(\lambda). \quad (8)$$

4 Witness Encryption over Smooth Projective Hashing

In this section, we first introduce witness encryption over smooth projective hashing and give the security game. Next, we construct generic witness encryption using NIZK and SPHF, and analyze the security of our scheme.

4.1 Definition

WE was initially defined in [1] and refined in [9] with a stronger concept of adaptive soundness, where the instance x output by the adversary may depend on the parameters pp. In our scheme, only adaptive soundness makes sense when WE defines a scheme for language families indexed by pp, i.e., the language is not fixed before the parameter pp is generated. In addition, in order to achieve effective encryption when the instance $x \in \mathcal{L}$, we add a Gen algorithm, which is used to generate a zero-knowledge proof for the witness w. Since our Setup and Gen algorithms are computationally expensive but only run once, which is similar to OWE, we follow the basis of [15] and add the Gen algorithm to define WE.

Definition 4 (Witness Encryption over Smooth Projective Hashing). *A witness encryption over smooth projective hashing scheme is defined by the following four PPT algorithms (Setup, Gen, Enc, Dec):*

- *Setup(1^λ): On input a security parameter 1^λ, Setup algorithm outputs a public parameters pp.*
- *Gen(pp, x', w'): On input a public parameter pp, an instance $x' \in \mathcal{X}$, a witness $w' \in \mathcal{W}$, Gen algorithm outputs $x = (x', \pi)$.*
- *Enc(pp, x, M): On input a public parameter pp, an instance x and a message $M \in \mathcal{M}$, Enc algorithm outputs a ciphertext C or $\perp$.*
- *Dec(C, w): On input a ciphertext C and a witness w, Dec algorithm outputs $M \in \mathcal{M}$ or $\perp$.*

We require the correctness and adaptive security of our WE to be defined as follows:

$\mathsf{Exp}^{Adp-b}_{\mathsf{WE},\mathcal{A}}(\lambda)$:

1. $pp \leftarrow \mathsf{Setup}\,(1^\lambda)$
2. $(x^*, w^*, M_0, M_1, st) \leftarrow \mathcal{A}(1^\lambda, pp)$
3. $x \leftarrow \mathsf{Gen}(pp, x^*, w^*)$
4. $b \leftarrow \{0,1\}; C_b \leftarrow \mathsf{Enc}(pp, x, M_b)$
5. $b^* \leftarrow \mathcal{A}(C_b, st)$
6. $return\ 1\ if\ (b^* = b) \wedge (x^* \notin \mathcal{L}) \wedge (x^*, w^*) \notin R$

Fig. 1. Adaptive-security game of witness encryption

Correctness. A WE scheme is correct, if for all $\lambda \in \mathbb{N}$, $M \in \mathcal{M}$, and for any $(x, w) \in R$ it holds that

$$\left| \Pr\left[\begin{array}{l} pp \leftarrow \mathsf{Setup}\,(1^\lambda)\,; \pi \leftarrow \mathsf{Gen}\,(pp, x, w)\,; \\ C \leftarrow \mathsf{Enc}\,(pp, x, M)\,; M' \leftarrow \mathsf{Dec}\,(C, w) \end{array} M = M' \right] - 1 \right| \leq \mu\,(\lambda)$$

Adaptive Security. A WE scheme is adaptive security, if for all PPT adversaries $\mathcal{A}$ in $\mathsf{Exp}_{\mathsf{WE},\mathcal{A}}^{Adp-b}(\lambda)$ (Fig. 1)it holds that

$$\left|\Pr[\mathsf{Exp}_{\mathsf{WE},\mathcal{A}}^{Adp-0}(\lambda)=1]-\Pr[\mathsf{Exp}_{\mathsf{WE},\mathcal{A}}^{Adp-1}(\lambda)=1]\right|\leqslant\mu(\lambda)$$

4.2 Our Construction 1

In Fig. 2, we present our general construction of WE that, besides an SPHF requires a non-interactive zero-knowledge protocol NIZK and the C-IND secure symmetric key encryption scheme SKE. Our construction work is as follows. First, a trusted third party generates public parameters by running the Setup algorithm. Subsequently, the decryptor uses NIZK to achieve zero-knowledge proof of witness w. After the encryption passes the verification, it means that $R(x, w) = 1$ is established, and then the hash value of SPHF is used as a random extractor to obtain the encryption key K of SKE. We are now ready to present our generic construction of WE = (Setup,Gen,Enc,Dec) from any SPHF and NIZK.

$\mathsf{Setup}(R, 1^\lambda)$: On input a security parameter 1^λ, do the following:

- Run $pp \leftarrow \mathsf{NIZK.Setup}(R, 1^\lambda)$ and output pp.

$\mathsf{Gen}(R, pp, x', w')$: On input a public parameter pp, a string x', and a string w, where $R(x', w') = 1$, do the following:

- Run $\pi \leftarrow \mathsf{NIZK.prove}(R, pp, x', w')$.
- Let $x = (x', \pi)$ and output x.

$\mathsf{Enc}(R, pp, x, M)$: On input pp, x and a message $M \in \mathcal{M}$, do the following:

- If $1 \leftarrow \mathsf{NIZK.Verify}(R, pp, x)$:
  - · Run $hk \leftarrow \mathsf{SPHF.HashKG}(pp)$, $hp \leftarrow \mathsf{SPHF}.ProjKG(pp, hk)$, and $K \leftarrow \mathsf{SPHF.Hash}(hk, x)$.
  - · Let $c = \mathsf{SKE.Enc}(K, M)$ and output $C = (c, x, hp)$.
- Else output $\perp$.

$\mathsf{Dec}(C, w)$: On input a ciphertext $C = (c, x, hp)$, $w =$, do the following:

- Run $K \leftarrow \mathsf{SPHF.ProjHash}(hp, x, w)$.
- Compute $M = \mathsf{SKE.Dec}(K, c)$ and output M.

Fig. 2. WE from SPHF and NIZK

Remark 1. In Fig 2, NIZK = (Setup,prove,Verify) be an NIZK scheme for a NP-language $\mathcal{L} = \{x' \mid \exists\ w' : R(x', w') = 1\}$, SKE = (Enc,Dec) be an SKE scheme,

SPHF = (Setup,HashKG,ProjKG,Hash,ProjHash) be an SPHF scheme for a NP-language $\mathcal{L}_R = \{x = (x', \pi) \mid \exists\ w = (w', r) : \pi = \mathsf{NIZK.prove}(R, x', w', r)\}$.

4.3 Correctness

Theorem 1. *If NIZK is perfect completeness and SPHF is correct, and SKE is correct then our witness encryption scheme is correct.*

Proof. If NIZK is computational knowledge soundness, for all $(R, w) \neq 1$, the generated proof π verification fails, and output $\perp$.

If NIZK is perfect completeness, for all $(R, w) = 1$, the generated proof π can be verified. After the verification is passed, the correctness of SPHF guarantees $H_{\mathsf{Hash}} = H_{\mathsf{ProjHash}}$. It is easy to see that our WE scheme is correct.

4.4 Security Proof

Theorem 2. *If NIZK is perfect zero-knowledge, SPHF is smooth, and SKE is C-IND secure, then our WE scheme is adaptively secure.*

Proof. We show that the distinguishing advantage between two experiments $\mathsf{Exp}^{Adp-0}_{\mathsf{WE},\mathcal{A}}(\lambda)$ and $\mathsf{Exp}^{Adp-1}_{\mathsf{WE},\mathcal{A}}(\lambda)$ (Fig. 1) for any PPT adversary $\mathcal{A}$ is negligible by defining the following a series of hybrid games $\mathcal{H}_i$ and proving the indistinguishability between them.

$\underline{\mathcal{H}_\mathbf{i}(1^\lambda):}$

$-pp \leftarrow \mathsf{NIZK.Setup}(1^\lambda)$

$\cdot\ if\ i \in \{0, 6\},\ pp = \delta \leftarrow \mathsf{NIZK.Setup}(1^\lambda)$

$\cdot\ else\ i \in \{1, 2, 3, 4, 5, 6\},\ pp = \tau \leftarrow \mathsf{NIZK.Setup}(1^\lambda)$

$-(x^*, w^*, M_0, M_1, st) \leftarrow \mathcal{A}^{\mathsf{Gen}}(1^\lambda, pp),\ where\ |M_0| = |M_1|$

$-x = (x^*, \pi) \leftarrow \mathsf{Gen}(pp, x^*, w^*)$

$\cdot\ if\ i \in \{0, 6\},\ \pi \leftarrow \mathsf{NIZK.prove}(\delta, x^*, w^*)$

$\cdot\ else\ i \in \{1, 2, 3, 4, 5\},\ \pi \leftarrow \mathsf{NIZK.Sim}(\tau, x^*)$

$-b \leftarrow \{0, 1\}; C_b \leftarrow \mathsf{Enc}(pp, x, M_b)$

$\cdot\ hk \leftarrow \mathsf{SPHF.HashKG}(pp),\ hp \leftarrow \mathsf{SPHF.ProjKG}(pp, hk)$

$\cdot\ if\ i \in \{0, 1, 5, 6\},\ K \leftarrow \mathsf{SPHF.Hash}(hk, x)$

$\cdot\ else\ i \in \{2, 3, 4\},\ K \leftarrow \Pi$

$\cdot\ if\ i \in \{0, 1, 2, 3\},\ c_0 \leftarrow \mathsf{SKE.Enc}(K, M_0)$

$\cdot\ else\ i \in \{4, 5, 6\},\ c_1 \leftarrow \mathsf{SKE.Enc}(K, M_1)$

$\cdot\ C_b = (c_b, x^*, hp)$

$-b^* \leftarrow \mathcal{A}(C_b, st); return\ 1\ if\ (b^* = b) \wedge (x^* \notin \mathcal{L}) \wedge (x^*, w^*) \notin R$

Fig. 3. Hybrid games $\mathcal{H}_i$ used in the proof of Theorem 2

Hybrid $\mathcal{H}_0$: The first hybrid game $\mathcal{H}_0$ is the original adaptive security experiment $\mathsf{Exp}_{\mathsf{WE},\mathcal{A}}^{Adp-0}(\lambda)$ described in Fig. 3.

It can be obtained from the above experiment that the output of experiment $\mathcal{H}_0(\lambda)$ is 1 if and only if $\mathsf{Exp}_{\mathsf{WE},\mathcal{A}}^{Adp-0}(1^\lambda)$ outputs 1, that is:

$$\Pr[\mathsf{Exp}_{\mathsf{WE},\mathcal{A}}^{Adp-0}(1^\lambda) = 1] = \Pr[\mathcal{H}_0(1^\lambda) = 1]$$

Hybrid $\mathcal{H}_1$: Hybrid game $\mathcal{H}_0$ differs from $\mathcal{H}_1$ in that the public parameter pp for the NIZK and the zero-knowledge proof π are simulated rather than honestly generated. The perfect zero-knowledge property of NIZK guarantees that honestly generated proof π is indistinguishable from simulated ones by PPT adversaries (Fig. 4).

Lemma 1. *$\mathcal{H}_0$ and $\mathcal{H}_1$ are computationally indistinguishable if NIZK is perfect zero-knowledge.*

Proof. Assume towards contradiction that there exists a polynomial $p(\cdot)$ such that for infinitely many λ

$$\left|\Pr[\mathcal{H}_0(1^\lambda) = 1] - \Pr[\mathcal{H}_1(1^\lambda) = 1]\right| \geqslant \mu(\lambda)$$

We use $\mathcal{A}$ to construct a non-uniform PPT adversary $\mathcal{B}$ against the perfect zero-knowledge security of NIZK (Formula 2) as follows: By construction, if (pp, π) is generated honestly then $\mathcal{B}$ simulates hybrid $\mathcal{H}_0$, and if (pp, π) is simulated then $\mathcal{B}$ simulates hybrid $\mathcal{H}_1$. Therefore, for infinitely many λ it holds that

$$\begin{aligned}\mu(\lambda) &\leqslant |\Pr[\mathcal{H}_0(\lambda) = 1] - \Pr[\mathcal{H}_1(\lambda) = 1]| \\ &= |\Pr[(\sigma, \tau) \leftarrow \mathsf{Setup}(1^\lambda); \pi \leftarrow \mathsf{prove}(\sigma, x, w) : \mathcal{A}(\sigma, \tau, \pi) = 1] \\ &- \Pr[(\sigma, \tau) \leftarrow \mathsf{Setup}(1^\lambda); \pi \leftarrow \mathsf{Sim}(\tau, x) : \mathcal{A}(\sigma, \tau, \pi) = 1]|.\end{aligned}$$

We therefore reach a contradiction to the perfect zero-knowledge security of NIZK, and conclude that

$$\Pr[\mathcal{H}_0(1^\lambda) = 1] - \Pr[\mathcal{H}_1(1^\lambda) = 1] = \mu(\lambda).$$

Hybrid $\mathcal{H}_2$: In this hybrid K is computed as $K \leftarrow \Pi$, rather than $K \leftarrow \mathsf{SPHF.Hash}(hk, x)$. The two hybrids are statistically indistinguishable by the smoothness of SPHF (Fig. 5).

Lemma 2. *$\mathcal{H}_1$ and $\mathcal{H}_2$ are statistically indistinguishable if SPHF is smoothness.*

Proof. Assume towards contradiction that there exists a polynomial $p(\cdot)$ such that for infinitely many λ

$$\left|\Pr[\mathcal{H}_1(1^\lambda) = 1] - \Pr[\mathcal{H}_2(1^\lambda) = 1]\right| \geqslant \mu(\lambda)$$

$\underline{\mathcal{B}(1^\lambda):}$
$-pp = (\delta, \tau) \leftarrow \mathsf{NIZK.Setup}(1^\lambda)$
$-(x^*, w^*, M_0, M_1, st) \leftarrow \mathcal{A}^{\mathsf{Gen}}(1^\lambda, pp)$
$-Submit\ (x^*, w^*)\ to\ the\ zero-knowledge\ game\ of\ (2)\ to\ obtain$
$\cdot\ An\ honest\ (pp, \pi):\ \pi \leftarrow \mathsf{NIZK.prove}(\delta, x^*, w^*), or$
$\cdot\ simulated\ (pp, \pi):\ \pi \leftarrow \mathsf{NIZK.Sim}(\tau, x^*)$
$-hk \leftarrow \mathsf{SPHF.HashKG}(pp)\ and\ hp \leftarrow \mathsf{SPHF.ProjKG}(pp, hk)$
$-K \leftarrow \mathsf{SPHF.Hash}(hk, x)$
$-c_0 \leftarrow \mathsf{SKE.Enc}(K, M_0)$
$-Set\ C_0 = (c_0, x^*, hp)$
$-Output\ b^* \leftarrow \mathcal{A}(C_0, st).$

Fig. 4. The NIZK-adversary $\mathcal{B}$ simulating hybrid game

We use $\mathcal{A}$ to construct a non-uniform PPT adversary $\mathcal{B}$ against the smoothness of SPHF (Formula 6) as follows:

By construction, if $K \leftarrow \mathsf{SPHF.Hash}(hp, x)$ then $\mathcal{B}$ simulates hybrid $\mathcal{H}_1$, and if $K \leftarrow \Pi$ then $\mathcal{B}$ simulates hybrid $\mathcal{H}_2$. Therefore, for infinitely many λ it holds that

$$\begin{aligned}\mu(\lambda) &\leqslant |\Pr[\mathcal{H}_1(\lambda) = 1] - \Pr[\mathcal{H}_2(\lambda) = 1]| \\ &= \left|\Pr_{\mathcal{D}_1}[H_{\mathsf{Hash}} = h] - \Pr_{\mathcal{D}_2}[H_{\mathsf{Hash}} = h]\right| \leqslant Adv_{\mathsf{SPHF}}^{Smooth}(\lambda).\end{aligned}$$

We therefore reach a contradiction to the smoothness of SPHF, and conclude that

$$\Pr[\mathcal{H}_1(1^\lambda) = 1] - \Pr[\mathcal{H}_2(1^\lambda) = 1] = \mu(\lambda).$$

Hybrid $\mathcal{H}_3$: In this hybrid K we are already free to randomly choose the key K for the SKE scheme. The two hybrids are statistically indistinguishable by the security of SKE (Fig. 6).

Lemma 3. *$\mathcal{H}_2$ and $\mathcal{H}_3$ are statistically indistinguishable if SKE is security.*

Proof. The difference between hybrid $\mathcal{H}_2$ and hybrid $\mathcal{H}_3$ is the different key K used to encrypt and generate $c = \mathsf{SKE.Enc}(K, M_0)$. Observe that both keys K are randomly selected from the key space of SKE, Therefore there exists a negligible function $\mu(\lambda) = 1/2^{l_{\mathsf{SKE}}}$ such that:

$$\Pr[\mathcal{H}_2(1^\lambda) = 1] - \Pr[\mathcal{H}_3(1^\lambda) = 1] = \mu(\lambda).$$

Hybrid $\mathcal{H}_4$: The only difference of this hybrid from $\mathcal{H}_3$ is that we compute $c_1 \leftarrow \mathsf{SKE.Enc}(K, M_1)$ instead of $c_0 \leftarrow \mathsf{SKE.Enc}(K, M_0)$. Therefore, $\mathcal{H}_3$ and $\mathcal{H}_4$ are computationally indistinguishable by the C-IND security of the SKE scheme.

$\underline{\mathcal{B}(1^\lambda):}$
$-pp = \tau \leftarrow \mathsf{NIZK.Setup}(1^\lambda)$
$-(x^*, w^*, M_0, M_1, st) \leftarrow \mathcal{A}^{\mathsf{Gen}}(1^\lambda, pp)$
$-\pi \leftarrow \mathsf{NIZK.Sim}(\tau, x^*)$
–Set $x = (x^*, \pi)$
$-hk \leftarrow \mathsf{SPHF.HashKG}(pp)$ *and* $hp \leftarrow \mathsf{SPHF.}ProjKG(pp, hk)$
–Submit (hk, x) *to the smoothness game of* (6) *to obtain*
  $\cdot\ K \leftarrow \mathsf{SPHF.Hash}(hk, x)$ *or*
  $\cdot\ K \leftarrow \Pi$
$-c_0 \leftarrow \mathsf{SKE.Enc}(K, M_0)$
–Set $C_0 = (c_0, x^*, hp)$
–Output $b^* \leftarrow \mathcal{A}(C_0, st)$.

Fig. 5. The Smooth-adversary $\mathcal{B}$ simulating hybrid game

Lemma 4. *$\mathcal{H}_3$ and $\mathcal{H}_4$ are computationally indistinguishable if SKE is C-IND.*

Proof. Assume towards contradiction that there exists a polynomial $p(\cdot)$ such that for infinitely many λ

$$|\Pr[\mathcal{H}_3(\lambda) = 1] - \Pr[\mathcal{H}_4(\lambda) = 1]| \geqslant \mu(\lambda)$$

We use $\mathcal{A}$ to construct a non-uniform PPT adversary $\mathcal{B}$ against the C-IND of SKE (Formula 8) as follows:

By construction, if $c_b \leftarrow \mathsf{SKE.Enc}(K, M_0)$ then $\mathcal{B}$ simulates hybrid $\mathcal{H}_3$, and if $c_b \leftarrow \mathsf{SKE.Enc}(K, M_1)$ then $\mathcal{B}$ simulates hybrid $\mathcal{H}_4$. Therefore, for infinitely many λ it holds that

$$\begin{aligned} \mu(\lambda) &\leqslant |\Pr[\mathcal{H}_3(\lambda) = 1] - \Pr[\mathcal{H}_4(\lambda) = 1]| \\ &= \left|\Pr[\mathcal{B}(1^\lambda, c_0) = 1] - \Pr[\mathcal{B}(1^\lambda, c_1) = 1]\right|. \end{aligned}$$

We therefore reach a contradiction to the C-IND security of SKE, and conclude that

$$\Pr[\mathcal{H}_3(1^\lambda) = 1] - \Pr[\mathcal{H}_4(1^\lambda) = 1] = \mu(\lambda).$$

Hybrid $\mathcal{H}_5$: The only difference of this hybrid from $\mathcal{H}_4$ is that we compute $K \leftarrow \mathsf{SPHF.Hash}(hk, x)$ instead of $K \leftarrow \Pi$. Therefore, $\mathcal{H}_4$ and $\mathcal{H}_5$ are statistically indistinguishable by the smoothness of the SPHF scheme.

Lemma 5. *$\mathcal{H}_3$ and $\mathcal{H}_4$ are statistically indistinguishable if SKE is C-IND.*

Proof. The proofs of Lemma 5 are analogous to those of Lemma 2.

Hybrid $\mathcal{H}_6$: The only difference of this hybrid from $\mathcal{H}_5$ is that we compute $\pi \leftarrow \mathsf{NIZK.prove}(pp, x, w)$ instead of $\pi \leftarrow \mathsf{NIZK.Sim}(pp, x)$. Therefore, $\mathcal{H}_5$ and $\mathcal{H}_6$ are computationally indistinguishable by the C-IND security of the SKE scheme.

$\underline{\mathcal{B}(1^\lambda):}$
$-pp = \tau \leftarrow \mathsf{NIZK.Setup}(1^\lambda)$
$-(x^*, w^*, M_0, M_1, st) \leftarrow \mathcal{A}^{\mathsf{Gen}}(1^\lambda, pp)$
$-\pi \leftarrow \mathsf{NIZK.Sim}(\tau, x^*)$
$-Set\ x = (x^*, \pi)$
$-hk \leftarrow \mathsf{SPHF.HashKG}(pp)$ *and* $hp \leftarrow \mathsf{SPHF}.ProjKG(pp, hk)$
$-K \leftarrow \mathsf{SPHF.Hash}(hk, x)$
$-Submit\ (1^\lambda, K)$ *to the* $C-IND$ *game of* (8) *to obtain*
 $\cdot\, c_0 \leftarrow \mathsf{SKE.Enc}(K, M_0)$ *or*
 $\cdot\, c_1 \leftarrow \mathsf{SKE.Enc}(K, M_1)$
$-Set\ C_b = (c_b, x^*, hp)$
$-Output\ b^* \leftarrow \mathcal{A}(C_b, st).$

Fig. 6. The SKE-adversary $\mathcal{B}$ simulating hybrid game

Lemma 6. *$\mathcal{H}_5$ and $\mathcal{H}_6$ are computationally indistinguishable if* NIZK *is perfect zero-knowledge.*

Proof. The proofs of Lemma 6 are analogous to those of Lemma 1.

It can be found that, in the hybrid $\mathcal{H}_6$, $\Pr[\mathsf{Exp}^{Adp-1}_{\mathsf{WE},\mathcal{A}}(1^\lambda) = 1] = \Pr[\mathcal{H}_6(1^\lambda) = 1]$, combining the results of Lemma 1 to Lemma 6, it holds that

$$\begin{aligned} Adv^{Adp-b}_{\mathsf{WE},\mathcal{A}}(1^\lambda) &= \left|\Pr[\mathsf{Exp}^{Adp-0}_{\mathsf{WE},\mathcal{A}}(1^\lambda) = 1] - \Pr[\mathsf{Exp}^{Adp-1}_{\mathsf{WE},\mathcal{A}}(1^\lambda) = 1]\right| \\ &= \left|\Pr[\mathcal{H}_0(1^\lambda) = 1] - \Pr[\mathcal{H}_6(1^\lambda) = 1]\right| = \mu(\lambda) \end{aligned}$$

5 Instantiating of SPHFfrom SNARK

SPHF is the key technology of our WE constructed in the previous section, and in this section we will mainly show how to instantiate SPHF from zk-SNARK and prove its smoothness under the standard assumption (DLP).

5.1 Tools

Bilinear Map. A bilinear map $e : \mathbb{G}_1 \times \mathbb{G}_2 \rightarrow \mathbb{G}_T$ has the following properties:

- $\mathbb{G}_1, \mathbb{G}_2, \mathbb{G}_T$ are groups of prime order p;
- $e : \mathbb{G}_1 \times \mathbb{G}_2 \rightarrow \mathbb{G}_T$ is a bilinear pairing, that is, $e(A^a, B^b) = e(A, B)^{ab}$ for all $A \in \mathbb{G}_1, B \in \mathbb{G}_2, a, b \in \mathbb{Z}_p$;
- If g_1 is a generator for $\mathbb{G}_1$ and g_2 is a generator for $\mathbb{G}_2$ then $e(g_1, g_2)$ is a generator for $\mathbb{G}_T$.

Galbraith, Paterson and Smart [30] classified bilinear groups as Type-1 where $\mathbb{G}_1 = \mathbb{G}_2$ (symmetric bilinear groups), Type-2 where there is an efficiently computable isomorphism $\psi : \mathbb{G}_2 \rightarrow \mathbb{G}_1$ (asymmetric bilinear groups), and Type-3 where no such efficiently computable isomorphism exists in either direction between $\mathbb{G}_1$ and $\mathbb{G}_2$. In our instantiations, we choose to present our results in the Type-1 symmetric bilinear groups.

SNARK for QAP. Our goal is to instantiate SPHF that can support all NP-languages $\mathcal{L}$ for encryption, so we use SNARKs for non-interactive zero-knowledge proof of NP-complete problem circuits SAT. To efficiently instantiate SPHF, we adopt the SNARK scheme based on the current state-of-the-art circuit SAT problem proposed by Groth [28] in 2016. Remarkably,the problem of converting from circuit SATto QAP is not the focus of this paper. Please refer to [28] for the specific conversion process.

We will now give a pairing-based NIZK argument for quadratic arithmetic programs. We consider relation generators $\mathcal{R}$ that return relations of the form

$$R = (p, \mathbb{G}_1, \mathbb{G}_T, , e, l, \{u_i(X), v_i(X), w_i(X)\}_{i=0}^{m}, t(X))$$

with $|p| = \lambda$. The relation defines a field $\mathbb{Z}_p$ and a language of statements $(a_1, \cdots, a_l) \in \mathbb{Z}_p^l$ and witnesses $(a_{l+1}, \cdots, a_m) \in \mathbb{Z}_p^{m-l}$ such that with $a_0 = 1$

$$\sum_{i=0}^{m} a_i u_i(X) \cdot \sum_{i=0}^{m} a_i v_i(X) = \sum_{i=0}^{m} a_i w_i(X) + h(X)t(X)$$

for some degree $n-2$ quotient polynomial $h(X)$.

- $\mathsf{Setup}(1^\lambda)$: Pick arbitrary generators g for $\mathbb{G}$. Pick$\alpha, \beta, \gamma, \delta, x \leftarrow$. Define $\tau = (\alpha, \beta, \gamma, \delta, x)$ and compute

$$\sigma = \left(\begin{array}{c} [\alpha], [\beta], [\gamma], [\delta], \left[x^i\right]_{i=0}^{n-1}, \left[\frac{x^i t(x)}{\delta}\right]_{i=0}^{n-1}, \\ \left[\frac{\beta u_i(x)+\alpha v_i(x)+w_i(x)}{\gamma}\right]_{i=0}^{l}, \left[\frac{\beta u_i(x)+\alpha v_i(x)+w_i(x)}{\delta}\right]_{i=l+1}^{m} \end{array} \right)$$

- $\mathsf{prove}(\sigma, x, w)$: Pick $r, s \leftarrow \mathbb{Z}_p$ and compute $\pi = (\pi_A, \pi_B, \pi_C)$, where

$$\pi_A = \left[\alpha + \sum_{i=0}^{m} a_i u_i(x) + r\delta\right], \pi_B = \left[\beta + \sum_{i=0}^{m} a_i v - i(x) + s\delta\right],$$

$$\pi_C = \left[\left(\sum_{i=l+1}^{m} a_i((\beta u_i(x) + \alpha v_i(x) + w_i(x)) + h(x)t(x))\right)/\delta + s\pi_A + r\pi_B - rs\delta\right].$$

- $\mathsf{Verify}(\sigma, x, \pi)$: Parse $\pi = (\pi_A, \pi_B, \pi_C) \in \mathbb{G} \times \mathbb{G} \times \mathbb{G}$. Accept the proof if and only if

$$e(\pi_A, \pi_B) = e([\alpha], [\beta]) e\left(\left[\left(\sum_{i=1}^{l} a_i(\beta u_i(x) + \alpha v_i(x) + w_i(x))\right)/\gamma\right], [\gamma]\right) e(\pi_C, [\delta]).$$

– $\mathsf{Sim}(\tau, x)$: Pick $r, s \leftarrow \mathbb{Z}_p$ and compute a simulated proof$\pi = (\pi_A, \pi_B, \pi_C)$ as

$$\pi_A = [r] \ , \ \pi_B = [s] \ , \ \pi_C = [(rs - \alpha\beta - \sum_{i=0}^{l} a_i(\beta u_i(x) + \alpha v_i(x) + w_i(x)))/\delta].$$

5.2 Our Construction 2: SPHFfor SNARK

To support all NP languages, we construct instantiations of SPHF from SNARKs. To ensure the efficiency of zero-knowledge verification, we use the current most effective zk-SNARKs for QAP. Specifically, our idea is to take the proof π generated by SNARK and the original NP problem instance x' as the SPHF instance x, and the generate random factor to prove π and the original witness w', as the new witness w. We now present the SPHF for SNARK, which borrows construction ideas from Cramer-Shoup encryption [31] (Fig. 7) .

$\mathsf{HashKG}(pp)$: On input the public parameter pp, choose $(r_1, r_2) \leftarrow \mathbb{Z}_p^2$, and output $hk \leftarrow r_1$.
$\mathsf{ProjKG}(pp)$: On input the public parameter pp, and output $hp \leftarrow (hp_1, hp_2, hp_3)$, where

$$hp_1 = [\alpha r_1], hp_2 = [\delta r_1], hp_3 = [r_1].$$

$\mathsf{Hash}(pp, hk, x)$: On input the public parameter pp, hash key hk, instance $x = (x', \pi)$, and output $H_h = \pi_A^{r_1}$.
$\mathsf{ProjHash}(hp, x, w)$: On input the public parameter pp, projhash key h, instance $x = (x', \pi)$,, $w = (w', r, s)$, and output H_p, where

$$H_h = hp_1 \cdot hp_2^{\sum_{i=0}^{m} a_i u_i(x)} \cdot hp_3^r.$$

Fig. 7. SPHF from SNARK

Remark 2. The public parameter pp involved in the above scheme generated by Setup algorithm of SNARK.

5.3 Correctness and Security of SPHF

Theorem 3. *If the DLP assumption holds, then the instantiating of SPHF scheme is correct and smooth secure.*

Proof (Correctness). If SNARK is perfect completeness, for all $(x, w) \in R$, the generated proof π can be verified. Perfect completeness follows by direct verification. After the verification is passed, the correctness of SPHF guarantees

$$\begin{aligned} H_h &= \pi_A^{r_1} \\ &= [(\alpha + \sum_{i=0}^{m} a_i u_i(x) + r\delta) \cdot r_1] = [\alpha r_1] \cdot ([r_1] \sum_{i=0}^{m} a_i u_i(x)) \cdot ([\delta r_1] r) \\ &= hp_1 \cdot hp_2^{\sum_{i=0}^{m} a_i u_i(x)} \cdot hp_3^r = H_p. \end{aligned}$$

It is easy to see that our instantiating of SPHF scheme is correct.

Proof (Smoothness). To prove smoothness, we simulated the following two distributions.
Distribution 0: Let D_0 be the distribution sampled according to the smoothness definition.
Distribution 1: As D_0, but we can get an invalid proof $\pi_A = [r] = x'$ by running the sim algorithm of SNARK. Therefore, it is not a valid instance in the language $\mathcal{L}$. The corresponding hash value is then of the form $H_{\mathsf{Hash}} = \pi_A^{r_1} = [r']$.

In D_1 we have a distribution the hash value is perfectly random. If the DLP assumption holds, D_0 and D_1 are computationally indistinguishable, which completes the proof.

6 Discussion

Cost of Enc and Dec. Subsequently, we would like to briefly demonstrate that our construction is very efficient (without MMap or $i\mathcal{O}$) and compare it with similar SPHF instantiation work.

In the encryption phase: we only need 4 bilinear mapping operations to perform zero-knowledge verification of the witness w (only run once), and only 4 exponentiation operations of the group $\mathbb{G}$ are used in the real encryption phase, and yields a constant ciphertext size (a symmetric encrypted ciphertext and 3 elements on the group $\mathbb{G}$).

In the decryption phase: we can decrypt quickly with only the exponentiation of 2 groups $\mathbb{G}$.

Similar of our scheme is the proposed by Derler and Slamanig [19] in 2018 DCC, but their SPHF instantiation is based on the GS proof system [24], only supports a limited algebraic language, and the instantiation of SPHF requires operations and pair product equations. The solutions are much smaller than their computational cost, and based on the SPHF instantiation implemented by SNARK, it supports NP-complete circuit SAT problems, that is, supports all NP-languages. The specific calculation cost is shown in Table 1, our instantiation from SPHF only requires fixed-size operations, while scheme [19] needs to vary according to the scale of NP languages.

Table 1. Computing cost comparison of SPHF

	HashKG	ProjKG	Hash	ProjHash
[19]	0	$(4(n+o)+1)_{\mathbb{G}}$	$(3n)_{\mathbb{G}}+(3o+1)_{\mathbb{G}_T}+1_e$	$(3(n+o)+o)_{\mathbb{G}}+(n+0)_e$
Our	0	$3_{\mathbb{G}}$	$1_{\mathbb{G}}$	$3_{\mathbb{G}}$

7 Conclusion

In this paper, We have shown a general framework for constructing witness encryption over smooth projective hashing. In terms of efficiency, we focus on schemes that produce efficient ciphertexts with efficient encryption and decryption stages. Specifically, we generate the proof π of the instance x corresponding to the witness w through SNARK. After the verification is passed, an efficient SPHF for SNARK is instantiated. In all cases, we have constant size ciphertext, one symmetric encrypted ciphertext and 3 group elements.

References

1. Garg, S., Gentry, C., Sahai, A., Waters, B.: Witness encryption and its applications. In Proceedings of the Forty-Fifth Annual ACM Symposium on Theory of Computing, pp. 467–476 (2013)
2. Garg, S., Gentry, C., Halevi, S.: Candidate multilinear maps from ideal lattices. In: Johansson, T., Nguyen, P.Q. (eds.) EUROCRYPT 2013. LNCS, vol. 7881, pp. 1–17. Springer, Heidelberg (2013). https://doi.org/10.1007/978-3-642-38348-9_1
3. Garg, S., Gentry, C., Halevi, S., Raykova, M., Sahai, A., Waters, B.: Candidate indistinguishability obfuscation and functional encryption for all circuits. In: 2013 IEEE 54th Annual Symposium on Foundations of Computer Science, pp. 40–49 (2013)
4. Barak, B., et al.: On the (im)possibility of obfuscating programs. In: Kilian, J. (ed.) CRYPTO 2001. LNCS, vol. 2139, pp. 1–18. Springer, Heidelberg (2001). https://doi.org/10.1007/3-540-44647-8_1
5. Bartusek, J., Ishai, Y., Jain, A., Ma, F., Sahai, A., Zhandry, M.: Affine determinant programs: a framework for obfuscation and witness encryption. In: 11th Innovations in Theoretical Computer Science Conference (2020)
6. Zhandry, M.: How to avoid obfuscation using witness PRFs. In: Kushilevitz, E., Malkin, T. (eds.) TCC 2016. LNCS, vol. 9563, pp. 421–448. Springer, Heidelberg (2016). https://doi.org/10.1007/978-3-662-49099-0_16
7. Goldwasser, S., Kalai, Y.T., Popa, R.A., Vaikuntanathan, V., Zeldovich, N.: How to run turing machines on encrypted data. In: Canetti, R., Garay, J.A. (eds.) CRYPTO 2013. LNCS, vol. 8043, pp. 536–553. Springer, Heidelberg (2013). https://doi.org/10.1007/978-3-642-40084-1_30
8. Gentry, C., Lewko, A., Waters, B.: Witness encryption from instance independent assumptions. In: Garay, J.A., Gennaro, R. (eds.) CRYPTO 2014. LNCS, vol. 8616, pp. 426–443. Springer, Heidelberg (2014). https://doi.org/10.1007/978-3-662-44371-2_24

9. Bellare, M., Hoang, V.T.: Adaptive witness encryption and asymmetric password-based cryptography. In: Katz, J. (ed.) PKC 2015. LNCS, vol. 9020, pp. 308–331. Springer, Heidelberg (2015). https://doi.org/10.1007/978-3-662-46447-2_14
10. Arita, S., Handa, S.: Two applications of multilinear maps: group key exchange and witness encryption. In: Proceedings of the 2nd ACM Workshop on ASIA Public-Key Cryptography, pp. 13–22 (2014)
11. Liu, J., Garcia, F., Ryan, M.: Time-release protocol from bitcoin and witness encryption for sat. Korean Circ. J. **40**(10), 530–535 (2015)
12. Liu, J., Jager, T., Kakvi, S.A., Warinschi, B.: How to build time-lock encryption. Des. Codes Crypt. **86**(11), 2549–2586 (2018)
13. Uberti, G., Luo, K., Cheng, O., Goh, W.: Building usable witness encryption. arXiv preprint arXiv:2112.04581 (2021)
14. Garg, S., Gentry, C., Halevi, S., Zhandry, M.: Fully secure attribute based encryption from multilinear maps. Cryptology ePrint Archive (2014)
15. Abusalah, H., Fuchsbauer, G., Pietrzak, K.: Offline witness encryption. In: Manulis, M., Sadeghi, A.-R., Schneider, S. (eds.) ACNS 2016. LNCS, vol. 9696, pp. 285–303. Springer, Cham (2016). https://doi.org/10.1007/978-3-319-39555-5_16
16. Pal, T., Dutta, R.: Offline witness encryption from witness PRF and randomized encoding in CRS model. In: Jang-Jaccard, J., Guo, F. (eds.) ACISP 2019. LNCS, vol. 11547, pp. 78–96. Springer, Cham (2019). https://doi.org/10.1007/978-3-030-21548-4_5
17. Chvojka, P., Jager, T., Kakvi, S.A.: Offline witness encryption with semi-adaptive security. In: Conti, M., Zhou, J., Casalicchio, E., Spognardi, A. (eds.) ACNS 2020. LNCS, vol. 12146, pp. 231–250. Springer, Cham (2020). https://doi.org/10.1007/978-3-030-57808-4_12
18. Pal, T., Dutta, R.: Semi-adaptively secure offline witness encryption from puncturable witness PRF. In: Nguyen, K., Wu, W., Lam, K.Y., Wang, H. (eds.) ProvSec 2020. LNCS, vol. 12505, pp. 169–189. Springer, Cham (2020). https://doi.org/10.1007/978-3-030-62576-4_9
19. Derler, D., Slamanig, D.: Practical witness encryption for algebraic languages or how to encrypt under Groth-Sahai proofs. Des. Codes Crypt. **86**(11), 2525–2547 (2018)
20. Cramer, R., Shoup, V.: Universal hash proofs and a paradigm for adaptive chosen ciphertext secure public-key encryption. In: Knudsen, L.R. (ed.) EUROCRYPT 2002. LNCS, vol. 2332, pp. 45–64. Springer, Heidelberg (2002). https://doi.org/10.1007/3-540-46035-7_4
21. Abdalla, M., Benhamouda, F., Pointcheval, D.: Disjunctions for hash proof systems: new constructions and applications. In: Oswald, E., Fischlin, M. (eds.) EUROCRYPT 2015. LNCS, vol. 9057, pp. 69–100. Springer, Heidelberg (2015). https://doi.org/10.1007/978-3-662-46803-6_3
22. Benhamouda, F., Blazy, O., Ducas, L., Quach, W.: Hash proof systems over lattices revisited. In: Abdalla, M., Dahab, R. (eds.) PKC 2018. LNCS, vol. 10770, pp. 644–674. Springer, Cham (2018). https://doi.org/10.1007/978-3-319-76581-5_22
23. Faonio, A., Nielsen, J.B., Venturi, D.: Predictable arguments of knowledge. In: Fehr, S. (ed.) PKC 2017. LNCS, vol. 10174, pp. 121–150. Springer, Heidelberg (2017). https://doi.org/10.1007/978-3-662-54365-8_6
24. Groth, J., Sahai, A.: Efficient non-interactive proof systems for bilinear groups. In: Smart, N. (ed.) EUROCRYPT 2008. LNCS, vol. 4965, pp. 415–432. Springer, Heidelberg (2008). https://doi.org/10.1007/978-3-540-78967-3_24

25. Campanelli, M., David, B., Khoshakhlagh, H., Konring, A., Nielsen, J.B. Encryption to the future: a paradigm for sending secret messages to future (anonymous) committees. Cryptology ePrint Archive (2021)
26. Escala, A., Herold, G., Kiltz, E., Ràfols, C., Villar, J.: An algebraic framework for Diffie-Hellman assumptions. In: Canetti, R., Garay, J.A. (eds.) CRYPTO 2013. LNCS, vol. 8043, pp. 129–147. Springer, Heidelberg (2013). https://doi.org/10.1007/978-3-642-40084-1_8
27. Ben-Sasson, E., Chiesa, A., Genkin, D., Tromer, E., Virza, M.: SNARKs for c: verifying program executions succinctly and in zero knowledge. In: Canetti, R., Garay, J.A. (eds.) CRYPTO 2013. LNCS, vol. 8043, pp. 90–108. Springer, Heidelberg (2013). https://doi.org/10.1007/978-3-642-40084-1_6
28. Groth, J.: On the size of pairing-based non-interactive arguments. In: Fischlin, M., Coron, J.-S. (eds.) EUROCRYPT 2016. LNCS, vol. 9666, pp. 305–326. Springer, Heidelberg (2016). https://doi.org/10.1007/978-3-662-49896-5_11
29. Benhamouda, F., Blazy, O., Chevalier, C., Pointcheval, D., Vergnaud, D.: New techniques for SPHFs and efficient one-round PAKE protocols. In: Canetti, R., Garay, J.A. (eds.) CRYPTO 2013. LNCS, vol. 8042, pp. 449–475. Springer, Heidelberg (2013). https://doi.org/10.1007/978-3-642-40041-4_25
30. Galbraith, S.D., Paterson, K.G., Smart, N.P.: Pairings for cryptographers. Discrete Appl. Math. **156**(6), 3113–3121 (2008). Applications of Algebra to Cryptography
31. Cramer, R., Shoup, V.: A practical public key cryptosystem provably secure against adaptive chosen ciphertext attack. In: Krawczyk, H. (ed.) CRYPTO 1998. LNCS, vol. 1462, pp. 13–25. Springer, Heidelberg (1998). https://doi.org/10.1007/BFb0055717

Post-quantum Cryptography

More Efficient Adaptively Secure Lattice-Based IBE with Equality Test in the Standard Model

Kyoichi Asano[1,2(✉)], Keita Emura[2], and Atsushi Takayasu[3]

[1] The University of Electro-Communications, 1-5-1, Chofugaoka, Chofu, Tokyo 182-8585, Japan
k.asano@uec.ac.jp

[2] National Institute of Information and Communications Technology, 4-2-1, Nukui-Kitamachi, Koganei, Tokyo 184-8795, Japan

[3] The University of Tokyo, 7-3-1, Hongo, Bunkyo-ku, Tokyo 113-8656, Japan

Abstract. Identity-based encryption with equality test (IBEET) is a variant of identity-based encryption (IBE), where any users who have trapdoors can check whether two ciphertexts are encryption of the same plaintext. Although several lattice-based IBEET schemes have been proposed, they have drawbacks in either security or efficiency. Specifically, most schemes satisfy only selective security, while adaptively secure schemes in the standard model suffer from large master public keys that consist of linear numbers of matrices. In other words, known lattice-based IBEET schemes perform poorly compared to the state-of-the-art lattice-based IBE schemes (without equality test). In this paper, we propose a semi-generic construction of CCA-secure lattice-based IBEET from a certain class of lattice-based IBE schemes. As a result, we obtain the first lattice-based IBEET schemes with adaptive security and CCA security in the standard model. Furthermore, our semi-generic construction can use several state-of-the-art lattice-based IBE schemes as underlying schemes. Then, we have adaptively secure lattice-based IBEET schemes whose public keys have only poly-log matrices.

Keywords: Identity-based encryption with equality test · Adaptive security · CCA security · Lattices

1 Introduction

Encryption is a fundamental tool for providing data confidentiality. On the other hand, it affects several functions such as searching, comparing, partitioning, and so on. Yang et al. [22] proposed public key encryption with equality test (PKEET) which allows us to check whether two plaintexts of two ciphertexts are the same or not. This equality check allows us to provide a keyword search on encrypted data, data partitioning on an encrypted database, and so on. Although anyone can run the test algorithm in the Yang's definition, a trapdoor for running the test algorithm is introduced in subsequent works, e.g., [12,13]. Identity-based

W. Susilo et al. (Eds.): ISC 2022, LNCS 13640, pp. 75–83, 2022.
https://doi.org/10.1007/978-3-031-22390-7_5

encryption with equality test (IBEET) [14] is an extension of PKEET that can simplify the certificate management of PKEET. As in identity-based encryption (IBE), an identity id is used as a public key for generating a ciphertext $\mathsf{ct}_{\mathsf{id}}$. A secret key $\mathsf{sk}_{\mathsf{id}}$ of an identity id can generate a trapdoor $\mathsf{td}_{\mathsf{id}}$. By using trapdoors $\mathsf{td}_{\mathsf{id}_0}$ and $\mathsf{td}_{\mathsf{id}_1}$, we can check whether $\mathsf{ct}_{\mathsf{id}_0}$ and $\mathsf{ct}_{\mathsf{id}_1}$ are encryptions of the same plaintexts.

Although several CCA-secure IBEET schemes have been proposed by assuming the hardness of Diffie-Hellman-type assumptions, e.g., [11,14], they are vulnerable against quantum attacks. To achieve post-quantum security, several lattice-based IBEET schemes have been proposed. There are two ways for constructing lattice-based IBEET schemes. One is instantiating lattice-based schemes from generic constructions of IBEET and the other is direct constructions by modifying known lattice-based IBE schemes.

At first, we review two known generic constructions of IBEET that can instantiate lattice-based schemes. Lin et al. [13] proposed a generic construction of CCA-secure IBEET from CCA-secure IBE in the random oracle model. Lee et al. [12] proposed a generic construction of CCA-secure IBEET from three-level CPA-secure hierarchical identity-based encryption (HIBE) and one-time signatures (OTSs) in the standard model, where OTSs are used for achieving CCA security via the Canetti-Halevi-Katz (CHK) transformation [6]. Lee et al.'s construction provides adaptively secure lattice-based schemes in the quantum random oracle model (QROM) based on adaptively secure lattice-based HIBE schemes in the QROM [2,7,23]. Lee et al.'s construction also provides selectively secure lattice-based schemes in the standard model based on selectively secure HIBE schemes in the standard model [1,7]. However, their construction does not provide *purely* adaptively secure lattice-based IBEET schemes in the standard model since there are no known adaptively secure lattice-based HIBE schemes in the standard model. Although Singh et al. [16] constructed an adaptively secure lattice-based HIBE scheme in the standard model based on Agrawal et al.'s adaptively secure non-hierarchical IBE scheme [1], the scheme achieves only bounded security in the sense that the size of a modulus q depends on the number of adversary's key extraction queries. Thus, the instantiation of the Lee et al.'s generic construction from the Singh et al.'s HIBE scheme does not satisfy purely adaptive security. Next, we review four known direct constructions of lattice-based IBEET schemes [8,15,17,20], where all known schemes were studied in the standard model. Duong et al.'s IBEET scheme [8] and Nguyen et al.'s IBEET scheme [15] are based on Agrawal et al.'s adaptively secure IBE scheme [1] achieving adaptive and CPA security. Unfortunately, due to the nature of Agrawal et al.'s IBE scheme, these IBEET schemes achieve only bounded security as the case of Singh et al.'s adaptively secure HIBE scheme [16]. Susilo et al.'s IBEET scheme [17] that is similar to Lee et al.'s generic construction [12] is based on Agrawal et al.'s selectively secure IBE scheme [1] achieving selective and CCA security. Wu et al.'s IBEET scheme [20] is based on Tsabary's IBE scheme [18] achieving adaptive and CPA security.

Summarizing the situation, almost all known lattice-based IBEET schemes in the standard model achieve only selective and CCA security [12,17] or adaptive and CPA security [8,15,20] with the only exception that Lee et al.'s generic construction [12] instantiated by Singh et al.'s HIBE scheme [16]. Moreover, almost all adaptively secure schemes achieve only bounded security with the only exception that Wu et al.'s CPA-secure scheme [20]. Therefore, constructing purely adaptive and CCA-secure lattice-based IBEET scheme is an interesting open problem. Moreover, known adaptively secure IBEET schemes have a common bottleneck in terms of efficiency. Although there are adaptively secure lattice-based IBE schemes such as Yamada's IBE scheme [21] and Jager-Kurek-Niehues's (JKN) IBE scheme [10][1] whose public keys consist of poly-log matrices, public keys of known adaptively secure lattice-based IBEET schemes [8,15,16,20] consist of matrices whose numbers are (almost) linear in the length of identities or the security parameter. Therefore, it is desirable to construct adaptively secure lattice-based IBEET schemes whose public keys consist of poly-log matrices.

1.1 Our Contribution

In this paper, we construct the first purely adaptive and CCA-secure lattice-based IBEET schemes in the standard model. One promising way for constructing such a desirable scheme is constructing adaptively secure lattice-based HIBE schemes based on known adaptively secure IBE schemes. Specifically, as the Waters pairing-based HIBE scheme [19], we can obtain such a HIBE scheme by sacrificing reduction loss. However, we take another approach to resolve the problem without sacrificing reduction loss very much. In particular, we propose a semi-generic construction of CCA-secure lattice-based IBEET from CPA-secure lattice-based IBE whose structure is similar to Agrawal-Boneh-Boyen (ABB)'s IBE scheme [1] which we call ABB-type IBE. The resulting IBEET schemes achieve adaptive security if the underlying IBE schemes satisfy adaptive security. Intuitively, a ciphertext and secret key for the same id of ABB-type IBE is associated with the same publicly computable matrix. Thanks to the semi-generic construction, we propose the first purely adaptive and CCA-secure lattice-based IBEET schemes. Moreover, since ABB-type IBE covers Yamada's IBE scheme [21] and JKN IBE scheme [10], we can obtain the first adaptive lattice-based IBEET schemes whose public keys consist of poly-log matrices. We note that the sizes of ciphertexts and secret keys are almost the same among all known lattice-based IBEET schemes.

The idea of our semi-generic construction is similar to Lee et al.'s generic construction [12] from three-level CPA-secure HIBE.[2] Recall that Lee et al. proved that adaptively secure three-level CPA-secure HIBE is sufficient for constructing adaptively and CCA-secure IBEET. Basically, ciphertexts of all IBEET schemes

[1] Although Yamada's scheme is purely secure under the LWE assumption, JKN scheme enjoys smaller LWE parameters at the expense of additionally employing near-collision resistance hash functions.

[2] In this paper, we do not follow Lee et al.'s argument [12] in a security proof but follow Asano et al.'s one [4] which is an attribute-based extension of Lee et al.'s work with a refined proof.

consist of two types of ciphertexts, one is responsible only for decryption and the other is also responsible for equality test. Lee et al. utilized each three hierarchical levels for id, ciphertext type 0 or 1, and verification keys of OTSs for the CHK transformation [6], respectively. Then, by using the CPA security of the underlying HIBE, Lee et al. hide the challenge plaintext for both types of ciphertexts one by one. Let's take a closer look at this proof strategy. It is widely known that the CHK transformation can convert CPA-secure IBE to CCA-secure public key encryption even when the underlying IBE satisfies only selective security. In other words, Lee et al.'s generic construction does not require HIBE with adaptive security for all hierarchical levels to construct adaptively secure and CCA-secure IBEET. In turn, a special three-level HIBE scheme that satisfies adaptive security only for the first level and selective security for the other levels is sufficient for our purpose. To this end, we construct such special three-level HIBE schemes from ABB-type IBE such as Yamada's scheme [21] and JKN scheme [10]. Briefly speaking, the first level and the other levels of our HIBE scheme are the same as those of the underlying IBE scheme, i.e., Yamada's scheme and the JKN scheme, and Agrawal-Boneh-Boyen's selectively secure HIBE scheme, respectively. Then, a slight modification of Agrawal et al.'s proof technique is applicable to the special three-level HIBE. Moreover, since we employ a semi-generic construction from ABB-type IBE, we do not need to make complex arguments to achieve adaptive security such as [10,21].

2 Identity-Based Encryption with Equality Test

In this section, we show a syntax of IBEET. The definitions for correctness and security are summarized in the full version of this paper.

An IBEET scheme Σ consists of the six algorithms (Setup, KeyGen, Enc, Dec, $\mathsf{Trapdoor}$, Test) as follows:

$\mathsf{Setup}(1^\lambda) \to (\mathsf{mpk}, \mathsf{msk})$: On input the security parameter 1^λ, it outputs a master public key mpk and a master secret key msk. We assume that mpk contains a description of a plaintext space $\mathcal{M}$ and an identity space $\mathcal{ID}$ that are determined only by the security parameter λ.

$\mathsf{KeyGen}(\mathsf{mpk}, \mathsf{msk}, \mathsf{id}) \to \mathsf{sk}_{\mathsf{id}}$: On input mpk, msk, and an identity $\mathsf{id} \in \mathcal{ID}$, it outputs a secret key $\mathsf{sk}_{\mathsf{id}}$.

$\mathsf{Enc}(\mathsf{mpk}, \mathsf{id}, \mathsf{M}) \to \mathsf{ct}_{\mathsf{id}}$: On input mpk, $\mathsf{id} \in \mathcal{ID}$, and a plaintext $\mathsf{M} \in \mathcal{M}$, it outputs a ciphertext $\mathsf{ct}_{\mathsf{id}}$.

$\mathsf{Dec}(\mathsf{mpk}, \mathsf{sk}_{\mathsf{id}}, \mathsf{ct}_{\mathsf{id}}) \to \mathsf{M}$ or $\perp$: On input mpk, $\mathsf{sk}_{\mathsf{id}}$, and $\mathsf{ct}_{\mathsf{id}}$, it outputs the decryption result M or $\perp$.

$\mathsf{Trapdoor}(\mathsf{mpk}, \mathsf{sk}_{\mathsf{id}}) \to \mathsf{td}_{\mathsf{id}}$: On input mpk and $\mathsf{sk}_{\mathsf{id}}$, it outputs the trapdoor $\mathsf{td}_{\mathsf{id}}$.

$\mathsf{Test}(\mathsf{mpk}, \mathsf{td}_{\mathsf{id}_0}, \mathsf{ct}_{\mathsf{id}_0}, \mathsf{td}_{\mathsf{id}_1}, \mathsf{ct}_{\mathsf{id}_1}) \to 1$ or 0: On input mpk, two trapdoors $\mathsf{td}_{\mathsf{id}_0}$ and $\mathsf{td}_{\mathsf{id}_1}$, and two ciphertexts $\mathsf{ct}_{\mathsf{id}_0}$ and $\mathsf{ct}_{\mathsf{id}_1}$, it outputs 1 or 0.

3 Construction

In this section, we give our semi-generic construction of IBEET from ABB-type IBE. At first, we define the ABB-type IBE in Sect. 3.1. Then, we show our semi-generic construction in Sect. 3.2. Due to the page limitation, we omit proofs of correctness and security. See the full version of this paper.

Preliminaries on Lattices. For all $\mathbf{V} \in \mathbb{Z}_q^{n\times m'}$, we let $\mathbf{A}_\tau^{-1}(\mathbf{V})$ denote the random variable whose distribution is a Gaussian $(D_{\mathbb{Z}^m,\tau})^{m'}$ conditioned on $\mathbf{A}\cdot\mathbf{A}_\tau^{-1}(\mathbf{V}) = \mathbf{V}$. A τ-trapdoor for $\mathbf{A}$ is a procedure that can sample from the distribution $\mathbf{A}_\tau^{-1}(\mathbf{V})$ in time $\mathsf{poly}(n, m, m', \log q)$, for any $\mathbf{V}$. We slightly overload the notation and denote a τ-trapdoor for $\mathbf{A}$ by $\mathbf{A}_\tau^{-1}$. We have the following:

Lemma 1 ([1–3,5,7,9], **Properties of Trapdoors).** *Lattice trapdoors exhibit the following properties.*

1. *Given $\mathbf{A}_\tau^{-1}$, one can obtain $\mathbf{A}_{\tau'}^{-1}$, for any $\tau' \geq \tau$.*
2. *Given $\mathbf{A}_\tau^{-1}$, one can deterministically obtain $[\mathbf{A}\|\mathbf{B}]_\tau^{-1}$ for any $\mathbf{B}$.*
3. *Given $\mathbf{A} \in \mathbb{Z}_q^{n\times m}$, $\mathbf{R} \in \mathbb{Z}^{m\times N}$ with $N > n\lceil\log q\rceil$, and a full-rank matrix $\mathbf{H} \in \mathbb{Z}_q^{n\times n}$, one can obtain $[\mathbf{A}\|\mathbf{AR} + \mathbf{HG}]_\tau^{-1}$ for $\tau = m\cdot\|\mathbf{R}\|\cdot\omega(\sqrt{\log m})$.*
4. *Given $\mathbf{A}_\tau^{-1}$, one can randomize it and obtain $\mathbf{A}_{\tau'}^{-1}$ for $\tau' = \tau\cdot\omega(\sqrt{m})$.*
5. *There exists an efficient procedure $\mathsf{TrapGen}(1^n, 1^m, q)$ that outputs $(\mathbf{A}, \mathbf{A}_{\tau_0}^{-1})$ where $\mathbf{A} \in \mathbb{Z}_q^{n\times m}$ for some $m = O(n\log q)$ and is 2^{-n}-close to uniform, where $\tau_0 = \omega(\sqrt{n\log q\log n})$.*
6. *For $\mathbf{A}_\tau^{-1}$ and $\mathbf{u} \in \mathbb{Z}_q^n$, it follows $\Pr[\|\mathbf{A}_\tau^{-1}(\mathbf{u})\| > \tau\sqrt{m}] = \mathsf{negl}(n)$.*

We also use the following full rank difference map.

Definition 1 ([1], **Full Rank Difference Map).** *Let q be a prime and n be a positive integer. We say that a function $\mathsf{FRD} : \mathcal{ID} \to \mathbb{Z}_q^{n\times n}$ is an encoding with full-rank differences if: for all distinct $\mathsf{id}, \mathsf{id}' \in \mathcal{ID}$, a matrix $\mathsf{FRD}(\mathsf{id}) - \mathsf{FRD}(\mathsf{id}') \in \mathbb{Z}_q^{n\times n}$ is full rank, and FRD is computable in polynomial time in $n\log q$.*

3.1 ABB-Type Identity-Based Encryption

At first, we briefly recall a multi-bit variant of the Agrawal-Boneh-Boyen selectively secure IBE scheme [1], where the plaintext is an ℓ-bit binary string. The IBE scheme has a master public key $(\mathbf{A}, \mathbf{B}, \mathbf{U}) \in (\mathbb{Z}_q^{n\times m})^2 \times \mathbb{Z}_q^{n\times\ell}$ and master secret key $\mathbf{A}_{\tau_0}^{-1}$. A ciphertext for id consists of three vectors $\mathbf{c}_0, \mathbf{c}_1, \mathbf{c}_2$ such that

$$\mathbf{c}_0^\top = \mathbf{s}^\top\mathbf{U} + \mathbf{e}_0^\top + \mathsf{M}\cdot\lceil q/2\rceil \in \mathbb{Z}_q^\ell,$$
$$\mathbf{c}_1^\top = \mathbf{s}^\top\mathbf{A} + \mathbf{e}_1^\top \in \mathbb{Z}_q^m, \qquad \mathbf{c}_2^\top = \mathbf{s}^\top[\mathbf{B} + \mathsf{FRD}(\mathsf{id})\mathbf{G}] + \mathbf{e}_2^\top \in \mathbb{Z}_q^m,$$

where $\mathbf{s}$ is a uniformly random vector and $\mathbf{e}_0, \mathbf{e}_1, \mathbf{e}_2$ are short vectors, e.g., sampled according to discrete Gaussian vectors. A secret key for id is $[\mathbf{A}\|\mathbf{B} + \mathsf{FRD}(\mathsf{id})\mathbf{G}]_\tau^{-1}(\mathbf{U})$ and decryption succeeds by using the relation

$$\mathbf{c}_0^\top - [\mathbf{c}_1^\top\|\mathbf{c}_2^\top]\cdot[\mathbf{A}\|\mathbf{B} + \mathsf{FRD}(\mathsf{id})\mathbf{G}]_\tau^{-1}(\mathbf{U}) = \mathsf{M}\cdot\lceil q/2\rceil + \mathsf{noise}.$$

Several improved variants which we call ABB-type IBE have been proposed to achieve adaptive security. To capture ABB-type IBE, we use the following auxiliary algorithm:

- $\mathsf{PubEval}(\{\mathbf{B}_i\}_{i\in[u]}, \mathsf{id}) \rightarrow \mathbf{B}_{\mathsf{id}}$: On input matrices $\{\mathbf{B}_i\}_{i\in[u]}$ and an identity $\mathsf{id} \in \mathcal{ID}$, it outputs $\mathbf{B}_{\mathsf{id}} \in \mathbb{Z}_q^{n\times m}$.

Intuitively, Agrawal et al.'s selectively secure IBE scheme uses a matrix $\mathbf{B}$ in a master public key to compute a matrix $\mathbf{B}_{\mathsf{id}} = \mathbf{B} + \mathsf{FRD}(\mathsf{id})\mathbf{G}$ that is associated with both ciphertext and secret key. To achieve adaptive security, we use u matrices $\{\mathbf{B}_i\}_{i\in[u]}$ in a master public key and compute a matrix $\mathbf{B}_{\mathsf{id}}$ by using the $\mathsf{PubEval}$ algorithm. Although the first (Q-bounded) adaptively secure IBE scheme of Agrawal et al. [1] uses $u = O(\lambda)$ matrices, there are a series of works to reduce u. Yamada's adaptively secure scheme [21] that is purely secure under the LWE assumption uses $u = O(\log^3 \lambda)$ matrices, while JKN's scheme [10] utilizes a near collision resistant hash function and further reduces u to be $O(\log \lambda)$.

Then, we formally define ABB-type IBE as follows.

$\mathsf{IBE.Setup}(1^\lambda) \rightarrow (\mathsf{IBE.mpk}, \mathsf{IBE.msk})$: On input the security parameter 1^λ, it chooses parameters n, m, q, τ_0, τ_1, α, α', ℓ, runs $(\mathbf{A}, \mathbf{A}_{\tau_0}^{-1}) \leftarrow \mathsf{TrapGen}(1^n, 1^m, q)$, and chooses random matrices $\{\mathbf{B}_i\}_{i\in[u]} \leftarrow_\$ (\mathbb{Z}_q^{n\times m})^u$ and $\mathbf{U} \leftarrow_\$ \mathbb{Z}_q^{n\times \ell}$. Finally, it outputs $\mathsf{IBE.mpk} := (\mathbf{A}, \{\mathbf{B}_i\}_{i\in[u]}, \mathbf{U})$ and $\mathsf{IBE.msk} := \mathbf{A}_{\tau_0}^{-1}$.

$\mathsf{IBE.Enc}(\mathsf{IBE.mpk}, \mathsf{id}, \mathsf{M}) \rightarrow \mathsf{IBE.ct}_{\mathsf{id}}$: Parse $\mathsf{IBE.mpk} = (\mathbf{A}, \{\mathbf{B}_i\}_{i\in[u]}, \mathbf{U})$. It samples $\mathbf{s} \leftarrow_\$ \mathbb{Z}_q^n$, $\mathbf{e}_0 \leftarrow D_{\mathbb{Z}^\ell, \alpha q}$ and $\mathbf{e}_1, \mathbf{e}_2 \leftarrow D_{\mathbb{Z}^m, \alpha' q}$, runs $\mathbf{B}_{\mathsf{id}} \leftarrow \mathsf{PubEval}(\{\mathbf{B}_i\}_{i\in[u]}, \mathsf{id})$, and sets

$$\mathbf{c}_0^\top = \mathbf{s}^\top \mathbf{U} + \mathbf{e}_0^\top + \mathsf{M} \cdot \lceil q/2 \rceil \in \mathbb{Z}_q^\ell,$$
$$\mathbf{c}_1^\top = \mathbf{s}^\top \mathbf{A} + \mathbf{e}_1^\top \in \mathbb{Z}_q^m, \qquad \mathbf{c}_2^\top = \mathbf{s}^\top \mathbf{B}_{\mathsf{id}} + \mathbf{e}_2^\top \in \mathbb{Z}_q^m.$$

Finally, it outputs $\mathsf{IBE.ct}_{\mathsf{id}} = (\mathbf{c}_0, \mathbf{c}_1, \mathbf{c}_2)$.

$\mathsf{IBE.KeyGen}(\mathsf{IBE.mpk}, \mathsf{IBE.msk}, \mathsf{id}) \rightarrow \mathsf{IBE.sk}_{\mathsf{id}}$: Parse $\mathsf{IBE.mpk} = (\mathbf{A}, \{\mathbf{B}_i\}_{i\in[u]}, \mathbf{U})$ and $\mathsf{IBE.msk} = \mathbf{A}_{\tau_0}^{-1}$. For an identity $\mathsf{id} \in \mathcal{ID}$, it runs $\mathbf{B}_{\mathsf{id}} \leftarrow \mathsf{PubEval}(\{\mathbf{B}_i\}_{i\in[u]}, \mathsf{id})$, obtains trapdoor $[\mathbf{A}\|\mathbf{B}_{\mathsf{id}}]_{\tau_1}^{-1}$ by using the trapdoor $\mathbf{A}_{\tau_0}^{-1}$ and Items 1 and 4 of Lemma 1, and outputs $\mathsf{sk}_{\mathsf{id}} := [\mathbf{A}\|\mathbf{B}_{\mathsf{id}}]_{\tau_1}^{-1}$.

$\mathsf{IBE.Dec}(\mathsf{IBE.mpk}, \mathsf{IBE.sk}_{\mathsf{id}}, \mathsf{IBE.ct}_{\mathsf{id}}) \rightarrow \mathsf{M}$ or $\perp$: Parse $\mathsf{IBE.mpk} = (\mathbf{A}, \{\mathbf{B}_i\}_{i\in[u]}, \mathbf{U})$, $\mathsf{IBE.sk}_{\mathsf{id}} = [\mathbf{A}\|\mathbf{B}_{\mathsf{id}}]_{\tau_1}^{-1}$, and $\mathsf{IBE.ct}_{\mathsf{id}} = (\mathbf{c}_0, \mathbf{c}_1, \mathbf{c}_2)$. It samples $\mathbf{E} \leftarrow [\mathbf{A}\|\mathbf{B}_{\mathsf{id}}]_{\tau_1}^{-1}(\mathbf{U})$, computes $\mathbf{m}^\top = \mathbf{c}_0^\top - [\mathbf{c}_1^\top \| \mathbf{c}_2^\top]\mathbf{E} \in \mathbb{Z}_q^\ell$, and sets i-th bit of ℓ bit string M as 1 if $|\mathbf{m}_i - \lceil q/2 \rceil| < \lceil q/4 \rceil$ and 0 otherwise. Finally, it outputs M.

3.2 Constructions of IBEET Schemes from ABB-Type IBE

We use ABB-type IBE to construct a lattice-based IBEET scheme. In addition to $\mathsf{IBE.mpk} = (\mathbf{A}, \{\mathbf{B}_i\}_{i\in[u]}, \mathbf{U})$, mpk has two random matrices $\mathbf{C}_1, \mathbf{C}_2 \in \mathbb{Z}_q^{n\times m}$. Before presenting our scheme, we introduce two auxiliary algorithms.

- $\widehat{\mathsf{Enc}}(\mathsf{mpk}, (\mathsf{id}, b, \mathsf{verk}), \mathsf{M}) \rightarrow \mathsf{ct}_{\mathsf{id},b}$: It runs $\mathsf{IBE.Enc}(\mathsf{IBE.mpk}, \mathsf{id}, \mathsf{M})$ to compute $\mathbf{c}_0, \mathbf{c}_1, \mathbf{c}_2$, samples $\mathbf{R} \leftarrow_\$ \{-1, 1\}^{m\times 2m}$ and computes

$$\mathbf{c}_3^\top = \mathbf{s}^\top [\mathbf{C}_1 + b\mathbf{G} \| \mathbf{C}_2 + \mathsf{FRD}(\mathsf{verk})\mathbf{G}] + \mathbf{e}_1^\top \mathbf{R} \in \mathbb{Z}_q^{2m},$$

where $\mathbf{s}, \mathbf{e}_1$ are sampled during $\mathsf{IBE.Enc}$ and $b \in \{0,1\}$. Finally, it outputs $\mathsf{ct}_{\mathsf{id},b} := (\mathbf{c}_0, \mathbf{c}_1, \mathbf{c}_2, \mathbf{c}_3)$.

- $\widehat{\mathsf{Dec}}(\mathsf{mpk}, \mathbf{E}_b, \mathsf{ct}_{\mathsf{id},b}) \to \mathsf{M}'$: It computes $\mathbf{m}^\top = \mathbf{c}_0^\top - [\mathbf{c}_1^\top \| \mathbf{c}_2^\top \| \mathbf{c}_3^\top]\mathbf{E}_b$ and recovers M' from $\mathbf{m}$ in the same way as $\mathsf{IBE.Dec}$.

Then, we show our IBEET scheme.

$\mathsf{Setup}(1^\lambda) \to (\mathsf{mpk}, \mathsf{msk})$: It runs $(\mathsf{IBE.mpk}, \mathsf{IBE.msk}) \leftarrow \mathsf{IBE.Setup}(1^\lambda)$, sample $\mathbf{C}_1, \mathbf{C}_2 \leftarrow_\$ \mathbb{Z}_q^{n\times m}$, selects a OTS scheme $\Gamma = (\mathsf{Sig.Setup}, \mathsf{Sig.Sign}, \mathsf{Sig.Vrfy})$ and a hash function H, and outputs $\mathsf{mpk} := (\mathsf{IBE.mpk}, \mathbf{C}_1, \mathbf{C}_2, \Gamma, \mathsf{H})$ and $\mathsf{msk} := \mathsf{IBE.msk}$.

$\mathsf{Enc}(\mathsf{mpk}, \mathsf{id}, \mathsf{M}) \to \mathsf{ct}_{\mathsf{id}}$: Parse $\mathsf{mpk} = (\mathsf{IBE.mpk}, \mathbf{C}_1, \mathbf{C}_2, \Gamma, \mathsf{H})$. It runs

- $(\mathsf{verk}, \mathsf{sigk}) \leftarrow \mathsf{Sig.Setup}(1^\lambda)$,
- $\mathsf{ct}_{\mathsf{id},0} \leftarrow \widehat{\mathsf{Enc}}(\mathsf{mpk}, (\mathsf{id}, 0, \mathsf{verk}), \mathsf{M})$,
- $\mathsf{ct}_{\mathsf{id},1} \leftarrow \widehat{\mathsf{Enc}}(\mathsf{mpk}, (\mathsf{id}, 1, \mathsf{verk}), \mathsf{H}(\mathsf{M}))$,
- $\sigma \leftarrow \mathsf{Sig.Sign}(\mathsf{sigk}, [\mathsf{ct}_{\mathsf{id},0} \| \mathsf{ct}_{\mathsf{id},1}])$.

Output $\mathsf{ct}_{\mathsf{id}} := (\mathsf{verk}, \mathsf{ct}_{\mathsf{id},0}, \mathsf{ct}_{\mathsf{id},1}, \sigma)$.

$\mathsf{KeyGen}(\mathsf{mpk}, \mathsf{msk}, \mathsf{id}) \to \mathsf{sk}_{\mathsf{id}}$: Parse $\mathsf{mpk} = (\mathsf{IBE.mpk}, \mathbf{C}_1, \mathbf{C}_2, \Gamma, \mathsf{H})$ and $\mathsf{msk} = \mathsf{IBE.msk}$. It runs $\mathsf{IBE.sk}_{\mathsf{id}} = [\mathbf{A}\|\mathbf{B}_{\mathsf{id}}]_{\tau_1}^{-1} \leftarrow \mathsf{IBE.KeyGen}(\mathsf{IBE.mpk}, \mathsf{IBE.msk}, \mathsf{id})$ and outputs $\mathsf{sk}_{\mathsf{id}} := \mathsf{IBE.sk}_{\mathsf{id}}$.

$\mathsf{Dec}(\mathsf{mpk}, \mathsf{sk}_{\mathsf{id}}, \mathsf{ct}_{\mathsf{id}}) \to \mathsf{M}$ or $\perp$: Parse $\mathsf{mpk} = (\mathsf{IBE.mpk}, \mathbf{C}_1, \mathbf{C}_2, \Gamma, \mathsf{H})$, $\mathsf{ct}_{\mathsf{id}} = (\mathsf{verk}, \mathbf{c}_{\mathsf{id},0}, \mathbf{c}_{\mathsf{id},1}, \sigma)$, and $\mathsf{sk}_{\mathsf{id}} = [\mathbf{A}\|\mathbf{B}_{\mathsf{id}}]_{\tau_1}^{-1}$. If $0 \leftarrow \mathsf{Sig.Vrfy}(\mathsf{verk}, [\mathbf{c}_{\mathsf{id},0}\|\mathbf{c}_{\mathsf{id},1}], \sigma)$, it outputs $\perp$. Otherwise, it computes $\mathbf{E}_b \leftarrow [\mathbf{A}\|\mathbf{B}_{\mathsf{id}}\|\mathbf{C}_1 + b\mathbf{G}\|\mathbf{C}_2 + \mathsf{FRD}(\mathsf{verk})\mathbf{G}]_{\tau_1}^{-1}(\mathbf{U})$ for $b \in \{0,1\}$ from $[\mathbf{A}\|\mathbf{B}_{\mathsf{id}}]_{\tau_1}^{-1}$ by using Item 2 of Lemma 1. It runs $\mathsf{M} \leftarrow \widehat{\mathsf{Dec}}(\mathsf{mpk}, \mathbf{E}_0, \mathsf{ct}_{\mathsf{id},0})$ and $h \leftarrow \widehat{\mathsf{Dec}}(\mathsf{mpk}, \mathbf{E}_1, \mathsf{ct}_{\mathsf{id},1})$. It outputs M if $\mathsf{H}(\mathsf{M}) = h$ and $\perp$ otherwise.

$\mathsf{Trapdoor}(\mathsf{mpk}, \mathsf{sk}_{\mathsf{id}}) \to \mathsf{td}_{\mathsf{id}}$: Parse $\mathsf{mpk} = (\mathsf{IBE.mpk}, \mathbf{C}_1, \mathbf{C}_2, \Gamma, \mathsf{H})$ and $\mathsf{sk}_{\mathsf{id}} = [\mathbf{A}\|\mathbf{B}_{\mathsf{id}}]_{\tau_1}^{-1}$. It computes $\mathsf{td}_{\mathsf{id}} := \mathbf{E} \leftarrow [\mathbf{A}\|\mathbf{B}_{\mathsf{id}}\|\mathbf{C}_1 + \mathbf{G}]_{\tau_1}^{-1}(\mathbf{U})$ from $[\mathbf{A}\|\mathbf{B}_{\mathsf{id}}]_{\tau_1}^{-1}$ by using Item 2 of Lemma 1. It outputs $\mathsf{td}_{\mathsf{id}}$.

$\mathsf{Test}(\mathsf{mpk}, \mathsf{td}_{\mathsf{id}}, \mathsf{ct}_{\mathsf{id}}, \mathsf{td}_{\mathsf{id}'}, \mathsf{ct}_{\mathsf{id}'}) \to 1$ or 0: Parse $\mathsf{td}_{\mathsf{id}} = \mathbf{E}_{\mathsf{id}} \in \mathbb{Z}_q^{3m\times\ell}$, $\mathsf{td}_{\mathsf{id}'} = \mathbf{E}_{\mathsf{id}'} \in \mathbb{Z}_q^{3m\times\ell}$, $\mathsf{ct}_{\mathsf{id}} = (\mathsf{verk}, \mathsf{ct}_{\mathsf{id},0}, \mathsf{ct}_{\mathsf{id},1}, \sigma)$, and $\mathsf{ct}_{\mathsf{id}'} = (\mathsf{verk}', \mathsf{ct}_{\mathsf{id}',0}, \mathsf{ct}_{\mathsf{id}',1}, \sigma')$. If $0 \leftarrow \mathsf{Sig.Vrfy}(\mathsf{verk}, [\mathsf{ct}_{\mathsf{id},0}\|\mathsf{ct}_{\mathsf{id},1}], \sigma) \vee 0 \leftarrow \mathsf{Sig.Vrfy}(\mathsf{verk}', [\mathsf{ct}_{\mathsf{id}',0}\|\mathsf{ct}_{\mathsf{id}',1}], \sigma')$, it outputs 0. Otherwise, it runs $h \leftarrow \widehat{\mathsf{Dec}}(\mathsf{mpk}, [\mathbf{E}_{\mathsf{id}}^\top \| \mathbf{O}_{\ell,m}]^\top, \mathsf{ct}_{\mathsf{id},1})$ and $h' \leftarrow \widehat{\mathsf{Dec}}(\mathsf{mpk}, [\mathbf{E}_{\mathsf{id}'}^\top \| \mathbf{O}_{\ell,m}]^\top, \mathsf{ct}_{\mathsf{id}',1})$, where $\mathbf{O}_{\ell,m}$ is an $\ell \times m$ zero matrix. It outputs 1 if $h = h'$ and 0 otherwise.

Acknowledgements. This paper is partially supported by JST CREST JP-MJCR2113, Japan.

References

1. Agrawal, S., Boneh, D., Boyen, X.: Efficient lattice (H)IBE in the standard model. In: Gilbert, H. (ed.) EUROCRYPT 2010. LNCS, vol. 6110, pp. 553–572. Springer, Heidelberg (2010). https://doi.org/10.1007/978-3-642-13190-5_28

2. Agrawal, S., Boneh, D., Boyen, X.: Lattice basis delegation in fixed dimension and shorter-ciphertext hierarchical IBE. In: Rabin, T. (ed.) CRYPTO 2010. LNCS, vol. 6223, pp. 98–115. Springer, Heidelberg (2010). https://doi.org/10.1007/978-3-642-14623-7_6
3. Ajtai, M.: Generating hard instances of lattice problems (extended abstract). In: 28th ACM STOC, pp. 99–108. ACM (1996)
4. Asano, K., Emura, K., Takayasu, A., Watanabe, Y.: A generic construction of CCA-secure attribute-based encryption with equality test. IACR Cryptology ePrint Archive, p. 1371 (2021). https://eprint.iacr.org/2021/1371
5. Brakerski, Z., Langlois, A., Peikert, C., Regev, O., Stehlé, D.: Classical hardness of learning with errors. In: 45th ACM STOC, pp. 575–584. ACM (2013)
6. Canetti, R., Halevi, S., Katz, J.: Chosen-ciphertext security from identity-based encryption. In: Cachin, C., Camenisch, J.L. (eds.) EUROCRYPT 2004. LNCS, vol. 3027, pp. 207–222. Springer, Heidelberg (2004). https://doi.org/10.1007/978-3-540-24676-3_13
7. Cash, D., Hofheinz, D., Kiltz, E., Peikert, C.: Bonsai trees, or how to delegate a lattice basis. J. Cryptol. **25**(4), 601–639 (2012)
8. Duong, D.H., Le, H.Q., Roy, P.S., Susilo, W.: Lattice-based IBE with equality test in standard model. In: Steinfeld, R., Yuen, T.H. (eds.) ProvSec 2019. LNCS, vol. 11821, pp. 19–40. Springer, Cham (2019). https://doi.org/10.1007/978-3-030-31919-9_2
9. Gentry, C., Peikert, C., Vaikuntanathan, V.: Trapdoors for hard lattices and new cryptographic constructions. In: 40th ACM STOC, pp. 197–206. ACM (2008)
10. Jager, T., Kurek, R., Niehues, D.: Efficient adaptively-secure IB-KEMs and VRFs via near-collision resistance. In: Garay, J.A. (ed.) PKC 2021. LNCS, vol. 12710, pp. 596–626. Springer, Cham (2021). https://doi.org/10.1007/978-3-030-75245-3_22
11. Lee, H.T., Ling, S., Seo, J.H., Wang, H.: Semi-generic construction of public key encryption and identity-based encryption with equality test. Inf. Sci. **373**, 419–440 (2016)
12. Lee, H.T., Ling, S., Seo, J.H., Wang, H., Youn, T.: Public key encryption with equality test in the standard model. Inf. Sci. **516**, 89–108 (2020)
13. Lin, X.J., Sun, L., Qu, H.: Generic construction of public key encryption, identity-based encryption and signcryption with equality test. Inf. Sci. **453**, 111–126 (2018)
14. Ma, S.: Identity-based encryption with outsourced equality test in cloud computing. Inf. Sci. **328**, 389–402 (2016)
15. Nguyen, G.L.D., Susilo, W., Duong, D.H., Le, H.Q., Guo, F.: Lattice-based IBE with equality test supporting flexible authorization in the standard model. In: Bhargavan, K., Oswald, E., Prabhakaran, M. (eds.) INDOCRYPT 2020. LNCS, vol. 12578, pp. 624–643. Springer, Cham (2020). https://doi.org/10.1007/978-3-030-65277-7_28
16. Singh, K., Pandurangan, C., Banerjee, A.K.: Adaptively secure efficient lattice (H)IBE in standard model with short public parameters. In: Bogdanov, A., Sanadhya, S. (eds.) SPACE 2012. LNCS, pp. 153–172. Springer, Heidelberg (2012). https://doi.org/10.1007/978-3-642-34416-9_11
17. Susilo, W., Duong, D.H., Le, H.Q.: Efficient post-quantum identity-based encryption with equality test. In: IEEE ICPADS, pp. 633–640 (2020)
18. Tsabary, R.: Fully secure attribute-based encryption for t-CNF from LWE. In: Boldyreva, A., Micciancio, D. (eds.) CRYPTO 2019. LNCS, vol. 11692, pp. 62–85. Springer, Cham (2019). https://doi.org/10.1007/978-3-030-26948-7_3

19. Waters, B.: Efficient identity-based encryption without random oracles. In: Cramer, R. (ed.) EUROCRYPT 2005. LNCS, vol. 3494, pp. 114–127. Springer, Heidelberg (2005). https://doi.org/10.1007/11426639_7
20. Wu, Z., et al.: Efficient and fully secure lattice-based IBE with equality test. In: Gao, D., Li, Q., Guan, X., Liao, X. (eds.) ICICS 2021. LNCS, vol. 12919, pp. 301–318. Springer, Cham (2021). https://doi.org/10.1007/978-3-030-88052-1_18
21. Yamada, S.: Asymptotically compact adaptively secure lattice IBEs and verifiable random functions via generalized partitioning techniques. In: Katz, J., Shacham, H. (eds.) CRYPTO 2017. LNCS, vol. 10403, pp. 161–193. Springer, Cham (2017). https://doi.org/10.1007/978-3-319-63697-9_6
22. Yang, G., Tan, C.H., Huang, Q., Wong, D.S.: Probabilistic public key encryption with equality test. In: Pieprzyk, J. (ed.) CT-RSA 2010. LNCS, vol. 5985, pp. 119–131. Springer, Heidelberg (2010). https://doi.org/10.1007/978-3-642-11925-5_9
23. Zhandry, M.: Secure identity-based encryption in the quantum random oracle model. In: Safavi-Naini, R., Canetti, R. (eds.) CRYPTO 2012. LNCS, vol. 7417, pp. 758–775. Springer, Heidelberg (2012). https://doi.org/10.1007/978-3-642-32009-5_44

QUIC Protocol with Post-quantum Authentication

Manohar Raavi(✉), Simeon Wuthier, Pranav Chandramouli, Xiaobo Zhou, and Sang-Yoon Chang(✉)

Department of Computer Science, University of Colorado, Colorado Springs, USA
{mraavi,swuthier,pchandra,xzhou,schang2}@uccs.edu

Abstract. Post-quantum ciphers (PQC) are designed to replace the current public-key ciphers which are vulnerable against the quantum-equipped adversaries, e.g., RSA. We study the incorporation of the PQC algorithms into the QUIC and TCP/TLS networking protocols and analyze the performances and overheads in authentication and connection establishment. To distinguish from previous research, we focus on the newer QUIC networking protocol while comparing it with TCP/TLS. The QUIC protocol builds on UDP and its superiority over TCP/TLS is highlighted by the quicker and lower-overhead connection establishments. QUIC is thus gaining wider deployment, including its planned standardization for HTTP/3. We implement and experiment in local networking environment which provides greater analyzability and control. We compare QUIC vs. TCP/TLS when using PQC and measure the handshake overhead in time duration while varying both the PQC security strength and the networking conditions. Our results show that the PQC overhead increases with the PQC cipher security strength (the key and signature sizes) and as the network condition worsens (greater occurrences of packet dropping). Comparing between the PQC and the classical cipher with comparable security strengths, the PQC ciphers outperform RSA in the handshake time duration; both Dilithium 2 and Falcon 512 handshakes are quicker than RSA 3072.

Keywords: QUIC · TCP · TLS · Post-quantum cryptography · Digital signatures

1 Introduction

Since the initialization and standardization of Hypertext Transfer Protocol (HTTP), the internet has seen a rising amount of web traffic over the years, driving the need for scalability and optimization. Over 70% of internet traffic [3] and 60% of internet connections [17] are secure HTTP (version 1 or 2) using Transmission Control Protocol with Transportation Layer Security (TCP/TLS) for transport layer communication. TCP/TLS's head-of-the-line blocking where a packet drop in a stream blocks all other streams limits its capabilities. Quick UDP Internet Connections (QUIC) transport protocol designed by Google [12]

W. Susilo et al. (Eds.): ISC 2022, LNCS 13640, pp. 84–91, 2022.
https://doi.org/10.1007/978-3-031-22390-7_6

and recently standardized by Internet Engineering Task Force (IETF) [10] is gaining popularity for removing head-of-the-line blocking as well as adding a plethora of new features for scalability and optimization. Google's implementations show that QUIC has 8% faster website search responses and 18% reduced re-buffer rates for YouTube over TCP/TLS [12]. QUIC carries more than 7% of internet traffic and is replacing TCP/TLS across major applications [12]. Works are in progress to standardize and replace TCP/TLS with QUIC as the primary transport for upcoming HTTP Version 3 (HTTP/3) [6]. Once HTTP/3 is standardized, majority of internet traffic ($\approx$70%) will be transported using QUIC. QUIC provides confidentiality and integrity within the authentication scheme for connections to ensure the security of the data packets.

Cryptographic ciphers are widely used in networking protocols. For example, well-known protocols like TLS [15], SSH [5], IPsec [9], etc., use digital signature cipher algorithms like Rivest-Shamir-Adleman (RSA) and Elliptic Curve Digital Signature Algorithm (ECDSA) with X.509 certificates for authentication of end-devices. Security of the protocols using RSA relies on integer factorization problem and ECDSA on discrete logarithm problem.

Recent advancements in quantum computing and Shor's algorithm (capable of solving integer factorization and discrete logarithm problem in polynomial time assuming quantum computer) cause a need to design and develop new post-quantum ciphers (PQC). National Institute of Science and Technology (NIST) launched a PQC standardization project [2], in December 2016, to identify and standardize cipher algorithms that can withstand the growing quantum threats. In August 2022, NIST PQC standardization project finished its third round [4] and selected algorithms for standardization. NIST selected the digital signature algorithms which are lattice-based (Dilithium and Falcon) and hash-based (SPHINCS$^+$). In our paper, we focus on the lattice-based schemes of Dilithium and Falcon as opposed to the hash-based algorithm of SPHINCS$^+$ because SPHINCS$^+$ produces long signatures which can challenge its deployment to many applications. To defend against the future quantum adversaries to protect the authenticity, the networking protocols (QUIC, TCP/TLS, SSH, IPsec) should transition from the classical ciphers to the PQC ciphers.

2 Background of QUIC and NIST PQC

2.1 QUIC Protocol

In contrast to TCP/TLS which has clear distinction between the OSI layers by design, the QUIC networking protocol has multi-layer connection that combines application and transport layers. QUIC builds on the faster UDP protocol. To add reliability to UDP, QUIC utilizes data fields for the connection state/identification in the application layer in the OSI model and a combination of cryptographic and transport-layer handshakes in the transport layer. QUIC's multi-layer connection helps in combining and negotiating both cryptographic and transport parameters during a handshake. In addition to the above differences with TCP/TLS, QUIC supports and requires clients in addition to servers to use error codes in application protocol negotiation failures. QUIC does not use TLS end-of-early data messages to signal key changes and it also does not need TLS middle-box compatibility mode that adds 32 byte legacy session id value in client and server hello messages.

2.2 NIST PQC Ciphers

We focus on the NIST standardization PQC cipher algorithms due to NIST's strong influence in standardizing cipher algorithms which impacts their future use in digital security, as demonstrated by the DES standardization in the 1970s and the AES standardization in the 1990s (popularly used globally in our current days). NIST PQC standardization project finished its third round, and the selected lattice-based digital signature algorithms are Dilithium and Falcon.

Dilithium. Crystals Dilithium uses "Fiat-Shamir with Aborts" approach, SHAKE or AES for its hashing algorithm. Dilithium introduces Dilithium 2, Dilithium 3 and Dilithium 5 which correspond to NIST post-quantum security levels 2, 3, and 5, respectively [7].

Falcon. Falcon stands for the acronym, Fast Fourier lattice-based compact signature scheme over a N-th Degree Truncated Polynomial Ring (NTRU). Falcon's security scheme is based on Gentry, Peikert and Vaikuntanathan (GPV), NTRU lattices, Fast Fourier sampling. Falcon introduces Falcon 512 and Falcon 1024 which correspond to NIST post-quantum security level 1 and 5 respectively [8].

3 Performance Analysis

In this section, First, we provide details of our experimentation and implementation in Sect. 3.1. Second, in Sect. 3.2, we analyze the TCP/TLS and QUIC connection establishment overheads induced by the PQC (Dilithium and Falcon) under no artificial network drop ($D = 0$). Later, in Subsect. 3.3, we analyze the behavior of both TCP/TLS and QUIC connections under different artificial packet dropping ($D \neq 0$) scenarios.

3.1 Implementation and Experimentation

We compare the NIST selected PQC ciphers described in Sect. 2.2 with the classical cipher RSA, which cipher is selected based on its popularity and since it supports digital signatures (it also supports key exchange and encryption for confidentiality). We implement the ciphers using Open-Quantum-Safe OpenSSL 1.1.1 [18]. We focus on our experiments based on the server and the client implementations on virtual machines (VM) on a single physical machine in this paper due to the following two reasons. First, the VM-based implementation enables a sharper focus on the comparative analyses of QUIC vs. TCP/TLS and excludes the other noise/random factors, such as the networking latency

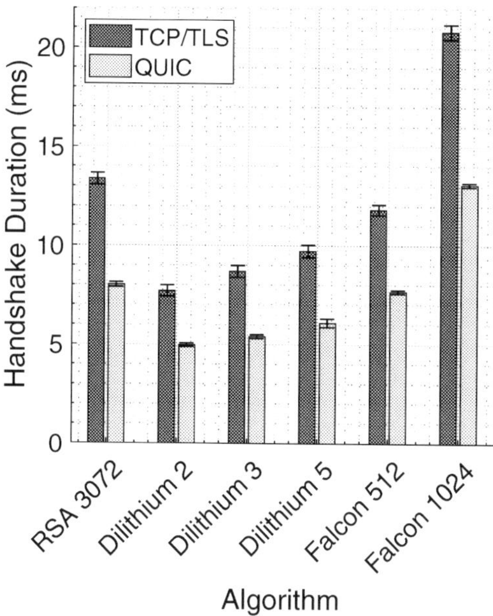

Fig. 1. The handshake duration while varying the PQC algorithms. The plot includes average values and the 95% confidence intervals.

variations between the local client and the remote server. Second, it enables the networking control between two machines, including enabling the networking condition simulation such as varying network drop rates and network delays.

Our virtual machine setup uses Ubuntu 18.04 with each VM containing 8 cores and 16 GB of RAM on an AMD Ryzen 9 3960x 24-core 48-thread processor with a base processor frequency of 3.8 GHz, and 64 GB of RAM. For the network control and simulation, we use the traffic control (*tc*) queuing discipline (*qdisc*) network emulator (*netem*) that selectively controls packets to be en-queued and modified when sent and received from the client machine. For networking, we implement the TCP/TLS 1.3 with Open-Quantum-Safe BoringSSL [18] and QUIC with LiteSpeed QUIC (*lsquic*) [1]. These protocols require multiple machines and, more specifically, a client to initiate the handshakes and a server to respond to TLS/QUIC connection requests. We run our experiments to establish 1,000 TCP/TLS and QUIC connections authenticated using PQC algorithms as well as classical RSA 3072. We use Python 3.9.7 for experimental automation and use *tcpdump* for packet capturing.

3.2 QUIC and TCP/TLS Performance

Experimental Design. Transitioning to PQC authentication impact the handshake duration between the client and the server. We test the performance of both TCP/TLS and QUIC connections and analyze their overheads with PQC authentication.

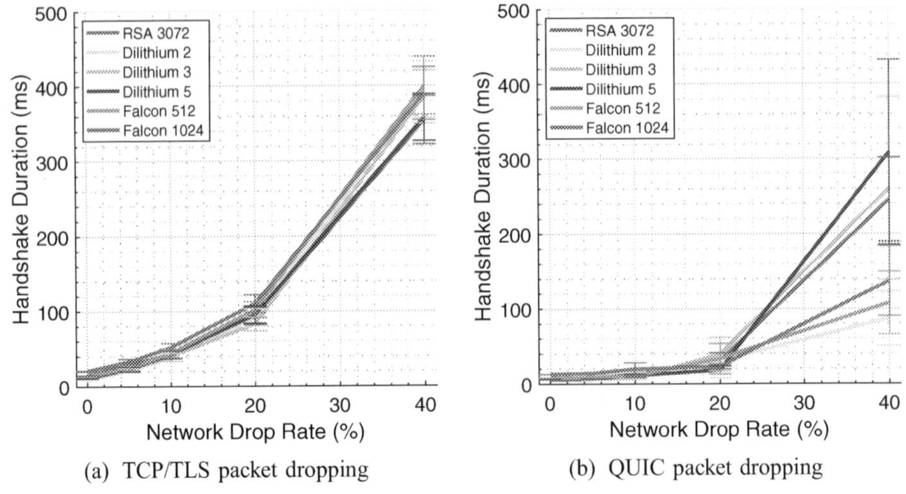

(a) TCP/TLS packet dropping

(b) QUIC packet dropping

Fig. 2. The handshake time duration while varying the packet drop rate D.

Experimental Results. Figure 1 plots the handshake duration for TCP/TLS and QUIC connections authenticated by classical RSA and NIST selected digital signatures for standardization. Our results show that, except for Falcon 1024, transitioning to PQC speeds up the handshake duration and connection establishment of both TCP/TLS and QUIC protocols. At comparable security of level 1, QUIC authentication with Dilithium 2 and Falcon 512 is 39.48% and 6.07% faster compared to RSA while it is 42.24% and 11.61% faster for TCP/TLS, respectively. Using Dilithium for authentication, QUIC is at least 35.40% faster than TCP/TLS. Using Falcon 1024 increases the handshake duration of QUIC by 69.46% and TCP/TLS by 76.27% compared to Falcon 512. Using Falcon 512 and Falcon 1024, QUIC is 34.49% and 37.01% faster when compared to TCP/TLS, respectively. Overall, Dilithium algorithms are most efficient and cause low handshake duration compared to RSA and Falcon in both QUIC and TCP/TLS protocols.

3.3 Performance with Packet Dropping (D)

Experimental Design. QUIC is designed to overcome TCP/TLS head of the line problem as discussed in Sect. 2. Our experiment targets to test the performance of QUIC when the network is lossy where not all the packets sent from the sender don't reach the receiver. We conduct lossy network experiment varying the droprate, $D \in \langle 0, 5, 10, 20, 40 \rangle$, which is the percentage of packet dropped by the network in uniform distribution. For example, when $D = 10$ network drops 10% of the packets during the connection.

Experimental Results. Figure 2a and Fig. 2b plots the average TCP/TLS and QUIC handshake times under varying network drop rates. As the drop rate increases, QUIC connection overheads increases but still are lower than TCP/TLS overheads with both the RSA and post-quantum algorithms for authentication. Using classical algorithm RSA, QUIC consistently outperforms TCP/TLS by 69% with $D = 5$ (i.e. dropping 5% traffic), 71.2% with $D = 10$, 65.7% with $D = 20$, and 31.3% with $D = 40$.

Using post-quantum authentication with Dilithium 2, QUIC is faster by 73.2% with $D = 5$, 70.8% with $D = 10$, 67.4% with $D = 20$, and 78.5% with $D = 40$ than TCP/TLS connections. When using post-quantum authentication with Dilithium 5, QUIC consistently outperforms TCP/TLS by 69.1% when $D = 5$ (0.1% improvement from RSA), 75.2% when $D = 10$, 81.6% when $D = 20$, and 16.3% when $D = 40$ (15% improvement from RSA). When using post-quantum authentication with Falcon 512, QUIC is 66.9% with $D = 5$, 75.8% with $D = 10$, 67.6% with $D = 20$, and 73.5% with $D = 40$ faster than TCP/TLS connections. QUIC remains the top performer throughout the varying D and is preferable over TCP/TLS.

4 Related Work

Related to our research are previous research works comparing QUIC vs. TCP/TLS and incorporating PQC on those protocols. Previous research compared the transport capabilities of QUIC and TCP protocols under different networking scenarios [16,19]. Yu et al. in [19] conducted an experimental study to evaluate the performance of QUIC and TCP protocols when competing for resources to deliver the application data. Their study shows that QUIC performs better than TCP in lossy networks and has no major advantage in loss-free networks. Seufert et al. [16] conducted a study to explore the application-level Quality of Experience (QoE) benefits of QUIC over TCP. Their works conclude that there are no QoE benefits from QUIC than TCP with respect to web browsing or video streaming unless there are bandwidth limitations. Our work studies the PQC integration on these networking protocols.

Other relevant research investigated the performance of the TCP/TLS using post-quantum authentication [11,13,14,17]. Kampanakis et al. in [11] investigated the viability of using post-quantum certificates in protocols including TLS and QUIC. They emulated large certificates by generating the certificates matching the sizes of the RSA keys (8192 and 16384 bits) and merging multiple certificates for certificate chains, as opposed to actually implementing the classical and PQC ciphers. They tested the protocol capabilities in handling such huge certificates chains up to 135 KB. Their emulation results show that TLS and QUIC can handle huge post-quantum certificates with minor implementation modifications. Sikeridis et al. [17] studied the throughput performance of TLS 1.3 when using post-quantum algorithms. Their results show that transitioning to post-quantum authentication in TLS induces latency overhead compared to classical algorithms. Our work implements the PQC ciphers in software and includes the analyses for both QUIC and TCP/TLS, including the comparisons between the two protocols. Our work also shows that the PQC ciphers in Dilithium and Falcon have smaller overheads in time duration than RSA when using security strength level 1 (Dilithium 2 vs. RSA-3072 and Falcon-512 vs. RSA 3072 in Sect. 3.2).

Our current work builds on our previous works of individual PQC algorithm performances [14] and PQC performance when integrated with PKI [13]. However, this paper focuses on understanding the behavior of QUIC when integrated with PQC authentication and compares its performance to that of TCP/TLS.

5 Conclusion

This paper analyzes the overheads of post-quantum authentication and connection establishments in the QUIC networking protocol. We compare the performance of QUIC and TCP/TLS in handshake duration times. We implement the protocols and the algorithms and analyze the behaviors under local environment that enables the control in networking, including the packet loss. Our implementation-based experimental results show that the connection overhead in handshake and PQC-based authentication increase with the cipher's security strength and with the deteriorating networking conditions. Our analyses results show that the PQC overheads in the handshake duration increases with the PQC cipher security strength (longer key and signature sizes) and as the network connection worsens (greater occurrences of packet dropping). The PQC ciphers also outperform RSA in the handshake time duration; both Dilithium 2 and Falcon 512 handshake is quicker than RSA-3072 while all of these algorithms are comparable in its security strength (security level 1).

Acknowledgement. This material is based upon work supported by the National Science Foundation under Grant No. 1922410 and by a grant from the U.S. Civilian Research & Development Foundation (CRDF Global).

References

1. lsquic github. https://github.com/litespeedtech/lsquic. Accessed 18 Apr 2022
2. NIST-call for proposals. https://csrc.nist.gov/CSRC/media/Projects/Post-Quantum-Cryptography/documents/call-for-proposals-final-dec-2016.pdf. Accessed 18 Apr 2022
3. Percentage of https (TLS) encrypted traffic on the internet? https://etherealmind.com/percentage-of-https-tls-encrypted-traffic-on-the-internet/. Accessed 10 Nov 2021
4. Alagic, G., et al.: Status report on the third round of the NIST post-quantum cryptography standardization process. US Department of Commerce, NIST (2022)
5. Bider, D.: Use of RSA keys with SHA-256 and SHA-512 in the Secure Shell (SSH) protocol. RFC 8332, March 2018. https://doi.org/10.17487/RFC8332, https://www.rfc-editor.org/info/rfc8332

6. Bishop, M.: Hypertext Transfer Protocol Version 3 (HTTP/3). Internet-Draft draft-ietf-quic-http-34, Internet Engineering Task Force, February 2021. https://datatracker.ietf.org/doc/html/draft-ietf-quic-http-34, work in Progress
7. Ducas, L., et al.: Crystals-dilithium: a lattice-based digital signature scheme. IACR Trans. Cryptogr. Hardware Embedded Syst., 238–268 (2018)
8. Fouque, P.A., et al.: Falcon: fast-Fourier lattice-based compact signatures over NTRU. Submission to the NIST's post-quantum cryptography standardization process (2018)
9. Frankel, S., Krishnan, S.: IP Security (IPsec) and Internet Key Exchange (IKE) Document Roadmap. RFC 6071, February 2011. https://doi.org/10.17487/RFC6071, https://www.rfc-editor.org/info/rfc6071
10. Iyengar, J., Thomson, M.: QUIC: a UDP-based multiplexed and secure transport. RFC 9000, May 2021. https://doi.org/10.17487/RFC9000, https://rfc-editor.org/rfc/rfc9000.txt
11. Kampanakis, P., Panburana, P., Daw, E., Van Geest, D.: The viability of post-quantum x. 509 certificates. IACR Cryptol. ePrint Arch. **2018**, 63 (2018)
12. Langley, A., et al.: The QUIC transport protocol: design and internet-scale deployment. In: Proceedings of the Conference of the ACM Special Interest Group on Data Communication, pp. 183–196 (2017)
13. Raavi, M., Chandramouli, P., Wuthier, S., Zhou, X., Chang, S.Y.: Performance characterization of post-quantum digital certificates. In: 2021 International Conference on Computer Communications and Networks (ICCCN), pp. 1–9. IEEE (2021)
14. Raavi, M., Wuthier, S., Chandramouli, P., Balytskyi, Y., Zhou, X., Chang, S.-Y.: Security comparisons and performance analyses of post-quantum signature algorithms. In: Sako, K., Tippenhauer, N.O. (eds.) ACNS 2021. LNCS, vol. 12727, pp. 424–447. Springer, Cham (2021). https://doi.org/10.1007/978-3-030-78375-4_17
15. Rescorla, E.: The Transport Layer Security (TLS) Protocol Version 1.3. RFC 8446, August 2018. https://doi.org/10.17487/RFC8446, https://www.rfc-editor.org/info/rfc8446
16. Seufert, M., Schatz, R., Wehner, N., Gardlo, B., Casas, P.: Is QUIC becoming the new TCP? On the potential impact of a new protocol on networked multimedia QoE. In: 2019 Eleventh International Conference on Quality of Multimedia Experience (QoMEX), pp. 1–6. IEEE (2019)
17. Sikeridis, D., Kampanakis, P., Devetsikiotis, M.: Post-quantum authentication in TLS 1.3: a performance study. IACR Cryptol. ePrint Arch. **2020**, 71 (2020)
18. Stebila, D., Mosca, M.: Post-quantum key exchange for the internet and the open quantum safe project. In: Avanzi, R., Heys, H. (eds.) SAC 2016. LNCS, vol. 10532, pp. 14–37. Springer, Cham (2017). https://doi.org/10.1007/978-3-319-69453-5_2
19. Yu, Y., Xu, M., Yang, Y.: When QUIC meets TCP: an experimental study. In: 2017 IEEE 36th International Performance Computing and Communications Conference (IPCCC), pp. 1–8. IEEE (2017)

Batched Fully Homomorphic Encryption from TFHE

Yuting Jiang[1(✉)] and Jianghong Wei[2]

[1] State Key Laboratory of Integrated Service Networks (ISN), Xidian University, Xi'an 710071, China
jiangyuting@foxmail.com

[2] State Key Laboratory of Mathematical Engineering and Advanced Computing, PLA Strategic Support Force Information Engineering University, Zhengzhou 450001, China

Abstract. A surge of interest in fully homomorphic encryption (FHE) has produced various FHE constructions in recent years. One of the main goals of these FHE schemes is to improve the efficiency when using the bootstrapping technique. Particularly, TFHE, a fast FHE scheme over the torus, decreases the running time of the bootstrapping significantly. However, it only supports a single-bit bootstrapping, and thus still has high computation cost. In this paper, we propose a batched FHE from TFHE, which can simultaneously bootstrap n torus-based LWE (TLWE) ciphertexts. In more detail, we employ a binary packing tree to pack several TLWE ciphertexts into one TLWE ciphertext, and further optimize the bootstrapping procedure with the homomorphic number theoretic transform (NTT). As a consequence, the amortized computation cost of our batched FHE scheme is reduced to $O(\log N)$ from $O(N)$ in the original TFHE scheme, where N is the dimension of the TLWE assumption. Moreover, we provide an implementation of the proposed FHE scheme with specific parameters, so as to demonstrate its practicability.

Keywords: Fully homomorphic encryption · TFHE · Bootstrapping · Batching · NTT

1 Introduction

Fully homomorphic encryption (FHE), first constructed by Gentry [20], allows anyone to perform arbitrary computations over encrypted data without the secret decryption key. Since Gentry's breakthrough work, research on FHE is booming due to its extensive applications [3,5–7,13,15,19,21]. To date, Gentry's bootstrapping technique [20], which supports to calculate arbitrary circuits by substantially calculating the decryption circuit on encrypted secret key, is still the only known method to achieve FHE. However, FHE is still far from practical since the bootstrapping technique is computationally expensive.

Towards improving the usability and efficiency of FHE, Chillotti et al. [13] proposed a fast fully homomorphic encryption scheme over the torus (TFHE).

W. Susilo et al. (Eds.): ISC 2022, LNCS 13640, pp. 92–109, 2022.
https://doi.org/10.1007/978-3-031-22390-7_7

Its security relies on the torus-based learning with errors (TLWE) and its ring variant. In particular, the elementary operations in the TFHE scheme are all the binary gates. Therefore, its bootstrapping procedure is greatly simplified to perform binary circuit tasks, which makes TFHE has better running time and easier to use compared to other FHE schemes. However, TFHE only supports a single-bit bootstrapping operation and thus the computation overhead grows linearly with the number of ciphertexts to be evaluated.

The way to solve the above problem is batching, namely, packing several messages into one ciphertext, and operate on them in parallel. This enables the client pack multiple encrypted messages into one ciphertext, and send it to a remote server to store and bootstrap. In this case, the boostrapping technique can simultaneously refresh a mass of ciphertexts in one bootstrapping procedure, although it may be still computation-expensive. Focusing on the standard lattice-based FHE scheme, there have been several well-studied solutions. For example, Brakerski et al. [4] packed Regev's encryption ciphertexts [27] to implement SIMD-type homomorphic operations. Chen et al. [11] showed a polynomial noise bootstrapping method with packed ciphertexts. Micciancio and Sorrell [24] introduced a new bootstrapping procedure that simultaneously refreshes N FHEW ciphertexts [19]. However, these works are all theoretical and far from practical implementation. Consequently, a natural problem is how to efficiently pack TFHE ciphertexts and bootstrap them simultaneously.

1.1 Our Contributions

In this paper, motivated by the merits of TFHE, we study the problem of packing TFHE ciphertexts, and propose a batced FHE scheme to reduce the amortized computation cost. More precisely, we conduct the following contributions:

- We propose a batched fully homomorphic encryption scheme from TFHE. Under the optimal conditions, the amortized computation complexity decreases from $O(N)$ in the original TFHE scheme to $O(\log N)$ in the proposed batched FHE. Furthermore, the amortized size of boostrapping keys decreases from $O(N^2)$ to $O(N \log N)$.
- In order to obtain our batched FHE scheme, we design a binary packing tree for TLWE samples, which is an efficient method to pack multiple TLWE ciphertexts to one ciphertext. We also use the homomorphic number theoretic transform (NTT) to optimize slow multiplication.
- We implement the batched FHE scheme on TFHE library and LatticeCrypto library with the concrete parameter sets, and compare it with the original TFHE. The experimental results are consistent with our expectations, and indicate its practicability.

1.2 Related Work

Since Gentry's breakthrough work [20], many constructions have been proposed to improve the efficiency with different manners. One of the important method to improve the efficiency is batching, namely, packing several messages into a single ciphertext and performing homomorphic computations on these encrypted messages simultaneously. Smart and Vercautren [28] first showed how to apply single-instruction-multiple-data (SIMD) operations to a ciphertext based on Chinese reminder theorem (CRT). Besides, two other matrix GSW packing techniques [4,22] exploited the matrix variant of [21] to implement SIMD homomorphic operations. However, the noise of these schemes increases quai-polynomial. Chen and Zhang [11] provided a polynomial noise bootstrapping method for the BGV-type FHE scheme with packed ciphertexts. Furthermore, they constructed a multi-key FHE scheme [12] based on ring-LWE assumption, which supports CRT-based ciphertext packing.

Besides the BGV-type scheme, there are some packing works related to homomorphic boolean circuit such as FHEW [19], TFHE [13]. Biasse and Ruiz [2] provided an extension of FHEW that allows to work with multibit message spaces. Micciancio and Sorrell [24] introduced a bootstrapping technique that can simultaneously refresh multiple FHEW ciphertexts. Chillotti et al. [14] proposed two packing methods to optimize the evaluation of random function in ring-GSW based homomorphic schemes. However, these works do not involve how to simultaneously perform bootstrapping on multiple TFHE ciphertexts.

Since TFHE was proposed in 2016 [13], researchers have refined and applied it from various perspectives. For bootstrapping, Okada et al. [25] implemented a functional bootstrapping on an integerwise variant of TFHE. Chillotti et al. provided a programmable bootstrapping [17] to handling the privacy-preserving inference with deep neural networks. Then Chillotti et al. improved the programmable bootstrapping with larger precision [18]. For application, Chen et al. [8] introduced an efficient oblivious RAM from TFHE. Morever, a TFHE-based multi-key FHE has been proposed [9].

1.3 Roadmap

Section 2 presents some TFHE's background and the related technologies involved in this paper. Section 3 constructs necessary building blocks of our construction. In Sect. 4, we propose a batched FHE scheme and analyze its computation complexity, noise growth, correctness condition and security. Section 5 gives the experimental results with concrete parameters. In Sect. 6, we conclude this paper.

2 Preliminaries

Throughout this paper, the index set $[N] = \{0, 1, \cdots, N-1\}$ and the set $\mathbb{B} = \{0, 1\}$. Vectors are in bold, e.g., $\boldsymbol{a}$, and matrices are in upper-case bold like $\boldsymbol{A}$. $\mathcal{M}_{u,v}(S)$ is a set of matrices $u \times v$ with entries in S. The i-th coefficient of the polynomial a is denoted as $a[i]$. The i-th entry of the vector $\boldsymbol{a}$ is denoted as $\boldsymbol{a}[i]$. The map $\iota : \boldsymbol{a} \mapsto \sum_{i\in[N]} \boldsymbol{a}[i]X^i$ represents the vector transform to a polynomial. Sampling x from a distribution D is written as $x \leftarrow D$. If D is uniform, then we write as $x \leftarrow U(D)$. We denote by $\mathcal{R} = \mathbb{Z}[X]/(X^N + 1)$ the polynomial ring with N power of 2. Let $\mathbb{B}_N[X]$ be the subset of $\mathcal{R}$ of polynomial with binary coefficients. Finally, $\|\cdot\|_1$ denotes l_1 norm and $\|\cdot\|_\infty$ denotes l_∞ norm.

2.1 Background on TFHE

The TFHE scheme, proposed by Chillotti et al. [13], is a fast fully homomorphic encryption scheme. It works over the real torus $\mathbb{T} = \mathbb{R}/\mathbb{Z}$ and the torus polynomial $\mathbb{T}_N[X] = \mathbb{R}[X]/(X^N + 1) \bmod 1$, where N is a power of 2. Its security depends on the torus variant of the LWE [27] problem and of the GSW construction [21], called TLWE and TGSW. Its homomorphic operations are all binary gates. So the running time is naturally proportional to the number of binary gates. In this section, we define TLWE and TGSW samples, and describe the controlled selector gate `CMux`, which will be adopted in this paper. Note that ciphertexts in TFHE are viewed as normal samples.

Definition 1 (TLWE [13]). *Let N be power of 2, $\alpha \geq 0$ be a noise parameter, and $k \geq 1$ be an integer. The vector of k binary polynomials $\boldsymbol{s} \in \mathbb{B}_N[X]^k$ be a TLWE secret key*[1]*, whose coefficients are chosen uniformly. A fresh TLWE ciphertext or sample $\boldsymbol{c} \in \mathbb{T}_N[X]^{k+1}$ of message m is a pair constructed as $(\boldsymbol{a}, b)$, where $\boldsymbol{a} \leftarrow U(\mathbb{T}_N[X]^k)$, b pursues a continuous Gaussian distribution of noise parameter α centered around $m + \boldsymbol{s} \cdot \boldsymbol{a}$. Furthermore, a trivial TLWE sample has $\boldsymbol{a} = \boldsymbol{0}$ and $b = m$. A noiseless TLWE sample has $\alpha = 0$.*

In the following, we write down as $\boldsymbol{c} = (\boldsymbol{a}, b) \in \mathsf{TLWE}_{\boldsymbol{s}}(m)$. The phase of a sample $\boldsymbol{c}$ is $\varphi_{\boldsymbol{s}}(\boldsymbol{c}) = b - \boldsymbol{s} \cdot \boldsymbol{a}$. The message $\mathsf{msg}(\boldsymbol{c}) \in \mathbb{T}_N[X]$ is the expectation of $\varphi_{\boldsymbol{s}}(\boldsymbol{c})$. The error $\mathsf{err}(\boldsymbol{c})$ is amount to $\varphi_{\boldsymbol{s}}(\boldsymbol{c}) - \mathsf{msg}(\boldsymbol{c})$.

For a degree $\ell \geq 1$, a base $B_g \geq 2$, and an integer $k \geq 1$, the canonical gadget matrix $\boldsymbol{G}_{k+1}$ is denoted as

$$\boldsymbol{G}_{k+1} = \left(\begin{array}{c|c|c} 1/B_g & \cdots & 0 \\ \vdots & \ddots & \vdots \\ 1/B_g^\ell & \cdots & 0 \\ \hline \vdots & \ddots & \vdots \\ \hline 0 & \cdots & 1/B_g \\ \vdots & \ddots & \vdots \\ 0 & \cdots & 1/B_g^\ell \end{array}\right) \in \mathcal{M}_{\ell(k+1),k+1}(\mathbb{T}_N[X]). \tag{1}$$

For any element $\boldsymbol{\mu} \in \mathbb{T}_N[X]^{k+1}$, it is possible to effectively decompose it as a small linear combination of lines of $\boldsymbol{G}_{k+1}$, namely, $\boldsymbol{v} = \boldsymbol{G}_{k+1}^{-1}(\boldsymbol{\mu})$, where $\|\boldsymbol{v}\|_\infty \leq B_g/2$ and the decomposition error $\|\boldsymbol{v}^T \cdot \boldsymbol{G}_{k+1} - \boldsymbol{\mu}^T\|_\infty$ is bounded by $1/2B_g^\ell$.

[1] Note that if $k = 1$ and N large, then TLWE problem is RingLWE problem. If k large and $N = 1$, then TLWE problem is the LWE problem. We use the former in this paper.

Definition 2 (TGSW [13]**).** *Let $\boldsymbol{G}_{k+1}$ be the gadget defined in* (1) *and $\boldsymbol{z} \in \mathbb{B}_N[X]^k$ be a TLWE secret key. A TGSW sample $\boldsymbol{C} \in \mathcal{M}_{(k+1)\ell,k+1}(\mathbb{T}_N[X])$ of $m \in \mathcal{R}$ is a matrix constructed as $\boldsymbol{C} = \boldsymbol{Z} + m \cdot \boldsymbol{G}_{k+1}$, where each line of the matrix $\boldsymbol{Z} \in \mathcal{M}_{(k+1)\ell,k+1}(\mathbb{T}_N[X])$ is a random TLWE ciphertext of 0 under the secret key $\boldsymbol{z}$.*

In the following, we write down as $\boldsymbol{C} \in \mathsf{TGSW}_{\boldsymbol{z}}(m)$. The phase $\varphi_{\boldsymbol{z}}(\boldsymbol{C})$ of a sample $\boldsymbol{C}$ is the list of the $\ell(k+1)$ TLWE phases of each row of $\boldsymbol{C}$. The error $\mathsf{err}(\boldsymbol{C})$ is the list of the $\ell(k+1)$ TLWE errors of each row of $\boldsymbol{C}$.

TGSW inherits some homomorphic properties, including the internal product and addition between two TGSW samples. Moreover, there is an external product $\boxdot$ between a TGSW sample and a TLWE sample under the same secret key. Details are as follows.

Lemma 1 ([15]**).** *Let $\boldsymbol{G}_{k+1}$ be the gadget defined in* (1) *and $\boldsymbol{s} \in \mathbb{B}_N[X]^k$ be a TLWE secret key, $\boldsymbol{A} \in \mathsf{TGSW}_{\boldsymbol{s}}(m_{\boldsymbol{A}})$, $\boldsymbol{b} \in \mathsf{TLWE}_{\boldsymbol{s}}(m_{\boldsymbol{b}})$. Then the external product $\boldsymbol{A} \boxdot \boldsymbol{b} = \boldsymbol{G}_{k+1}^{-1}(\boldsymbol{b}) \cdot \boldsymbol{A} \in \mathsf{TLWE}_{\boldsymbol{s}}(m_{\boldsymbol{A}} \cdot m_{\boldsymbol{b}})$ and*

$$\|\mathsf{err}(\boldsymbol{A}\boxdot\boldsymbol{b})\|_\infty \le \frac{\ell N B_g(k+1)\|\mathsf{err}(\boldsymbol{A})\|_\infty}{2} + \frac{\|m_{\boldsymbol{A}}\|_1(kN+1)}{2B_g^\ell} + \|m_{\boldsymbol{A}}\|_1\|\mathsf{err}(\boldsymbol{b})\|_\infty.$$

If $\boldsymbol{A} \boxdot \boldsymbol{b}$ is a valid TLWE sample, then $\|\mathsf{err}(\boldsymbol{A} \boxdot \boldsymbol{b})\|_\infty \le 1/4$[2]*.*

More high level circuits can be generated with the external product, such as the controlled selector gate (`CMux`).

Lemma 2 ([15]**).** *Let $\boldsymbol{C} \in \mathsf{TGSW}_{\boldsymbol{s}}(\{0,1\})$ and $\mathsf{ct}_1, \mathsf{ct}_0 \in \mathsf{TLWE}_{\boldsymbol{s}}(\mathbb{T}_N[X])$. The controlled selector gate `CMux`$(\boldsymbol{C}, \mathsf{ct}_1, \mathsf{ct}_0)$ takes input two data $\mathsf{ct}_1, \mathsf{ct}_0$ and one control $\boldsymbol{C}$, and returns $\boldsymbol{C}\boxdot(\mathsf{ct}_1 - \mathsf{ct}_0) + \mathsf{ct}_0$. Then the message of `CMux`$(\boldsymbol{C}, \mathsf{ct}_1, \mathsf{ct}_0)$ is $\mathsf{msg}(\boldsymbol{C})?\mathsf{msg}(\mathsf{ct}_1) : \mathsf{msg}(\mathsf{ct}_0)$*[3]*. In the conditions of Lemma 1, we have*

$$\|\mathsf{err}(\mathtt{CMux}(\boldsymbol{C}, \mathsf{ct}_1, \mathsf{ct}_0))\|_\infty \le \max(\|\mathsf{err}(\mathsf{ct}_1)\|_\infty, \|\mathsf{err}(\mathsf{ct}_0)\|_\infty) + \zeta(\boldsymbol{C}), \tag{2}$$

where $\zeta(\boldsymbol{C}) = \ell N B_g(1+k)\|\mathsf{err}(\boldsymbol{C})\|_\infty/2 + (1+kN)/2B_g^\ell$.

2.2 Number Theoretic Transform

The Number theoretic transform (NTT) [26] is a fast convolution technique that has a structure similar to the discrete Fourier transform (DFT), but with complex exponential roots of unity replaced by integer roots from a finte ring.

Let $h = \{h_0, \cdots, h_{N-1}\}$ be a N-point integer sequence with elements in $\mathbb{Z}_q$, where N is power of 2 and prime modulo $q \equiv 1 \bmod 2N$. Let $g \in \mathbb{Z}_q$ be a primitive N-th root of unity. The direct NTT of h is $\bar{h}_i = \sum_{j=0}^{N-1} h_j g^{ij} \bmod q$

[2] To ensure successful decryption, the noise must be small enough in the rounding procedure. This value is usually 1/4.

[3] It means $\mathsf{msg}(\boldsymbol{C})(\mathsf{msg}(\mathsf{ct}_1) - \mathsf{msg}(\mathsf{ct}_0)) + \mathsf{msg}(\mathsf{ct}_0)$. If $\mathsf{msg}(\boldsymbol{C}) = 1$, then the message of `CMux`$(\boldsymbol{C}, \mathsf{ct}_1, \mathsf{ct}_0)$ is $\mathsf{msg}(\mathsf{ct}_1)$; If $\mathsf{msg}(\boldsymbol{C}) = 0$, then the message is $\mathsf{msg}(\mathsf{ct}_0)$.

for $i \in [N]$. Since q is prime, N has an inverse $N^{-1} \bmod q$, then the inverse transformation INTT of $\bar{h}$ is denoted as $h_i = N^{-1}\sum_{j=0}^{N-1} \bar{h}_j g^{-ij} \bmod q$ for $i \in [N]$. For two polynomials a, b of degree N, the polynomial multiplication in $\mathcal{R}_q = \mathbb{Z}_q/(X^N+1)$, namely, $c = a \cdot b \bmod (X^N+1)$, is equivalent to negative wrapped convolution [29], which can be efficiently computed by NTT.

Lemma 3 (Negative Wrapped Convolution [29]**).** *Let two vectors* $\boldsymbol{a} = (a_0, \cdots, a_{N-1})$ *and* $\boldsymbol{b} = (b_0, \cdots, b_{N-1})$ *of length* N *be the vector representations of the polynomial* $a = \sum_{i=0}^{N_1} a_i X^i$ *and* $b = \sum_{i=0}^{N_1} b_i X^i$*, respectively, where* $a, b \in \mathcal{R}_q$*. Let* $g \in \mathbb{Z}_q$ *be a primitive* N*-th root of unity and* $\eta^2 = g$*. Vectors* $\hat{\boldsymbol{a}}$ *and* $\hat{\boldsymbol{b}}$ *are defined as* $(a_0, \eta a_1, \cdots, \eta^{N-1} a_{N-1})$*,* $(b_0, \eta a_1, \cdots, \eta^{N-1} b_{N-1})$*. The negative wrapped convolution of* a *and* b *is computed by* $(1, \eta^{-1}, \eta^{-2}, \cdots, \eta^{-(N-1)}) \circ \mathrm{INTT}(\mathrm{NTT}(\hat{\boldsymbol{a}}) \circ \mathrm{NTT}(\hat{\boldsymbol{b}}))$*, where* $\circ$ *means componentwise multiplication. This operation is equivalent to* $a \cdot b$ *in* $\mathcal{R}_q$*.*

2.3 Homomorphic Evalutation of Automorphisms

As shown in [10], for a power-of-2 integer N, $K = \mathbb{Q}/(X^N+1)$, the Galois group $\mathrm{Gal}(K/\mathbb{Q})$ contains the automorphisms $\tau_d : a(X) \mapsto a(X^d)$ for $d \in \mathbb{Z}_{2N}^\times$, the invertible residues modulo $2N$. Algorithm 1 describes a notable approach to homomorphically evaluate the automorphisms. Given a TLWE sample $\mathsf{ct} \in \mathsf{TLWE}_s(m)$ and an integer $d \in \mathbb{Z}_{2N}^\times$, the message of the output ciphertext in Algorithm 1 is $\tau_d(m)$, which has been proved in [10]. Furthermore, the security of the Algorithm 1 depends on the security of subroutines `KSKeyGen` and `KeySwitch`, which are common key switching methods in FHE schemes. We describe a key switching algorithm for TLWE samples and prove its security in Sect. 3.1.

Algorithm 1. `EvalAuto`$(\mathsf{ct} \in \mathbb{T}_N[X]^2, d \in \mathbb{Z}_{2N}^\times)$

Input: A TLWE ciphertext $\mathsf{ct} = (a, b) \in \mathsf{TLWE}_s(m)$, an integer $d \in \mathbb{Z}_{2N}^\times$
Output: A TLWE ciphertext $\mathsf{ct}' \in \mathsf{TLWE}_{\tau_d(s)}(\tau_d(m))$
1: Run $\boldsymbol{K}_d \leftarrow$ `KSKeyGen`$(s, \tau_d(s))$
2: Compute the ciphertext $\mathsf{ct}' \leftarrow$ `KeySwitch`$((\tau_d(a), \tau_d(b)), \boldsymbol{K}_d)$
3: **return** ct'

Note that when the automorphism $\tau_d(\cdot)$ acts on the monomials for $d = 2^l + 1$, $1 \le l \le \log N$, then the map $m \mapsto m + \tau_d(m)$ makes the coefficients $m[i]$ double if $2^{\log N - l + 1} | i$, and the coefficients $m[i]$ zero if $2^{\log N - l} | i \wedge 2^{\log N - l + 1} \nmid i$. For example, if $N = 8$, $d = 5$, then $m = \sum_{i=0}^{7} m[i]X^i$ and $\tau_d(m) = m[0]X^0 - m[5]X - m[2]X^2 + m[7]X^3 + m[4]X^4 + m[1]X^5 - m[6]X^6 - m[3]X^7$. Therefore, $m + \tau_d(m) = 2m[0]X^0 + (m[1] - m[5])X + (m[3] + m[7])X^3 + 2m[4]X^4 + (m[1] + m[5])X^5 + (m[7] - m[3])X^7)$. We can see that the coefficients $m[0]$ and $m[4]$ are double, and the coefficients $m[2]$ and $m[6]$ are zero.

3 Building Blocks

3.1 Key Switching on TLWE Ciphertexts

The key switching algorithm is used to transform a ciphertext with the secret key z into another ciphertext with the different secret key z' while the phase remains almost constant. Based on the external product, we provide a key-switching algorithm for TLWE ciphertexts.

- $\texttt{KSKeyGen}(z \in \mathbb{B}_N[X], z' \in \mathbb{B}_N[X])$: Given TLWE secrets $z, z' \in \mathbb{B}_N[X]$, it returns the key-switching key $\mathsf{KS} = \mathsf{TGSW}_{z'}(z) \in \mathbb{T}_N[X]^{2\ell \times 2}$ from z to z'.
- $\texttt{KeySwitch}(\texttt{ct}, \mathsf{KS})$: Given an TLWE ciphertext $\mathsf{ct} = (a, b) \in \mathbb{T}_N[X]^2$ and a key-switching key $\mathsf{KS} \in \mathbb{T}_N[X]^{2\ell \times 2}$, let $(0, a), (0, b) \in \mathbb{T}_N[X]^2$ be two noiseless trivial TLWE samples of a and b, respectively. Output the ciphertext $\mathsf{ct}' = (0, b) - \mathsf{KS} \boxdot (0, a)$.

Correctness. Note that $(0, a), (0, b)$ are the trivial TLWE encryption of a and b, respectively, namely, $(0, a) \in \mathsf{TLWE}_{z'}(a), (0, b) \in \mathsf{TLWE}_{z'}(b)$. The following equation proves the correctness of the algorithm:

$$\mathsf{TLWE}_{z'}(b) - \mathsf{TGSW}_{z'}(z) \boxdot \mathsf{TLWE}_{z'}(a) = \mathsf{TLWE}_{z'}(b - a \cdot z) = \mathsf{TLWE}_{z'}(m).$$

Hence, ct' is a TLWE ciphertext under new secret key z' while preserving the phase of ct. The computation complexity is one external product. Due to $(0, a), (0, b)$ are noiseless and secret key z is binary polynomial, the additional noise added by the key switching algorithm is bounded by $\ell N B_g \|\mathsf{err}(\mathsf{KS})\|_\infty + \frac{N(1+N)}{2B_g^\ell}$ according to Lemma 1. Plus the noise e_{ct} carried by the original TLWE ciphertext, the output ciphertext noise is $\ell N B_g \|\mathsf{err}(\mathsf{KS})\|_\infty + \frac{N(1+N)}{2B_g^\ell} + \|e_{\mathsf{ct}}\|_\infty$.

Security. The key switching key KS from $\texttt{KSKeyGen}(z \in \mathbb{B}_N[X], z' \in \mathbb{B}_N[X])$ is a TGSW sample, which are essential vectors of TLWE samples. The entries of KS are TLWE samples under the secret z', which are computationally indistinguishable from the uniform distribution over $\mathbb{T}_N[X]^{2\ell}$ under the TLWE assumption.

3.2 Binary Packing Tree

Ciphertext packing is a method that packs multiple LWE ciphertexts into a ring-LWE encryption to improve the effectiveness of HE, since ring-based HE systems have shown remarkable performance in real-world applications. Micciancio and Sorrell [24] described a variant of the key-switching technique to realize it, and Chen et al. [10] achieved better amortized complexity based on iterative mode.

Motivated by Chen et al.'s work [10], we design a binary packing tree for TLWE ciphertexts. In a binary packing tree, the inputs placed at the leaves are TLWE ciphertexts ready to be packed. The value of each node is the result of the packing operation of its two children's values. In the following, we will explain how to pack two TLWE ciphertexts and how to pack multiple TLWE ciphertexts by binary packing tree.

Paking Two TLWE Samples. Recall that the phase m of N-dimensional TLWE ciphertext holds the valid message only in the constant term, so the critical point is how to annihilate useless coefficient of m except $m[0]$ and how to aggregate other useful values at the appropriate position in the phase. Note that the map $m \mapsto m + \tau_d(m)$ can zeroize the coefficient $m[i]$ if $2^{\log N - l} \| i$[4] for $d = 2^l + 1$, namely, zeroize $m[N/2^l]$. And the phase multiplied by $X^{N/2^l}$ moves valid value $m[0]$ from position 0 to position $N/2^l$. Hence, for two TLWE ciphertexts ct_0 and ct_1 with phase m_0 and m_1, respectively, one can zeroize $m_0[N/2^l]$, and the other can shift $m_1[0]$ to poisiton $N/2^l$. Combined with the ideas mentioned above, we can pack two TLWE ciphertexts into a single TLWE ciphertext, where the valid value of the phase of the output TLWE ciphertext lies in the constant term and the monomial $X^{N/2^l}$. See Algorithm 2 for details.

Algorithm 2. $\texttt{Pack2TLWEs}(\mathsf{ct}_0, \mathsf{ct}_1, \mathsf{KS}, d)$

Input: Two TLWE ciphertexts $\mathsf{ct}_j \in \mathsf{TLWE}_s(\frac{1}{4} m_j[0])$ with $m_j[0] \in \mathbb{B}$ for $j \in \{0, 1\}$, an integer $d = 2^l + 1$, and a key-switching key $\mathsf{KS} \leftarrow \texttt{KSKeyGen}(s, \texttt{EvalAuto}(s, d))$

Output: A TLWE ciphertext $\mathsf{ct}_{01} \in \mathsf{TLWE}_{\tilde{s}}(\frac{1}{2} m_0[0] X^0 + \frac{1}{2} m_1[0] X^{N/2^l})$

1: Set $\mathsf{ct}_{add} \leftarrow \mathsf{ct}_0 + X^{N/2^l} \mathsf{ct}_1$
2: $\mathsf{ct}_{add} \leftarrow \texttt{KeySwitch}(\mathsf{ct}_{add}, \mathsf{KS})$
3: $\mathsf{ct}_{sub} \leftarrow \texttt{EvalAuto}(\mathsf{ct}_0 - X^{N/2^l} \mathsf{ct}_1, d)$
4: **return** $\mathsf{ct}_{01} \leftarrow \mathsf{ct}_{add} + \mathsf{ct}_{sub}$

Correctness. In Algorithm 2, the output ciphertext $\mathsf{ct}_{01} = \texttt{KeySwitch}(\mathsf{ct}_0 + X^{N/2^l}, \mathsf{KS}) + \texttt{EvalAuto}(\mathsf{ct}_0 - X^{N/2^l} \mathsf{ct}_1, d)$, then $\langle \mathsf{ct}_{01}, (-\tilde{s}, 1)\rangle \approx \langle (\mathsf{ct}_0 + X^{N/2^l}, \mathsf{KS}), (-s, 1)\rangle + \tau_d(\langle (\mathsf{ct}_0 - X^{N/2^l} \mathsf{ct}_1), (-s, 1)\rangle)$ by algorithm $\texttt{KeySwitch}$ and $\texttt{EvalAuto}$. Note that $\tau_d(X^i) = X^i$ for $2^{\log N - l + 1} | i$ and $\tau_d(X^i) = -X^i$ for $2^{\log N - l} \| i$. Thereby the value at position 0 of $m_0 + \tau_d(m_0)$ is $\frac{1}{2} m_0[0]$, at position $N/2^l$ is 0. The value at position $N/2^l$ of $X^{N/2^l}(m_1 + \tau_d(m_1)))$ is $\frac{1}{2} m_1[0]$, at position $N/2^{l-1}$ is 0. Hence, the phase of ct_{01} is

$$
\begin{aligned}
m_{01} &\approx \langle (\mathsf{ct}_0 + \tau_d(\mathsf{ct}_0)), (-s, 1)\rangle + X^{N/2^l} \cdot \langle (\mathsf{ct}_1 + \tau_d(\mathsf{ct}_1)), (-s, 1))\rangle \\
&\approx 2 \cdot \frac{1}{4} m_0[0] X^0 + 0 \cdot \frac{1}{4} m_0[N/2^l] X^{N/2^l} + X^{N/2^l} (2 \cdot \frac{1}{4} m_1[0] X^0) \\
&= \frac{1}{2} m_0[0] X^0 + \frac{1}{2} m_1[0] X^{N/2^l}.
\end{aligned} \tag{3}
$$

The phase of the output ciphertext is as desired. Note that the $\texttt{EvalAuto}$ algorithm is a signed permutation that incuring no noise growth and homomorphic

[4] $2^t \| i$ is equivalent to $2^t | i \wedge 2^{t+1} \nmid i$.

operation. Hence, the computation complexity of Algorithm 2 is one external product and the noise is bounded by $\ell N B_g \|\mathsf{err}(\mathsf{KS})\|_\infty + \frac{N(1+N)}{2B_g^\ell} + 2\|e_{\mathsf{ct}}\|_\infty$ from subroutine `KeySwitch`.

Paking multiple TLWE samples. On input n TLWE ciphertexts $\{\mathsf{ct}_j \in \mathsf{TLWE}_{s_0}(\frac{m_j[0]}{2n})\}_{j\in[n]}$ under the same secret $s_0 \in \mathbb{B}_N[X]$ for $n = 2^l \le N$, where $m_j[0] \in \mathbb{B}$, Algorithm 3 merges them into a TLWE ciphertext that can store all n valid values in the coefficients of its phase by binary packing tree of depth $\log n$. Figure 1 gives a case of $n = 8$.

Algorithm 3. $\mathtt{PackTLWEs}(\{\mathsf{ct}_j \in \mathsf{TLWE}_{s_0}(\frac{m_j[0]}{2n})\}_{j\in[n]}, \{\mathsf{KS}_k\}_{k\in\{1,\cdots,l\}})$

Input: n TLWE ciphertexts $\mathsf{ct}_j \in \mathsf{TLWE}_{s_0}(\frac{m_j[0]}{2n})$ with $m_j[0] \in \mathbb{B}$ for $j \in [2^l]$, key-switching keys $\mathsf{KS}_k \leftarrow \mathtt{KSKeyGen}(s_{k-1}, s_k)$ where $s_k \leftarrow \mathtt{EvalAuto}(s_{k-1}, 2^k+1)$ for $k \in \{1, \cdots, l\}$

Output: A TLWE ciphertext $\widetilde{\mathsf{ct}} \in \mathsf{TLWE}_{s_l}(\frac{1}{2}m_j \cdot Y^j)$ where $Y = X^{N/n}$

if $l = 0$ **then**
  return $\widetilde{\mathsf{ct}} \leftarrow \mathsf{ct}_0$
else
  for $k = 1$ to l **do**
    for $i = 0$ to $2^{l-k} - 1$ **do**
      $\mathsf{ct}_{left} \leftarrow \mathsf{ct}_i$
      $\mathsf{ct}_{right} \leftarrow \mathsf{ct}_{i+2^{l-k}}$
      $\mathsf{ct}_i \leftarrow \mathtt{Pack2TLWEs}(\mathsf{ct}_{left}, \mathsf{ct}_{right}, \mathsf{KS}_k, 2^k+1)$
    end for
  end for
end if

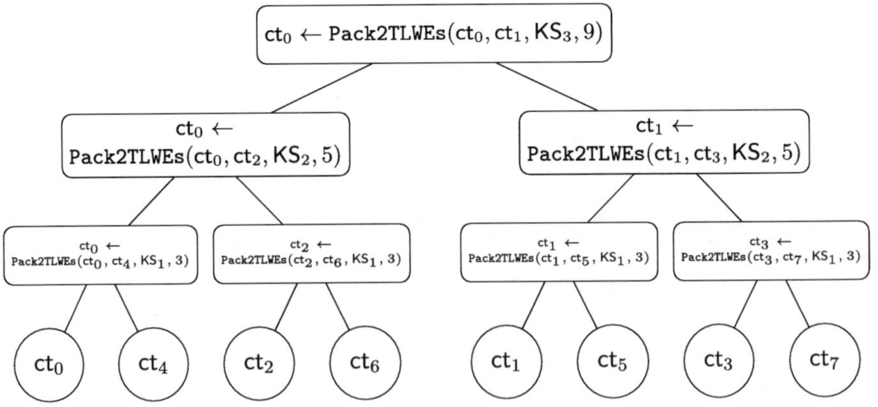

Fig. 1. A binary packing tree of $n = 8$.

Correctness. In Algorithm 3, the base $l = 0$ is trivial since $m = \frac{m_0[0]}{2n} X^0 \bmod 1$. At level k, there are $2^{l-k} = n/2^k$ TLWE samples running circularly in the program. Let $N = 2^t$, $r = N/n$, we inductively show the phase m_i of the return ciphertext ct_i satisfies

$$m_i \approx 2^k \sum_{N/2^k | j \in [N]} \frac{m_{i+j/r}[0]}{2n} X^j \bmod 1 \text{ for } i \in [n/2^k] \tag{4}$$

at iteration k. Now we assume that (4) is true for $k-1$. From the induction hypothesis,

$$m_{left} = m_i \approx 2^{k-1} \cdot \sum_{N/2^{k-1} | j \in [N]} m_{i+j/r}[0] X^j \bmod 1,$$

$$m_{right} = m_{i+n/2^k} \approx 2^{k-1} \cdot \sum_{N/2^{k-1} | j \in [N]} m_{i+n/2^k+j/r}[0] X^j \bmod 1.$$

In k-th iteration, we compute the procedure $\mathtt{Pack2TLWEs}(\mathsf{ct}_{left}, \mathsf{ct}_{right}, \mathsf{KS}, 2^k + 1)$. For m_{right}, $N/2^{k-1} = 2^{t-k+1} | j$, e.g., $2^{t-k} | (2^{t-k} + j) \wedge 2^{t-k+1} \nmid (2^{t-k} + j)$, so $2^{t-k} = N/2^k \| (N/2^k + j)$. Hence, for $j \in [N]$, we obtain that

$$\begin{aligned} m_i &= 2^k \Big(\sum_{\frac{N}{2^{k-1}} | j} \frac{m_{i+j/r}[0]}{2n} X^j + 0 \sum_{\frac{N}{2^k} \| j} \frac{m_{left}[j]}{2n} X^j + X^{\frac{N}{2^k}} \sum_{\frac{N}{2^{k-1}} | j} \frac{m_{i+n/2^k+j/r}[0]}{2n} X^j \Big) \\ &= 2^k \sum_{N/2^{k-1} | j} \frac{m_{i+j/r}[0]}{2n} X^j + 2^k \sum_{N/2^k \| j} \frac{m_{i+n/2^k+j/r}[0]}{2n} X^{j+N/2^k} \\ &= 2^k \sum_{N/2^k | j} \frac{m_{i+j/r}[0]}{2n} X^j. \end{aligned}$$

After last interation l, the output ciphertext $\widetilde{\mathtt{ct}}$'s phase is $\tilde{m} = \sum_{r | j \in [N]} \frac{m_{j/r}[0]}{2} X^j \bmod 1$, namely, $\tilde{m} = \frac{1}{2} \sum_{j \in [n]} m_j[0] Y^j$, where $Y = X^{N/n}$.

When packing n TLWE ciphertexts, the $\mathtt{PackTLWEs}$ algorithm needs to call $2^{l-1} + 2^{l-2} + \cdots + 2^0 = n - 1$ $\mathtt{Pack2TLWEs}$ subroutine, namely, $n-1$ external product. We remark that then asymptotically optimal amortized complexity $O(1)$ is achieved.

Each $\mathtt{Pack2TLWEs}$ subroutine adds extra noise $\ell N B_g \|\mathsf{err}(\mathsf{KS})\|_\infty + \frac{N(1+N)}{2B_g^\ell}$. The total additional noise is $(n-1)(\ell N B_g \|\mathsf{err}(\mathsf{KS})\|_\infty + \frac{N(1+N)}{2B_g^\ell})$. So the noise of the final ciphertext is bounded by $(n-1)(\ell N B_g \|\mathsf{err}(\mathsf{KS})\|_\infty + \frac{N(1+N)}{2B_g^\ell}) + n\|e_{\mathsf{ct}}\|_\infty$.

Security. The $\mathtt{Pack2TLWEs}$ algorithm, consisting of $\mathtt{KeySwith}$ and $\mathtt{EvalAuto}$ subroutines, is a simple application of key switching algorithm. The security of the key switching algorithm for TLWE ciphertexts has been proved in Sect. 3.1. So the algorithm $\mathtt{PackTLWEs}$ is secure relied on the security of the key switching algorithm.

3.3 Homomorphic Ring Decryption

On input a single TLWE ciphertext $(a, b) \in \mathsf{TLWE}_s(\frac{1}{2}m_j Y^j)$ for $j \in [n]$ and encryption of the binary representation of the secret key $s \in \mathbb{B}_N[X]$, the homomorphic ring decryption algorithm computes the ring element $b - a \cdot s \bmod (X^N + 1)$ homomorphically, and then extracts the result to n TLWE ciphertexts. In this section, we first describe a slow multiplication algorithm with homomorphic NTT to compute $a \cdot s \bmod X^N + 1$ homomorphically. Following by the description, we design a homomorphic ring decryption procedure and give a analysis.

Slow Multiplication with Homomorphic NTT. Proposed by Micciancio and Sorrell [24], slow multiplication algorithm computes $a \cdot s$ homomorphically using only the operations of addition and subtraction. In this section, we designed an efficient slow multiplication algorithm with homomorphic NTT to compute the polynomial product $a \cdot s \bmod X^N + 1$.

Let prime modulo $q \equiv 1 \bmod 2N$ with N power-of-two, $g \in \mathbb{Z}_q$ be a primitive N-th root of unity and $\eta^2 = g$. As in Sect. 2.2, the polynomial product $a \cdot s \bmod (X^N + 1)$ for $a, s \in \mathcal{R}_q$ may be computed as

$$a \cdot s \bmod (X^N + 1) = (1, \eta^{-1}, \cdots, \eta^{-(N-1)}) \circ \mathrm{INTT}(\mathrm{NTT}(\hat{\boldsymbol{a}}) \circ \mathrm{NTT}(\hat{\boldsymbol{s}})) \in \mathcal{R}_q,$$

where $\hat{\boldsymbol{a}} = (a[0], \eta a[1], \cdots, \eta^{N-1} a[N-1])$ and $\hat{\boldsymbol{s}} = (s[0], \eta s[1], \cdots, \eta^{N-1} s[N-1])$. We write as $\bar{\boldsymbol{a}} = \mathrm{NTT}(\hat{\boldsymbol{a}})$ and $\bar{\boldsymbol{s}} = \mathrm{NTT}(\hat{\boldsymbol{s}})$, then we need to compute $\mathrm{NTT}(\hat{\boldsymbol{a}}) \circ \mathrm{NTT}(\hat{\boldsymbol{s}}) = (\bar{\boldsymbol{a}}[0] \cdot \bar{\boldsymbol{s}}[0], \cdots, \bar{\boldsymbol{a}}[N-1] \cdot \bar{\boldsymbol{s}}[N-1])$ homomorphically. To do this, we use bit decomposition technique [6] that widely adopted in FHE schemes.

Assume that $q = 2tN + 1$ and $\iota = \lceil \log q \rceil$, $\bar{s}_{i,k}$ be the kth bit in $\bar{\boldsymbol{s}}[i]$'s binary representation, namely, $\bar{\boldsymbol{s}}[i] = \sum_{j=0}^{\iota-1} \bar{s}_{i,k} 2^k$. We may express multiplication of $\bar{\boldsymbol{a}}[i]$ by $\bar{\boldsymbol{s}}[i]$ by computing $\bar{\boldsymbol{a}}[i] \cdot \bar{\boldsymbol{s}}[i] = \sum_{j=0}^{\iota-1} \bar{\boldsymbol{a}}[i] 2^k \cdot \bar{s}_{i,k}$. Set the bootstrapping key as $\mathsf{BK}_{i,k} = \mathsf{TGSW}(\bar{s}_{i,k})$ for $i \in [N], k \in [\iota]$. Define $\sum_{j=0}^{\iota-1} \bar{\boldsymbol{a}}[i] 2^k \cdot \mathsf{TGSW}(\bar{s}_{i,k})$ to be a circuit computing this multiplication homomorphically using only additions, as the $\bar{s}_{i,k}$ values are binary. In Algorithm 4, we describe the slow multiplication algorithm to compute $a \cdot s \bmod X^N + 1$ homomorphically.

Algorithm 4. `SlowMult`$(\bar{\boldsymbol{a}}, \{BK_{i,k}\}_{i \in [N], k \in [\iota]}, v)$

Input: $\bar{\boldsymbol{a}} = \mathrm{NTT}(\hat{\boldsymbol{a}})$, bootstrapping keys $\mathsf{BK}_{i,k} = \mathsf{TGSW}_z(\bar{s}_{i,k})$ for $i \in [N]$ and $k \in [\iota]$, a test polynomial $v \in \mathbb{T}_{tN}[X]$

Output: TLWE samples of $X^{\rho_i} \cdot v$ where ρ_i is the ith coefficient of $a \cdot s \bmod X^N + 1$

for $i = 0$ to $N - 1$ **do**
  Initialize the noiseless TLWE sample as $\overline{ACC}_i = (0, v) \in \mathbb{T}_{tN}^2[X]$
  for $k = 0$ to $\iota - 1$ **do**
    $\overline{ACC}_i \leftarrow \mathtt{CMux}(\mathsf{BK}_{i,k}, X^{\bar{\boldsymbol{a}}[i] \cdot 2^k \bmod q} \cdot \overline{ACC}_i, \overline{ACC}_i)$
  end for
end for
$ACC_i \leftarrow X^{\varphi^{-i}} \mathrm{INTT}(\overline{ACC})_i$ for $i \in [N]$
return ACC_i

Homomorphic Ring Decryption. Given a TLWE sample $\mathsf{TLWE}_s(\frac{1}{2}m_jY^j) = (a, b) \in \mathbb{T}_N^2[X]$ for $j \in [n]$, the homomorphic ring decryption algorithm constructs n encryptions of m_j under a fixed amount of noise, which is summarized in Algorithm 5. The `SampleExtract` subroutine used in the algorithm comes from [15]. It is a method that homomorphically extracts the constant term of message in polynomial form as a TLWE ciphertext under the same secret key.

Algorithm 5. $\texttt{RingDecrypt}(\mu_1, \mathsf{ct}, \{BK_{i,k}\}_{i\in[N],k\in[\iota]})$

Input: A TLWE ciphertext $\mathsf{ct} = (a, b) \in \mathsf{TLWE}_{s_0}(\frac{1}{2}m_jY^j)$ with $m_j \in \mathbb{B}$ for $j \in [n]$, bootstrapping keys $\mathsf{BK}_{i,k} = \mathsf{TGSW}(\bar{s}_{i,k})$ for $i \in [N]$ and $k \in [\iota]$, a constant $\mu_1 \in \mathbb{T}$,

Output: n TLWE ciphertexts $\mathsf{ct}_j = (\boldsymbol{a}_j, b_j) \in \mathsf{TLWE}_z(\mu_1 \cdot m_j)$ for all $j \in [n]$

$\mu = \frac{1}{2}\mu_1 \in \mathbb{T}$

$\hat{\boldsymbol{a}} = (\lfloor 2tNa[0] \rceil, \psi\lfloor 2tNa[1] \rceil, \cdots, \psi^{N-1}\lfloor 2tNa[N-1] \rceil)$

$\bar{\boldsymbol{a}} = \mathrm{NTT}(\hat{\boldsymbol{a}})$

Let test polynomial $v := (1 + X + \cdots + X^{tN-1}) \cdot X^{\frac{tN}{2}} \cdot \mu \in \mathbb{T}_{tN}[X]$

$ACC_i \leftarrow \texttt{SlowMult}(\bar{\boldsymbol{a}}, \{\mathsf{BK}_{i,k}\}_{i\in[N],k\in[l]}, v)$

$b'[j] = \lfloor 2tNb[j] \rceil$

for $j = 0$ to $n - 1$ **do**

  $\mathsf{ct}'_j = X^{-b'[j]} \cdot ACC_j$

  $\mathsf{ct}_j = (0, \mu) + \texttt{SampleExtract}(\mathsf{ct}'_j)$

end for

return $\{\mathsf{ct}_j\}_{j\in[n]}$

Correctness. Let $a'[i] = \lfloor 2tNa[i] \rceil \in \mathbb{Z}_q$ for $i \in [N]$ and $a' \cdot s \bmod X^N + 1 = c'[0]X^0 + \cdots + c'[N-1]X^{N-1}$. As shown in `SlowMult` subroutine, $ACC_i = \mathsf{TLWE}_z(X^{c'[i]} \cdot v)$. We get that

$$\mathsf{ct}'_j = X^{-b'[j]} \cdot ACC_j = \mathsf{TLWE}_z(X^{c'[j]-b'[j]} \cdot v) = \mathsf{TLWE}_z(X^{-tN\cdot m_j} \cdot v).$$

If $m_j = 0$, then the contant term of the messge of ct'_j is $-\mu$. If $m_j = 1$, then is μ. So the message of the output ciphertext ct_j is $\mu_1 \cdot m_j$ as desired.

Note that multiplications by X^i is only the shifts of polynomial coefficients of the ciphertext, so we ignore this computational complexity. So the `RingDecrypt` algorithm needs to $N\lceil \log(tN+1) \rceil$ `CMux` gates, namely, $\tilde{O}(N)$ external products. And the sample output by `SampleExtract` encodes the constant term with at most the same noise variance as the original sample. Hence, the noise of the output ciphertext is $\lceil \log(tN+1) \rceil (\ell N B_g \|\mathsf{err}(\mathsf{BK})\|_\infty + \frac{N+1}{2B_g^\ell})$ according to Lemma 2.

4 Batched FHE from TFHE

In this section, we translate TFHE [15] into be a batched FHE, which can reduce the amortized bootstrapping complexity efficiently.

4.1 The Construction

Here we present our batched FHE scheme from TFHE. The key difference between our scheme and the original TFHE in [13] is that we can do bootstrapping batching after the homomorphic circuits. The details of our construction are specified as follows.

- $\texttt{FHE.Setup}(1^\lambda)$: On input the security parameter λ, the algorithm set TLWE dimension N of the power of two, set the decomposition degree ℓ and the base $B_g \geq 2$ for the gadget matrix $\boldsymbol{G}_2$ defined in (1), set the error gaussian distribution D_α over $\mathbb{T}$ with parameter α, set the prime modulo of NTT $q \equiv 1 \bmod 2N$ and $\iota = \lceil \log q \rceil$, set a constant $\mu_1 \in \mathbb{T}$. Let $g \in \mathbb{Z}_q$ be a primitive N-th root of unity and $\eta^2 = g$. Output the public parameter $pp = (N, B_g, \ell, D_\alpha, \alpha, q, \iota, \eta, \mu_1)$.
- $\texttt{FHE.Gen}(pp)$: Sample a secret key $s_0 \leftarrow U(\mathbb{B}_N[X])$. Let $n = 2^l \leq N$, sample n random polynomials $a_j \leftarrow U(\mathbb{T}_N[X])$ and n error polynomials $e_j \leftarrow U(D_\alpha^N)$ for $j \in [n]$. Generate n TLWE samples $\texttt{tl}_j = (a_j, a_j \cdot s_0 + e_j) \in \mathbb{T}_N^2[X]$. Generate l key switching keys $\mathsf{KS}_r \leftarrow \texttt{KSKeyGen}(s_{r-1}, s_r)$ where $s_r \leftarrow \texttt{EvalAuto}(s_{r-1}, 2^r + 1)$ for $r \in \{1, \cdots, l\}$. Let $\hat{\boldsymbol{s}} = (s_l[0], \eta s_l[1], \cdots, \eta^{N-1} s_l[N-1])$ and $\bar{\boldsymbol{s}} = \mathrm{NTT}(\hat{\boldsymbol{s}})$, where $\bar{\boldsymbol{s}}[i] = \sum_{k=0}^{\iota-1} \bar{s}_{i,k} 2^k$. Generate bootstrapping keys $\mathsf{BK}_{i,k} = \mathsf{TGSW}_z(\bar{s}_{i,k})$ for $k \in [\iota]$ and $i \in [N]$. Generate another key switching key $\mathsf{KS}_0 \leftarrow \texttt{KSKeyGen}(z, s_0)$. So, the algorithm returns n TLWE samples $\{\texttt{tl}_j\}_{j \in [n]}$, key switching keys $\{\mathsf{KS}_r\}_{r \in [l+1]}$ and bootstrapping keys $\{\mathsf{BK}_{i,k}\}_{i \in [N], k \in [\iota]}$.
- $\texttt{FHE.Enc}(\{m_j\}_{j \in [n]}, \{\texttt{tl}_j\}_{j \in [n]})$: Given n messages $\{m_j\}_{j \in [n]}$ where $m_j \in \mathbb{B}_j$, output n TLWE ciphertexts $\mathsf{ct}_j = (0, \frac{m_j}{2n}) + \texttt{tl}_j$.
- $\texttt{FHE.Eval}(\{\mathsf{ct}_j\}_{j \in [n]})$: For arbitrary TLWE ciphertexts ct, $\mathsf{ct}_1, \mathsf{ct}_2 \in \{\mathsf{ct}_j\}_n$, the homomorphically evaluate the basic gates as follows:
  - $\mathrm{HomNot}(\mathsf{ct}) = (0, \frac{1}{2n})\text{-}\mathsf{ct}$;
  - $\mathrm{HomAND}(\mathsf{ct}_1, \mathsf{ct}_2) = (0, -\frac{1}{4n}) + \mathsf{ct}_1 + \mathsf{ct}_2$;
  - $\mathrm{HomOR}(\mathsf{ct}_1, \mathsf{ct}_2) = (0, \frac{1}{4n}) + \mathsf{ct}_1 + \mathsf{ct}_2$;
  - $\mathrm{HomNAND}(\mathsf{ct}_1, \mathsf{ct}_2) = (0, \frac{5}{4n})\text{-}\mathsf{ct}_1 - \mathsf{ct}_2$;
  - $\mathrm{HomXOR}(\mathsf{ct}_1, \mathsf{ct}_2) = \mathsf{ct}_1 - \mathsf{ct}_2$.
- $\texttt{FHE.Pack}(\{\mathsf{ct}_j\}_n, \{\mathsf{KS}_r\}_{r \in \{1, \cdots, l\}})$: Packing the input ciphertexts by running $\widetilde{\mathsf{ct}} \leftarrow \texttt{PackTLWEs}(\{\mathsf{ct}_j\}_n, \{\mathsf{KS}_r\}_{r \in \{1, \cdots, l\}})$. Return the TLWE ciphertext $\widetilde{\mathsf{ct}}$.
- $\texttt{FHE.Boot}(pp, \widetilde{\mathsf{ct}}, \{\mathsf{BK}_{i,k}\}_{i \in [N], k \in [\iota]}, \mathsf{KS}_0)$: To get refresh ciphertexts ct'_j for $j \in [n]$, run $\texttt{RingDecrypt}(\mu_1, \widetilde{\mathsf{ct}}, \{\mathsf{BK}_{i,k}\}_{i \in [N], k \in [\iota]})$. Return n TLWE ciphertexts $\mathsf{ct}_j \leftarrow \texttt{KeySwitch}(\mathsf{ct}'_j, \mathsf{KS}_0)$.
- $\texttt{FHE.Dec}(s_0, \{\mathsf{ct}_j\}_{j \in [n]})$: To decrypt ciphertexts $\mathsf{ct}_j = (a_j, b_j)$, we compute the phase $\varphi_{s_0}(\mathsf{ct}_j) = b - as$, and round it to the nearest element in $\{0, \mu_1\}$. If it is close to μ_1, then $m_j = 1$. Otherwise, $m_j = 0$.

4.2 Analysis

In the following, we will analyze the computation complexity, noise growth, correctness conditions and security of our batched FHE scheme.

Lemma 4. *The computation complexity of the batched FHE scheme described above is no more than $\tilde{O}(N)$. Suppose the bootstrapping key carries the same noise as the key switching key carries, then the noise of the output ciphertext is $\tilde{O}(N^2)$.*

Proof. The computation complexity of the batched FHE scheme mainly comes from external products, which appear in `FHE.Pack` step and `FHE.Boot` step. The computation complexity of `PackTLWEs` subroutine is $n-1$ while `RingDecrypt` is $N\lceil\log q\rceil$. Finally, we also need n external products to perform `KeySwitch`$(\mathsf{ct}'_j, \mathsf{KS}_0)$. Therefore, the computation computation of the batched FHE is $2n-1+N\lceil\log(tN+1)\rceil = \tilde{O}(N)$ in summary.

After `RingDecrypt` subroutine in `FHE.Boot` step, the noise is $\lceil\log(tN+1)\rceil(\ell N B_g\|\mathsf{err}(\mathsf{BK})\|_\infty + \frac{N+1}{2B_g^\ell})$ according to Sect. 3.3. The `KeySwitch`$(\mathsf{ct}'_j, \mathsf{KS}_0)$ will add extra noise $\ell N B_g\|\mathsf{err}(\mathsf{KS})\|_\infty + \frac{N(1+N)}{2B_g^\ell}$. Therefore, the noise of final output ciphertext is $(\lceil\log q\rceil+1)\ell N B_g\|\mathsf{err}(\mathsf{BK})\|_\infty + (\lceil\log q\rceil + N)\frac{N+1}{2B_g^\ell} = \tilde{O}(N^2)$.

Correctness Conditions. To make decryption algorithm works successfully for the worst case, our batched FHE scheme should satisfy the following requirement:

$$(\lceil\log q\rceil+1)\ell N B_f g\|\mathsf{err}(\mathsf{BK})\|_\infty + (\lceil\log q\rceil + N)\frac{N+1}{2B_g^\ell} \leq \frac{1}{4}. \tag{5}$$

Therefore, the noise of key switching keys and bootstrapping keys is bounded by $\frac{B_g^\ell - 2(\lceil\log q\rceil+N)(N+1)}{4(\lceil\log q\rceil+1)\ell N B_g^{\ell+1}}$.

Security. From the attacker's point of view, it obtains the the distribution of key switching keys $\{\mathsf{KS}_r\}_{r\in[l+1]}$, bootstrapping keys $\{\mathsf{BK}_{i,k}\}_{i\in[N],k\in[\iota]}$ and TLWE ciphertexts $\{\mathsf{ct}_j\}_{j\in[n]}$. In the following hybrids, we will prove semantic security of the batched FHE scheme depending on the semantic security of the TLWE assumption.

- First, the key switching keys $\{\mathsf{KS}_r\}_{r\in[l+1]}$ and the bootstrapping keys $\{\mathsf{BK}_{i,k}\}_{i\in[N],k\in[\iota]}$ generated by `FHE.Gen` are changed to random matrices in $\mathcal{M}_{2\ell\times 2}(\mathbb{T}_N[X])$ according to the TLWE assumption.
- Second, the ciphertexts $\{\mathsf{ct}_j\}_{j\in[n]}$ generated by `FHE.Enc` are changed to n TLWE samples of 0.

Finally, these distributions are completely independent of the message $\{m_j\}_{j\in[n]}$.

4.3 Comparisons

We compare the proposed batched FHE scheme with three existing FHE schemes, where Chillotti et al.' FHE [13] is the original TFHE, Chen et al.' work [11] with BGV-type packing, and Miccianco et al.' work [24] with FHEW-ciphertext packing. The comparisons of the computation complexity, the size of

Table 1. Computation cost, boostrapping keys size and noise overhead comparisons. N denotes the dimension of the TLWE assumption. # of ciphers indicates the number of packed ciphertexts. Parameter $0 < \varepsilon < 1/2$.

Schemes	# of ciphers	Computation cost		Bootstrapping keys		Noise overhead
		Total cost	Amortized cost	Total cost	Amortized cost	
Chillotti et al. [13]	1	$O(N)$	$O(N)$	$O(N^2)$	$O(N^2)$	$\tilde{O}(N)$
Chen et al. [11]	N	$\tilde{O}(N^3)$	$\tilde{O}(N^2)$	$\tilde{O}(N^2)$	$\tilde{O}(N)$	$\tilde{O}(N^3)$
Miccianco et al. [24]	N	$\tilde{O}(3^{1/\varepsilon}N^{1+2\varepsilon})$	$\tilde{O}(3^{1/\varepsilon}N^{2\varepsilon})$	$\tilde{O}(N^2)$	$\tilde{O}(N)$	$\tilde{O}(N^{3/\varepsilon-2})$
This work	n	$\tilde{O}(N)$	$\tilde{O}(N/n)$	$\tilde{O}(N^2)$	$\tilde{O}(N^2/n)$	$\tilde{O}(N^2)$

bootstrapping keys and noise overhead are provided in Table 1. As of now, the work of Chen et al. [11] and Miccianco et al. [24] remains theoretical.

As shown in Table 1, the total cost of our work is less than [11] and [24], but more than [13]. When $n > \log tN$ (modulo $q = tN + 1$ for NTT), our scheme has lower amortized complexity than [13]. In particular, when $n = N$, we get the optimal amortized computation complexity $O(\log N)$, which is better than the other three schemes. We have a clear advantage in terms of noise overhead excluding the work of Chillotti et al. [13]

The size of bootstrapping keys of our work is equal to [11] and [24] , but more than [13]. Same as amortized computation cost, when $n > \log tN$, our scheme has lower amortized bootstrapping sizes than [13]. When $n = N$, we get the optimal amortized computation complexity $\widetilde{O}(N)$, which is identical to Chen et al.'s [11] and Miccianco et al.'s work [24]. Note that the number of packing ciphertexts of our scheme is more flexible. Miccianco et al.' FHE [24] can only pack fixed $\varphi(N)$ ciphertexts where φ is Euler's totient function. Chen et al.'s FHE [11] can only pack N messages. We can pack the n TLWE ciphertexts as long as n is power of two and less than N.

Another advantage of our work is that with the increase in the number of ciphertexts, our ciphertext size remains constant while the ciphertext size of [13] increases linearly.

5 Performance Evaluation

We performed our batched FHE scheme in C/C++ based on the TFHE library [16] and the LatticeCrypto library [23] for NTT. All experiments were conducted with a standard desktop computer (Lenovo Intel CoreTM i7-4710MQ CPU @2.5 GHZ) on Ubuntu. The running time, ciphertexts size and amortized bootstrapping keys of experiments are presented in Fig. 2. We also compared with original TFHE [13] under the same conditions. The details of the experiment are as follows.

The modulo of ring LWE-based cryptosystem satisfies the form $q = t \cdot 2N + 1$, where $t \geq 3$ is a very small integer. Typical parameter choices might be $N = 1024$ and $q = 12289 = 12 \cdot N + 1$, as used in the NewHope proposal [1], in which case a 2048-th root of unity would be 9098. In our experiments, we choose the security parameter $\lambda = 128$, then the concrete parameters are shown in Table 2. The parameter α of error Gaussian distribution satisfies Eq. (5).

Table 2. Parameters of our batched FHE scheme.

λ	N	q	ℓ	B_g	α
128	1024	12289	3	256	1.85×10^{-8}

Figure 2 illustrates the expected behavior of our batched FHE scheme. We measured running time (s), boostrapping key size (MB) and ciphertext size (KB) for $n \in \{2, 4, 8, 16, 32, 64, 128, 256, 512, 1024\}$, respectively. These measurements are almost kept in a constant range since the dimension N of TLWE sample remains constant. Therefore, the amortized complexity decreases with the increase of the number of the packing ciphertexts. We can see that when $n > 2^5$, our total running time is less than TFHE. When $n > 2^2$, our amortized bootstrapping key is smaller than TFHE. When $n = N$, we can get the optimal amortized complexity.

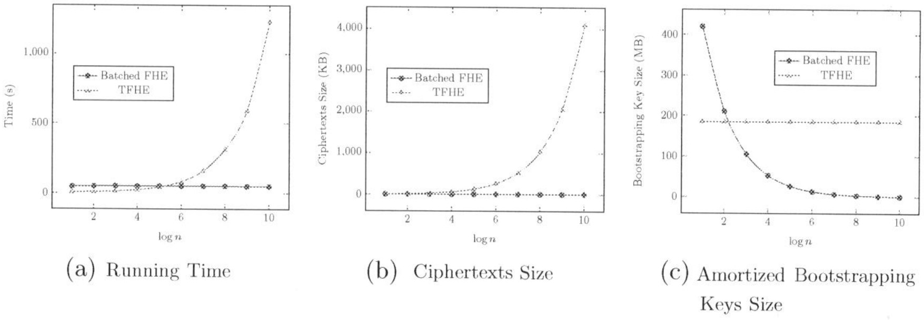

(a) Running Time (b) Ciphertexts Size (c) Amortized Bootstrapping Keys Size

Fig. 2. Experimental results

6 Conclusion

In this paper, we combine the advantages of TFHE and ciphertexts packing, and propose a batched fully homomorphic encryption scheme. Our work reduces the amortized computation complexity from $O(N)$ in the original TFHE cryptosystem to $O(\log N)$ in the proposed batched FHE. Furthermore, it can reduce the amortized size of boostrapping keys from $O(N^2)$ to $\tilde{O}(N)$. To obtain our batched FHE scheme, we use a binary packing tree for TLWE samples and NTT for slow multiplication. We also implement our batched FHE scheme. The experimental results indicate the metrics of the proposed FHE scheme.

Acknowledgements. This work was supported by the National Nature Science Foundation of China under Grant 62172434.

References

1. Alkim, E., Ducas, L., Pöppelmann, T., Schwabe, P.: Post-quantum key exchange - A new hope. In: 25th USENIX Security Symposium, USENIX Security 16, pp. 327–343. USENIX Association (2016)
2. Biasse, J.-F., Ruiz, L.: FHEW with efficient multibit bootstrapping. In: Lauter, K., Rodríguez-Henríquez, F. (eds.) LATINCRYPT 2015. LNCS, vol. 9230, pp. 119–135. Springer, Cham (2015). https://doi.org/10.1007/978-3-319-22174-8_7
3. Brakerski, Z.: Fully homomorphic encryption without modulus switching from classical GapSVP. In: Safavi-Naini, R., Canetti, R. (eds.) CRYPTO 2012. LNCS, vol. 7417, pp. 868–886. Springer, Heidelberg (2012). https://doi.org/10.1007/978-3-642-32009-5_50
4. Brakerski, Z., Gentry, C., Halevi, S.: Packed ciphertexts in LWE-based homomorphic encryption. In: Kurosawa, K., Hanaoka, G. (eds.) PKC 2013. LNCS, vol. 7778, pp. 1–13. Springer, Heidelberg (2013). https://doi.org/10.1007/978-3-642-36362-7_1
5. Brakerski, Z., Gentry, C., Vaikuntanathan, V.: (Leveled) fully homomorphic encryption without bootstrapping. In: Innovations in Theoretical Computer Science 2012, pp. 309–325. ACM (2012). https://doi.org/10.1145/2090236.2090262
6. Brakerski, Z., Vaikuntanathan, V.: Efficient fully homomorphic encryption from (standard) LWE. In: IEEE 52nd Annual Symposium on Foundations of Computer Science, FOCS 2011, pp. 97–106. IEEE Computer Society (2011). https://doi.org/10.1109/FOCS.2011.12
7. Brakerski, Z., Vaikuntanathan, V.: Fully homomorphic encryption from ring-LWE and security for key dependent messages. In: Rogaway, P. (ed.) CRYPTO 2011. LNCS, vol. 6841, pp. 505–524. Springer, Heidelberg (2011). https://doi.org/10.1007/978-3-642-22792-9_29
8. Chen, H., Chillotti, I., Ren, L.: Onion ring ORAM: efficient constant bandwidth oblivious RAM from (leveled) TFHE. In: Proceedings of the 2019 ACM SIGSAC Conference on Computer and Communications Security, CCS 2019, pp. 345–360. ACM (2019). https://doi.org/10.1145/3319535.3354226
9. Chen, H., Chillotti, I., Song, Y.: Multi-Key homomorphic encryption from TFHE. In: Galbraith, S.D., Moriai, S. (eds.) ASIACRYPT 2019. LNCS, vol. 11922, pp. 446–472. Springer, Cham (2019). https://doi.org/10.1007/978-3-030-34621-8_16
10. Chen, H., Dai, W., Kim, M., Song, Y.: Efficient homomorphic conversion between (ring) LWE ciphertexts. In: Sako, K., Tippenhauer, N.O. (eds.) ACNS 2021. LNCS, vol. 12726, pp. 460–479. Springer, Cham (2021). https://doi.org/10.1007/978-3-030-78372-3_18
11. Chen, L., Zhang, Z.: Bootstrapping fully homomorphic encryption with ring plaintexts within polynomial noise. In: Okamoto, T., Yu, Y., Au, M.H., Li, Y. (eds.) ProvSec 2017. LNCS, vol. 10592, pp. 285–304. Springer, Cham (2017). https://doi.org/10.1007/978-3-319-68637-0_18
12. Chen, L., Zhang, Z., Wang, X.: Batched multi-hop multi-key FHE from Ring-LWE with compact ciphertext extension. In: Kalai, Y., Reyzin, L. (eds.) TCC 2017. LNCS, vol. 10678, pp. 597–627. Springer, Cham (2017). https://doi.org/10.1007/978-3-319-70503-3_20
13. Chillotti, I., Gama, N., Georgieva, M., Izabachène, M.: Faster fully homomorphic encryption: bootstrapping in less than 0.1 seconds. In: Cheon, J.H., Takagi, T. (eds.) ASIACRYPT 2016. LNCS, vol. 10031, pp. 3–33. Springer, Heidelberg (2016). https://doi.org/10.1007/978-3-662-53887-6_1

14. Chillotti, I., Gama, N., Georgieva, M., Izabachène, M.: Faster packed homomorphic operations and efficient circuit bootstrapping for TFHE. In: Takagi, T., Peyrin, T. (eds.) ASIACRYPT 2017. LNCS, vol. 10624, pp. 377–408. Springer, Cham (2017). https://doi.org/10.1007/978-3-319-70694-8_14
15. Chillotti, I., Gama, N., Georgieva, M., Izabachène, M.: TFHE: fast fully homomorphic encryption over the torus. J. Cryptol. **33**(1), 34–91 (2019). https://doi.org/10.1007/s00145-019-09319-x
16. Chillotti, I., Gama, N., Georgieva, M., Izabachène, M.: TFHE: fast fully homomorphic encryption library (2016). https://tfhe.github.io/tfhe/
17. Chillotti, I., Joye, M., Paillier, P.: Programmable bootstrapping enables efficient homomorphic inference of deep neural networks. In: Dolev, S., Margalit, O., Pinkas, B., Schwarzmann, A. (eds.) CSCML 2021. LNCS, vol. 12716, pp. 1–19. Springer, Cham (2021). https://doi.org/10.1007/978-3-030-78086-9_1
18. Chillotti, I., Ligier, D., Orfila, J.-B., Tap, S.: Improved programmable bootstrapping with larger precision and efficient arithmetic circuits for TFHE. In: Tibouchi, M., Wang, H. (eds.) ASIACRYPT 2021. LNCS, vol. 13092, pp. 670–699. Springer, Cham (2021). https://doi.org/10.1007/978-3-030-92078-4_23
19. Ducas, L., Micciancio, D.: FHEW: bootstrapping homomorphic encryption in less than a second. In: Oswald, E., Fischlin, M. (eds.) EUROCRYPT 2015. LNCS, vol. 9056, pp. 617–640. Springer, Heidelberg (2015). https://doi.org/10.1007/978-3-662-46800-5_24
20. Gentry, C.: Fully homomorphic encryption using ideal lattices. In: Proceedings of the 41st Annual ACM Symposium on Theory of Computing, STOC 2009, pp. 169–178. ACM (2009). https://doi.org/10.1145/1536414.1536440
21. Gentry, C., Sahai, A., Waters, B.: Homomorphic encryption from learning with errors: conceptually-simpler, asymptotically-faster, attribute-based. In: Canetti, R., Garay, J.A. (eds.) CRYPTO 2013. LNCS, vol. 8042, pp. 75–92. Springer, Heidelberg (2013). https://doi.org/10.1007/978-3-642-40041-4_5
22. Hiromasa, R., Abe, M., Okamoto, T.: Packing messages and optimizing bootstrapping in GSW-FHE. In: Katz, J. (ed.) PKC 2015. LNCS, vol. 9020, pp. 699–715. Springer, Heidelberg (2015). https://doi.org/10.1007/978-3-662-46447-2_31
23. Longa, P., Naehrig, M.: Latticecrypto (2016). https://www.microsoft.com/en-us/research/project/lattice-cryptography-library/
24. Micciancio, D., Sorrell, J.: Ring packing and amortized FHEW bootstrapping. In: 45th International Colloquium on Automata, Languages, and Programming, ICALP 2018. LIPIcs, vol. 107, pp. 100:1–100:14. Schloss Dagstuhl - Leibniz-Zentrum für Informatik (2018). https://doi.org/10.4230/LIPIcs.ICALP.2018.100
25. Okada, H., Kiyomoto, S., Cid, C.: Integerwise functional bootstrapping on TFHE. In: Susilo, W., Deng, R.H., Guo, F., Li, Y., Intan, R. (eds.) ISC 2020. LNCS, vol. 12472, pp. 107–125. Springer, Cham (2020). https://doi.org/10.1007/978-3-030-62974-8_7
26. Pollard, J.M.: The fast Fourier transform in a finite field. Math. Comput. **25**(114), 365–374 (1971). https://doi.org/10.2307/2004932
27. Regev, O.: On lattices, learning with errors, random linear codes, and cryptography. In: Proceedings of the 37th Annual ACM Symposium on Theory of Computing, pp. 84–93. ACM (2005). https://doi.org/10.1145/1060590.1060603
28. Smart, N.P., Vercauteren, F.: Fully homomorphic SIMD operations. Des. Codes Crypt. **71**(1), 57–81 (2012). https://doi.org/10.1007/s10623-012-9720-4
29. Winkler, F.: Polynomial Algorithms in Computer Algebra. Springer, Heidelberg (1996). https://doi.org/10.1007/978-3-7091-6571-3

Implicit Rejection in Fujisaki-Okamoto: Framework and a Novel Realization

Zhao Chen[1,2], Xianhui Lu[1,2](✉), Dingding Jia[1], and Bao Li[1]

[1] State Key Laboratory of Information Security, Institute of Information Engineering, Chinese Academy of Sciences, Beijing, China

[2] School of Cyber Security, University of Chinese Academy of Sciences, Beijing, China

luxianhui@iie.ac.cn

Abstract. The generic IND-CCA secure key encapsulation mechanism (KEM) constructions in the quantum random oracle model (QROM) attract much attention due to the NIST post-quantum competition. Most of the NIST KEM submissions follow the generic Fujisaki-Okamoto transformation with implicit rejection (FO-IR). We propose a framework for the construction of quantum random oracles that supports implicit rejection, and prove that the KEMs satisfying our framework are IND-CCA secure in the QROM. Specifically, we use the idea of hash combination to eliminate the requirement for checking the validity of ciphertexts, which is the key point to achieve IND-CCA security. We show that the existing FO-IR widely used in the NIST KEM submissions can be explained by our framework. Additionally, we also propose a novel realization which exploits the verifiability of the private key.

Keywords: IND-CCA security · Key encapsulation mechanism · Quantum random oracle model · Implicit rejection

1 Introduction

The Fujisaki-Okamoto (FO) transformation [9,10] is one of the most important transformations to construct an indistinguishability against chosen-ciphertext attacks (IND-CCA) [20] secure public-key encryption (PKE) scheme. First introduced by Fujisaki and Okamoto [9] in 1999 and revisited by Dent [5] and Hofheinz et al. [12], there are many variants [3,8,12,14,15,17,18,21] that are widely used in the submissions to the National Institute of Standard and Technology (NIST) post-quantum competition [19]. The main function of the FO transformation [9,10] is to convert a PKE scheme with a weaker security property (i.e., one-way against chosen-plaintext attacks (OW-CPA)) into an IND-CCA secure one in the random oracle model (ROM) [2]. The core idea of realizing the transformation is to use "re-encryption" in the decryption algorithm to verify the validity of ciphertexts, thereby rejecting invalid ciphertexts that may reveal information of the private key. Specifically, the decryption algorithm outputs a rejection symbol for an invalid ciphertext, which is called explicit rejection.

W. Susilo et al. (Eds.): ISC 2022, LNCS 13640, pp. 110–130, 2022.
https://doi.org/10.1007/978-3-031-22390-7_8

With the development of quantum computation [11,22], we have to consider the cryptographic constructions that are secure against quantum adversaries. Particularly, the NIST launched the Post-Quantum Cryptography (PQC) standardization project, which called for candidates of quantum-resistant public-key cryptographic primitives [19]. Note that a quantum adversary may execute public cryptographic components such as hash functions in superposition on his own quantum computer. In order to capture this ability of quantum adversaries, Boneh et al. [4] introduced the quantum random oracle model (QROM), where hash functions are modeled as public random oracles similarly as in the ROM [2] but with **quantum** access. Now, it is generally believed that the security of post-quantum cryptographic constructions should be established in the QROM.

Unfortunately, proving the IND-CCA security of the PKE scheme obtained by applying the FO transformation [9,10] in the QROM is quite challenging, as many classical ROM proof techniques cannot carry over to the quantum settings [4]. For example, to implement the security reduction, the simulator needs to simulate the decryption oracle without knowing the private key. Then, the simulator has to first verify the validity of ciphertexts during the decryption queries. In the ROM, the adversary's queries to random oracle (RO) can be recorded by a list, the simulator can easily check the validity of ciphertexts by scanning over the RO-query list. However, such an RO-query list does not exist in the QROM since quantum adversaries can evaluate the random oracle on a superposition state of exponential many states [4].

Considering the problem of ciphertext validity verification, Hofheinz et al. [12] revisited the key encapsulation mechanism (KEM) version of the FO transformation [9,10] and provided an "implicit rejection" variant of the KEM construction, where a pseudorandom key is returned instead of a rejection symbol $\bot$ for an invalid ciphertext c in the decapsulation algorithm. Particularly, Hofheinz et al. [12] provided several generic FO-KEM constructions with implicit rejection, e.g., $\mathsf{FO}_m^{\not\bot}$ and $\mathsf{FO}^{\not\bot}$, where $\not\bot$ means implicit rejection and the pseudorandom key $K := \mathsf{H}(s, c)$, where s is a random seed which is contained in the private key, thus the adversary cannot verify the validity of ciphertexts by querying the decapsulation oracle. Thereby, it is possible that the simulator can simulate the decapsulation oracle in the security reduction without the requirement for checking the validity of ciphertexts. Subsequently, Jiang et al. [15] extended the technique in [4] to prove that the KEMs obtained by applying $\mathsf{FO}_m^{\not\bot}$ and $\mathsf{FO}^{\not\bot}$ are both IND-CCA secure in the QROM. Recently, the NIST announced the finalist KEM algorithm and Round-4 submissions, all of which follow the implicit rejection variants of the FO-KEM to achieve IND-CCA security in the QROM.

Although existing KEMs with implicit rejection [12] can be shown to be IND-CCA secure in the QROM [3,8,14,15,17,18,21], they need to introduce an additional secret information (i.e., the s) in the construction compared with FO-KEM with explicit rejection [5,12]. In terms of the functionality of the KEM, the additional secret information is unnecessary, and it is more like only serving for the security proof in the QROM. From a design point of view, it is natural to ask whether there is a better solution to achieving "implicit rejection"?

1.1 Our Contributions

In this paper, we answer the question above in the affirmative. At first, we can utilize the secrecy of the private key to hide the validity of ciphertexts. Then, we can also achieve implicit rejection and without requirement for the additional secret information. Furthermore, we abstract out a framework that supports implicit rejection.

(1) We propose a framework for the construction of quantum random oracles that supports implicit rejection, and then prove that the KEMs satisfying our framework are IND-CCA secure in the QROM. The key observation is that we can use the idea of hash combination to eliminate the requirement for checking the validity of ciphertexts. Specifically, we combine multiple internal independent hash functions to construct the key-derivation-function H (KDF in the KEM, modeled as a random oracle), and then simulate the decapsulation oracle by only using one of the internal hash functions whether the ciphertext is valid or not. As a consequence, it is easy to prove the IND-CCA security of the KEMs. Moreover, we notice that the generic transfomation $\mathsf{FO}^{\not\perp}$ [12] satifies our framework.

(2) We present a novel realization $\mathsf{FO}^{\not\perp,sk}$ for constructing an IND-CCA secure KEM scheme in the QROM by exploiting the verifiability of the private key, where sk (the secret key of the underlying PKE scheme) means a pseudo-random key $K := \mathsf{H}(sk, c)$ is returned for an invalid ciphertext c. Our new realization no longer requires additional secret information in the construction, thus it is more concise compared with $\mathsf{FO}^{\not\perp}$ [12]. We can apply our new realization to NIST KEM submissions to simplify the constructions.

1.2 Technical Overview

Before showing our framework in detail, we first review the original FO-KEM with implicit rejection. To simplify the presentation of $\mathsf{FO}^{\not\perp}$, we decompose $\mathsf{FO}^{\not\perp}$ into two separate transformations [12], i.e., T and $\mathsf{U}^{\not\perp}$[1], and $\mathsf{FO}^{\not\perp} := \mathsf{U}^{\not\perp} \circ \mathsf{T}$.

- The transformation T converts a randomized PKE (rPKE) into a deterministic PKE (dPKE) scheme $\mathsf{PKE}' := \mathsf{T}[\mathsf{PKE}, \mathsf{G}]$ by using a random oracle G. The encryption of PKE' is defined by $\mathsf{Enc}'(pk, m) := \mathsf{Enc}(pk, m; \mathsf{G}(m))$ and $\mathsf{Dec}'(sk, c)$ invokes $m' := \mathsf{Dec}(sk, c)$ and rejects (outputs $\perp$) if $m' = \perp$ or $\mathsf{Enc}(pk, m'; \mathsf{G}(m')) \neq c$.

- The transformation $\mathsf{U}^{\not\perp}$ converts PKE' into a KEM scheme $\mathsf{KEM} := \mathsf{U}^{\not\perp}[\mathsf{PKE}', \mathsf{H}]$ with "implicit rejection". The encapsulation of KEM is defined by

$$\mathsf{Encaps}(pk) := (c \leftarrow \mathsf{Enc}'(pk, m), K := \mathsf{H}(m, c)),$$

[1] There are some variants of $\mathsf{U}^{\not\perp}$ including $\mathsf{U}^{\not\perp}_{m}$, $\mathsf{U}^{\perp}$ and $\mathsf{U}^{\perp}_{m}$ [12], where $\perp$ means explicit rejection, and m (without m) means $K := \mathsf{H}(m)$ ($K := \mathsf{H}(m, c)$).

where m is picked at random from the message space. The decapsulation of KEM is defined by

$$\mathsf{Decaps}^{\not\perp}(sk, c) := \begin{cases} \mathsf{H}(m, c) & m \neq \perp \\ \mathsf{H}(s, c) & m = \perp, \end{cases}$$

where $m := \mathsf{Dec}'(sk, c)$ and s is a random seed as part of the private key.

1.2.1 Our Framework for Implicit Rejection To show our framework more clearly, we consider a $\mathsf{U}^{\not\perp}$-like transformation which converts the dPKE scheme PKE' into a KEM scheme $\mathsf{KEM} := \mathsf{U}^{\not\perp,\mathrm{DS}}[\mathsf{PKE}', \mathsf{H}]$, where "DS"[2] means $K := \mathsf{H}(\mathrm{DS}, c)$ is returned for an invalid ciphertext c in the decapsulation algorithm. We first propose the framework for constructing a structured H via domain separation, and then prove that if the simulator can construct such an H without possessing the private key, then $\mathsf{KEM} := \mathsf{U}^{\not\perp,\mathrm{DS}}[\mathsf{PKE}', \mathsf{H}]$ is $\mathsf{IND\text{-}CCA}$ secure in the QROM. Finally, we analyze the specific properties that DS needs to satisfy, which also helps us construct $\mathsf{IND\text{-}CCA}$ secure KEM schemes.

According to the responses of the decapsulation algorithm to valid ciphertexts and invalid ciphertexts[3], we first define two sets that contain all possible queries to H during the decapsulation queries:

$$\mathcal{D}_{valid} := \{(m, c) | \mathsf{Dec}'(sk, c) = m\} \text{ and } \mathcal{D}_{invalid} := \{(\mathrm{DS}, c) | \mathsf{Dec}'(sk, c) = \perp\}.$$

Next, we divide the domain of H (i.e., $\mathcal{D}$) into $\mathcal{D}_1$ and $\mathcal{D}_2 := \mathcal{D} \backslash \mathcal{D}_1$, where $\mathcal{D}_1 := \mathcal{D}_{valid} \bigcup \mathcal{D}_{invalid}$. Let $\mathsf{H}_1 : \mathcal{C} \rightarrow \mathcal{K}$ and $\mathsf{H}_2 : \{0,1\}^* \rightarrow \mathcal{K}$ be two independent internal random oracles that cannot be accessed directly by the adversary, we construct H as follows:

$$\mathsf{H}(A) := \begin{cases} \mathsf{H}_1(c) & A \in \mathcal{D}_1 \\ \mathsf{H}_2(A) & A \in \mathcal{D}_2. \end{cases}$$

Note that every c in $(\cdot, c) \in \mathcal{D}_{valid}$ is valid and every c in $(\cdot, c) \in \mathcal{D}_{invalid}$ is invalid, and the decryption of PKE' is deterministic, thus it is not possible for two distinct $A_1 \in \mathcal{D}_1$ and $A_2 \in \mathcal{D}_1$ to result in a same output $\mathsf{H}_1(c)$. Therefore, such a construction of H is a purely conceptual change and it is still a random oracle in the adversary's view.

If the simulator can construct such an H without possessing the private key and PKE' is one-way secure, then we can prove that $\mathsf{KEM} := \mathsf{U}^{\not\perp,\mathrm{DS}}[\mathsf{PKE}', \mathsf{H}]$ is $\mathsf{IND\text{-}CCA}$ secure in the QROM. Specifically, we first replace the truly quantum random oracle with our structured H. Then, the simulator can simulate the decapsulation oracle by only using H_1, without the requirement for the private key. Thus, the decapsulation oracle completely hides the information of the

[2] Here, "DS" is a domain separator, and it should be a bit string of sufficient length, otherwise it is easy to be guessed by the adversary.

[3] For any fixed key pair (pk, sk), we say that a ciphertext c is invalid if $\mathsf{Dec}'(sk, c) = \perp$, and valid otherwise.

private key. As a consequence, the IND-CCA adversary against KEM cannot distinguish the real key $K_0^* := \mathsf{H}(m^*, c^*)$ from a uniform random key K_1^* unless the adversary queries H on (m^*, c^*). In the QROM, the probability can easily be bounded by reducing a distinguishing problem to the one-way security of PKE′ via one-way to hiding (OW2H) lemma [1,3,18,24].

Obviously, the key point to construct such an H is that the simulator can effectively check whether A belongs to $\mathcal{D}_1$. If the underlying encryption scheme is perfectly correct, the simulator can check whether (m, c) belongs to $\mathcal{D}_{valid}$ by testing whether $c = \mathsf{Enc}'(pk, m)$. Thus, the only problem is how the simulator checks that A belongs to $\mathcal{D}_{invalid}$. For our purposes, we require that $A \in \mathcal{D}_{invalid}$ satisfies the following intuitive property:

Property 1. (**Public Verifiability.**) *For any fixed key pair $(pk, sk) \leftarrow$ Gen, given any input $A \in \mathcal{D}$, there is a quantum polynomial-time adversary $\mathcal{A}(pk)$ that can effectively check whether A belongs to $\mathcal{D}_{invalid}$.*

In this case, the simulator can explicitly check whether A belongs to $\mathcal{D}_{invalid}$ and construct such an H without possessing the private key. Meanwhile, we notice that if DS $:= sk$ (the secret key of PKE′), i.e., $\mathcal{D}_{invalid} := \{(sk, c) | \mathsf{Dec}'(sk, c) = \perp\}$, then $A \in \mathcal{D}_{invalid}$ is publicly verifiable (see Sect. 1.3 for details).

However, it is obvious that the property is too strict for the selection of DS. Actually, an H^* that is indistinguishable from H in the adversary's view also satisfies our requirement. We just need to replace H with H^* after simulating the decapsulation oracle with H_1, then we can also prove the IND-CCA security. Therefore, we define another property that the simulator can implicitly check whether A belongs to $\mathcal{D}_{invalid}$:

Property 2. (**Hiding.**) *We say $A \in \mathcal{D}_{invalid}$ is hidden from the adversary's view, if for any fixed key pair $(pk, sk) \leftarrow$ Gen, for any quantum polynomial-time adversary $\mathcal{A}(pk)$ against* KEM, *the advantage* $\mathsf{Adv}(\mathcal{A}) := \Pr[A \in \mathcal{D}_{invalid} : A \leftarrow \mathcal{A}(pk)]$ *is negligible.*

In general, it is easy to find an invalid ciphertext c, thus we essentially require that "DS" is hidden from the adversary's view. In this case, informally, the probability that the adversary queries H on $(\mathrm{DS}, \cdot)$ is negligible. The simulator can implicitly consider that each A does not belongs to $\mathcal{D}_{invalid}$ and construct an H^* as follows:

$$\mathsf{H}^*(A) := \begin{cases} \mathsf{H}_1(c) & A \in \mathcal{D}_{valid} \\ \mathsf{H}_2(A) & otherwise. \end{cases}$$

Note that H^* is equal to H except on input $A \in \mathcal{D}_{invalid}$, we can apply OW2H lemma [1,3] to bound the advantage that the adversary distinguishes H from H^*.

Remark. In our framework, the internal random oracles cannot be accessed by adversaries, which is different from the indifferentiability framework [26].

1.2.2 Explanation for $\mathsf{FO}^{\not\perp}$ by Using Our Framework We notice that the widely used generic transfomation $\mathsf{FO}^{\not\perp} := \mathsf{U}^{\not\perp} \circ \mathsf{T}$ [12] satifies our framework.

In transfomation $\mathsf{U}^{\not\perp}$, we have DS $:= s$, where s is picked at random from the message space $\mathcal{M}$ of PKE' and is part of the private key. Thus, the simulator cannot check whether A belongs to $\mathcal{D}_{invalid}$ because it does not know s. However, it is easy to see that the transfomation $\mathsf{U}^{\not\perp}$ satisfies **Property 2** and we have $\mathsf{Adv}(\mathcal{A}) := \Pr[A \in \mathcal{D}_{invalid} : A \leftarrow \mathcal{A}(pk)] \leq 1/|\mathcal{M}|$. Applying OW2H lemma [1,3], we can bound the probability that the IND-CCA adversary distinguishes H from H^* by $2q/\sqrt{|\mathcal{M}|}$ if it performs at most q oracle queries.

1.3 A New Realization for Our Framework

We present a novel realization $\mathsf{U}^{\not\perp,sk}$, i.e., DS $:= sk$ (the secret key of PKE'), that satisfies our framework. Moreover, we analyze the cases where pk (the public key of PKE') corresponds to only one private key and n private keys:

(1) If pk corresponds to only one private key, then $\mathsf{U}^{\not\perp,sk}$ satisfies **Property 1**, i.e., $A \in \mathcal{D}_{invalid}$ is publicly verifiable. Parse $A = (A_1, c)$, the simulator can use pk to check whether $A_1 = sk$ by testing whether $\mathsf{Gen.keygen}(A_1) = pk$[4]. Furthermore, the simulator can use A_1 to check if c is valid if $A_1 = sk$. In this case, the simulator can effectively construct the H.

(2) If pk corresponds to n private keys, then $\mathsf{U}^{\not\perp,sk}$ only satisfies **Property 2** since all private keys are functionally equivalent. In this case, H^* is computationally indistinguishable from H in the adversary's view since sk is secret. Furthermore, if n is sufficiently large, i.e., private keys still have sufficiently high entropy when pk is determined, then sk works like s in the $\mathsf{U}^{\not\perp}$.

We can easily prove the IND-CCA security of $\mathsf{KEM} := \mathsf{U}^{\not\perp,sk}[\mathsf{PKE}', \mathsf{H}]$ by using our framework. Surprisingly, the previous proof technique in [3,14,15,17,18,21] does not apply to $\mathsf{U}^{\not\perp,sk}$, and there is a technical hurdle for simulating the decapsulation oracle due to the re-use of sk. In the previous proofs, they first replaced $\mathsf{H}(s, \cdot)$ with an internal random oracle $\mathsf{H}_1(\cdot)$ during the simulation of the decapsulation oracle. In $\mathsf{U}^{\not\perp,sk}$, since sk is used to decrypt ciphertexts and hide the validity of ciphertexts simultaneously, the two roles of sk become intertwined in the security reduction. Specifically, the simulator needs to simulate the decapsulation oracle without the secret key, then we must replace $\mathsf{H}(sk, \cdot)$ with $\mathsf{H}_1(\cdot)$ first. However, in the present game, we need sk to decrypt ciphertexts, which would leak information on the private key. Thus one cannot claim that the replacement of $\mathsf{H}_1(\cdot)$ for $\mathsf{H}(sk, \cdot)$ will not be noticed by an adversary.

1.4 Related Works

In this section, we briefly introduce related works on IND-CCA secure KEM in the QROM. Hofheinz et al. [12] first followed Targhi and Unruh's technique

[4] Since quantum adversaries may evaluate random oracles on quantum superposition states, the simulator can only **test** whether $A_1 = sk$ and cannot extract sk, which means the simulator need to measure the quantum queries.

[23] and provided two variants of the original FO-KEM transformations, i.e., $\mathsf{QFO}_m^{\not\perp}$ and $\mathsf{QFO}_m^{\perp}$, where Q means adding an additional length-preserving hash to the ciphertext. Although $\mathsf{QFO}_m^{\not\perp}$ and $\mathsf{QFO}_m^{\perp}$ [12] can be shown to be IND-CCA secure in the QROM, there are two obvious drawbacks: the ciphertext size increases significantly and the security bounds are far from tight. The subsequent works are mainly to remove the additional hash and improve the tightness of the security reduction.

For the KEM with implicit rejection, Jiang et al. [15] and Saito et al. [21] extended the technique in [4] to prove the QROM security without suffering any ciphertext overhead. Subsequent works [3,14,17,18] improved the tightness of the security reduction by using some generalized versions of the OW2H lemma [24]. Jiang et al. [17] and Bindel et al. [3] applied the semi-classical OW2H lemma [1] to give a security proof for transformation T without the square-root advantage loss. Kuchta et al. [18] applied Measure-Rewind-Measure OW2H (MRM OW2H) lemma to prove the transformation $\mathsf{U}^{\not\perp}$ from an OW-CPA secure dPKE, without the square-root advantage loss for the first time.

For the KEM with explicit rejection, Jiang et al. [16] developed a novel verification method for the validity of ciphertexts, and replaced the additional length-preserving hash [12,23] with a traditional hash to reduce the ciphertext size. Recently, Don et al. [7] developed a new generic "online-extractability" technique by using Zhandry's compressed-oracle technique [25]. Moreover, Don et al. [7] and Hövelmanns et al. [13] applied the new technique to verify the validity of ciphertexts and proved the IND-CCA security of the original FO-KEM with explicit rejection (i.e., $\mathsf{FO}_m^{\perp}$) in the QROM, without the requirement for an additional hash.

1.5 Paper Organization

The rest of this paper is organized as follows. In Sect. 2, some notations and lemmas are introduced. In Sect. 3, we propose a framework for the construction of quantum random oracles that supports implicit rejection, and prove that the KEMs with implicit rejection satisfying our framework are IND-CCA secure in the QROM. Meanwhile, we explain the generic transfomation $\mathsf{FO}^{\not\perp}$ [12] by using our new framework. In Sect. 4, we present a novel realization $\mathsf{FO}^{\not\perp,sk}$ that satisfies our framework. The conclusions are drawn in Sect. 5.

2 Preliminaries

Notations. For a finite set S, let $|S|$ denotes the cardinality of S, let $x \xleftarrow{\$} S$ denote the sampling of a uniform random element x, while we denote the sampling according to some distribution D by $x \leftarrow D$. For the Boolean statement E, $[\![E]\!]$ denotes the bit that is 1 if E is true, and 0 otherwise. We denote deterministic (probabilistic) computation of an algorithm $\mathcal{A}$ on input x by $y := \mathcal{A}(x)$ $(y \leftarrow \mathcal{A}(x))$. We denote algorithm $\mathcal{A}$ with access to an oracle H by $\mathcal{A}^{\mathsf{H}}$.

2.1 Public-Key Encryption

A public-key encryption $\mathsf{PKE} = (\mathsf{Gen}, \mathsf{Enc}, \mathsf{Dec})$ consists of three polynomial-time algorithms and a finite message space $\mathcal{M}$:

- $\mathsf{Gen}(1^k) \rightarrow (pk, sk)$: a key generation algorithm that on input 1^k, where k is the security parameter, outputs a key pair (pk, sk), where pk defines a randomness space $\mathcal{R} = \mathcal{R}(pk)$.
- $\mathsf{Enc}(pk, m) \rightarrow c$: an encryption algorithm that on input pk and a message $m \in \mathcal{M}$, outputs a ciphertext $c \leftarrow \mathsf{Enc}(pk, m)$. If necessary, we make the used randomness of encryption explicit by writing $c := \mathsf{Enc}(pk, m; r)$, where $r \xleftarrow{\$} \mathcal{R}$ and $\mathcal{R}$ is the randomness space.
- $\mathsf{Dec}(sk, c) \rightarrow m/\bot$: a decryption algorithm that on input decryption key sk and ciphertext c, outputs either a message $m := \mathsf{Dec}(sk, c)$ or a special symbol $\bot \notin \mathcal{M}$ to indicate that c is an invalid ciphertext.

Remark. We follow the definition of key generation algorithm that was proposed in [6,28]. Let $\mathsf{Gen}(1^k)$ invoke $\mathsf{Gen.keygen}(\cdot)$, whose input is $sk \in \mathcal{SK}$ and output is the corresponding pk. The security parameter k defines a secret key space $\mathcal{SK} = \mathcal{SK}(k)$. Moreover, $\mathsf{Gen.keygen}(\cdot)$ is public and visible to everyone [28].

Definition 1 (Correctness [12]**).** *We call a Public-Key Encryption scheme* PKE *δ-correct if*

$$\mathbf{E}[\max_{m \in \mathcal{M}} \Pr[\mathsf{Dec}(sk, c) \neq m : c \leftarrow \mathsf{Enc}(pk, m)]] \leq \delta,$$

where the expectation is taken over $(pk, sk) \leftarrow \mathsf{Gen}$.

Security. We now define two security notions for public-key encryption: One-Way against Quantum Plaintext Checking Attacks (OW-qPCA) and Indistinguishbility against Chosen Plaintext Attacks (IND-CPA).

Definition 2 (OW-qPCA). *For any adversary $\mathcal{A}$, we define its* OW-qPCA *advantage against* PKE *as follows:*

$$\mathsf{Adv}_{\mathsf{PKE}}^{\mathsf{OW\text{-}qPCA}}(\mathcal{A}) := \Pr\left[\mathsf{OW\text{-}qPCA}^{\mathcal{A}} \Rightarrow 1\right],$$

where OW-qPCA *game is defined as in the left-hand of Fig. 1, and the adversary $\mathcal{A}$ can query the oracle* Pco *with quantum state.*

Definition 3 (IND-CPA). *For any adversary $\mathcal{A} = (\mathcal{A}_1, \mathcal{A}_2)$, we define its* IND-CPA *advantage against* PKE *as follows:*

$$\mathsf{Adv}_{\mathsf{PKE}}^{\mathsf{IND\text{-}CPA}}(\mathcal{A}) := |\Pr\left[\mathsf{IND\text{-}CPA}^{\mathcal{A}} \Rightarrow 1\right] - 1/2|,$$

where IND-CPA *game is defined as in the right-hand of Fig. 1.*

GAME OW-qPCA	**GAME** IND-CPA
$(pk, sk) \leftarrow \mathsf{Gen}$	$(pk, sk) \leftarrow \mathsf{Gen}$
$m^* \xleftarrow{\$} \mathcal{M}$	$b \xleftarrow{\$} \{0,1\}$
$c^* \leftarrow \mathsf{Enc}(pk, m^*)$	$(m_0^*, m_1^*, st) \leftarrow \mathcal{A}_1(pk)$
$m' \leftarrow \mathcal{A}^{\mathsf{Pco}}(pk, c^*)$	$c^* \leftarrow \mathsf{Enc}(pk, m_b^*)$
return $[\![m' = m]\!]$	$b' \leftarrow \mathcal{A}_2(pk, c^*, st)$
	return $[\![b' = b]\!]$
$\mathsf{Pco}(m \in \mathcal{M}, c)$	
return $[\![\mathsf{Dec}(sk, c) = m]\!]$	

Fig. 1. Games OW-qPCA and IND-CPA for PKE. Note that in game OW-qPCA, we allow the adversary $\mathcal{A}$ to evaluate the oracle Pco on quantum states.

2.2 Key Encapsulation Mechanism

A key encapsulation mechanism KEM = (Gen, Encaps, Decaps) consists of three polynomial-time algorithms:

- $\mathsf{Gen}(1^k) \rightarrow (pk, sk)$: a key generation algorithm that on input 1^k, where k is the security parameter, outputs a key pair (pk, sk).
- $\mathsf{Encaps}(pk) \rightarrow (K, c)$: an encapsulation algorithm that on input encapsulation key pk, outputs a tuple (K, c), where c is called an encapsulation of the key K which is contained in the key space $\mathcal{K}$.
- $\mathsf{Decaps}(sk, c) \rightarrow K$: a decapsulation algorithm that on input decapsulation key sk and an encapsulation ciphertext c, outputs a key K associated with c or a pseudorandom key (implicit rejection), which implies that c is an invalid encapsulation ciphertext.

Remark. Implicit (Explicit) rejection means a pseudorandom key K (a rejection symbol $\perp \notin \mathcal{K}$, resp.) is returned for an invalid encapsulation ciphertext. In this paper, we only consider the KEM with implicit rejection.

Security. We now define Indistinguishability against Chosen Ciphertext Attacks (IND-CCA) security for key encapsulation mechanism.

GAME IND-CCA	$\mathsf{Decaps}(c)$
$(pk, sk) \leftarrow \mathsf{Gen}$	**if** $c = c^*$
$b \xleftarrow{\$} \{0,1\}$	**return** $\perp$
$(K_0^*, c^*) \leftarrow \mathsf{Encaps}(pk)$	**else return**
$K_1^* \xleftarrow{\$} \mathcal{K}$	$K := \mathsf{Decaps}(sk, c)$
$b' \leftarrow \mathcal{A}^{\mathsf{Decaps}}(pk, c^*, K_b^*)$	
return $[\![b' = b]\!]$	

Fig. 2. Game IND-CCA for KEM.

Definition 4 (IND-CCA). *For any adversary $\mathcal{A}$, we define its* IND-CCA *advantage against* KEM *as follows:*

$$\mathsf{Adv}_{\mathsf{KEM}}^{\mathsf{IND\text{-}CCA}}(\mathcal{A}) := |\Pr\left[\mathsf{IND\text{-}CCA}^{\mathcal{A}} \Rightarrow 1\right] - 1/2|,$$

where IND-CCA *game is defined as in Fig. 2.*

2.3 Quantum Random Oracle Model

We prove security in the QROM [4] where adversaries are given quantum access to the random oracles, and classical access to all the other oracles.

Simulating Quantum Random Oracle. Zhandry [27] proved that for at most q queries, no quantum algorithm $\mathcal{A}^{\mathcal{O}}$ can distinguish a truly random function $\mathsf{H}: \mathcal{X} \to \mathcal{Y}$ from a $2q$-wise independent function f_{2q}, where $f_{2q}: \mathcal{X} \to \mathcal{Y}$ is a random polynomial of degree $2q$ over the finite field $F_{|\mathcal{Y}|}$.

Lemmas. We now review several important lemmas in the QROM, including original One-Way to Hiding (OW2H) lemma [1,3,24] and Measure-Rewind-Measure OW2H (MRM OW2H) lemma [18], which we will use in our proof.

Lemma 1 (Original OW2H [1,3,24]). *Let $S \subseteq X$ be a random set, let z be a random bit string. Let* G, H*: $X \to Y$ be random functions satisfying $\forall x \notin S$, $\mathsf{G}(x) = \mathsf{H}(x)$, the tuple $(\mathsf{G}, \mathsf{H}, S, z)$ may have arbitrary joint distribution. Let $\mathcal{A}^{\mathsf{H}}$ be a q-query quantum oracle algorithm with depth d. Let* Ev *be an arbitrary classical event. Define an oracle algorithm $\mathcal{B}^{\mathsf{H}}(z)$ as follows: Pick $i \xleftarrow{\$} \{1, ..., d\}$, run $\mathcal{A}^{\mathsf{H}}$ until (just before) the i-th query. Measure all query input registers in the computational basis, and output the set T of measurement outcomes. Let*

$$P_{left} := \Pr[\mathsf{Ev} : \mathcal{A}^{\mathsf{H}}(z)], \quad P_{right} := \Pr[\mathsf{Ev} : \mathcal{A}^{\mathsf{G}}(z)],$$

$$P_{guess} := \Pr[S \cap T \neq \varnothing : T \leftarrow \mathcal{B}^{\mathsf{H}}(z)] = \Pr[S \cap T \neq \varnothing : T \leftarrow \mathcal{B}^{\mathsf{G}}(z)].$$

Then $|P_{left} - P_{right}| \leq 2d\sqrt{P_{guess}}$.

We say that $\mathcal{A}$ is a q-query oracle algorithm [1] if it performs at most q oracle queries (counting parallel queries as separate queries), and has query depth d if it invokes the oracle at most d times (counting parallel queries as one query).

Lemma 2 (Double-sided OW2H with Measure-rewind-Measure [18]). *Let $S \subseteq X$ be a random set, let z be a random bit string. Let* G, H*: $X \to Y$ be random functions satisfying $\forall x \notin S$, $\mathsf{G}(x) = \mathsf{H}(x)$, the tuple $(\mathsf{G}, \mathsf{H}, S, z)$ may have arbitrary joint distribution. Furthermore, let $\mathcal{A}^{\mathsf{O}}$ be a quantum oracle algorithm with depth d, we can construct an algorithm $\mathcal{D}^{\mathsf{G},\mathsf{H}}$ such that $\mathcal{T}_{\mathcal{D}^{\mathsf{G},\mathsf{H}}} \leq 3 \cdot \mathcal{T}_{\mathcal{A}^{\mathsf{O}}}$ and*

$$|\Pr_{\mathsf{H},z}[1 \leftarrow \mathcal{A}^{\mathsf{H}}(z)] - \Pr_{\mathsf{G},z}[1 \leftarrow \mathcal{A}^{\mathsf{G}}(z)]| \leq 4d \cdot \Pr_{\mathsf{G},\mathsf{H},S,z}[S \cap T \neq \varnothing : T \leftarrow \mathcal{D}^{\mathsf{G},\mathsf{H}}(z)].$$

3 Our Framework

To simplify the presentation of our framework, we analyze the FO-like KEM with implicit rejection in a modular way. We first review the transformation T [12], then propose a framework for constructing quantum random oracles that supports $\mathsf{U}^{\not\perp}$-like transformation. Moreover, we prove that the KEMs with implicit rejection satisfying our framework are IND-CCA secure in the QROM. Finally, we show that the generic transformation $\mathsf{FO}^{\not\perp}$ [12] satifies our framework.

3.1 Transformation T: From IND-CPA to OW-qPCA

The transformation T [12] converts a rPKE scheme into a dPKE scheme by using a random oracle. To a rPKE scheme $\mathsf{PKE} = (\mathsf{Gen}, \mathsf{Enc}, \mathsf{Dec})$ with message space $\mathcal{M}$, randomness space $\mathcal{R}$ and a random oracle $\mathsf{G} : \mathcal{M} \to \mathcal{R}$, the dPKE scheme $\mathsf{PKE}' = (\mathsf{Gen}, \mathsf{Enc}', \mathsf{Dec}') := \mathsf{T}[\mathsf{PKE}, \mathsf{G}]$ is defined in Fig. 3.

$\mathsf{Enc}'(pk, m)$	$\mathsf{Dec}'(sk, c)$
$c := \mathsf{Enc}(pk, m; \mathsf{G}(m))$	$m' := \mathsf{Dec}(sk, c)$
return c	**if** $m' = \perp$ **or** $\mathsf{Enc}(pk, m'; \mathsf{G}(m')) \neq c$
	return $\perp$
	else return m'

Fig. 3. OW-qPCA secure dPKE scheme $\mathsf{PKE}' := \mathsf{T}[\mathsf{PKE}, \mathsf{G}]$

If the underlying rPKE scheme PKE is IND-CPA secure, Jiang et al. [17] and Bindel et al. [3] proved that $\mathsf{PKE}' := \mathsf{T}[\mathsf{PKE}, \mathsf{G}]$ is OW-qPCA secure and OW-CPA secure in the QROM, respectively. We use the result from [17], since the resulting OW-qPCA[5] security is our desired security property.

Theorem 1 (IND-CPA PKE $\overset{QROM}{\Rightarrow}$ OW-qPCA PKE′ [17]). *If* PKE *is δ-correct, for any* OW-qPCA *adversary $\mathcal{B}$ against* $\mathsf{PKE}' := \mathsf{T}[\mathsf{PKE}, \mathsf{G}]$, *issuing at most q_{G} quantum queries to the random oracle* G *and at most q_{p} quantum queries to the plaintext checking oracle* Pco, *there exists an* IND-CPA *adversary $\mathcal{A}$ against* PKE *such that* $\mathsf{Adv}^{\text{OW-qPCA}}_{\mathsf{PKE}'}(\mathcal{B}) \leq 2(d_{\mathsf{G}}+2) \cdot \mathsf{Adv}^{\text{IND-CPA}}_{\mathsf{PKE}}(\mathcal{A}) + \frac{4(q_{\mathsf{G}}+2)^2}{|\mathcal{M}|} + 16 q_{\mathsf{G}}\sqrt{\delta}$ *and the running time of $\mathcal{A}$ is about that of $\mathcal{B}$.*

3.2 Our Framework for Implicit Rejection

We now state our framework for the construction of quantum random oracles that supports $\mathsf{U}^{\not\perp}$-like transformation. To a public-key encryption scheme $\mathsf{PKE}' = (\mathsf{Gen}, \mathsf{Enc}', \mathsf{Dec}')$ with message space $\mathcal{M}$ and a random oracle H :

[5] We will explain in Sect. 3.2 why we require the intermediate scheme to be OW-qPCA secure.

$\mathsf{Encaps}(pk)$	$\mathsf{Decaps}^{\not\perp}(sk,c)$
$m \xleftarrow{\$} \mathcal{M}$	$m' := \mathsf{Dec}'(sk,c)$
$c \leftarrow \mathsf{Enc}'(pk,m)$	**if** $m' = \perp$
$K := \mathsf{H}(m,c)$	**return** $K := \mathsf{H}(\mathrm{DS},c)$
return (K,c)	**else return** $K := \mathsf{H}(m',c)$

Fig. 4. IND-CCA secure KEM scheme $\mathsf{KEM} := \mathsf{U}^{\not\perp,\mathrm{DS}}[\mathsf{PKE}',\mathsf{H}]$

$\{0,1\}^* \to \mathcal{K}$, we associate $\mathsf{KEM} = (\mathsf{Gen},\mathsf{Encaps},\mathsf{Decaps}^{\not\perp}) := \mathsf{U}^{\not\perp,\mathrm{DS}}[\mathsf{PKE}',\mathsf{H}]$, see Fig. 4.

Next, we construct a structured H. Specifically, we first define two sets that contain all possible queries to random oracle H during the decapsulation queries:

$$\mathcal{D}_{valid} := \{(m,c)|\mathsf{Dec}'(sk,c) = m\} \text{ and } \mathcal{D}_{invalid} := \{(\mathrm{DS},c)|\mathsf{Dec}'(sk,c) = \perp\},$$

Then, we divide the domain of H (i.e., $\mathcal{D}$) into $\mathcal{D}_1$ and $\mathcal{D}_2 := \mathcal{D}\backslash\mathcal{D}_1$, where $\mathcal{D}_1 := \mathcal{D}_{valid} \bigcup \mathcal{D}_{invalid}$. Let $\mathsf{H}_1 : \mathcal{C} \to \mathcal{K}$ and $\mathsf{H}_2 : \{0,1\}^* \to \mathcal{K}$ be two independent internal random oracles, we construct the H as follows:

$$\mathsf{H}(A) := \begin{cases} \mathsf{H}_1(c) & A \in \mathcal{D}_1 \\ \mathsf{H}_2(A) & A \in \mathcal{D}_2. \end{cases}$$

The core idea of our framework is to construct such an H or an H^* that is indistinguishable from H in the adversary's view, without possessing the private key. Obviously, the key point to construct H is that the simulator can effectively check whether A belongs to $\mathcal{D}_1$. For our purpose, we require that $A \in \mathcal{D}_{invalid}$ satisfies one of the following properties:

Property 1. (Public Verifiability.) *For any fixed key pair $(pk,sk) \leftarrow \mathsf{Gen}$, given any input $A \in \mathcal{D}$, there is a quantum polynomial-time adversary $\mathcal{A}(pk)$ that can effectively check whether A belongs to $\mathcal{D}_{invalid}$.*

Property 2. (Hiding.) *We say $A \in \mathcal{D}_{invalid}$ is hidden from the adversary's view, if for any fixed key pair $(pk,sk) \leftarrow \mathsf{Gen}$, for any quantum polynomial-time adversary $\mathcal{A}(pk)$ against* KEM*, the advantage* $\mathsf{Adv}(\mathcal{A}) := \Pr[A \in \mathcal{D}_{invalid} : A \leftarrow \mathcal{A}(pk)]$ *is negligible.*

If a KEM scheme satisfies **Property 1**, then the simulator can explicitly check whether A belongs to $\mathcal{D}_1$ and effectively construct such an H without possessing the private key. If a KEM scheme satisfies **Property 2**, the simulator can implicitly consider that each A does not belongs to $\mathcal{D}_{invalid}$. Moreover, the simulator can construct an H^* as follows:

$$\mathsf{H}^*(A) := \begin{cases} \mathsf{H}_1(c) & A \in \mathcal{D}_{valid} \\ \mathsf{H}_2(A) & otherwise. \end{cases}$$

Note that $\mathsf{H}^*(A) = \mathsf{H}(A)$ except on input $A \in \mathcal{D}_{invalid}$, we can apply OW2H lemma [1,3] to argue the indistinguishability.

Our framework allows the underlying PKE to be non-perfectly correct since many practical lattice-based encryption schemes have a small probability of decryption failure. However, if we use "re-encryption" to check whether (m, c) belongs to $\mathcal{D}_{valid}$, it is possible that $c = \mathsf{Enc}'(pk, m)$ but $\mathsf{Dec}'(sk, c) \neq m$ due to the decryption errors. In order to handle decryption errors, we assume that PKE' is $\mathsf{OW\text{-}qPCA}$ secure. Then, the simulator can easily check whether (m, c) belongs to $\mathcal{D}_{valid}$ by querying oracle $\mathsf{Pco}(m, c)$. Particularly, we give a equivalent definition, i.e., $\mathcal{D}_{valid} := \{(m, c) | \mathsf{Pco}(m, c) = 1\}$ and $\mathcal{D}_{invalid} := \{(\mathrm{DS}, c) | c \; is \; invalid\}$.

Next, we prove the $\mathsf{IND\text{-}CCA}$ security of the KEMs with implicit rejection that satisfy our framework. The following theorem shows that $\mathsf{KEM} := \mathsf{U}^{\not\perp,\mathrm{DS}}[\mathsf{PKE}', \mathsf{H}]$ is $\mathsf{IND\text{-}CCA}$ secure in the QROM if PKE' is $\mathsf{OW\text{-}qPCA}$ secure.

Theorem 2 (OW-qPCA PKE′ $\overset{QROM}{\Rightarrow}$ IND-CCA KEM). *Let* PKE' *be a dPKE scheme obtained by applying the transformation* T *to* δ*-correct rPKE* PKE. *If* $\mathsf{KEM} := \mathsf{U}^{\not\perp,\mathrm{DS}}[\mathsf{PKE}', \mathsf{H}]$ *satisfies our framework and* $\mathsf{DS} \in \{0,1\}^l$, *for any* $\mathsf{IND\text{-}CCA}$ *adversary* $\mathcal{B}$ *against* $\mathsf{KEM} := \mathsf{U}^{\not\perp,\mathrm{DS}}[\mathsf{PKE}', \mathsf{H}]$, *issuing at most* q_{D} *classical queries to the decapsulation oracle* $\mathsf{Decaps}^{\not\perp}$ *and at most* q_{H} *quantum queries to the random oracle* H *with query depth at most* d_{H}, *there exist an* $\mathsf{OW\text{-}qPCA}$ *adversary* $\mathcal{A}$ *against* PKE' *such that*

$$\mathsf{Adv}_{\mathsf{KEM}}^{\mathsf{IND\text{-}CCA}}(\mathcal{B}) \leq 2d_{\mathsf{H}} \cdot \mathsf{Adv}_{\mathsf{PKE}'}^{\mathsf{OW\text{-}qPCA}}(\mathcal{A}) + (2d_{\mathsf{H}} + 1) \cdot \delta \tag{1}$$

$$\mathsf{Adv}_{\mathsf{KEM}}^{\mathsf{IND\text{-}CCA}}(\mathcal{B}) \leq 2d_{\mathsf{H}} \cdot \mathsf{Adv}_{\mathsf{PKE}'}^{\mathsf{OW\text{-}qPCA}}(\mathcal{A}) + (2d_{\mathsf{H}} + 1) \cdot \delta + 2d_{\mathsf{H}}\sqrt{negl(\lambda)} \tag{2}$$

$$\mathsf{Adv}_{\mathsf{KEM}}^{\mathsf{IND\text{-}CCA}}(\mathcal{B}) \leq 2d_{\mathsf{H}} \cdot \mathsf{Adv}_{\mathsf{PKE}'}^{\mathsf{OW\text{-}qPCA}}(\mathcal{A}) + (2d_{\mathsf{H}} + 1) \cdot \delta + 2\sqrt{q_{\mathsf{H}} d_{\mathsf{H}}/2^l}, \tag{3}$$

and the running time of $\mathcal{A}$ *is* $\lesssim 3T_{\mathcal{B}}$.

We obtain Eq. (1) if KEM satisfies **Property 1**. If KEM only satisfies **Property 2**, we obtain Eq. (2) or Eq. (3). Note that bound Eq. (3) is meaningless for small values l, thus we require that l is sufficiently large in this case. The proof of Eq. (1) can be divided into two steps: we first replace the quantum random oracle with our structured H, then we can simulate the oracle $\mathsf{Decaps}^{\not\perp}$ such that it no longer uses sk. Finally, we apply MRM OW2H lemma [18] to argue key indistinguishability. The proof of Eq. (2, 3) is the same as the proof of Eq. (1) except that we need to replace H with H^* after simulating the oracle $\mathsf{Decaps}^{\not\perp}$ without requirement for sk.

Proof . We first define some notations. Let Ω_1, Ω_2 and Ω_3 be the sets of all functions $\mathsf{H}_1 : \mathcal{C} \to \mathcal{K}$, $\mathsf{H}_2 : \mathcal{M} \times \mathcal{C} \to \mathcal{K}$ and $\mathsf{H}_3 : \{0,1\}^l \times \mathcal{C} \to \mathcal{K}$, respectively. Consider the games $G_0 - G_2$ in Fig. 5, we will prove security through a sequences of games.

Game $\mathbf{G_0}$: The game G_0 is the original $\mathsf{IND\text{-}CCA}$ game, then we have

$$|\Pr[G_0 \Rightarrow 1] - 1/2| = \mathsf{Adv}_{\mathsf{KEM}}^{\mathsf{IND\text{-}CCA}}(\mathcal{B}).$$

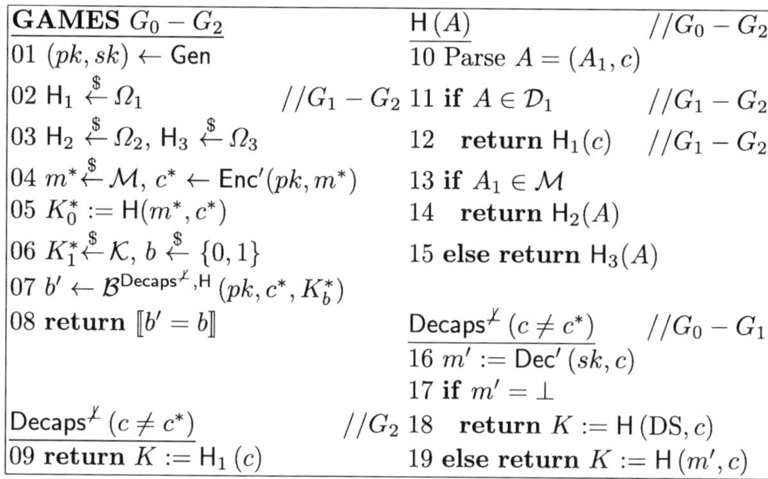

Fig. 5. Games $G_0 - G_2$ for the proof of Theorem 2

Game $\mathbf{G_1}$: This game is identical to game G_0, except that we replace the truly quantum random oracle H with our structured H. Following our framework, we define $\mathcal{D}_{valid} := \{(m, c) | \mathsf{Pco}(m, c) = 1\}$ and $\mathcal{D}_{invalid} := \{(\mathrm{DS}, c) | c \textit{ is invalid}\}$.

Let $\mathsf{H}_1 \xleftarrow{\$} \Omega_1$, $\mathsf{H}_2 \xleftarrow{\$} \Omega_2$ and $\mathsf{H}_3 \xleftarrow{\$} \Omega_3$ be three independent internal random functions, let $\mathcal{D}_1 := \mathcal{D}_{valid} \bigcup \mathcal{D}_{invalid}$, $\mathcal{D}_2 := \mathcal{M} \times \mathcal{C} \backslash \mathcal{D}_{valid}$ and $\mathcal{D}_3 := \{0,1\}^l \times \mathcal{C} \backslash \mathcal{D}_{invalid}$, we construct the structured H as follows:

$$\mathsf{H}(A) := \begin{cases} \mathsf{H}_1(c) & A \in \mathcal{D}_1 \\ \mathsf{H}_2(A) & A \in \mathcal{D}_2 \\ \mathsf{H}_3(A) & A \in \mathcal{D}_3, \end{cases}$$

Note that every c in $(\cdot, c) \in \mathcal{D}_{valid}$ is valid and every c in $(\cdot, c) \in \mathcal{D}_{invalid}$ is invalid, and $\mathsf{Pco}(m_0, c) = \mathsf{Pco}(m_1, c) = 1$ for $m_0 \neq m_1$ is impossible, thus it is not possible for two distinct $A_1 \in \mathcal{D}_1$ and $A_2 \in \mathcal{D}_1$ to result in a same output $\mathsf{H}_1(c)$. Therefore, this is a purely conceptual change and the distribution of H in G_0 and G_1 are identical. Thus we have

$$\Pr[G_0 \Rightarrow 1] = \Pr[G_1 \Rightarrow 1].$$

Game $\mathbf{G_2}$: This game is identical to game G_1, except that the oracle $\mathsf{Decaps}^{\not\perp}$ is modified such that it does not make use of sk any longer: $\mathsf{H}_1(c)$ is returned as long as $c \neq c^*$.

In the decapsulation algorithm, since (m', c) and $(\mathrm{DS}, \textit{invalid } c)$ are both members of $\mathcal{D}_1$, we can rewrite $\mathsf{H}(m', c) = \mathsf{H}_1(c)$ and $\mathsf{H}(\mathrm{DS}, c) = \mathsf{H}_1(c)$, which is a purely written change, thus it does not change $\mathcal{B}$'s advantage. We have

$$\Pr[G_1 \Rightarrow 1] = \Pr[G_2 \Rightarrow 1].$$

Remark: If KEM satisfies **Property 1**, i.e., $A \in \mathcal{D}_{invalid}$ is publicly verifiable, then the OW-qPCA adversary $\mathcal{A}$ can construct such an H perfectly, and we can directly apply MRM OW2H lemma [18] to argue key indistinguishability.

Game $\mathbf{G_3}$: In game G_3, we choose K^* uniformly at random from $\mathcal{K}$. Additionally, let $\mathcal{S} := \{(m, c^*) : \mathsf{Pco}(m, c^*) = 1\}$, we define a new random oracle H':

$$\mathsf{H}'(A) := \begin{cases} K^* & if\ A \in \mathcal{S} \\ \mathsf{H}(A) & otherwise. \end{cases}$$

Then, we run $b' \leftarrow \mathcal{B}^{\mathsf{Decaps}^{\not\perp}, \mathsf{H}'}(pk, c^*, K^*)$ if $b = 0$, and $b' \leftarrow \mathcal{B}^{\mathsf{Decaps}^{\not\perp}, \mathsf{H}}(pk, c^*, K^*)$ otherwise.

If $\mathcal{S} := \{(m^*, c^*)\}$, then the change from game G_2 to game G_3 is purely conceptual. However, PKE' is not perfectly correct since it is derived from δ-correct PKE. Thus, it is possible that $\mathsf{Dec}'(sk, c^*) \neq m^*$ and $\mathcal{S} \neq \{(m^*, c^*)\}$. Thus we define a bad event,

$$\mathsf{BadEv} := [\mathsf{Dec}'(sk, c^*) \neq m^* | (pk, sk) \leftarrow \mathsf{Gen}, m^* \xleftarrow{\$} \mathcal{M}, c^* \leftarrow \mathsf{Enc}'(pk, m^*)].$$

Moreover, we have

$$\begin{aligned} \Pr[\mathsf{BadEv}] &= \Pr[\mathsf{Dec}'(sk, c^*) \neq m^* | (pk, sk) \leftarrow \mathsf{Gen}, m^* \xleftarrow{\$} \mathcal{M}, c^* \leftarrow \mathsf{Enc}'(pk, m^*)] \\ &= \mathop{\mathbf{E}}_{(pk,sk) \leftarrow \mathsf{Gen}} \left[\mathop{\mathbf{E}}_{m^* \xleftarrow{\$} \mathcal{M}} \Pr[\mathsf{Dec}'(sk, c^*) \neq m^* | c^* \leftarrow \mathsf{Enc}'(pk, m^*)] \right] \\ &\leq \mathop{\mathbf{E}}_{(pk,sk) \leftarrow \mathsf{Gen}} \left[\mathop{max}_{m \in \mathcal{M}} \Pr[\mathsf{Dec}'(sk, c) \neq m | c \leftarrow \mathsf{Enc}'(pk, m)] \right]. \end{aligned}$$

By the definitions of PKE'[6] and δ-correct, we have

$$\Pr[\mathsf{BadEv}] \leq \mathop{\mathbf{E}}_{(pk,sk) \leftarrow \mathsf{Gen}} \left[\mathop{max}_{m \in \mathcal{M}} \Pr[\mathsf{Dec}(sk, c) \neq m | c \leftarrow \mathsf{Enc}(pk, m)] \right] \leq \delta.$$

If BadEv doesn't happen, then $\mathcal{S} := \{(m^*, c^*)\}$ and the change from game G_2 to game G_3 is purely conceptual. By the difference lemma, we have

$$|\Pr[G_2 \Rightarrow 1] - \Pr[G_3 \Rightarrow 1]| \leq \Pr[\mathsf{BadEv}].$$

Next, we will bound $\mathcal{B}$'s advantage in game G_3. First, we have

$$\begin{aligned} \left| \Pr[G_3 \Rightarrow 1] - \frac{1}{2} \right| &= \left| \frac{1}{2} \Pr[1 \leftarrow \mathcal{B} : b = 1] + \frac{1}{2} \Pr[0 \leftarrow \mathcal{B} : b = 0] - \frac{1}{2} \right| \\ &= \frac{1}{2} \left| \Pr[0 \leftarrow \mathcal{B} : b = 0] - \Pr[0 \leftarrow \mathcal{B} : b = 1] \right|. \end{aligned}$$

6 By the definitions of Dec' and condition on $c \leftarrow \mathsf{Enc}'(pk, m)$, if $\mathsf{Dec}'(sk, c) \neq m$, then we must have $\mathsf{Dec}(sk, c) = m' \neq m$ or $\mathsf{Dec}(sk, c) = \perp$, i.e., $\mathsf{Dec}(sk, c) \neq m$.

Then, note that H' is equal to H except on input $(m,c) \in \mathcal{S}$. Let $z = (pk, c^*, K^*)$, by Lemma 2, there is an algorithm $\mathcal{D}$, with run-time $\lesssim 3\mathcal{T}_{\mathcal{B}}$ and making oracle calls to H' and H, such that

$$\begin{aligned} & |\Pr[0 \leftarrow \mathcal{B} : b = 0] - \Pr[0 \leftarrow \mathcal{B} : b = 1]| \\ = & |\Pr[0 \leftarrow \mathcal{B}^{\mathsf{H}'}(z)] - \Pr[0 \leftarrow \mathcal{B}^{\mathsf{H}}(z)]| \\ \leq & \ 4d_{\mathsf{H}} \cdot \Pr[S \cap T \neq \varnothing : T \leftarrow \mathcal{D}^{\mathsf{H}',\mathsf{H}}(z)]. \end{aligned}$$

Finally, we can construct an adversary $\mathcal{A}(pk, c^*)$ against the OW-qPCA security of PKE' that simulates H' and H for $\mathcal{D}$ simultaneously. Suppose that BadEv doesn't happen, then $\mathcal{S}$ has only one tuple (m^*, c^*). In this case, the adversary $\mathcal{A}$ can return the right m^* as long as $S \cap T \neq \varnothing$. Therefore, we have

$$\Pr[S \cap T \neq \varnothing : T \leftarrow \mathcal{D}^{\mathsf{H}',\mathsf{H}}(z)] \leq \mathrm{Adv}_{\mathsf{PKE}'}^{\mathsf{OW-qPCA}}(\mathcal{A}) + \Pr[\mathsf{BadEv}].$$

Combining above formulas, we obtain Eq. (1):

$$\begin{aligned} \mathsf{Adv}_{\mathsf{KEM}}^{\mathsf{IND\text{-}CCA}}(\mathcal{B}) &= |\Pr[G_0 \Rightarrow 1] - 1/2| \\ &= |\Pr[G_1 \Rightarrow 1] - 1/2| \\ &= |\Pr[G_2 \Rightarrow 1] - 1/2| \\ &= |\Pr[G_2 \Rightarrow 1] - \Pr[G_3 \Rightarrow 1] + \Pr[G_3 \Rightarrow 1] - 1/2| \\ &\leq |\Pr[G_3 \Rightarrow 1] - 1/2| + \Pr[\mathsf{BadEv}] \\ &\leq 2d_{\mathsf{H}} \cdot \Pr[S \cap T \neq \varnothing : T \leftarrow \mathcal{D}^{\mathsf{H}',\mathsf{H}}(z)] + \Pr[\mathsf{BadEv}] \\ &\leq 2d_{\mathsf{H}} \cdot (\mathsf{Adv}_{\mathsf{PKE}'}^{\mathsf{OW\text{-}qPCA}}(\mathcal{A}) + \Pr[\mathsf{BadEv}]) + \Pr[\mathsf{BadEv}] \\ &\leq 2d_{\mathsf{H}} \cdot \mathsf{Adv}_{\mathsf{PKE}'}^{\mathsf{OW\text{-}qPCA}}(\mathcal{A}) + (2d_{\mathsf{H}} + 1) \cdot \delta\ . \end{aligned}$$

Remark: Note that in game G_3, the OW-qPCA adversary $\mathcal{A}(pk, c^*)$ needs to simulate H for $\mathcal{D}$. Thus, if KEM only satisfies **Property 2**, then we must insert game $G_{2.5}$ after game G_2 to replace H with H^*, which can be simulated by $\mathcal{A}$.

Game $\mathbf{G_{2.5}}$: This game is identical to game G_2, except that we replace H with H^*, which is defined by

$$\mathsf{H}^*(A) := \begin{cases} \mathsf{H}_1(c) & A \in \mathcal{D}_{valid} \\ \mathsf{H}_2(A) & A \in \mathcal{D}_2 \\ \mathsf{H}_3(A) & otherwise. \end{cases}$$

Note that H is equal to H^* except on input $A \in \mathcal{D}_{invalid}$. Applying Lemma 1 with $S := \mathcal{D}_{invalid}$ and $z := (pk, c^*, K_b^*, \mathsf{Decaps}^{\not\perp})^7$, we have

$$|\Pr[b = b' : \mathcal{B}^{\mathsf{H}}(z)] - \Pr[b = b' : \mathcal{B}^{\mathsf{H}^*}(z)]| \leq 2d_{\mathsf{H}}\sqrt{P_{guess}},$$

[7] In Lemma 1, since there is no assumption on the size of z, the additional oracles can simply be encoded as part of z [1,3].

where $P_{guess} := \Pr[S \cap T \neq \varnothing : T \leftarrow \mathcal{C}^{\mathsf{H}^*}(z)]$ for a random measurement outcome T. By **Property 2**, we have $P_{guess} \leq negl(\lambda)$ for a negligible function $negl(\lambda)$. Thus, we have

$$|\Pr[G_2 \Rightarrow 1] - \Pr[G_{2.5} \Rightarrow 1]| \leq 2d_{\mathsf{H}}\sqrt{negl(\lambda)}.$$

Remark: More specifically, if DS is independent of $\mathcal{B}^{\mathsf{H}^*}(z)$'s view (e.g., DS $:= s$ in $\mathsf{U}^{\not\perp}$), then $\mathcal{B}^{\mathsf{H}^*}(z)$ has no information about DS, we can directly obtain

$$P_{guess} \leq \Pr[\exists(\mathrm{DS}, \cdot) \in T : T \leftarrow \mathcal{C}^{\mathsf{H}^*}(z)] \leq q_{\mathsf{H}}/(d_{\mathsf{H}} \cdot 2^l)$$

since set T contains $q_{\mathsf{H}}/d_{\mathsf{H}}$ parallel queries. Thus, we have

$$|\Pr[G_2 \Rightarrow 1] - \Pr[G_{2.5} \Rightarrow 1]| \leq 2\sqrt{q_{\mathsf{H}} d_{\mathsf{H}}/2^l}.$$

Game $\mathbf{G_{3'}}$: The game $G_{3'}$ is tha same as game G_3 except that the new random oracle H' is defined by

$$\mathsf{H}'(A) := \begin{cases} K^* & if\ A \in \mathcal{S} \\ \mathsf{H}^*(A) & otherwise, \end{cases}$$

and we run $b' \leftarrow \mathcal{B}^{\mathsf{Decaps}^{\not\perp}, \mathsf{H}'}(pk, c^*, K^*)$ if $b = 0$, and $b' \leftarrow \mathcal{B}^{\mathsf{Decaps}^{\not\perp}, \mathsf{H}^*}(pk, c^*, K^*)$ otherwise. Similar to the case from game G_2 to game G_3, we can obtain

$$|\Pr[G_{2.5} \Rightarrow 1] - \Pr[G_{3'} \Rightarrow 1]| \leq \Pr[\mathsf{BadEv}]$$

and

$$|\Pr[G_{3'} \Rightarrow 1] - 1/2| \leq 2d_{\mathsf{H}} \cdot (\mathsf{Adv}_{\mathsf{PKE}'}^{\mathsf{OW\text{-}qPCA}}(\mathcal{A}) + \Pr[\mathsf{BadEv}]).$$

Combining above formulas, if KEM only satisfies **Property 2**, we have

$$\mathsf{Adv}_{\mathsf{KEM}}^{\mathsf{IND\text{-}CCA}}(\mathcal{B}) \leq 2d_{\mathsf{H}} \cdot \mathsf{Adv}_{\mathsf{PKE}'}^{\mathsf{OW\text{-}qPCA}}(\mathcal{A}) + (2d_{\mathsf{H}} + 1) \cdot \delta + 2d_{\mathsf{H}}\sqrt{negl(\lambda)}.$$

Furthermore, if DS is independent of $\mathcal{B}$'s view, we obtain Eq. (3):

$$\mathsf{Adv}_{\mathsf{KEM}}^{\mathsf{IND\text{-}CCA}}(\mathcal{B}) \leq 2d_{\mathsf{H}} \cdot \mathsf{Adv}_{\mathsf{PKE}'}^{\mathsf{OW\text{-}qPCA}}(\mathcal{A}) + (2d_{\mathsf{H}} + 1) \cdot \delta + 2\sqrt{q_{\mathsf{H}} d_{\mathsf{H}}/2^l}.$$

3.3 Explanation for $\mathsf{FO}^{\not\perp}$ by Using Our Framework

We now show that the generic transfomation $\mathsf{FO}^{\not\perp} := \mathsf{U}^{\not\perp} \circ \mathsf{T}$ [12] satifies our framework, thus $\mathsf{KEM} := \mathsf{FO}^{\not\perp}[\mathsf{PKE}, \mathsf{G}, \mathsf{H}]$ is IND-CCA secure in the QROM.

Following our framework, in transfomation $\mathsf{U}^{\not\perp}$, we have DS $:= s$ and

$$\mathcal{D}_{valid} := \{(m, c) | \mathsf{Pco}(m, c) = 1\} \text{ and } \mathcal{D}_{invalid} := \{(s, c) | c\ is\ invalid\},$$

where s is picked at random from $\mathcal{M}$ and is part of the private key. Thus, the simulator cannot effectively check whether A belongs to $\mathcal{D}_{invalid}$ because it does not know s. However, it is obvious that the transfomation $\mathsf{U}^{\not\perp}$ satisfies **Property 2** since s is independent of $\mathcal{B}$'s view. By Eq. (3) of Theorem 2, we have

$$\mathsf{Adv}_{\mathsf{KEM}}^{\mathsf{IND\text{-}CCA}}(\mathcal{B}) \leq 2d_{\mathsf{H}} \cdot \mathsf{Adv}_{\mathsf{PKE}'}^{\mathsf{OW\text{-}qPCA}}(\mathcal{A}) + (2d_{\mathsf{H}} + 1) \cdot \delta + 2\sqrt{q_{\mathsf{H}} d_{\mathsf{H}}/|\mathcal{M}|}.$$

4 Our New Realization

In this section, we present a novel realization $\mathsf{U}^{\not\perp,sk}$, see Fig. 6. We analyze the cases where pk corresponds to only one private key and n private keys. In either case, we can explain $\mathsf{U}^{\not\perp,sk}$ by using our framework. Combining our realization $\mathsf{U}^{\not\perp,sk}$ with transformation T, we can obtain a variant of the FO-KEM, i.e., $\mathsf{FO}^{\not\perp,sk} := \mathsf{U}^{\not\perp,sk} \circ \mathsf{T}$, which converts an IND-CPA secure PKE into an IND-CCA secure KEM in the QROM. Compared with $\mathsf{FO}^{\not\perp}$ [12], $\mathsf{FO}^{\not\perp,sk}$ no longer requires additional secret informations, thus it is more concise. We can apply our new realization to NIST Round-4 KEM submissions to simplify the constructions.

$\mathsf{Encaps}(pk)$	$\mathsf{Decaps}^{\not\perp}(sk, c)$
$m \xleftarrow{\$} \mathcal{M}$	$m' := \mathsf{Dec}'(sk, c)$
$c \leftarrow \mathsf{Enc}'(pk, m)$	**if** $m' = \perp$
$K := \mathsf{H}(m, c)$	**return** $K := \mathsf{H}(sk, c)$
return (K, c)	**else return** $K := \mathsf{H}(m', c)$

Fig. 6. IND-CCA secure KEM scheme $\mathsf{KEM} := \mathsf{U}^{\not\perp,sk}[\mathsf{PKE}', \mathsf{H}]$

- **Case 1 (one to one)**: In this case, $\mathsf{U}^{\not\perp,sk}$ satisfies **Property 1**. Following our framework, we have DS $:= sk$ and $\mathcal{D}_{invalid} := \{(sk, c) | c\ is\ invalid\}$. For the adversary's queries $A = (A_1, c)$ to random oracle, the simulator can use pk to check whether $A_1 = sk$ by testing whether $\mathsf{Gen.keygen}(A_1) = pk$[8]. If $A_1 = sk$, then the simulator can use A_1 to check if c is valid. Therefore, $A \in \mathcal{D}_{invalid}$ is publicly verifiable. By Eq. (1) of Theorem 2, we have

$$\mathsf{Adv}_{\mathsf{KEM}}^{\mathsf{IND\text{-}CCA}}(\mathcal{B}) \leq 2d_{\mathsf{H}} \cdot \mathsf{Adv}_{\mathsf{PKE}'}^{\mathsf{OW\text{-}qPCA}}(\mathcal{A}) + (2d_{\mathsf{H}} + 1) \cdot \delta.$$

- **Case 2 (one to many)**: In this case, $\mathsf{U}^{\not\perp,sk}$ only satisfies **Property 2**. Without loss of generality, let pk corresponds to n private keys, i.e., there are $sk_i \in \mathcal{SK}$ such that $\mathsf{Gen.keygen}(sk_i) = pk$ for $i \in \{1, ..., n\}$, let pseudorandom key $K := \mathsf{H}(sk_1, c)$. Following our framework, we have DS $:= sk_1$ and $\mathcal{D}_{invalid} := \{(sk_1, c) | c\ is\ invalid\}$. Since all private keys are functionally equivalent, the simulator will recognize that $A \in \{(sk_i, c) | i \in \{2, .., n\}, c\ is\ invalid\}$ belongs to $\mathcal{D}_{invalid}$. Thus, the simulator cannot construct H perfectly. Meanwhile, since sk_1 is (computationally) hidden from view of any adversary, $\mathsf{U}^{\not\perp,sk}$ satisfies **Property 2**.

For **Case 2**, by Theorem 2, we have $P_{guess} := \Pr[S \cap T \neq \varnothing : T \leftarrow \mathcal{C}^{\mathsf{H}^*}(z)]$. Note that sk_1 is not independent of the adversary's view, there may be information of sk_1 in pk. We need to construct another OW-qPCA adversary $\mathcal{A}(pk, c^*)$

[8] In addition, the simulator can also test whether $A_1 = sk$ by repeated random encryption and trial decryption.

that simulates H^* for $\mathcal{C}$, and obtain $P_{guess} \leq \mathsf{Adv}_{\mathsf{PKE}'}^{\mathsf{OW-qPCA}}(\mathcal{A})$. By Eq. (2) of Theorem 2, we can obtain

$$\mathsf{Adv}_{\mathsf{KEM}}^{\mathsf{IND\text{-}CCA}}(\mathcal{B}) \leq 4d_{\mathsf{H}}\sqrt{\mathsf{Adv}_{\mathsf{PKE}'}^{\mathsf{OW\text{-}qPCA}}(\mathcal{A})} + (2d_{\mathsf{H}}+1)\cdot\delta.$$

Moreover, if n is sufficiently large, i.e., private keys still have sufficiently large entropy when pk is determined. Note that all private keys are functionally equivalent (information-theoretically), thus sk_1 works like s in the $\mathsf{U}^{\not\perp}$, we can directly obtain $P_{guess} \leq q_{\mathsf{H}}/(d_{\mathsf{H}}\cdot n)$. By Eq. (3) of Theorem 2, we have

$$\mathsf{Adv}_{\mathsf{KEM}}^{\mathsf{IND\text{-}CCA}}(\mathcal{B}) \leq 2d_{\mathsf{H}}\cdot\mathsf{Adv}_{\mathsf{PKE}'}^{\mathsf{OW\text{-}qPCA}}(\mathcal{A}) + (2d_{\mathsf{H}}+1)\cdot\delta + 2\sqrt{q_{\mathsf{H}}d_{\mathsf{H}}/n}.$$

5 Conclusions

In this paper, we propose a framework for constructing quantum random oracle that supports implicit rejection, and prove that the KEMs with implicit rejection satisfying our framework are IND-CCA secure in the QROM. Moreover, we present a novel realization $\mathsf{U}^{\not\perp,sk}$ for our framework. Compared with existing KEMs with implicit rejection [12], $\mathsf{U}^{\not\perp,sk}$ is more concise, and it can be applied to NIST KEM submissions to simplify the constructions.

Acknowledgments. We thank the anonymous ISC2022 reviewers for their helpful comments. This work was supported by the National Natural Science Foundation of China (Grant Nos. 61972391).

References

1. Ambainis, A., Hamburg, M., Unruh, D.: Quantum security proofs using semi-classical oracles. In: Boldyreva, A., Micciancio, D. (eds.) CRYPTO 2019. LNCS, vol. 11693, pp. 269–295. Springer, Cham (2019). https://doi.org/10.1007/978-3-030-26951-7_10
2. Bellare, M., Rogaway, P.: Random oracles are practical: a paradigm for designing efficient protocols. In: Proceedings of the 1st ACM Conference on Computer and Communications Security, pp. 62–73 (1993)
3. Bindel, N., Hamburg, M., Hövelmanns, K., Hülsing, A., Persichetti, E.: Tighter proofs of CCA security in the quantum random oracle model. In: Hofheinz, D., Rosen, A. (eds.) TCC 2019. LNCS, vol. 11892, pp. 61–90. Springer, Cham (2019). https://doi.org/10.1007/978-3-030-36033-7_3
4. Boneh, D., Dagdelen, Ö., Fischlin, M., Lehmann, A., Schaffner, C., Zhandry, M.: Random oracles in a quantum world. In: Lee, D.H., Wang, X. (eds.) ASIACRYPT 2011. LNCS, vol. 7073, pp. 41–69. Springer, Heidelberg (2011). https://doi.org/10.1007/978-3-642-25385-0_3
5. Dent, A.W.: A designer's guide to KEMs. In: Paterson, K.G. (ed.) Cryptography and Coding 2003. LNCS, vol. 2898, pp. 133–151. Springer, Heidelberg (2003). https://doi.org/10.1007/978-3-540-40974-8_12
6. Diffie, W., Hellman, M.E.: New directions in cryptography. IEEE Trans. Inf. Theory **22**(6), 644–654 (1976)

7. Don, J., Fehr, S., Majenz, C., Schaffner, C.: Online-extractability in the quantum random-oracle model. In: Dunkelman, O., Dziembowski, S. (eds) Advances in Cryptology – EUROCRYPT 2022. EUROCRYPT 2022. LNCS, vol. 13277, pp. 677–706. Springer, Cham (2022). https://doi.org/10.1007/978-3-031-07082-2_24
8. Duman, J., Hövelmanns, K., Kiltz, E., Lyubashevsky, V., Seiler, G.: Faster lattice-based KEMs via a generic Fujisaki-Okamoto transform using prefix hashing. In: Proceedings of the 2021 ACM SIGSAC Conference on Computer and Communications Security, pp. 2722–2737 (2021)
9. Fujisaki, E., Okamoto, T.: Secure integration of asymmetric and symmetric encryption schemes. In: Wiener, M. (ed.) CRYPTO 1999. LNCS, vol. 1666, pp. 537–554. Springer, Heidelberg (1999). https://doi.org/10.1007/3-540-48405-1_34
10. Fujisaki, E., Okamoto, T.: Secure integration of asymmetric and symmetric encryption schemes. J. Cryptol. **26**(1), 80–101 (2011). https://doi.org/10.1007/s00145-011-9114-1
11. Grover, L.K.: A fast quantum mechanical algorithm for database search. In: Miller, G.L. (ed.) The Twenty-Eighth Annual ACM Symposium on the Theory of Computing, pp. 212–219 (1996)
12. Hofheinz, D., Hövelmanns, K., Kiltz, E.: A modular analysis of the Fujisaki-Okamoto transformation. In: Kalai, Y., Reyzin, L. (eds.) TCC 2017. LNCS, vol. 10677, pp. 341–371. Springer, Cham (2017). https://doi.org/10.1007/978-3-319-70500-2_12
13. Hövelmanns, K., Hülsing, A., Majenz, C.: Failing gracefully: decryption failures and the Fujisaki-Okamoto transform. arXiv preprint arXiv:2203.10182 (2022)
14. Hövelmanns, K., Kiltz, E., Schäge, S., Unruh, D.: Generic authenticated key exchange in the quantum random oracle model. In: Kiayias, A., Kohlweiss, M., Wallden, P., Zikas, V. (eds.) PKC 2020. LNCS, vol. 12111, pp. 389–422. Springer, Cham (2020). https://doi.org/10.1007/978-3-030-45388-6_14
15. Jiang, H., Zhang, Z., Chen, L., Wang, H., Ma, Z.: IND-CCA-secure key encapsulation mechanism in the quantum random oracle model, revisited. In: Shacham, H., Boldyreva, A. (eds.) CRYPTO 2018. LNCS, vol. 10993, pp. 96–125. Springer, Cham (2018). https://doi.org/10.1007/978-3-319-96878-0_4
16. Jiang, H., Zhang, Z., Ma, Z.: Key encapsulation mechanism with explicit rejection in the quantum random oracle model. In: Lin, D., Sako, K. (eds.) PKC 2019. LNCS, vol. 11443, pp. 618–645. Springer, Cham (2019). https://doi.org/10.1007/978-3-030-17259-6_21
17. Jiang, H., Zhang, Z., Ma, Z.: Tighter security proofs for generic key encapsulation mechanism in the quantum random oracle model. In: Ding, J., Steinwandt, R. (eds.) PQCrypto 2019. LNCS, vol. 11505, pp. 227–248. Springer, Cham (2019). https://doi.org/10.1007/978-3-030-25510-7_13
18. Kuchta, V., Sakzad, A., Stehlé, D., Steinfeld, R., Sun, S.-F.: Measure-rewind-measure: tighter quantum random oracle model proofs for one-way to hiding and CCA security. In: Canteaut, A., Ishai, Y. (eds.) EUROCRYPT 2020. LNCS, vol. 12107, pp. 703–728. Springer, Cham (2020). https://doi.org/10.1007/978-3-030-45727-3_24
19. NIST: National institute for standards and technology. In: Post Quantum Crypto Project (2021). https://csrc.nist.gov/Projects/post-quantum-cryptography/round-3-submissions
20. Rackoff, C., Simon, D.R.: Non-interactive zero-knowledge proof of knowledge and chosen ciphertext attack. In: Feigenbaum, J. (ed.) CRYPTO 1991. LNCS, vol. 576, pp. 433–444. Springer, Heidelberg (1992). https://doi.org/10.1007/3-540-46766-1_35

21. Saito, T., Xagawa, K., Yamakawa, T.: Tightly-secure key-encapsulation mechanism in the quantum random oracle model. In: Nielsen, J.B., Rijmen, V. (eds.) EUROCRYPT 2018. LNCS, vol. 10822, pp. 520–551. Springer, Cham (2018). https://doi.org/10.1007/978-3-319-78372-7_17
22. Shor, P.W.: Polynomial-time algorithms for prime factorization and discrete logarithms on a quantum computer. SIAM J. Comput. **26**(5), 1484–1509
23. Targhi, E.E., Unruh, D.: Post-quantum security of the Fujisaki-Okamoto and OAEP transforms. In: Hirt, M., Smith, A. (eds.) TCC 2016. LNCS, vol. 9986, pp. 192–216. Springer, Heidelberg (2016). https://doi.org/10.1007/978-3-662-53644-5_8
24. Unruh, D.: Revocable quantum timed-release encryption. In: Advances in Cryptology - EUROCRYPT 2014, pp. 129–146 (2014)
25. Zhandry, M.: How to record quantum queries, and applications to quantum indifferentiability. In: Boldyreva, A., Micciancio, D. (eds.) CRYPTO 2019. LNCS, vol. 11693, pp. 239–268. Springer, Cham (2019). https://doi.org/10.1007/978-3-030-26951-7_9
26. Zhandry, M.: Redeeming reset indifferentiability and applications to post-quantum security. In: Tibouchi, M., Wang, H. (eds.) ASIACRYPT 2021. LNCS, vol. 13090, pp. 518–548. Springer, Cham (2021). https://doi.org/10.1007/978-3-030-92062-3_18
27. Zhandry, M.: Secure identity-based encryption in the quantum random oracle model. In: CRYPTO 2012, pp. 758–775 (2012)
28. Zhandry, M., Zhang, C.: Indifferentiability for public key cryptosystems. In: Micciancio, D., Ristenpart, T. (eds.) CRYPTO 2020. LNCS, vol. 12170, pp. 63–93. Springer, Cham (2020). https://doi.org/10.1007/978-3-030-56784-2_3

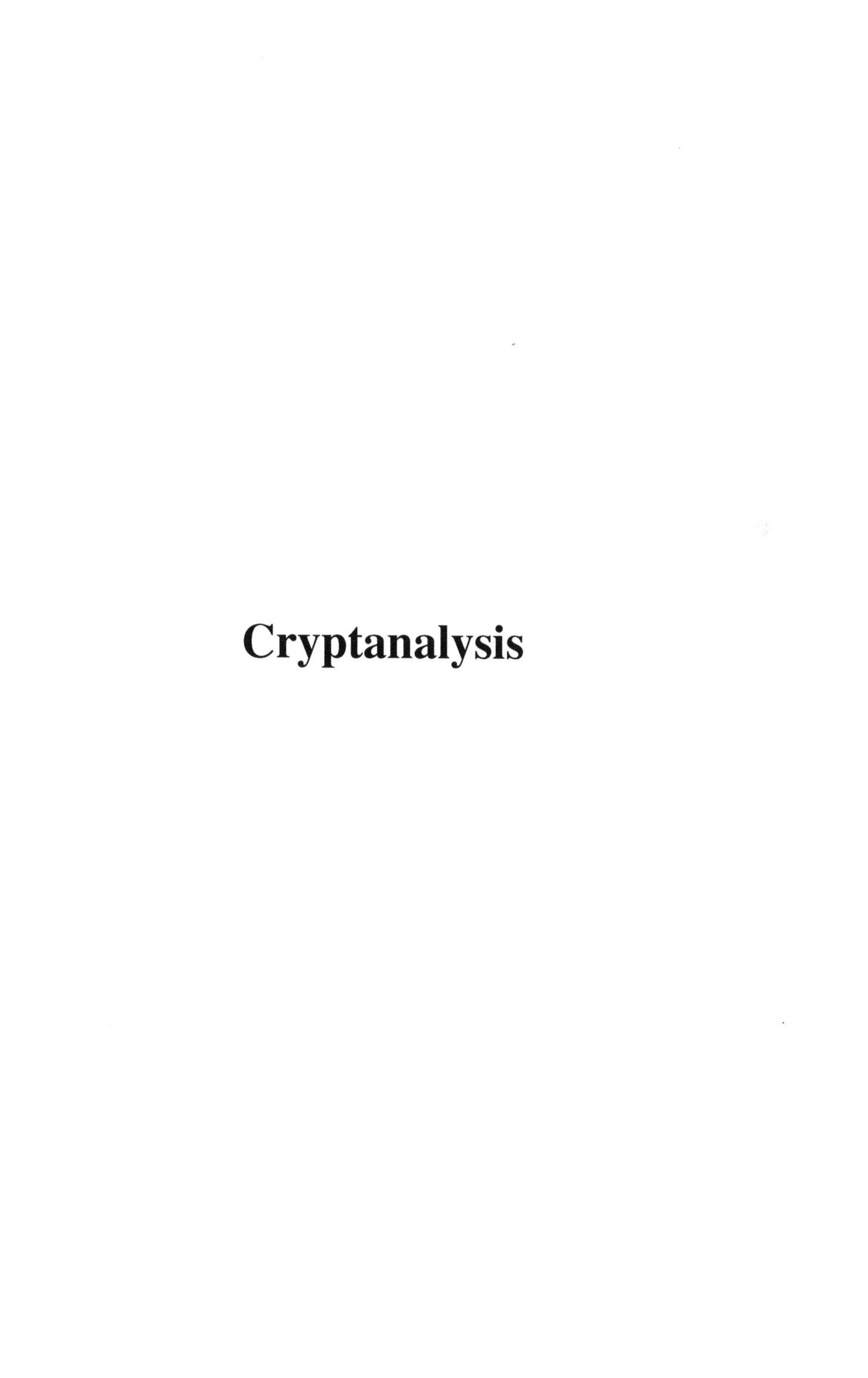

Cryptanalysis

Further Cryptanalysis of a Type of RSA Variants

Gongyu Shi, Geng Wang(✉), and Dawu Gu(✉)

School of Electronic Information and Electrical Engineering,
Shanghai Jiao Tong University, Shanghai 200240, People's Republic of China
{gy_shi,wanggxx,dwgu}@sjtu.edu.cn

Abstract. To enhance the security or the efficiency of the standard RSA cryptosystem, some variants have been proposed based on elliptic curves, Gaussian integers or Lucas sequences. A typical type of these variants which we called Type-A variants have the specified modified Euler's totient function $\psi(N) = (p^2 - 1)(q^2 - 1)$. But in 2018, based on cubic Pell equation, Murru and Saettone presented a new RSA-like cryptosystem, and it is another type of RSA variants which we called Type-B variants, since their scheme has $\psi(N) = (p^2 + p + 1)(q^2 + q + 1)$. For RSA-like cryptosystems, four key-related attacks have been widely analyzed, i.e., the small private key attack, the multiple private keys attack, the partial key exposure attack and the small prime difference attack. These attacks are well-studied on both standard RSA and Type-A variants. Recently, the small private key attack on Type-B variants has also been analyzed. In this paper, we make further cryptanalysis of Type-B variants, that is, we propose the first theoretical results of multiple private keys attack, partial key exposure attack as well as small prime difference attack on Type-B variants, and the validity of our attacks are verified by experiments. Our results show that for all three attacks, Type-B variants are less secure than standard RSA.

Keywords: Cryptanalysis · RSA variants · Coppersmith's method · Lattice reduction

1 Introduction

1.1 Background

Rivest, Shamir and Adleman [24] proposed the RSA cryptosystem in 1978, which is one of the oldest public-key cryptosystems and is still widely used nowadays.

In the standard RSA cryptosystem, the public modulus N is a product of two large primes p, q, namely, $N = pq$. Then select two integers e, d such that $ed \equiv 1 \pmod{\varphi(N)}$, where $\varphi(N) = (p-1)(q-1)$ is Euler's totient function. And (N, e) is the public key used to encrypt, (p, q, d) is the private key used to decrypt. To encrypt a message $m < N$, one computes $c := m^e \mod N$, while to decrypt the ciphertext c, one needs to compute $c^d \mod N$. It is recommended to choose p

W. Susilo et al. (Eds.): ISC 2022, LNCS 13640, pp. 133–152, 2022.
https://doi.org/10.1007/978-3-031-22390-7_9

and q of the same size such that $q < p < 2q$, which is called balanced RSA. In this paper, we only consider the balanced cases of the RSA cryptosystem and its variants. For convenience, we may represent the public exponent e as well as the secret exponent d with $e = N^\alpha$ and $d = N^\beta$ respectively.

To enhance the security or improve the efficiency, some researchers proposed variants of the standard RSA cryptosystem by modifying the underlying group, e.g., Elliptic curves based [18], Gaussian integers based [11] and Lucas sequences based [7]. In fact, all the variants proposed in [7,11,18] have the same modified Euler's totient function $\psi(N) = (p^2 - 1)(q^2 - 1)$, while the modulus $N = pq$ remains unchanged as the standard RSA. And we call these typical schemes with that specified Euler's totient function Type-A variants in the following texts.

But recently, Murru and Saettone, two Italian researchers from the University of Turin, proposed a new RSA variant with the modified Euler's totient function $\psi(N) = (p^2 + p + 1)(q^2 + q + 1)$ [21]. This cryptosystem is based on the cubic Pell equation, and it defines a non-standard product over a particular group. The authors claimed their scheme is more secure than standard RSA in some circumstances, as this variant scheme is robust against Hastad's broadcast attack [13] and Wiener's small private key attack [30]. And in this paper, we call the variants with $\psi(N) = (p^2 + p + 1)(q^2 + q + 1)$ Type-B variants. Note that one may create new Type-B cryptosystems based on other algebra structure, but it will also suffer from the attacks proposed in this paper, as our attacks do not rely on the structure of the underlying group and are general for Type-B variants.

The following paragraphs introduce four common key-related attacks on RSA-like cryptosystems, e.g., the small private key attack, the multiple private keys attack, the partial key exposure attack and the small prime difference attack.

Small Private Key Attack. In 1990, Wiener showed that if the private key d of an RSA cryptosystem is less than $\frac{1}{3}N^{0.25}$, then one can easily recover d using continued fraction. Specifically, one may find d from the continued fraction expansion of $\frac{e}{N}$. Later, Wiener's bound was improved by Boneh and Durfee [4] to $N^{0.284}$, respectively $N^{0.292}$. They used Coppersmith's lattice-based method [9] to find small roots of the modular equation $x(y + \frac{N+1}{2}) + 1 \equiv 0 \pmod{e}$. In 2010, Herrmann and May [14] obtained the same bound $d < N^{0.292}$, but with a smaller lattice dimension using the technique of unravelled linearization.

The small private key attack on Type-A variants has also been studied. Bunder et al. [6] proposed the first attack based on continued fraction, and the attack was improved in [6,23] using Coppersmith's method, which yields the best bound so far $d < N^{0.585}$.

Recently, the small private key attack on Type-B variants has been analyzed in several papers. In [22,26], it was found that Wiener's method still works. Furthermore, the use of Coppersmith's method has also been explored. Nitaj et al. [22] showed Type-B variants can be broken if $d < N^{0.569}$, and Zheng et al. [32] got a higher bound $d < N^{0.585}$ using an optimized construction.

Multiple Private Keys Attack. Howgrave-Graham and Seifert [16] first studied the case when given multiple public keys with the same modulus $(e_i \approx N^\alpha, N)$ that correspond to some small private keys $d_i \approx N^\beta$ in 1999. Later, their attack was improved successively by Sarkar and Maitra [25] and Aono [1] using Coppersmith's method. In 2014, Takayasu and Kunihiro [27] proposed the best bound so far, their attack works if $\beta < 1 - \sqrt{\frac{2}{3l+1}}$ and l is the number of obtained keys. When $l = 1$, one can find their attack achieves Boneh and Durfee's stronger bound $\beta < 0.292$.

The multiple private keys attack on Type-A variants has been studied by Zheng et al. [31]. Their attack works if $\beta < 2 - 2\sqrt{\frac{2}{3l+1}}$, and the bound is exactly twice of that on standard RSA.

Partial Key Exposure Attack. In 1998, Boneh et al. [5] first introduced the partial key exposure attack on standard RSA [5], where the attackers are given some most/least significant bits (MSBs/LSBs) of the private key d. The original attack only works for small e, but in 2003, Blömer and May [3] showed that there exists attack for larger e up to $N^{\frac{7}{8}}$. Then, in 2005, Ernst et al. [12] extended the bound to full size e. Later, the partial key exposure attack for small d has been improved by Takayasu and Kunihiro [28], which can achieve Boneh and Durfee's stronger bound in both MSBs and LSBs leakage scenarios.

Zheng et al. [31] studied the partial key exposure attack on Type-A variants. And their attack only covers a weaker bound $d < N^{0.569}$ instead of the best bound of small private key attack on Type-A variants $d < N^{0.585}$.

Small Prime Difference Attack. In 2002, de Weger [10] proposed an attack on standard RSA where the difference of prime factors $|p-q|$ is small. His results showed that under this specified scenario, the small private key attack based on Wiener's method, as well as Boneh and Durfee's method, can both obtain a better bound.

Recently, Cherkaoui-Semmouni et al. [8] studied the small prime difference attack on Type-A variants. And their attack can retrieve the best bound of small private key attack on Type-A variants $d < N^{0.585}$ under the common condition $|p - q| \approx N^{\frac{1}{2}}$.

As stated above, one can find Type-A variants are less secure than standard RSA against all four attacks. And Type-B variants are weaker than standard RSA on small private key attack. Note that the multiple private keys attack, the partial key exposure attack as well as the small prime difference attack on Type-B variants have not been studied yet.

1.2 Our Contributions

In this paper, we make a further cryptanalysis of Type-B RSA variants (i.e., RSA variants with the Euler's totient function $\psi(N) = (p^2 + p + 1)(q^2 + q + 1)$), that is, we propose the theoretical bounds of the multiple private keys attack, the partial key exposure attack, as well as the small prime difference attack on Type-B variants for the first time, and we verify the validity of all three attacks with experiments. What's more, for all three attacks, we consider a more general case for arbitrary α[1].

The results of our three attacks, in addition with the bounds of those attacks as well as the small private key attack on standard RSA and Type-A variants are given in Table 1.

Table 1. Summary of four attacks on standard RSA, Type-A and Type-B variants

	Standard RSA [24]	Type-A [7,11,18]	Type-B [21]
Euler's totient function	$\varphi(N)=(p-1)(q-1)$	$\psi(N)=(p^2-1)(q^2-1)$	$\psi(N)=(p^2+p+1)(q^2+q+1)$
Small private key attack	$\beta<1-\frac{\sqrt{2}}{2}$ [2,4]	$\beta<2-\sqrt{2}$ [23,31]	$\beta<2-\sqrt{2}$ [32]
Multiple private keys attack[a]	$\beta<1-\sqrt{\frac{2}{3l+1}}$ [27]	$\beta<2-2\sqrt{\frac{2}{3l+1}}$ [31]	$\beta<\frac{3}{2}-\frac{4}{3l+1}$ [**Sect.** 3]
Partial key exposure attack[b]	$\beta<\frac{\gamma+2-\sqrt{2-3\gamma^2}}{2}$ [28]	$\beta<\frac{3\gamma+7-2\sqrt{3\gamma+7}}{3}$ [31]	$\beta<\frac{3\gamma+7-2\sqrt{3\gamma+7}}{3}$ [**Sect.** 4]
Small prime difference attack[c]	$\beta<1-\sqrt{2\delta-\frac{1}{2}}$ [10]	$\beta<2-2\sqrt{\delta}$ [8]	$\beta<2-\sqrt{8\delta-2}$ [**Sect.** 5]

* $e=N^\alpha$ is the public exponent, $d=N^\beta$ is the secret exponent. For comparison, we take $\alpha=1$ for standard RSA, $\alpha=2$ for Type-A and Type-B variants, since some previous works only give the results for fixed α.
[a] l is the number of keys obtained.
[b] $\tilde{d}=N^\gamma$ and $\bar{d}=N^{\beta-\gamma}$ are the known leaked part and the unknown part of d respectively.
[c] $|p-q|=N^\delta$ is the prime difference.

From the table above, we can learn that Type-B variants are weaker against all four attacks compared with standard RSA, and this property is similar as Type-A variants. Especially for the small prime difference attack, Type-B variants are even less secure than Type-A variants. We will give a detailed analysis and discussion later in the main body.

1.3 Organization

The rest of this paper is organized as follows. In Sect. 2, we give some notations and describe some important lemmas used in our attacks. From Sect. 3 to Sect. 5, we propose our multiple private keys attack, partial key exposure attack and small prime difference attack on Type-B RSA variants respectively. In Sect. 6, we verify the validity of all three attacks by computer experiments. Finally, we conclude the paper in Sect. 7.

2 Preliminaries

In this section, we first give some notations, then introduce the lattice reduction technique and Coppersmith's method used in our attack.

[1] Since e is typically of the same order of magnitude as $\psi(N)$ for small d, we can fix $\alpha=2$ in our case. But Wiener [30] suggests one can add extra $\psi(N)$ to e, which yields larger α.

Minkowski Sum. Let $\mathcal{A}$ and $\mathcal{B}$ be two finite subsets of $\mathbb{Z}^n$, their Minkowski sum is denoted by $\mathcal{A} \boxplus \mathcal{B} := \{(a_1+b_1, \ldots, a_n+b_n) : (a_1, \ldots, a_n) \in \mathcal{A}, (b_1, \ldots, b_n) \in \mathcal{B}\}$. And it can be similarly extended to three or more sets.

Multivariate Terms Order. In this paper, polynomials and monomials are ordered in *lexicographic* order by default. For example, $x_1^{i_1} x_2^{i_2} \prec x_1^{i'_1} x_2^{i'_2} \Leftrightarrow i_1 < i'_1$ or $i_1 = i'_1, i_2 < i'_2$. The maximum monomial of each polynomial f in lexicographic order is called the head term, and its coefficient is called the head coefficient, denoted as $\mathrm{HC}(f)$.

Euclidean Norm. For a vector $\mathbf{b} = (b_1, \ldots, b_n) \in \mathbb{R}^n$, its Euclidean norm is denoted as $\|\mathbf{b}\| := \sqrt{\sum_{i=1}^{n} b_i^2}$. For a polynomial $f(x_1, \ldots, x_n) := \sum a_{i_1,\ldots,i_n} x_1^{i_1} \ldots x_n^{i_n}$, its Euclidean norm is defined as the Euclidean norm of its coefficients vector: $\|f(x_1, \ldots, x_n)\| := \sqrt{\sum |a_{i_1,\ldots,i_n}|^2}$, while its infinity norm is defined as the maximum term of its coefficients vector: $\|f(x_1, \ldots, x_n)\|_\infty := \max\{|a_{i_1,\ldots,i_n}|\}$.

Lattice. A lattice $\mathcal{L}$ spanned by ω linearly independent row vectors $\mathbf{b}_1, \ldots, \mathbf{b}_\omega \in \mathbb{R}^n$ is the set of their integer linear combinations, denoted as $\mathcal{L}(\mathbf{b}_1, \ldots, \mathbf{b}_\omega) := \{\sum_{i=1}^{\omega} z_i \mathbf{b}_i : z_i \in \mathbb{Z}\}$. The vectors $(\mathbf{b}_1, \ldots, \mathbf{b}_\omega)$ are called a basis of $\mathcal{L}$, and it can be represented with the basis matrix $\mathbf{B} \in \mathbb{R}^{\omega \times n}$ which contains $\mathbf{b}_1, \ldots, \mathbf{b}_\omega$ in each row. We call n the dimension of $\mathcal{L}$, and ω the rank of $\mathcal{L}$. If $\omega = n$, we call $\mathcal{L}$ is a full-rank lattice. The determinant of $\mathcal{L}$ is defined as $\det(\mathcal{L}) := \sqrt{\det(\mathbf{B}\mathbf{B}^T)}$, where $\mathbf{B}^T$ is the transpose of $\mathbf{B}$. We have $\det(\mathcal{L}) = |\det(\mathbf{B})|$ for a full-rank lattice.

In 1982, Lenstra, Lenstra and Lovász [19] proposed the LLL algorithm to find non-zero short lattice vectors in polynomial time, which is widely used in lattice-based cryptanalysis. And according to [20], the output of the LLL algorithm satisfies the following property.

Lemma 1 (LLL algorithm). *Let $\mathcal{L}$ be a lattice spanned by a basis $(\boldsymbol{b}_1, \ldots, \boldsymbol{b}_\omega)$, the LLL algorithm finds a reduced basis $(\tilde{\boldsymbol{b}}_1, \ldots, \tilde{\boldsymbol{b}}_\omega)$ of $\mathcal{L}$ satisfying*

$$\|\tilde{\boldsymbol{b}}_1\| \leq \cdots \leq \|\tilde{\boldsymbol{b}}_i\| \leq 2^{\frac{\omega(\omega-1)}{4(\omega+1-i)}} \det(\mathcal{L})^{\frac{1}{\omega+1-i}}, \textit{for } i = 1, 2, \ldots, \omega$$

in time polynomial in the dimension n and the size of entries in the basis matrix of $\mathcal{L}$.

One of the applications of the LLL algorithm in cryptanalysis is Coppersmith's method. In [9], Coppersmith proposed rigorous techniques to find small integer solutions of a univariate modular equation $f(x) = 0 \pmod{N}$ and a bivariate integer equation $f(x, y) = 0$. Both can be heuristically extended to more multivariate cases with reasonable assumptions.

We focus on the modular equation case here. Howgrave-Graham [15] reformulated this method and showed how to judge whether the roots of a modular equation are also roots over integers as follows:

Lemma 2 (Howgrave-Graham). *Let $h(x_1, \ldots, x_n) \in \mathbb{Z}[x_1, \ldots, x_n]$ be a polynomial with at most ω monomials and M be a positive integer. Suppose that*

1) $h(x'_1, \ldots, x'_n) \equiv 0 \pmod{M}$ where $|x'_1| < X_1, \ldots, |x'_n| < X_n$, and
2) $\|h(x_1X_1, \ldots, x_nX_n)\| < \frac{M}{\sqrt{\omega}}$.

Then $h(x'_1, \ldots, x'_n) = 0$ holds over the integers.

The main idea of Coppersmith's method is to construct a set of so-called shift polynomials that have the common small roots modular an integer, then apply the LLL algorithm to reduce them to several new polynomials over integers which are easier to solve.

Specifically, we can construct a lattice with the basis containing the coefficients vectors of each shift polynomials, and the LLL reduction algorithm may output several short vectors in the lattice corresponding to the norm of polynomials. If they are small enough to satisfy the bound in Lemma 2, then these equations will hold over integers. Combing with Lemma 1, we obtain

$$2^{\frac{\omega(\omega-1)}{4(\omega+1-i)}} \det(\mathcal{L})^{\frac{1}{\omega+1-i}} < \frac{M}{\sqrt{\omega}}.$$

Since the value of the determinant and M grows significantly faster than the other terms in our case, it can be transformed to the simplified condition

$$\det(\mathcal{L}) < M^{\omega}. \tag{1}$$

Finally, we can use the resultant technique or the Gröbner basis technique to extract the common roots. Note that both techniques require the polynomials we get after reduction are algebraic independent. But no existed method can guarantee the algebraic independence, thus Coppersmith's method is heuristic in this case. In this paper, we make the following assumption just as numerous previous works [1,4,22,27,32].

Assumption 1. *The reduced lattice basis yields algebraically independent polynomials.*

The following lemma proposed by de Weger [10] gives a range of the sum of two integers when their difference is known.

Lemma 3. *Let $N = pq$ be a product of two integers p, q and $\delta = p - q$ is their difference. Then*

$$0 < p + q - 2N^{\frac{1}{2}} < \frac{\delta^2}{4N^{\frac{1}{2}}}.$$

3 Multiple Private Keys Attack

In this section, we propose the multiple private keys attack on Type-B RSA variants.

We consider the situation where the attacker obtained l public key pairs $(e_1, N), \ldots, (e_l, N)$ with a common modulus N, and they correspond to some small $d_1, \ldots, d_l$. All the public exponents e_k and the secret exponents d_k are assumed to be the same size respectively. The goal is to factor N efficiently.

Theorem 1. *Let $N = pq$ be a modulus of Type-B RSA variants with $q < p < 2q$. For integers $l \geq 2$, $1 \leq k \leq l$, let $e_k = N^{\alpha}, d_k = N^{\beta}$ be a valid pair of public and secret exponents such that $e_k d_k \equiv 1 \mod (p^2+p+1)(q^2+q+1)$. Then for $\frac{1}{2} + \frac{1}{3l-1} < \alpha < \frac{3}{4} + \frac{9l}{4}$, one can factor N in polynomial time if*

$$\beta < \frac{3}{2} - \frac{2\alpha}{3l+1}.$$

Proof. We can rewrite the known equations as

$$\begin{aligned} & e_k d_k \equiv 1 \pmod{(p^2+p+1)(q^2+q+1)} \\ \Rightarrow \quad & e_k d_k = r_k(N^2 + (N+1)(p+q) + p^2 + q^2 + N + 1) + 1 \\ \Rightarrow \quad & e_k d_k = r_k((p+q)^2 + a(p+q) + b) + 1, \end{aligned}$$

where $a := N+1, b := N^2 - N + 1$.

Then we need to solve the following modular equations simultaneously:

$$\begin{cases} f_1(x_1, y) := x_1(y^2 + ay + b) + 1 \equiv 0 \pmod{e_1}, \\ f_2(x_2, y) := x_2(y^2 + ay + b) + 1 \equiv 0 \pmod{e_2}, \\ \quad \vdots \\ f_l(x_l, y) := x_l(y^2 + ay + b) + 1 \equiv 0 \pmod{e_l}, \end{cases} \tag{2}$$

where the roots $(x_1, x_2, \ldots, x_l, y)$ are $(r_1, r_2, \ldots, r_l, p+q)$, and their values are bounded with $X_1 = X_2 = \cdots = X_l = N^{\alpha+\beta-2}$ and $Y \approx N^{0.5}$.

To solve this problem, we use the Minkowski sum based lattice construction technique proposed by Aono [1].

At first, we define the set of shift polynomials $\mathcal{G}_k (1 \leq k \leq l)$ and its index set $\mathcal{I}_k$ as

$$\begin{aligned} & j_k' := 2j_k + h_k, \\ & g_{i_k, j_k'}^{(k)}(x_k, y) := x_k^{i_k - j_k} f_k(x_k, y)^{j_k} e_k^{m - j_k} y^{h_k}, \\ & \mathcal{G}_k := \{g_{i_k, j_k'}^{(k)} : 0 \leq i_k \leq m, 0 \leq j_k \leq i_k, 0 \leq h_k \leq 1\}, \\ & \mathcal{I}_k := \{(\underbrace{0, \ldots, 0}_{k-1}, i_k, \underbrace{0, \ldots, 0}_{l-k}, j_k') : 0 \leq i_k \leq m, 0 \leq j_k \leq i_k, 0 \leq h_k \leq 1\}, \end{aligned}$$

where i_k, j_k, h_k are non-negative integers and m is a fixed positive integer. It is clear that $g_{i_k, j_k'}^{(k)} \equiv 0 \pmod{e_k^m}$. And each index vector stores the maximum exponents of variables x_k, y in the corresponding polynomials.

Then, the Minkowski sum of all index set in our case is defined as

$$\mathcal{I}_+ := \mathcal{I}_1 \boxplus \cdots \boxplus \mathcal{I}_l = \{(i_1, \ldots, i_l, j) : 0 \leq i_1, \ldots, i_l \leq m, 0 \leq j \leq 2\sum\nolimits_{k=1}^{l} i_k + l\}.$$

For each $(i_1, \ldots, i_l, j) \in \mathcal{I}_+$, we can define a corresponding polynomial and obtain a new polynomial set:

$$g_{i_1,\ldots,i_l,j} := \sum_{\sum_{k=1}^{l} j'_k = j} c_{j'_1,\ldots,j'_l} g^{(1)}_{i_1,j'_1} \cdots g^{(l)}_{i_l,j'_l},$$

$$\mathcal{G}_+ := \{g_{i_1,\ldots,i_l,j} : (i_1, \ldots, i_l, j) \in \mathcal{I}_+\}.$$

According to the definition of the Minkowski sum lattice, $c_{j'_1,\ldots,j'_l}$ are some selected integers such that the following equation holds:

$$\begin{aligned} \mathrm{HC}(g_{i_1,\ldots,i_l,j}) &= \operatorname*{GCD}_{\sum_{k=1}^{l} j'_k = j} (\mathrm{HC}(g^{(1)}_{i_1,j'_1} \cdots g^{(l)}_{i_l,j'_l})) \\ &= \operatorname*{GCD}_{\sum_{k=1}^{l} j'_k = j} (e_1^{m-\lfloor \frac{j'_1}{2} \rfloor} \cdots e_l^{m-\lfloor \frac{j'_l}{2} \rfloor}), \end{aligned} \tag{3}$$

where $\mathrm{HC}(f)$ means the coefficient of the head term of f in lexicographic order.

Each j'_k can move from 0 to $\min(2i_k + 1, j)$, so we can transform Eq. (3) to

$$\mathrm{HC}(g_{i_1,\ldots,i_l,j}) = e_1^{m-\min(i_1,\lfloor \frac{j}{2} \rfloor)} \cdots e_l^{m-\min(i_l,\lfloor \frac{j}{2} \rfloor)}. \tag{4}$$

Now, consider the lattice basis matrix of each $\mathcal{G}_k$, which is generated by taking the coefficients vector of $g^{(k)}_{i_k,j'_k}(X_k x_k, Yy)$ for each $g^{(k)}_{i'_k,j'_k} \in \mathcal{G}_k$. By ordering polynomials corresponding to rows and monomials corresponding to columns in lexicographic order, as shown in [22], the basis matrix will be lower triangular. Then, according to [1], the Minkowski sum lattice basis matrix of $\mathcal{G}_+$ is also lower triangular. Furthermore, we can learn the diagonal element in this basis matrix are exactly the result of Eq. (4) multiple with the powers of the bounds of each variable, so the determinant will be

$$\det(\mathcal{L}) = \prod_{(i_1,\ldots,i_l,j) \in \mathcal{I}_+} e_1^{m-\min(i_1,\lfloor \frac{j}{2} \rfloor)} \cdots e_l^{m-\min(i_l,\lfloor \frac{j}{2} \rfloor)} X_1^{i_1} \cdots X_l^{i_l} Y^j.$$

Notice that each polynomial in the form $g^{(k)}_{i_k,j'_k}$ equals to zero modulo e_k^m, thus, for each $g_{i_1,\ldots,i_l,j} \in \mathcal{G}_+$, we have $g_{i_1,\ldots,i_l,j} \equiv 0 \pmod{(e_1 \cdots e_l)^m}$.

Then substitute the above $\det(\mathcal{L})$ into Eq. (1), and set $e_k = N^{\alpha}$, $X_k = N^{\alpha+\beta-2}$, $Y = N^{0.5}$, $M = (e_1 \cdots e_l)^m$, after some computations (details can be found in Appendix A), we may obtain the condition

$$-\alpha(\frac{l^2}{2} - \frac{l}{6}) + (\alpha + \beta - 2)(\frac{l^2}{2} + \frac{l}{6}) + (\frac{l^2}{4} + \frac{l}{12}) < 0, \tag{5}$$

which yields the bound of β as

$$\beta < \frac{3}{2} - \frac{2\alpha}{3l+1}. \tag{6}$$

On the other hand, we must have $\beta > 0$ and $\alpha + \beta > 2$, which gives the range of valid α as

$$\frac{1}{2} + \frac{1}{3l-1} < \alpha < \frac{3}{4} + \frac{9l}{4}. \tag{7}$$

If the conditions in Eq. (7) and Eq. (6) are satisfied, with Assumption 1, we may construct $l+1$ polynomials over integers from the reduced lattice, then extract the shared common root $(x_1, x_2, \ldots, x_l, y) = (r_1, r_2, \ldots, r_l, p+q)$ using the Gröbner basis method. And the knowledge of $p+q$ yields a factorization of N. This terminates the proof. □

The validity of our multiple private keys attack has been verified by experiments, and the results are given in Table 2 in Sect. 6.

Comparison with Small Private Key Attack Using Coppersmith's Method on Type-B Variants. Set $l = 1$ in our attack, the bound becomes $\beta < \frac{3}{2} - \frac{\alpha}{2}$, which is weaker than the bound in [22,32], thus our attack is not a tight extension of the small private key attack. This is mainly because they use several extra y-shift polynomials and the number is related to a tweakable parameter τ. By optimizing the value of τ, one can always get the best bound. In our attack, we just pick the basic shift polynomials, as many previous works involving the Minkowski sum lattice construction [1,27,31].

Comparison with Multiple Private Keys Attack on Standard RSA and Type-A Variants. According to Table 1, the bound of small private key attack on Type-A and Type-B variants are exactly the same. So we may expect they also have the same bound on multiple private keys attack. However, this is not the case in our attack. Typically, when d is small, e will be of the same order of magnitude as $\psi(N)$, which implies $\alpha = 2$ in our case, the bound of β becomes $\beta < \frac{3}{2} - \frac{4}{3l+1}$, which is exactly twice the bound of multiple private keys attack on standard RSA obtained by Aono [1]. Note that Aono's original attack has been improved by Takayasu and Kunihiro [27] with an optimized construction. Using their method, one may obtain the results of multiple private keys attack on standard RSA and Type-A variants in Table 1. However, we find it is hard to apply their strategy directly on Type-B variants. The main idea of their method is to determine whether a polynomial is helpful or not by comparing its corresponding diagonal value in the lattice basis matrix with the modulus $(e_1 \ldots e_l)^m$, then try to collect as many helpful polynomials as possible and as few unhelpful polynomials as possible during the lattice construction. They claimed the lattice basis matrix can still be triangular if $l \geq 3$, and for $l = 1, 2$ one may use the unravelled linearization technique [14] to transform it to be triangular. As a result, they obtain the same result $\beta < 0.292$ as [4] when $l = 1$. But if we apply the same method in our attack, i.e., we add some extra y-shift polynomials into each $\mathcal{G}_k$ and modify the range of j in $\mathcal{I}_+$ from $2\sum_{k=1}^{l} i_k + l$ to $2(2-\beta)\sum_{k=1}^{l} i_k$. When $l \geq 3$, the lattice can not be full-rank even use the unravelled linearization $z_i = x_i y^2 + 1$. Furthermore, we find if setting the upper bound of j as $2\lfloor(2-\beta)\rceil \sum_{k=1}^{l} i_k$, the lattice basis matrix can be triangular again, but we carried out some experiments for small l, m and the results suggest this method gets a lower bound than our original one. Thus, how to improve our attack is still an open problem.

4 Partial Key Exposure Attack

In this section, we propose the partial key exposure attack on Type-B RSA variants. Same as [31], we consider the general case where some MSBs and LSBs of the private key are leaked, so the unknown part is in the middle.

Theorem 2. *Let $N = pq$ be a modulus of Type-B RSA variants with $q < p < 2q$. Let $e = N^{\alpha}, d = N^{\beta}$ be a valid pair of public and secret exponents such that $ed \equiv 1 \mod (p^2+p+1)(q^2+q+1)$. Given some MSBs $d_M = N^{\gamma_M}$ and some LSBs $d_L = N^{\gamma_L}$ of the secret exponent, and let $\gamma = \gamma_M + \gamma_L$ satisfying $\gamma < \frac{15}{4}$. Then for $1-\gamma < \alpha < \frac{15}{4} - \gamma$, one can factor N in polynomial time if*

$$\beta < \frac{3\gamma + 7 - 2\sqrt{3\gamma + 3\alpha + 1}}{3}.$$

Proof. Let $\bar{d}$ denotes the unknown middle part of private key which is bounded by $N^{\beta-\gamma}$, we have

$$d = Md_M + L\bar{d} + d_L,$$

where $M := 2^{(\beta-\gamma_M)\log_2 N}$, $L := 2^{(\beta-\gamma_L)\log_2 N}$.

Thus, we can rewrite the key equation as

$$\begin{aligned} ed &= r((p+q)^2 + a(p+q) + b) + 1 \\ \Rightarrow \quad e(L\bar{d} + \tilde{d}) &= r((p+q)^2 + a(p+q) + b) + 1, \end{aligned}$$

where $a := N+1, b := N^2 - N + 1$, and $\tilde{d} := Md_M + d_L$, which denotes the leaked value of d.

Now, consider the integer equation

$$\bar{f}(x,y,z) := 1 - e\tilde{d} - eLx + y(z^2 + az + b), \tag{8}$$

which has a small root $(x,y,z) = (\bar{d}, r, p+q)$ bounded by $X = N^{\beta-\gamma}, Y = N^{\alpha+\beta-2}, Z \approx N^{0.5}$.

To solve Eq. (8) using Coppersmith's method, we apply Jochemsz and May's strategy [17]. First, we need to define a parameter as $W := \|f(Xx, Yy, Zz)\|_{\infty}$, and in our case, that's

$$W = \max\{|1 - e\tilde{d}|, eLX, YZ^2, aYZ, bY\} = bY = N^{\alpha+\beta}.$$

Then, set $R := WX^{m-1}Y^{m-1}Z^{2(m-1)+\tau m}$, where m is a fixed positive integer and $0 \le \tau \le 1$ is a parameter to be optimized later. And we can transform Eq. (8) to the modular equation

$$f(x,y,z) := (1 - e\tilde{d})^{-1} f(x,y,z) \pmod{R}. \tag{9}$$

We define the set of shift polynomials as

$$\begin{aligned}
&g_{i,j,k}(x,y,z) := x^i y^j z^k f(x,y,z) X^{m-1-i} Y^{m-1-j} Z^{2(m-1)-k+\tau m},\\
&h_{i,j,k}(x,y,z) := x^i y^j z^k R,\\
&\mathcal{G} := \{g_{i,j,k} : 0 \le i \le m-1, 0 \le j \le m-1-i, 0 \le k \le 2j+\tau m\},\\
&\mathcal{H} := \{h_{i,j,k} : 0 \le i \le m, j = m-i, 0 \le k \le 2j+\tau m\},\\
&\mathcal{F} := \mathcal{G} \cup \mathcal{H},
\end{aligned}$$

where i, j, k are non-negative integers. Note that all polynomials in $\mathcal{F}$ share the common root $(\bar{d}, r, p+q)$ modular R.

Consider the basis matrix generated by taking the coefficients vector of $F(Xx, Yy, Zz)$ for each $F \in \mathcal{F}$. By sorting all the monomials (each corresponds to a column in the matrix) with the order mentioned in [17], we may get an upper triangular matrix.

Let $\mathcal{L}$ be the lattice corresponding to that triangular basis matrix and ω be its dimension. In our construction, the diagonal entries of this matrix are $X^{m-1}Y^{m-1}Z^{2(m-1)+\tau m}$ for polynomials in $\mathcal{G}$ and $WX^{m-1+i}Y^{m-1+j}Z^{2(m-1)+\tau m+k}$ for polynomials in $\mathcal{H}$. So, we have

$$\det(\mathcal{L}) = \prod_{\substack{(i,j,k):\\ g_{i,j,k}\in\mathcal{G}}} X^{m-1}Y^{m-1}Z^{2(m-1)+\tau m} \prod_{\substack{(i,j,k):\\ h_{i,j,k}\in\mathcal{H}}} WX^{m-1+i}Y^{m-1+j}Z^{2(m-1)+\tau m+k}.$$

Next, we can set $X = N^{\beta-\gamma}, Y = N^{\alpha+\beta-2}, Z = N^{0.5}, W = N^{\alpha+\beta}$, $M = WX^{m-1}Y^{m-1}Z^{2(m-1)+\tau m}$, and the condition in Eq. (1) can be simplified to (details of computation are given in Appendix B)

$$3\tau^2 + (6\beta - 6\gamma - 6)\tau + 4\alpha + 8\beta - 4\gamma - 12 < 0. \tag{10}$$

By setting $\tau = 1 - \beta + \gamma$, the left-hand side of Eq. (10) reaches its minimum, and we get

$$-3(1-\beta+\gamma)^2 + 4\alpha + 8\beta - 4\gamma - 12 < 0.$$

Thus, we get the bound of β as

$$\beta < \frac{3\gamma + 7 - 2\sqrt{3\gamma + 3\alpha + 1}}{3}. \tag{11}$$

On the other hand, we require $0 \le \tau \le 1$, which indicates $0 \le \beta \le 1+\gamma$. We consider the case $\beta < \min(\frac{3\gamma+7-2\sqrt{3\gamma+3\alpha+1}}{3}, 1+\gamma) = \frac{3\gamma+7-2\sqrt{3\gamma+3\alpha+1}}{3}$, which implies $\alpha > 1 - \gamma$. Combing with the condition $0 < \gamma \le \beta$ and $\alpha + \beta \ge 2$, we can get the range of valid α as

$$1 - \gamma < \alpha < \frac{15}{4} - \gamma. \tag{12}$$

If the conditions in Eq. (11) and Eq. (12) are satisfied, with Assumption 1, similar as the previous attack, we can extract the shared common root $(x, y, z) = (\bar{d}, r, p+q)$. And the knowledge of $p+q$ yields a factorization of N. This terminates the proof. □

We verify the validity of our partial key exposure attack with experiments, and the results can be found in Table 3 of Sect. 6.

Comparison with Small Private Key Attack Using Coppersmith's Method on Type-B Variants. Set $\gamma = 0, \alpha = 2$ in our attack, the bound becomes $\beta < \frac{7-2\sqrt{7}}{3} \approx 0.569$, which is same as the bound obtained by Nitaj et al. [22]. This implies our construction can only achieve the weaker bound instead of the stronger bound $\beta < 0.585$, so it is an open problem for how to optimize our attack to cover the stronger bound. As our attack corresponds to the general case when both some MSBs and LSBs are leaked, there may be some loss of precision. One can consider the MSBs and LSBs cases separately with some different ad-hoc optimized constructions.

Comparison with Partial Key Exposure Attack on Standard RSA and Type-A Variants. According to Table 1, our attack yields the same bound as that on Type-A variants. This is mainly because the $\psi(N)$ of both Type-A and Type-B variants are of the same order of magnitude as N^2 and Zheng et al. [31] as well as we use the general construction proposed by Jochemsz and May [17]. But this result is not twice as the partial key exposure attack bound on standard RSA. Just as the former analysis, Takayasu and Kunihiro [28] choose some ad-hoc and well-optimized constructions instead of general constructions, which makes it possible to fully cover Boneh and Durfee's bound.

5 Small Prime Difference Attack

In this section, we propose the small prime difference attack on Type-B RSA variants with a modulus $N = pq$ where the primes difference $|p-q|$ is sufficiently small.

Note that when $|p-q| \leq N^{\frac{1}{4}}$, the attack is trivial, since one may find $p+q$ is equal to $2N^{\frac{1}{2}}$ according to Lemma 3, which yields a factorization. So, we only consider the case $\delta > \frac{1}{4}$.

Theorem 3. *Let $N = pq$ be a modulus of Type-B RSA variants with $q < p < 2q$ and $p - q < N^{\delta}$ where $\frac{1}{4} < \delta < \frac{1}{2}$. Let $e = N^{\alpha}, d = N^{\beta}$ be a valid pair of public and secret exponents such that $ed \equiv 1 \mod (p^2+p+1)(q^2+q+1)$. Then for $4\delta - 1 < \alpha < 9\delta - \frac{36\delta-9}{4}$, one can factor N in polynomial time if*

$$\beta < 2 - \sqrt{\alpha(4\delta - 1)}.$$

Proof. Similar as the multiple private keys attack, the key equation is

$$ed = r((p+q)^2 + a(p+q) + b) + 1,$$

where $a := N+1, b := N^2 - N + 1$. And it corresponds to the modular equation

$$\bar{f}(x,y) := x(y^2 + ay + b) + 1 \equiv 0 \pmod{e},$$

which has a root $(x,y) = (r, p+q)$.

According to Lemma 3, we have $p+q=c+\Delta$ where $c:=2N^{\frac{1}{2}}, \Delta<\frac{N^{2\delta}}{4N^{\frac{1}{2}}}\approx N^{2\delta-\frac{1}{2}}$. To make the desired root of variable y becomes Δ, we just replace y in $\bar{f}(x,y)$ with $y+c$, and obtain the new equation

$$f(x,y):=x(y^2+Ay+B)+1\equiv 0 \pmod{e},$$

where $A:=2c+a, B:=c^2+ac+b$. Obviously, $f(x,y)$ has a small root (r,Δ), which are bounded by $X=N^{\alpha+\beta-2}$ and $Y=N^{2\delta-\frac{1}{2}}$.

Notice that f and $\bar{f}$ only differ at some coefficients, thus, to find the small roots of f, we may refer to the lattice construction used to find the small roots of $\bar{f}$ in [32] by Zheng et al.

Let $z:=xy^2+1$, then we transform $f(x,y)$ into

$$f^*(x,y,z):=z+x(Ay+B)\equiv 0 \pmod{e}.$$

We define the set of shift polynomials as

$$\begin{aligned}
&g_{i,j,k}(x,y,z):=x^{i-j}f^*(x,y,z)^j e^{m-j}y^k,\\
&h_{j,k}(x,y,z):=f^*(x,y,z)^j e^{m-j}y^k,\\
&\mathcal{G}:=\{g_{i,j,k}:0\le i\le m, 0\le j\le i, 0\le k\le 1\},\\
&\mathcal{H}:=\{h_{j,k}:0\le j\le m, 2\le k\le \tau m\},\\
&\mathcal{F}:=\mathcal{G}\cup\mathcal{H},
\end{aligned}$$

where i,j,k are non-negative integers, m is a fixed positive integer and $0\le\tau\le 1$ is a parameter to be optimized later.

Now, for each polynomial $F\in\mathcal{F}$, we just apply the unravelled linearization technique, by replacing terms in the form $(xy^2)^t$ to $(z-1)^t$ for any $t\in\mathbb{N}$ to get F'. Consider the basis matrix generated by taking the coefficients vector of each $F'(Xx,Yy,Zz)$, by sorting the rows and columns using the rules described in [32], we may obtain a triangular matrix.

Let $\mathcal{L}$ be the lattice corresponding to that triangular matrix, following a similar computation in previous attacks, we get its dimension ω and its determinant:

$$\begin{aligned}
\omega&=\frac{\tau+2}{2}m^2+o(m^2),\\
\det(\mathcal{L})&=X^{\frac{1}{3}m^3+o(m^3)}Y^{\frac{\tau^2}{6}m^3+o(m^3)}Z^{\frac{\tau+1}{3}m^3+o(m^3)}e^{\frac{\tau+4}{6}m^3+o(m^3)}.
\end{aligned}$$

In our construction, each polynomial F' satisfies that $F'(r,\Delta,r\Delta^2+1)\equiv 0 \pmod{e^m}$. Thus, substitute the above $\det(\mathcal{L})$ into Eq. 1, and set $e=N^{\alpha}$, $X=N^{\alpha+\beta-2}$, $Y=N^{2\delta-\frac{1}{2}}$, $Z=N^{\alpha+\beta+4\delta-3}$, $M=e^m$, we will obtain the condition

$$\begin{aligned}
&N^{(\alpha+\beta-2)(\frac{1}{3}m^3+o(m^3))}\cdot N^{(2\delta-\frac{1}{2})(\frac{\tau^2}{6}m^3+o(m^3))}\cdot\\
&N^{(\alpha+\beta+4\delta-3)(\frac{\tau+1}{3}m^3+o(m^3))}\cdot N^{\alpha(\frac{\tau+4}{6}m^3+o(m^3))}<N^{\alpha(\frac{\tau+2}{2}m^3+o(m^3))}
\end{aligned}$$

When m is sufficient large, we may omit all terms in $o(m^3)$, then take the exponents part of N, and we can transform the condition to

$$(4\delta - 1)\tau^2 + (4\beta + 16\delta - 12)\tau + 4\alpha + 8\beta + 16\delta - 20 < 0. \tag{13}$$

By setting $\tau = \frac{-2\beta-8\delta+6}{4\delta-1}$, the left-hand side of Eq. (13) reaches its minimum, and we obtain

$$\beta^2 - 4\beta - 4\alpha\delta + \alpha + 4 > 0,$$

which gives the upper bound of β as

$$\beta < 2 - \sqrt{\alpha(4\delta - 1)}. \tag{14}$$

On the other hand, we require $0 \leq \tau \leq 1$, which implies $\frac{7}{2} - 6\delta \leq \beta \leq 3 - 4\delta$. We consider the case $\beta < \min(2 - \sqrt{\alpha(4\delta - 1)}, 3 - 4\delta) = 2 - \sqrt{\alpha(4\delta - 1)}$, which always holds if $\alpha > 4\delta - 1$. Combing with $\alpha + \beta > 2$, we can get the range of solvable α as

$$4\delta - 1 < \alpha < 9\delta - \frac{9}{4}. \tag{15}$$

If the conditions in Eq. (14) and Eq. (15) are satisfied, with Assumption 1, similar as the previous attack, we may extract the shared common root $(x, y, z) = (r, \Delta, r\Delta^2 + 1)$. Then, we get $p+q$ as $p+q = c+\Delta$, which yields a factorization of N. This terminates the proof. □

We carried out some experiments to verify the validity of our small prime difference attack, one may check Table 4 in Sect. 6 for details.

Comparison with Small Private Key Attack Using Coppersmith's Method on Type-B Variants. Set $\delta = \frac{1}{2}, \alpha = 2$ in our attack, the bound becomes $\beta < 2 - \sqrt{2}$, which is same as the best bound so far obtained by Zheng et al. [32]. This is reasonable, as one can find the modular equation we construct (i.e., equation f in Therorem 3) only differs from that constructed in [32] (i.e., equation $\bar{f}$ in Therorem 3) at two coefficients and the same lattice constructions are used in these two attacks. Thus, for Type-B variants, the small prime difference attack is a tight extension of the small private key attack.

Comparison with Small Prime Difference Attack on Standard RSA and Type-A Variants. If we set $\alpha = 2$, one can verify that our bound is exactly twice as the bound on standard RSA obtained by de Weger [10]. This is reasonable, as the small primes difference attack is a specified version of the small private key attack. But one may find the bound on Type-A and Type-B variants are different. This is mainly due to the difference between the modular equation construction. The $\psi(N)$ of Type-A variants can be represented as a function of $p-q$ directly (i.e., $\psi(N) = (p^2-1)(q^2-1) = -(p-q)^2 + N^2 - 2N + 1$), while for Type-B we can only represent $\psi(N)$ as a function of $p+q$. Specifically, Type-B variants are weaker than Type-A variants on small prime difference attack, since the upper bound of solvable β in our attack on Type-B is always higher than the bound obtained by Cherkaoui-Semmouni et al. [8] on Type-A for any valid $\frac{1}{4} < \delta < \frac{1}{2}$ with the same valid α.

6 Experimental Results

In this section, we verify the validity of the all three attacks proposed in this paper.

Experiments are carried out using SageMath 9.4 [29] with a single process on an Ubuntu 20.04.3 LTS workstation with Intel(R) Xeon(R) Gold 5218 CPU @ 2.30 GHz.

For each test, we first generate two 512-bit primes p, q and compute the 1024-bit modulus $N = pq$, then randomly choose secret exponent(s) bounded by N^{β} and computes the corresponding public exponent(s).

In the following tables, ω is the lattice dimension, β_{thm} means the bound computed from the theorems, β_{exp} indicates the experimental bounds, that's if we increase β_{exp} by 0.01, our attacks will fail to factor the modulus N. And Time_{LLL}, Time_{GB} are the time cost of the LLL reduction and the Gröbner basis computation respectively.

For all three attacks, we can find that there are some differences between the theoretical bounds and our experimental results. In fact, this is reasonable, since we assume m can be sufficiently large and employ lots of approximation when computing the theoretical bound.

Due to the constrained computer resources, the lattice reduction process becomes the bottleneck of our attacks, for the time cost of the Gröbner basis

Table 2. Experiment results of multiple private keys attack

l	m	ω	β_{thm}	β_{exp}	Time_{LLL}	Time_{GB}
2	1	20	0.93	0.54	0.14 s	0.01 s
2	2	63	0.93	0.69	64.69 s	0.09 s
2	3	144	0.93	0.75	18608.71 s	2.77 s
3	1	56	1.10	0.76	3.41 s	0.30 s
3	2	270	1.10	0.82	98643.22 s	38.31 s
4	1	144	1.19	0.86	226.32 s	6.73 s
5	1	352	1.25	0.93	19154.73 s	3919.37 s

Table 3. Experiment results of partial key exposure attack

γ	m	ω	β_{thm}	β_{exp}	Time_{LLL}	Time_{GB}
0.05	3	50	0.60	0.43	28.16 s	0.01 s
0.10	3	50	0.63	0.45	27.65 s	0.01 s
0.20	3	60	0.69	0.49	56.14 s	0.01 s
0.40	3	60	0.82	0.59	60.18 s	0.01 s
0.40	4	115	0.82	0.63	1538.38 s	0.02 s
0.40	5	175	0.82	0.66	18763.19 s	0.05 s
0.80	3	60	1.09	0.81	48.91 s	0.02 s

Table 4. Experiment results of small prime difference attack

δ	m	ω	β_{thm}	β_{exp}	Time_{LLL}	Time_{GB}
0.30	3	26	1.37	1.10	1.49 s	0.03 s
0.30	5	57	1.37	1.12	73.04 s	0.12 s
0.30	7	100	1.37	1.14	1385.02 s	0.39 s
0.30	9	155	1.37	1.16	17616.57 s	1.12 s
0.34	5	57	1.15	0.99	67.36 s	0.10 s
0.38	5	57	0.98	0.86	65.34 s	0.10 s
0.42	5	57	0.83	0.73	53.96 s	0.08 s
0.46	5	57	0.70	0.60	120.49 s	0.07 s

computation is substantially less than that of the LLL algorithm. Even if we slightly increase m, the time cost will increase significantly, making it difficult to reach the bound β_{thm} in practice.

7 Conclusion

In this paper, we study the multiple private keys attack, the partial key exposure attack, as well as the small prime difference attack on a new type of RSA variants with the modified Euler's totient function $\psi(N) = (p^2+p+1)(q^2+q+1)$ for the first time. Our results imply this type of variants are less secure than standard RSA under these attacks. And according to the previous researches, one can find another typical type of RSA variants with $\psi(N) = (p^2-1)(q^2-1)$ are also weaker than standard RSA against these attacks. Thus, it seems that one should not pick the groups with larger Euler's totient function when designing RSA-like cryptosystems, since this will reduce the security against some key-related attacks.

Acknowledgments. We thank the anonymous reviewers for insightful comments. This work was partially supported by the National Natural Science Foundation of China (Grant Number 62072307), the National Key Research and Development Project of China (Grant Number 2020YFA0712300) as well as the Science and Technology Innovation Action Plan of Shanghai (Grant Number 22511101300).

Appendix A: Details of the Computation of Eq. (5)

According to Eq. (1), we have

$$\prod_{(i_1,\ldots,i_l,j)\in\mathcal{I}_+} e_1^{m-\min(i_1,\lfloor\frac{j}{2}\rfloor)}\cdots e_l^{m-\min(i_l,\lfloor\frac{j}{2}\rfloor)} X_1^{i_1}\cdots X_l^{i_l} Y^j < (e_1\ldots e_l)^{m|\mathcal{I}_+|}$$

$$\Rightarrow \prod_{(i_1,\ldots,i_l,j)\in\mathcal{I}_+} N^{-\alpha\sum_{k=1}^{l}\min(i_k,\lfloor\frac{j}{2}\rfloor)} N^{(\alpha+\beta-2)\sum_{t=1}^{l} i_t} N^{0.5j} < 1$$

$$\Rightarrow \sum_{(i_1,\ldots,i_l,j)\in\mathcal{I}_+} -\alpha\sum_{k=1}^{l}\min(i_k,\lfloor\frac{j}{2}\rfloor)+(\alpha+\beta-2)\sum_{t=1}^{l}i_t+0.5j \qquad <0. \tag{16}$$

Let $\dot{\sum}$ denotes the sum $\sum_{i_1=0}^{m}\cdots\sum_{i_l=0}^{m}$, $\bar{i}$ denotes the sum $\sum_{k=1}^{l}i_k$.
For any $l,m\in\mathbb{N}$ and $1\le a\le b\le l$, the following formulas hold:

$$\dot{\sum} i_a i_b = \begin{cases} m^{l-1}\dfrac{m(m+1)(2m+1)}{6} & = \dfrac{m^{l+2}}{3}+o(m^{l+2}) \quad (a=b),\\ m^{l-2}\dfrac{m^2(m+1)^2}{4} & = \dfrac{m^{l+2}}{4}+o(m^{l+2}) \quad (a\ne b).\end{cases}$$

Then,

$$\dot{\sum}\bar{i}^2=(\frac{l^2}{4}+\frac{l}{12})m^{l+2}+o(m^{l+2}).$$

Thus,

$$\sum_{(i_1,\ldots,i_l,j)\in\mathcal{I}_+} j=\dot{\sum}\sum_{j=0}^{l+2\bar{i}}j=\dot{\sum}(2\bar{i}^2+o(m))=(\frac{l^2}{2}+\frac{l}{6})m^{l+2}+o(m^{l+2}),$$

$$\sum_{(i_1,\ldots,i_l,j)\in\mathcal{I}_+} \bar{i}=\dot{\sum}\sum_{j=0}^{l+2\bar{i}}\bar{i}=\dot{\sum}(2\bar{i}^2+o(m))=(\frac{l^2}{2}+\frac{l}{6})m^{l+2}+o(m^{l+2}),$$

$$\begin{aligned}\sum_{(i_1,\ldots,i_l,j)\in\mathcal{I}_+}\sum_{k=1}^{l}\min(i_k,\lfloor\frac{j}{2}\rfloor)&=l\sum_{(i_1,\ldots,i_l,j)\in\mathcal{I}_+}\min(i_1,\lfloor\frac{j}{2}\rfloor)=l\dot{\sum}\sum_{j=0}^{l+2\bar{i}}\min(i_1,\lfloor\frac{j}{2}\rfloor)\\&=l\dot{\sum}(\sum_{j=0}^{2i_1}\lfloor\frac{j}{2}\rfloor+\sum_{j=2i_1+1}^{l+2\bar{i}}i_1)=l\dot{\sum}(i_1(i_1+1)+i_1(l+2\sum_{t=2}^{l}i_t))\\&=(\frac{l^2}{2}-\frac{l}{6})m^{l+2}+o(m^{l+2}).\end{aligned}$$

Now, just substitute the above results into the left-hand side of Eq. (16), we get

$$-\alpha(\frac{l^2}{2}-\frac{l}{6})m^{l+2}+(\alpha+\beta-2)(\frac{l^2}{2}+\frac{l}{6})m^{l+2}+(\frac{l^2}{4}+\frac{l}{12})m^{l+2}+o(m^{l+2})<0.$$

When m is sufficient large, we may omit the term $o(m^{l+2})$, which yields the new condition in Eq. (5)

Appendix B: Details of the Computation of Eq. (10)

First, we can rewrite the condition in Eq. (1) as

$$X^{n_X}Y^{n_Y}Z^{n_Z}<W^{n_W}. \tag{17}$$

We can compute the value of $\omega, n_X, n_Y, n_Z, n_W$ as follows:

$$\omega = |\mathcal{G}| + |\mathcal{H}| = \sum_{\substack{(i,j,k):\\ g_{i,j,k}\in\mathcal{G}}} 1 + \sum_{\substack{(i,j,k):\\ h_{i,j,k}\in\mathcal{H}}} 1 = \frac{3\tau+2}{6}m^3 + o(m^3)$$

$$n_X = \sum_{\substack{(i,j,k):\\ g_{i,j,k}\in\mathcal{G}}} (m-1) + \sum_{\substack{(i,j,k):\\ h_{i,j,k}\in\mathcal{H}}} (m-1+i) - (m-1)\omega = \sum_{\substack{(i,j,k):\\ h_{i,j,k}\in\mathcal{H}}} i = \frac{3\tau+2}{6}m^3 + o(m^3)$$

$$n_Y = \sum_{\substack{(i,j,k):\\ g_{i,j,k}\in\mathcal{G}}} (m-1) + \sum_{\substack{(i,j,k):\\ h_{i,j,k}\in\mathcal{H}}} (m-1+j) - (m-1)\omega = \sum_{\substack{(i,j,k):\\ h_{i,j,k}\in\mathcal{H}}} j = \frac{3\tau+4}{6}m^3 + o(m^3)$$

$$\begin{aligned} n_Z &= \sum_{\substack{(i,j,k):\\ g_{i,j,k}\in\mathcal{G}}} (2(m-1)+\tau m) + \sum_{\substack{(i,j,k):\\ h_{i,j,k}\in\mathcal{H}}} (2(m-1)+\tau m+k) - (2(m-1)+\tau m)\omega \\ &= \sum_{\substack{(i,j,k):\\ h_{i,j,k}\in\mathcal{H}}} k = \frac{3\tau^2+6\tau+4}{6}m^3 + o(m^3) \end{aligned}$$

$$n_W = \omega - \sum_{\substack{(i,j,k):\\ h_{i,j,k}\in\mathcal{H}}} 1 = \frac{3\tau+2}{6}m^3 + o(m^3)$$

Substitute the above results and $X = N^{\beta-\delta}, Y = N^{\alpha+\beta-2}, Z = N^{0.5}, W = N^{\alpha+\beta}$ into Eq. (17), then take the exponents part, we can obtain

$$\begin{aligned} &(\beta-\delta)(\frac{3\tau+2}{6}m^3 + o(m^3)) + (\alpha+\beta-2)(\frac{3\tau+4}{6}m^3 + o(m^3)) \\ &\quad + 0.5(\frac{3\tau^2+6\tau+4}{6}m^3 + o(m^3)) < (\alpha+\beta)(\frac{3\tau+2}{6}m^3 + o(m^3)). \end{aligned}$$

When m is sufficient large, we may omit the term $o(m^3)$, and get the new condition in Eq. (10).

References

1. Aono, Y.: Minkowski sum based lattice construction for multivariate simultaneous Coppersmith's technique and applications to RSA. In: Boyd, C., Simpson, L. (eds.) ACISP 2013. LNCS, vol. 7959, pp. 88–103. Springer, Heidelberg (2013). https://doi.org/10.1007/978-3-642-39059-3_7
2. Blömer, J., May, A.: Low secret exponent RSA revisited. In: Silverman, J.H. (ed.) CaLC 2001. LNCS, vol. 2146, pp. 4–19. Springer, Heidelberg (2001). https://doi.org/10.1007/3-540-44670-2_2
3. Blömer, J., May, A.: New partial key exposure attacks on RSA. In: Boneh, D. (eds) Advances in Cryptology - CRYPTO 2003. CRYPTO 2003. LNCS, vol. 2729, pp. 27–43. Springer, Heidelberg (2003). https://doi.org/10.1007/978-3-540-45146-4_2
4. Boneh, D., Durfee, G.: Cryptanalysis of RSA with private key d less than $N^{0.292}$. IEEE Trans. Inform. Theory **46**(4), 1339–1349 (2000)

5. Boneh, D., Durfee, G., Frankel, Y.: An attack on RSA given a small fraction of the private key bits. In: Ohta, K., Pei, D. (eds.) ASIACRYPT 1998. LNCS, vol. 1514, pp. 25–34. Springer, Heidelberg (1998). https://doi.org/10.1007/3-540-49649-1_3
6. Bunder, M., Nitaj, A., Susilo, W., Tonien, J.: A new attack on three variants of the RSA cryptosystem. In: Liu, J.K., Steinfeld, R. (eds.) ACISP 2016. LNCS, vol. 9723, pp. 258–268. Springer, Cham (2016). https://doi.org/10.1007/978-3-319-40367-0_16
7. Castagnos, G.: An efficient probabilistic public-key cryptosystem over quadratic fields quotients. Finite Fields Their Appl. **13**(3), 563–576 (2007)
8. Cherkaoui-Semmouni, M., Nitaj, A., Susilo, W., Tonien, J.: Cryptanalysis of RSA variants with primes sharing most significant bits. In: Liu, J.K., Katsikas, S., Meng, W., Susilo, W., Intan, R. (eds.) ISC 2021. LNCS, vol. 13118, pp. 42–53. Springer, Cham (2021). https://doi.org/10.1007/978-3-030-91356-4_3
9. Coppersmith, D.: Small solutions to polynomial equations, and low exponent RSA vulnerabilities. J. Cryptol. **10**(4), 233–260 (1997). https://doi.org/10.1007/s001459900030
10. De Weger, B.: Cryptanalysis of RSA with small prime difference. Appl. Algebra Eng. Commun. Comput. **13**(1), 17–28 (2002)
11. Elkamchouchi, H., Elshenawy, K., Shaban, H.: Extended RSA cryptosystem and digital signature schemes in the domain of Gaussian integers. In: The 8th International Conference on Communication Systems (2002). ICCS 2002, vol. 1, pp. 91–95. IEEE (2002)
12. Ernst, M., Jochemsz, E., May, A., de Weger, B.: Partial key exposure attacks on RSA up to full size exponents. In: Cramer, R. (ed.) EUROCRYPT 2005. LNCS, vol. 3494, pp. 371–386. Springer, Heidelberg (2005). https://doi.org/10.1007/11426639_22
13. Hastad, J.: N using RSA with low exponent in a public key network. In: Williams, H.C. (ed.) CRYPTO 1985. LNCS, vol. 218, pp. 403–408. Springer, Heidelberg (1986). https://doi.org/10.1007/3-540-39799-X_29
14. Herrmann, M., May, A.: Maximizing small root bounds by linearization and applications to small secret exponent RSA. In: Nguyen, P.Q., Pointcheval, D. (eds.) PKC 2010. LNCS, vol. 6056, pp. 53–69. Springer, Heidelberg (2010). https://doi.org/10.1007/978-3-642-13013-7_4
15. Howgrave-Graham, N.: Finding small roots of univariate modular equations revisited. In: Darnell, M. (ed.) Cryptography and Coding 1997. LNCS, vol. 1355, pp. 131–142. Springer, Heidelberg (1997). https://doi.org/10.1007/BFb0024458
16. Howgrave-Graham, N., Seifert, J.-P.: Extending Wiener's attack in the presence of many decrypting exponents. In: CQRE 1999. LNCS, vol. 1740, pp. 153–166. Springer, Heidelberg (1999). https://doi.org/10.1007/3-540-46701-7_14
17. Jochemsz, E., May, A.: A strategy for finding roots of multivariate polynomials with new applications in attacking RSA variants. In: Lai, X., Chen, K. (eds.) ASIACRYPT 2006. LNCS, vol. 4284, pp. 267–282. Springer, Heidelberg (2006). https://doi.org/10.1007/11935230_18
18. Kuwakado, H., Koyama, K., Tsuruoka, Y.: A new RSA-type scheme based on singular cubic curves $y^2 \equiv x^3 + bx^2 (\bmod n)$. IEICE Trans. Fundam. Electron. Comput. Sci. **78**(1), 27–33 (1995)
19. Lenstra, A.K., Lenstra, H.W., Lovász, L.: Factoring polynomials with rational coefficients. Math. Ann. **261**, 515–534 (1982)
20. May, A.: New RSA vulnerabilities using lattice reduction methods. Ph.D. thesis, Citeseer (2003)

21. Murru, N., Saettone, F.M.: A novel RSA-like cryptosystem based on a generalization of the Rédei rational functions. In: Kaczorowski, J., Pieprzyk, J., Pomykała, J. (eds.) NuTMiC 2017. LNCS, vol. 10737, pp. 91–103. Springer, Cham (2018). https://doi.org/10.1007/978-3-319-76620-1_6
22. Nitaj, A., Ariffin, M.R.B.K., Adenan, N.N.H., Abu, N.A.: Classical attacks on a variant of the RSA cryptosystem. In: Longa, P., Ràfols, C. (eds.) LATINCRYPT 2021. LNCS, vol. 12912, pp. 151–167. Springer, Cham (2021). https://doi.org/10.1007/978-3-030-88238-9_8
23. Peng, L., Hu, L., Lu, Y., Wei, H.: An improved analysis on three variants of the RSA cryptosystem. In: Chen, K., Lin, D., Yung, M. (eds.) Inscrypt 2016. LNCS, vol. 10143, pp. 140–149. Springer, Cham (2017). https://doi.org/10.1007/978-3-319-54705-3_9
24. Rivest, R.L., Shamir, A., Adleman, L.: A method for obtaining digital signatures and public-key cryptosystems. Commun. ACM **21**(2), 120–126 (1978)
25. Sarkar, S., Maitra, S.: Cryptanalysis of RSA with more than one decryption exponent. Inf. Process. Lett. **110**(8–9), 336–340 (2010)
26. Susilo, W., Tonien, J.: A Wiener-type attack on an RSA-like cryptosystem constructed from cubic Pell equations. Theoret. Comput. Sci. **885**, 125–130 (2021)
27. Takayasu, A., Kunihiro, N.: Cryptanalysis of RSA with multiple small secret exponents. In: Susilo, W., Mu, Y. (eds.) ACISP 2014. LNCS, vol. 8544, pp. 176–191. Springer, Cham (2014). https://doi.org/10.1007/978-3-319-08344-5_12
28. Takayasu, A., Kunihiro, N.: Partial key exposure attacks on RSA: achieving the Boneh-Durfee bound. In: Joux, A., Youssef, A. (eds.) SAC 2014. LNCS, vol. 8781, pp. 345–362. Springer, Cham (2014). https://doi.org/10.1007/978-3-319-13051-4_21
29. The Sage Developers: SageMath, the Sage Mathematics Software System (Version 9.4) (2021). https://www.sagemath.org
30. Wiener, M.J.: Cryptanalysis of short RSA secret exponents. IEEE Trans. Inf. Theory **36**(3), 553–558 (1990)
31. Zheng, M., Kunihiro, N., Hu, H.: Cryptanalysis of RSA variants with modified Euler quotient. In: Joux, A., Nitaj, A., Rachidi, T. (eds.) AFRICACRYPT 2018. LNCS, vol. 10831, pp. 266–281. Springer, Cham (2018). https://doi.org/10.1007/978-3-319-89339-6_15
32. Zheng, M., Kunihiro, N., Yao, Y.: Cryptanalysis of the RSA variant based on cubic Pell equation. Theoret. Comput. Sci. **889**, 135–144 (2021)

The SAT-Based Automatic Searching and Experimental Verification for Differential Characteristics with Application to Midori64

Yingying Li and Qichun Wang(✉)

School of Computer and Electronic Information, Nanjing Normal University, Nanjing, China
yyli@nnu.edu.cn, qcwang@fudan.edu.cn

Abstract. In this paper, we show that it is inaccurate to apply the hypothesis of independent round keys to search for differential characteristics of a block cipher with a simple key schedule. Therefore, the derived differential characteristics may be valid. We develop a SAT-based algorithm to verify the validity of differential characteristics. Furthermore, we take the key schedule into account and thus put forward an algorithm to directly find the valid differential characteristics. All experiments are performed on Midori64 and we find some interesting results.

Keywords: Lightweight block cipher · Differential characteristic · SAT · Midori64 · Hypothesis of independent round keys

1 Introduction

Midori [2] presented at ASIACRYPT 2015 is a family of lightweight block ciphers with low energy consumption. The family is composed of two versions Midori64 and Midori128, which encrypt 64-bit and 128-bit plaintexts, respectively. Due to the small state space of Midori64, we focus on Midori64 in this paper.

The most critical step of differential cryptanalysis is to obtain the differential characteristics with high probability. In general, automatic search methods based on MILP and SAT/SMT are utilized to find them under the hypothesis of independent round keys [1,3,8]. However, for Midori64, its round keys are not independent because of its simple key schedule. Furthermore, there are no right pairs that follow the expected propagation of the differential characteristic [4]. That is, the differential characteristic is invalid.

This inspires us to develop an accurate SAT-based method for verifying the validity of the differential characteristics and encourages us to improve the existing algorithms for directly finding the valid differential characteristics. Our main contributions are listed in the following:

W. Susilo et al. (Eds.): ISC 2022, LNCS 13640, pp. 153–161, 2022.
https://doi.org/10.1007/978-3-031-22390-7_10

- Using the SAT-based method under the hypothesis of independent round keys, see Algorithm 1, we obtain the upper bounds on the probability of the best differential characteristics for full-round Midori64.
- We propose a SAT-based method to verify the validity of a differential characteristic, see Algorithm 2. For Midori64, we apply this method to test whether the differential characteristics obtained by Algorithm 1 are valid.
- In knowing the upper bounds on the probability of the best differential characteristics, we take the key schedule into account and thus put forward an algorithm to directly search for valid characteristics of a block cipher, see Algorithm 3. As a result, we improve some previous results.

The rest of this paper is organized as follows. In Sect. 2, we give a brief description of Midori64. In Sect. 3, the SAT-based method under the hypothesis of independent round keys is used for Midori64. In Sect. 4, we present an accurate SAT-based algorithm to verify the validity of differential characteristics. In Sect. 5, we give the algorithm directly finding the valid differential characteristics with application to Midori64. In Sect. 6, we conclude this paper.

2 A Brief Description of Midori64

Midori64 has a SPN structure, whose state size is 64 bits, key size is 128 bits and round number R is 16.

Each round function of Midori64 is composed of the following four operations. SubCell (SC) is the only nonlinear operation where 16 4-bit S-boxes are applied to each nibble of the state in parallel. ShuffleCell (SFC) applies a nibble-wise permutation to the state. MixColumn (MC) performs a linear transformation on each 4-nibble column of the state. KeyAdd (KA) uses a XOR operation, which bitwise XORs the i-th 64-bit round key RK_i to each bit of the state.

The data encryption process of Midori64 is as follows: Firstly, using KA, a 64-bit whitening key WK is XORed to each bit of the state. Then, the round function is performed $R-1$ times. Finally, SC is executed, and again KA using WK is carried out.

The key schedule of Midori64 is relatively simple and uses a 128-bit master key K that is composed of two 64-bit keys K_0 and K_1: $K = K_0||K_1$. The whitening key WK is computed as $WK = K_0 \oplus K_1$ and the round key is $RK_i = K_{i \bmod 2} \oplus \alpha_i$, $0 \leq i \leq 14$, where α_i is the round constant. More details about Midori64 are depicted in design documentation [2].

3 The Method Proposed by Sun et al. with Application to Midori64

In this section, we apply the SAT-based method proposed by Sun et al. to find the upper bounds on the probability of the best differential characteristics for full-round Midori64. We use the SAT solver called Cryptominisat [6] to do our work. It accepts CNF (Conjunctive Normal Form) files as the standard input, which is equivalent to the product-of-sum representation of Boolean functions.

In the following, we give a general framework of the SAT-based method proposed by Sun et al. [8], see Algorithm 1. However, we emphasize that this approach is based on the hypothesis of independent round keys. If this hypothesis of a block cipher is weak, the derived differential characteristics may be invalid. Thus, the probability of the best differential characteristics is only the upper bound. It depends on whether the derived characteristics are valid. If valid, the bound is tight; otherwise, is not tight.

Algorithm 1. The SAT-based search algorithm under the hypothesis of independent round keys

```
Require: the total round R
Ensure: the upper bounds bound on the best probability for a R-round primitive
 1: bound ← list([0,0,···])                          ▷ store R-round information
 2: result ← - 1                                ▷ the weight of the best probability
 3: for r ← 0 to R − 1 do
 4:     flag ← false
 5:     while flag is false do
 6:         result ← result + 1
 7:         model1 ← ()
 8:         model1 ← BuildModel1(r, model1, result,bound)
 9:         Flag ← the result obtained by solving the model1
10:         if Flag is "SAT" then
11:             flag ← true
12:         end if
13:     end while
14:     bound[r] ← result
15: end for
16: return bound
17:
18: function BuildModel1(r, model1, result, bound)
19:     for i ← 0 to r - 1 do
20:         model1 += the differential propagation rules for the i-th round primitive
21:     end for
22:     model1 += the model of objective function about the weight result
23:     model1 += the model of Matsui's bounding conditions created with bound
24:     return model1
25: end function
```

In lines 7–9 of Algorithm 1, the process of searching with the SAT solver can be summarized as follows: Firstly, the search problem is expressed as a set of CNF clauses, and thus the SAT model is established. Then, the model is solved by the solver. Finally, if there is a solution, then the solver returns “SAT” and a solution is extracted; otherwise, returns “UNSAT”.

For different block ciphers, BUILDMODEL1() is the only different part. To apply Algorithm 1 to Midori64, we need to establish the differential propagation models for all the operations that include XOR, S-box, SFC, and MC.

For bitwise XOR operation $\alpha_0 \oplus \alpha_1 \oplus \cdots \oplus \alpha_{n-1} = \beta$, we define a $(n+1)$-bit Boolean function $f(\alpha_0||\alpha_1||\cdots||\alpha_{n-1}||\beta)$ as

$$f(\alpha_0||\alpha_1||\cdots||\alpha_{n-1}||\beta) = \begin{cases} 1, \; if \; \alpha_0 \oplus \alpha_1 \oplus \cdots \oplus \alpha_{n-1} = \beta \\ 0, \; else \end{cases}.$$

For 4-bit S-box operation, let $x \in F_2^4$ and $y \in F_2^4$ be the input and output differences of differential distribution table (DDT) of S-box, respectively. And p is the probability of a differential propagation in the DDT. We introduce 3 extra binary variables w_0, w_1, w_2 to encode the weight of probability, as follows:

$$w = (w_0, w_1, w_2) = \begin{cases} (0,0,0), \; if \; p = 2^{-0} \\ (0,1,1), \; if \; p = 2^{-2} \\ (1,1,1), \; if \; p = 2^{-3} \end{cases}.$$

We define a 11-bit Boolean function $f(x||y||w)$ as

$$f(x||y||w) = \begin{cases} 1, \; if \; x \rightarrow y \; is \; a \; possible \; propagation \; with - log_2 \, p = \sum_{k=0}^{2} w_k \\ 0, \; else \end{cases}.$$

For SFC operation, we only need to change the positions of bits, which indicates that the extra CNF clauses are not required.

For MC operation, we can find its primitive representation [7]. Thus, the 4×4 involutive matrix over field F_2^4 can be converted to a 16×16 binary matrix. And the MC operation is converted to 64 XOR operations.

Use the software Logic Friday [5] to obtain the minimum product-of-sum representations of all operations and thus generate a set of smaller CNF clauses.

Our goal is the r-round upper bounds of probability. Express the extra variable of the j-th S-box in the i-th round as $w_k^{(i,j)}$, where $0 \le i \le r-1$, $0 \le j \le 15$, and $0 \le k \le 2$. Thus, the objective function is expressed as $\sum_{i=0}^{r-1} \sum_{j=0}^{15} \sum_{k=0}^{2} w_k^{(i,j)}$. It can be abstracted as the Boolean cardinality constraint $\sum_{i=0}^{n-1} x_i \le z$, where z is a non-negative integer. This requires the solver to find such a differential characteristic that the weight of differential probability is less than or equal to z. For more information about the modeling of this constraint, see [8].

Matsui's bounding conditions are encoded to the SAT model for accelerating the search. These conditions take full advantage of the fact that the upper bounds on the probability of short characteristics are known. Similarly, for more information about the modeling of those conditions, see [8].

Thus, the involved SAT model has been completed. Using Algorithm 1, we find the upper bounds on the probability of the best differential characteristics for full-round Midori64, as shown in Table 1. It more accurately evaluates the

Table 1. The weight of the upper bounds on the probability of the best differential characteristics for full-round Midori64.

Round	1	2	3	4	5	6	7	8	9	10	11	12	13	14	15
$-log_2\ p$	2	8	14	32	46	60	70	76	82	100	114	124	134	144	150

security of Midori64 against single-key differential cryptanalysis, which is roughly estimated by the low bounds on the number of differential active S-boxes in the design document of Midori64 [2]. Notice the fact that the block size for Midori64 is 64 bits. From Table 1, 7-round Midori64 is sufficient to resist single-key differential cryptanalysis, because $2^{-70} \leq 2^{-64} \leq 2^{-60}$.

4 Verifying the Validity of Differential Characteristics Based on SAT

In this section, we show that the derived differential characteristics under the hypothesis of independent round keys may be invalid because round keys of Midori64 are not independent. As the work in [4], we only focus on whether a differential characteristic is valid and ignore the value of its non-zero probability. If the characteristic Q with non-zero probability is invalid, the work based on Q cannot reflect the security of a block cipher against differential cryptanalysis.

Therefore, we present an accurate SAT-based algorithm to verify the validity of a differential characteristic, see Algorithm 2. It encrypts separately a pair of plaintexts with a key for the primitive and thus it can be used to check whether the XOR value of two plaintexts in each round satisfies the difference value in each round. If the SAT model has a solution, then a valid key and the corresponding right pairs following the differential characteristic are output; otherwise, the differential characteristic will be invalid, which also indicates that there are no valid keys that follow the propagation of Q.

Next, we give a specific description of BUILDMODEL2() for Midori64. We need to establish the value propagation models for all operations. Then, according to the structure of the block cipher, the model of each operation is connected to establish the r-round propagation model of a pair of plaintexts. XOR, SFC, and MC of all operations are linear and can be modeled similarly to the corresponding differential propagations in Sect. 3. Here, we introduce the SAT model for the value propagations of the non-linear operation S-box.

For 4-bit S-box operation $y = S(x)$, where $x \in F_2^4$ and $y \in F_2^4$ are the input and the output values of S-box, respectively. We define a 8-bit Boolean function $f(x||y)$ as

$$f(x||y) = \begin{cases} 1, & if\ x \rightarrow y\ is\ a\ possible\ propagation\ with\ y = S(x) \\ 0, & else \end{cases}.$$

Similarly, use Logic Friday to generate a set of smaller CNF clauses. So far, the SAT model of each operation of Midori64 has been completed. Thus, we can use Algorithm 2 to verify some of the characteristics obtained by Algorithm 1.

Algorithm 2. The SAT-based algorithm to verify the validity of a differential characteristic

Require: a r-round differential characteristic Q
Ensure: The validity of Q

$model2 \leftarrow ()$
$model2 \leftarrow$ BUILDMODEL2(r, $model2$)
$Flag \leftarrow$ the result obtained by solving the $model2$
if $Flag$ is "SAT" **then**
  $solution \leftarrow$ a valid key and corresponding right pairs following characteristic Q
  return ["SAT", $solution$] ▷ Q is valid
else
  return "UNSAT" ▷ Q is invalid
end if

function BUILDMODEL2(r, $model2$)
  for $i \leftarrow 0$ to r - 1 **do**
    $model2$ += the constraint rules of characteristic Q on intermediate states of a pair of plaintexts in the i-th round
    $model2$ += the value propagation rules of the encryption part for a pair of plaintexts in the i-th round
    $model2$ += the value propagation rules of the key schedule part for a pair of plaintexts in the i-th round
    $model2$ += the rules of linking both parts via the round key k_i
  end for
  return $model2$
end function

We modified Algorithm 1 to output multiple differential characteristics of r-round Midori64, where $1 \leq r \leq 6$. Usually, the solver only outputs one solution. To find multiple solutions, we utilize its incremental property, which allows the solver to record the current information. After the solver outputs a solution, an additional CNF clause is added to the SAT model to prohibit this solution. Then, the solver is asked to give a solution again, and so on, until the solver returns "UNSAT". Specifically, for a n-bit variable $(x_0, x_1, \cdots, x_{n-1})$ with its specific solution $(k_0, k_1, \cdots, k_{n-1})$, the CNF clause $\bigvee_{i=0}^{n-1} (x_i \oplus k_i) = 1$ is appended.

We apply Algorithm 2 to verify the validity of these differential characteristics. The results show that some of them are valid, which indicates that the upper bounds of $1 \leq r \leq 6$ rounds obtained by Algorithm 1 are tight. However, some of them are invalid, which also indicates that the hypothesis of independent round keys is inaccurate for Midori64.

Such experimental results remind us that we can use this hypothesis to roughly assess the resistance of a block cipher against differential cryptanalysis. However, when we want to obtain specific differential characteristics for differential attacks, we should pay attention to the validity of characteristics.

5 Our New Algorithm for Finding Valid Differential Characteristics

The first two sections explain that the derived differential characteristics under the hypothesis of independent round keys may be invalid. In the following, we build a SAT model that involves both the differential and value propagations of a primitive to directly search for valid differential characteristics.

In knowing the upper bounds on the best probability of the r-round primitive, we take the key schedule into account and thus propose an improved search method for directly finding a valid characteristic, see Algorithm 3.

Algorithm 3. The improved SAT-based search algorithm for directly finding a valid r-round characteristic

Require: the target round r
Ensure: a valid r-round differential characteristic

```
 1: bound ← list(R)   ▷ store the known upper bounds on the probability of R rounds
 2: result ← bound[r]                   ▷ the weight of the best r-round probability
 3: MAX_WEIGHT ← 10000
 4: while result < MAX_WEIGHT do
 5:     model3 ← ()
 6:     model3 ← BuildModel3(model3, result, bound)
 7:     Flag ← the result obtained by solving the model3
 8:     if Flag is "SAT" then
 9:         solution ← a valid r-round characteristic
10:         return ["SAT", solution]
11:     end if
12:     result ← result + 1
13: end while
14:
15: function BuildModel3(model3, result, bound)
16:     BuildModel1(r, model3, result, bound)       ▷ the differential propagations
17:     BuildModel2(r, model3)                          ▷ the value propagations
18:     return model3
19: end function
```

To improve efficiency of the search, we use the upper bounds obtained by Algorithm 1 to avoid the search in the probability space for which no characteristics exist, as shown in the 1-th row of Algorithm 3. The BUILDMODEL3() part not only searches for a characteristic but also verifies its validity. Similarly, incremental property of the solver can be used to obtain multiple valid characteristics.

The greater probability of two 5-round characteristics was 2^{-52} in [9]. Using our Algorithm 3, we search for the best valid differential characteristics of Midori64. We find some 5-round characteristics with probability 2^{-46}, which increases a factor of 2^6 than the probability 2^{-52}. Furthermore, we also find some 6-round characteristics with probability 2^{-60}, which means that we may attack Midori64 with one more round than the result of [9].

These multiple valid characteristics may be used to launch better differential attacks than the existing ones. And for Midori64, the fewer active nibbles of the input and output differences of a characteristic, the more conducive to a differential key recovery attack. Note that we did not consider this factor when searching for characteristics. Thus, we can continue the study of selecting advantageous ones among these multiple valid characteristics.

6 Conclusion and Future Work

In this paper, we show by experimentation that the derived characteristics for Midori64 under the hypothesis of independent round keys may be invalid. Furthermore, we propose a new algorithm to directly search for valid characteristics. Using it, we obtain some better valid characteristics, which may improve the complexity of existing key recovery attacks of Midori64.

In the future, on the one hand, we can search for advantageous characteristics to perform better differential key recovery attacks on Midori64. On the other hand, we need to be careful in presuming that the hypothesis of independent round keys applies to a block cipher.

Acknowledgement. We would like to thank the anonymous reviewers for their helpful comments. This work was supported by National Natural Science Foundation of China (No. 62172230), National Natural Science Foundation of Jiangsu Province (No. BK20201369) and Open Research Program of Shanghai Key Lab of Intelligent Information Processing (No. IIPL201901).

References

1. Ankele, R., Kölbl, S.: Mind the gap - a closer look at the security of block ciphers against differential cryptanalysis. In: Cid, C., Jacobson, M.J., Jr. (eds.) SAC 2018. LNCS, vol. 11349, pp. 163–190. Springer, Cham (2019). https://doi.org/10.1007/978-3-030-10970-7_8
2. Banik, S., et al.: Midori: a block cipher for low energy. In: Iwata, T., Cheon, J.H. (eds.) ASIACRYPT 2015. LNCS, vol. 9453, pp. 411–436. Springer, Heidelberg (2015). https://doi.org/10.1007/978-3-662-48800-3_17
3. Lai, X., Massey, J.L., Murphy, S.: Markov ciphers and differential cryptanalysis. In: Davies, D.W. (ed.) EUROCRYPT 1991. LNCS, vol. 547, pp. 17–38. Springer, Heidelberg (1991). https://doi.org/10.1007/3-540-46416-6_2
4. Liu, Y., et al.: The phantom of differential characteristics. Des. Codes Crypt. **88**(11), 2289–2311 (2020). https://doi.org/10.1007/s10623-020-00782-3
5. Rickmann, S.: Logic Friday (version 1.1. 3) [computer software] (2011)
6. Soos, M.: Cryptominisat SAT solver (2009). https://github.com/msoos/cryptominisat
7. Sun, B., Liu, Z., Rijmen, V., Li, R., Cheng, L., Wang, Q., Alkhzaimi, H., Li, C.: Links among impossible differential, integral and zero correlation linear cryptanalysis. In: Gennaro, R., Robshaw, M. (eds.) CRYPTO 2015. LNCS, vol. 9215, pp. 95–115. Springer, Heidelberg (2015). https://doi.org/10.1007/978-3-662-47989-6_5

8. Sun, L., Wang, W., Wang, M.: Accelerating the search of differential and linear characteristics with the SAT method. IACR Trans. Symmetric Cryptol. **2021**(1), 269–315 (2021)
9. Zhao, H., Han, G., Wang, L., Wang, W.: MILP-based differential cryptanalysis on round-reduced Midori64. IEEE Access **8**, 95888–95896 (2020). https://doi.org/10.1109/ACCESS.2020.2995795

Efficient Scalar Multiplication on Koblitz Curves with Pre-computation

Xiuxiu Li[1,2,3], Wei Yu[1,2,3](✉), and Kunpeng Wang[1,3]

[1] State Key Laboratory of Information Security, Institute of Information Engineering, CAS, Beijing, China

[2] State Key Laboratory of Cryptology, P. O. Box 5159, Beijing 100878, China

[3] School of Cyberspace Security, University of Chinese Academy of Sciences, Beijing, China

yuwei@iie.ac.cn,yuwei_1_yw@163.com

Abstract. Scalar multiplication is the basic operation in elliptic curve cryptography. The double-base number system (DBNS) is an effective tool for speeding up scalar multiplication on elliptic curves. This paper proposes a novel decomposition algorithm for scalar n based on the specific double bases $(\overline{\tau}, \tau)$ instead of the ordinary window τ-NAF. On μ_4-Koblitz curves, we evaluate the cost of our scalar multiplication method and compare it to related work. We also consider scalar multiplication using LD coordinates. Experiment results show that μ_4-Koblitz curves perform well.

Keywords: Elliptic curve cryptography · Scalar multiplication · Koblitz curves · Double-base number system · Width-ω τ-NAF

1 Introduction

Elliptic curve cryptography (ECC) is an asymmetric cryptographic algorithm based on the hardness of the elliptic curve discrete logarithm problem. The most expensive part of the elliptic curve cryptography is computing the scalar multiplication nP that can be evaluated as a Horner scheme, where n is a non-negative integer and P is a point on the elliptic curve.

Generally, there are two ways to speed up scalar multiplication algorithms: either reducing the complexity of curve operations or designing decomposition algorithms with lower density for scalar n. This work selects the Koblitz curve E_a [12] for the former case because it has more efficient curve operations. For the latter case, we design a double-base decomposition algorithm for n that requires fewer point additions by invoking the width-ω τ-NAF.

Koblitz curves defined over $\mathbb{F}_{2^m}$ are an essential family of elliptic curves to optimize the scalar multiplication algorithm. The computational advantage of

Supported by the National Natural Science Foundation of China (No. 62272453, U1936209, 61872442, and 61502487).

W. Susilo et al. (Eds.): ISC 2022, LNCS 13640, pp. 162–172, 2022.
https://doi.org/10.1007/978-3-031-22390-7_11

Koblitz curves is that replacing the point doubling with the Frobenius endomorphism τ enables faster scalar multiplication. The set of all endomorphism τ on E_a is the Euclidean domain $\mathbb{Z}[\tau] = \mathbb{Z} + \tau\mathbb{Z}$. To compare the cost of the different curve operations and scalar multiplication algorithms, let **M** denote the cost of a multiplication and **S** denote the cost of a squaring in $\mathbb{F}_{2^m}$.

In 1998, Dimitrov et al. [10] first introduced double bases in elliptic curve cryptography. Later, many works have improved and applied DBNS [2,9,11,20] to speed up scalar multiplications. In 2006, Avanzil et al. [3] gave an efficient DBNS$(\overline{\tau}, \tau)$ recoding algorithm for integer n in López-Dahab (LD) coordinates, where $\overline{\tau}$ is the complex conjugate of τ. The fly in the ointment is that the cost for evaluating $\overline{\tau}$ is expensive with $4\mathbf{M} + 4\mathbf{S}$. Later, Doche et al. [11] presented a new way to compute $\overline{\tau}(P)$ in LD coordinates with $2\mathbf{M} + \mathbf{S}$ when $a = 1$ and $2\mathbf{M} + 2\mathbf{S}$ when $a = 0$.

Various techniques have been proposed using memory and pre-computation to speed up scalar multiplication. For window τ-NAF with width ω, one needs to store $2^{\omega-2} - 1$ pre-computed points in memory. Blake and Murty et al. [7] established a framework to make the pre-computation of window τ-NAF more flexible. In their follow-up work [8], authors studied the fast scalar multiplication by performing basis-τ expansions for integers. Recently, Yu et al. [21] proposed $\mu\overline{\tau}$-operations and applied them to the pre-computation scheme to speed up scalar multiplication. In addition, Aranha et al. [1] give a faster implementation of scalar multiplication on Koblitz curves by using the $\tau^{\lfloor m/3 \rfloor}$ and $\tau^{\lfloor m/4 \rfloor}$ maps to create analogs of the 3-and 4-dimensional GLV decompositions.

Our Contributions. This paper investigates the efficiency of scalar multiplication on Koblitz curves over F_{2^m} using DBNS$(\overline{\tau}, \tau)$ expansion. The main contributions are described as follows.

1. We propose a new double-base decomposition algorithm for an integer n. Considering the high efficiency of τ-operation and $\overline{\tau}$-operation on the Koblitz curve, we present the scalar multiplication using DBNS$(\overline{\tau}, \tau)$ expansion.
2. We give the cost of scalar multiplication on different curves. We consider two coordinate systems denoted by μ_4-Koblitz curves [14] and LD coordinates [17]. Meanwhile, we compare the scalar multiplication cost on four Koblitz curves recommended by NIST [4,5,18] K-233, K-283, K-409, and K-571 with $a = 0$. We also analyze the cost on Koblitz curves with $a = 1$ denoted by: K1-163, K1-283, K1-359, and K1-701.

The rest of this paper is organized as follows. Section 2 discusses the notation and basics behind the elliptic curve scalar multiplication. We present the theoretical basis and double-base recoding algorithm in Sect. 3. The cost of scalar multiplications in different cases is analyzed in Sect. 4. Finally, we conclude the paper in Sect. 5.

2 Preliminary

This section includes the definitions of DBNS and Koblitz curves and some technical preparation.

2.1 Double Bases

Following [9], an integer can be represented as $A^{s_i}B^{t_i}$ with (A, B) as a suitable integer pair, and s_i, t_i are nonnegative integers. This research uses a more general definition. Precisely, $A, B \in \mathbb{Z}[\tau]$ are algebraic integers. The DBNS(A, B) expansion of an integer n as shown below:

$$n = \sum_{i=0}^{k-1} (-1)^{e_i} A^{s_i} B^{t_i}, \quad \text{where } e_i \in \{0, 1\}.$$

2.2 Koblitz Curves

In [12], Koblitz introduced a new normal form for elliptic curves called Koblitz curves, which benefit from fast curve operations. The Koblitz curve E_a defined over $\mathbb{F}_{2^m}$ is given as

$$y^2 + xy = x^3 + ax^2 + 1 \tag{1}$$

with $a \in \{0, 1\}$. $E_a(\mathbb{F}_{2^m})$ is the rational point group. For cryptographic security, the order $\#E_a(\mathbb{F}_{2^m})$ should be a prime or the product of a prime and small integer. There exists an equation $\#E_a(\mathbb{F}_{2^m}) = \#E_a(\mathbb{F}_2) \cdot p$ due to $E_a(\mathbb{F}_2)$ is a subgroup of $E_a(\mathbb{F}_{2^m})$, where $\#E_a(\mathbb{F}_2) = 2$ if $a = 1$ (resp. $\#E_a(\mathbb{F}_2) = 4$ if $a = 0$). This article only considers p as a prime.

The definition of a Frobenius map τ is $\tau(x, y) = (x^2, y^2)$. Let $\mathcal{O}$ denotes the point at infinity, there exists $\tau(\mathcal{O}) = \mathcal{O}$. Let $\mu = (-1)^{1-a}$, there is an equation

$$\tau^2(P) + 2P = \mu\tau(P),$$

that is true for every point P in $E_a(\mathbb{F}_{2^m})$. τ's complex conjugate is $\overline{\tau} = \mu - \tau$.

The main subgroup of $E_a(\mathbb{F}_{2^m})$ is M. For every point $P \in M$, there exists a $\delta = \frac{\tau^m - 1}{\tau - 1}$ that satisfies $\delta(P) = \mathcal{O}$. The norm function N defined as $N(n_0 + n_1\tau) = n_0^2 + \mu n_0 n_1 + 2n_1^2$ satisfies $N(\delta) = p$. It implies that $\rho P = nP$ if $\rho \equiv n \pmod{\delta}$.

2.3 The Width-ω τ-NAF

The τ-NAF of an integer n can be expressed as $n = \sum_{i=0}^{k-1} \epsilon_i \tau^i$ where $\epsilon_i \in \{0, \pm 1\}$ with the *non-adjacency* property $\epsilon_j \epsilon_{j+1} = 0$. The average Hamming weight among length-k τ-NAF is $k/3$, and such a representation is unique.

In [12], Koblitz proposed an approach to calculate scalar multiplication nP, where n's representation using τ-NAF. Subsequently, Solinas [19] developed a high-efficiency window τ-NAF to accelerate scalar multiplication by reducing the nonzero terms. He gives a general signed version of width-ω τ-NAF coding on $E_a(\mathbb{F}_{2^m})$, which average has $\frac{m}{\omega+1}$ non-zero terms. Blake and Murty et al. [7,8] have obtained some refinements and extensions to Solinas' method.

2.4 Curve Operations' Costs on Koblitz Curves

The cost of scalar multiplication varies depending on the coordinate system. Table 1 summarizes the costs of curve operations in two coordinate systems: μ_4-Koblitz curve [14] and LD coordinates [17].

Table 1. Curve operations' costs on the Koblitz curves [21]

Coordinates	$\tau(P)$	τ-affine operation	Addition	Mixed addition
μ_4-Koblitz curve ($a = 0$) [13]	4**S**	3**S**	7**M** + 2**S**	6**M** + 2**S**
μ_4-Koblitz curve ($a = 1$) [14,16]	4**S**	3**S**	8**M** + 2**S**	7**M** + 2**S**
LD coordinates [15,17]	3**S**	2**S**	13**M** + 4**S**	8**M** + 5**S**

The μ_4-Koblitz curve is defined by

$$X_0^2 + X_2^2 = X_1X_3 + aX_0X_2,\ X_1^2 + X_3^2 = X_0X_2.$$

The identity is $(1 : 1 : 0 : 1)$, and the inverse morphism is $[-1](X_0 : X_1 : X_2 : X_3) = (X_0 : X_3 : X_2 : X_1)$. Frobenius map $\tau(X_0 : X_1 : X_2 : X_3) = (X_0^2 : X_1^2 : X_2^2 : X_3^2)$. On a μ_4-Koblitz curve, the cost of τ-operation is 4**S**, and the cost of τ-affine operation is 3**S**.

In 1998, López and Dahab [17] proposed the LD coordinates system, in which a τ-operation costs 3**S**, the cost of one mixed addition is 8**M** + 5**S**, and the cost of one addition is 13**M** + 4**S**. Table 2 gives the costs of $\mu\overline{\tau}(P)$ on the μ_4-Koblitz curve and LD coordinates.

Table 2. $\mu\overline{\tau}(P)$ costs on μ_4-Koblitz curves and LD coordinates.

	μ_4-Koblitz curves	LD coordinates ($a = 0/a = 1$)
$\mu\overline{\tau}(P)$	2**M** + 2**S**	2**M** + 2**S**/2**M** + **S**
$(\mu\overline{\tau})^i(P)$, $i \geq 2$	2**M** + 2**S**	2**M** + 2**S**/2**M** + **S**

3 DBNS Recoding and Scalar Multiplication

3.1 Theoretical Background

All the new results about DBNS($\overline{\tau}, \tau$) expansion are based on the following Lemma, which appears in $\mathbb{Z}[\tau]$.

Lemma 1. *Let* $\overline{\tau} \in \mathbb{Z}[\tau]$ *and* $\omega \geq 3$. *Then* $(\overline{\tau})^i \neq \pm(\overline{\tau})^j (mod\ 2^\omega)$ *with* $0 \leq i < j < 2^{\omega-2}$.

Proof. Suppose that $(\overline{\tau})^i \equiv \pm(\overline{\tau})^j (mod\ 2^\omega)$ with $0 \leq i < j < 2^{\omega-2}$. According to Corollary 1 in [3], which gives the order of $\overline{\tau}$ modulo τ^ω is $2^{\omega-2}$, we get that $i = j$. There is a contradiction. □

3.2 Our New Recoding Algorithms

Algorithm 1 provides a newly signed decompositions algorithm using τ and its complex conjugate $\overline{\tau}$ on E_a. This work proceeds from right to left and is not greedy.

Algorithm 1. Signed right-to-left DBNS($\overline{\tau}, \tau$)

Input: An integer $\rho \in \mathbb{Z}[\tau]$, a parameter ω.
Output: Three arrays $s[\,], t[\,], e[\,]$ and their common length k. The arrays are sequences of exponents in the decomposition $n = \sum_{i=0}^{k-1} (-1)^{e[i]}\, \overline{\tau}^{s[i]} \tau^{t[i]}$

1: $N \leftarrow \rho,\ i \leftarrow 0,\ t \leftarrow 0$
2: $t[\,] \leftarrow 0,\ s[\,] \leftarrow 0,\ e[\,] \leftarrow 0$
3: **while** $|N| \geq 2^{2^{\omega-3}}$ **do**
4:     **while** $\tau \mid N$ **do**
5:         $N \leftarrow N/\tau,\ t \leftarrow t+1$
6:     Find $0 \leq j < 2^{\omega-2}$ and $e = 0, 1$ with $N \equiv (-1)^e \overline{\tau}^j \pmod{\tau^\omega}$
7:     $N \leftarrow (N - (-1)^e \overline{\tau}^j)/\tau^\omega$
8:     $s[i] \leftarrow j,\ t[i] \leftarrow t,\ e[i] \leftarrow e$
9:     $t \leftarrow t + \omega,\ i \leftarrow i+1$
10: **while** $|N| > 0$ **do**
11:     **while** $\tau \mid N$ **do**
12:         $N \leftarrow N/\tau,\ t \leftarrow t+1$
13:     Find $0 \leq j < 4$ and $e = 0, 1$ with $N \equiv (-1)^e \overline{\tau}^j \pmod{\tau^4}$
14:     $N \leftarrow (N - (-1)^e \overline{\tau}^j)/\tau^4$
15:     $s[i] \leftarrow j,\ t[i] \leftarrow t,\ e[i] \leftarrow e$
16:     $t \leftarrow t + 4,\ i \leftarrow i+1$
17: **return** $s[\,], t[\,], e[\,], i$

According to Lemma 1, we can find j in Step 6. Besides, the termination of the algorithm is easily obtained. Since in Step 7, N is positive and becomes strictly smaller. As soon as entering Step 10, the algorithm performs the width-4 τ-NAF for the remainder. [7] has provided proof for the termination of the ordinary width-ω τ-NAF. Notice that if $|N| \geq 2^{2^{\omega-3}}$, then

$$|(-1)^e \overline{\tau}^j| \leq 2^{j/2} < 2^{2^{\omega-3}} \leq |N| \tag{2}$$

hence in Step 7

$$\left| \frac{N - (-1)^e \overline{\tau}^j}{\tau^\omega} \right| < \frac{2|N|}{|\tau^\omega|} = \frac{|N|}{|\tau^{\omega-2}|} < |N| \tag{3}$$

since $\omega \geq 3$. Because of $|N|^2 \in \mathbb{N}$, eventually $|N| < 2^{2^{\omega-3}}$. Here $\mathbb{N}$ is the norm of the algebraic integer N. Thus our algorithm is correct. All computations in Algorithm 1 are done for ρ, the modular reduction of n in the ring $\mathbb{Z}[\tau]$.

Then we discuss the Hamming weight of Algorithm 1 on Koblitz curves standardized by NIST. When ω is given, according to (3), the upper bound on the

---

Algorithm 2. Scalar Multiplication using DBNS($\overline{\tau}, \tau$) expansion

---

Input: A point P on the curve E_a and the arrays $e[\,], s[\,], t[\,]$ of length k such that $t[i+1] \geq t[i]$ and $s[i+1] > s[i]$ whenever $t[i+1] = t[i]$, the pre-computation points $P_h = (\mu\overline{\tau})^h P$ with $h \in \{0, 1, \cdots, 2^{\omega-2} - 1\}$.

Output: The point R on E_a such that $R = \sum_{i=0}^{k-1} (-1)^{e[i]} \overline{\tau}^{s[i]} \tau^{t[i]} P$

for all $i = 0$ to $k-1$ **do**
  Find $h \in \{0, 1, \cdots, 2^{\omega-2} - 1\}$ s.t. $s[i] = h$
  if $a = 1$ or $s[i]$ is even **then**
    $Q_i = P_h$
  else
    $Q_i = (-1)P_h$
$i \leftarrow k-1$
$t[-1] \leftarrow 0,$
$Q_{-1} \leftarrow \mathcal{O}$
$R \leftarrow (-1)^{e[i]} Q_i$
while $i \geq 0$ **do**
  $R \leftarrow \tau^{t[i]-t[i-1]} R + (-1)^{e[i-1]} Q_{i-1}$
  $i \leftarrow i - 1$
return R

---

number of iterations of the main loop is number c that satisfies $|\rho| = |\tau^{\omega-2}|^c = 2^{\frac{c}{2}(\omega-2)}$. It follows that

$$c = \frac{2\log_2|\rho|}{\omega - 2} = \frac{m}{\omega - 2}$$

is the expected Hamming weight. However, N's new value in (3) has an absolute value much closer to $|N|/|\tau^\omega|$ when N is large. Thus we should use a Hamming weight $\frac{m}{\omega}$. Furthermore, during Steps 4 to 5, the probability that N is divided by τ is 1/2, thus we have to take this part into account when evaluating the average Hamming weight. Consequently, the main body's average Hamming weight is $\frac{m}{\omega+1}$.

Besides, the remainder (Steps 10 to 16) is an integer in $\mathbb{Z}[\tau]$ with a norm less than $2^{2^{\omega-3}}$. In this part, the window width $\omega' = 4$ is fixed. Its Hamming weight is not greater than $\frac{2^{\omega-3}}{(\omega'+1)}$. Combining the above two parts, we can get the whole algorithm' average Hamming weight is

$$\frac{m}{\omega + 1} + \frac{2^{\omega-3}}{\omega' + 1} \tag{4}$$

The following Algorithm 2 computes the scalar multiplication based on the result of Algorithm 1.

4 Costs of Scalar Multiplications

The **S**/**M** ratio has an effect on the cost of scalar multiplication. According to the cases suggested by Bernstein and Lange [6] and the experiments of our environments, we consider three cases **S**/**M** $= 0$, **S**/**M** $= 0.2$, and **S**/**M** $= 0.5$.

4.1 Scalar Multiplications on μ_4-Koblitz Curves

We precompute and store a point corresponding to each odd congruence class (mod τ^ω) for the DBNS($\overline{\tau}, \tau$) expansion. Table 3 summarizes the pre-computation cost for several window widths.

Table 3. The pre-computation cost for width from 4 to 7.

	μ_4-Koblitz curves	LD coordinates ($a = 0/a = 1$)
$\omega = 4$	$6\mathbf{M} + 6\mathbf{S}$	$6\mathbf{M} + 6\mathbf{S}/6\mathbf{M} + 3\mathbf{S}$
$\omega = 5$	$14\mathbf{M} + 14\mathbf{S}$	$14\mathbf{M} + 14\mathbf{S}/14\mathbf{M} + 7\mathbf{S}$
$\omega = 6$	$30\mathbf{M} + 30\mathbf{S}$	$30\mathbf{M} + 30\mathbf{S}/30\mathbf{M} + 15\mathbf{S}$
$\omega = 7$	$62\mathbf{M} + 62\mathbf{S}$	$62\mathbf{M} + 62\mathbf{S}/62\mathbf{M} + 31\mathbf{S}$

Theorem 1. *Let* Pre_ω *denotes the cost of pre-computation part for scalar multiplication using DBNS($\overline{\tau}, \tau$) expansion with variable window widths ω and fixed window widths $\omega' = 4$ on μ_4-Koblitz Curves.*

1. According to Algorithm 2, on μ_4-Koblitz curves the total cost of scalar multiplication in projective coordinates is calculated as follows:

$$\mathrm{Pre}_\omega + 4\mathrm{m}\mathbf{S} + (\frac{\mathrm{m}}{\omega+1} + \frac{2^{\omega-3}}{\omega'+1}) \cdot ((7+\mathrm{a})\mathbf{M} + 2\mathbf{S} - \frac{1}{2^{\omega-2}}\mathbf{M})$$

2. According to Algorithm 2, on μ_4-Koblitz curves the total cost of scalar multiplication in affine coordinates is calculated as follows:

$$\mathrm{Pre}_\omega + \mathbf{I} + (6 \cdot 2^{\omega-2} - 9)\mathbf{M} + 4\mathrm{m}\mathbf{S} + (\frac{\mathrm{m}}{\omega+1} + \frac{2^{\omega-3}}{\omega'+1}) \cdot ((6+\mathrm{a})\mathbf{M} + 2\mathbf{S})$$

Proof. 1. The average Hamming weight of the new representation given in Algorithm 1 is $\frac{m}{\omega+1} + \frac{2^{\omega-3}}{\omega'+1}$ (formula 4). The implementation of scalar multiplication in our Algorithm 2 requires the pre-computation, m τ-operations, $(\frac{m}{\omega+1} + \frac{2^{\omega-3}}{\omega'+1}) \cdot \frac{2^{\omega-2}-1}{2^{\omega-2}}$ point additions, and $(\frac{m}{\omega+1} + \frac{2^{\omega-3}}{\omega'+1}) \cdot \frac{1}{2^{\omega-2}}$ mixed additions. The calculation of $\overline{\tau}$ is included in the pre-computation. In projective coordinates, by adding up the costs of the above four parts with $a \in \{0, 1\}$, we obtain the cost of scalar multiplication:

$$\mathrm{Pre}_\omega + 4\mathrm{m}\mathbf{S} + (\frac{\mathrm{m}}{\omega+1} + \frac{2^{\omega-3}}{\omega'+1}) \cdot ((7+\mathrm{a})\mathbf{M} + 2\mathbf{S} - \frac{1}{2^{\omega-2}}\mathbf{M}).$$

2. The point additions of scalar multiplication in affine coordinates entirely use mixed additions. In this case, computing scalar multiplication requires the pre-computation, m τ-projective operations, the Montgomery trick, and $\frac{m}{\omega+1} + \frac{2^{\omega-3}}{(\omega'+1)}$ mixed additions. The Montgomery trick that translates the points in

projective coordinates to affine coordinates needs $3(n-1)$ multiplication and one inversion. The total cost of scalar multiplication in affine coordinates is expected to be:

$$\mathrm{Pre}_\omega + \mathbf{I} + (6 \cdot 2^{\omega-2} - 9)\mathbf{M} + 4\mathrm{m}\mathbf{S} + (\frac{\mathrm{m}}{\omega+1} + \frac{2^{\omega-3}}{\omega'+1}) \cdot ((6+\mathrm{a})\mathbf{M} + 2\mathbf{S}).$$

□

Table 4 summarizes the costs of our scalar multiplication method on Koblitz curves with $a = 0$. Table 5 summarizes that on Koblitz curves with $a = 1$. The most efficient in our new method is the μ_4-Koblitz curves. In Appendix A, we give our scalar multiplication implementation using LD coordinates.

Table 4. The scalar multiplications costs on K-233, K-283, K-409, and K-571 using μ_4-Koblitz curves

		K-233(ω)	K-283(ω)	K-409(ω)	K-571(ω)
S = 0M	Yu et al. [21]	274.9(6)	324.5(6)	444.3(7)	585.4(7)
	Ours	270.6(6)	320.2(6)	439.2(7)	580.3(7)
S = 0.2M	Yu et al. [21]	481(6)	573.4(6)	804.3(7)	1083.1(7)
	Ours	476.9(6)	569.3(6)	800.4(7)	1079.2(7)
S = 0.5M	Yu et al. [21]	790.2(6)	946.9(6)	1341.8(6)	1829.8(7)
	Ours	786.3(6)	943.0(6)	1337.9(6)	1825.7(7)

Table 5. The scalar multiplications costs on K1-163, K1-283, K1-359, and K1-701 using μ_4-Koblitz curves

		K1-163(ω)	K1-283(ω)	K1-359(ω)	K1-701(ω)
S = 0M	Yu et al. [21]	231.8(6)	367.9(6)	450.6(7)	791.3(7)
	Ours	225.9(6)	362.0(6)	443.5(7)	784.2(7)
S = 0.2M	Yu et al. [21]	377.9(6)	616.9(6)	768.1(7)	1399.5(7)
	Ours	372.2(6)	611.1(6)	762.2(7)	1393.6(7)
S = 0.5M	Yu et al. [21]	594.6(5)	990.3(6)	1239.4(6)	2311.9(7)
	Ours	591.6(6)	984.8(6)	1233.8(6)	2307.8(7)

4.2 Comparison with Other Methods

Compared with previous results in the literature, the novelties of our work are to give a new double-base decomposition algorithm for scalar n and a more efficient scalar multiplication algorithm. On the whole, our implementations of scalar multiplication save 24% more time than [3] and 16% more than [11] in LD coordinates, and 3% more than [21] on μ_4-Koblitz curves.

The experimental results are consistent with the theoretical analysis within the allowable error range. The reason for the slight differences is that some field additions have been omitted.

5 Conclusion

This paper presents an up-to-date scalar multiplication algorithm on Koblitz curves employing DBNS($\overline{\tau}, \tau$) expansion, where n is represented as $\sum_{i=0}^{k-1}(-1)^{e_i}\overline{\tau}^{s_i}\tau^{t_i}$. Our new method requires fewer point operations and improves the work of Doche et al. [11] and Yu et al. [21].

We give the cost of scalar multiplication on various Koblitz curves recommended by NIST. Overall, our work improves the efficiency of scalar multiplication on Koblitz curves.

A Scalar Multiplications Using LD Coordinates

Let PreLD_ω denote the pre-computation costs. Table 6 gives the scalar multiplications costs on several Koblitz curves using LD coordinates. Using a proof similar to Theorem 1, we also obtain the formulas for the costs of scalar multiplication in LD coordinates.

1. Scalar multiplication in LD coordinates. This case requires the pre-computation, m τ-operations, $(\frac{m}{\omega+1}+\frac{2^{\omega-3}}{\omega'+1})\cdot\frac{2^{\omega-2}-1}{2^{\omega-2}}$ point additions, and $(\frac{m}{\omega+1}+\frac{2^{\omega-3}}{\omega'+1})\cdot\frac{1}{2^{\omega-2}}$ mixed additions. The costs of scalar multiplication are expected to be

$$\text{PreLD}_\omega+(2^{\omega-2}-1)\mathbf{M}+3\text{m}\mathbf{S}+(\frac{\text{m}}{\omega+1}+\frac{2^{\omega-3}}{\omega'+1})\cdot(13\mathbf{M}+4\mathbf{S}-\frac{1}{2^{\omega-2}}(5\mathbf{M}-\mathbf{S}))$$

2. Scalar multiplication in affine coordinates. It requires the pre-computation, the Montgomery trick, m τ-operations, and $\frac{m}{\omega+1}+\frac{2^{\omega-3}}{(\omega'+1)}$ mixed additions. The cost of Montgomery trick is $\mathbf{I}+(5n-3)\mathbf{M}+n\mathbf{S}$. The cost of scalar multiplication is expected to be

$$\text{PreLD}_\omega+\mathbf{I}+(5\cdot2^{\omega-2}-8)\mathbf{M}+(2^{\omega-2}-1)\mathbf{S}+3\text{m}\mathbf{S}+(\frac{\text{m}}{\omega+1}+\frac{2^{\omega-3}}{\omega'+1})\cdot(8\mathbf{M}+5\mathbf{S}).$$

Table 6. The scalar multiplications costs in LD coordinates on K1-163, K-233, K-283, K1-283, K-409, and K-571

		K1-163(ω)	K-233(ω)	K-283(ω)	K1-283(ω)	K-409(ω)	K-571(ω)
S = 0M	Doche et al. [11]	326.5(6)	431.5(6)	506.5(6)	506.5(6)	687.8(7)	896.1(7)
	Aranha et al. [1]	277.0(5)	373.0(5)	437.0(5)	437.0(5)	606.0(5)	823.1(5)
	Yu et al. [21]	276.3(5)	369.7(5)	436.3(5)	436.3(5)	598.4(6)	783.6(6)
	Ours	276.1(5)	369.5(5)	436.1(5)	436.1(5)	588.6(6)	773.7(6)
S = 0.2M	Doche et al. [11]	460.0(6)	621.9(6)	735.2(6)	732.0(6)	1015.2(7)	1343.8(7)
	Aranha et al. [1]	404.4(5)	553.4(5)	656.4(5)	656.4(5)	921.0(5)	1261.2(5)
	Yu et al. [21]	405.3(5)	553.5(5)	658.5(5)	657.3(5)	913.3(6)	1218.7(6)
	Ours	404.5(5)	552.9(5)	657.9(5)	656.5(5)	902.8(6)	1208.3(6)
S = 0.5M	Doche et al. [11]	660.3(6)	907.4(6)	1078.3(6)	1070.3(6)	1506.1(7)	2015.2(7)
	Aranha et al. [1]	594.0(5)	824.0(5)	983.0(5)	983.0(5)	1392.5(5)	1920.0(5)
	Yu et al. [21]	598.8(5)	829.3(5)	991.8(5)	988.8(7)	1385.5(6)	1871.5(6)
	Ours	597.0(5)	828.0(5)	990.5(5)	987.0(5)	1374.2(6)	1860.2(6)

References

1. Aranha, D.F., Faz-Hernández, A., López, J., Rodríguez-Henríquez, F.: Faster implementation of scalar multiplication on Koblitz curves. In: Hevia, A., Neven, G. (eds.) LATINCRYPT 2012. LNCS, vol. 7533, pp. 177–193. Springer, Heidelberg (2012). https://doi.org/10.1007/978-3-642-33481-8_10
2. Avanzi, R., Sica, F.: Scalar multiplication on Koblitz curves using double bases. In: Nguyen, P.Q. (ed.) VIETCRYPT 2006. LNCS, vol. 4341, pp. 131–146. Springer, Heidelberg (2006). https://doi.org/10.1007/11958239_9
3. Avanzi, R., Dimitrov, V., Doche, C., Sica, F.: Extending scalar multiplication using double bases. In: Lai, X., Chen, K. (eds.) ASIACRYPT 2006. LNCS, vol. 4284, pp. 130–144. Springer, Heidelberg (2006). https://doi.org/10.1007/11935230_9
4. Barker, E.: Draft NIST special publication 800–57 part 1, revision 5: recommendation for key management: part 1-general, May 2020
5. Barker, E., Chen, L., Keller, S., Roginsky, A., Vassilev, A., Davis, R.: NIST special publication 800-56A revision 3-recommendation for pair-wise key-establishment schemes using discrete logarithm cryptography, April 2018. https://doi.org/10.6028/NIST.SP.800-56Ar3
6. Bernstein, D.J.: Explicit-formulas database (2015). http://www.hyperelliptic.org/EFD
7. Blake, I., Murty, V., Xu, G.: A note on window τ-NAF algorithm. Inf. Process. Lett. **95**, 496–502 (2005)
8. Blake, I., Murty, V., Xu, G.: Nonadjacent radix-τ expansions of integers in Euclidean imaginary quadratic number fields. Can. J. Math.-journal Canadien De Mathematiques - CAN J MATH **60** (2008). https://doi.org/10.4153/CJM-2009-055-6
9. Dimitrov, V., Imbert, L., Mishra, P.K.: Efficient and secure elliptic curve point multiplication using double-base chains. In: Roy, B. (ed.) ASIACRYPT 2005. LNCS, vol. 3788, pp. 59–78. Springer, Heidelberg (2005). https://doi.org/10.1007/11593447_4
10. Dimitrov, V.S., Jullien, G.A., Miller, W.C.: An algorithm for modular exponentiation. Inf. Process. Lett. **66**, 155–159 (1998)
11. Doche, C., Kohel, D.R., Sica, F.: Double-base number system for multi-scalar multiplications. In: Joux, A. (ed.) EUROCRYPT 2009. LNCS, vol. 5479, pp. 502–517. Springer, Heidelberg (2009). https://doi.org/10.1007/978-3-642-01001-9_29
12. Koblitz, N.: CM-curves with good cryptographic properties. In: Feigenbaum, J. (ed.) CRYPTO 1991. LNCS, vol. 576, pp. 279–287. Springer, Heidelberg (1992). https://doi.org/10.1007/3-540-46766-1_22
13. Kohel, D.: Efficient arithmetic on elliptic curves in characteristic 2 (2016). https://arxiv.org/abs/1601.03669
14. Kohel, D.: Twisted μ_4-normal form for elliptic curves. In: Coron, J.-S., Nielsen, J.B. (eds.) EUROCRYPT 2017. LNCS, vol. 10210, pp. 659–678. Springer, Cham (2017). https://doi.org/10.1007/978-3-319-56620-7_23
15. Lange, T.: A note on López-Dahab coordinates. IACR Cryptology ePrint Archive 2004, 323 (January 2004)
16. Li, W., Yu, W., Li, B., Fan, X.: Speeding up scalar multiplication on Koblitz curves using μ_4 coordinates. In: Jang-Jaccard, J., Guo, F. (eds.) ACISP 2019. LNCS, vol. 11547, pp. 620–629. Springer, Cham (2019). https://doi.org/10.1007/978-3-030-21548-4_34

17. López, J., Dahab, R.: Improved algorithms for elliptic curve arithmetic in $GF(2^n)$. In: Tavares, S., Meijer, H. (eds.) SAC 1998. LNCS, vol. 1556, pp. 201–212. Springer, Heidelberg (1999). https://doi.org/10.1007/3-540-48892-8_16
18. National Institute of Standards and Technology(NIST): Digital signature standard (DSS). FIPS PUB 186–5(Draft), October 2019. https://doi.org/10.6028/NIST.FIPS.186-5-draft
19. Solinas, J.A.: Efficient arithmetic on Koblitz curves. Des. Codes Cryptogr. **19**(2/3), 195–249 (2000). https://doi.org/10.1023/A:1008306223194
20. Yu, W., Musa, S.A., Li, B.: Double-base chains for scalar multiplications on elliptic curves. In: Canteaut, A., Ishai, Y. (eds.) EUROCRYPT 2020. LNCS, vol. 12107, pp. 538–565. Springer, Cham (2020). https://doi.org/10.1007/978-3-030-45727-3_18
21. Yu, W., Xu, G.: Pre-computation scheme of window τNAF for Koblitz curves revisited. In: Canteaut, A., Standaert, F.-X. (eds.) EUROCRYPT 2021. LNCS, vol. 12697, pp. 187–218. Springer, Cham (2021). https://doi.org/10.1007/978-3-030-77886-6_7

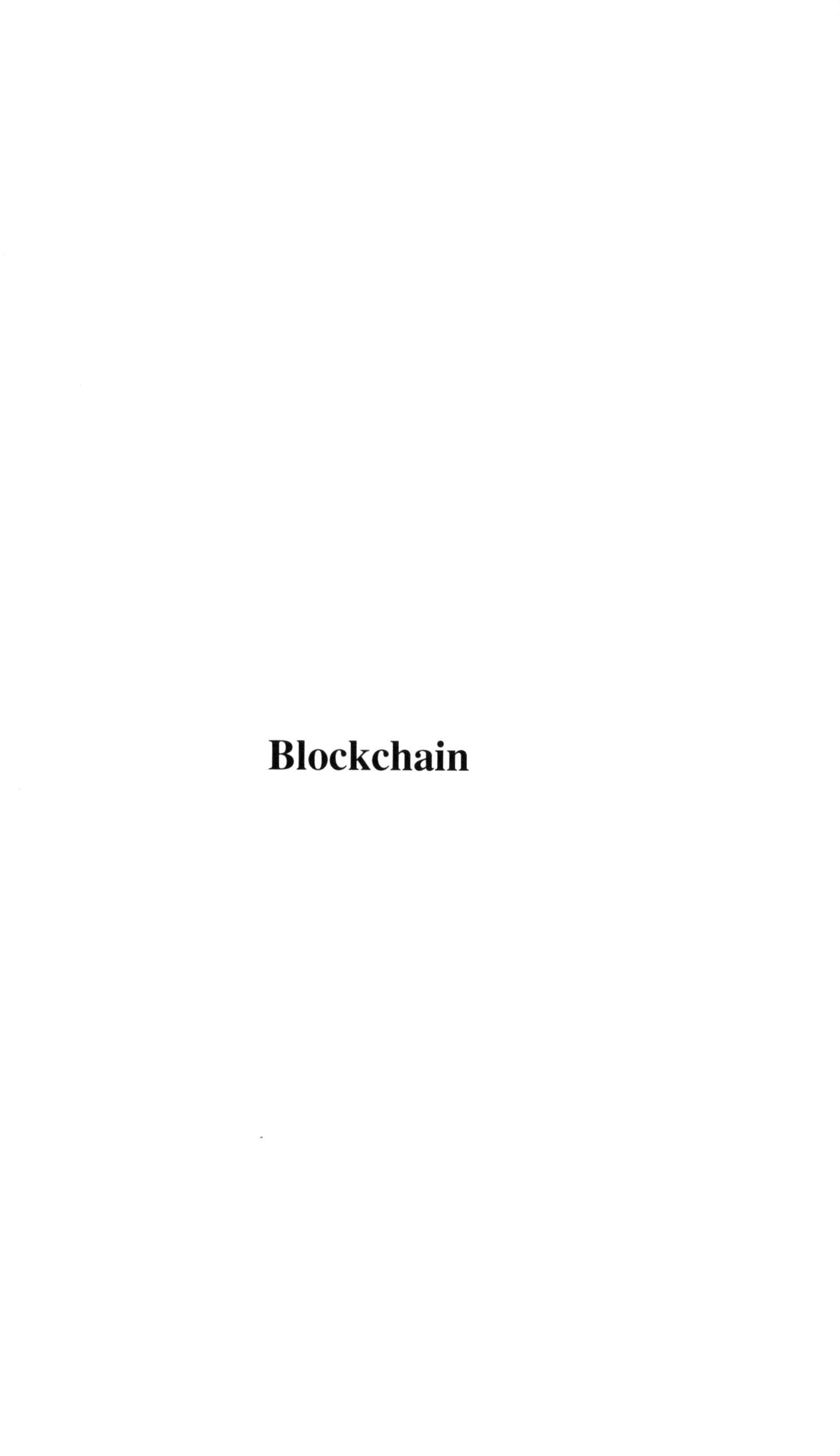

Blockchain

Efficient ECDSA-Based Adaptor Signature for Batched Atomic Swaps

Binbin Tu[1,2,3], Min Zhang[1,2,3], and Chen Yu[1,2,3](✉)

[1] School of Cyber Science and Technology, Shandong University, Qingdao 266237, China
{tubinbin,zm_min}@mail.sdu.edu.cn, yuchen@sdu.edu.cn

[2] State Key Laboratory of Cryptology, P.O. Box 5159, Beijing 100878, China

[3] Key Laboratory of Cryptologic Technology and Information Security, Ministry of Education, Shandong University, Qingdao 266237, China

Abstract. Adaptor signature is a novel cryptographic primitive which ties together the signature and the leakage of a secret value. It has become an important tool for solving the scalability and interoperability problems in the blockchain. Aumayr et al. (Asiacrypt 2021) recently provide the formalization of the adaptor signature and present a provably secure ECDSA-based adaptor signature, which requires zero-knowledge proof in the pre-signing phase to ensure the signer works correctly. However, the number of zero-knowledge proofs is linear with the number of participants. In this paper, we propose efficient ECDSA-based adaptor signature schemes and give security proofs based on ECDSA. In our schemes, the zero-knowledge proofs in the pre-signing phase can be generated in a batch and offline. Meanwhile, the online pre-signing algorithm is similar to the ECDSA signing algorithm and can enjoy the same efficiency as ECDSA. In particular, considering specific verification scenarios, such as (batched) atomic swaps, our schemes can reduce the number of zero-knowledge proofs in the pre-signing phase to one, independent of the number of participants. Last, we conduct an experimental evaluation, demonstrating that the performance of our ECDSA-based adaptor signature reduces online pre-signing time by about 60% compared with the state-of-the-art ECDSA-based adaptor signature.

Keywords: Adaptor signature · ECDSA-based adaptor signature · Batched atomic swaps · Blockchain

1 Introduction

Adaptor signatures (AS), also known as scriptless scripts, are introduced by Poelstra [19] and recently formalized by Aumayr et al. [2]. It can be seen as an extension over a digital signature with respect to leaking a secret to certain parties. Namely, the signer uses a signing key to compute a pre-signature of a message and a statement of a hard relation (e.g., the discrete logarithm), such that the pre-signature can be adapted into a (full) signature by the witness of the

W. Susilo et al. (Eds.): ISC 2022, LNCS 13640, pp. 175–193, 2022.
https://doi.org/10.1007/978-3-031-22390-7_12

hard relation. Meanwhile, the witness can be extracted from the pre-signature and the full signature. AS provides the following intuitive properties: (i) Only the user knowing the signing key can generate a pre-signature; (ii) Only the user knowing the witness of the hard relation can convert a pre-signature into a full signature; (iii) Anyone holding a pre-signature and corresponding full signature can extract the witness.

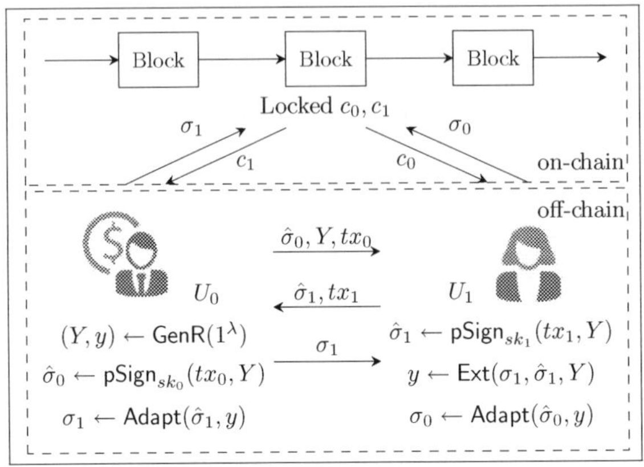

Fig. 1. The atomic swap protocol based on adaptor signature

To demonstrate the idea of AS, we introduce its key application atomic swaps in Fig. 1. An atomic swap [10] can be defined between two users U_0 and U_1 who want to exchange two different cryptocurrencies c_0 and c_1. The crucial point of the exchange is ensuring fairness, i.e., both parties receive their expected output or nothing. Two parties U_0 and U_1 first set the time-lock for c_0 with the timeout t_0 and c_1 with the timeout t_1 on-chain[1]. Then, U_0 chooses a hard relation $(Y, y) \in R$ and pre-signing a transaction tx_0 for spending the coins c_0 to U_1, and then sends the pre-signature $\hat{\sigma}_0$, tx_0, Y to U_1. U_1 can check the validity of $\hat{\sigma}_0$ and pre-signing a transaction tx_1 for spending the coins c_1 to U_0 and then sends the pre-signature $\hat{\sigma}_1$, tx_1 to U_0. U_0 can check the validity of $\hat{\sigma}_1$ and adapts $\hat{\sigma}_1$ into the full signature σ_1 by the witness y, and then publishes σ_1 on the blockchain to get the coin c_1 within t_1. U_1 can extract the witness y from σ_1 and $\hat{\sigma}_1$ and adapts $\hat{\sigma}_0$ into σ_0, then publishes σ_0 on the blockchain to get the coin c_0 within t_0. As we can see, the pre-signature and the cryptographic condition need not to be published on-chain, compared with using the *Hash Time-Lock Contracts* (HTLCs) [15,20], AS reduces the operations on-chain and weaken scripting restrictions on the underlying blockchain.

By tying the signing processing to the revelation of a secret value, AS brings about various advantages as follows: (i) Reducing the operations on-chain; (ii)

[1] Both parties use time-lock to lock the exchange coins on-chain, and the timeouts $t_1 < t_0$ to ensure that U_1 can have enough time to react.

Supporting advanced functionality beyond the limitation of the blockchain's scripting language; (iii) Improving fungibility of transactions. To be specific, the pre-signature is generated and verified off-chain and only the full signature is published on-chain, so AS reduces the additional storage and verification costs greatly on-chain, meanwhile, it is not limited by the blockchain's scripting language. Based on this advantage, Aumayr et al. [2] give a generalized channel construction by using AS as a key technique, which is compatible with any blockchain supporting transaction authorization, time-locks, and constant number of Boolean $\wedge$ and $\vee$ operations - requirements fulfilled by many (non-Turing-complete) blockchains including the Bitcoin. The fungibility property is said that the pre-signature embedded the cryptographic condition (hard relations) inside is indistinguishable from a regular signature, and it can be used to hide payment channel network transactions among any other transactions [16]. Benefiting from above advantages, AS has also been shown highly useful in many blockchain applications such as payment channels [2–4,7,20], payment routing in payment channel networks [9,10,16,17], and atomic swaps [8,10,13].

Poelstra [19] first gives a Schnorr-based AS that is limited to cryptocurrencies using Schnorr signatures [21]. Moreno-Sanchez and Kate [18] present an ECDSA-based AS and its two-party version without provable security. Malavolta et al. [16] present two-party AS based on ECDSA [1], but they do not define AS as a stand-alone primitive and formalize the security definition for the threshold primitive and hence the security of their schemes has not been analyzed completely, such as the lack of the witness extractability. Until Aumayr et al. [2] first formalize AS as a standalone primitive and prove the security of their ECDSA-based AS based on the strong unforgeability of positive ECDSA in the Universal Composability (UC) framework [5]. They exquisitely modify the hard relation in [18], by adding a zero-knowledge proof such that the witness can be extracted in the random oracle model [12]. For convenience, we name this modification as "self-proving structure". However, their ECDSA-based AS is not entirely satisfactory. In the pre-signing phase, the signer uses the random value as a witness to compute a pre-signing public parameter and a corresponding zero-knowledge proof. Especially, in the case of multiple participants, such as (batched) atomic swaps or multi-hop payments [10,16], the number of zero-knowledge proofs is *linear* with the number of participants. Therefore, we consider the following question in this work:

Is it possible to design an efficient ECDSA-based AS in which the number of zero-knowledge proofs in the pre-signing phase is independent of the number of participants?

1.1 Our Contributions

In this paper, we give an affirmative answer to the above question. First, we propose an ECDSA-based AS (ECDSA-AS) and prove the security based on positive ECDSA in UC framework following [2]. Then, we develop more efficient ECDSA-AS schemes in which the zero-knowledge proofs in the pre-signing phase can be generated in a batch and offline. In particular, considering *specific verification scenarios*[2], in which only the participants verify the pre-signatures, our ECDSA-AS can reduce the number of zero-knowledge proofs in pre-signing phase to *one*.

ECDSA-Based Adaptor Signature. ECDSA-AS can be seen as an extension of ECDSA with a hard relation $(I_Y = (Y = yG, \pi_Y), y)$, where $\pi_Y \leftarrow \mathsf{P}_Y(Y, y)$, P_Y denotes the proving algorithm[3]. We briefly introduce our ECDSA-AS as follows: Let $(Q = xG, x)$ denote ECDSA verification key and signing key. The signer computes a pre-signing public parameter $Z = xY$ and uses x as the witness to compute $\pi_Z \leftarrow \mathsf{P}_Z((G, Q, Y, Z), x)$[4], then chooses a random value $k \leftarrow \mathbb{Z}_q$, computes $r = f(kY)$, $\hat{s} = k^{-1}(h(m) + rx) \bmod q$, and outputs the pre-signature $\hat{\sigma} = (r, \hat{s}, Z, \pi_Z)$. The verification algorithm verifies π_Z and $r \stackrel{?}{=} f(\hat{s}^{-1} \cdot h(m) \cdot Y + \hat{s}^{-1} \cdot r \cdot Z)$. The adaptor algorithm takes the witness y and the pre-signature $\hat{\sigma}$ as inputs to compute $s = \hat{s} \cdot y^{-1} \bmod q$, and outputs ECDSA signature $\sigma = (r, s)$. The extraction algorithm can extract the witness by computing $y = \hat{s}/s$.

Following [2], we use "self-proving structure" $(I_Y = (Y, \pi_Y), y)$ to give security proofs. Intuitively speaking, since the zero-knowledge proof system holds straight-line extractability, the simulator can extract the witness y from the instance (Y, π_Y), then it can use ECDSA signing oracle to obtain ECDSA signature $\sigma = (r, s)$ and simulates the pre-signing oracle by computing the pre-signature $\hat{s} = s \cdot y \bmod q$.

Then, we develop two efficient ECDSA-AS schemes called ECDSA-AS$_{sk}$ and ECDSA-AS$_{wit}$ by computing the pre-signing public parameter and corresponding zero-knowledge proof offline, where ECDSA-AS$_{sk}$ uses signing key x as a witness to compute $(Z = xY, \pi_Z)$, and ECDSA-AS$_{wit}$ uses the witness y of hard relation (I_Y, y) as a witness to compute $(Z = yQ, \pi_Z)$.

Offline/Online Pre-signing. In ECDSA-AS [2,18], the signer computes the pre-signing public parameter $K = kY$ and proves the hard relation $((G, \hat{K} = kG, Y, K), k)$ satisfies equality of discrete logarithms $\pi_K \leftarrow \mathsf{P}_K((G, \hat{K}, Y, K), k)$, that is, there exists a witness k that is the *random value* used in the pre-signing algorithm, such that $\hat{K} = kG$ and $K = kY$.

[2] Common verification scenarios require that everyone can verify signatures. However, the pre-signature of the adaptor signature is not published on the blockchain, so it is always used in the specific verification scenarios where only the participants verify the pre-signatures off-chain and others (such as miners) need not verify pre-signatures.

[3] The zero-knowledge proof system requires straight-line extractor, also namely online extractor [12]. The straight-line extractability property allows for extraction of a witness y for a statement Y from a proof π_Y in the random oracle model and is useful for models where the rewinding proof technique is not allowed, such as UC [2].

[4] This zero-knowledge proof system does not require straight-line extractor. Such a proof can be derived by applying the Fiat-Shamir heuristic [11] to Chaum-Pedersen $\sum$-protocol [6] for the language comprising valid DDH tuples.

In our ECDSA-AS$_{sk}$, the signer computes $Z = xY$ and proves the hard relation $((G, Q, Y, Z), x)$ satisfies equality of discrete logarithms $\pi_Z \leftarrow \mathsf{P}_Z((G, Q, Y, Z), x)$, that is, there exists a witness x that is the *signing key*, such that $Q = xG$ and $Z = xY$. In our ECDSA-AS$_{wit}$, the signer[5] computes $Z = yQ$ and proves the hard relation $((G, Y, Q, Z), y)$ satisfies equality of discrete logarithms $\pi_Z \leftarrow \mathsf{P}_Z((G, Y, Q, Z), y)$, that is, there exists a witness y that is the *witness of hard relation* (I_Y, y), such that $Y = yG$ and $Z = yQ$. By using y as the witness, the signer (hard relation chooser) holding y can generate all pre-signing public parameters $Z_i = yQ_i$ and zero-knowledge proofs π_{Z_i} *in a batch* and *offline* for all other participants. Other participants can compute $Z_i = x_iY$ by using the signing key x_i and the instance Y.

Performance. We show the theoretical and experimental analysis of ECDSA-AS [2,18] and our ECDSA-AS$_{sk/wit}$. In the offline phase, all parties in ECDSA-AS$_{sk/wit}$ generates and checks the hard relation $I_Y = (Y, \pi_Y \leftarrow \mathsf{P}_Y(Y, y), y)$. In the online phase, the signer uses Y and $Z_i = yQ_i$ to run the online pre-signing algorithm to generate the pre-signature which can be verified by Y and $Z_i = x_iY$. Thus, the online pre-signing algorithm is similar to the original ECDSA signing algorithm except for modifying parameters by using (Z, Y) as the verification key and base point instead of (Q, G). To be specific, ECDSA-AS$_{sk/wit}$ only computes once point multiplication operation online, while ECDSA-AS in [2,18] need four times point multiplication operation. The experimental results show that ECDSA-AS$_{wit}$ reduces online pre-signing time by about 60% compared with the state-of-the-art ECDSA-AS [2] in a two-party case.

Applications. AS can be divided into off-chain and on-chain two phases. In the off-chain phase, all participants generate and verify the pre-signatures from each other, and adapt the pre-signatures into full signatures. In the on-chain phase, all participants use the time-lock to lock their coins and then publish full signatures to achieve the exchange within the timeouts. Therefore, the pre-signatures are not published on the blockchain and are only verified by the participants that satisfy special verification scenarios. Our ECDSA-AS$_{sk/wit}$ can reduce all zero-knowledge proof in the pre-signing phase, except one zero-knowledge proof of the hard relation chooser. Since other participants can compute the pre-signing public parameters $Z_i = x_iY$ and the hard relation chooser can compute the pre-signing public parameters $Z_i = yQ_i$, there is no need to use zero-knowledge proofs to ensure the correctness of pre-signing public parameters.

To our knowledge, atomic swaps are mostly for two-party exchange scenarios to ensure fairness. We consider the special batched case in which one party with many addresses (accounts) or one party with a lot of transactions that need to exchange with many users at once, such as the scenario of the Exchange. For this scenario, we develop *batched atomic swaps*, in which all parties first set the

[5] The signer can be seen as a hard relation chooser who is the protocol initiator and holds the witness y.

time-lock for the exchange coins on-chain[6] and then one user U_0 can exchange its coins with many users (addresses) U_i, $i \in [n]$ in a batch. Compared with running independently n times atomic swaps between U_0 and U_i, $i \in [n]$, batched atomic swaps can reduce the number of hard relations (Y, y) from n to *one*. In particular, constructing batched atomic swaps based on ECDSA-AS$_{sk/wit}$ only transmits one zero-knowledge proof, while using ECDSA-AS [2,18] requires $2n$ zero-knowledge proofs, where n denotes the number of parties in batched atomic swaps.

2 Preliminaries

2.1 Notations

For $n \in \mathbb{N}$, $[n]$ denotes the set $\{1, 2, \cdots, n\}$, 1^λ denotes the string of λ ones. Throughout, we use λ to denote the security parameter. A function is negligible in λ, written $\mathsf{negl}(\lambda)$, if it vanishes faster than the inverse of any polynomial in λ. We denote a probabilistic polynomial-time algorithm by PPT. If S is a set then $s \leftarrow S$ denotes the operation of sampling an element s of S at random.

2.2 Hard Relation and Zero-Knowledge Proof

We recall the definition of a hard relation R with statement/witness pairs $(stat = (G,\ Y = yG), y)$ [2]. Let $\mathsf{L_R}$ be the associated language defined as $\mathsf{L_R} = \{(G, Y) | \exists\ y \text{ s.t. } ((G, Y), y) \in \mathsf{R}\}$. We say that R is a hard relation if the following holds: (i) There exists a PPT sampling algorithm $\mathsf{GenR}(1^\lambda)$ that on input 1^λ outputs a statement/witness pair $((G, Y), y) \in \mathsf{R}$; (ii) The relation is poly-time decidable; (iii) For all PPT $\mathcal{A}$, the probability of $\mathcal{A}$ on input (G, Y) outputting y is negligible.

We recall the definition of a non-interactive zero-knowledge proof of knowledge (NIZKPoK) with straight-line extractors as introduced in [12]. More formally, a pair (P, V) of PPT algorithms is called a NIZKPoK with a straight-line extractor for a relation R, random oracle $\mathcal{H}$ and security parameter λ if the following holds: (i) Completeness: For any $((G, Y), y) \in \mathsf{R}$, it holds that $\mathsf{V}((G, Y), \pi \leftarrow \mathsf{P}((G, Y), y)) = 1$; (ii) Zero knowledge: There exists a PPT simulator $\mathcal{S}$, which on input (G, Y) can simulate the proof π for any $((G, Y), y) \in \mathsf{R}$. (iii) Straight-line extractability: There exists a PPT straight-line extractor K with access to the sequence of queries to the random oracle and its answers, such that given $((G, Y), \pi)$, the algorithm K can extract the witness y with $((G, Y), y) \in \mathsf{R}$. For convenience, we omit the parameter G in this paper.

[6] All parties use time-lock to lock the exchange coins c_0 with the timeouts t_0 and c_i with the timeouts t_i, and the timeouts $t_i < t_0$, $i \in [n]$ to ensure that U_i can have enough time to react.

2.3 Adaptor Signature Scheme

An adaptor signature scheme [2] w.r.t. a hard relation $\mathsf{R} = \{Y, y\}$ and a signature scheme $\sum = (\mathsf{Gen}, \mathsf{Sign}, \mathsf{Vrfy})$ consists of four algorithms $\Pi_{\mathsf{R},\sum} = (\mathsf{pSign}, \mathsf{pVrfy}, \mathsf{Adapt}, \mathsf{Ext})$ defined as:

- $\mathsf{pSign}_{sk}(m, Y) \to \hat{\sigma}$: On input a signing key sk, an instance Y and a message $m \in \{0,1\}^*$, outputs a pre-signature $\hat{\sigma}$.
- $\mathsf{pVrfy}_{vk}(m, Y, \hat{\sigma}) \to 0/1$: On input a verification key vk, a pre-signature $\hat{\sigma}$, an instance Y and a message $m \in \{0,1\}^*$, outputs a bit $b \in \{0,1\}$.
- $\mathsf{Adapt}(\hat{\sigma}, y) \to \sigma$: On input a pre-signature $\hat{\sigma}$ and a witness y, outputs a signature σ.
- $\mathsf{Ext}(\sigma, \hat{\sigma}, Y) \to y$: On input a signature σ, a pre-signature $\hat{\sigma}$ and an instance Y, outputs a witness y such that $(Y, y) \in \mathsf{R}$, or $\perp$.

Definition 1 (Pre-signature correctness). *An adaptor signature scheme $\Pi_{\mathsf{R},\sum}$ satisfies pre-signature correctness if for every λ, every message $m \in \{0,1\}^*$ and every statement/witness pair $(Y, y) \in \mathsf{R}$, the following holds:*

$$\Pr\left[\begin{array}{c|c} \mathsf{pVrfy}_{vk}(m, Y, \hat{\sigma}) \to 1 \wedge & \mathsf{Gen}(1^\lambda) \to (sk, vk) \\ \mathsf{Vrfy}_{vk}(m, \sigma) \to 1 \wedge & \mathsf{pSign}_{sk}(m, Y) \to \hat{\sigma} \\ (Y, y') \in \mathsf{R} & \mathsf{Adapt}(\hat{\sigma}, y) \to \sigma \\ & \mathsf{Ext}(\sigma, \hat{\sigma}, Y) \to y' \end{array}\right] = 1$$

We review the existential unforgeability under chosen message attack for AS (aEUF-CMA), pre-signature adaptability, and witness extractability [2].

Definition 2 (aEUF-CMA security). *An adaptor signature scheme $\Pi_{\mathsf{R},\sum}$ is aEUF-CMA secure if for every PPT adversary $\mathcal{A}$ there exists a negligible function* negl *such that:*

$$\Pr[aSigForge_{\mathcal{A},\Pi_{\mathsf{R},\sum}}(\lambda) = 1] \leq \mathsf{negl}(\lambda),$$

where the experiment $aSigForge_{\mathcal{A},\Pi_{\mathsf{R},\sum}}$ is defined as follows:

$\text{aSigForge}_{\mathcal{A},\Pi_{\mathsf{R},\sum}}(\lambda)$	$\mathcal{O}_{\text{Sign}_{sk}}(m)$
$\mathcal{Q} = \emptyset$	$\sigma \leftarrow \mathsf{Sign}_{sk}(m)$
$(vk, sk) \leftarrow \mathsf{Gen}(1^\lambda)$	$\mathcal{Q} = \mathcal{Q} \cup \{m\}$
$m \leftarrow \mathcal{A}^{\mathcal{O}_{\text{Sign}_{sk}}(\cdot), \mathcal{O}_{\text{pSign}_{sk}}(\cdot)}(vk)$	return σ
$(Y, y) \leftarrow \mathsf{GenR}(1^\lambda)$	
$\hat{\sigma} \leftarrow \mathsf{pSign}_{sk}(m, Y)$	$\mathcal{O}_{\text{pSign}_{sk}}(m, Y)$
$\sigma \leftarrow \mathcal{A}^{\mathcal{O}_{\text{Sign}_{sk}}(\cdot), \mathcal{O}_{\text{pSign}_{sk}}(\cdot)}(\hat{\sigma}, Y)$	$\hat{\sigma} \leftarrow \mathsf{pSign}_{sk}(m, Y)$
return $(m \notin \mathcal{Q} \wedge \mathsf{Vrfy}_{vk}(m, \sigma))$	$\mathcal{Q} = \mathcal{Q} \cup \{m\}$
	return $\hat{\sigma}$

Definition 3 (Pre-signature adaptability). *An adaptor signature scheme* $\Pi_{\mathsf{R},\Sigma}$ *satisfies pre-signature adaptability if for any* λ, *any message* $m \in \{0,1\}^*$, *any statement/witness pair* $(Y, y) \in \mathsf{R}$, *any key pair* $(vk, sk) \leftarrow \mathsf{Gen}(1^\lambda)$ *and any pre-signature* $\hat{\sigma}$ *with* $\mathsf{pVrfy}_{vk}(m, Y, \hat{\sigma}) \rightarrow 1$, *we have* $\mathsf{Vrfy}_{vk}(m, \mathsf{Adapt}(\hat{\sigma}, y)) \rightarrow 1$.

The aEUF-CMA security together with the pre-signature adaptability ensures that a pre-signature for Y can be transferred into a valid signature if and only if the corresponding witness y is known [2].

Definition 4 (Witness extractability). *An adaptor signature scheme* $\Pi_{\mathsf{R},\Sigma}$ *is witness extractable if for every PPT adversary* $\mathcal{A}$, *there exists a negligible function* negl *such that:*

$$\Pr[aWitExt_{\mathcal{A},\Pi_{\mathsf{R},\Sigma}}(\lambda) = 1] \leq \mathsf{negl}(\lambda),$$

where the experiment $aWitExt_{\mathcal{A},\Pi_{\mathsf{R},\Sigma}}$ *is defined as follows*

$\text{aWitExt}_{\mathcal{A},\Pi_{\mathsf{R},\Sigma}}(\lambda)$	$\mathcal{O}_{\text{Sign}_{sk}}(m)$
$\mathcal{Q} = \emptyset$	$\sigma \leftarrow \mathsf{Sign}_{sk}(m)$
$(vk, sk) \leftarrow \mathsf{Gen}(1^\lambda)$	$\mathcal{Q} = \mathcal{Q} \cup \{m\}$
$(m, Y) \leftarrow \mathcal{A}^{\mathcal{O}_{\text{Sign}_{sk}}(\cdot), \mathcal{O}_{\text{pSign}_{sk}}(\cdot)}(vk)$	return σ
$\hat{\sigma} \leftarrow \mathsf{pSign}_{sk}(m, Y)$	
$\sigma \leftarrow \mathcal{A}^{\mathcal{O}_{\text{Sign}_{sk}}(\cdot), \mathcal{O}_{\text{pSign}_{sk}}(\cdot)}(\hat{\sigma})$	$\mathcal{O}_{\text{pSign}_{sk}}(m, Y)$
$y' \leftarrow \mathsf{Ext}(\sigma, \hat{\sigma}, Y)$	$\hat{\sigma} \leftarrow \mathsf{pSign}_{sk}(m, Y)$
return $m \notin \mathcal{Q} \wedge (Y, y') \notin \mathsf{R}$	$\mathcal{Q} = \mathcal{Q} \cup \{m\}$
$\wedge \mathsf{Vrfy}_{vk}(m, \sigma)$	return $\hat{\sigma}$

The witness extractability guarantees that a valid signature/pre-signature pair $(\sigma, \hat{\sigma})$ for message/statement (m, Y) can be used to extract the corresponding witness y. There is one crucial difference between aWitExt and aSigForge: The adversary is allowed to choose the challenge instance Y. Hence, he knows a witness for Y and can generate a valid signature on the forgery message m. However, this is not sufficient to win the experiment aWitExt. The adversary wins only if the valid signature does not reveal a witness for Y [2].

2.4 ECDSA

We review the ECDSA scheme [1] $\sum_{\text{ECDSA}} = (\mathsf{Gen}, \mathsf{Sign}, \mathsf{Vrfy})$ on a message $m \in \{0,1\}^*$ as follows. Let $\mathbb{G}$ be an Elliptic curve group of order q with base point (generator) G and let $pp = (\mathbb{G}, G, q)$ be the public parameter.

- $\mathsf{Gen}(pp) \rightarrow (Q, x)$: The key generation algorithm uniformly chooses a secret signing key $x \leftarrow \mathbb{Z}_q$, calculates the verification key $Q = x \cdot G$, and outputs $(sk = x, vk = Q)$.

- $\mathsf{Sign}_{sk}(m) \rightarrow (r, s)$. The signing algorithm chooses $k \leftarrow \mathbb{Z}_q$ randomly and computes $r = f(kG)$[7] and $s = k^{-1}(h(m) + rx)$, where h is a hash function and f is defined as the projection to the x-coordinate.
- $\mathsf{Vrfy}_{vk}(m, \sigma) \rightarrow 0/1$. The verification algorithm computes $r' = f(s^{-1} \cdot (h(m) \cdot G + r \cdot Q))$. If $r = r' \bmod q$, outputs 1, otherwise, outputs 0.

We use the *positive* ECDSA [2,14,16] which guarantees that if (r, s) is a valid signature, then $|s| \leq (q-1)/2$, to prove the security of our ECDSA-AS.

3 ECDSA-Based Adaptor Signature

In this section, we present a construction of ECDSA-AS $\Pi_{\mathsf{R},\sum} = (\mathsf{pSign}, \mathsf{pVrfy}, \mathsf{Adapt}, \mathsf{Ext})$ w.r.t. a hard relation R and a ECDSA signature $\sum = (\mathsf{Gen}, \mathsf{Sign}, \mathsf{Vrfy})$. Let $(Q = xG, x)$ be the verification key and signing key of ECDSA. We define hard relations $\mathsf{R} = \{(I_Y = (Y, \pi_Y \leftarrow \mathsf{P}_Y(Y, y)), y) | \ Y = yG \wedge \mathsf{V}_Y(I_Y) = 1\}$ and $\mathsf{R}_Z = \{(I_Z = (G, Q, Y, Z), x) | Q = xG \wedge Z = xY\}$ where P_Y and V_Y denotes the proving and verification algorithm of a NIZKPoK with straight-line extractability [12], P_Z and V_Z denotes the proving and verification algorithm of a NIZK.

- $\mathsf{pSign}_{(vk,sk)}(m, I_Y) \rightarrow \hat{\sigma}$: On input a key-pair $(vk, sk) = (Q, x)$, a message m and an instance $I_Y = (Y, \pi_Y)$, the algorithm computes the pre-signing public parameter $Z = xY$, runs $\pi_Z \leftarrow \mathsf{P}_Z(I_Z = (G, Q, Y, Z), x)$, and chooses $k \leftarrow \mathbb{Z}_q$, computes $r = f(kY)$, $\hat{s} = k^{-1}(h(m) + rx) \bmod q$ and outputs the pre-signature $\hat{\sigma} = (r, \hat{s}, Z, \pi_Z)$.
- $\mathsf{pVrfy}_{vk}(m, I_Y, \hat{\sigma}) \rightarrow 0/1$: On input the verification key $vk = Q$, a message m, an instance I_Y, and a pre-signature value $\hat{\sigma}$, the algorithm outputs 0, if $\mathsf{V}_Z(I_Z) \rightarrow 0$, otherwise, it computes $r' = f(\hat{s}^{-1} \cdot (h(m) \cdot Y + r \cdot Z)) \bmod q$, and if $r' = r$, outputs 1, else outputs 0.
- $\mathsf{Adapt}(y, \hat{\sigma}) \rightarrow \sigma$: On input the witness y, and pre-signature $\hat{\sigma}$, the algorithm computes $s = \hat{s} \cdot y^{-1} \bmod q$ and outputs the signature $\sigma = (r, s)$.
- $\mathsf{Ext}(\sigma, \hat{\sigma}, I_Y) \rightarrow y$: On input the signature σ, the pre-signature $\hat{\sigma}$ and the instance I_Y, it computes $y = \hat{s}/s \bmod q$. If $(I_Y, y) \in \mathsf{R}$, it outputs y, else outputs $\perp$.

Note that in the pre-signing phase, our ECDSA-AS uses the signing key x as the witness to compute the pre-signing public parameter $Z = xY$ and zero-knowledge proof π_Z, then the later pre-signing operation is similar to original ECDSA signing algorithm except for modifying some parameters by using (Z, Y) as the verification key and base point instead of (Q, G).

Theorem 1. *Assuming that the positive ECDSA $\sum$ is SUF-CMA secure, and R is a hard relation, NIZKPoK and NIZK are secure, above ECDSA-AS $\Pi_{\mathsf{R},\sum}$ is secure in random oracle model.*

[7] The function f is defined as the projection to x-coordinate.

Following [2], we use self-proving structure in our ECDSA-AS and prove that our ECDSA-AS scheme satisfies pre-signature adaptability, pre-signature correctness, aEUF-CMA security, and witness extractability.

Lemma 1. (Pre-signature adaptability) *Above ECDSA-AS* $\Pi_{\mathsf{R},\sum}$ *satisfies pre-signature adaptability.*

Proof. For any $(I_Y, y) \in \mathsf{R}$, $m \in \{0,1\}^*$, $G, Q, Y, Z \in \mathbb{G}$ and $\hat{\sigma} = (r, \hat{s}, Z, \pi_Z)$. For $\mathsf{pVrfy}_{vk}(m, I_Y, \hat{\sigma}) \to 1$. That is, $Y = yG, Z = xyG$, $\hat{K} = (h(m) \cdot \hat{s}^{-1})Y + r \cdot \hat{s}^{-1}Z = kY$, $r' = f(\hat{K}) = f(kY) = r$. By definition of Adapt, we know that $\mathsf{Adapt}(\hat{\sigma}, y) \to \sigma$, where $\sigma = (r, s), s = \hat{s} \cdot y^{-1} = (yk)^{-1}(h(m) + rx) \bmod q$. Hence, we have

$$K' = (h(m) \cdot s^{-1})G + r \cdot s^{-1}Q = kY.$$

Therefore, $r' = f(K') = r$. That is, $\mathsf{Vrfy}_{vk}(m,\sigma) \to 1$.

Lemma 2. (Pre-signature correctness) *Above ECDSA-AS* $\Pi_{\mathsf{R},\sum}$ *satisfies pre-signature correctness.*

Proof. For any $x, y \in \mathbb{Z}_q$, $Q = xG, Y = yG$ and $m \in \{0,1\}^*$. For $\mathsf{pSign}_{(vk,sk)}(m, I_Y) \to \hat{\sigma} = (r,\ \hat{s},\ Z,\ \pi_Z)$, it holds that $Y = yG, Z = xY$, $\hat{s} = k^{-1}(h(m) + rx) \bmod q$ for some $k \leftarrow \mathbb{Z}_q$. Set $\hat{K} = (h(m) \cdot \hat{s}^{-1})Y + r \cdot \hat{s}^{-1}Z = kY$. Therefore, $r' = f(\hat{K}) = f(kY) = r$, we have $\mathsf{pVrfy}_{vk}(m, I_Y, \hat{\sigma}) \to 1$. By Lemma 1, this implies that $\mathsf{Vrfy}_{vk}(m, \sigma) \to 1$, for $\mathsf{Adapt}(\hat{\sigma}, y) \to \sigma = (r, s)$. By the definition of Adapt, we know that $s = \hat{s} \cdot y^{-1}$ and $y' = \mathsf{Ext}(\sigma, \hat{\sigma}, I_Y) = \hat{s}/s = \hat{s}/(\hat{s}/y) = y$. Hence, $(I_Y, y') \in \mathsf{R}$.

Lemma 3. (aEUF-CMA security) *Assuming that the positive ECDSA signature scheme* $\sum$ *is SUF-CMA secure,* R *is a hard relation, NIZKPoK and NIZK are secure, above ECDSA-AS* $\Pi_{\mathsf{R},\sum}$ *is aEUF-CMA secure.*

Proof. We prove the aEUF-CMA security by reduction to the strong unforgeability of positive ECDSA signatures. Following [2], our ECDSA-AS uses the same hard relation $(I_Y = (Y, \pi_Y), y)$, where NIZKPoK_Y satisfies straight-line extractability, so the simulator can extract the witness from I_Y. Our proof works by showing that, for any PPT adversary $\mathcal{A}$ breaking aEUF-CMA security of the ECDSA-AS, we construct a PPT simulator $\mathcal{S}$ who breaks the SUF-CMA security of ECDSA. $\mathcal{S}$ has access to the signing oracle $\mathcal{O}_{\text{ECDSA-Sign}}$ of ECDSA and the random oracle $\mathcal{H}_{\text{ECDSA}}$. It needs to simulate oracle for $\mathcal{A}$, namely random oracle ($\mathcal{H}$), signing oracle ($\mathcal{O}_{\text{Sign}}$) and pre-signing oracle ($\mathcal{O}_{\text{pSign}}$).

The simulator $\mathcal{S}$ can use its oracle $\mathcal{O}_{\text{ECDSA-Sign}}$ and $\mathcal{H}_{\text{ECDSA}}$ to simulate $\mathcal{O}_{\text{Sign}}$ and $\mathcal{H}$. The main challenge is simulating $\mathcal{O}_{\text{pSign}}$ queries. Because $\mathcal{S}$ can extract the witness from I_Y, it uses its oracle $\mathcal{O}_{\text{ECDSA-Sign}}$ to get a full signature on m which is queried by $\mathcal{A}$, and transform the full signature into a pre-signature. What's more, $\mathcal{S}$ can use the zero-knowledge property of NIZK_Z to simulate π_Z for a statement (G, Q, Y, Z) without knowing the corresponding witness x.

We prove security by describing a sequence of games $G_0, \cdots, G_4$, where G_0 is the original aSigForge game. Then we show that for all $i = 0, \cdots, 3$, G_i and G_{i+1} are indistinguishable.

- Game G_0: This game corresponds to the original aSigForge game.
- Game G_1: This game works as G_0 with the exception that upon the adversary outputting a forgery σ^*. It checks that if completing the pre-signature $\hat{\sigma}$ using the secret value y results in σ^*. If yes, it aborts.
- Game G_2: This game works as G_1 excepting that in $\mathcal{O}_{\text{pSign}}$, it extracts a witness y' by executor K. It aborts if $(I_Y, y') \notin \mathsf{R}$.
- Game G_3: This game works as G_2 excepting that it extracts a witness y and calculates $Z = yQ$, and simulates a zero-knowledge proof π_S.
- Game G_4: In this game, upon receiving the challenge message m^* from $\mathcal{A}$, it creates a full signature by executing the Sign algorithm and transforms the resulting signature into a pre-signature in the same way as in the previous game G_3 during the $\mathcal{O}_{\text{pSign}}$ execution.

There exists a simulator that perfectly simulates G_4 and uses $\mathcal{A}$ to win a positive ECDSA strongSigForge game.

- Signing oracle queries: Upon $\mathcal{A}$ querying $\mathcal{O}_{\text{Sign}}$ on input m, $\mathcal{S}$ forwards m to its oracle $\mathcal{O}_{\text{ECDSA-sign}}$ and forwards its response to $\mathcal{A}$.
- Random oracle queries: Upon $\mathcal{A}$ querying $\mathcal{H}$ on input x, if $H[x] = \perp$, then $\mathcal{S}$ queries $\mathcal{H}_{\text{ECDSA}}(x)$, otherwise the simulator returns $\mathcal{H}[x]$.
- Pre-signing oracle queries: Upon $\mathcal{A}$ querying $\mathcal{O}_{\text{pSign}}$ on input (m, I_Y), the simulator extracts y, and forwards m to $\mathcal{O}_{\text{ECDSA-sign}}$ and gets (r, s), then $\mathcal{S}$ computes $\hat{s} = s \cdot y$, $Z = yQ = xY$ and simulates a zero-knowledge proof π_S, and outputs $(r, \hat{s}, Z, \pi_S)$.
- In the challenge phase: Upon $\mathcal{A}$ outputting the challenge message m^*, $\mathcal{S}$ generates $(I_Y, y) \leftarrow \mathsf{GenR}(1^\lambda)$, forwards m^* to $\mathcal{O}_{\text{ECDSA-sign}}$ and gets (r, s). And then, $\mathcal{S}$ generates the pre-signature $\hat{\sigma}^*$ in the same way as during $\mathcal{O}_{\text{pSign}}$. Upon $\mathcal{A}$ outputting σ^*, the simulator outputs (m^*, σ^*) as its own forgery.

Therefore, the simulator $\mathcal{S}$ can simulate the views of $\mathcal{A}$. It remains to show that the forgery output by $\mathcal{A}$ can be used by the simulator to win the positive ECDSA strongSigForge game.

Claim 1. *Let Bad_1 be the event that G_1 aborts, then* $\Pr[Bad_1] \leq \mathsf{negl}_1(\lambda)$.

Proof. We prove this claim using a reduction to the hardness of the relation R. The simulator gets a challenge I_Y^*, and it generates a key pair $(vk, sk) \leftarrow \mathsf{Gen}(1^\lambda)$ to simulate $\mathcal{A}$'s queries of $\mathcal{H}$, $\mathcal{O}_{\text{Sign}}$ and $\mathcal{O}_{\text{pSign}}$. This simulation of the oracles works as described in G_1. Upon receiving challenge message m^* from $\mathcal{A}$, $\mathcal{S}$ computes a pre-signature $\hat{\sigma} \leftarrow \mathsf{pSign}_{(vk,sk)}(m^*, I_Y^*)$, returns $\hat{\sigma}$ to $\mathcal{A}$ who outputs a forgery σ^*.

Assuming that Bad_1 happened (i.e. $\mathsf{Adapt}(\hat{\sigma}, y) = \sigma^*$), the simulator can extract $y^* \leftarrow \mathsf{Ext}(\sigma^*, \hat{\sigma}, I_Y^*)$. Since the challenge I_Y^* is an instance of the hard relation R and hence equally distributed to the public output of GenR. Hence the probability of $\mathcal{S}$ breaking the hardness of the relation is equal to the probability of the Bad_1 event.

Claim 2. *G_0, G_1, G_2, G_3 and G_4 are computationally indistinguishable.*

Proof. Since G_1 and G_0 are equivalent except if event Bad_1 occurs, it holds that $|\Pr[G_0 = 1] - \Pr[G_1 = 1]| \le \mathsf{negl}_1(\lambda)$.

According to the straight-line extractability of the NIZKPoK_Y, for a witness y extracted from a proof π_Y of the instance I_Y such that $\mathsf{V}_Y(I_Y, \pi_Y) \to 1$, it holds that $(I_Y, y) \in \mathsf{R}$ except with negligible probability. It holds that $|\Pr[G_2 = 1] - \Pr[G_1 = 1]| \le \mathsf{negl}_2(\lambda)$.

Due to the zero-knowledge property of the NIZK_Z, the simulator can compute a proof π_S which is computationally indistinguishable from a proof $\pi_Z \leftarrow \mathsf{P}_Z((G, Q, Y, Z), x)$. Hence, it holds that $|\Pr[G_3 = 1] - \Pr[G_2 = 1]| \le \mathsf{negl}_3(\lambda)$.

Following above proof, due to the zero-knowledge property of the NIZK_Z, G_4 is indistinguishable from G_3 and it holds that $|\Pr[G_4 = 1] - \Pr[G_3 = 1]| \le \mathsf{negl}_2(\lambda)$.

Claim 3. (m^*, σ^*) *constitutes a valid forgery in positive ECDSA strongSigForge game.*

Proof. We show that (m^*, σ^*) has not been output by the oracle $\mathcal{O}_{\text{ECDSA-Sign}}$ before. Note that $\mathcal{A}$ has not previously made a query on the challenge message m^* to either $\mathcal{O}_{\text{Sign}}$ or $\mathcal{O}_{\text{pSign}}$. Hence, $\mathcal{O}_{\text{ECDSA-Sign}}$ is only queried on m^* during the challenge phase. As shown in game G_1, the adversary outputs a forgery σ^* which is equal to the signature σ output by $\mathcal{O}_{\text{ECDSA-Sign}}$ during the challenge phase only with negligible probability. Hence, $\mathcal{O}_{\text{ECDSA-Sign}}$ has never output σ^* on query m^* before and consequently (m^*, σ^*) constitutes a valid forgery for positive ECDSA strongSigForge game.

From the games G_0 to G_4, we get that $|\Pr[G_0 = 1] - \Pr[G_4 = 1]| \le \mathsf{negl}_1(\lambda) + \mathsf{negl}_2(\lambda) + \mathsf{negl}_3(\lambda) + \mathsf{negl}_4(\lambda) \le \mathsf{negl}(\lambda)$. Since $\mathcal{S}$ provides a perfect simulation of game G_4, we obtain:

$$\begin{aligned}\Pr[\text{aSigForge}_{\mathcal{A},\Pi_{\mathsf{R},\Sigma}}(\lambda) = 1] = \Pr[G_0 = 1] &\le \Pr[G_4 = 1] + \mathsf{negl}(\lambda)\\ &\le \Pr[\text{sSigForge}_{\mathcal{A},\Sigma}(\lambda) = 1] + \mathsf{negl}(\lambda).\end{aligned}$$

Lemma 4. (Witness extractability). *Assuming that the positive ECDSA is SUF-CMA secure,* R *is a hard relation, NIZKPoK and NIZK are secure, above ECDSA-AS* $\Pi_{\mathsf{R},\Sigma}$ *is witness extractable.*

Proof. Our proof is to reduce the witness extractability to the strong unforgeability of the positive ECDSA. Following the proof of Lemma 3, the simulator $\mathcal{S}$ can use its oracle $\mathcal{O}_{\text{ECDSA-Sign}}$ and $\mathcal{H}_{\text{ECDSA}}$ to simulate $\mathcal{O}_{\text{Sign}}$ and $\mathcal{H}$ of $\mathcal{A}$.

The main challenge in this proof is to simulate the pre-signing oracle $\mathcal{O}_{\text{pSign}}$. The crucial difference between aWitExt and aSigForge is that in the challenge phase of aSigForge, I_Y is chosen by challenger, but in the challenge phase of aWitExt, I_Y is chosen by $\mathcal{A}$. That is, $\mathcal{S}$ can not choose (I_Y, y). Following [2], our ECDSA-AS uses the same hard relation $(I_Y = (Y, \pi_Y), y)$, where NIZKPoK_Y satisfies straight-line extractability, so $\mathcal{S}$ can extract the witness y from challenge instance $I_Y = (Y, \pi_Y)$. And then, $\mathcal{S}$ forwards m to $\mathcal{O}_{\text{ECDSA-sign}}$ and gets the signature $\sigma = (r, s)$, then $\mathcal{S}$ computes $\hat{s} = s \cdot y$, $Z = yQ$ and simulates a zero-knowledge proof π_S, and outputs the pre-signature $\hat{\sigma} = (r, \hat{s}, Z, \pi_S)$.

Therefore, we can construct a simulator $\mathcal{S}$ following the proof of Lemma 3 excepting that in the challenge phase, $\mathcal{S}$ does not generate the hard relation (I_Y, y) to get the witness y, but obtains the witness from the instance I_Y chosen by $\mathcal{A}$ based on the straight-line extractability. $\mathcal{S}$ can simulate the views of $\mathcal{A}$. The simulator can win the positive ECDSA strongSigForge game if $\mathcal{A}$ can break the witness extractability of ECDSA-AS.

4 Fast ECDSA-Based Adaptor Signature Schemes with Offline/Online Pre-signing

In this section, we show two fast ECDSA-AS schemes called ECDSA-AS$_{sk}$ and ECDSA-AS$_{wit}$ with offline/online pre-signing, where ECDSA-AS$_{sk}$ uses the signing key x as the witness to compute $Z = xY$, and ECDSA-AS$_{wit}$ uses the witness y of hard relation (I_Y, y) as the witness to compute $Z = yQ$.

In our ECDSA-AS, the pre-signing public parameter $Z = xY$ and the zero-knowledge proof $\pi_Z \leftarrow \mathsf{P}_Z(I_Z = (G, Q, Y, Z), x)$ are independent of the message m and the random value k, so the signer can compute the pre-signing public parameter and the zero-knowledge proof *offline* before getting the message. ECDSA-AS$_{sk}$ can be designed from our ECDSA-AS directly with offline computing $Z = xY$ and π_Z. Refer to the Sect. 3 for specific construction which is ignored here.

We construct efficient ECDSA-AS$_{wit}$ as follows. Formally, Let $(Q = xG, x)$ be the verification key and signing key of ECDSA. We define hard relations $\mathsf{R} = \{(I_Y = (Y, \pi_Y \leftarrow \mathsf{P}_Y(Y, y)), y) |\ Y = yG \wedge \mathsf{V}_Y(I_Y) = 1\}$, $\mathsf{R}_Z = \{(I_Z = (G, Y, Q, Z), y) | Y = yG \wedge Z = yQ\}$ and $I = (I_Y, I_Z)$.

- $\mathsf{pSign}_{(vk,sk)}(m, I) \rightarrow \hat{\sigma}$: On input a key-pair $(vk, sk) = (Q, x)$, a message m and an instance I, the algorithm chooses $k \leftarrow \mathbb{Z}_q$, computes $r = f(kY)$, $\hat{s} = k^{-1}(h(m) + rx) \bmod q$ and outputs $\hat{\sigma} = (r, \hat{s})$.
- $\mathsf{pVrfy}_{vk}(m, I, \hat{\sigma}) \rightarrow 0/1$: On input the verification key $vk = Q$, a message m, an instance I, and a pre-signature value $\hat{\sigma}$, the algorithm computes $r' = f(\hat{s}^{-1} \cdot (h(m) \cdot Y + r \cdot Z))$, and if $r' = r$, outputs 1, else outputs 0.
- $\mathsf{Adapt}(y, \hat{\sigma}) \rightarrow \sigma$: On input the witness y, and pre-signature $\hat{\sigma}$, the algorithm computes $s = \hat{s} \cdot y^{-1} \bmod q$ and outputs the signature $\sigma = (r, s)$.
- $\mathsf{Ext}(\sigma, \hat{\sigma}, I) \rightarrow y$: On input the signature σ, the pre-signature $\hat{\sigma}$ and the instance I, it computes $y = \hat{s}/s \bmod q$. If $(I, y) \in \mathsf{R}$, it outputs y, else outputs $\perp$.

Note that ECDSA-AS$_{wit}$ is similar to our ECDSA-AS excepting that the signer can compute $Z = yQ$ and $\pi_Z \leftarrow \mathsf{P}_Z(I_Z = (G, Y, Q, Z), y)$ offline. Before running the online pre-signing algorithm, the signer should *check the validity* of π_Y and π_Z offline to ensure that Y and Z are correct.

Correctness. Following the proofs of Lemma 1 and Lemma 2, our ECDSA-$AS_{sk/wit}$ schemes also satisfy pre-signature adaptability and pre-signature correctness.

Security. Our ECDSA-$AS_{sk/wit}$ schemes embed the hard relation ($I_Y = (Y, \pi_Y)$, y) [2]. In the security proof, the simulator can extract the witness y and simulate the pre-signing oracle. Following the proofs of Lemma 3 and Lemma 4, our ECDSA-$AS_{sk/wit}$ schemes also satisfy aEUF-CMA security and witness extractability.

Comparisons with ECDSA-AS [2]**.** Our ECDSA-AS_{wit} use y as the witness, so the signer (hard relation chooser) can help all other participants compute the pre-signing public parameter $Z_i = yQ_i$ and the zero-knowledge proofs π_{Z_i} in a batch and offline. In particular, consider the special verification scenario, such as (batched) atomic swaps, ECDSA-AS_{wit} only transmits *one* zero-knowledge proof π_{Z_0} which is independent of the number of participants, since all participants can compute the pre-signing public parameter locally.

Our ECDSA-$AS_{sk/wit}$ can be seen as an adaptor signature that specifies the signer, since the hard relation chooser requires the verification key Q_i of other parties to compute $Z_i = yQ_i$ and π_{Z_i}, while ECDSA-AS [2] dose not restrict the signer's verification key. However, this does not affect the application of ECDSA-$AS_{sk/wit}$ in atomic swaps, because the verification keys are public before the protocol begins. In addition, consider special verification scenarios, ECDSA-$AS_{sk/wit}$ can remove above restriction because the zero-knowledge proofs of other parties can be removed.

5 Performance and Experimental Results

5.1 Theoretical Analysis

As is shown in Table 1, we give the theoretical analysis of communication cost and efficiency of ECDSA-AS [2,18] and our schemes, respectively. The first ECDSA-AS proposed by Moreno-Sanchez et al. [18] does not provide provable security. Then Aumayr et al. [2] uses self-proving structure $(I_Y = (Y, \pi_Y), y)$ to give a provably secure ECDSA-AS. But this scheme requires that proving $\hat{K} = kG$ and $K = kY$ satisfy equality of discrete logarithms with the witness k. For each message to be signed, the signer needs to choose new random values and computes new pre-signing public parameters and zero-knowledge proofs.

Our ECDSA-$AS_{sk/wit}$ can use the witness x or y to prove $(Z = xY, Q = xG)$ or $(Z = yQ, Y = yG)$ satisfy equality of discrete logarithms offline. The online pre-signing algorithm is similar to ECDSA signing algorithm and can enjoy the same efficiency as ECDSA. In ECDSA-AS_{wit}, the hard relation chooser can compute all pre-signing public parameters $Z_i = yQ_i$ and zero-knowledge proofs for all other participants *in a batch* and *offline*. In particular, consider special verification scenarios, such as (batched) atomic swaps, ECDSA-$AS_{sk/wit}$ can reduce the number of zero-knowledge proofs to one, since all parties can compute public pre-signing parameters locally, but ECDSA-AS [2,18] requires the number of zero-knowledge proofs is linear with the number of participants.

Table 1. Communication cost and efficiency comparison

Schemes	PK Size	SK Size	Online Pre-signature size	The number of zk proofs	The number of Pre-signing parameter	Batched pre-signing parameter	Provable security
ECDSA-AS [18]	$\|\mathbb{G}\|$	$\|\mathbb{Z}_q\|$	$\|\mathbb{G}\| + 4\|\mathbb{Z}_q\|$	$2n$	$2n$	×	?
ECDSA-AS [2]	$\|\mathbb{G}\|$	$\|\mathbb{Z}_q\|$	$\|\mathbb{G}\| + 4\|\mathbb{Z}_q\|$	$2n$	$2n$	×	√
Our ECDSA-AS$_{sk}$	$\|\mathbb{G}\|$	$\|\mathbb{Z}_q\|$	$2\|\mathbb{Z}_q\|$	n	$n+1$	×	√
Our ECDSA-AS$_{wit}$	$\|\mathbb{G}\|$	$\|\mathbb{Z}_q\|$	$2\|\mathbb{Z}_q\|$	1	$n+1$	√	√

‡ $|\mathbb{G}|$ and $|\mathbb{Z}_q|$ denotes the size of the element in the group $\mathbb{G}$ and $\mathbb{Z}_q$, respectively. n denotes the number of parties in the one-to-n atomic swaps. ? denotes unclear.

5.2 Experimental Analysis

In order to evaluate the practical performance of our schemes, we implement the ECDSA-AS [2], our ECDSA-AS, and ECDSA-AS$_{wit}$ based on the OpenSSL library. All experiments are carried out on an Intel Core i5 CPU 2.3 GHz and 8 GB RAM running macOS High Sierra 10.13.3 system.

We run ECDSA-AS [2], our ECDSA-AS and ECDSA-AS$_{wit}$ on the standard NIST curve NID.X9.62.prime256v1. Since the verification algorithm, the adaptor algorithm and the extraction algorithm are rough same, we omit the comparison. We show the efficiency of the online pre-signing algorithm in Table 2. The average running times over 1000 executions of the online pre-signing operation in ECDSA-AS [2], our ECDSA-AS and ECDSA-AS$_{wit}$ are 173.65 µs, 189.72 µs and 71.64 µs. The experimental results show that our ECDSA-AS$_{wit}$ reduces online pre-signing time by about 60% compared with the state-of-the-art ECDSA-AS [2].

Table 2. Runtime of the online pre-signing operation comparing our ECDSA-AS and ECDSA-AS$_{wit}$ to ECDSA-AS [2]

Schemes	ECDSA-AS [2]	Our ECDSA-AS	Our ECDSA-AS$_{wit}$
Runtime (online)	173.65 µs	189.72 µs	71.64 µs

6 Application

6.1 Verification Scenario

According to the definition of AS [2], the verification of pre-signature does not limit the verifier, so it can be verified by *anyone*. However, the pre-signature of AS is generated and verified off-chain and is not published on the blockchain, so AS does not require such a strong property and the pre-signature satisfies the specific verification scenario in which it is only verified by the participants.

As mentioned in Fig. 1, in the atomic swaps, the pre-signatures are only generated and verified by participants U_0 and U_1 off-chain. Thus, ECDSA-AS$_{sk/wit}$ can reduce the number of zero-knowledge proofs. To be specific, the zero-knowledge proof π_{Z_1} of U_1 can be removed, because U_0 can use the witness y to compute $Z_1 = yQ_1$. The zero-knowledge proof π_{Z_0} of U_0 cannot be removed, since U_1 does not know the signing key x_0 and the witness y of U_0, and requires π_{Z_0} to ensure U_0 generates Z_0 correctly. In particular, even if U_0 runs an atomic swap protocol with many parties U_i, $i \in [n]$, it still only needs one zero-knowledge proof π_{Z_0}. Note that these modifications do not affect correctness or security, since the simulator can extract the witness y from I_Y and simulates the pre-signing public parameter $Z_1 = yQ_1$.

6.2 Batched Atomic Swaps

We develop batched atomic swaps from one-to-one atomic swaps: U_0 (hard relation chooser) spends c_{0i} (transaction tx_{0i}) to U_i, $i \in [n]$ in a batch and U_i spends each c_i (transaction tx_i) to U_0. It can be applied to one party with many addresses (accounts) or one party with a lot of transactions that need to exchange with many users once, such as the scenario of the Exchange. Compared with running independently n times one-to-one atomic swaps between U_0 and U_i, $i \in [n]$, batched atomic swaps reduce the number of hard relations (Y, y) from n to *one*.

We introduce batched atomic swaps as follows: All parties U_0 and U_i, $i \in [n]$ first set the time-lock for c_{0i} and c_i on-chain, where the timeouts $t_i < t_0$ such that U_i can have enough time to react. Then, U_0 chooses one hard relation $(Y, y) \in R$ and pre-signing the transactions tx_{0i} for spending the coins c_{0i} to U_i in a batch, and sends the pre-signature $\hat{\sigma}_{0i}$, tx_{0i}, Y to U_{0i}. Then, U_i checks the validity of $\hat{\sigma}_{0i}$ and pre-signing a transaction tx_i for spending the coins c_i to U_0 and sends the pre-signature $\hat{\sigma}_i$, tx_i to U_0. U_0 can check the validity of all pre-signatures $\hat{\sigma}_i$[8] and adapts $\hat{\sigma}_i$ into the full signature σ_i by the witness y, and publishes all σ_i on the blockchain to get the coin c_i in a batch. U_i can extract the witness y from σ_i and $\hat{\sigma}_i$ and adapts $\hat{\sigma}_{0i}$ into σ_{0i}, and publishes σ_{0i} on the blockchain to get the coin c_{0i} before timeouts t_0.

$U_0((Q_0, x_0), Q_i, tx_{0i}), i \in [n]$		$U_i((Q_i, x_i), Q_0, tx_i), i \in [n]$
	Offline phase	
$\mathsf{GenR}(1^\lambda) \rightarrow (Y, y)$, $\mathsf{P}_Y(Y, y) \rightarrow \pi_Y$, $Z_i = yQ_i$, $\mathsf{P}_Z(I_Z = (G, Y, Q_0, Z_0), y) \rightarrow \pi_{Z_0}$	$\xrightarrow{I_Y, Z_0, \pi_{Z_0}}$	If $\mathsf{V}_Y(I_Y) \rightarrow 0$, or $\mathsf{V}_Z((G, Y, Q_0, Z_0), \pi_{Z_0}) \rightarrow 0$, output $\perp$
	Online phase	
$\hat{\sigma_{0i}} \leftarrow \mathsf{pSign}((Q_0, x_0), (Y, Z_0), tx_{0i})$	$\xrightarrow{\hat{\sigma_{0i}}, tx_{0i}}$	If $\mathsf{pVrfy}(Q_0, tx_{0i}, (Y, Z_0), \hat{\sigma_{0i}}) \rightarrow 0$, output $\perp$
If $\exists\, i \in [n]$, $\mathsf{pVrfy}(Q_i, tx_i, (Y, Z_i), \hat{\sigma}_i) \rightarrow 0$, output $\perp$, else, $\sigma_i \leftarrow \mathsf{Adapt}(\hat{\sigma}_i, y)$.	$\xleftarrow{\hat{\sigma}_i, tx_i}$	else, $\hat{\sigma}_i \leftarrow \mathsf{pSign}((Q_i, x_i), (Y, Z_i), tx_i)$
Publish all σ_i, $i \in [n]$ on blockchain	$\xrightarrow{\sigma_i}$	$y \leftarrow \mathsf{Ext}(\sigma_i, \hat{\sigma}_i, (I_Y, I_Z))$ $\sigma_{0i} \leftarrow \mathsf{Adapt}(\hat{\sigma_{0i}}, y)$. Publish σ_{0i} on blockchain

Fig. 2. Batched atomic swap based on ECDSA-AS$_{wit}$

[8] U_0 must check all pre-signatures, because any full signature is published on blockchain, the witness y can be extracted, and all coins can be taken.

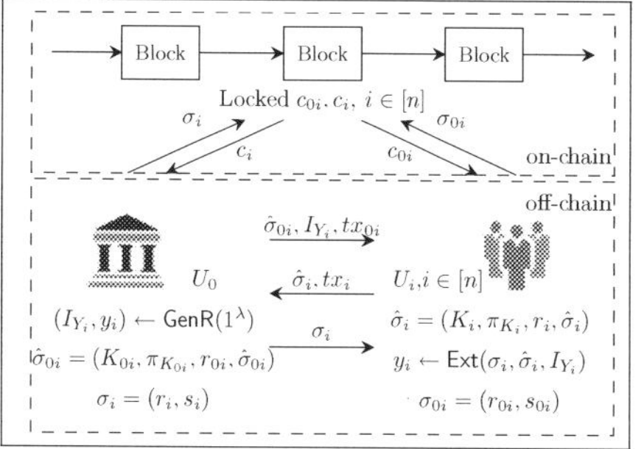

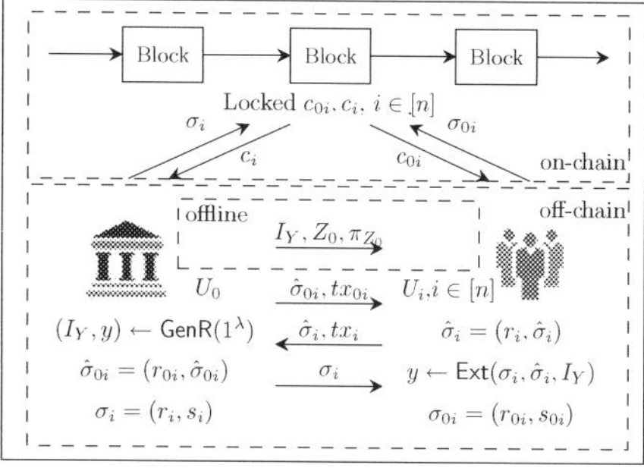

Fig. 3. n times independent ECDSA-based atomic swaps (left) and once ECDSA-based batched atomic swap (right)

Constructions Based on ECDSA-AS. Our ECDSA-AS$_{wit}$ is more efficient for using in batched atomic swaps than ECDSA-AS [2,18]. We show the batched atomic swap protocol based on ECDSA-AS$_{wit}$ in Fig. 2, and give the comparison of n times independent ECDSA-based atomic swaps and once ECDSA-based batched atomic swap in Fig. 3. To be specific, in the offline phase, U_0 computes $Z_0 = yQ_0$, $\pi_{Z_0} \leftarrow \mathsf{P}_Z((G, Y, Q_0, Z_0), y)$, and n pre-signing public parameters $Z_i = yQ_i$ in a batch and offline. U_i checks $\mathsf{V}_Z((G, Y, Q_0, Z_0), \pi_{Z_0}) \to 1$ and computes $Z_i = x_i Y$. In the online phase, U_0 runs n times AS$_{wit}$.pSign and AS$_{wit}$.pVrfy and each U_i runs once AS$_{wit}$.pSign and AS$_{wit}$.pVrfy, where AS$_{wit}$.pSign and AS$_{wit}$.pVrfy is same as original ECDSA signing and verification algorithms.

In ECDSA-AS [2,18], each user uses the random value k as the witness to generate the pre-signing public parameter $K = kY$ and zero-knowledge proof π_K. For a batch of transactions, U_0 needs to choose n random values to generate individual pre-signing public parameter $K_{0i} = k_{0i}Y$ and zero-knowledge proof $\pi_{K_{0i}} \leftarrow \mathsf{P}_K(G, \hat{K}_{0i} = k_{0i}G, Y, K_{0i})$ for U_i, and U_i uses different random value k_i to compute pre-signing public parameter $K_i = k_i Y$ and zero-knowledge proof $\pi_{K_i} \leftarrow \mathsf{P}_K(G, \hat{K}_i = k_i G, Y, K_i)$. What's more, U_0 needs to check the validity of all n proofs π_{K_i}, and U_i also needs to check the validity of $\pi_{K_{0i}}$.

As depicted in Table 3, we give a comparison of (batched) atomic swaps based on ECDSA-AS [2,18] or ECDSA-AS$_{sk/wit}$. Batched atomic swaps based on ECDSA-AS [2,18] need to compute $2n$ pre-signing public parameters and $2n$ zero-knowledge proofs. The batched atomic swaps can be seen as specific verification scenarios. Since U_0 computes all pre-signing public parameters $Z_i = yQ_i$ and U_i computes each pre-signing public parameter $Z_i = x_i Y$ locally, batched atomic swaps based on ECDSA-AS$_{wit}$ only requires one zero-knowledge proof π_{Z_0}. Compared with [2,18], ECDSA-AS$_{wit}$ reduces $2n-1$ zero-knowledge proofs.

Table 3. Comparison of ECDSA-AS [2,18] and our ECDSA-AS$_{sk/wit}$ used in (batched) atomic swaps

Schemes	Users	Atomic swaps ($i=1$)			Batched atomic swaps ($i \in [n]$)		
		Hard Relation	Pre-signing		Hard Relations	Pre-signing	
			Offline	Online		Offline	Online
ECDSA-AS [18]	U_0	(Y_i, y_i)	—	$\hat{\sigma_0} = (K_0, \pi_{K_0}, r_0, \hat{s_0})$	(Y, y)	—	$\hat{\sigma_{0i}} = (K_{0i}, \pi_{K_{0i}}, r_{0i}, \hat{s_{0i}})$
	U_i	—	—	$\hat{\sigma}_i = (K_i, \pi_{K_i}, r_i, \hat{s}_i)$	—	—	$\hat{\sigma}_i = (K_i, \pi_{K_i}, r_i, \hat{s}_i)$
ECDSA-AS [2]	U_0	(I_{Y_i}, y_i)	—	$\hat{\sigma_0} = (K_0, \pi_{K_0}, r_0, \hat{s_0})$	(I_Y, y)	—	$\hat{\sigma_{0i}} = (K_{0i}, \pi_{K_{0i}}, r_{0i}, \hat{s_{0i}})$
	U_i	—	—	$\hat{\sigma}_i = (K_i, \pi_{K_i}, r_i, \hat{s}_i)$	—	—	$\hat{\sigma}_i = (K_i, \pi_{K_i}, r_i, \hat{s}_i)$
Our ECDSA-AS$_{sk}$	U_0	(I_{Y_i}, y_i)	$Z_0 = x_0Y, \pi_{Z_0}$	$\hat{\sigma_0} = (r_0, \hat{s_0})$	(I_Y, y)	$Z_0 = x_0Y, \pi_{Z_0}$	$\hat{\sigma_{0i}} = (r_{0i}, \hat{s_{0i}})$
	U_i	—	$Z_i = x_iY$	$\hat{\sigma}_i = (r_i, \hat{s}_i)$	—	$Z_i = x_iY$	$\hat{\sigma}_i = (r_i, \hat{s}_i)$
Our ECDSA-AS$_{wit}$	U_0	(I_{Y_i}, y_i)	$Z_0 = yQ_0, Z_i = yQ_i, \pi_{Z_0}$	$\hat{\sigma_0} = (r_0, \hat{s_0})$	(I_Y, y)	$Z_0 = yQ_0, Z_i = yQ_i, \pi_{Z_0}$	$\hat{\sigma_{0i}} = (r_{0i}, \hat{s_{0i}})$
	U_i	—	—	$\hat{\sigma}_i = (r_i, \hat{s}_i)$	—	—	$\hat{\sigma}_i = (r_i, \hat{s}_i)$

‡—denotes no such operation, Q_i denotes the verification key, Z_i and K_i denote the pre-signing public parameters of our ECDSA-AS$_{sk/wit}$ and ECDSA-AS [2,18], π_{Z_i} and π_{K_i} denote the zero-knowledge proofs of proving Z_i and K_i are generated correctly. n denotes the number of parties in batched atomic swaps. $Z_i = x_iY$ and $Z_i = yQ_i$, $i \in [n]$ don't need to be transmitted.

7 Conclusion

In this paper, we propose an ECDSA-based adaptor signature and give the security proof based on ECDSA. And then, we develop two ECDSA-AS schemes called ECDSA-AS$_{sk}$ and ECDSA-AS$_{wit}$ with offline/online pre-signing which are more efficient than the state-of-the-art ECDSA-AS [2]. In particular, considering specific verification scenarios, ECDSA-AS$_{wit}$ reduces the number of zero-knowledge proofs in the pre-signing phase to one, independent of the number of participants. Furthermore, we develop batched atomic swaps which can reduce the number of hard relations in a batch compared with independently running one-to-one atomic swaps. Finally, we use our ECDSA-AS$_{wit}$ to construct the batched atomic swaps, it can reduce the number of zero-knowledge proofs into one compared with [2,18].

Acknowledgements. We thank the anonymous reviewers for their helpful feedback. This work is supported by the National Key Research and Development Program of China (Grant No. 2021YFA1000600) and the National Natural Science Foundation of China (Grant No. 62272269).

References

1. American National Standards Institute: X9.62: Public key cryptography for the financial services industry: the elliptic curve digital signature algorithm (ECDSA) (2005)
2. Aumayr, L., Ersoy, O., Erwig, A., Faust, S., Hostáková, K., Maffei, M., Moreno-Sanchez, P., Riahi, S.: Generalized channels from limited blockchain scripts and adaptor signatures. In: Tibouchi, M., Wang, H. (eds.) ASIACRYPT 2021. LNCS, vol. 13091, pp. 635–664. Springer, Cham (2021). https://doi.org/10.1007/978-3-030-92075-3_22
3. Aumayr, L., et al.: Bitcoin-compatible virtual channels. In: 42nd IEEE Symposium on Security and Privacy, SP 2021, pp. 901–918 (2021)
4. Bitcoin Wiki: Payment channels (2018). https://en.bitcoin.it/wiki/Paymentchannels

5. Canetti, R.: Universally composable security: a new paradigm for cryptographic protocols. In: 42nd Annual Symposium on Foundations of Computer Science, FOCS 2001. pp. 136–145. IEEE Computer Society (2001)
6. Chaum, D., Pedersen, T.P.: Wallet databases with observers. In: Brickell, E.F. (ed.) CRYPTO 1992. LNCS, vol. 740, pp. 89–105. Springer, Heidelberg (1993). https://doi.org/10.1007/3-540-48071-4_7
7. Decker, C., Wattenhofer, R.: A fast and scalable payment network with bitcoin duplex micropayment channels. In: Pelc, A., Schwarzmann, A.A. (eds.) SSS 2015. LNCS, vol. 9212, pp. 3–18. Springer, Cham (2015). https://doi.org/10.1007/978-3-319-21741-3_1
8. Deshpande, A., Herlihy, M.: Privacy-preserving cross-chain atomic swaps. In: Bernhard, M., et al. (eds.) FC 2020. LNCS, vol. 12063, pp. 540–549. Springer, Cham (2020). https://doi.org/10.1007/978-3-030-54455-3_38
9. Eckey, L., Faust, S., Hostáková, K., Roos, S.: Splitting payments locally while routing interdimensionally. IACR Cryptology ePrint Archive 2020, 555 (2020)
10. Esgin, M.F., Ersoy, O., Erkin, Z.: Post-quantum adaptor signatures and payment channel networks. In: Chen, L., Li, N., Liang, K., Schneider, S. (eds.) ESORICS 2020. LNCS, vol. 12309, pp. 378–397. Springer, Cham (2020). https://doi.org/10.1007/978-3-030-59013-0_19
11. Fiat, A., Shamir, A.: How to prove yourself: practical solutions to identification and signature problems. In: Odlyzko, A.M. (ed.) CRYPTO 1986. LNCS, vol. 263, pp. 186–194. Springer, Heidelberg (1987). https://doi.org/10.1007/3-540-47721-7_12
12. Fischlin, M.: Communication-efficient non-interactive proofs of knowledge with online extractors. In: Shoup, V. (ed.) CRYPTO 2005. LNCS, vol. 3621, pp. 152–168. Springer, Heidelberg (2005). https://doi.org/10.1007/11535218_10
13. Gugger, J.: Bitcoin-monero cross-chain atomic swap. IACR Cryptology ePrint Archive 2020, 1126 (2020)
14. Lindell, Y.: Fast secure two-party ECDSA signing. In: Katz, J., Shacham, H. (eds.) CRYPTO 2017. LNCS, vol. 10402, pp. 613–644. Springer, Cham (2017). https://doi.org/10.1007/978-3-319-63715-0_21
15. Malavolta, G., Moreno-Sanchez, P., Kate, A., Maffei, M., Ravi, S.: Concurrency and privacy with payment-channel networks. In: Thuraisingham, B.M., Evans, D., Malkin, T., Xu, D. (eds.) Proceedings of the 2017 ACM SIGSAC Conference on Computer and Communications Security, CCS 2017, pp. 455–471. ACM (2017)
16. Malavolta, G., Moreno-Sanchez, P., Schneidewind, C., Kate, A., Maffei, M.: Anonymous multi-hop locks for blockchain scalability and interoperability. In: 26th Annual Network and Distributed System Security Symposium, NDSS 2019 (2019)
17. Miller, A., Bentov, I., Bakshi, S., Kumaresan, R., McCorry, P.: Sprites and state channels: payment networks that go faster than lightning. In: Goldberg, I., Moore, T. (eds.) FC 2019. LNCS, vol. 11598, pp. 508–526. Springer, Cham (2019). https://doi.org/10.1007/978-3-030-32101-7_30
18. Moreno-Sanchez, P., Kate, A.: Scriptless scripts with ECDSA. Lightning-dev mailing list https://lists.linuxfoundation.org/pipermail/lightning-dev/attachments/20180426/fe978423/attachment-0001.pdf
19. Poelstra, A.: Lightning in scriptless scripts. mimblewimble team mailing list (2017). https://lists.launchpad.net/mimblewimble/msg00086.html
20. Poon, J., Dryja, T.: The bitcoin lightning network: scalable off-chain instant payments. https://lightning.network/lightning-network-paper.pdf
21. Schnorr, C.P.: Efficient identification and signatures for smart cards. In: Brassard, G. (ed.) CRYPTO 1989. LNCS, vol. 435, pp. 239–252. Springer, New York (1990). https://doi.org/10.1007/0-387-34805-0_22

Searching for Encrypted Data on Blockchain: An Efficient, Secure and Fair Realization

Jianzhang Chen[1,2], Haibo Tian[1,2], and Fangguo Zhang[1,2(✉)]

[1] School of Computer Science and Engineering, Sun Yat-sen University, Guangzhou 510006, China
isszhfg@mail.sysu.edu.cn

[2] Guangdong Province Key Laboratory of Information Security Technology, Guangzhou 510006, China

Abstract. Searchable symmetric encryption (SSE) is a research hotspot in applied cryptography, with the purpose of protecting outsourced data while enabling querying of encrypted data. However, the majority of current research focuses on the scenario in which data is stored on a single server and disregards the possibility that both the clients and servers are malicious. While several existing blockchain-based SSE schemes provide solutions to the issues above, they do not simultaneously achieve security, fairness, and decentralized storage.

In this paper, we explore how to efficiently solve the above problems in the blockchain setting. We build up a decentralized fair SSE framework in a layered fashion. First, we present a practical and efficient method for accessing data on the blockchain. Based on this, we craft a decentralized publicly verifiable SSE scheme in which encrypted indexes are stored on the blockchain and search operations are shifted to be executed off-chain for lightweight decentralized storage and efficient query performance. Then, we use smart contracts to confer fairness to SSE by constructing a game model that makes each party prefer to cooperate. Finally, we implement and evaluate our framework on Ethereum. The experimental results demonstrate that our design is effective and practical.

Keywords: Searchable symmetric encryption · Blockchain · Fairness

1 Introduction

Symmetric searchable encryption (SSE), a cryptographic primitive aimed at enabling the search function of encrypted data while guaranteeing data confidentiality, has received considerable attention. It was initially proposed by Song *et al.* [16]. Since Curtmola *et al.* [7] developed a better definition of the functionality and security of SSE, numerous feature-rich schemes have emerged in recent years, including dynamic SSE [5] and verifiable SSE [3].

However, the majority of SSE schemes store data on a single server, making the single point of failure one of the obstacles to the deployment of SSE schemes.

W. Susilo et al. (Eds.): ISC 2022, LNCS 13640, pp. 194–213, 2022.
https://doi.org/10.1007/978-3-031-22390-7_13

Even though most cloud providers offer redundant backup services, it remains an unresolved question how to fully utilize these backup servers for search. To compound the issue, when users find that the data stored on the server has been altered or deleted, it is difficult to migrate the data to other cloud providers without ensuring the completeness and accuracy of their data.

Beyond that, most SSE schemes are based on the assumption that data users are trustworthy and servers are honest but curious. However, the usability and security of SSE will be significantly weakened if both data users and servers are malicious. Even though verifiable SSE schemes are reasonable solutions to the problem that a malicious server returns incorrect results, it is impossible to prevent a malicious data user from claiming that the server returned incorrect results to avoid paying the remuneration, even if the server performs the search honestly.

Blockchain has emerged in the last decade and has brought the possibility of decentralization and fairness to SSE. Originating from Bitcoin, blockchain is a cryptographic technology that maintains a reliable and tamper-evident database through decentralization. In recent years, some works have been utilizing blockchain to ensure fairness for SSE. Li *et al.* [14,15] first proposed a blockchain-based searchable symmetric encryption scheme whose construction is based on a blockchain transaction paradigm. Zhang *et al.* [22] proposed a fair SSE scheme called TKSE based on the same transaction paradigm and claimed to achieve two-party verifiability and better compatibility with blockchain platforms. These schemes assume that the documents and encrypted indexes are placed on the server, and the blockchain acts as a fair judge, ensuring that all parties behave honestly. However, the introduction of the transaction paradigm makes the construction of SSE nonintuitive and poorly scalable. Moreover, these schemes do not implement decentralized storage because the encrypted indexes are still stored on a single server.

The advent of smart contracts provides solutions to the aforementioned issues. Hu *et al.* [8] proposed the first smart contract-based SSE scheme, in which the index storage and search operations are performed by the smart contract, ensuring fair transactions for all parties. Following the work of Hu *et al.* [8], some efficient schemes (*e.g.*, [6,9,10,13,19]) were proposed to enhance security and functionality. The introduction of smart contracts brings inherent fairness and decentralized storage to the schemes but at the expense of a significant overhead that limits the utility of SSE.

Consequently, some works (*e.g.*, [20,21]) still store encrypted indexes on cloud servers, while smart contracts are responsible for result verification. Essentially, these works replace the transaction paradigms of [15,22] with smart contracts to shield the details of transaction-related operations. However, it remains controversial whether these schemes achieve fairness. Even though these works use MACs or digital signatures to ensure verifiability of results, if a data owner uploads faulty tags (or proofs) in the setup phase, the judge may wrongly conclude that the server is dishonest even if it returns the correct result. Cai *et al.* [4] proposed a fair SSE framework based on smart contracts, in which a voluntary "arbitration panel" is responsible for verifying the results by simulating the index and search process. The dishonest party is determined by voting. This scheme is effective against the malicious behavior of both users and servers. However, it is an open problem to ensure the motivation and majority reliability of the arbiters continuously. Tang *et al.* [17] shift the responsibility of arbitration to a smart contract, eliminating the need to rely on volunteers to ensure fairness. However, the index reconstructions and search simulations of the smart contract incur a significant validation overhead.

In general, existing SSE schemes do not provide efficiency, fairness, and decentralized storage concurrently.

Contribution. This paper uses the aforementioned challenges as a springboard for proposing a decentralized and fair searchable symmetric encryption system based on blockchain. We choose to store the encrypted index on the blockchain for decentralized storage and try to alleviate the storage and search burdens. In this paper, we build up the decentralized fair SSE framework in a hierarchical manner and conduct experiments to evaluate its practical performance. Specifically, our work makes the following contributions.

- We suggest a practical and efficient way to store and read data on blockchain. We first provide an abstract model of blockchain storage called Append-only Block Storage (ABS), on which the subsequent designs will depend. Subsequently, we present a lookup table data structure Π_{LT} based on ABS and an implementation of it, a B$'$ tree, which is a minor modification of the B$^+$ tree where nodes are stored via ABS blocks. The B$'$ trees enable high fanout and low tree height to alleviate the performance bottleneck caused by reading ABS blocks.
- Based on ABS and Π_{LT}, we devise a decentralized publicly verifiable SSE scheme $\Pi_{\mathsf{PVSSE}}^{\mathsf{ABS}}$. The proposed scheme integrates the design ideas of [3] and [5] and uses digital signatures to enable data confidentiality and public verifiability. In our design, encrypted indexes are organized as ABS-based lookup tables, and search operations are shifted off the chain, which ensures lightweight on-chain storage and efficient query performance.
- We develop a decentralized fair SSE framework Π_{fair} based on Ethereum [18], which empowers $\Pi_{\mathsf{PVSSE}}^{\mathsf{ABS}}$ with fairness. It uses smart contracts to guarantee fair transactions between data users and service providers. We build a game paradigm in which all participants tend to behave faithfully, thereby avoiding deliberate fraud and resource waste.

2 Overview

2.1 System Model

We employ smart contracts to devise the decentralized fair SSE framework Π_{fair}. The framework consists of three types of entities: (i) data users (DUs), (ii) service providers (SPs), and (iii) a smart contract (SC). A data user is an entity that wants to store its sensitive data on the blockchain and enjoy encrypted search services. The DU does not store the complete blockchain data locally, so it needs to outsource the query operation to SPs, which are full nodes. To ensure the fairness of the outsourced search, the DU submits a query request as a task on the SC with remuneration and the task deadline. The SP decides whether to participate in the task based on the task information and pays a deposit if it does. All the participants compete to find the desired result for remuneration. When one of them successfully finds the data from the blockchain, it sends the result and the corresponding proof to the SC for verification. If the validation succeeds (*i.e.*, the result and the proof match), the SC returns the result to the DU and issues the remuneration to the winning SP.

If the SP finds a problem with the outsourced task, it declares the task invalid to seek compensation. When the task deadline passes and none of the participants can find the result, the SC checks whether any SP has declared the task invalid. If so, the data user's remuneration is seized and compensated to the SP who declared the task invalid, and all the SPs' deposits are refunded; if not, the remuneration is returned to the DU, and the deposits of participants are refunded to their original location. To prevent dishonest SPs from maliciously declaring a task invalid, if there exists an SP who finds the result and passes the verification, the SC seizes the dishonest complainants' deposit and releases it to the winner.

2.2 Threat Model

Considering the realistic scenarios, we assume that SPs and DUs are potentially malicious: 1) the SP may return incorrect results in an attempt to cheat the remuneration, 2) the DU may submit an incorrect query request to squander the SPs' computational resources or reject the correct result to refuse to pay the remuneration.

In addition, all blockchain peers can monitor the traffic flowing through the smart contract, including search tokens, results, and proofs, from which they may learn some sensitive information of data.

2.3 Append-Only Block Store

We turn our focus to the study of efficient storage on blockchain. In the literature, most SSE schemes work on random access storage devices. Although there exist some blockchain-based SSE schemes whose underlying storage does not support random access, they are built on a higher-level abstraction, making them work on "virtual" random access storage devices. Expressly, these studies assume that the fragmented append-only data storage has been transformed into a "random access" view of storage through some protocol, such as smart contracts.

However, existing storage abstractions are inefficient due to the performance drain caused by their conversion mechanism. For instance, some SSE schemes that use smart contracts to store indexes generate many transactions in the setup phase, burdening the blockchain network and costing the data owner a significant amount of money. Our goal is to propose a simple and efficient storage abstraction that can be built on top of blockchain transactions or other types of data shards while avoiding the enormous overhead associated with complex conversion operations.

We introduce an append-only block store (ABS) as a storage abstraction for blockchains. ABS is a subset of the block storage model, where anyone cannot alter previously written blocks and can only add new ones to ABS. ABS returns the block address when a block is appended, which is used to access the data later. The ABS block is limited in length by the public parameter γ. When the length of written data exceeds γ, ABS stops writing rather than slicing the data, requiring the caller to slice the data itself. Without sacrificing generality, we will assume that the length of a block address is constant, denoted by l_{addr}.

We now define the ABS model with a modification of the ADS model proposed by [1] to explicitly constrain the block size. An append-only block store $\Pi_{\mathsf{ABS}} = (\mathsf{Init}, \mathsf{Get}, \mathsf{Put})$ consists of three algorithms:

- $\mathsf{ABS} \leftarrow \mathsf{Init}(\gamma)$: is an initialization algorithm that takes as input a public parameter γ specifying the maximum block length and outputs an empty append-only block store ABS.
- $v/\bot \leftarrow \mathsf{Get}(\mathsf{ABS}, \mathsf{addr})$: is an algorithm that takes as input an append-only block store ABS and an address addr. If the block specified by addr exists, it returns the block content v; otherwise, it returns $\bot$.
- $(\mathsf{ABS}', \mathsf{addr}) \leftarrow \mathsf{Put}(\mathsf{ABS}, v)$: is an algorithm that takes as input an append-only block store ABS and a value v to be written. If the length of v is greater than the public parameter γ, the algorithm aborts. Otherwise, it outputs the address addr associated with v and the updated append-only block store ABS'.

In our design, when someone wants to write data into the ABS, it needs to broadcast the data through some API in some medium (*e.g.*, transactions). Then, the entire blockchain network writes the data to the ABS through mining.

To read data from ABS, full-node SPs can call the method Get efficiently because they store the complete blockchain data locally, which is an off-chain operation. DUs can also implement the method through some API to establish a connection to a full node, which leads to high latency. Therefore, weighing performance and security, we assume that DUs call the method Put by themselves to guarantee the integrity of written data, outsource heavy operations involving multiple Get method calls to SPs for efficient reads, and take some measures to guarantee reliable reads, which we will describe below.

2.4 ABS-Based Lookup Table

Further, we propose a lookup table data structure Π_{LT} adapted to the ABS model. Π_{LT} provides two algorithms: the initialization algorithm LTInit and the query algorithm LTGet. Unlike conventional lookup tables, Π_{LT} writes data to the ABS only once during initialization and does not permit update operations.

Formally, an ABS-based lookup table $\Pi_{\mathsf{LT}} \triangleq (\mathsf{LTInit}, \mathsf{LTGet})$ contains two algorithms:

- $(\mathsf{LT}, \mathsf{ABS}') \leftarrow \mathsf{LTInit}(\{(l_1, v_1), \ldots, (l_n, v_n)\}, \mathsf{ABS})$: is an algorithm that takes as input n label/value pairs and an append-only block store ABS, then it outputs the updated append-only block store ABS′ and a lookup table stored on ABS′.
- $v/\perp \leftarrow \mathsf{LTGet}(l, \mathsf{LT}, \mathsf{ABS})$: is an algorithm that takes as input a label, an append-only block store ABS and a lookup table LT stored on ABS. If the label l exists in LT, it outputs the corresponding value stored in LT; otherwise, it returns $\perp$.

Recall that the algorithm LTGet is off-chain for full nodes such as SPs. In the whole paper, the lengths of keys and values in Π_{LT} are fixed, denoted by l_{key} and l_{value}, respectively.

2.5 ABS-Based Publicly Verifiable Searchable Symmetric Encryption

Assume that there is a collection of D documents with identifiers id_1, id_2, ..., id_D. A database $\mathsf{DB} = (id_i, W_i)_{i=1}^{D}$ is a tuple of identifier/keyword-set pairs where $id_i \in \{0,1\}^{l_{id}}$ and $W_i \subseteq \{0,1\}^*$, such that keyword $w \in W_i$ if and only if the file identified by id_i contains the keyword w. The set of keywords contained in DB is $W = \bigcup_{i=1}^{D} W_i$. Let $\mathsf{DB}(w) = \{id_i | w \in W_i\}$ denote the set of documents containing keyword w, and N the number of document/keyword pairs (*i.e.*, $N = \sum_{i=1}^{D} |W_i|$).

We devise an ABS-based publicly verifiable SSE (PVSSE) scheme without considering fairness, which we will introduce in the next section. The blockchain nodes are only regarded as ordinary servers storing encrypted indexes and performing search operations without the function of arbiters, which is consistent with the traditional system model. In our setting, the search results are publicly verifiable, *i.e.*, all entities can use the DU's public key to verify the correctness of the results, which lays the foundation for our fair SSE framework construction.

An ABS-based publicly verifiable SSE scheme $\Pi_{\mathsf{PVSSE}}^{\mathsf{ABS}} = (\mathsf{KeyGen}, \mathsf{EDBSetup}, \mathsf{TokGen}, \mathsf{Search}, \mathsf{Verify})$ contains five algorithms:

- $(PK, SK) \leftarrow \mathsf{KeyGen}(1^\lambda)$: is a key generation algorithm run by the DU. It takes as input a security parameter λ and then outputs a public key PK and a secret key SK, where PK is open to the public, and SK is kept in secret by the user.
- $(\mathsf{EDB}, \mathsf{ABS}') \leftarrow \mathsf{EDBSetup}(SK, \mathsf{DB}, \mathsf{ABS})$: is run by the DU to encrypt the given database. It takes as input a secret key SK, a database DB, and an append-only block store ABS and then outputs an encrypted database EDB stored on the updated store ABS′.
- $\tau \leftarrow \mathsf{TokGen}(SK, w)$: is a token generation algorithm run by the DU to generate a token for a keyword. It takes as input a string w and a secret key SK and outputs a search token τ.

- $(\mathcal{R}, \mathsf{prf}) \leftarrow \mathsf{Search}(\mathsf{EDB}, \tau, \mathsf{ABS})$: is a search algorithm run by the SP to search for the files that contains the keyword w. It takes as input τ, EDB, and ABS and then outputs the result $\mathcal{R}$ and the corresponding proof prf. Note that the search operations are off-chain.
- $\mathsf{accept/reject} \leftarrow \mathsf{Verify}(PK, \tau, \mathcal{R}, \mathsf{prf})$: is a verification algorithm run by any entity to check whether $\mathcal{R}$ is correct and complete. It takes as input a public key PK, a token τ, a set of results $\mathcal{R}$, and a proof prf, and outputs accept if $\mathcal{R}$ matches prf. Otherwise, it outputs reject.

The definition of ABS-based PVSSE is almost the same as that of traditional SSE, except that the storage model is changed to ABS. Moreover, the security and soundness definitions of ABS-based PVSSE are also compatible with those of the traditional verifiable SSEs, which will not be discussed in detail due to space constraints.

For simplicity, the formalization of PVSSE here does not involve modeling the storage of the actual file payloads. There is no agreement in the literature of SSE in dealing with this issue. Considering the case of decentralized environments, we argue that the encrypted files can be stored in any decentralized file system, such as IPFS.

2.6 Cryptographic Primitives

Pseudo-random Function. A pseudo-random function (PRF) $F : \mathcal{K} \times \mathcal{X} \rightarrow \mathcal{Y}$ is a polynomial-time computable function that cannot be distinguished from a truly random function by any polynomial-time adversary. The formal definition of PRFs is given in [11].

Digital Signature. A digital signature scheme is a triple of algorithms $\Pi_{\mathrm{sig}} = (\mathsf{KeyGen}, \mathsf{Sign}, \mathsf{Verify})$. The probabilistic key generation algorithm KeyGen takes as input a security parameter and outputs a pair (pk, sk), where sk is called a secret signing key, and pk is called a public verification key. The probabilistic signing algorithm Sign takes as input a secret key sk and a string m and then outputs a signature σ. The deterministic verification algorithm Verify takes as input a public key pk, a message m, and a signature σ and then outputs either accept or reject. Informally, a digital signature scheme is secure if any polynomial-time adversary cannot forge a valid message/signature pair. We refer the reader to [11] for a formal definition of digital signatures.

Symmetric Encryption. We follow the definition of symmetric encryption in [5]. A symmetric encryption scheme is a pair of algorithms (E, D). The encryption algorithm E takes as input a key K and a plain text m and outputs a ciphertext c. The decryption algorithm D takes as input a key K and a ciphertext c, then it outputs m if c was produced by $E(K, m)$. We say that a symmetric encryption scheme is RCPA-secure (a stronger notion than CPA-secure) if the ciphertexts are computationally indistinguishable from truly random strings. The concrete definition of RCPA can be found in [5].

3 The Proposed Constructions

In this section, we give the specific constructions of the ABS-based lookup table, the publicly verifiable SSE, and the final fair SSE framework, respectively, in a step-by-step manner.

3.1 B′ Tree: An Implementation of the ABS-Based Lookup Table

We first propose read-only B′ trees based on the design concept of B^+ trees to instantiate the ABS-based lookup table, where the nodes can be stored via ABS blocks. Similar to B^+ trees, B′ trees store all satellite data in the leaf nodes and only keywords and child pointers in the internal nodes. The difference is that B′ trees do not support update operations and require that all data be written simultaneously in the setup phase. We retain the links between the leaf nodes to facilitate range queries.

We define that an internal node of an M-order B′ tree can hold up to M children. Each node x of a B′ tree has $x.n$ fixed-length keys $x.key_1, \ldots, x.key_{x.n}$ in non-descent order and a boolean $x.leaf$ that marks whether x is a leaf node. Furthermore, if x is an internal node, it also contains $x.n + 1$ children $x.child_1, \ldots, x.child_{x.n+1}$, satisfying that if k_i be any key stored in a subtree rooted at $x.child_i$, then $k_1 < x.key_1 \leq k_2 < x.key_2 \leq \cdots \leq k_{x.n} < x.key_{x.n} \leq k_{x.n+1}$; if x is a leaf node, it additionally contains $x.n$ fixed-length values labeled by keys and a pointer $x.ptr_{next}$ to the next leaf node. For any node x, the lengths of its contained keys, values (if any), $x.n$, and $x.leaf$ are fixed and the same as those of other nodes, which we denote by l_{key}, l_{value}, l_n, and l_{bool}, respectively.

Other properties of B′ trees, as well as the search algorithm LTGet, are consistent with those of B^+ trees, and the reader is referred to [12] for more details.

Initialization Algorithm. Given n key/value pairs $(l_1, v_1), \ldots, (l_n, v_n)$, the initialization algorithm LTInit for constructing an M-order B′ tree is as follows:

1. If $n = 0$, return $\perp$; otherwise:
2. Sort key/value pairs $(l_1, v_1), \ldots, (l_n, v_n)$ in non-descent order according to the key. The result is $(l'_1, v'_1), \ldots, (l'_n, v'_n)$.
3. Slice the ordered key/value pair $\{(l'_1, v'_1), \ldots, (l'_n, v'_n)\}$ into $\lceil n/(M-1) \rceil$ subsets $\{B_1, B_2, \ldots, B_{\lceil n/(M-1) \rceil}\}$ evenly, which means that the size of the last two subsets satisfies $\left|B_{\lceil n/(M-1) \rceil - 1}\right| - \left|B_{\lceil n/(M-1) \rceil}\right| \leq 1$, while the size of the rest is $M - 1$.
4. For subsets $\mathbf{B} = \{B_1, B_2, \ldots, B_{\lceil n/(M-1) \rceil}\}$, call the algorithm $\mathsf{LeafBuild}$ shown in Fig. 1 to generate a B′ tree from the bottom up and return the address of the root node as LT.

3.2 $\Pi^{\mathsf{ABS}}_{\mathsf{PVSSE}}$ Construction

Based on the ABS-based lookup table, we further illustrate the detailed construction of $\Pi^{\mathsf{ABS}}_{\mathsf{PVSSE}}$, which combines with the ideas of Π_{bas} in [5] and the verifiable

LeafBuild $(\mathbf{B} = \{B_1, B_2, \ldots, B_m\}, \mathsf{ABS})$

If $\mathbf{B}$ is empty, then return $\perp$; otherwise:
Initialize m empty leaf nodes $x_1, \ldots, x_m$
$p \leftarrow \perp$
for $i \leftarrow m$ **to** 1 **do**
  Write the key/value pairs contained in B_i to the leaf node x_i
  $x.ptr_{next} \leftarrow p, \quad x.n \leftarrow |B_i|$
  $addr_i \leftarrow \mathsf{Put}(\mathsf{ABS}, x_i)$
  $p \leftarrow addr_i$
Let κ_i be the smallest key of the subset B_i, where $2 \leq i \leq m$
return $\mathsf{InternalBuild}(\{\kappa_2, \ldots, \kappa_m\}, \{addr_1, \ldots, addr_m\}, \mathsf{ABS})$

InternalBuild $(\mathbf{K} = \{k_1, \ldots, k_m\}, \mathbf{ADDR} = \{addr_1, \ldots, addr_{m+1}\}, \mathsf{ABS})$

If $\mathbf{K}$ is empty, then return $addr_1$; otherwise:
Initialize $\lfloor m/M \rfloor$ empty internal nodes $x_1, \ldots, x_{\lfloor m/M \rfloor}$
Initialize two empty lists $\mathbf{K}', \mathbf{ADDR}'$
$i \leftarrow 0, j \leftarrow 1$
while $m - i \geq M$ **do**
  $i' \leftarrow i$
  $i \leftarrow i + \min(M - 1, \lceil (m - i)/2 \rceil)$
  $\kappa_j \leftarrow k_i$
  $x_j.n \leftarrow i - i' - 1$
  Write $k_{i'+1}, \ldots, k_{i-1}$ to $x_j.key_1, \ldots, x_j.key_{x_j.n}$
  Write $addr_{i'+1}, \ldots, addr_i$ to $x_j.child_1, \ldots, x_j.child_{x_j.n+1}$
  $(\mathsf{ABS}, addr'_j) \leftarrow \mathsf{Put}(\mathsf{ABS}, x)$
  Push κ_j to $\mathbf{K}'$, and push $addr'_j$ to $\mathbf{ADDR}'$
  $j \leftarrow j + 1$
$x_{\lfloor m/M \rfloor}.n \leftarrow m - i$
Write $k_{i+1}, \ldots, k_m$ to $x_{\lfloor m/M \rfloor}.key_1, \ldots, x_{\lfloor m/M \rfloor}.key_{x_{\lfloor m/M \rfloor}.n}$
Write $addr_{i+1}, \ldots, addr_{m+1}$ to $x_{\lfloor m/M \rfloor}.child_1, \ldots, x_{\lfloor m/M \rfloor}.child_{x_{\lfloor m/M \rfloor}.n+1}$
$(\mathsf{ABS}, addr'_{\lfloor m/M \rfloor}) \leftarrow \mathsf{Put}(\mathsf{ABS}, x_{\lfloor m/M \rfloor})$
Push $addr'_{\lfloor m/M \rfloor}$ to $\mathbf{ADDR}'$
return $\mathsf{InternalBuild}(\mathbf{K}', \mathbf{ADDR}', \mathsf{ABS})$

Fig. 1. Tree build algorithm of B′ Tree.

hash table (VHT) in [3]. Let $F : \{0,1\}^\lambda \times \{0,1\}^* \rightarrow \{0,1\}^\lambda$ be a variable-input-length PRF, $\mathsf{LT} = (\mathsf{LTInit}, \mathsf{LTGet})$ be an ABS-based lookup table, Π_{sig} be a digital signature scheme, and $\mathcal{E} = (E, D)$ be a symmetric encryption scheme. The detailed construction is given in Fig. 2.

Unlike previous verifiable SSE schemes, our design uses digital signatures instead of MACs to enable public verifiability by DUs' public keys. On the skeleton of Π_{bas}, we embed the VHT into the construction, replace MACs with

$\mathsf{KeyGen}(1^\lambda)$

$K \leftarrow \$ \{0,1\}^\lambda, K' \leftarrow \$ \{0,1\}^\lambda$
$(pk, sk) \leftarrow \Pi_{\text{sig}}.\mathsf{KeyGen}(1^\lambda)$
return $(PK = pk, SK = (K, K', sk))$

$\mathsf{EDBSetup}(SK, \mathsf{DB}, \mathsf{ABS})$

Parse SK as (K, K', sk)
Initialize three empty lists L, L', L''
foreach $w \in W$ **do**
 $K_1 \leftarrow F(K, 1\|w), K_2 \leftarrow F(K, 2\|w)$
 $K_3 \leftarrow F(K', 1\|w), \mathsf{wtag} \leftarrow F(K', 2\|w)$
 Initialize a counter $c \leftarrow 0$
 foreach $id \in \mathsf{DB}(w)$ **do**
  $l \leftarrow F(K_1, c), d \leftarrow E(K_2, id)$
  $c \leftarrow c + 1$
  Push (l, d) to L
 $\widetilde{id} \leftarrow id_1\|id_2\|\ldots\|id_{N_w}$, where $id_i \in \mathsf{DB}(w)$
 $\mathsf{prf} \leftarrow \Pi_{\text{sig}}.\mathsf{Sign}(\mathsf{wtag}\|\widetilde{id})$
 $d_{\mathsf{prf}} \leftarrow E(K_3, \mathsf{prf})$
 Push $(\mathsf{wtag}, d_{\mathsf{prf}})$ to L'
$(\mathsf{LT}_{\mathsf{in}}, \mathsf{ABS}) \leftarrow \mathsf{LTInit}(L, \mathsf{ABS})$
Sort L' in ascending lexicographic order of keys
$i \leftarrow 0$
for $(\mathsf{wtag}, d_{\mathsf{prf}}) \in L'$ **do**
 $\mathsf{prf}' \leftarrow \Pi_{\text{sig}}.\mathsf{Sign}(sk, \mathsf{wtag}\|i)$
 Push $(\mathsf{wtag}, d_{\mathsf{prf}}, i, \mathsf{prf}')$ to L''
 $i \leftarrow i + 1$
$(\mathsf{LT}_{\mathsf{prf}}, \mathsf{ABS}) \leftarrow \mathsf{LTInit}(L'', \mathsf{ABS})$
return $(\mathsf{EDB} = (\mathsf{LT}_{\mathsf{in}}, \mathsf{LT}_{\mathsf{prf}}), \mathsf{ABS})$

$\mathsf{TokGen}(SK, w)$

Parse SK as (K, K', sk)
$K_1 \leftarrow F(K, 1\|w), K_2 \leftarrow F(K, 2\|w)$
$K_3 \leftarrow F(K', 1\|w), \mathsf{wtag} \leftarrow F(K', 2\|w)$
return $\tau = (K_1, K_2, K_3, \mathsf{wtag})$

$\mathsf{Search}(\mathsf{EDB}, \tau, \mathsf{ABS})$

Parse EDB as $(\mathsf{LT}_{\mathsf{in}}, \mathsf{LT}_{\mathsf{prf}})$ and τ as $(K_1, K_2, K_3, \mathsf{wtag})$
Initialize an empty list $\mathcal{R}$
for $c \leftarrow 0$ **until** LTGet returns $\perp$ **do**
 $d \leftarrow \mathsf{LTGet}(F(K_1, c), \mathsf{LT}_{\mathsf{in}}, \mathsf{ABS})$
 $id \leftarrow D(K_2, d)$
 Push id to $\mathcal{R}$
if $\mathcal{R} \neq \emptyset$ **do**
 $(d_{\mathsf{prf}}, i, \mathsf{prf}') \leftarrow \mathsf{LTGet}(\mathsf{wtag}, \mathsf{LT}_{\mathsf{prf}}, \mathsf{ABS})$
 $\mathsf{prf} \leftarrow D(K_3, d_{\mathsf{prf}})$
else
 Find i such that $\mathsf{wtag}_i < \mathsf{wtag} < \mathsf{wtag}_{i+1}$
 $(d_{\mathsf{prf}_i}, i, \mathsf{prf}'_i) \leftarrow \mathsf{LTGet}(\mathsf{wtag}_i, \mathsf{LT}_{\mathsf{prf}}, \mathsf{ABS})$
 $(d_{\mathsf{prf}_{i+1}}, i+1, \mathsf{prf}'_{i+1}) \leftarrow \mathsf{LTGet}(\mathsf{wtag}_{i+1}, \mathsf{LT}_{\mathsf{prf}}, \mathsf{ABS})$
 $\mathsf{prf} \leftarrow (\mathsf{wtag}_i, i, \mathsf{prf}'_i, \mathsf{wtag}_{i+1}, \mathsf{prf}'_{i+1})$
return $(\mathcal{R}, \mathsf{prf})$

$\mathsf{Verify}(PK, \tau, \mathcal{R}, \mathsf{prf})$

Parse τ as $(K_1, K_2, K_3, \mathsf{wtag})$
if $\mathcal{R} \neq \emptyset$ **do**
 Parse $\mathcal{R}$ as $(id_1, id_2, \ldots, id_{|\mathcal{R}|})$
 $\widetilde{id} \leftarrow id_1\|id_2\|\ldots\|id_{|\mathcal{R}|}$
 return $\Pi_{\text{sig}}.\mathsf{Verify}(PK, \mathsf{wtag}\|\widetilde{id}, \mathsf{prf})$
else
 Parse prf as $(\mathsf{wtag}_i, i, \mathsf{prf}'_i, \mathsf{wtag}_{i+1}, \mathsf{prf}'_{i+1})$
 if $\mathsf{wtag}_i < \mathsf{wtag} < \mathsf{wtag}_{i+1}$ **do**
  return $\Pi_{\text{sig}}.\mathsf{Verify}(PK, \mathsf{wtag}_i\|i, \mathsf{prf}'_i)$ and $\Pi_{\text{sig}}.\mathsf{Verify}(PK, \mathsf{wtag}_{i+1}\|i+1, \mathsf{prf}'_{i+1})$
 else
  return reject

Fig. 2. The detailed construction of $\Pi_{\mathsf{PVSSE}}^{\mathsf{ABS}}$.

digital signatures, and simplify some operations to meet the smart contract environment.

Specifically, to build the encrypted database, the key generation algorithm KeyGen called by the DU selects two keys K, K', where K is used to derive keys for PRF (to derive the retrieving labels) and encryption (to encrypt the identifiers) per keyword, and similarly K' is used to derive keys for PRF (to derive the proof labels) and encryption (to encrypt the proof information) per keyword. In addition, KeyGen invokes the underlying digital signature scheme to obtain the signing key and verification key. Subsequently, the setup algorithm $\mathsf{EDBSetup}$ iterates over the identifiers in $\mathsf{DB}(w)$ for each keyword w. For each identifier, it computes a retrieving label by applying the PRF to a counter, encrypts the identifier, and adds the retrieving label/ciphertext pair to a list L. To achieve public verifiability, it also uses PRF to derive a proof label wtag for each keyword w, concatenates and signs all the document identifiers in $\mathsf{DB}(w)$, and then creates a list L' of all label/signature pairs. In order to prevent malicious services from returning faulty empty results, it sorts the list L', assigns the ordinal, and generates another signature on the ordinal and the label wtag for each item. Finally, it obtains a list L'' of quadruples of the form (wtag, a signature on the result, an ordinal, a signature on the ordinal) and creates two ABS-based lookup tables $\mathsf{LT}_{\mathsf{in}}$ and $\mathsf{LT}_{\mathsf{prf}}$ from L and L'', respectively.

To search for keyword w, the DU re-derives the keys and the proof label wtag for w and sends them to the SP. The search algorithm called by the SP starts by computing retrieving labels and decrypting the result. If the result is not empty, it looks up the signature prf corresponding to the result from $\mathsf{LT}_{\mathsf{prf}}$ and returns the result and signature. By contrast, if the result is empty, the algorithm queries $\mathsf{LT}_{\mathsf{prf}}$ for the two labels wtag_i and wtag_{i+1} adjacent to wtag, and returns the two labels, their ordinals, and the corresponding signatures.

The verification algorithm takes the following checks depending on whether the result is empty. If the result is not empty, it verifies the signature on the result. Otherwise, it checks whether wtag is between wtag_i and wtag_{i+1}, and verifies the signatures on the ordinals of these two labels. If the verification passes, wtag does not exist in $\mathsf{LT}_{\mathsf{prf}}$, and hence the result does not exist.

We argue that for SPs, the search algorithm involving multiple Get calls of ABS is off-chain, which significantly costs less time than the counterparts where the search operations are executed by smart contracts.

3.3 Π_{fair} Construction

Based on the ABS-based PVSSE scheme, we finally give the specific construction of the fair SSE framework. Let $\Pi_{\mathsf{PVSSE}}^{\mathsf{ABS}}$ be an ABS-based PVSSE scheme, of which the digital signature scheme Π_{sig} is provided by the specific blockchain platform. We give a formal construction of Π_{fair} in Fig. 3, where the global variable `msg.sender` denotes the method caller, `msg.value` denotes the fee attached to the call, and `currentTime` denotes the current time. The smart contract maintains a dictionary T, where the key is the task tag and the value is the task information, including the search token, the address of the encrypted index, and the task remuneration.

Setup. In the setup phase, each participant generates a public/private key pair (pk, sk) using a wallet program. Any peer node can deploy a smart contract of Π_{fair} on the blockchain. After being created, the smart contract initializes an empty dictionary T.

Subsequently, the DU generates an SSE key by calling $\Pi_{\mathsf{PVSSE}}^{\mathsf{ABS}}.\mathsf{KeyGen}$, then it generates and uploads the encrypted database by calling $\Pi_{\mathsf{PVSSE}}^{\mathsf{ABS}}.\mathsf{EDBSetup}$.

PublishTask(tag, tk, tx, ddl)

Assert $T[tag] == \perp$
Assert $ddl >$ `currentTime`
$P_{all} \leftarrow \emptyset, P_{cit} \leftarrow \emptyset$
$issuer \leftarrow$ `msg.sender`
$\$remuneration \leftarrow$ `msg.value`
Generate a tuple $\tau \leftarrow (tk, tx, ddl, issuer, \$remuneration, P_{all}, P_{cit})$
Put the key/value pair $[tag : t]$ to T
Broadcast the event of the arrival of a new task

Withdraw(tag)

Assert $T[tag] \neq \perp$
$(tk, tx, ddl, issuer, \$remuneration, P_{all}, P_{cit}) \leftarrow T[tag]$
Assert $issuer ==$ `msg.sender`
Assert $ddl >$ `currentTime` `and` $P_{all} = \emptyset$
Delete $T[tag]$
Send $\$remuneration$ to `msg.sender`

AnnounceResult$(tag, result, prf)$

Assert $T[tag] \neq \perp$
$(tk, tx, ddl, issuer, \$remuneration, P_{all}, P_{cit}) \leftarrow T[tag]$
Assert $issuer \neq$ `msg.sender`
Assert $ddl >$ `currentTime`
Assert `msg.sender` $\in P_{all}$
Assert `msg.sender` $\notin P_{cit}$
Assert $\Pi^{\mathsf{ABS}}_{\mathsf{PVSSE}}.\mathsf{Verify}(pk_{issuer}, tk, result, prf)$ returns accept
$\$award \leftarrow \$remuneration$
foreach $p \in P_{all}$ **do**
  if $p \in P_{cit}$ **then**
    $\$award \leftarrow \$award + \$remuneration$
  else Send $\$remuneration$ to p
Send $\$award$ to `msg.sender` and inform `issuer` of the result
Delete $T[tag]$

Participate(tag)

Assert $T[tag] \neq \perp$
$(tk, tx, ddl, issuer, \$remuneration, P_{all}, P_{cit}) \leftarrow T[tag]$
Assert $issuer \neq$ `msg.sender`
Assert $ddl >$ `currentTime`
Assert $\$remuneration \leq$ `msg.value`
Assert `msg.sender` $\notin P_{all}$
$P_{all} \leftarrow P_{all} \cup \{$`msg.sender`$\}$
$\$change \leftarrow$ `msg.value` $- \$remuneration$
Send $\$change$ to `msg.sender`
$T[tag] \leftarrow (tk, tx, ddl, issuer, \$remuneration, P_{all}, P_{cit})$

ClaimInvalid(tag)

Assert $T[tag] \neq \perp$
$(tk, tx, ddl, issuer, \$remuneration, P_{all}, P_{cit}) \leftarrow T[tag]$
Assert $issuer \neq$ `msg.sender`
Assert $ddl >$ `currentTime`
Assert `msg.sender` $\in P_{all}$
Assert `msg.sender` $\notin P_{cit}$
$P_{cit} \leftarrow P_{cit} \cup \{$`msg.sender`$\}$

ClaimTimeout(tag)

Assert $T[tag] \neq \perp$
$(tk, tx, ddl, issuer, \$remuneration, P_{all}, P_{cit}) \leftarrow T[tag]$
Assert $ddl \leq$ `currentTime`
if $P_{cit} \neq \emptyset$ **then**
  $\$refund \leftarrow \$remuneration/|P_{cit}|$
  foreach $p \in P_{cit}$ **then**
    Send $\$refund$ to p
else
  Send $\$remuneration$ to $issuer$
foreach $p \in P_{all}$ **then**
  Send $\$remuneration$ to p
Delete $T[tag]$

Fig. 3. The detailed construction of Π_{fair}.

Recall that in order to enable fairness, when generating the encrypted index, the DU needs to sign the $\mathsf{DB}(w)$ for each keyword w in DB as proof of faithful search execution by SPs.

Task Publishing and Withdrawl. The DU who wants to search for its data on the blockchain publishes a search task by calling $\Pi_{\mathsf{fair}}.\mathsf{PublishTask}$ with arguments (tag, tk, tx, ddl), where tag is the task identifier generated by the DU, tk

is the search token generated by calling the method $\Pi^{\mathsf{ABS}}_{\mathsf{PVSSE}}.\mathsf{TokGen}$, tx is the address of the encrypted index, and ddl is the task deadline. In addition, the DU needs to set a fee for the task, which will be included in the message sent to the SC.

The SC initially checks if the task tag exists in the dictionary T (*i.e.*, another task with the same tag has not finished) and if the task deadline is valid. Subsequently, the SC creates two empty sets P_{all} and P_{cit} and extracts the issuer and the task remuneration. Then the SC creates a tuple to record the task detail and adds the tuple as a value and tag as a key to the dictionary T. Finally, it broadcasts the arrival of the new task to the peers.

When the issuer stops outsourcing the search, it can submit a task withdrawal request by calling $\Pi_{\mathsf{fair}}.\mathsf{Withdraw}$ with argument tag. The SC will check the validity of the task and the canceler. If no SP has participated in the task, the SC permits the task cancellation, deletes the corresponding item from T, and refunds the remuneration to the issuer.

Task Participation. When a task is published, the SC broadcasts an event including the above task arguments to all subscribed SPs. Based on the content, the SP determines whether to participate. If it decides to participate and compete for the reward, it can call $\Pi_{\mathsf{fair}}.\mathsf{Participate}$ with the argument tag and attach the message with its deposit equivalent to the remuneration. The SC will check if the task, the participant, and the deposit meet the conditions. If the above conditions are satisfied, the SC adds the participant to the P_{all} and refunds the excess deposit.

After participating in the task, the SP utilizes the search token tk provided by the DU to search over the EDB whose address is specified by tx stored on the blockchain. When the SP finds the result and the related proof successfully, denoted by $result$ and prf respectively, it verifies whether $\Pi^{\mathsf{ABS}}_{\mathsf{PVSSE}}.\mathsf{Verify}(pk_{\mathrm{DU}}, tk, result, prf)$ returns accept using the public key pk_{DU} of the DU. If the equation holds, the SP calls $\Pi_{\mathsf{fair}}.\mathsf{AnnounceResult}$ with arguments $(tag, result, prf)$ to announce the successful completion of the task. After the SC receives the message, it first checks that the task and the participant are valid and verifies that the result returned by the SP is correct and complete by calling $\Pi^{\mathsf{ABS}}_{\mathsf{PVSSE}}.\mathsf{Verify}(pk_{\mathrm{DU}}, tk, result, prf)$. If the validation succeeds, which means that the SP performed the search honestly and returned the correct result, the SC performs a series of monetary operations and returns the deposit to the honest SPs (*i.e.*, those who have not invalidated the task). As for dishonest complainants, the SC seizes their deposits and sends them to the winner as a reward. Finally, the SC informs the DU of the correct result and removes the task information from T.

When the SP finds that the search token or encrypted index provided by the DU is wrong, or the proof previously incorporated in the encrypted index is invalid, it can raise a task invalidity complaint by calling $\Pi_{\mathsf{fair}}.\mathsf{ClaimInvalid}$ with parameter tag. The SC performs a series of validity checks and adds the complainant to P_{cit}. Once the task has expired and no SP has found the result, the SC divides the remuneration equally as compensation to each complainant.

Task Expiration Without Any Winner. When the current time exceeds the deadline, anyone can raise a task expiration declaration to the SC. The SC validates the existence of the task and ensures that it has indeed expired. If no SP claims the task is invalid, the task remuneration is refunded; otherwise, the task remuneration is shared equally among the SPs that declared the task invalid. Finally, all SPs have their deposits refunded.

4 Security Analysis

In this section, we discuss the security of our proposed framework in terms of confidentiality, soundness, and fairness.

4.1 Confidentiality

We first discuss the confidentiality of the proposed ABS-based PVSSE construction $\Pi_{\mathsf{PVSSE}}^{\mathsf{ABS}}$, which is the basis for that of the fair SSE framework Π_{fair}.

We follow the ideal/real simulation paradigm of SSE [2,5] to demonstrate the confidentiality of the scheme. We define the leakage function $\mathcal{L}$ of scheme $\Pi_{\mathsf{PVSSE}}^{\mathsf{ABS}}$ as

$$\mathcal{L}(\mathsf{DB}, \boldsymbol{w}) = \left(N, \{\mathsf{DB}(w)\}_{w \in \boldsymbol{w}}, |W|\right),$$

where the leakage function $\mathcal{L}$ takes as input a database DB and a list of queries $\boldsymbol{w}$ and outputs the size of the database N, the plain file identifiers contained in the database DB for each query w, and the number of keywords $|W|$.

Theorem 1. *If F is a secure PRF and $\mathcal{E} = (E, D)$ is RCPA-secure, then $\Pi_{\mathsf{PVSSE}}^{\mathsf{ABS}}$ is $\mathcal{L}$-secure against non-adaptive attacks.*

The proof of the theorem is basically identical to [5], and the sketch is given later; a complete and formal proof can be found in [5].

Proof Sketch: To prove non-adaptive security, we give the construction of the simulator $\mathcal{S}$, which takes as input the return value of the leak function $\mathcal{L}$ (*i.e.*, the size N of the database, $\mathsf{DB}(w)$ for each query keyword w, and the number of keywords $|W|$) and outputs the view of the server (*i.e.*, EDB) and the corresponding search token for each query. Without loss of generality, we assume that the adversary's queries $\boldsymbol{w}$ are non-repeating.

The simulator $\mathcal{S}$ iterates over the queries and generates $K_{i,1}, K_{i,2}, K_{i,3}, \mathsf{wtag}_i \leftarrow_{\$} \{0,1\}^{\lambda}$ for the i-th query w_i. Next, for each $id \in \mathsf{DB}(w_i)$, $\mathcal{S}$ calculates l, d, and d_{prf}, then it adds (l, d) to L and $(\mathsf{wtag}_i, d_{\mathsf{prf}})$ to L' as $\mathsf{EDBSetup}$ does. Subsequently, $\mathcal{S}$ adds random pairs to L until L has N items and creates $\mathsf{LT}_{\mathsf{in}}$ by calling $\mathsf{LTInit}(L, \mathsf{ABS})$. Similarly, $\mathcal{S}$ adds random pairs to L' until L' has $|W|$

items and creates $\mathsf{LT}_{\mathsf{prf}}$ (as in lines 16 to 22 of EDBSetup). Finally, $\mathcal{S}$ outputs $\mathsf{EDB} = (\mathsf{LT}_{\mathsf{in}}, \mathsf{LT}_{\mathsf{prf}})$ and $\boldsymbol{\tau} = (\tau_1, \ldots, \tau_q)$, where $\tau_i = (K_{i,1}, K_{i,2}, K_{i,3}, \mathsf{wtag}_i)$.

The hybrid argument given in [5] can also be applied to this proof. The first hybrid shows that selecting $K_{i,1}, K_{i,2}$ randomly is indistinguishable from deriving them from the secure PRF $F(K, \cdot)$. Similarly, the second hybrid shows that selecting $K_{i,3}, \mathsf{wtag}_i$ randomly is indistinguishable from deriving them from the secure PRF $F(K', \cdot)$. The third hybrid states that the unqueried k-v pairs in $\mathsf{LT}_{\mathsf{in}}$ and $\mathsf{LT}_{\mathsf{prf}}$ are pseudo-random. Therefore, the output produced by $\mathcal{S}$ is indistinguishable from the view of the real world. □

We turn to the confidentiality analysis of Π_{fair}. The confidentiality of Π_{fair} relies on the underlying PVSSE scheme $\Pi^{\mathsf{ABS}}_{\mathsf{PVSSE}}$. SPs cannot sniff any information other than the leakage $\mathcal{L}$. It is noted that the scope of the leakage is extended from a single server to all peers of the blockchain network since the state of the smart contract is public.

4.2 Soundness

Intuitively, the soundness of PVSSE signifies that the server cannot forge a result/proof pair $(\mathcal{R}, \mathsf{prf})$ where $\mathcal{R}$ has not been previously signed by the user such that $\Pi^{\mathsf{ABS}}_{\mathsf{PVSSE}}.\mathsf{Verify}$ returns accept. Our design relies on the security of the underlying PRF and digital signature. Depending on whether the result forged by the server is empty, we analyze the soundness separately. On the one hand, if the forged result is not empty, the server cannot forge evidence unless it knows the signing key owned by the user or finds a collision of the retrieving labels computed by F. On the other hand, if the forged result is empty, the server needs to provide the two adjacent wtags, their ordinals, and the corresponding signatures, which is also a difficult problem for a server that does not know the secret signing key. Therefore, if the underlying PRF F and the digital signature scheme are secure, our scheme can be inferred to be sound.

The soundness of Π_{fair} is dependent on $\Pi^{\mathsf{ABS}}_{\mathsf{PVSSE}}$. As long as $\Pi^{\mathsf{ABS}}_{\mathsf{PVSSE}}$ is sound, Π_{fair} is equally sound, *i.e.*, a malicious SP cannot forge proof for a wrong result to deceive the smart contract.

4.3 Fairness

Π_{fair} achieves fairness by constructing a multi-party game in which both SPs and DUs tend to cooperate. We discuss the fairness of the scheme in several cases as follows.

- If DUs and SPs are honest, the scheme will work appropriately, the remuneration will be awarded to the winning SP, and all SPs will be returned their deposits.
- Malicious DUs may refuse to pay the remuneration, send a faulty search request, or upload fraudulent proof in the setup phase (*i.e.*, the proof and the result may not match, even if the result is correct). Refusal to pay is impossible because our scheme requires the DU to pay the remuneration beforehand.

The complaint mechanism can solve the latter two cases, *i.e.*, SPs can file a complaint if they find something wrong with the request or the proof. If none of the SPs finds the result until the end of the task, the smart contract can conclude that the task is wrong and seize the remuneration to recompense the complainants. Under the stimulation of the penalty mechanism, DU tends to behave honestly.

- Malicious SPs may send incorrect results or directly claim the task is invalid without performing any substantive operation. The former is impossible due to the soundness of $\Pi^{\mathsf{ABS}}_{\mathsf{PVSSE}}$. For the latter case, whenever an honest SP succeeds in finding the result and proof within the time limit, the deposits of the malicious SPs will be seized and compensated to the honest winner by the SC. With the combination of penalty and incentive mechanisms, SPs tend to behave honestly.
- It is crucial to set the task time appropriately to ensure fairness. Too short task time will lead to fraud from dishonest SPs, whereas too long task time may lead to the decline of user experience. Therefore, the task time needs to be set according to the specific network situation, the number of nodes, and the performance of each node.

5 Implementation and Experimental Results

5.1 Implementation Details

We implement the proposed schemes in Python and Solidity and conduct the experiments on a computer with an AMD Ryzen 5700G CPU, 32 GB of RAM, running Ubuntu 22.04. Inspired by [1], we use Ethereum to instantiate ABS by storing blocks via transactions, whose hashes are used for block addresses. We conduct our experiments on the Ganache test network and interface with the network via Metamask and the Ethereum API `web3.py`. The Init method of ABS is instantiated by generating a Metamask wallet, while the Put and Get methods are instantiated using the Ethereum APIs `web3.eth.sendTransaction` and `web3.eth.getTransaction`, respectively.

For cryptographic primitives, we use the Python cryptography package to implement symmetric encryption via AES-256 and PRF via HMAC-SHA-256. Furthermore, we implement Π_{sig} using Web3 APIs `web3.eth.accounts.sign` and `web3.eth.accounts.recover`, whose underlying signature algorithm is ECDSA with SHA3-256. Thus, the data user's signature key corresponds to the key pair of the Metamask wallet. For the fair SSE framework Π_{fair}, we program a smart contract `FairContract` using the Solidity language and deploy it to the Ganache test network at the cost of $2,946.65$k gas.

For full implementation, we set the parameters as follows: we set γ to 64 KB for ABS implementation, $l_{key} = l_{value} = l_{addr} = 32$ bytes (the hash length of an Ethereum transaction), $l_{bool} = 1$ byte and $l_n = 4$ bytes for B$'$ tree implementation, and $l_{id} = 8$ bytes for SSE implementation.

5.2 Performance Evaluation

For comparison, we implement the scheme of [8], where the storage and search of data are performed by the smart contract. We modify the scheme of [8] by removing the `Add` and `Delete` methods and restricting the writing of encrypted indexes to the setup phase. Due to the gas limit, we slice the massive $\mathsf{DB}(w)$ into multiple chunks of size $1,000$ and send each chunk to the smart contract in turn. We program a smart contract `SSEContract` and deploy it to the same test network at the cost of 930.89k gas.

Table 1. Database properties in our experiment.

DB name	(w, id) pairs	Distinct keywords
DB_1	100,381	1,000
DB_2	100,180	10,000
DB_3	99,596	5,000
DB_4	500,012	25,000

Using the Python Faker library and the `os.random` method, we generate four databases whose main properties are summarized in Table 1.

We measure the gas used, the number of transactions, the running time in the setup phase, and the running time and the gas used by each participant in the query phase.

Setup Performance. Figure 4(a)–(c) depict the time costs, gas usage, and transaction counts for Π_{fair} and `SSEContract` on various datasets. We can see that our design reduces the initialization time and gas consumption by about 90% and the number of transactions by approximately 80%. Specifically, when deploying DB_4 with large amounts of data, `SSEContract` requires more than 30 min, whereas our solution requires less than 3 min. The results demonstrate that our design achieves a significantly lower initialization overhead than `SSEContract`, indicating that Π_{fair} will reduce deployment costs significantly and be suitable for a wider range of use cases.

Table 2. The gas consumption of different entities for search in the unit of 10^3 gas.

	Gas Used By the DU				Gas Used By the winning SP				Gas Used By other SPs
	DB_1	DB_2	DB_3	DB_4	DB_1	DB_2	DB_3	DB_4	DB_1-DB_4
Π_{fair}	116.3				180.0	160.9	164.3	163.2	92.7
`SSEContract`	$2,400.9$	368.8	625.9	665.4					

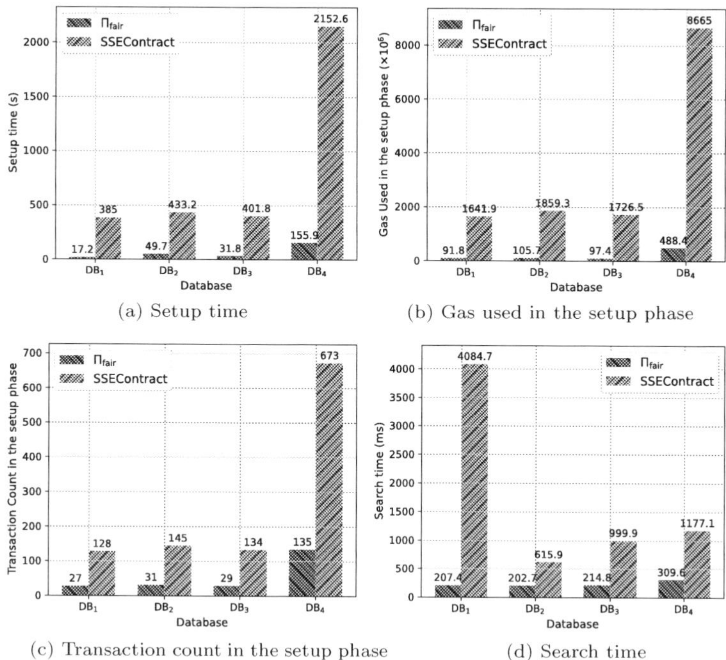

(a) Setup time

(b) Gas used in the setup phase

(c) Transaction count in the setup phase

(d) Search time

Fig. 4. Efficiency evaluations.

Query Performance. In the query phase, we further measure the time cost and the gas usage of each party, averaging the results over 100 randomly selected queries. Figure 4(d) shows the "entire search time" for both schemes, which refers to the time interval between when the DU posts a search task and when it receives the correct result. Overall, our design outperforms `SSEContract` and performs substantially better on databases containing high-frequency keywords, owing to the underlying B′ tree, which reduces the frequency of reading ABS blocks per search.

Table 2 shows the comparison of the gas consumption of different entities for search between the two schemes. In our design, the gas consumption varies between different entities. For `SSEContract`, only the DU executing the smart contract method consumes gas. As Table 2 shows, in our design, the DU consumes only 116.3k of gas to publish the search task, and the SP uses 92.7k of gas for participation. In addition, the SP that finds the result consumes more gas due to the additional call to the AnnounceResult method, the amount of which varies depending on the size of the result. As for `SSEContract`, the gas consumed by the DU is positively correlated with the size of the result. Overall, our scheme efficiently reduces the amount of gas consumed for search compared to `SSEContract`, since the search operation with high consumption is shifted to off-chain execution, while the smart contract is only used for the lifecycle of the task.

6 Conclusion

Existing blockchain-based SSE schemes cannot simultaneously achieve high efficiency and fairness. This paper uses the aforementioned issue as a springboard to provide an effective and fair solution for searching for encrypted data on the blockchain. We first build a generic abstraction model ABS for blockchain storage, compatible with the majority of blockchain platforms. Based on ABS, we propose a lookup table data structure and an implementation of it to achieve efficient storage and search. We further propose a publicly verifiable SSE scheme in which indexes are organized as ABS-based lookup tables, and the search operations are shifted to be executed off the chain, thereby significantly reducing the time overhead and gas usage. Then, we use smart contracts to introduce fairness to SSE via multi-party gaming. We implement our scheme in Solidity and Python and deploy it on Ethereum. The experimental results show that our design is effective and practical.

Acknowledgement. This work is supported by Guangdong Major Project of Basic and Applied Basic Research (2019B030302008) and the National Natural Science Foundation of China (No. 61972429).

References

1. Adkins, D., Agarwal, A., Kamara, S., Moataz, T.: Encrypted blockchain databases. In: Proceedings of the 2nd ACM Conference on Advances in Financial Technologies, pp. 241–254 (2020)
2. Asharov, G., Naor, M., Segev, G., Shahaf, I.: Searchable symmetric encryption: optimal locality in linear space via two-dimensional balanced allocations. In: Proceedings of the Forty-Eighth Annual ACM Symposium on Theory of Computing, pp. 1101–1114 (2016)
3. Bost, R., Fouque, P.A., Pointcheval, D.: Verifiable dynamic symmetric searchable encryption: optimality and forward security. Cryptology ePrint Archive (2016)
4. Cai, C., Weng, J., Yuan, X., Wang, C.: Enabling reliable keyword search in encrypted decentralized storage with fairness. IEEE Trans. Depend. Secure Comput. (2018)
5. Cash, D., et al.: Dynamic searchable encryption in very-large databases: data structures and implementation. In: NDSS, vol. 14, pp. 23–26. Citeseer (2014)
6. Chen, L., Lee, W.K., Chang, C.C., Choo, K.K.R., Zhang, N.: Blockchain based searchable encryption for electronic health record sharing. Futur. Gener. Comput. Syst. **95**, 420–429 (2019)
7. Curtmola, R., Garay, J., Kamara, S., Ostrovsky, R.: Searchable symmetric encryption: improved definitions and efficient constructions. In: Proceedings of the 13th ACM Conference on Computer and Communications Security, pp. 79–88 (2006)
8. Hu, S., Cai, C., Wang, Q., Wang, C., Luo, X., Ren, K.: Searching an encrypted cloud meets blockchain: a decentralized, reliable and fair realization. In: IEEE INFOCOM 2018-IEEE Conference on Computer Communications, pp. 792–800. IEEE (2018)
9. Jiang, S., et al.: Privacy-preserving and efficient multi-keyword search over encrypted data on blockchain. In: 2019 IEEE International Conference on Blockchain (Blockchain), pp. 405–410. IEEE (2019)

10. Jiang, S., Liu, J., Wang, L., Yoo, S.M.: Verifiable search meets blockchain: a privacy-preserving framework for outsourced encrypted data. In: ICC 2019–2019 IEEE International Conference on Communications (ICC), pp. 1–6. IEEE (2019)
11. Katz, J., Lindell, Y.: Introduction to Modern Cryptography. Chapman and Hall/CRC Press, Hoboken (2007)
12. Leiserson, C.E., Rivest, R.L., Cormen, T.H., Stein, C.: Introduction to Algorithms, vol. 3. MIT Press, Cambridge (1994)
13. Li, H., Gu, C., Chen, Y., Li, W.: An efficient, secure and reliable search scheme for dynamic updates with blockchain. In: Proceedings of the 2019 the 9th International Conference on Communication and Network Security, pp. 51–57 (2019)
14. Li, H., Tian, H., Zhang, F., He, J.: Blockchain-based searchable symmetric encryption scheme. Comput. Electr. Eng. **73**, 32–45 (2019)
15. Li, H., Zhang, F., He, J., Tian, H.: A searchable symmetric encryption scheme using blockchain. arXiv preprint arXiv:1711.01030 (2017)
16. Song, D.X., Wagner, D., Perrig, A.: Practical techniques for searches on encrypted data. In: Proceeding 2000 IEEE Symposium on Security and Privacy. S&P 2000, pp. 44–55. IEEE (2000)
17. Tang, Q.: Towards blockchain-enabled searchable encryption. In: Zhou, J., Luo, X., Shen, Q., Xu, Z. (eds.) ICICS 2019. LNCS, vol. 11999, pp. 482–500. Springer, Cham (2020). https://doi.org/10.1007/978-3-030-41579-2_28
18. Wood, G., et al.: Ethereum: a secure decentralised generalised transaction ledger. In: Ethereum Project Yellow Paper, vol. 151, pp. 1–32 (2014)
19. Xu, C., Yu, L., Zhu, L., Zhang, C.: A blockchain-based dynamic searchable symmetric encryption scheme under multiple clouds. Peer-to-Peer Network. Appl. **14**(6), 3647–3659 (2021). https://doi.org/10.1007/s12083-021-01202-6
20. Yan, X., Yuan, X., Ye, Q., Tang, Y.: Blockchain-based searchable encryption scheme with fair payment. IEEE Access **8**, 109687–109706 (2020)
21. Yang, Y., Lin, H., Liu, X., Guo, W., Zheng, X., Liu, Z.: Blockchain-based verifiable multi-keyword ranked search on encrypted cloud with fair payment. IEEE Access **7**, 140818–140832 (2019)
22. Zhang, Y., Deng, R.H., Shu, J., Yang, K., Zheng, D.: TKSE: trustworthy keyword search over encrypted data with two-side verifiability via blockchain. IEEE Access **6**, 31077–31087 (2018)

GRUZ: Practical Resource Fair Exchange Without Blockchain

Yongqing Xu, Kaiyi Zhang(✉), and Yu Yu

Shanghai Jiao Tong University, Shanghai, China
{yvonna,kzoacn,yyuu}@sjtu.edu.cn

Abstract. A fair exchange protocol allows two parties to exchange their secret messages fairly. The protocol is said to be fair if either both parties receive secrets from each other or neither of them does. However, complete fairness was proven not always possible by Cleve (STOC 1986) as a corrupted party can always abort early to obtain more advantages than the other party. Thus, we should consider partial fairness. In this paper, we specifically discuss resource fairness (one of partial fairness), which means parties require similar computation resources to recover secrets even if the protocol is aborted at an arbitrary round. One of the methods used to achieve resource fairness is gradual release, where two parties gradually release their private information. We put forward a protocol named GRUZ (Gradual Release Using Zero-knowledge) to realize gradual release in the two-party exchange problem using zero-knowledge from garbled circuits (ZKGC) without blockchain that many past works rely on. Two parties first encrypt messages with their secret keys. Then they gradually release their secret keys one bit at a time alternately so that either party gains an advantage of at most one bit if he/she aborts. The authenticity of the exchanged keys is guaranteed by zero-knowledge proof. We implement this protocol with standard primitives AES, SHA256, and ECDSA, which are compatible with real-world applications such as digital currency exchange. We show that our protocol is practical by analyzing its running time and communication costs.

Keywords: Fair exchange · Zero-knowledge · Garbled circuits · Digital currency

1 Introduction

Fair exchange protocols enable the fair exchange of secrets between the two parties, where fairness refers to either both parties receive the intended messages, or neither of them does. Fairness was first considered in the exchange problem [41], and it is later extended to secure multiparty computation [48].

Ideally, fairness should guarantee the atomicity of the exchange. Despite this ideal definition of fairness, Cleve [13] proved that complete fairness is impossible in general when there are half or more dishonest parties. But there are also works showing that complete fairness is possible in secure two-party and multiparty

W. Susilo et al. (Eds.): ISC 2022, LNCS 13640, pp. 214–228, 2022.
https://doi.org/10.1007/978-3-031-22390-7_14

computation without an honest majority for certain functions [21,23]. Gordon, Liu, and Shi [25] discussed the round complexity of MPC with fairness. Besides, Gordon et al. [22] studied primitives for fair computation.

Since complete fairness is not always attainable, partial fairness [24] seems to be the best one can hope for in many scenarios. There are a few definitions and approaches [26] to partial fairness. One is probabilistic fairness, in which case parties should know the correct answer with higher confidence as the protocol progresses. Another type of fairness is resource fairness put forward by Garay et al. [17,38,44,45], which guarantees that both parties need a similar amount of resources to recover the secrets.

Blum [8] introduces a method to achieve resource fairness, which Brickell et al. [9] referred to as "gradual release", and they constructed a protocol based on discrete logarithm. In addition, Even [15] realizes the protocol with partial fairness using Merkle puzzles. Informally speaking, gradual release let the two parties disclose their secrets one bit (block) at a time in an alternating fashion. As a result, at any point during the protocol execution, if a malicious party chooses to abort, he gains an advantage of at most one bit (block) over the other party. Therefore, two parties always need similar resources to reveal the other party's secret.

In this paper, we focus on the concept of resource fairness. Under this concept, fair exchange of digital signatures is discussed by Garay and Pomerance [18] with applications to digital currency exchange (also known as Interchain Swap). For instance, suppose Alice plans to trade x BTC for y ETH from Bob by exchanging the digital signatures of the corresponding transfers. The message to be exchanged to be digitally signed writes something like "Alice sends x BTC to Bob" (or "Bob sends y ETH to Alice", respectively).

To solve the above problem, most of the works relied on smart contracts [1–4] running over blockchains. In this case, the smart contracts are conditioned that both parties agree on the exchange before timeout. Besides, Choudhuri et al. [12] used the public bulletin property of blockchain to build fair exchange protocols. Later, Paul and Shrivastava [40] improved the performance using blockchain and trusted hardware.

Although blockchain-based exchange protocols are becoming increasingly practical, those protocols rely on infrastructures such as smart contracts or public bulletins which may not always be possible. Further, previous protocols realizing partial fairness without blockchains either used zero-knowledge proof in a black box way [17] or relied on number theoretic and assumptions such as factorization and quadratic residuosity [8,9]. We present a novel and practical way to achieve resource fairness for the secret exchange problem without using blockchain.

In this work, we design and realize GRUZ (Gradual Release Using Zero-knowledge), a "gradual release"-based contract signing protocol with resource fairness, which is based on zero-knowledge proof from garbled circuits (ZKGC) [29]. Let Alice and Bob first encrypt their signatures using the respective private keys and then exchange their keys bit by bit alternatively. In this way, even if one party chooses to abort the protocol at any point, he or she will only gain an advantage of at most one bit in terms of the uncertainty about the space to be enumerated by brute force. During the exchange, zero-knowledge proofs are used to prove the validity of the keys to be revealed. A zero-knowledge proof (ZKP) protocol [20] allows a prover to prove some NP statement to a verifier without revealing anything substantial beyond the validity of the statement. A garbled circuit (GC), introduced by Yao [47], is widely used as a way to realize two-party secure computation. Zero-knowledge from garbled circuits (ZKGC) combines the two techniques and realizes zero-knowledge proofs using GCs. A good advantage of this method is that it is easy to express NP relations using Boolean circuits. Our contributions can be summarized as follows:

- We design a practical resource-fair exchange protocol without relying on blockchains, which follows the "gradual release" approach and is based on zero-knowledge proof from garbled circuits.
- We instantiate this protocol with standard and widely deployed cryptographic primitives, i.e. `AES`, `SHA256` and `ECDSA`. Especially, we instantiate `ECDSA` with `secp256k1` which is used in Bitcoin and Ethereum. Therefore, our implementation is compatible with and can be directly applied to real-world applications such as digital currency exchange.
- We provide an implementation of the protocol along with performance evaluation. Our protocol exhibits affordable performance in terms of the running time and communication cost.

Our protocol has many potential applications, such as contract signing and electronic cheque deposit by exchanging the corresponding signatures. Furthermore, it can also be used for fair exchange of digital assets, which we will discuss in Sect. 3.1.

2 Preliminaries

The following Table 1 concludes frequently used mathematical notations.

Table 1. Mathematical notations

Notation	Meaning
n	Input size
w	Prover's input as witness
$\{C_n\}$	Circuit family
$\mathcal{R}(x; w)$	$\mathcal{NP}$ relation where $(x, w) \in \mathcal{R}$ iff. $C(x, w) = 1$
(K_i^0, K_i^1)	True and false input labels for wire i
Δ	Global offset under free-XOR
σ	Signature
k	Private key
κ	Computational security parameter
$\{r_i\}_{i\in[\kappa]}$	a sequence of random strings

2.1 Relation and Language

An $\mathcal{NP}$ relation $\mathcal{R}(x; w)$ is defined by a polynomial-sized uniform circuit family $\{C_n\}$ and $(x, w) \in \mathcal{R}$ iff. $C(x, w) = 1$. We then define the corresponding language $L(\mathcal{R})$ induced by this relation as $L(\mathcal{R}) = \{x : \exists w \text{ s.t. } C(x, w) = 1\}$.

2.2 Zero-Knowledge Proof

Zero-knowledge proof was put forward by Goldwasser et al. [20] Prover P uses a witness w to prove an NP statement to verifier V. In brief, a pair of algorithms (P,V) is said to be zero-knowledge if for every PPT verifier V, there exists a PPT simulator Sim such that the views $\mathsf{View}_{\mathsf{P,V}}(\mathsf{x})$, $\mathsf{Sim}(x)$ are computationally indistinguishable for every input x.

We define some ideal functionality of our zero-knowledge from garbled circuits (ZKGC) protocol described in Sect. 3.

Ideal Functionality $\mathcal{F}^{\mathsf{cho}}$

- Receiver sends (choose, b) where $b \in \{0, 1\}$ as input. Sender inputs m_0, m_1.
- Receiver receives m_b.
- On receiving **open** instruction from sender, send m_0,m_1 to receiver.

Fig. 1. Ideal functionality $\mathcal{F}^{\mathsf{cho}}$ for oblivious transfer

Ideal Functionality $\mathcal{F}^{\mathsf{com}}$

- Sender inputs (commit, m), committing to message m.
- On receiving **open** instruction from the sender, send message m to receiver.

Fig. 2. Ideal functionality $\mathcal{F}^{\mathsf{com}}$ for commitment

The above figures Fig. 1 and Fig. 2 define ideal functionalities for choosing input and committing messages respectively. The OT (Oblivious Transfer) [41] we use is weak committing OT instead of standard OT since it requires an open command.

2.3 Garbling Scheme

In this section, we describe the privacy-free garbling scheme [16], which is a kind of garbling scheme designed for ZKGC.

A garbling scheme [6] is defined as a tuple $\mathcal{G} = (\mathsf{Gb}, \mathsf{En}, \mathsf{Ev}, \mathsf{De}, \mathsf{Ve})$:

- $(\mathsf{GC}, e, d) \leftarrow \mathsf{Gb}(1^\kappa, f)$. This algorithm takes as input security parameter κ, boolean function $f : \{0,1\}^n \to \{0,1\}$ and some randomness. Then it generates garbled circuit GC, decoding information d and encoding information $e = \{K_i^0, K_i^1\}_{i\in[n]}$ where n is the input size and K_i^0, K_i^1 are input labels.
- $X := \mathsf{En}(e, x)$, which generates garbled input X using encoding information e and input x.
- $Y := \mathsf{Ev}(GC, X)$. It evaluates the garbled circuit GC using garbled input X and outputs garbled output Y.
- $y := \mathsf{De}(d, Y)$. The algorithm decodes garbled output Y using decoding information d and outputs the final output y.

To let prover believe in the correctness of the garbled circuit, another algorithm Ve is required [29].

- $\{0,1\} \leftarrow \mathsf{Ve}(\mathsf{GC}, e, f)$. It outputs accept if the garbled circuit is indeed a description of f.

A garbling scheme should meet the following properties:

Definition 1. *A garbling scheme $\mathcal{G}$ satisfies* **correctness** *if for any boolean function $f : \{0,1\}^n \to \{0,1\}$ and $x \in \{0,1\}^n$, the probability that*

$$(\mathsf{GC}, e, d) \leftarrow \mathsf{Gb}(1^\kappa, f), f(x) \neq \mathsf{De}(d, \mathsf{Ev}(\mathsf{GC}, \mathsf{En}(e, x)))$$

is negligible.

Definition 2. *A garbling scheme $\mathcal{G}$ has* **authenticity** *if for every boolean function $f : \{0,1\}^n \to \{0,1\}$ and input $x \in \{0,1\}^n$, the probability that any PPT adversary $\mathcal{A}$ outputs the following is negligible:*

$$(\mathsf{GC}, e, d) \leftarrow \mathsf{Gb}(1^\kappa, f), X = \mathsf{En}(e, x), Y \leftarrow \mathcal{A}(\mathsf{GC}, d, X), \mathsf{De}(d, Y) \notin \{f(x), \perp\}$$

Definition 3. *A garbling scheme $\mathcal{G}$ has* **verifiability** *if for every boolean function $f : \{0,1\}^n \to \{0,1\}$ and input $x \in \{0,1\}^n$ such that $f(x) = 1$, and for any PPT adversary $\mathcal{A}$ there exists an expected polynomial time algorithm* Ext *such that the following is negligible:*

$$(\mathsf{GC}, e, d) \leftarrow \mathcal{A}(1^\kappa, f), \mathsf{Ve}(GC, e, d) = 1, \mathsf{Ext}(\mathsf{GC}, e) \neq \mathsf{Ev}(\mathsf{GC}, \mathsf{En}(e, x))$$

2.4 Garbled Circuits and Elliptic Curves Group

Garbled circuits was proposed by Yao [47] as a way to perform secure two-party computation. It has gone through lots of improvements, such as point-and-permute [5], free-XOR [34], row reduction method [36], half-gates [49] and the state-of-the-art three halves protocol [43]. Here, we describe free-XOR briefly since it is important in our protocol. Besides, we also introduce elliptic curves group as in Sect. 3.3 we will discuss how to use free-XOR on elliptic curves group, which is an essential technique of our paper.

Free-XOR. We use (K_i^0, K_i^1) to denote the wire labels indicating true and false respectively for the ith wire. There is a global offset Δ under the free-XOR setting. And two labels for any wire i satisfy $K_i^0 = K_i^1 \oplus \Delta$.

For an XOR gate in Fig. 3, suppose A and $A \oplus \Delta$ are wire labels corresponding to 0 and 1 for one input, and B, $B \oplus \Delta$ are 0,1 wire labels for the other input. Then $C = A \oplus B = (A \oplus \Delta) \oplus (B \oplus \Delta)$ and $C \oplus \Delta = A \oplus (B \oplus \Delta) = (A \oplus \Delta) \oplus B$.

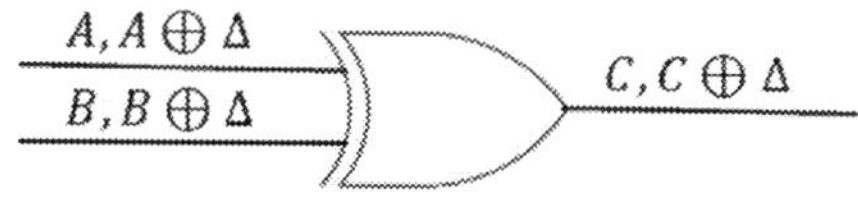

Fig. 3. Wire Labels under free-XOR setting

Elliptic Curves Group. Koblitz [33] and Miller [35] use elliptic curves cryptosystems. An elliptic E curve over a field $\mathbb{F}$ meet the condition of an abelian group. Its group identity is ∞, a point at infinity. And for a point on the curve $(x, y) \in E$, its negative is $(x, -y)$ since $(x, y) + (x, -y) = \infty$.

2.5 Symmetric Encryption

Encryption algorithms can be broadly divided into symmetric (private) encryption and asymmetric (public) encryption. Specifically, AES (the Advanced Encryption Standard) is a famous symmetric encryption scheme designed by Daemen and Rijmen [14]. The syntax of symmetric key encryption is:

- $k \leftarrow \mathsf{KeyGen}(\kappa)$ where κ is the security parameter. The output k is the secret key.
- $c \leftarrow \mathsf{Enc}(k, m)$ where m is the message to be encrypted and c is the ciphertext.
- $m \leftarrow \mathsf{Dec}(k, c)$ is the decryption algorithm.

Any adversary can not break an ideal symmetric encryption scheme better than enumerating the key space. Ideally, any x bits leakage on the encryption key should reduce the key space exactly to its $1/2^x$.

2.6 Commitment

A commitment scheme that commits to message m should meet the following requirements [31]:

Hiding. Any PPT adversary $\mathcal{A}$ can not win the following experiment with probability more than $\frac{1}{2}+\mathsf{negl}(\kappa)$ for a commitment scheme meeting hiding property:

$\mathcal{C}$		$\mathcal{A}$
		choose m_0, m_1
$b \leftarrow \{0,1\}$	$\xleftarrow{(m_0, m_1)}$	
$c = \mathsf{Com}(m_b, r)$		
	$\xrightarrow{c}$	
		compute b'
$b \stackrel{?}{=} b'$	$\xleftarrow{b'}$	

Binding. If $c = \mathsf{Com}(m, r)$ is the commitment of message m, then for any PPT adversary $\mathcal{A}$, binding ensures the possibility that he/she outputs $m' \neq m, r'$ such that $c = \mathsf{Com}(m, r) = \mathsf{Com}(m', r')$ is negligible.

2.7 ECDSA

ECDSA (Elliptic Curve Digital Signature Algorithm) [42], which is an elliptic curve analogue of DSA (Digital Signature Algorithm) [37]. It [30] is a signature protocol based on elliptic curves group.

Suppose $\mathbb{G}$ is an elliptic curve group with generator g over $\mathbb{Z}_q$. ECDSA consists of the following PPT algorithms [31]:

- $(pk, sk) \leftarrow \mathsf{KeyGen}(1^\kappa)$: choose a random $x \in \mathbb{Z}_q$ and let $y = g^x$. The public key and private key are $pk := (\mathbb{G}, q, g, y)$, $sk := x$. Besides, function $H : \{0,1\}^* \rightarrow \mathbb{Z}_q$ is a hash function. $F : \mathbb{G} \rightarrow \mathbb{Z}_q$ outputs the x part of a point on elliptic curve.
- $\sigma \leftarrow \mathsf{Sign}(sk, m)$: choose a uniform $k \in \mathbb{Z}_q$ and let $r = F(g^k)$, $s = k^{-1}(H(m) + xr) \bmod q$. If $r = 0$ or $s = 0$, restart with another choice of k, otherwise output signature $\sigma = (r, s)$.
- $\{0,1\} \leftarrow \mathsf{Verify}(pk, m, \sigma)$: check if $r = F(g^{H(m)\cdot s^{-1}} y^{r \cdot s^{-1}})$. Output 1 if they are the same, otherwise output 0.

3 Construction

In this section, we will describe our protocol for realizing fair exchange using zero-knowledge from garbled circuits (ZKGC). First, we will give the intuitions followed by a concrete description of the protocol.

3.1 Intuitions

Consider the contract-signing [7] case where two parties Alice and Bob wish to exchange their respective signatures σ of contracts. They decide to first encrypt their signatures using private keys k. After encryption $\mathsf{Enc}(k, \sigma) = ct$, they then exchange their private keys k bit by bit. In this way, if either Alice or Bob chooses to abort the protocol, she or he will only obtain an advantage of at most one bit of k. To realize the protocol, they need to also prove the validity of the signature σ and make commitments of each bit of key k, $c_i = \mathtt{Com}(k_i, r_i), \cdots, c_\kappa = \mathtt{Com}(k_\kappa, r_\kappa)$ where κ is the length of private keys and computational security parameter. Overall, the following relation needs to be met:

$$\mathcal{R}^{\mathrm{ZK}}(ct, pk, \{c_i\}_{i\in[\kappa]}; k, \sigma, \{r_i\}_{i\in[\kappa]}): \quad \begin{array}{l} \mathtt{Enc}(k, \sigma) = ct \text{ and } \mathsf{Verify}(pk, \sigma) = 1 \\ \text{and } \left\{\mathtt{Com}(k_i, r_i) = c_i\right\}_{i\in[\kappa]} \end{array}$$

Here, the relation $\mathcal{R}(x; w)$ is defined in Sect. 2.1. The semicolon separates x and witnesses w.

This scenario is not the only application since our protocol can also be used for exchanging any digital goods by replacing the second equation $\mathsf{Verify}(pk, \sigma) = 1$ with $C(\sigma) = 1$, where $C(\cdot)$ is a function that checks the validity of the corresponding message. Although the exchanged messages are not limited to signatures, in our protocol, we focus on exchanging signatures.

The instantiation of this zero-knowledge proof is not trivial, we have to handle both large Boolean circuits and algebra computation. The symmetric encryption and the commitment are naturally Boolean circuits. However, the ECDSA signature involves elliptic curve operations, which can not be garbled directly. Fortunately, ZKGC, with the combination of Free-XOR on elliptic curves group, meets all of our need. In the following parts, we will show the technique we use to realize $\mathsf{Verify}(pk, \sigma) = 1$ in $\mathcal{R}^{\mathrm{ZK}}$ by realizing ECDSA in garbled circuits.

3.2 Zero-Knowledge Verification of ECDSA

Recall the verification of ECDSA in Sect. 2.7. The verifier checks whether $r = F(g^{H(m)\cdot s^{-1}} y^{r\cdot s^{-1}})$, where F outputs the x part of a group element. Although we can represent the whole function in Boolean circuits to garble it, the size of the circuit will be considerably large.

To reduce the circuit size, we make some slight modifications. The verifier first computes (two possible) g^k from r and checks if $g^k = g^{H(m)\cdot s^{-1}} y^{r\cdot s^{-1}} = (g^{H(m)} y^r)^{s^{-1}}$. This will reject for only a negligible fraction of valid signatures and does not accept any invalid signatures. This is because the field size does not match the group order.

To zero-knowledge prove that the prover has a valid signature, the prover first opens r as a public parameter. This will not harm the security because any algorithm which can compute a valid s from r will break the EUF-CMA property of ECDSA. Thus, consider $g^k = (g^{H(m)}y^r)^{s^{-1}}$, where $g^k, H(m), y, r$ are all public, and only s is private. Now the statement is a proof of knowledge for the discrete logarithm problem. We show how to prove it on garbled circuits in the next subsection.

3.3 Free-XOR on Elliptic Curves Group

We extend the usage of free-XOR to elliptic curve groups where the ideas come from Garillot et al. [19] and Chase et al. [10]. Under the setting of free XOR on elliptic curve group over $\mathbb{Z}_q$, suppose $A + a\Delta$ is the wire label corresponding to truth value a for one input wire, and $B + b\Delta$ is the wire label of value b for the other input wire where truth values $a, b \in \mathbb{Z}_q$. Since $(A + a\Delta) + (B + b\Delta) = (A + B) + (a + b)\Delta$, free-XOR on an elliptic curve group with generator g over $\mathbb{Z}_q$ can be expressed as:

$$g^{A+a\Delta} \cdot g^{B+b\Delta} = g^{(A+B)+(a+b)\Delta}$$

where $(A+B)+(a+b)\Delta$ is the wire label of the output wire indicating truth value $a+b \in \mathbb{Z}_q$. On the elliptic curve, the output label has the form of $g^{(A+B)+(a+b)\Delta}$.

Next, we will show how to apply this method in detail. If prover needs to prove his knowledge of a secret m to verifier, parties can first exchange a value $c = g^m$ and let prover show that g^m is indeed c through a garbled circuit constructed by verifier. Meanwhile, the validity of this message m is also guaranteed through commitment. To prove $c = g^m$, prover can first express m as a binary $m = m_{n-1} \cdots m_1 m_0$. Verifier, who generates the garbled circuit, also generates random labels $A_i, i \in [n]$ for these values. Through oblivious transfer [41], prover gets garbled values $A_{n-1} + m_{n-1}\Delta, \cdots, A_0 + m_0\Delta$ as inputs for the garbled circuit. During circuit evaluation, for each bit i of message m, prover receives the following ciphertexts, where the hash functions are circular correlation robustness (CCR) hash functions [11,27] (or simply, random oracle) and $B_i, i \in [n]$ are randomly generated labels:

$$\begin{cases} H(A_i + 0\Delta) \oplus g^{B_i + 2^i \cdot 0\Delta} \\ H(A_i + 1\Delta) \oplus g^{B_i + 2^i \cdot 1\Delta} \end{cases}$$

Prover can decrypt one of them and gets $g^{B_i + 2^i m_i \Delta}$, the garbled value of the corresponding value on elliptic curve. Adding all these values, prover gets:

$$g^{B_{n-1}+2^{n-1}m_{n-1}\Delta} \cdots g^{B_1+2^1 m_1\Delta} \cdot g^{B_0+2^0 m_0\Delta} = g^{(B_{n-1}+\cdots+B_1+B_0)+m\Delta = g^{C+m\Delta}}$$

which is the garbled output. Verifier receives this value from prover and compares it with her garbled value of m on elliptic curve using public value $c = g^m$ and accepts if they are the same.

Protocol $\Pi_{\mathbf{ZK}}$

Suppose $\mathcal{G} = (\mathsf{Gb}, \mathsf{En}, \mathsf{Ev}, \mathsf{De}, \mathsf{Ve})$ is a garbling scheme meeting the requirements in Sect. 2.3. The length of prover's witness $w = (w_1, \cdots, w_n)$ is n.

1. Prover sends (choose, w_i) for $i \in [n]$ to $\mathcal{F}^{\mathsf{cho}}$.
2. Verifier generates garbled circuit $(\mathsf{GC}, e, d) \leftarrow \mathsf{Gb}(1^\kappa, f)$ where $e = \{K_i^0, K_i^1\}_{i\in[n]}$ are input wire labels.
3. Verifier sends $e = \{K_i^0, K_i^1\}_{i\in[n]}$ as messages to $\mathcal{F}^{\mathsf{cho}}$.
4. Prover receives input wire labels $X = \{K_i^{w_i}\}_{i\in[n]}$ corresponding to his input $w = (w_1, \cdots, w_n)$ from $\mathcal{F}^{\mathsf{cho}}$.
5. Verifier sends the garbled circuit GC to prover.
6. Prover evaluates the garbled circuit and gets garbled output (output wire label) $Y = \mathsf{Ev}(GC, \mathsf{En}(e, w))$.
7. Prover sends (commit, Y) to $\mathcal{F}^{\mathsf{com}}$.
8. Verifier sends **open** instruction to $\mathcal{F}^{\mathsf{cho}}$. Prover receives all input labels $e = \{K_i^0, K_i^1\}_{i\in[n]}$.
9. Prover verifies the validity of garbled circuit $\{0,1\} \leftarrow \mathsf{Ve}(\mathsf{GC}, e, f)$. If the result is 0, he terminates the protocol.
10. Prover sends **open** instruction to $\mathcal{F}^{\mathsf{com}}$. Verifier receives garbled output Y.
11. Verifier checks if the output label Y is the same as the true label. She accepts if they are the same.

Fig. 4. Zero-knowledge from Garbled Circuits (ZKGC) Protocol

3.4 Protocol Description

The protocol of performing zero-knowledge from garbled circuits [29] is described in Fig. 4, where verifier acts as the garbled circuit constructor and prover is the circuit evaluator. Ideal functionality $\mathcal{F}^{\mathsf{cho}}$ and $\mathcal{F}^{\mathsf{com}}$ are described in Sect. 2.2.

The full protocol Fig. 5 is divided into three stages. Two parties Alice and Bob first do some preparation work. Then they run the ZKGC protocol in Fig. 4 and at last reveal their secrets.

3.5 Security Analysis

In this section, we show a proof sketch about the security of our protocol. Our protocol achieves resource fairness as follows:

1. Any party who aborts at the preparation phase or ZK phase, learns nothing about the private message and private key of the other party.
2. Any party who aborts at the exchange phase, can obtain at most one bit advantage on enumerating the remaining keys.
3. Any party who doesn't follow the protocol, will be caught by the other party.

As stated above, we also assume that the commitment scheme and symmetric encryption are ideal. We leave it as an open problem whether a security proof can be obtained in the standard model.

Protocol $\Pi_{\mathbf{GRUZ}}$

Preparation. Alice encrypts her private messages σ^A with her private key k^A as $ct^A = \mathsf{Enc}(k^A, \sigma^A)$ and commits to Bob each bit of their private keys k^A as $c_i^A = \mathsf{Com}(k_i^A, r_i^A)$. Bob does the same with σ^B, k^B, ct^B and c_i^B respectively.

ZK Phase. Alice first plays as the prover while Bob acts as the verifier. They run protocol Π_{ZK} together for the first time. Then they exchange their roles and run protocol Π_{ZK} again. In this way, they prove to the other party the validity of their secret keys and messages.

Exchange Phase. Alice and Bob exchange their secrets (k_i^A, r_i^A) and (k_i^B, r_i^B), $i \in [\kappa]$, one pair at a time alternately. Each round they check that $k_i^{\{A,B\}}$ and $r_i^{\{A,B\}}$ are the decommitment of $c_i^{\{A,B\}}$ in the ZK phase. If one party finds the commitment inconsistent or receiving time goes out, he or she will abort and enumerate the remaining keys. At last, they decrypt the ciphertext to recover the private messages $\sigma^{\{A,B\}}$ using secret keys.

Fig. 5. The GRUZ protocol

For the first claim, the transcripts during the first two phases are a ciphertext, commitments and a zero-knowledge proof. Intuitively they do not leak any information about the private message and private key, because of the ideal cipher, the (ideal) hiding property of commitment scheme and the zero-knowledge property, respectively. The second claim is straightforward. Both parties exchange keys bit by bit alternately. One party can obtain at most one bit advantage if he or she aborts at any point. The third claim is guaranteed by the soundness property of ZK and the binding property of commitment scheme.

4 Implementation and Experimental Results

We have implemented the protocol in Sect. 3 by instantiating the symmetric encryption with `AES128` in ECB mode, the commitment scheme with `SHA256` and the signature scheme with `ECDSA` where the elliptic curve is `secp256k1`. The oblivious transfer is instantiated by actively secure IKNP protocol [28,32]. Our implementation relies on emp-toolkit [46] library and can be found at github.com/kzoacn/emp-swap. Based on this implementation, we conducted experiments on the following relations:

$$\mathcal{R}^{\mathrm{ZK}}(ct, pk, \{c_i\}_{i\in[\kappa]}; k, \sigma, \{r_i\}_{i\in[\kappa]}) : \begin{array}{l} \mathtt{AES}(k,\sigma) = ct \text{ and } \mathsf{Verify}(pk,\sigma) = 1 \\ \text{and } \left\{\mathtt{SHA256}(k_i, r_i) = c_i\right\}_{i\in[\kappa]} \end{array}$$

We run the experiments on a Ubuntu 20.04 LTS machine with AMD® Ryzen 5600X CPU and 16GB of RAM in LAN setting. The simulated communication channel has 10Gbps bandwidth and 1ms delay. Parameters and results for the experiments are reported in Table 2.

Table 2. Experiments Result. Enc refers to the symmetric encryption part. Verify refers to the verification part. Com refers to the commitment part, which repeats `SHA256` 128 times. $\mathcal{R}^{\text{ZK}}$ refers to the whole execution.

Circuit	Circuit size	#AND gates	Prover time	Verifier time	Communication size
Enc	67,232	13,602	–	–	–
Verify	8,192	2,048	–	–	–
Com	30,222,336	11,625,600	–	–	–
$\mathcal{R}^{\text{ZK}}$	30,297,889	11,641,379	4.20 s	4.21 s	187.9 MB

Zero-knowledge phase plays the main role in our protocol, thus we analyze this phase only. From the table we can see the major cost is the commitment, which is dominated by the size of the circuit. The execution time and communication time are acceptable for practice use.

5 Conclusion and Future Directions

Our GRUZ (Gradual Release Using Zero-knowledge) protocol uses zero-knowledge from garbled circuits (ZKGC) [29] to realize gradual release in the fair exchange problem without using blockchain. We also implement it with standard cryptographic primitives AES, SHA256, and ECDSA. Our results show that our protocol is acceptable for practice.

In the future, we plan to investigate making zero-knowledge proof more succinct and using zk-friendly primitives, which can reduce proof size and improve running time and communication costs. Besides, we can generalize our protocol to secure multiparty computation with resource fairness.

References

1. Decred adds atomic swap support for exchange-free cryptocurrency trading nasdaq. https://www.nasdaq.com/articles/decred-adds-atomic-swap-support-for-exchange-free-cryptocurrency-trading-2017-09-20
2. First btc-ltc lightning network swap completed, huge potential. https://cointelegraph.com/news/first-btc-ltc-lightning-network-swap-completed-huge-potential
3. Github-decred/atomicswap: On-chain atomic swaps for decred and other cryptocurrencies. https://github.com/decred/atomicswap
4. Xmr. developer announces bitcoin to monero atomic swap capabilities-privacy bitcoin news. https://news.bitcoin.com/xmr-developer-announces-bitcoin-to-monero-atomic-swap-capabilities/

5. Beaver, D., Micali, S., Rogaway, P.: The round complexity of secure protocols (extended abstract). In: 22nd ACM STOC, pp. 503–513. ACM Press, May 1990. https://doi.org/10.1145/100216.100287
6. Bellare, M., Hoang, V.T., Rogaway, P.: Foundations of garbled circuits. In: Yu, T., Danezis, G., Gligor, V.D. (eds.) ACM CCS 2012, pp. 784–796. ACM Press, October 2012. https://doi.org/10.1145/2382196.2382279
7. Ben-Or, M., Goldreich, O., Micali, S., Rivest, R.L.: A fair protocol for signing contracts. IEEE Trans. Inf. Theory **36**(1), 40–46 (1990)
8. Blum, M.: How to exchange (secret) keys (extended abstract). In: 15th ACM STOC, pp. 440–447. ACM Press, April 1983. https://doi.org/10.1145/800061.808775
9. Brickell, E.F., Chaum, D., Damgård, I.B., van de Graaf, J.: Gradual and verifiable release of a secret (extended abstract). In: Pomerance, C. (ed.) CRYPTO 1987. LNCS, vol. 293, pp. 156–166. Springer, Heidelberg (1988). https://doi.org/10.1007/3-540-48184-2_11
10. Chase, M., Ganesh, C., Mohassel, P.: Efficient zero-knowledge proof of algebraic and non-algebraic statements with applications to privacy preserving credentials. In: Robshaw, M., Katz, J. (eds.) CRYPTO 2016. LNCS, vol. 9816, pp. 499–530. Springer, Heidelberg (2016). https://doi.org/10.1007/978-3-662-53015-3_18
11. Choi, S.G., Katz, J., Kumaresan, R., Zhou, H.-S.: On the security of the "Free-XOR" technique. In: Cramer, R. (ed.) TCC 2012. LNCS, vol. 7194, pp. 39–53. Springer, Heidelberg (2012). https://doi.org/10.1007/978-3-642-28914-9_3
12. Choudhuri, A.R., Green, M., Jain, A., Kaptchuk, G., Miers, I.: Fairness in an unfair world: fair multiparty computation from public bulletin boards. In: Thuraisingham, B.M., Evans, D., Malkin, T., Xu, D. (eds.) ACM CCS 2017, pp. 719–728. ACM Press, October/November 2017. https://doi.org/10.1145/3133956.3134092
13. Cleve, R.: Limits on the security of coin flips when half the processors are faulty (extended abstract). In: 18th ACM STOC, pp. 364–369. ACM Press, May 1986. https://doi.org/10.1145/12130.12168
14. Daemen, J., Rijmen, V.: The design of Rijndael, vol. 2. Springer
15. Even, S.: Protocol for signing contracts. In: Gersho, A. (ed.) CRYPTO'81. vol. ECE Report 82–04, pp. 148–153. U.C. Santa Barbara, Dept. of Elec. and Computer Eng. (1981)
16. Frederiksen, T.K., Nielsen, J.B., Orlandi, C.: Privacy-free garbled circuits with applications to efficient zero-knowledge. In: Oswald and Fischlin [39], pp. 191–219. https://doi.org/10.1007/978-3-662-46803-6_7
17. Garay, J., MacKenzie, P., Prabhakaran, M., Yang, K.: Resource fairness and composability of cryptographic protocols. In: Halevi, S., Rabin, T. (eds.) TCC 2006. LNCS, vol. 3876, pp. 404–428. Springer, Heidelberg (2006). https://doi.org/10.1007/11681878_21
18. Garay, J.A., Pomerance, C.: Timed fair exchange of standard signatures. In: Wright, R.N. (ed.) FC 2003. LNCS, vol. 2742, pp. 190–207. Springer, Heidelberg (2003). https://doi.org/10.1007/978-3-540-45126-6_14
19. Garillot, F., Kondi, Y., Mohassel, P., Nikolaenko, V.: Threshold schnorr with stateless deterministic signing from standard assumptions. In: Malkin, T., Peikert, C. (eds.) CRYPTO 2021. LNCS, vol. 12825, pp. 127–156. Springer, Cham (2021). https://doi.org/10.1007/978-3-030-84242-0_6
20. Goldwasser, S., Micali, S., Rackoff, C.: The knowledge complexity of interactive proof-systems (extended abstract). In: 17th ACM STOC, pp. 291–304. ACM Press, May 1985. https://doi.org/10.1145/22145.22178

21. Gordon, S.D., Hazay, C., Katz, J., Lindell, Y.: Complete fairness in secure two-party computation. In: Ladner, R.E., Dwork, C. (eds.) 40th ACM STOC, pp. 413–422. ACM Press, May 2008. https://doi.org/10.1145/1374376.1374436
22. Gordon, D., Ishai, Y., Moran, T., Ostrovsky, R., Sahai, A.: On Complete Primitives for Fairness. In: Micciancio, D. (ed.) TCC 2010. LNCS, vol. 5978, pp. 91–108. Springer, Heidelberg (2010). https://doi.org/10.1007/978-3-642-11799-2_7
23. Gordon, S.D., Katz, J.: Complete fairness in multi-party computation without an honest majority. In: Reingold, O. (ed.) TCC 2009. LNCS, vol. 5444, pp. 19–35. Springer, Heidelberg (2009). https://doi.org/10.1007/978-3-642-00457-5_2
24. Gordon, S.D., Katz, J.: Partial fairness in secure two-party computation. In: Gilbert, H. (ed.) EUROCRYPT 2010. LNCS, vol. 6110, pp. 157–176. Springer, Heidelberg (2010). https://doi.org/10.1007/978-3-642-13190-5_8
25. Dov Gordon, S., Liu, F.-H., Shi, E.: Constant-round MPC with fairness and guarantee of output delivery. In: Gennaro, R., Robshaw, M. (eds.) CRYPTO 2015. LNCS, vol. 9216, pp. 63–82. Springer, Heidelberg (2015). https://doi.org/10.1007/978-3-662-48000-7_4
26. Gordon, S.D.: On fairness in secure computation. Ph.D. thesis (2010)
27. Guo, C., Katz, J., Wang, X., Yu, Y.: Efficient and secure multiparty computation from fixed-key block ciphers. In: 2020 IEEE Symposium on Security and Privacy, pp. 825–841. IEEE Computer Society Press, May 2020. https://doi.org/10.1109/SP40000.2020.00016
28. Ishai, Y., Kilian, J., Nissim, K., Petrank, E.: Extending oblivious transfers efficiently. In: Boneh, D. (ed.) CRYPTO 2003. LNCS, vol. 2729, pp. 145–161. Springer, Heidelberg (2003). https://doi.org/10.1007/978-3-540-45146-4_9
29. Jawurek, M., Kerschbaum, F., Orlandi, C.: Zero-knowledge using garbled circuits: how to prove non-algebraic statements efficiently. In: Sadeghi, A.R., Gligor, V.D., Yung, M. (eds.) ACM CCS 2013, pp. 955–966. ACM Press, November 2013. https://doi.org/10.1145/2508859.2516662
30. Johnson, D., Menezes, A., Vanstone, S.: The elliptic curve digital signature algorithm (ecdsa). Int. J. Inf. Secur. **1**(1), 36–63 (2001)
31. Katz, J., Lindell, Y.: Introduction to Modern Cryptography. CRC Press (2014)
32. Keller, M., Orsini, E., Scholl, P.: Actively secure OT extension with optimal overhead. In: Gennaro, R., Robshaw, M. (eds.) CRYPTO 2015. LNCS, vol. 9215, pp. 724–741. Springer, Heidelberg (2015). https://doi.org/10.1007/978-3-662-47989-6_35
33. Koblitz, N.: Elliptic curve cryptosystems. Math. Comput. **48**(177), 203–209 (1987)
34. Kolesnikov, V., Schneider, T.: Improved garbled circuit: free XOR gates and applications. In: Aceto, L., Damgård, I., Goldberg, L.A., Halldórsson, M.M., Ingólfsdóttir, A., Walukiewicz, I. (eds.) ICALP 2008. LNCS, vol. 5126, pp. 486–498. Springer, Heidelberg (2008). https://doi.org/10.1007/978-3-540-70583-3_40
35. Miller, V.S.: Use of elliptic curves in cryptography. In: Williams, H.C. (ed.) CRYPTO 1985. LNCS, vol. 218, pp. 417–426. Springer, Heidelberg (1986). https://doi.org/10.1007/3-540-39799-X_31
36. Naor, M., Pinkas, B., Sumner, R.: Privacy preserving auctions and mechanism design. In: Proceedings of the 1st ACM Conference on Electronic Commerce, pp. 129–139 (1999)
37. Nist, C.: The digital signature standard. Commun. ACM **35**(7), 36–40 (1992)
38. Okamoto, T., Ohta, K.: How to simultaneously exchange secrets by general assumptions. In: Denning, D.E., Pyle, R., Ganesan, R., Sandhu, R.S. (eds.) ACM CCS 94, pp. 184–192. ACM Press, November 1994. https://doi.org/10.1145/191177.191221

39. Oswald, E., Fischlin, M. (eds.): EUROCRYPT 2015. LNCS, vol. 9057. Springer, Heidelberg (2015). https://doi.org/10.1007/978-3-662-46803-6
40. Paul, S., Shrivastava, A.: Efficient fair multiparty protocols using blockchain and trusted hardware. In: Schwabe, P., Thériault, N. (eds.) LATINCRYPT 2019. LNCS, vol. 11774, pp. 301–320. Springer, Cham (2019). https://doi.org/10.1007/978-3-030-30530-7_15
41. Rabin, M.O.: How to exchange secrets with oblivious transfer. Cryptology ePrint Archive, Report 2005/187 (2005). http://eprint.iacr.org/2005/187
42. Rivest, R.L., Hellman, M.E., Anderson, J.C., Lyons, J.W.: Responses to nist's proposal. Commun. ACM **35**(7), 41–54 (1992)
43. Rosulek, M., Roy, L.: Three halves make a whole? beating the half-gates lower bound for garbled circuits. In: Malkin, T., Peikert, C. (eds.) CRYPTO 2021. LNCS, vol. 12825, pp. 94–124. Springer, Cham (2021). https://doi.org/10.1007/978-3-030-84242-0_5
44. Tedrick, T.: How to exchange half a bit. In: Chaum, D. (ed.) CRYPTO'83, pp. 147–151. Plenum Press, New York (1983)
45. Tedrick, T.: Fair exchange of secrets. In: Blakley, G.R., Chaum, D. (eds.) CRYPTO'84. LNCS, vol. 196, pp. 434–438. Springer, Heidelberg (1984)
46. Wang, X., Malozemoff, A.J., Katz, J.: EMP-toolkit: Efficient MultiParty computation toolkit. https://github.com/emp-toolkit (2016)
47. Yao, A.C.C.: Protocols for secure computations (extended abstract). In: 23rd FOCS, pp. 160–164. IEEE Computer Society Press, November 1982. https://doi.org/10.1109/SFCS.1982.38
48. Yao, A.C.C.: How to generate and exchange secrets (extended abstract). In: 27th FOCS, pp. 162–167. IEEE Computer Society Press, October 1986. https://doi.org/10.1109/SFCS.1986.25
49. Zahur, S., Rosulek, M., Evans, D.: Two halves make a whole - reducing data transfer in garbled circuits using half gates. In: Oswald and Fischlin [39], pp. 220–250. https://doi.org/10.1007/978-3-662-46803-6_8

Daric: A Storage Efficient Payment Channel with Punishment Mechanism

Arash Mirzaei(✉), Amin Sakzad, Jiangshan Yu, and Ron Steinfeld

Faculty of Information Technology, Monash University, Melbourne, Australia
{arash.mirzaei,amin.sakzad,jiangshan.yu,ron.steinfeld}@monash.edu

Abstract. Lightning Network (LN), the most widely deployed payment channel for Bitcoin, requires channel parties to generate and store distinct revocation keys for all n payments of a channel to resolve fraudulent channel closures. To reduce the required storage in a payment channel, eltoo introduces a new signature type for Bitcoin to enable payment versioning. This allows a channel party to revoke all old payments by using a payment with a higher version number, reducing the storage complexity from $\mathcal{O}(n)$ to $\mathcal{O}(1)$. However, eltoo fails to achieve bounded closure, enabling a dishonest channel party to significantly delay the channel closure process. Eltoo also lacks a punishment mechanism, which may incentivize profit-driven channel parties to close a payment channel with an old state, to their own advantage.

This paper introduces Daric, a payment channel with unlimited lifetime for Bitcoin that achieves optimal storage and bounded closure. Moreover, Daric implements a punishment mechanism and simultaneously avoids the methods other schemes commonly use to enable punishment: 1) state duplication which leads to exponential increase in the number of transactions with the number of applications on top of each other or 2) dedicated design of adaptor signatures which introduces compatibility issues with BLS or most post-quantum resistant digital signatures. We also formalise Daric and prove its security in the Universal Composability model.

Keywords: Bitcoin · Scalability · Payment channel · Lightning network · Watchtower

1 Introduction

Due to its permissionless nature, Bitcoin suffers from poor transaction throughput [9,14,25]. Payment channel constitutes a promising solution, which allows two parties to perform several transactions without touching the blockchain except for creating and closing the channel. In more details, two parties create a payment channel by locking Bitcoins in a shared address. Then, they pay each other arbitrarily many times by exchanging authenticated off-chain transactions that spend the shared address and split the channel funds among parties. Each

W. Susilo et al. (Eds.): ISC 2022, LNCS 13640, pp. 229–249, 2022.
https://doi.org/10.1007/978-3-031-22390-7_15

party can finally close the channel by publishing the last authenticated transactions on the blockchain. Payment channels can also be linked to form a payment channel network (PCN) where each payment can be routed via intermediaries.

Since each party's share of coins in a channel changes over time, one might attempt to close the channel with an old state to maximize her profit. Lightning Network [24]–the most popular payment channel network– adopts a punishment mechanism to prevent parties from acting dishonestly. In this network, upon authorizing a new state, channel parties exchange some revocation secrets to revoke the previous state. Then, if a party publishes a revoked state, her counterparty, who is supposed to be always online, uses the corresponding revocation secrets to take all the channel funds. Parties might also delegate the punishing job to a third party, called the *watchtower* [24].

Although elegantly designed, the Lightning Network has some shortcomings. Firstly, since channel parties must store all the revocation secrets, received from their counter-parties, their storage amount increases linearly with the number of channel updates. Moreover, to detect and punish the misbehaving party, the channel state is duplicated meaning each party has its own copy of the state. Then, when for adding an application (e.g. *Virtual channel* [6]) on top of the channel, parties have to split their channel into sub-channels, the state of each sub-channel is duplicated and it must propagate on both duplicates of the parent channel. Thus, state duplication causes the number of transactions to exponentially rise with the number of applications k built on top of each other [5].

Towards a different direction, the payment channel eltoo [12] introduces `ANYPREVOUT` [13] (also known as `NOINPUT`) as a new Bitcoin signature type to deploy the concept of versioning. This allows channel parties to override the current channel state by creating a state with a higher version number, which can be published upon fraud. So, channel parties in eltoo do not store any revocation secrets from old channel states. This simplifies the key management and offers more affordable watchtowers as the transaction with the highest version invalidates all previous states. Furthermore, if an honest party forgets about an update and publishes an outdated state, it does not result in the loss of funds.

However, eltoo is incentive incompatible because its lack of punishment might encourage a dishonest party to publish an old state; Either the other side corrects it or the dishonest party wins [23]. The only discouraging factor–the fee for publishing the old state–is also determined by the dishonest party. Thus, she can set it to the minimum possible value, i.e. few cents for some blockchains such as Bitcoin hard forks (e.g. Litecoin and Bitcoin Cash) and less than 1 USD for Bitcoin. Moreover, the transaction fee is independent of the channel *capacity* (i.e. the total funds in the channel). Therefore, even for payment channels with huge capacity of several BTCs (e.g., channels listed in [1]), the dishonest party's cost will be still below 1 USD (See Sect. 6.2 for detailed analysis). Additionally, enforcing a large transaction fee or restricting the channel capacity (proposed in [3]) might be unfavourable to the honest party.

Furthermore, a dishonest party in eltoo might publish multiple outdated states to delay the channel closure process [2]. Thus, eltoo fails to achieve *bounded closure*, i.e. honest party is not guaranteed that the channel closure completes within a bounded time. This compromises the security of time-based payments, e.g. *Hash-Time Lock Contract* (HTLC) (See Sect. 6.1 for further analysis).

Therefore, the main motivation of this paper is designing a Bitcoin payment channel that (1) provides optimal storage, (2) achieves bounded closure, (3) provides incentive compatibility, and (4) avoids state duplication.

1.1 Contributions

The contributions of the paper are as follows:

- We present a new Bitcoin payment channel, called Daric, which (i) is provably secure in the Universal Composability (UC) framework, (ii) achieves constant size storage for both channel parties and the watchtower, (iii) provides bounded closure, (iv) provides punishment mechanism and hence achieves incentive compatibility, (v) avoids state duplication without needing any particular property (e.g. adaptor signature properties) for the underlying digital signature, and (vi) attains unlimited lifetime, given that channel parties on average pay each other at most once per second. Table 1 compares Daric with other Bitcoin payment channels.

Table 1. Comparison of different payment channels with n channel updates and k recursive channel splitting.

Scheme	Party's St. Req.	Watch. St. Req.	Lifetime	Incent. Compat.	# of Txs	Ada. Sig. Avoid.	Bnd. Cls.
Lightning† [24]	$\mathcal{O}(n)$	$\mathcal{O}(n)$	Unlimited	Yes	$\mathcal{O}(2^k)$	Yes	Yes
Generalized† [5]	$\mathcal{O}(n)$	$\mathcal{O}(n)$	Unlimited	Yes	$\mathcal{O}(1)$	No	Yes
Outpost [18]	$\mathcal{O}(n)$	$\mathcal{O}(\log(n))$	Limited	Yes	$\mathcal{O}(2^k)$	Yes	Yes
FPPW [20]	$\mathcal{O}(n)$	$\mathcal{O}(n)$	Unlimited	Yes	$\mathcal{O}(1)$	No	Yes
Cerberus [8]	$\mathcal{O}(n)$	$\mathcal{O}(n)$	Unlimited	Yes	$\mathcal{O}(2^k)$	Yes	Yes
Sleepy† [7]	$\mathcal{O}(n)$	N/A	Limited	Yes	$\mathcal{O}(2^k)$	Yes	Yes
eltoo [12]	$\mathcal{O}(1)$	$\mathcal{O}(1)$	Unlimited§	No	$\mathcal{O}(1)$	Yes	No
Daric (this work)	$\mathcal{O}(1)$	$\mathcal{O}(1)$	Unlimited§	Yes	$\mathcal{O}(1)$	Yes	Yes

†: If parties pre-generate n keys in a merkle tree, their storage requirements decrease to $\mathcal{O}(\log(n))$ but the channel lifetime becomes limited to n channel updates.
§: Given that the channel update rate is at most one update per second.

- We compare Daric and eltoo and show Daric is robust against an attack [2] to eltoo, that we also formalize in this paper. We further perform a cost benefit analysis to assess the attacker's revenue in practice. We also show (i) Daric provides a higher deterrent effect against profit-driven attackers than eltoo and (ii) unlike eltoo, Daric's deterrent effect is flexible.

- We compare Daric, eltoo, Lightning, Generalized, Sleepy, Cerberus, FPPW and Outpost channels with respect to the amount of data that is published on the blockchain in different channel closure scenarios (See Table 3). We show that Daric in the dishonest closure scenario outperforms Lightning with at least 1 HTLC output as well as all other schemes. In the non-collaborative closure scenario, Daric outperforms Lightning with at least 7 HTLC outputs as well as Generalized, eltoo and FPPW. Moreover, we compute the number of operations required for each channel update and show that (i) Unlike Lightning, Daric values are independent of the number of HTLC outputs m and (ii) Daric is comparable with other schemes (see Table 3).

1.2 Related Works

The first payment channel [26] is unidirectional and hence cannot continue working if the payer's balance is depleted. DMC [14] uses decrementing timelocks but suffers from limited channel lifetime. For Lightning channel [24], an existing state is replaced upon authorizing a new state and then revoking the previous one where each party has his own version of transactions. *Generalized channel* [5] uses *adaptor signatures* to distinguish the publisher of a revoked state from her counter-party. In this way, Generalized channel avoids state duplication.

Outpost [18], Cerberus [8], FPPW [20] and the very recent work Garrison [22] are other payment channels, which improve their watchtower properties. Sleepy channel [7] is a bi-directional payment channel without watchtowers where parties can go offline for prolonged periods. Towards a different direction, Teechain [19] requires channel parties to possess Trusted Execution Environment (TEE).

2 Background and Notations

2.1 Outputs and Transactions

Throughout this work, we define different attribute tuples. Let U be a tuple of multiple attributes including the attribute attr. To refer to this attribute, we use $U.\mathsf{attr}$. Our focus in this work is on Bitcoin or any other blockchains with *Unspent Transaction Output* (UTXO) model. In this model, units of value–which we call coins–are held in *outputs*. Each output contains a condition that needs to be fulfilled to spend the output. Satisfying a condition might require one or multiple parties' signatures. Such a condition contains public keys of all the involved parties and we say those parties own the output. A condition might also have several subconditions, one of which must be satisfied to spend the output.

A transaction changes ownership of coins, meaning it takes a list of existing outputs and transfers their coins to a list of new outputs. To distinct between these two lists, we refer to the list of existing outputs as *inputs*. A transaction TX is formally defined as the tuple $(\mathsf{txid}, \mathsf{Input}, \mathsf{nLT}, \mathsf{Output}, \mathsf{Witness})$. The identifier $\mathsf{TX}.\mathsf{txid} \in \{0,1\}^*$ is computed as $\mathsf{TX}.\mathsf{txid} := \mathcal{H}([\mathsf{TX}])$, where $[\mathsf{TX}]$ is called the *body* of the transaction defined as $[\mathsf{TX}] := (\mathsf{TX}.\mathsf{Input}, \mathsf{TX}.\mathsf{nLT}, \mathsf{TX}.\mathsf{Output})$ and $\mathcal{H}$

is a hash function, which is modeled as a random oracle. The attribute $\mathsf{TX.nLT}$ denotes the value of the parameter $nLockTime$, where $\mathtt{TX}$ is invalid unless its $nLockTime$ is in the past. The attribute $\mathsf{TX.Input}$ is a list of identifiers for all inputs of $\mathtt{TX}$. The attribute $\mathsf{TX.Output}$ is a list of new outputs. The attribute $\mathsf{TX.Witness}$ is a list where its ith element authorizes spending the output that is taken as the ith input of $\mathtt{TX}$. We also use $\overline{[\mathtt{TX}]}$ and $\overline{\mathtt{TX}}$ to denote ($\mathsf{TX.nLT}$, $\mathsf{TX.Output}$) and ($\mathsf{TX.nLT}, \mathsf{TX.Output}, \mathsf{TX.Witness}$), respectively.

Floating Transactions. Each signature in a Bitcoin transaction contains a flag, called SIGHASH, which specifies which part of the transaction has been signed. Typically, signatures are of type SIGHASH_ALL, meaning the signature authorizes all inputs (i.e. references to previous outputs) and outputs. The SIGHASH of type ANYPREVOUT indicates that the signature does not authorize the inputs. This allows the signer to refer to any arbitrary UTXO whose condition is met by the transaction witness data. Such a transaction is called a *floating* transaction.

Timelocks. The relative timelock of T rounds (a round in our paper is considered the same as the round in [5,7]) in an output condition is denoted by T^+ and means the output cannot be spent unless at least T rounds passed since the output was recorded on the blockchain. The absolute timelock of i in an output condition is shown by $i^{\geq}$ and means the output cannot be spent unless the $nLockTime$ parameter in the spending transaction is equal to or greater than i. Since a transaction may only be recorded on the blockchain if its $nLockTime$ is in the past, $i^{\geq}$ in an output condition ensures the output cannot be spent unless i is expired (i.e. i is in the past). Table 2 summarizes the notations.

Table 2. Summary of notations

Notation	Description
$\mathtt{TX}$	Transaction $\mathtt{TX} = (\mathsf{txid}, \mathsf{Input}, \mathsf{nLT}, \mathsf{Output}, \mathsf{Witness})$
$\overline{\mathtt{TX}}$	Tuple ($\mathsf{TX.nLT}, \mathsf{TX.Output}, \mathsf{TX.Witness}$)
$[\mathtt{TX}]$	Tuple ($\mathsf{TX.Input}, \mathsf{TX.nLT}, \mathsf{TX.Output}$)
$\overline{[\mathtt{TX}]}$	Tuple ($\mathsf{TX.nLT}, \mathsf{TX.Output}$)
T^+	The relative timelock of T rounds
$i^{\geq}$	The absolute timelock of i

Representation of Transaction Flows. We use charts to illustrate transaction flows. As Fig. 1 shows, doubled edge and single edge rectangles represent published and unpublished transactions, respectively. Since the output of $\mathtt{TX}$

with the value of $a + b$ has two subconditions, it is denoted by a diamond shape with two arrows. One of the subconditions can be fulfilled by both A and B and is relatively timelocked by T rounds and another subcondition can be fulfilled by C and contains an absolute timelock of i. Dotted arrow to $\mathtt{TX}''$ shows it is a floating transaction whose signature matches the public key pk_C. This transaction is denoted by $\overline{\mathtt{TX}''}$ to emphasize that since it is a floating transaction, its input is unspecified and can be any output with matching condition. The $nLockTime$ parameter for $\mathtt{TX}$ and $\mathtt{TX}'$ is 0, so it is not shown inside these transactions.

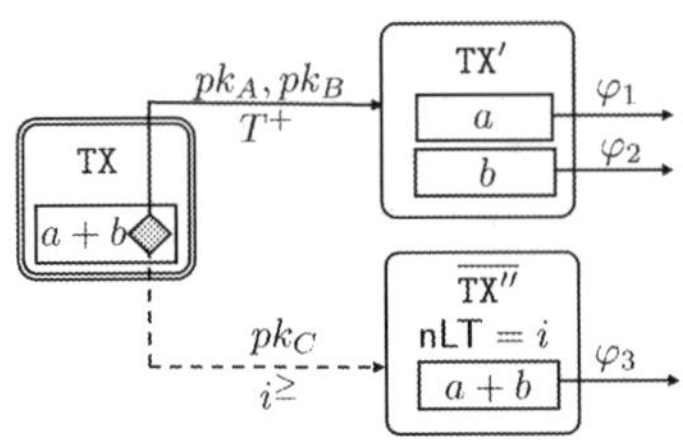

Fig. 1. A sample transaction flow.

2.2 Payment Channel

A payment channel between two parties Alice (or A) and Bob (or B) allows them to perform a number of transactions without publishing every single transaction on the blockchain. To create a channel with channel capacity of $a + b$ coins, A and B respectively deposit a and b coins into a joint address that is controlled by both parties. Parties can update their balance in the channel off-chain by agreeing on a new way to split the channel funds. Each party can close the channel at any time by enforcing the latest channel state on the blockchain where dispute between channel parties are resolved on the blockchain.

Lightning Channels [24]. To create a Lightning channel, A and B publish a *funding* transaction to respectively deposit a and b coins into a joint address. Each party also has its own copy of an off-chain transaction, called the *commit* transaction, that spends the joint address and splits the channel funds between A and B accordingly, i.e. each commit transaction has two outputs: one output holding a coins owned by A and the other output holding b coins owned by B. Each party can publish the commit transaction to close the channel, but parties typically create new commit transactions to update their shares in the channel.

As one may submit an intermediate state (which is already replaced by a later state) to the blockchain, the channel parties will need to punish such misbehaviours. Thus, after each channel update, parties revoke their previous state by exchanging two *revocation* transactions (one version for each party) that take the output of the old commit transactions and give the balance of the dishonest party to the honest party. However, the honest party (e.g. A) must publish the revocation transaction before the dishonest party (e.g. B) can claim his balance. So, to give precedence to the revocation transaction, B has to wait for a relative timelock of T rounds (in practice, one day) before he can claim his output. This gives some time to A to publish the revocation transaction.

eltoo [12]. An eltoo channel is created like a Lightning channel, but each state is represented by two transactions: (i) the *update* transaction and (ii) the *settlement* transaction, where both parties have the same version of these two transactions. Each update transaction is a floating transaction that transfers all the channel funds to a new joint address. The update transaction's output can be spent by its corresponding settlement transaction, which splits the channel funds among parties. If A submits an old update transaction, she has to wait for a relative timelock of T rounds before she can publish the corresponding settlement transaction. It gives some time to B to publish the latest update transaction (which is a floating transaction) and override the already published update transaction.

3 Solution Overview

To provide a high level overview of our solution, we start by reviewing the limitations of the Lightning channel and then gradually present our work.

Revocation per State. Parties' and their watchtower's storage in a Lightning channel increases over time as they should store some revocation-related data for each revoked state. Our main idea to reduce their storage is transforming the revocation transactions into floating transactions. Thereby, participants only need to store the latest revocation transaction with the largest version number and use it upon fraud. However, for a Lightning channel, (i) the monetary value of each revocation transaction typically differs from one state to another, and (ii) each commit transaction might have multiple HTLC outputs and hence the number of revocation transactions might also differ from one state to another. So, since revocation transactions of different states differ in value and number, it is infeasible to replace them all with the latest revocation transactions.

Therefore, our first modification is following the *punish-then-split* mechanism, introduced in [5]. According to this mechanism, the commit transaction sends the channel funds to a new joint output, which is controlled by both parties. Output of this commit transaction can be spent by its corresponding split transaction after T rounds where outputs of the split transaction split the channel funds between A and B. If A publishes a revoked commit transaction, B must spend its output within T rounds with the corresponding revocation transaction. This revocation transaction gives all the channel funds to B. Figure 2 depicts the transaction flows for this channel where each party stores a single revocation transaction with fixed monetary value (i.e. $a + b$ coins) per state.

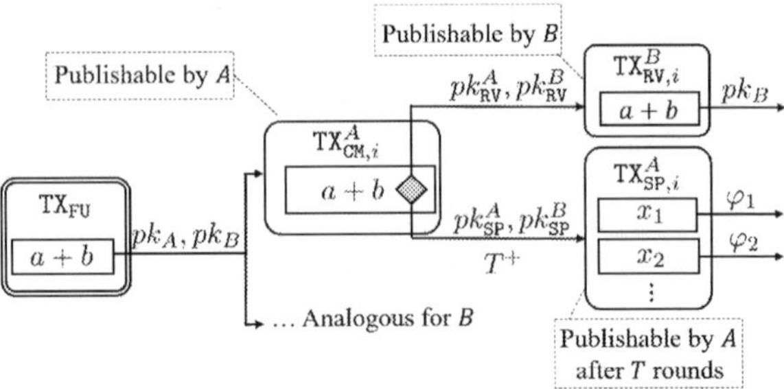

Fig. 2. Transaction flows for a Lightning channel with punish-then-split mechanism where TX_{FU} denotes the funding transaction and $\text{TX}_{\text{CM},i}^{A}$, $\text{TX}_{\text{SP},i}^{A}$ and $\text{TX}_{\text{RV},i}^{A}$ (or respectively $\text{TX}_{\text{CM},i}^{B}$, $\text{TX}_{\text{SP},i}^{B}$ and $\text{TX}_{\text{RV},i}^{B}$) denote the commit, split and revocation transactions held by A (or respectively held by B) for state i.

Revocation per Channel. In the scheme, depicted in Fig. 2, channel parties need to store a revocation transaction for each revoked state. Therefore, storage requirements of channel parties (or their watchtower) increase with each channel update. To solve this issue, we transform revocation transactions into floating transactions, i.e. the signatures in a revocation transaction, held by A, are of type `ANYPREVOUT` and meet the output condition of all commit transactions, held by B, and vice versa. It allows parties to only store the last revocation transaction.

Avoiding State Duplication. Since each state in the introduced scheme contains two split transactions (one for each party), the scheme suffers from state duplication. To avoid this, we transform split transactions into floating transactions. Then, each state contains one split transaction (held by both parties), which spends any of two commit transactions of that state.

State Ordering. Since split and revocation transactions are floating, it must be guaranteed that the latest commit transaction cannot be spent using any split or revocation transaction from previous states. Otherwise, the honest party, who has published the latest commit transaction, might lose some funds in the channel. To achieve this requirement, we repurpose [12] the *nLockTime* parameter of split and revocation transactions to store the *state number*: the number of times the channel has been updated to date. Furthermore, we add the state number to the output condition of each commit transaction as an absolute timelock. Then, since the absolute timelock in output condition of the last commit transaction would be larger than the *nLockTime* parameter in any split or revocation transaction from previous states, the mentioned requirement is met.

Putting Pieces Together. The transaction flow for state i of Daric is depicted in Fig. 3. Let channel be in state n. To close the channel, each party (e.g. A) can

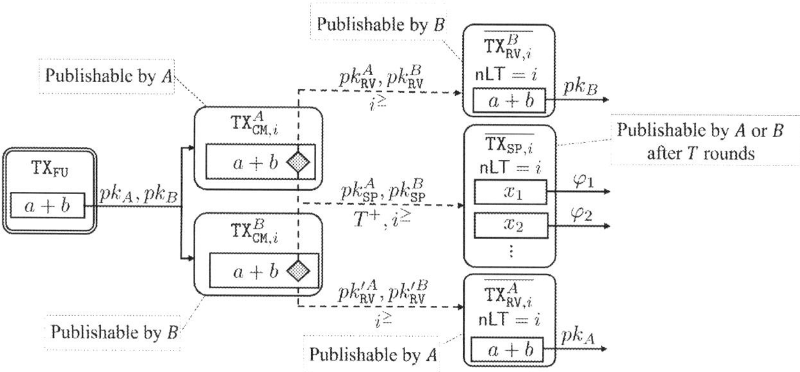

Fig. 3. Transaction flows for state i of a Daric channel.

publish the latest commit transaction (e.g. $\text{TX}^A_{\text{CM},n}$), wait for T rounds and finally publish the latest split transaction $\text{TX}_{\text{SP},n}$. There is no revocation transaction for the latest state. If party B publishes a revoked commit transaction (i.e. $\text{TX}^B_{\text{CM},i}$ with $i < n$), then party A instantly publishes the latest revocation transaction $\text{TX}^A_{\text{RV},n-1}$ to take all the channel funds.

4 Protocol Description

This section presents our protocol using the transaction flows depicted in Fig. 3. The lifetime of a Daric channel can be divided into 4 phases including "create", "update", "close, and "punish". We introduce these phases through Sects. 4.1 to 4.4. The technical report [21] provides the formal description of the protocol.

4.1 Create

To create the channel, A and B sign and publish the funding transaction TX_{FU} on the blockchain. By publishing this transaction, A and B fund the channel with a and b coins, respectively, but since output of the funding transaction can only be spent if both parties agree, one party might become unresponsive to raise a hostage situation. To avoid this, before signing the funding transaction, parties commit to the initial channel state, i.e. state 0, by exchanging signatures for the corresponding commit and split transactions. Let us explain different steps of the channel creation phase in more details.

Step 1: At the first step, A and B send their funding sources (i.e. $txid_A$ and $txid_B$) to each other. This enables them to create the body of the funding transaction $[\text{TX}_{\text{FU}}]$. **Step 2:** Having the transaction identifier of TX_{FU}, parties create the body of the commit transactions, i.e. $[\text{TX}^A_{\text{CM},0}]$ and $[\text{TX}^B_{\text{CM},0}]$. **Steps 3:** Parties exchange the required signatures (with SIGHASH of type ANYPREVOUT) to create the floating transaction $\overline{\text{TX}_{\text{SP},0}}$. This floating transaction could take output of $\texttt{TX}^{A}_{\texttt{CM},0}$ or $\texttt{TX}^{B}_{\texttt{CM},0}$ as its input. **Step 4:** Parties exchange the required signatures to create the commit transactions $\texttt{TX}^{A}_{\texttt{CM},0}$ and $\texttt{TX}^{B}_{\texttt{CM},0}$. **Step 5:** Parties exchange the required signatures to create the funding transactions $\texttt{TX}_{\texttt{FU}}$. **Step 6:** Parties publish the funding transaction on the blockchain.

The absolute timelock in output script of commit transactions and correspondingly the *nLockTime* parameter in the split transaction must be in the past. Otherwise, parties have to wait to publish such transactions. As explained in Sect. 3, the timelock is set to the state number and hence its value increases with each channel update. Absolute timelocks lower than 500,000,000 specify the block number after which the transaction can be included in a block. According to the value of the current block height, if we set the initial timelock to the first state number, i.e. 0, the channel can be updated around 700,000 times. However, absolute timelocks equal to or larger than 500,000,000 specify the UNIX timestamp after which the transaction will be valid. According to the value of the current timestamp, if we set the initial timelock (and correspondingly *nLockTime* parameter) to 500,000,000, the channel can be updated around 1 billion times [12]. Moreover, the current timestamp increases one unit per second, meaning if the average rate of the channel update is up to once per second, the channel can be updated an infinite number of times.

4.2 Update

Let the channel be in state $i \geq 0$ and channel parties decide to update it to state $i+1$. The update process is performed in two sub-phases. The first subphase is similar to steps 2 to 4 of channel creation phase where channel parties create two new commit transactions $\texttt{TX}^{A}_{\texttt{CM},i+1}$ and $\texttt{TX}^{B}_{\texttt{CM},i+1}$ as well as a new split transaction $\overline{\texttt{TX}_{\texttt{SP},i+1}}$ for the new state. In the second sub-phase, channel parties revoke the state i by signing two revocation transactions $\overline{\texttt{TX}^{A}_{\texttt{RV},i}}$ and $\overline{\texttt{TX}^{B}_{\texttt{RV},i}}$. The revocation transaction $\overline{\texttt{TX}^{A}_{\texttt{RV},i}}$ (or respectively $\overline{\texttt{TX}^{B}_{\texttt{RV},i}}$) contains no input yet and can spend output of any commit transaction $\overline{\texttt{TX}^{B}_{\texttt{CM},j}}$ (or respectively $\overline{\texttt{TX}^{A}_{\texttt{CM},j}}$) with $j \leq i$. With each channel update, the state number and hence the timelock value in the output condition of each commit transaction and *nLockTime* in split and revocation transactions increase by one unit. Let us explain different steps of the channel update phase in more details.

Step 1: Parties create the body of the commit transactions, i.e. $[\texttt{TX}^{A}_{\texttt{CM},i+1}]$ and $[\texttt{TX}^{B}_{\texttt{CM},i+1}]$. **Steps 2:** Parties exchange the required signatures (with `SIGHASH` of type `ANYPREVOUT`) to create the floating transaction $\overline{\texttt{TX}_{\texttt{SP},i+1}}$. This floating transaction takes output of $\texttt{TX}^{A}_{\texttt{CM},i+1}$ or $\texttt{TX}^{B}_{\texttt{CM},i+1}$ as its input. **Step 3:** Parties exchange the required signatures to create the commit transactions $\texttt{TX}^{A}_{\texttt{CM},i+1}$ and $\texttt{TX}^{B}_{\texttt{CM},i+1}$. **Step 4:** Parties exchange the required signatures (with `SIGHASH` of type `ANYPREVOUT`) to create the floating transactions $\overline{\texttt{TX}^{A}_{\texttt{RV},i}}$ and $\overline{\texttt{TX}^{B}_{\texttt{RV},i}}$.

In [21], we discuss the cases where a party misbehaves during the update.

4.3 Close

Assume while the channel between A and B is in state n, they decide to collaboratively close it. To do so, A and B exchange signatures for a new transaction, called modified split transaction $\mathtt{TX}_{\overline{\mathtt{SP}}}$, and publish it on the blockchain. This transaction takes the funding transaction's output as its input and splits the channel funds among channel parties. If one of the channel parties, e.g. party B, becomes unresponsive, its counter-party A can still non-collaboratively close the channel by publishing $\mathtt{TX}^{A}_{\mathtt{CM},n}$, adding the output of $\mathtt{TX}^{A}_{\mathtt{CM},n}$ as an input to $\overline{\mathtt{TX}_{\mathtt{SP},n}}$ to transform it into $\mathtt{TX}_{\mathtt{SP},n}$, and finally publishing $\mathtt{TX}_{\mathtt{SP},n}$ after T rounds.

4.4 Punish

Let the channel be in state n. If a dishonest channel party, let's say A, publishes an old commit transaction $\mathtt{TX}^{A}_{\mathtt{CM},i}$ with $i < n$ on the ledger, party B transforms $\overline{\mathtt{TX}^{B}_{\mathtt{RV},n-1}}$ into $\mathtt{TX}^{B}_{\mathtt{RV},n-1}$ and instantly publishes it on the blockchain.

5 Security Analysis

In this section, we firstly provide some payment channel notations as well as our security model, which follow previous works on *layer-2* solutions [5,15–17]. Then, we present desired properties of a payment channel and an ideal functionality $\mathcal{F}$ that attains those properties. Finally, we show Daric protocol is a realization of the ideal functionality $\mathcal{F}$ and hence achieves its desired properties.

5.1 Notation and Security Model

We use an extended version of the *universal composability* framework [10] to formally model the security of our construction. This extended version [11], called Global Universal Composability framework (GUC), supports a global setup. To simplify our model, we assume that the communication network is synchronous, meaning that the protocol is executed through multiple rounds and parties in the protocol are connected to each other via an authenticated communication channel which guarantees 1-round delivery. Transactions are recorded by a global ledger $\mathcal{L}(\Delta, \Sigma)$, where Σ is a signature scheme used by the blockchain and Δ is an upper bound on the blockchain delay: the number of rounds it takes a transaction to be accepted by the ledger. The technical report [21] provides more details on our security model.

A payment channel γ is defined as an attribute tuple $\gamma := (\mathsf{id}, \mathsf{users}, \mathsf{cash}, \mathsf{st}, \mathsf{sn}, \mathsf{flag}, \mathsf{st}')$, where $\gamma.\mathsf{id} \in \{0,1\}^*$ defines the channel identifier, $\gamma.\mathsf{users}$ represents the identities of the channel users, $\gamma.\mathsf{cash} \in \mathbb{R}^{\geq 0}$ is the total funds locked in the channel, $\gamma.\mathsf{st} := (\theta_1, \ldots, \theta_l)$ is a list of l outputs defining the channel state after the last complete channel update and $\gamma.\mathsf{sn}$ is the state number. The flag $\gamma.\mathsf{flag} \in \{1,2\}$ and the state $\gamma.\mathsf{st}'$ will be explained below.

The initial value of $\gamma.\mathsf{flag}$ and $\gamma.\mathsf{st}'$ are 1 and $\perp$, respectively. Assume that the channel has been updated $n \geq 0$ times and the channel state after the nth update is st and hence we have $\gamma.\mathsf{st} = st$. Now, assume that parties start the update process to update the state of the channel from state st to st'. From a particular point in the channel update process onward, at least one of the parties has sufficient data to enforce the new state st' on the blockchain when parties have not completely revoked the state $\gamma.\mathsf{st}$ yet. The flag $\gamma.\mathsf{flag}$ is set to 2 to identify such occasions and $\gamma.\mathsf{st}'$ is set to st' to maintain the new state. Thus, when $\gamma.\mathsf{flag} = 2$, the channel might be finalized with either $\gamma.\mathsf{st}$ or $\gamma.\mathsf{st}'$. At the end of the channel update process, once the state st was revoked by both parties, $\gamma.\mathsf{st}$ and $\gamma.\mathsf{st}'$ are set to st' and $\perp$, respectively, and $\gamma.\mathsf{flag}$ is set to 1.

5.2 Ideal Functionality

This section closely follows [5] to introduce desired security and efficiency properties of a payment channel as following:

- **Consensus on creation:** A channel γ is created only if both channel parties in the set $\gamma.\mathsf{users}$ agree to create it.
- **Consensus on update:** A channel γ is updated only if both channel parties in the set $\gamma.\mathsf{users}$ agree to update it. Also, parties reach agreement on update acceptance or rejection within a bounded number of rounds (the bound might depend on the ledger delay Δ).
- **Bounded closure with punish:** An honest user $P \in \gamma.\mathsf{users}$ has the assurance that within a bounded number of rounds (the bound might depend on the ledger delay Δ), she can finalize the channel state on the ledger either by enforcing a state that gives her $\gamma.\mathsf{cash}$ coins, or by enforcing $\gamma.\mathsf{st}$ if $\gamma.\mathsf{flag} = 1$ or by enforcing either $\gamma.\mathsf{st}$ $\gamma.\mathsf{st}'$ otherwise.
- **Optimistic update:** If both parties in $\gamma.\mathsf{users}$ are honest, the channel update completes with no ledger interaction.

Appendix A introduces an ideal functionality $\mathcal{F}$ that achieves these properties. Theorem 1 shows Daric protocol, denoted by π, is a realization of $\mathcal{F}$ and hence achieves its desired properties. It follows from 14 Lemmas. Due to space limits, we refer readers to the technical report [21] for the full security proof.

Theorem 1. *Let Σ be an* $\mathsf{EUF-CMA}$ *secure signature scheme. Then, for any ledger delay $\Delta \in \mathbb{N}$, the protocol π UC-realizes the ideal functionality $\mathcal{F}(T)$ with any $T > \Delta$.*

In the technical report [21], we formally define π and provide a simulator $\mathcal{S}$ where $\mathcal{S}$ has interaction with $\mathcal{F}$ and $\mathcal{L}$. The simulator simulates content and timing of all messages of the honest party to the adversary and also translates any message from the adversary into a message to the ideal functionality, such that an indistinguishable execution of the protocol in the ideal world is emulated. Thus, our protocol would be as secure as the ideal functionality $\mathcal{F}$. We also prove for any action that causes the ideal functionality to output Error with non-negligible probability, the simulator constructs a reduction against the existential unforgeability of the underlying signature scheme Σ with non-negligible success probability, which contradicts with our assumption regarding the security of Σ. This proves our protocol provides the desirable properties of $\mathcal{F}$.

6 Daric Versus Eltoo

In Sect. 6.1, we present an attack to eltoo whose main purpose is to postpone the channel closure. We show this attack is practically profitable when applied to eltoo but it cannot be applied to Daric. In Sect. 6.2, we analyze Daric and eltoo to compare their robustness against profit-driven attackers. We use the statistical data derived from the Lightning network to enable such an analysis.

6.1 HTLC Security

This section presents an attack against HTLC security in eltoo (previously informally discussed in [2]) and analyzes the attacker's revenue. Let the adversary represent two nodes on the PCN: node M_1 and node M_2. Assume that the adversary has established N channels from M_1 to victim nodes $V_1, \ldots, V_N$ and N channels from victim nodes to M_2. The channel between M_1 and V_i is denoted with γ_i. The adversary performs N simultaneous HTLC payments from M_1 to M_2 through $V_1, \ldots, V_N$. Let the payment value for all HTLCs be A coins and the timelock for all these payments for M_1's channels be T. Assume that M_2 accepts the payments and provides the required secrets for all HTLC payments and hence M_2 is paid $N \cdot A$ coins in total. Then, victims provide the secrets to the node M_1. However, M_1 does not update her channels with victims. Therefore, victims attempt to claim all HTLCs on-chain. To prevent victims from closing their channels in time, M_1 takes the following steps:

1. Submit a valid *Delay* transaction $\texttt{TX}_{\texttt{De}}$ with $N+1$ inputs and $N+1$ outputs where the ith input-output pair corresponds with an outdated state of the channel γ_i and the last input-output pair adds further funds to be used as the transaction fee, which is set to any value larger than A.
2. If $\texttt{TX}_{\texttt{De}}$ is published and the timelock T is still unexpired, go to step 1.
3. Once the timelock T is expired, submit the latest channel state for all channels and claim their HTLC outputs.

In the explained scenario, to replace the already submitted transaction $\texttt{TX}_{\texttt{De}}$ with the latest state of the channel γ_i, V_i has to set a transaction fee that is larger than the total absolute transaction fee of $\texttt{TX}_{\texttt{De}}$ [27]. But since the transaction fee for $\texttt{TX}_{\texttt{De}}$ is larger than A, V_i will be unwilling to pay such a transaction fee.

Once the HTLC timelock is expired and the latest channel state is added to the ledger, there will be a race between M_1 and each victim to claim the HTLC output. The adversary will have a better chance to win the race if she has a better network connection with a higher number of nodes.

Now we perform a cost benefit analysis to determine if the attack is profitable to the attacker. For a fixed value of A, with setting N to the largest possible value, the adversary 1) reduces the fee per channel for each delay transaction and 2) reduces the pace at which outdated states are added to the blockchain. A Bitcoin transaction can contain up to 100,000 VBytes (where each VByte equals four weight units) and each input-output pair contains 222 bytes of witness data and 84 bytes of non-witness data [21]. Therefore, $\mathtt{TX_{De}}$ can cover up to around $\frac{100,000}{0.25\times 222+84} \approx 715$ eltoo channels. The minimum possible fee rate is 1 Satoshi per VByte. Thus, if A is set to 100,000 Satoshi, the total fee for each delay transaction would be 100,000 Satoshi.

At the time of writing this paper (in April 2022), the average transaction fee is quite low and hence transactions with the minimum fee rate are added to the blockchain in 30 min. It means if HTLC timelocks are set to 3 days, 144 delay transactions are published before timelocks getting expired. In other words, the adversary pays $144A$ as transaction fee to earn up to $715A$. In more congested times, it might take several hours for a transaction with minimum fee rate to be added to the blockchain. Thus, the attack could be even more profitable to the attacker. This attack is inapplicable to Daric because once the attacker publishes an old commit transaction, the only valid transactions are the revocation transactions held by her counter-party.

6.2 Punishment Mechanism

Prior to providing a formal analysis, we provide intuitions as follows. The only cost for a dishonest party in eltoo is the fee for publishing the old state, which could be (i) less than 1 USD for Bitcoin and (ii) independent of the channel capacity. However, given that the balance of each party in a Daric channel cannot be less than 1% of the channel capacity (which is currently deployed in the Lightning network), the minimum amount that a dishonest party might lose would have the following properties: (i) It is proportional to the channel capacity, (ii) Its value (around 20 USD on average in the Lightning network in April 2022) is typically significantly larger than the transaction fee and (iii) It is easily raised by increasing the minimum possible balance of each channel party from 1% of the channel capacity to a higher proportion. Therefore, Daric's deterrent effect against profit-driven attackers is higher and more flexible than that of eltoo.

Now, we perform a more formal comparison between eltoo and Daric. We assume the channel party either stays online or employs a watchtower that is fair w.r.t the hiring party [20] (i.e. the watchtower guarantees its client's funds in the channel). For the former case, let p denote the probability that the honest channel party successfully reacts upon fraud, i.e. $1-p$ is the probability that the honest party, due to crash failures or DoS attacks, fails to react. We show that (i) to discourage attacks by profit-driven parties, p for eltoo must be more significant than that of Daric, and (ii) unlike Daric, increase in the channel capacity in eltoo channels raises the minimum value of p that is required to prevent fraud. However, achieving large values of p (e.g. 0.9999) could be difficult for ordinary users. This indicates eltoo needs a way to punish profit-driven attackers.

To monitor a channel, the watchtower's collateral equals the channel capacity [8,20]. Let C denote the total capacity of Bitcoin payment channel network and C_W denote the total capital that fair watchtowers have spent to watch their clients' channels. Then, the probability that a randomly selected payment channel is monitored by a fair watchtower is roughly computed as $\frac{C_W}{C}$.

Assume that a dishonest party $\mathcal{A}$ creates an eltoo channel with channel capacity of $C_\mathcal{A}$ coins, where the initial balance of $\mathcal{A}$ and her counter-party are $C_\mathcal{A}$ and 0, respectively. For now, we assume that parties know if their counter-parties are using a fair watchtower. We will relax this assumption later. If the channel is being monitored by a fair watchtower, $\mathcal{A}$ continues using the channel in an honest way. Otherwise, she sends all her balance to her counter-party in exchange for some products or services and then submits the initial channel state to the blockchain. In such a case, with probability of $1-p$ and p, $\mathcal{A}$'s revenue and her loss would be $C_\mathcal{A} - f$ and f, respectively, where f denotes the transaction fee. Thus, $\mathcal{A}$ is discouraged to attack iff:

$$(C_\mathcal{A} - f)(1-p) - f \cdot p < 0 \Leftrightarrow p > 1 - \frac{f}{C_\mathcal{A}}.$$

For a Daric channel, $\mathcal{A}$ is discouraged to attack iff:

$$0.99 \cdot C_\mathcal{A} \cdot (1-p) - 0.01 \cdot C_\mathcal{A} \cdot p < 0 \Leftrightarrow p > 0.99.$$

The threshold value for eltoo is typically more significant than that of Daric. At the time of writing this paper, the average values of f for a transaction and $C_\mathcal{A}$ for a Lightning channel are around 0.000055 BTC and 0.04 BTC, respectively, leading to $1 - \frac{f}{C_\mathcal{A}} \approx 0.999$. But the adversary can practically set f to the lowest possible value (i.e. 1 Satoshi per VByte) leading to $f \approx 0.0000021$ and $1 - \frac{f}{C_\mathcal{A}} \approx 0.9999$ for eltoo [21]. Therefore, (i) to discourage attacks, the honest party would require to meet a higher p in eltoo than in Daric, (ii) the threshold for eltoo depends on the channel capacity, and (iii) the threshold for Daric can simply decrease from 0.99 to lower values.

In the above analysis, we assumed that $\mathcal{A}$ knows whether her counter-party is hiring any fair watchtower. Considering the opposite case, the probability that the channel is not being monitored by any fair watchtower and the honest party fails to react upon fraud would be $p_0 := (1 - \frac{C_W}{C})(1-p)$. Thus, with probability of p_0 and $1 - p_0$, $\mathcal{A}$'s revenue and her loss in an eltoo channel would be $C_\mathcal{A} - f$ and f, respectively. Thus, $\mathcal{A}$ is discouraged to attack iff:

$$(C_\mathcal{A} - f) \cdot p_0 - f \cdot (1 - p_0) < 0 \Leftrightarrow p > 1 - \frac{\frac{f}{C_\mathcal{A}}}{1 - \frac{C_W}{C}}.$$

Similarly, for a Daric channel we have:

$$0.99 \cdot C_\mathcal{A} \cdot p_0 - 0.01 \cdot C_\mathcal{A} \cdot (1 - p_0) < 0 \Leftrightarrow p > 1 - \frac{0.01}{1 - \frac{C_W}{C}}.$$

As explained earlier, the threshold value for eltoo depends on $C_\mathcal{A}$ and is typically more significant than that of Daric.

7 Performance Analysis

Table 3 shows the total number of weight units of transactions, published on the blockchain for different payment channels in different channel closure scenarios. Since the weight units of a transaction directly impacts its fee, we use this parameter to compare different schemes. Payment channels perform similarly in the collaborative channel closure, so we do not consider this scenario in our analysis. Since the funding transaction is the same in all schemes, we do not involve it in our comparison results either. To do a consistent comparison, we assume that each transaction output is either P2WSH[1] or P2WPKH[2] , each public key and signature are respectively 33 bytes and 73 bytes, shared outputs are implemented using the `OP_CHECKMULTSIG` opcode (rather than using multi-party signing), and each state contains m HTLC outputs with $0 \leq m \leq 966$ [4] where each party is the payer for $\frac{m}{2}$ HTLC outputs and the payee for the rest.

Once a dishonest party in a Lightning channel publishes a revoked commit transaction, $m + 1$ revoked outputs are created. For simplicity, we assume that the victim claims all the revoked outputs through one transaction. Cerberus [8], Sleepy [7] and Outpost [18] have not explained ways HTLC is added to these schemes and discussing it is out of the scope of this paper, so Table 3 contains their figures with $m = 0$.

As Table 3 shows, in the dishonest closure scenario, (1) the weight units for Lightning and eltoo increase linearly with the number of HTLC outputs m compared to Daric, Generalized and FPPW and (2) Daric (with weight unit equal to 1239) is more cost effective than other schemes with $m \geq 1$. In the non-collaborative closure scenario with $m \neq 0$, Daric outperforms Generalized, eltoo and FPPW channels with any value of m and Lightning channel with $m > 6$.

Table 3 also compares the number of operations performed by each party for a channel update. To count the operations, we additionally assume that i) channel parties delegate the monitoring task to a watchtower and ii) they do not compute a signature unless it is supposed to be sent to their counter-party or their watchtower. The technical report [21] provides complete details regarding the way figures of Table 3 have been computed.

A Ideal Functionality

This section defines an ideal functionality $\mathcal{F}(T)$ with $T > \Delta$ that achieves the desired properties stated in Sect. 5.2. To simplify the notations, we abbreviate $\mathcal{F} := \mathcal{F}(T)$. The ideal functionality $\mathcal{F}$ stores a set Γ of all the created channels and their corresponding funding transactions. The set Γ can also be treated as a function s.t. $\Gamma(id) = (\gamma, \mathtt{TX})$ with $\gamma.\mathsf{id} = id$ if γ exists and $\Gamma(id) = \perp$ otherwise. Before presenting the ideal functionality $\mathcal{F}$ in details, we briefly introduce its different phases and explain the way $\mathcal{F}$ achieves the desired properties.

[1] Pay-to-Witness-Script-Hash: Used to lock bitcoin to a SegWit script hash.

[2] Pay-to-Witness-Public-Key-Hash: Used to lock bitcoin to a SegWit public key hash.

Table 3. On-chain cost of different closure scenarios and number of operations performed by each party for a channel update for different payment channels with m HTLC outputs ($0 \leq m \leq 966$). Cerberus [8], Sleepy [7] and Outpost [18] have not explained ways that HTLC outputs can be added to their schemes, so their figures in this table are for $m = 0$ only.

	Dishonest closure		Non-coll. closure		Num. of operations		
Scheme	#Tx	weight units	#Tx	weight units	Sign	Verify	Exp.
Lightning [24]	≥ 2	$\geq$1209+582.5 m	$1+m$	724+793 m	2+2 m	$1+\frac{m}{2}$	2
Generalized [5]	2	1342	$2+m$	1432+696 m	3	2	1
FPPW [20]	2	2045	$2+m$	1562+696 m	6	10	1
Cerberus [8]	2	1798	1	772	3	6	0
Outpost [18]	3	2632	3	3018	4	4	0
Sleepy [7]	3	2172	3	2558	5	5	0
eltoo [12]	3	2268+696 m	$2+m$	1588+696 m	2	2	1
Daric (this work)	2	1239	$2+m$	1363+696 m	4	3	0

a) Create: In this phase, $\mathcal{F}$ receives messages $(\texttt{INTRO}, \gamma, tid_P)$ and $(\texttt{CREATE}, \gamma.\mathsf{id})$ from both parties in rounds τ_0 and $\tau_0 + 1$, respectively, where tid_P specifies the funding source of the user P. Then, if the corresponding funding transaction appears on the ledger $\mathcal{L}$ within $2+\Delta$ rounds, $\mathcal{F}$ sends the message $(\texttt{CREATED}, \gamma.\mathsf{id})$ to both parties and stores γ and the funding transaction in $\Gamma(\gamma.\mathsf{id})$. If the CREATE message is not received from both parties but the funding transaction appears on $\mathcal{L}$ within $2 + \Delta$ rounds, $\mathcal{F}$ outputs Error. Since the message CREATED might be sent to the parties only if they both have sent the message CREATE to $\mathcal{F}$, the ideal functionality achieves "consensus on creation".

b) Update: One of the parties, denoted by P, initiates this phase by sending the message $(\texttt{UPDATE}, id, \boldsymbol{\theta}, t_{stp})$ to $\mathcal{F}$, where id is the channel identifier, $\boldsymbol{\theta}$ is the new channel state and t_{stp} is the number of rounds needed to prepare prerequisites of the channel update (e.g. preparing the needed HTLCs). Due to disagreeing with the new state or failure in preparing its prerequisites, party Q can stop it by not sending the message $(\texttt{UPDATE} - \texttt{OK}, id)$ in step 2. Abort by P or Q in next steps causes the procedure $\texttt{ForceClose}(id)$ to be executed. The property "optimistic update" is satisfied because if both parties act honestly, the channel can be updated without any blockchain interaction. Furthermore, if P or Q disagree to update the channel, they can stop sending the UPDATE or UPDATE − OK messages, respectively. This stops the channel update process without changing the latest channel state. Also, in cases where either P or Q stop cooperating, the procedure $\texttt{ForceClose}(id)$ is executed. This procedure takes at most Δ rounds to complete. This also guarantees "consensus on update".

c) Close: If $\mathcal{F}$ receives the message $(\texttt{CLOSE}, id)$ from both parties, a transaction TX is expected to appear on $\mathcal{L}$ within $\Delta + 1$ rounds. This transaction spends the output of the funding transaction and its outputs equal the latest channel state $\gamma.\mathsf{st}$. If the CLOSE message is received only from one of the parties,

$\mathcal{F}$ executes the procedure ForceClose(id). In both cases, output of the funding transaction must be spent within $\Delta + 1$ rounds. Otherwise, $\mathcal{F}$ outputs Error.

d) Punish: If a transaction TX spends the funding transaction's output of a channel γ, one of the following events is expected to occur: 1) another transaction appears on $\mathcal{L}$ within Δ rounds where this transaction spends output of TX and sends γ.cash coins to the honest party P; or 2) another transaction whose outputs correspond to the channel state γ.st or γ.st$'$ appears on $\mathcal{L}$ within $T + \Delta$ rounds. Otherwise, $\mathcal{F}$ outputs Error. According to its definition, "bounded closure with punish" is achieved, if $\mathcal{F}$ returns no Error in the close and punish phases.

We describe the ideal functionality below. Normally, once $\mathcal{F}$ receives a message, it performs several validations on the message. But to simplify the description, we assume that messages are well-formed. Data exchange between $\mathcal{F}$ and other parties is represented by directed arrows. If $\mathcal{F}$ sends the message m to party P in round τ_0, we denote it with $m \xhookrightarrow{\tau_0} P$. Similarly, if $\mathcal{F}$ is supposed to receive the message m from party P in round τ_0, we denote it with $m \xhookleftarrow{\tau_0} P$.

Ideal Functionality $\mathcal{F}(T)$

Create

upon $(\texttt{INTRO}, \gamma, tid_P) \xhookleftarrow{\tau_0} P$:

- If $(\texttt{INTRO}, \gamma, tid_Q) \xhookleftarrow{\tau_0} Q$, then continue. Else stop.
- If $(\texttt{CREATE}, id) \xhookleftarrow{\tau_0+1} \gamma.users$:
  - Wait if in round $\tau_1 \leq \tau_0 + 3 + \Delta$ a transaction $\texttt{TX}_{\texttt{FU}}$ with $\texttt{TX}_{\texttt{FU}}$.Input $=$ (tid_P, tid_Q) and $\texttt{TX}_{\texttt{FU}}$.Output $= \{(\gamma.\mathsf{cash}, \varphi)\}$ appears on the ledger $\mathcal{L}$. If yes, set $\Gamma(\gamma.\mathsf{id}) := (\gamma, \texttt{TX}_{\texttt{FU}})$ and $(\texttt{CREATED}, \gamma.\mathsf{id}) \xhookrightarrow{\tau_1} \gamma.users$. Else stop.

  Otherwise:
  - Wait if in round $\tau_1 \leq \tau_0 + 3 + \Delta$ a transaction $\texttt{TX}_{\texttt{FU}}$ with $\texttt{TX}_{\texttt{FU}}$.Input $=$ (tid_P, tid_Q) and $\texttt{TX}_{\texttt{FU}}$.Output $= \{(\gamma.\mathsf{cash}, \varphi)\}$ appears on the ledger $\mathcal{L}$. If yes, Output Error $\xhookrightarrow{\tau_1} \gamma$.users. Else, stop.

Update

Upon $(\texttt{UPDATE}, id, \boldsymbol{\theta}, t_{stp}) \xhookleftarrow{\tau_0} P$, parse $(\gamma, \texttt{TX}) := \Gamma(id)$ and proceed as follows:

1. Send $(\texttt{UPDATE}-\texttt{REQ}, id, \boldsymbol{\theta}, t_{stp}) \xhookrightarrow{\tau_0+1} Q$.
2. If $(\texttt{UPDATE}-\texttt{OK}, id) \xhookleftarrow{\tau_1 \leq \tau_0+1+t_{stp}} Q$, then set $\gamma.\mathsf{flag} := 2$ and $\gamma.\mathsf{st}' := \boldsymbol{\theta}$ and send $(\texttt{SETUP}, id) \xhookrightarrow{\tau_1+1} P$. Else stop.
3. If $(\texttt{SETUP}-\texttt{OK}, id) \xhookleftarrow{\tau_1+1} P$, then $(\texttt{SETUP}', id) \xhookrightarrow{\tau_1+2} Q$. Else ForceClose($id$) and stop.
4. If $(\texttt{SETUP}'-\texttt{OK}, id) \xhookleftarrow{\tau_1+2} Q$, then $(\texttt{UPDATE}-\texttt{OK}, id) \xhookrightarrow{\tau_1+3} P$. Else execute ForceClose(id) and stop.
5. If $(\texttt{REVOKE}, id) \xhookleftarrow{\tau_1+3} P$, then $(\texttt{REVOKE}-\texttt{REQ}, id) \xhookrightarrow{\tau_1+4} Q$. Else execute ForceClose(id) and stop.

6. If $(\texttt{REVOKE}', id) \xleftrightarrow{\tau_1+4} Q$, set $\gamma.st := \boldsymbol{\theta}$, $\gamma.\mathsf{flag} := 1$, $\gamma.\mathsf{st}' :=\perp$, $\gamma.\mathsf{sn} := \gamma.\mathsf{sn} + 1$, $\Gamma(id) := (\gamma, \texttt{TX})$, $(\texttt{UPDATED}, id) \xhookrightarrow{\tau_1+5} \gamma.\mathsf{Users}$ and stop. Else execute $\texttt{ForceClose}(id)$ and stop.

Close

upon $(\texttt{CLOSE}, id) \xhookleftarrow{\tau_0} P$, distinguish:

Both agreed: If $(\texttt{CLOSE}, id) \xhookleftarrow{\tau_0} Q$, let $(\gamma, \texttt{TX}_{\texttt{FU}}) := \Gamma(id)$ and distinguish:

- If in round $\tau_1 \leq \tau_0 + 1 + \Delta$, $\texttt{TX}_{\overline{\texttt{SP}}}$, with $\texttt{TX}_{\overline{\texttt{SP}}}.\mathsf{Output} = \gamma.\mathsf{st}$ and $\texttt{TX}_{\overline{\texttt{SP}}}.\mathsf{Input} = \texttt{TX}_{\texttt{FU}}.\mathsf{txid}||1$ appears on $\mathcal{L}$, set $\Gamma(id) := (\perp, \texttt{TX}_{\texttt{FU}})$, $(\texttt{CLOSED}, id) \xhookrightarrow{\tau_1} \gamma.\mathsf{users}$ and stop.
- If in round $\tau_0+1+\Delta$, the $\texttt{TX}_{\texttt{FU}}$ is still unspent, output $\texttt{Error} \xhookrightarrow{\tau_0+1+\Delta} \gamma.\mathsf{users}$ and stop.

Q **disagreed:** Else, execute $\texttt{ForceClose}(id)$ in round $\tau_0 + 1$.

Punish (executed at the end of every round τ_0)

For each $(\gamma_i, \texttt{TX}_i) \in \Gamma$ check if there is a transaction $\texttt{TX}$ on the ledger $\mathcal{L}$ s.t. $\texttt{TX}.\mathsf{Input} = \texttt{TX}_i.\mathsf{txid}||1$ and $\gamma_i \neq \perp$. If yes, distinguish:

1. **Punish**: For the honest $P \in \gamma_i.\mathsf{users}$, in round $\tau_1 \leq \tau_0 + \Delta$, a transaction $\texttt{TX}_j$ with $\texttt{TX}_j.\mathsf{Input} = \texttt{TX}.\mathsf{txid}||1$ and $\texttt{TX}_j.\mathsf{Output} = (\gamma.\mathsf{cash}, pk_P)$ appears on $\mathcal{L}$. Then, $(\texttt{PUNISHED}, id) \xhookrightarrow{\tau_1} P$, set $\Gamma(id) := (\perp, \texttt{TX}_i)$ and stop.
2. **Close**: In round $\tau_1 \leq \tau_0 + T + \Delta$ a transaction $\texttt{TX}_j$ appears on $\mathcal{L}$ where one of the following two sets of conditions hold: 1) $\gamma.\mathsf{flag} = 1$, $\texttt{TX}_j.\mathsf{Input} = \texttt{TX}.\mathsf{txid}||1$ and $\texttt{TX}_j.\mathsf{Output} = \gamma.\mathsf{st}$ or 2) $\gamma.\mathsf{flag} = 2$, $\texttt{TX}_j.\mathsf{Input} = \texttt{TX}.\mathsf{txid}||1$ and either $\texttt{TX}_j.\mathsf{Output} = \gamma.\mathsf{st}$ or $\texttt{TX}_j.\mathsf{Output} = \gamma.\mathsf{st}'$. Then, set $\Gamma(id) := (\perp, \texttt{TX}_i)$ and $(\texttt{CLOSED}, id) \xhookrightarrow{\tau_1} \gamma.\mathsf{users}$.
3. **Error**: Otherwise, $\texttt{Error} \xhookrightarrow{\tau_0+T+\Delta} \gamma.\mathsf{users}$.

Subprocedure $\texttt{ForceClose}(id)$

Let τ_0 be the current round and $(\gamma, \texttt{TX}_{\texttt{FU}}) := \Gamma(id)$. If within Δ rounds, $\texttt{TX}_{\texttt{FU}}.\mathsf{Output}$ is still an unspent output on $\mathcal{L}$, then output $\texttt{Error} \xhookrightarrow{\tau_0+\Delta} \gamma.\mathsf{users}$.

References

1. Lightning channels - top capacity. https://1ml.com/channel?order=capacity
2. eltoo: A simplified update mechanism for lightning and off-chain contracts (2018). https://lists.linuxfoundation.org/pipermail/lightning-dev/2018-June/001313.html
3. Using per-update credential to enable eltoo-penalty (2019). https://lists.linuxfoundation.org/pipermail/lightning-dev/2019-July/002068.html

4. Bolt 5: Recommendations for on-chain transaction handling (2021). https://github.com/lightningnetwork/lightning-rfc/blob/master/05-onchain.md
5. Aumayr, L., Ersoy, O., Erwig, A., Faust, S., Hostáková, K., Maffei, M., Moreno-Sanchez, P., Riahi, S.: Generalized channels from limited blockchain scripts and adaptor signatures. In: Tibouchi, M., Wang, H. (eds.) ASIACRYPT 2021. LNCS, vol. 13091, pp. 635–664. Springer, Cham (2021). https://doi.org/10.1007/978-3-030-92075-3_22
6. Aumayr, L., Maffei, M., Ersoy, O., Erwig, A., Faust, S., Riahi, S., Hostáková, K., Moreno-Sanchez, P.: Bitcoin-compatible virtual channels. In: 2021 IEEE Symposium on Security and Privacy (SP), pp. 901–918. IEEE (2021)
7. Aumayr, L., Thyagarajan, S.A., Malavolta, G., Moreno-Sanchez, P., Maffei, M.: Sleepy channels: Bitcoin-compatible bi-directional payment channels without watchtowers. Cryptology ePrint Archive (2021)
8. Avarikioti, G., Litos, O.S.T., Wattenhofer, R.: Cerberus channels: Incentivizing watchtowers for bitcoin. Financial Cryptography and Data Security (FC) (2020)
9. Bamert, T., Decker, C., Elsen, L., Wattenhofer, R., Welten, S.: Have a snack, pay with bitcoins. In: IEEE P2P 2013 Proceedings, pp. 1–5. IEEE (2013)
10. Canetti, R.: Universally composable security: a new paradigm for cryptographic protocols. In: Proceedings 42nd IEEE Symposium on Foundations of Computer Science, pp. 136–145. IEEE (2001)
11. Canetti, R., Dodis, Y., Pass, R., Walfish, S.: Universally composable security with global setup. In: Vadhan, S.P. (ed.) TCC 2007. LNCS, vol. 4392, pp. 61–85. Springer, Heidelberg (2007). https://doi.org/10.1007/978-3-540-70936-7_4
12. Decker, C., Russell, R., Osuntokun, O.: eltoo: A simple layer2 protocol for bitcoin. White paper. https://blockstream.com/eltoo.pdf (2018)
13. Decker, C., Towns, A.: Bip 118: Sighash_anyprevout for taproot scripts (2017). https://github.com/bitcoin/bips/blob/master/bip-0118.mediawiki
14. Decker, C., Wattenhofer, R.: A fast and scalable payment network with bitcoin duplex micropayment channels. In: Pelc, A., Schwarzmann, A.A. (eds.) SSS 2015. LNCS, vol. 9212, pp. 3–18. Springer, Cham (2015). https://doi.org/10.1007/978-3-319-21741-3_1
15. Dziembowski, S., Eckey, L., Faust, S., Hesse, J., Hostáková, K.: Multi-party virtual state channels. In: Ishai, Y., Rijmen, V. (eds.) EUROCRYPT 2019. LNCS, vol. 11476, pp. 625–656. Springer, Cham (2019). https://doi.org/10.1007/978-3-030-17653-2_21
16. Dziembowski, S., Eckey, L., Faust, S., Malinowski, D.: Perun: virtual payment hubs over cryptocurrencies. In: 2019 IEEE Symposium on Security and Privacy (SP), pp. 106–123. IEEE (2019)
17. Dziembowski, S., Faust, S., Hostáková, K.: General state channel networks. In: Proceedings of the 2018 ACM SIGSAC Conference on Computer and Communications Security, pp. 949–966 (2018)
18. Khabbazian, M., Nadahalli, T., Wattenhofer, R.: Outpost: a responsive lightweight watchtower. In: Proceedings of the 1st ACM Conference on Advances in Financial Technologies, pp. 31–40 (2019)
19. Lind, J., Naor, O., Eyal, I., Kelbert, F., Sirer, E.G., Pietzuch, P.: Teechain: a secure payment network with asynchronous blockchain access. In: Proceedings of the 27th ACM Symposium on Operating Systems Principles, pp. 63–79 (2019)
20. Mirzaei, A., Sakzad, A., Yu, J., Steinfeld, R.: FPPW: a fair and privacy preserving watchtower for bitcoin. In: Borisov, N., Diaz, C. (eds.) FC 2021. LNCS, vol. 12675, pp. 151–169. Springer, Heidelberg (2021). https://doi.org/10.1007/978-3-662-64331-0_8

21. Mirzaei, A., Sakzad, A., Yu, J., Steinfeld, R.: Daric: a storage efficient payment channel with punishment mechanism. Cryptology ePrint Archive, Report 2022/1295 (2022). https://eprint.iacr.org/2022/1295
22. Mirzaei, A., Sakzad, A., Yu, J., Steinfeld, R.: Garrison: a novel watchtower scheme for bitcoin. Cryptology ePrint Archive, Report 2022/1300 (2022). https://eprint.iacr.org/2022/1300
23. Pickhardt, R.: Does eltoo eliminate the need to watch the blockchain/implement watchtowers (2019). https://bitcoin.stackexchange.com/questions/84846/does-eltoo-eliminate-the-need-to-watch-the-blockchain-implement-watchtowers
24. Poon, J., Dryja, T.: The bitcoin lightning network: Scalable off-chain instant payments (2016)
25. Sompolinsky, Y., Zohar, A.: Accelerating bitcoin's transaction processing. Fast money grows on trees, not chains (2013)
26. Spilman, J.: [bitcoin-development] anti dos for tx replacement (2013). https://lists.linuxfoundation.org/pipermail/bitcoin-dev/2013-April/002433.html
27. Todd, P., Harding, D.A.: Bip 125: Opt-in full replace-by-fee signaling (2015). https://github.com/bitcoin/bips/blob/master/bip-0125.mediawiki

A Blockchain-Based Mutual Authentication Protocol for Smart Home

Biwen Chen[1,2,3], Bo Tang[1], Shangwei Guo[1], Jiyun Yang[1(✉)], and Tao Xiang[1]

[1] College of Computer Science, Chongqing University, Chongqing 400044, China
{macrochen,202014021073t,swguo,yangjy,txiang}@cqu.edu.cn
[2] Key Laboratory of Aerospace Information Security and Trusted Computing, Ministry of Education, Wuhan University, Wuhan, China
[3] State Key Laboratory of Cryptology, P.O. Box 5159, Beijing 100878, China

Abstract. Smart home is an emerging paradigm that facilitates the user to control remotely appliances and devices from anywhere through the internet connection using a networked device. The privacy-preserving authentication protocol is an important way for the security and privacy of remote access in the smart home. Recently, Lin *et al.* proposed a blockchain-based mutual authentication (HomeChain) protocol to achieve reliable auditing and anonymous authentication. Their work has drawn wide attention and continues to be widely cited. However, we propose two universal attacks against HomeChain and demonstrate that in Homechain, a malicious home gateway can break the anonymity of users and a malicious authorized user can break the traceability. Meanwhile, to address the above problems, we design a new secure and privacy-preserving blockchain-based authentication protocol by leveraging a secure short group signature scheme. Finally, we conduct extensive experiments and compare our performance with that of HomeChain. The experiment results show that our protocol achieves stronger security and privacy at the expense of a slightly higher computation and communication cost.

Keywords: Smart homes · Blockchain · Privacy-preserving authentication · Group signature

1 Introduction

With the development of communication and sensor technologies, the smart home as an emerging paradigm of the Internet of Things (IoT) has aroused

This work was supported by the National Natural Science Foundation of China under Grants U20A20176, 62072062, 62102050, the Natural Science Foundation of Chongqing, China, under Grant cstc2022ycjh-bgzxm0031, China Postdoctoral Science Foundation under Grant BX2021399, State Key Laboratory of Cryptology under Grant MMK-FKT202118, Sichuan Science and Technology Program under Grant 2021YFQ0056, CCF-AFSG Research Fund under Grant CCF-AFSG RF20220009.

W. Susilo et al. (Eds.): ISC 2022, LNCS 13640, pp. 250–265, 2022.
https://doi.org/10.1007/978-3-031-22390-7_16

wide attention from academia and industry [24]. Smart home is an intelligent residence that uses internet-connected devices to enable the remote control and automatic management of appliances and systems. Its application gives tremendous convenience to homeowner's work, study and lifestyle. For example, in a smart home environment, users can program their lights to go on and the garage door to open, regardless of the user's location.

While smart home technology had made great progress, its network security and information privacy risks had become obstacles to hinder its further application [26]. As an example, the sensors and the wireless communication channel in the smart home networks may be subject to exploitation [20]. Without the security and privacy guarantee, attackers can introduce serious financial and health problems through tampering, modifying, or intercepting transmitting information. Statistically, a smart home could suffer from over ten thousand hacking attempts in a single week[1]. Therefore, how to improve system security and privacy has become a fundamental requirement in the smart home environment.

Identity authentication [6,9,17,22,30] is a promising cryptographic primitive that can mitigate the above communication issues [1,18,23,29]. Vaidya *et al.* [1] presented a secure one-time password-based authentication scheme using the smart card in smart home environments. Luo *et al.* [17] proposed a secure gateway-based two-factor authentication framework to enhance the security of smart home. Guo *et al.* [6] designed an efficient remote authentication scheme for fog-enabled smart home, which has the feature of low latency. However, most of these schemes were designed with no consideration of the anonymity in the smart home, that is, a malicious attacker can easily obtain the real identities of devices and users, thereby threatening users' privacy. Clearly, it is urgently needed to design a secure framework in the smart home to realize its privacy protection for individuals.

Recently, some researchers [10,19,21,25] have proposed privacy-preserving authentication protocols that not only achieve the authenticity and validity of transmitting messages, but also support the anonymity of honest users and traceability of malicious users. Shuai *et al.* [19] proposed a two-factor-based anonymous authentication protocol for smart homes using elliptic curve cryptography. Poh *et al.* [21] proposed a privacy-preserving scheme that provides data confidentiality as well as entity and data authentication to prevent an outsider from learning or modifying the data communicated between the device service provider, gateway, and the user. Generally, based on the technical characteristics, existing privacy-preserving authentication protocols could be divided into several types, including multi-factor-based [19,33], PKI/ID-based [8,16], certificateless-based [12,31] and blockchain-based [4,5,15].

While existing privacy-preserving authentication protocols solve the basic security and privacy problems to a certain extent, there are still some challenges requiring urgent solutions. For example, the multi-factor-based protocols are generally simple to realize, but most of them need to equip with hardware

[1] https://www.which.co.uk/news/2021/07/how-the-smart-home-could-be-at-risk-from-hackers/.

equipment to ensure their security. However, some existing PKI/ID-based protocols have to suffer from the issues of certificate management or key escrow [15]. In addition, most protocols are based on single-server architecture, which may raise a significant limitation [13], i.e. single point of failure.

Blockchain [28] as an emerging technology has been considered to be one of the most promising technologies because of its properties such as decentralization, verifiability, and immutability. Currently, blockchain technology is widely introduced by scholars [3,27] to ensure the security of systems. For example, Zhang *et al.* [32] applied blockchain in electronic auctions to solve the problems of auction opacity and data security. Feng *et al.* [4] introduced a novel blockchain-assisted privacy-preserving authentication system, in which the blockchain is used to preserve users' privacy and provide automatic authentication. Lin *et al.* [14] presented a conditional privacy-preserving authentication protocol by leveraging a digital signature scheme and Ethereum technology. However, both Feng *et al.* [4] and Lin *et al.* [14] can not trace the real identity of malicious behaviors or verify the integrity of transmitted messages. Moreover, affected by the blockchain, some blockchain-based protocols [11,34] introduce frequent interactions or high communication/computation overhead. To overcome the above problems, Lin *et al.* [13] proposed a blockchain-based secure mutual authentication system that can be applied in smart homes and other applications. They proved that HomeChain satisfies security and privacy requirements in authenticating the users' access. Currently, their work has been widely cited in three years.

However, in this paper, our cryptanalysis shows that in Homechain, the user privacy may be compromised during the authenticating signatures phase. It is because a malicious or compromised home gateway can judge whether two signatures are from the same group user. Moreover, we observe that HomeChain cannot trace the users' real identity as they claimed, that is, a malicious authenticated user can generate a special group signature that can be successfully verified but cannot trace the real identity from the signature. Hence, our work will be able to help cryptographers and engineers design more secure and efficient authentication schemes for IoT by avoiding these two vulnerabilities.

1.1 Contributions

The main contributions of this paper are summarized as follows:

- We propose two universal attacks against Lin *et al.*'s HomeChain protocol to demonstrate that a malicious authenticated user or home gateway can break the anonymity and traceability of their protocol.
- We propose an enhanced protocol based on their original framework, based on an efficient short group signature scheme. The scheme is leveraged to ensure the security and privacy of the whole authentication process.
- We implement our protocol and test the time costs of main operations and analyze the performance of both HomeChain and enhanced protocol.

1.2 Organization

The organization of the rest sections is listed below. In Sect. 2, we briefly review Lin *et al.* 's HomeChain protocol. In Sect. 3, we focus on our attacks against HomeChain protocols, describing in detail their process. In Sects. 4 and 5, we propose an enhanced solution and compare it with HomeChain in terms of performance. Finally, we provide a conclusion to this paper.

2 Review of HomeChain

In this section, we give a brief overview of the HomeChain protocol introduced by Lin *et al.* [13]. HomeChain mainly contains four roles that are group manager, group member, home gateway, and consensus node. And, it includes five main phases, namely *System Setup*, *Request Control*, *State Delivery*, *Chain Transaction* and *Handle Dispute*.

System Setup. This step is executed by the group manager and mainly contains two processes: **parameter initialization** and **member registration**.

Parameter Initialization: In this step, the group manager generates the system parameter and the main secret key. It first chooses a security parameter λ, and then produces the group public parameters $GPP = (q, \mathbb{G}_1, \mathbb{G}_2, \mathbb{G}_T, e, P_1, P_2, H(\cdot))$, where $\mathbb{G}_1, \mathbb{G}_2$, and $\mathbb{G}_T$ are cyclic groups of order q (of length λ bits), $e : \mathbb{G}_1 \times \mathbb{G}_2 \rightarrow \mathbb{G}_T$ is a bilinear pairing, P_1, P_2 are two generators of $\mathbb{G}_1$ and $\mathbb{G}_2$, and $H : \{0,1\}^* \rightarrow \{0,1\}^{256}$ is a secure hash function, respectively. Then, it performs as follows.

- choose three random numbers $d, s, u \leftarrow \mathbb{Z}_q^*$ and compute $D = dP_1$, $S = sP_2$, $U = uP_1$.
- set $msk = (d, s)$ as the group main private key, $u \leftarrow \mathbb{Z}_q^*$ as the tracing key, and $gpk = (D, S, U)$ as the group public key.

In addition, it also needs to invoke the parameter generation algorithm in ECIES [7] to generate the parameters $EPP = \{E, \mathbb{G}, p, q, a, b, P, h\}$, where a, b are the elliptic curve parameter, P is a generator of $\mathbb{G}$, and h is a secure hash function. Finally, the public system parameter is (gpk, GPP, EPP), while the main private key is gsk.

Member Registration: Once receiving the registration request from the user with identity ID, the group manager needs to generate a group private key $gsk_i = (x_i, Z_i)$ for the group member by executing the following steps:

- choose $x_i \leftarrow \mathbb{Z}_q^*$ and compute $Z_i = (d - x_i)(sx_i)^{-1}P_1$.
- compute $tag_i = H(x_iZ_i)$ as user's tag. Meanwhile, the group manager maintains tag_i in a member list List $= (ID_i, GU_i, tag_i)$.

Then, each group member allocates its individual group private key to sign a transaction. Correspondingly, the home gateway as a verifier holds the group public key for the transaction verification. In addition, the home gateway needs to generate a public/private key pair ($Q = dP, d \in \mathbb{Z}_q^*$) by invoking the key generation algorithm KGen in ECIES, where the public key Q is used to encrypt the group member's public key.

Request Control. To publish a request with the home gateway, a group member first generates a fresh public/private key pair (pk, sk) by invoking the KGen algorithm in ECIES, which is a suggested way to avoid replay attacks. Then, it constructs the transaction from his requirements and invokes the Enc algorithm in ECIES to encrypt the request information $inf = (transaction\_version \| public\_key \| device\_information \| control\_order)$, and obtains the corresponding ciphertext $ciphertext = Enc_{pk}(inf)$. Next, to obtain a valid transaction, it signs the ciphertext under the group public key gpk by using the group member's private key gsk_i:

- choose $k \leftarrow \mathbb{Z}_q^*$ and compute $C_1 = kP_1$, $C_2 = x_i Z_i + kU$, and $Q = e(U, S)^k$.
- compute the $digest = H(transaction\_version \| public\_key \| device\_information \| control\_order)$, $c = H(C_1, C_2, Q, digest)$, and $w = kc + x_i$.
- return $TX_{access} = (C_1, C_2, c, w)$ as the signature of request information.

Finally, the group member constructs the request information and a group signature into a transaction TX_{access}, and then uploads this access request into the smart contract via calling a function **uploadRequest**.

State Delivery. Once receiving the new requests from the group member, the home gateway can retrieve the request via the function **getRequest** and verify the availability of this request by executing the following steps:

$$Q^* = \frac{e(C_2, S)e(wP_1, P_2)}{e(cC_1 + D, P_2)} \tag{1}$$

and a digest $digest = H(msg)$ of messages msg. Then it checks that

$$c^* = H(C_1, C_2, Q^*, digest) \tag{2}$$

In addition, the home gateway needs to determine whether the transaction has appeared in the existing revocation list. If not, it decrypts the message via the decryption algorithm in ECIES using its private key, which aims to obtain the group member's information such as the public key. Then it responds to the request by connecting to the target home device. Note that the home gateway will encrypt the feedback from the target device using the group member's fresh public key pk and generate the corresponding MAC using its private key sk_{hg}, which can ensure the confidentiality and validity of returned information.

Chain Transaction. Consensus nodes are responsible for retrieving all valid transactions within the transaction collection period in the smart contract via the **getRequest** algorithm. The consensus nodes use the PBFT consensus mechanism to reach a consensus on the pending block, that is, there are no less than two-thirds of the total consensus nodes approving this block. Finally, this block will be chained to the blockchain.

Handle Dispute. Group manager can trace the transaction $Tx_{unusual}$ back to the actual group member when unusual/abnormal behaviors are detected. The group manager first retrieves the transaction associated with such behavior, and then invokes the **GTrace** algorithm for revealing the real identity of the requester, where the main calculation is as follows:

$$tag_i = H(x_i Z_i) = H(C_2 - uC_1) \tag{3}$$

After this, the group manager can obtain the real identity of the signer by searching the whole List $= (ID_i, GU_i, tag_i)$ via tag_i.

3 Cryptanalysis of HomeChain

According to the work [13], Lin *et al.* claimed that HomeChain satisfies the security and privacy requirements in verifying the group members and home gateway. In this section, we will analyze the security of the HomeChain protocol and point out two concrete attacks against HomeChain, namely linkable message attack, and untraceable signature attack. In the linkable message attack, a malicious home gateway can determine whether the two signatures are from the same group user. In the untraceable signature attack, a user can generate a special group signature that can be verified successfully, but the group manager cannot trace the real identity of the signer through the signature. The detailed attacks are presented as follows.

3.1 Linkable Message Attack

If a malicious home gateway can determine whether group signatures are from the same user, it can link multiple messages from the same user, which may cause privacy leakage through the association of multiple messages. For convenience, we suppose that A is a malicious or compromised home gateway and B is a usual group member. Let TX_1, TX_2 be two access request transactions and $\sigma_1 = (C_1, C_2, c, w), \sigma_2 = (C_1^*, C_2^*, c^*, w^*)$ be the corresponding signature. Then, A can implement the linkable message attack through the following steps:

1. Suppose B initiates a request to access the temperature sensor at time TS_1. B first generates a signature σ_1 on the request information, and then constructs the request information and signature σ_1 into a transaction TX_1. The information is uploaded to the smart contract via **uploadRequest** algorithm.

2. A monitors the smart contract for retrieving the new access request and can obtain $B's$ access request transaction TX_1 and the corresponding signature σ_1. Since A is curious about $B's$ behavior, it will record the signature σ_1.
3. After obtaining the TX_1 from B, A performs the Eq. (4) for each subsequent signature retrieved.

$$wP_1 - cC_1 \stackrel{?}{=} w^*P_1 - c^*C_1^* \tag{4}$$

By Eq. 4, A can determine whether two messages are from the same group user. If yes, which means (σ_1, σ_2) are from the same group user. Otherwise, this means that two signatures are from different users.
4. B initiates a request to turn on the conditioner at time TS_2. Similarly, B generates a signature σ_2 on the request information and constructs the request information and signature σ_2 into a transaction TX_2 followed by uploading it to the smart contract via the **uploadRequest** algorithm.
5. After A retrieves the TX_2, it can know that TX_2 is from B via Eq. (4). We present the proof of Eq. (4) below:

$$\begin{aligned} Left &= wP_1 - cC_1 \\ &= (kc + x_i)P_1 - cC_1 \\ &= kcP_1 + x_iP_1 - ckP_1 \\ &= x_iP_1 \end{aligned} \tag{5}$$

$$\begin{aligned} Right &= w^*P_1 - c^*C_1^* \\ &= (k^*c^* + x_i^*)P_1 - c^*C_1^* \\ &= k^*c^*P_1 + x_i^*P_1 - c^*k^*P_1 \\ &= x_i^*P_1 \end{aligned} \tag{6}$$

According to Eq. (5) and Eq. (6), we know that the Eq. (4) holds if x_i and x_i^* are equal. Because Each x_i corresponds to a specific user, and then which indicates that TX_1, TX_2 are from the same group user.

By launching the linkable message attack, A can know that B accesses the temperature sensor at TS_1 and turns on the conditioner at TS_2. Even worse, A can make a prediction that B is going home if possible. Moreover, since all requests are structured as transactions and stored on the blockchain, which makes it easier for A to obtain the user's request. If A records $B's$ behavior for several days in a row, in this case, A can easily predict the $B's$ daily activities.

3.2 Untraceable Signature Attack

Besides, Lin *et al.* claimed that the HomeChain satisfies traceability, that is, the group manager can reveal the real identity of the user from the signature. However, we observe that their protocol may be not available at the identity tracing phase, because an authorized group user can easily generate a special signature that can be successfully verified but can not be traced. In this subsection, we give a detailed description to further illustrate the attack.

Assuming that a user B wants to frequently change the device's state or maliciously publish revocation transactions without being tracked by the group manager. B holds the secret key (x_i, Z_i), and it performs untraceable signature attack in the following steps:

1. B generates a fresh public/private key pair (pk, sk), and obtains the *ciphertext* by encrypting the $request\_information = (transaction\_version \,\|public\_key \,\|\, device\_information \,\|control\_order)$.
2. It constructs the transaction from his/her requirement by performing the following three steps. 1) it randomly chooses $k, t \leftarrow \mathbb{Z}_q^*$ and computes $C_1^* = ktP_1$, $C_2 = x_iZ_i + kU$, and $Q = e(U, S)^k$. 2) it computes a digest $digest = H(msg)$ of the message, a hash value $c = H(C_1^*, C_2, Q, digest)$, and $w = ktc + x_i$. 3) It outputs $\sigma^* = (C_1, C_2, c, w)$ and uploads the request into smart contract via the **uploadRequest** algorithm.
3. The home gateway monitors the smart contract to retrieve the new request, and then it executes the verification process as follows:

$$\begin{aligned} Q^* &= \frac{e(C_2, S)e(wP_1, P_2)}{e(cC_1^* + D, P_2)} \\ &= \frac{e(x_iZ_i + kU, S)e((ktc + x_i)P_1, P_2)}{e(cktP_1 + D, P_2)} \\ &= \frac{e((d - x_i)s^{-1}P_1, S)e(kU, S)e(ktcP_1, P_2)e(x_iP_1, P_2)}{e(cktP_1, P_2)e(D, P_2)} \\ &= \frac{e(dP_1, P_2)e(kU, S)e(kctP_1, P_2)}{e(cktP_1, P_2)e(dP_1, P_2)} \\ &= e(U, S)^k \end{aligned} \tag{7}$$

$$c^* = H(C_1^*, C_2, Q^*, digest) \tag{8}$$

According to Eq. (7) and Eq. (8), since $Q = Q^*$ and $c = c^*$, and thus the signature sent by the user can pass the verification. However, the signature can not be traced, with details as follows:

$$\begin{aligned} tag^* &= H(C_2 - uC_1^*) \\ &= H(x_iZ_i + kU - uktP_1) \\ &= H(x_iZ_i + (1 - t)kU) \end{aligned} \tag{9}$$

According to Eq. (9), we observe that $tag \neq tag^*$. As a result, the signature corresponding to B's misbehavior passes the verification, but the real identity of the B cannot be traced by the group manager. Therefore, an authorized user can perform malicious behavior and cannot be traced by launching this attack, however, which is a fatal drawback for the anonymous system.

4 The Enhanced Protocol

To solve the above vulnerabilities in the HomeChain protocol analyzed in Sect. 3, we design a new blockchain-based mutual authentication protocol based on an efficient and secure group signature scheme [2]. The new protocol follows the framework of Homechain and mainly includes five phases, namely **System Setup**, **User Initialization**, **Request Control**, **State Delivery**, **Chain Transaction**, and **Handle Dispute**. In addition, we also adopt the same smart contract functions as the Homechain, and see Reference [13] for details.

System Setup. This phase is primarily targeted towards the group manager and is used to initialize the whole system. The group manager obtains the group public key gpk and the group private key gsk by executing the following steps:

- select the system parameters $(G_1, G_2, G_T, p, g_1, g_2, e)$, where G_1, G_2, G_T are multiplicative cyclic groups of prime order p, g_1 is a generator of G_1, g_2 is a generator of G_2, and e is a computable map $e : G_1 \times G_2 \rightarrow G_T$. Then, it chooses a secure hash function H: $\{0,1\}^* \rightarrow \mathbb{Z}_p^*$.
- select $h \leftarrow G_1 \setminus \{1_{G_1}\}$ and $\xi_1, \xi_2 \leftarrow \mathbb{Z}_p^*$, and set $(u, v) \in G_1$ such that $u^{\xi_1} = v^{\xi_2} = h \in G_1$.
- select $\gamma \leftarrow \mathbb{Z}_p^*$ and set $w = g_2^{\gamma} \in G_2$.
- generate the public parameters of ECIES, like Homechain. In addition, let $MAC = MAC_{key}(msg)$ denote the MAC generation function, where msg is the message to be sent, key is the negotiated key, and MAC is the MAC for authenticating message.

where the group public key is $gpk = (g_1, g_2, h, u, v, w)$ and the group private key is $gsk = (\xi_1, \xi_2, \gamma)$. Finally, the group manager publishes the group public key to the participants.

User Initialization. This phase is used to initialize the new group member and generate the public/private key pair of the home gateway, which mainly includes two processes.

- *Group Member Join.* Any user who wants to join the group needs to be authenticated by the group manager. For each user i, the group manager proceeds as follows:
  - select a random number $x_i \leftarrow \mathbb{Z}_p^*$ and compute the value $A_i = g_1^{1/(\gamma + x_i)}$, where γ is the main group private key.
  - set the private key $gsk[i] = (A_i, x_i)$ of the user i.
- *Home Gateway Setup.* In our system, each home gateway needs to keep the group public key $gpk = (g_1, g_2, h, u, v, w)$ for transaction verification. In addition, the home gateway needs to generate his/her public/private key pair (pk_{hg}, sk_{hg}) by invoking the key generation algorithm KGen in ECIES.

Request Control. If a group member i tries to publish a request, it needs to execute the following steps:

- generate a new public/private key pair $(pk_i = y_i P \in \mathbb{G}, sk_i = y_i \in \mathbb{Z}_q^*)$ by invoking the KeyGen algorithm in ECIES.

- construct a requirement information $info$, where the public key must be included. For example, the group member tries to switch off the lights in the room, then the information is $info = (01||pk||l01||to)$, where 01 is current version, $l01$ is the light identity, to is the control order of "switch off".
- encrypt the requirement information using the public key pk_{hg} of the home gateway to generate the transaction information $ciphertext = Enc_{pk_{hg}}(01||pk||l01||to)$.
- sign the transaction information to generate the transaction TX_{access} using the group member's private key $gsk[i] = (A_i, x_i)$ and perform the following steps:
  - it first selects exponents $\alpha, \beta \leftarrow \mathbb{Z}_p^*$, and computes $T_1 = u^{\alpha}$, $T_2 = v^{\beta}$, $T_3 = A_i h^{\alpha+\beta}$, $\delta_1 = x_i\alpha$, $\delta_2 = x_i\beta$.
  - it randomly picks blinding values $(r_{\alpha}, r_{\beta}, r_{x_i}, r_{\delta_1}, r_{\delta_2}) \leftarrow \mathbb{Z}_p^*$, and computes $R_1 = u^{r_{\alpha}}, R_2 = v^{r_{\beta}}, R_3 = e(T_3, g_2)^{r_{x_i}} \cdot e(h, w)^{-r_{\alpha}-r_{\beta}} \cdot e(h, g_2)^{-r_{\delta_1}-r_{\delta_2}}$, $R_4 = T_1^{r_{x_i}} \cdot u^{-r_{\delta_1}}$, and $R_5 = T_2^{r_{x_i}} \cdot v^{-r_{\delta_2}}$.
  - it computes $c = H(ciphertext, T_1, T_2, T_3, R_1, R_2, R_3, R_4, R_5)$, $s_{\alpha} = r_{\alpha} + c\alpha$, $s_{\beta} = r_{\beta} + c\beta$, $s_{x_i} = r_{x_i} + cx_i$, $s_{\delta_1} = r_{\delta_1} + c\delta_1$, $s_{\delta_2} = r_{\delta_2} + c\delta_2$.
  - it outputs a signature $\sigma = (T_1, T_2, T_3, c, s_{\alpha}, s_{\beta}, s_{x_i}, s_{\delta_1}, s_{\delta_2})$ and constructs an access transaction $TX_{access} = (ciphertext, \sigma)$.
- upload this request into the smart contract via the **uploadRequest** algorithm.

State Delivery. In our system, the home gateway will monitor the smart contract for processing new requests. If a request is monitored, the home gateway will retrieve the request via the algorithm **getRequest**. Then, it first verifies the validity of this transaction $TX_{access} = (ciphertext, T_1, T_2, T_3, c, s_{\alpha}, s_{\beta}, s_{x_i}, s_{\delta_1}, s_{\delta_2})$ by the following steps:

- it needs to rederive $\tilde{R}_1 = u^{s_{\alpha}}/T_1^c$, $\tilde{R}_2 = v^{s_{\beta}}/T_2^c$, $\tilde{R}_3 = e(T_3, g_2)^{s_{x_i}} \cdot e(h, w)^{-s_{\alpha}-s_{\beta}} \cdot e(h, g_2)^{-s_{\delta_1}-s_{\delta_2}} \cdot (e(T_3, w)/e(g_1, g_2))^c$, $\tilde{R}_4 = T_1^{s_{x_i}}/u^{s_{\delta_1}}$, and $\tilde{R}_5 = T_2^{s_{x_i}}/v^{s_{\delta_2}}$.
- it checks that:

$$c \stackrel{?}{=} H(ciphertext, T_1, T_2, T_3, \tilde{R}_1, \tilde{R}_2, \tilde{R}_3, \tilde{R}_4, \tilde{R}_5) \tag{10}$$

- the transaction is valid if this check succeeds.

If the transaction is valid and has not appeared in existing revocation transaction list which can be obtained by calling the **getRL** algorithm, then the home gateway can obtain the public key pk_i of the group member by decrypting the transaction information $version||public\_key||device\_information\ ||control\_order\}$, including the group member's public key, the target device information, and control order. Then, similar to Homechain, the home gateway responds to the request by connecting to the devices. To protect the privacy of the feedback, the home gateway encrypts it using the group member's public key pk_i. In addition, it also computes a MAC using the private key sk_{hg}. Thus, the final response is $Data = Enc_{pk_i}(feedback)$ and

$MAC = MAC_{key}(Data)$, where $feedback$ is the execution result or the device's status information and $key = pk_i^{sk_{hg}}$. As a result, $(Data, MAC)$ is uploaded into the smart contract via the **uploadResponse** algorithm. After the response has been received by the group member via the **getResult** algorithm, he/she uses his/her private key sk_i to recompute $MAC^{'} = \mathrm{MAC}_{key'}(\mathrm{Data})$, where $\mathrm{key}' = pk_{hg}^{sk_i}$. If $MAC' = MAC$ holds, then it implies that the response is not from an impersonator. Hence, it can obtain the response information about the request by decrypting the $Data$ via the Dec algorithm using sk_i.

Chain Transaction. This phase is the same as Homechain. Specifically, consensus nodes are responsible for retrieving transactions in the smart contract via the **getRequest** algorithm, and compete with each other for chaining the block to the blockchain. The process is described as follows.

- Collect all valid transactions $(Tx_1, Tx_2, ..., Tx_n)$ within the transaction collection period (a certain system period of time). Note that the invalid transactions to be illegitimate signatures will be discarded.
- The consensus nodes use the PBFT consensus mechanism for chaining the valid transactions. Namely, the present recorder first pends some valid transactions into a block. Then, all the consensus nodes reach a consensus on this pending block when there are no less than two-third of total consensus nodes approving this block. Hence, this block is finally chained into the blockchain.

Handle Dispute. This phase is used to handle the disputes of users by breaking the anonymity. In our system, the group manager can trace the real identity of the group member by using the transaction $Tx_{unusual}$. When a malicious behavior is detected, the group manager can then retrieve the transaction associated with such behavior and reveal the real identity

by performing the following steps:

- it takes as input a group public key $gpk = (g_1, g_2, u, v, w)$ and the corresponding group manager's private key $gmsk = (\xi_1, \xi_2)$, together with a message $ciphtext$ and a transaction $TX_{access} = (ciphertext, T_1, T_2, T_3, c, s_\alpha, s_\beta, s_{x_i}, s_{\delta_1}, s_{\delta_2})$.
- it verifies that TX_{access} is a valid signature on $ciphtext$.
- it uses the three elements (T_1, T_2, T_3) and recovers the user's identity A_i as $A_i = T_3/(T_1^{\xi_1} \cdot T_2^{\xi_2})$.
- it looks up the user index corresponding to the identity A_i to trace the real identity.

Here, the group manager can periodically and selectively revoke illegal group members' private key (A_i, x_i) into a Revocation List $revoList$ followed by updating the $revoList$ via the **addRL** algorithm.

4.1 Correctness and Security Analysis

Correctness. It is straightforward to see that correctness can be guaranteed as long as the authorized participants execute correctly. For authorized users, they have the signature secret key (A_i, x_i) distributed by the key authorization center, and thus always generate valid group signatures $\sigma = (T_1, T_2, T_3, c, s_\alpha, s_\beta, s_{x_i}, s_{\delta_1}, s_{\delta_2})$ to achieve anonymous authentication.

Security. To address the problems of Homechain, our enhanced protocol adopts a new security group signature scheme based on its original framework. Specifically, for the linkable message attack, the signing key (A_i, x_i) in our enhanced protocol is encrypted using the linear encryption scheme, which can break the link of different signatures from the same user. For example, the value A_i is encrypted to generate the *ciphertext* $T_3 = A_i h^{\alpha+\beta}$ under the *public key h*. For the untraceable signature attack, our enhanced protocol can resist this attack through the group signature scheme. In our protocol, the users can be anonymously authenticated only through generating a valid group signature σ that contains a real identity. According to the correctness and security of the based group signature scheme, the group manager can decrypt the ciphertext of identity using the main group secret key, i.e., $A_i = T_3/(T_1^{\xi_1} \cdot T_2^{\xi_2})$. Therefore, our protocol can ensure the traceability. Note that we omit other security analyses that have been proven in the work [13], because the processes are the same for both our protocol and Homechain.

Table 1. The execution time of different cryptographic operations in milliseconds.

Operation	The notations of operations	Execution time
T_{G1a}	A point addition in G_1	0.006 ms
T_{G1pm}	A point multiplication in G_1	1.320 ms
T_{G2pm}	A point multiplication in G_2	16.550 ms
T_{GTpm}	A point multiplication in G_T	0.004 ms
T_{G1ep}	A one exponentiation in G_1	1.317 ms
T_{G2ep}	An exponentiation in G_2	17.902 ms
T_{GTep}	An exponentiation in G_T	6.057 ms
T_{GTbp}	A bilinear pairing in G_T	17.886 ms
T_{G1m}	A multiplication in G_T	0.006 ms
T_{GTm}	A multiplication in G_T	0.029 ms
T_{mi}	A modular inversion in $\mathbb{Z}_q$	0.003 ms
T_h	A general hash function	0.001 ms

5 Experiment Analysis

In this section, we give a performance analysis between HomeChain and our improved HomeChain in terms of computation and communication overhead.

The computation overhead and communication overhead experiments are conducted with a desktop owning a 3.4 GHz Inter(R) Core(TM) i5-7500 CPU

Table 2. The comparison between HomeChain and improved HomeChain in computation cost and communication cost.

Phase	Computation cost		Communication cost	
	HomeChain	Improved HomeChain	HomeChain	Improved HomeChain
System Setup	$(2+2t)T_{G1pm} + tT_h + T_{G2pm} + tT_{mi}$	$tT_{G1ep} + T_{G2ep}$	$t\lvert G_1\rvert + t\lvert \mathbb{Z}_q\rvert$	$t\lvert G_1\rvert + t\lvert \mathbb{Z}_q\rvert$
Request Control	$6T_{G1pm} + T_{G1a} + 4T_h + T_{GTep} + T_{enc} + uploadRequest$	$3T_{G1pm} + 9T_{G1ep} + 3T_{G1m} + 3T_{GTbp} + 3T_{GTep} + 2T_{GTm} + 3T_h + uploadRequest$	$3\lvert G_1\rvert + 2\lvert hash\rvert + \lvert \mathbb{Z}_q\rvert + \lvert c_{AES}\rvert$	$4\lvert G_1\rvert + 2\lvert hash\rvert + 5\lvert \mathbb{Z}_q\rvert + \lvert c_{AES}\rvert$
State Delivery	$3T_{GTbp} + 8T_{G1pm} + T_{G1a} + 10T_h + getResult + getRL + uploadResponse + getRequest$	$8T_{G1ep} + 4T_{G1m} + 5T_{GTbp} + 4T_{GTep} + 4T_{Gtm} + 6T_{g1pm} + 9T_h + getResult + getRL + uploadResponse + getRequest$	$4\lvert G_1\rvert + 4\lvert hash\rvert + \lvert \mathbb{Z}_q\rvert + \lvert c_{AES}\rvert$	$5\lvert G_1\rvert + 4\lvert hash\rvert + 5\lvert \mathbb{Z}_q\rvert + 2\lvert c_{AES}\rvert$
Chain Transaction	$3T_{GTbp} + 2T_{G1pm} + T_{G1a} + 2T_h + getRL$	$8T_{G1ep} + 4T_{G1m} + 5T_{GTbp} + 4T_{GTep} + 4T_{GTm} + T_h + getRL$	$3\lvert G_1\rvert + 2\lvert hash\rvert + \lvert \mathbb{Z}_q\rvert + \lvert c_{AES}\rvert$	$4\lvert G_1\rvert + 2\lvert hash\rvert + 5\lvert \mathbb{Z}_q\rvert + \lvert c_{AES}\rvert$
Handle Dispute	$T_{G1pm} + T_{G1a} + T_h + addRL$	$2T_{G1ep} + 2T_{G1m} + addRL$	$3\lvert G_1\rvert + 2\lvert hash\rvert + \lvert \mathbb{Z}_q\rvert + \lvert c_{AES}\rvert$	$4\lvert G_1\rvert + 2\lvert hash\rvert + 5\lvert \mathbb{Z}_q\rvert + \lvert c_{AES}\rvert$

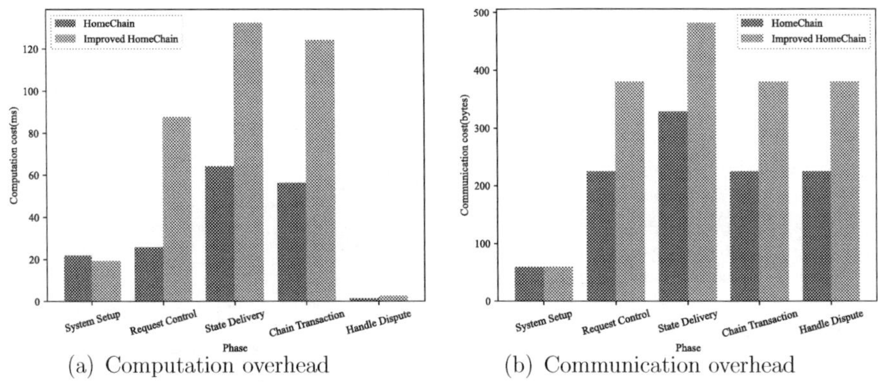

(a) Computation overhead (b) Communication overhead

Fig. 1. The comparison of HomeChain and improved HomeChain in computation and communication overhead

and 8 GB of RAM. We use Pairing-Based Cryptography Library (PBC) with version 0.4.7. For bilinear pairing is a map e: $\mathbb{G}_1 \times \mathbb{G}_2 \rightarrow \mathbb{G}_T$, in which Type-D Pairing is utilized. In practices, the order of all groups is 160 bits and the SHA-256 is choosen as the basic hash function. To compare the communication overhead, we first count the byte size of different elements. The size of the element in $\mathbb{G}_1$ is 40 bytes, the size of a one-way hash value is 32 bytes. At the same time, it is assumed that the original messages sent in different scenarios are all included in the finite field $\mathbb{Z}_q^*$ and have a size of 20 bytes. In additon, these messages are encrypted by the AES algorithm.

We first summarize the time-consuming cryptographic operations and list the notations and relevant execution time in Table 1, where each of these results is an average result of 1000 times. Then, we theoretically analyze the computation and communication overhead of HomeChain and improved HomeChain, the results are shown in Table 2. For further comparison, the numerical analysis results are shown in Fig. 1. The results show that the improved HomeChain is inferior to HomeChain in terms of computation cost and communication cost, but the improved HomeChain provides higher security. The computation and communication costs of the improved HomeChain are within acceptable limits, but higher security is a priority.

6 Conclusions

In this paper, we first reviewed the HomeChain protocol, and then pinpointed the vulnerabilities in both the State Delivery phase and the Handle Dispute phase. The cryptanalysis demonstrates that HomeChain is vulnerable to two universal attacks: 1) a malicious home gateway can determine whether the two signatures are from the same user. 2) an authorized user can generate a special signature that can be verified but the group manager cannot trace the real identity. To solve the two vulnerabilities in the HomeChain protocol, we introduce a new authentication protocol by leveraging a new group signature. Finally, the experimental results show that our enhanced protocol achieves stronger security at the expense of slightly higher storage and computing costs.

References

1. Vaidya, B., Park, J.H., Yeo, S.S., Rodrigues, J.J.: Robust one-time password authentication scheme using smart card for home network environment. Comput. Commun. **34**(3), 326–336 (2011)
2. Boneh, D.: Short group signatures. Advances in Crypto Crypto (2004)
3. Esposito, C., Ficco, M., Gupta, B.B.: Blockchain-based authentication and authorization for smart city applications. Inf. Process. Manage. **58**(2), 102468 (2021)
4. Feng, Q., He, D., Zeadally, S., Liang, K.: Bpas: blockchain-assisted privacy-preserving authentication system for vehicular ad hoc networks. IEEE Trans. Industr. Inf. **16**(6), 4146–4155 (2019)
5. Feng, X., Shi, Q., Xie, Q., Liu, L.: An efficient privacy-preserving authentication model based on blockchain for vanets. J. Syst. Architect. **117**, 102158 (2021)
6. Guo, Y., Zhang, Z., Guo, Y.: Secfhome: Secure remote authentication in fog-enabled smart home environment. Comput. Netw. **207**, 108818 (2022)
7. Hankerson, D., Menezes, A.J., Vanstone, S.: Guide to elliptic curve cryptography. Springer Science & Business Media (2006)
8. He, D., Zeadally, S., Xu, B., Huang, X.: An efficient identity-based conditional privacy-preserving authentication scheme for vehicular ad hoc networks. IEEE Trans. Inf. Forensics Secur. **10**(12), 2681–2691 (2015)
9. Kumar, P., Chouhan, L.: A secure authentication scheme for iot application in smart home. Peer-to-Peer Networking Appl. **14**(1), 420–438 (2021)
10. Kumar, P., Braeken, A., Gurtov, A., Iinatti, J., Ha, P.H.: Anonymous secure framework in connected smart home environments. IEEE Trans. Inf. Forensics Secur. **12**(4), 968–979 (2017)

11. Li, L., Liu, J., Cheng, L., Qiu, S., Wang, W., Zhang, X., Zhang, Z.: Creditcoin: a privacy-preserving blockchain-based incentive announcement network for communications of smart vehicles. IEEE Trans. Intell. Transp. Syst. **19**(7), 2204–2220 (2018)
12. Li, Q., He, D., Yang, Z., Xie, Q., Choo, K.K.R.: Lattice-based conditional privacy-preserving authentication protocol for the vehicular ad hoc network. IEEE Trans. Veh. Technol. **71**(4), 4336–4347 (2022)
13. Lin, C., He, D., Kumar, N., Huang, X., Vijayakumar, P., Choo, K.: Homechain: a blockchain-based secure mutual authentication system for smart homes. IEEE Internet Things J. (2020)
14. Lin, C., He, D., Huang, X., Kumar, N., Choo, K.K.R.: Bcppa: a blockchain-based conditional privacy-preserving authentication protocol for vehicular ad hoc networks. IEEE Trans. Intell. Transp. Syst. **22**(12), 7408–7420 (2020)
15. Lin, C., Huang, X., He, D.: Ebcpa: efficient blockchain-based conditional privacy-preserving authentication for vanets. IEEE Trans. Dependable Secure Comput. (2022)
16. Lu, R., Lin, X., Zhu, H., Ho, P.H., Shen, X.: Ecpp: efficient conditional privacy preservation protocol for secure vehicular communications. In: IEEE INFOCOM 2008-The 27th Conference on Computer Communications, pp. 1229–1237. IEEE (2008)
17. Luo, H., Wang, C., Luo, H., Zhang, F., Lin, F., Xu, G.: G2f: a secure user authentication for rapid smart home iot management. IEEE Internet Things J. **8**(13), 10884–10895 (2021)
18. Mansoor, K., Ghani, A., Chaudhry, S.A., Shamshirband, S., Mosavi, A.: Securing iot-based rfid systems: a robust authentication protocol using symmetric cryptography. Sensors **19**(21), 4752- (2019)
19. Ms, A., Ny, A., Hw, B., Ling, X.C.: Anonymous authentication scheme for smart home environment with provable security. Comput. Secur. **86**, 132–146 (2019)
20. Nyangaresi, V.O., Rodrigues, A.J., Abeka, S.O.: Efficient group authentication protocol for secure 5g enabled vehicular communications. In: 2020 16th International Computer Engineering Conference (ICENCO) (2020)
21. Poh, G.S., Gope, P., Ning, J.: Privhome: privacy-preserving authenticated communication in smart home environment. IEEE Trans. Dependable Secure Comput. **PP**(99), 1 (2019)
22. Poh, G.S., Gope, P., Ning, J.: Privhome: privacy-preserving authenticated communication in smart home environment. IEEE Trans. Dependable Secure Comput. **18**(3), 1095–1107 (2019)
23. Satapathy, U., Mohanta, B.K., Jena, D., Sobhanayak, S.: An ecc based lightweight authentication protocol for mobile phone in smart home. In: 2018 IEEE 13th International Conference on Industrial and Information Systems (ICIIS) (2018)
24. Shuai, M., Yu, N., Wang, H., Xiong, L.: Anonymous authentication scheme for smart home environment with provable security. Comput. Secur. **86**, 132–146 (2019)
25. Song, L., Sun, G., Yu, H., Du, X., Guizani, M.: Fbia: a fog-based identity authentication scheme for privacy preservation in internet of vehicles. IEEE Trans. Veh. Technol. **69**(5), 5403–5415 (2020)
26. Touqeer, H., Zaman, S., Amin, R., Hussain, M., Al-Turjman, F., Bilal, M.: Smart home security: challenges, issues and solutions at different iot layers. J. Supercomput. **77**(12), 14053–14089 (2021)

27. Vangala, A., Sutrala, A.K., Das, A.K., Jo, M.: Smart contract-based blockchain-envisioned authentication scheme for smart farming. IEEE Internet Things J. **8**(13), 10792–10806 (2021)
28. Wang, W., Huang, H., Zhang, L., Su, C.: Secure and efficient mutual authentication protocol for smart grid under blockchain. Peer-to-Peer Networking Appl. **14**(5), 2681–2693 (2021)
29. Wazid, M., Das, A.K., Odelu, V., Kumar, N., Susilo, W.: Secure remote user authenticated key establishment protocol for smart home environment. IEEE Trans. Dependable Secure Comput., 1 (2017)
30. Xiao, Y., Jia, Y., Liu, C., Alrawais, A., Rekik, M., Shan, Z.: Homeshield: a credential-less authentication framework for smart home systems. IEEE Internet Things J. **7**(9), 7903–7918 (2020)
31. Xu, J., Zhang, D., Xiong, G., Zhang, H.: CPBA: an efficient conditional privacy-preserving batch authentication scheme for VANETs. In: Yu, D., Dressler, F., Yu, J. (eds.) WASA 2020. LNCS, vol. 12384, pp. 555–567. Springer, Cham (2020). https://doi.org/10.1007/978-3-030-59016-1_46
32. Zhang, M., Yang, M., Shen, G.: Ssbas-fa: a secure sealed-bid e-auction scheme with fair arbitration based on time-released blockchain. J. Syst. Architect. **129**, 102619 (2022)
33. Zhang, Y., Li, B., Wu, J., Liu, B., Chen, R., Chang, J.: Efficient and privacy-preserving blockchain-based multi-factor device authentication protocol for cross-domain iiot. IEEE Internet of Things Journal (2022)
34. Zheng, D., Jing, C., Guo, R., Gao, S., Wang, L.: A traceable blockchain-based access authentication system with privacy preservation in vanets. IEEE Access **7**, 117716–117726 (2019)

Email and Web Security

OblivSend: Secure and Ephemeral File Sharing Services with Oblivious Expiration Control

Yanjun Shen[1], Bin Yu[1], Shangqi Lai[1](✉), Xingliang Yuan[1], Shi-Feng Sun[2], Joseph K. Liu[1], and Surya Nepal[1,2,3]

[1] Monash University, Melbourne, Australia
shangqi.lai@monash.edu
[2] Shanghai Jiao Tong University, Shanghai, China
[3] Data61, CSIRO, Sydney, Australia

Abstract. Users have personal or business need to share most private and confidential documents; however, often at the expense of privacy and security. A sought after feature in the trending ephemeral context is to set download constraints of a particular file - a file can only be downloaded a limited number of times and/or for a limited period of time. Emerging end-to-end encrypted file sharing services with enhanced expiration control are attempts to meet the needs. Although such new services have drawn much attention, their server can still observe and control metadata of such download constraints, which could reveal partial data information. To address this challenge, we propose OblivSend, a privacy-preserving file sharing web service that 1) supports end-to-end encryption, 2) allows a limited period of time and a limited number of downloads at users' control, and 3) protects expiration control metadata from the server efficiently by lightweight cryptographic primitives. We develop a proof of concept prototype implemented in Hyperledger Fabric on a Research Cloud and evaluations demonstrate that our prototype can function as intended to achieve privacy of metadata without sacrificing user experience.

Keywords: Security and privacy protection · Web application security · Privacy-preserving protocols · Metadata protection · Smart contract

1 Introduction

Individuals' security and privacy are fundamental rights, not only in the real world but also the digital universe. Far-too-frequent high-profile data leakages and mass surveillance projects [24,36] remind people of the vulnerability and sensitivity of personal data, hence the increasing privacy awareness brings up a growing group of privacy concerned users, who demand safe and private services including file sharing services. Existing regulations and acts to protect personal data, such as the General Data Protection Regulation (GDPR) [9] and the California Consumer Privacy Act (CCPA) [41], also impose on service providers to

W. Susilo et al. (Eds.): ISC 2022, LNCS 13640, pp. 269–289, 2022.
https://doi.org/10.1007/978-3-031-22390-7_17

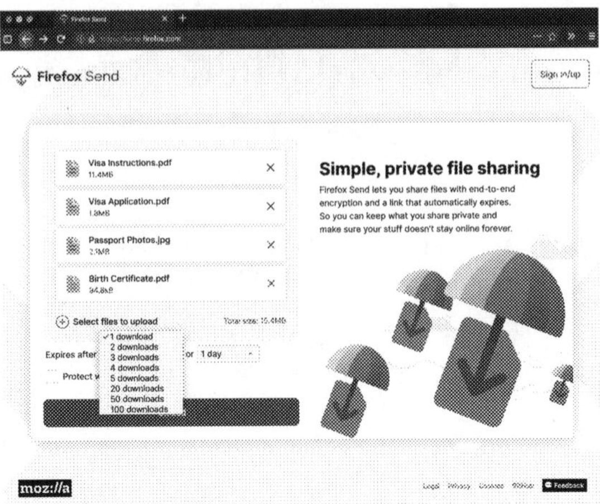

Fig. 1. Firefox Send. Choose when a file expires and the number of downloads [27].

grant individuals control over their private information. There are a quantity of file sharing services in the market, such as *Gmail*, *DropBox*, even instant messaging tools like *WhatsApp*, but these services often have constraints: emails and instant messengers have harsh attachment size limit that a 30-s 1080p footage can easily exceed; and most file hosting services do not support client-side encryption or self-destruct, which means your long-lived files can be decrypted any time simply by a rogue employee or if cooperated with government surveillance.

Among existing services, *Firefox Send* [27], officially launched by Mozilla in March 2019, allows to share files up to 2.5 GB at a time with end-to-end encryption (E2EE) from any modern browsers. *Send* empowers a user to encrypt a file and its metadata including file name, size and type before uploading (see Fig. 1); then send the file link (via a secure channel of the user's choice) to dedicated receiver(s) who can then request the service for downloading. In addition, it offers extra security control to users over the files they share: setting files to expire after a certain period of time or number of downloads. *Send* incorporates two most desired features, **E2EE** and **ephemeral**, which meets personal needs of more secure connections and intimate sharing.

However, limitations of *Send* are also apparent: 1) Users have to fully trust the service to honestly check if a file has expired. 2) Users send expiration control metadata, i.e. download number and time limits that are used to check if a file has expired on a download request, to *Send* in plaintext, which can be used to indicate the popularity and sensitivity of specific file(s).

Metadata privacy has drawn increasingly attention after the Edward Snowden leaks. "If you have enough metadata, you don't really need content", "we kill people based on metadata" [32,33]. Since sharing a file is similar to calling and messaging someone, metadata access in file sharing is also concerning.

1.1 Motivation

To illustrate the motivation of hiding the expiration control metadata (expiration metadata for short in the rest of the paper), we present some privacy issues resulted from potential leakage of expiration metadata, even with E2EE file sharing systems.

User Story 1: Sensitivity Derived from Expiration Metadata. Alice is an oncologist. Due to COVID-19, she shares files with patients and other contacts in an E2EE system. Alice shares electronic medical records with her patients and sets each to expire after 1 download or 1 day. With the knowledge of the expiration metadata, a curious server knows that Alice shares some files of strict access, hence deduces they are sensitive. Bob is a patient of Alice and downloads his report from the system. With Alice's identity and the sensitivity of the file, the server thus infers Bob is suspected to have cancer, which has implications on his insurance and other indemnities.

User Story 2: Frequency Derived from Expiration Metadata. A medical institution distributes confidential reports to different teams of professionals using an E2EE system and sets the download number limit as the number of team members. For instance, a cancer service team has 6 doctors and all files shared to the team are set to expire after 6 downloads. With side information about the institution's teams, likely available via a web search from its homepage, a server can infer the disease in each file. Bob visits Alice in the institution, even without Alice's identity, a server can reasonably deduce Bob's disease from the file Alice downloads without decryption.

User-input expiration metadata by itself may not be damaging; however, when combined with other metadata, scaling to a great population, and observed in aggregate, it can be meaningful and reveal sensitive information [23,33].

1.2 Our Contributions

We propose OblivSend, a secure and ephemeral file-sharing system that for the first time provides users with advanced and oblivious expiration control. OblivSend puts forward a new framework of a file-sharing service that not only supports comprehensive file expiration control, but is also expiration-metadata-private, which is a generic solution that can be integrated into other file sharing services. To understand our contribution, we now outline the main challenges OblivSend aims to address.

Challenge 1: How to Achieve Expiration Control over Protected Expiration Metadata? We define expiration metadata as a download number limit and a download time limit to ensure expiration control of a file sharing service. Users are not able to download a file upon exceeding the pre-set number of downloads or elapse time. Unfortunately, though more secure file sharing services promise expiration control as a premium feature [15,27,34], inadequate discussion has since occurred to understand the privacy of expiration metadata and how they impact the way people experience file sharing over the network. To the best of our knowledge, whereas many scholars focus on protection of general

Table 1. Secure file sharing services.

Product	E2EE	Time Lim.	No. Lim.	Oblivious
OblivSend	✓	✓	✓	✓
Firefox Send [27]	✓	✓	✓	✗
DropSecure [15]	✓	✓	Future	✗
SendSafely [34]	✓	✓	✗	✗
WhatsApp [45]	✓	Future	✗	✗
Digify [17]	✗	✓	✗	✗
Dropbox [14]	✗	✗	✗	✗

security control metadata in file sharing such as user identity and access pattern [6], there is no prior research aiming to prevent leakage of expiration metadata, hence a gap exists to address such expiration-metadata-privacy.

Challenge 2: How to Grant Expiration Control Power to a User Rather than a Service Provider? Users pursue E2EE file sharing services because they do NOT trust a service provider to keep their encryption keys. Therefore, it is an obvious defect that users adopt an E2EE service, but completely trust the service to check the expiration conditions and control if a file can be downloaded and decrypted. We assume a server that provides file storage services and fulfils upload and download requests; but wants to learn the expiration metadata, furthermore, actively manipulate its internal download state that is compared to expiration conditions.

OblivSend supports E2EE meanwhile protects the expiration metadata through the entire course with oblivious expiration control. Overall, our contributions are:

1 **Hiding expiration metadata.** We hide expiration metadata of file sharing services, both download number and time limits, through the entire life cycle by adopting cryptographic secret sharing scheme and garbled Bloom filter.
2 **Oblivious expiration control.** We enforce oblivious expiration control by transferring the responsibility for checking expiration conditions from a server to clients.
3 **Precautionary detection.** We audit and precautionarily detect forged download state at a serve side leveraging the immutability of smart contract.
4 **Implementation.** We implement a OblivSend prototype and develop a smart contract program cover a Hyperledger Fabric network. We use them to evaluate the performance of OblivSend and show that OblivSend has negligible extra computation and communication overhead on top of a traditional E2EE file sharing system.

2 Related Work

2.1 Existing Secure File Sharing Services

Table 1 compares several existing secure file sharing applications or web services. We organise the comparison by the following properties: 1) Does the service support E2EE? 2) Does the service support user-controlled file expiration? 3) Is the server oblivious of the expiration control?

While E2EE has become increasingly preferred when users choose a web service, additional impermanence or ephemeral feature, such as *Telegram Secret Chat* [40] and *Gmail confidential mode* [18], inspired and pioneered by *SnapChat* is another highly pursued trend that dominates the internet [15,27,34,45]. With certain expiration control, people can be confident that what they share is only accessible to dedicated users for a limited period of time or number of times, and they are able to wipe out all their "secrets" with a Thanos snap so that nothing will stay in a server for longer than necessary and become a vulnerability later. Emerging file sharing services that grant users expiration control are the file-sharing versions of *Snapchat*.

In addition to *Send*, *DropSecure* and *SendSafely* claim to offer zero-knowledge E2EE. *DropSecure* (premium) automatically destroys files from the servers after seven days and plans to support download number limit in the future. As an instant messaging service, *WhatsApp* also supports E2EE attachments, and has been developing its "Expiring Messages" feature. Services such as *Dropbox* and *Digify* provide an addition layer of security on top of server-side encryption, which enables a user to double encrypt files or folders by setting a password.

Some email services also support E2EE but the size of attachments is limited to 25 MB per email [30,42], and other approaches to share file securely online have low usability for none technical users [19,28,38].

2.2 Privacy-Preserving Web Services

In recent literature, researchers and practitioners have made great efforts to propose and promote privacy-preserving systems. [4,20,29] allow privacy-preserving data aggregation that enables monitoring, collection and analysis of statistics on the population without explicitly learning each user's individual contribution. [11,16,20] offers privacy-preserving safe browsing experience, while the former two protect sensitive user information entered into a browser and cached from auto-filled forms from sophisticated attackers and malware without trusting any part of the web applications, and the latter detects and blocks unsafe websites without leaking either users' browsing history or the lists of unsafe URLs maintained by third-party blacklist providers. [7] enables privacy-preserving smart contracts that address blockchain's lack of confidentiality by separating consensus from execution. Similar attempts have been made to develop metadata-private systems, but with a limited focus on secure messaging, either group messaging [10,46], or private messaging [2,22,43,44], and private presence and notification [5].

OblivSend is aiming to strike a good balance of the above desired features and usability; further, address the security challenges mentioned in Sect. 1.

3 Preliminaries

OblivSend makes black box use of secret sharing, garbled Bloom filter, smart contract, collision-resistant pseudorandom functions and hash functions.

Table 2. Notation

Notation	Description
λ, σ, l	Security parameters
N (T)	A finite set of integers from 1 to n (or t) that denotes all download *numbers* (or *time units*) allowed by OblivSend
L_N (L_T)	A finite set of integers from 1 to l_N (or l_T) where l_N (l_T) is the download *number* (or *time*) limit
S_U	A user secret shared securely between a data owner and clients
E_N (E_T)	A key element bound to download *number* (or *time*)
FK	A secret key used for file encryption that is composed of E_N and E_T
K_N (K_T)	A finite set of protection keys to cipher a *number* (or *time*) key element
C_{E_N} (C_{E_T})	A finite set of cipher *number* (or *time*) elements encrypted using each element in K_N (or K_T)
AB_N (AB_T)	A finite set of encrypted payload messages used for GBF_N (or GBF_T)
M_N (M_T)	A map of all elements in N (or T) paired with their hash values
k	Number of hash functions in a garbled Bloom filter
m	Length of a garbled Bloom filter
H	A set of k independent hash functions $\{h_0, ..., h_{k-1}\}$ each $h_i(j)$ on input j outputs an index number over $[0, m-1]$ uniformly
GBF_N (GBF_T)	A garbled Bloom filter encoding a set N (or T)
PRF	A pseudorandom function $\{0,1\}^{2\sigma} \xleftarrow{\$} \{0,1\}^{\sigma} \times \{0,1\}^{*}$ that on input a σ-bit key and some string, outputs a 2σ-bit pseudorandom string

Notation. We define parameters, entities, denotations in OblivSend in Table 2.

Secret Sharing [35] is a fundamental cryptographic primitive that splits a secret s into n shares such that the secret s can be recovered efficiently with any subset of t or more shares. With any subset of less than t shares, the secret is unrecoverable and the shares give no information about the secret. A scenario when $t = n$ is applied in this scheme, and a secret related to a file encryption key can be restored via simple $\oplus(XOR)$ operations.

The scheme generates $n-1$ random bit strings $r_1, r_2, ..., r_{n-1}$ of the same length as the secret s, and computing $r_n = r_1 \oplus r_2 \oplus, ..., \oplus r_{n-1} \oplus s$. Each r_i is a share of the secret s. It is apparent that s can be recovered by (XOR)ing all the shares $r_1 \oplus r_2 \oplus, ..., \oplus r_{n-1} \oplus r_n$ and any subset of less than n shares reveals no information about the secret and the secret is unrecoverable.

Garbled Bloom Filter (GBF) is a data structure introduced in [13] that encodes a set of at most n λ-bit strings in an array of length m, which supports membership query with no false negative and negligible false positive. Instead of generating an array of bits of 0 and 1 in a standard Bloom filter [3], a GBF adds secrets of $x \in S$ using the XOR-based secret sharing scheme depicted above. While querying the GBF for membership checking, only if $y \in S$, the XOR operations will recover y from the GBF.

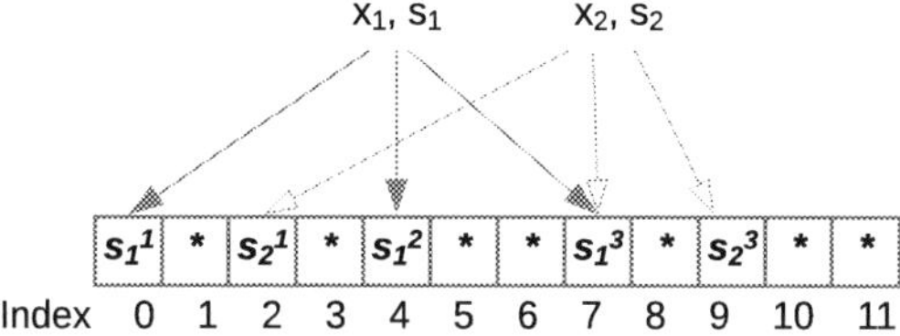

Fig. 2. Adding secrets into a GBF. x_1 is hashed into 3 numbers 0, 4, 7, and 3 shares of s_1 are allocated to index 0, 4, 7; x_2 is mapped to 2, 7, 9, where an existing share s_1^3 is reused at index 7.

To add an element $x \in S$ to a garbled Bloom filter, the element x is first split into k λ-bit strings using the XOR-based secret sharing scheme depicted in the previous paragraph, then is mapped by k hash functions into k index numbers and each location $h_i(x)$ is allocated with one secret share to form an array of λ-bit strings. To query an element y, the element y is mapped by the same k hash functions into k index numbers and all bit strings at the corresponding array locations $h_i(y)$ are collected and XORed together. To query an element y, the element y is mapped by the same k hash functions into k index numbers and all bit strings at the corresponding array locations $h_i(y)$ are collected and XORed together. If $y \in S$, the XOR operation will recover y as a result of XORing its k shares retrieved from the garbled Bloom filter by their indices. If $y \notin S$, then the probability of the XOR result is the same as y is negligible in λ.

Remark: During the course, a specific location $j \leftarrow h_i(x)$ may have been occupied by a share of a previously added secret, and in this case the existing share stored at $GBF[j]$ is reused (line 18 in Algorithm 2), otherwise, the previously added secret will not be recoverable in the query phase. For instance, in Fig. 2, when we add s_2, $GBF[7]$ has already been occupied by s_1^3 and reused as a share of s_2, since $s_2^3 = s_2^1 \oplus s_1^3 \oplus s_2$, $s_2 = s_2^1 \oplus s_1^3 \oplus s_2^3$ still stands.

According to [13], the false positive probability of a garbled Bloom filter, which is the probability that for $y \notin S$, the recovered string from XORing all $GBF_S[h_i(y)]$ is the same as y coincidentally, is at most $2^{-\lambda}$.

In our proposed framework, x is either a download number or time unit, and the secret whose shares are added is either a cipher key element or a payload message. When y, which is the current download count or elapse time unit, is within the corresponding download limit, the cipher key element can be recovered.

Smart Contract is a "computerised transaction protocol" first coined by Nick Szabo in 1997 [39] that digitally enforces secure relationships and credible transactions over public networks via a blockchain. It intends to minimises trust and eliminates needs for third parties, and common application of a smart contract ranges from financial to logistics, healthcare to energy resources. [1,25,47].

Since blockchain is a massive decentralised ledger by nature, once a transaction is validated and written to the blockchain, it can neither be deleted nor modified without a majority of collusion, which makes the blockchain immutable.

Our proposed scheme builds smart contract into the framework because it is automatic and direct, fast and cheap, and tamper-proof.

4 System Overview

In OblivSend, when a data owner uploads a file, the data owner is able to set the file to expire after a number of downloads or period of time. When a client makes a download request to OblivSend, OblivSend sends the encrypted file to the client, and the client can only decrypt the file if it has not expired. To understand how OblivSend performs these operations securely, we present an overview of OblivSend's design, threats and security goals.

4.1 Intuition

We now present several attempts, beginning with naive approaches that are obviously insecure and proceeding to a practical version of our proposed scheme.

Attempt #1: Client-End Encryption of Expiration Metadata. A natural approach is to simply encrypt the expiration metadata and send the resulting ciphertext to a server. Assuming we use proper encryption schemes so that the server is able to verify a client's download request by comparing its current internal download state with the ciphertext of download limits. Based on the comparison results, the server determines to send the encrypted file to the client or not. This design should offer metadata privacy even when they are held by a malicious server.

It is obvious that although it prevents tampering with the stored metadata, it does not prevent a malicious server from manipulating the comparison result. Such an attacker can allow downloads after a file has expired by using an old internal state, and vice versa. Further, the server is able to deduce the expiration metadata based on its internal download state on the boundary if a new download request fails the comparison.

Attempt #2: Server is Oblivious of the Comparison. Instead of comparing the its internal download state with encrypted download limits, a server computes an output using its internal download state, and sends the output and the encrypted file to the client. Only if the internal download state fulfils the pre-set expiration conditions, the output can unveil the file encryption key.

This approach deprives the server of the ultimate power to grant or deny a download request. The server is oblivious of the comparison outcome, moreover not able to learn about the expiration metadata. However, it still requires a single trust party, the server, to compute the output using the correct internal download state. It is apparently not desirable because a single authority is easy to attack and collude. Besides, this protocol does not prevent the server from replaying an old computation result to the client. In practice, such an attacker can always permit a download request regardless of the pre-set expiration conditions.

Attempt #3: Use Smart Contract to Audit State. In order to address the single trust issue, we require decentralised trust that reduces the trust level of a single server. We use a public ledger on a blockchain to keep a world download state, and a client interacts with a smart contract to post and get the world download state. The server still computes an output but the output is encrypted using its internal download state. The client requests the world download state from the smart contract, and only if the world download state in the ledger is consistent with the internal state used by the server, the output can be recovered. It is impossible for an adversary to tamper the world download state in the ledger without a majority of collusion because of the immutable nature of a blockchain. This is a practical and more accepting setting, and exposes no extra trace on the blockchain by publishing hashed digests rather than real data.

Remark. Like the previous attempt, the protocol described above does not prevent a server from replaying old computation results. However, it precautionarily detects such replaying attack, and indeed prevents a client from downloading an expired file even if the server keeps replaying old computation results, and hopefully ensures that the server gains nothing from such attacks.

Our Design Intuition. The above attempts provide an intuition for our ideas, and OblivSend uses the following techniques to realise our intuition. OblivSend hides expiration metadata leveraging secret sharing and GBF. It first maps the download count and time unit up to system default download limit (i.e. the maximum download count or time unit allowed by OblivSend) into a GBF's locations, and puts secret shares of a cipher key element in locations mapped from counts or time units under the download limit but a payload message in those over the limit. OblivSend builds two GBFs for number and time limits respectively. On a download request, an OblivSend's server computes both GBFs using its internal download state and sends the result to a client. If its internal download state does not exceed either limit, shares from corresponding locations of each GBF result recover the corresponding cipher key element.

Further, OblivSend takes advantage of the immutability of a blockchain to audit the server integrity. The client requests for the world download state on a blockchain via a smart contract, and validates the server's internal state. Only if the states are consistent can a client decrypt the cipher key element, and with both key elements, the client can rebuild the file decryption key and decrypt the file. The server is oblivious of all the subsequent validation and decryption operations after handing over the GBF computation results, hence is no longer a central authority to grand or deny a download request and never knows if the expiration conditions have reached or not. Note this is a loose description, the detailed construction is elaborated in Sect. 5.

4.2 Framework

Figure 3 shows that OblivSend consists of four parties and three phases:

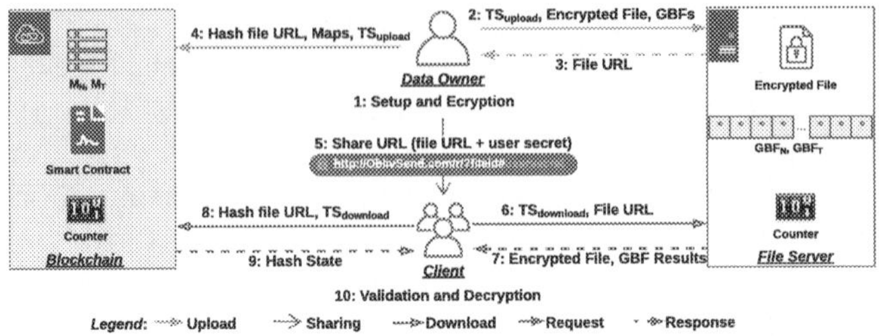

Fig. 3. High-level framework. Shaded areas are components introduced by OblivSend.

- **Data Owner** is a sender of file(s), who generates keys, encrypts the file(s), sets download limits, and encodes the file encryption key and expiration metadata into GBFs before uploading them to a server.
- **Server** is where the encrypted files and GBFs are stored, who computes the GBFs using its internal download state and returns the GBF results and encrypted files on download requests.
- **Smart Contract** on a blockchain is a program that truthfully receives, updates, and returns the world download state.
- **Client** is the file(s) recipient who retrieves the encrypted file(s) and GBF results from the server, and the world download state from the smart contract. The client validates the GBF results before it decrypts the file(s).

Upload consists of 4 steps according to Fig. 3: 1) Data Owner generates a file encryption key composed of a *number* and a *time* key element, and encrypts a file; then populates hashes for each allowed download count and time unit and puts them into two maps; it generates a user secret and ciphers the two key elements using the user secret and hashes, then put the cipher key elements into two GBFs based on the download limits accordingly. 2) Data Owner uploads the GBFs, the encrypted file and an upload timestamp to Server. 3) Server returns a file URL. 4) Data Owner sends a hash value of the file URL as a unique identifier, two maps of hashes, and an upload timestamp to Smart Contract.

During **Sharing**, Data Owner appends a user secret to the file URL and sends the share URL to trusted Client(s) via some out-of-band communication independent of OblivSend (as discussed in Sect. 4.3).

Download includes the following operations shown on Fig. 3: 6) Client renders the share URL, and requests Server for the encrypted file by the file URL and an download timestamp. 7) Server returns the encrypted file and the GBF computation results using its internal download state. 8) Client queries Smart Contract for hashes of the world download state by the hash file URL and the download timestamp. 9) Smart Contract returns the hashes by looking up the world download count number and elapse time unit in the maps on the blockchain. 10) Client imports the user secret from the share URL and validates Server's download state by decrypting the GBF results with the user secret and hashes. If Server's internal state is consistent with the world state on the blockchain, Client can decipher the GBF results. If neither the current download count nor the elapse time unit has exceeded the pre-set download limits, the deciphered GBF results are the two key elements, and Client can rebuild the file encryption key to decrypt the file.

OblivSend changes *Send*'s framework to a minimal extend while improving its security performance. A notable variation is the usage of GBF to hide expiration metadata and ensure server obliviousness. Another extension is the introduction of Smart Contract on the left hand side of Fig. 3, which provides a mechanism to audit the server integrity to detect any forged download state. We make such minimal extension on purpose so as OblivSend's oblivious expiration control is generic and can be applied to other file sharing services.

4.3 Threat Models and Security Goals

Threat Models. We assume that an attacker can compromise any set of users and an OblivSend server, while at least one client is honest. In particular, OblivSend considers the following threats:

(a) The server would sniff the expiration metadata, hence deduces valuable information of encrypted data.
(b) The server would forge its internal download state. A replay attack is typical that allows a client to download after a file has expired.
(c) An attacker controlling a client tries to compromise the privacy of data that is not shared with him/her.

Assumptions. *Out-of-band communication.* A data owner in OblivSend shares a URL with client(s) through third party end-to-end secured channels of their own control, such as *Telegram* [40], *Signal* [31]. The share URL can be sent via secure messages similar to communicating user identities or notifications in [6,21]. OblivSend only uses such out-of-band communication once at the sharing stage, which is the same as *Send* and a common practice of other secure file sharing systems [14,27], keeping all other activities within OblivSend.

Blockchain. OblivSend makes black-box use of a blockchain and a standard assumption that a blockchain is immutable. If any set of peer nodes are compromised or an attacker seeks membership of a blockchain, who attempt to mutate the world download state on a blockchain, it becomes visible to all participants who, by a simple majority of votes [8], can prevent such unlawful actions from happening. We also inherent general blockchain security assumptions, which is not narrated in this paper.

Anonymous Network. In order to hide other metadata during file sharing, OblivSend assumes the data owner and clients communicate with the server in an anonymous manner that does not reveal their network information via existing tools such as Tor [12] or secure messaging [10,43,44] based on decentralised trust.

Algorithm 1: Upload.Generate

Input: σ, N, T
Output: FK, S_U, C_{E_N}, C_{E_T}, AB_N, AB_T, M_N, M_T
1 Initialisation;
2 Generate $S_U, E_N, E_T \xleftarrow{\$} \{0,1\}^\sigma$;
3 Compute $FK \leftarrow hash(E_N||E_T)$;
4 **for** $p \in N$ **do**
5 $\quad \hat{p} \leftarrow hash(p)$, $M_N[p] \leftarrow \hat{p}$;
6 $\quad K_N[p] \leftarrow PRF_{S_U}(\hat{p})$;
$\quad$ // protect the key element
7 $\quad C_{E_N}[p] \leftarrow Enc_{K_N[p]}(E_N)$;
8 $\quad AB_N[p] \leftarrow Enc_{K_N[p]}(\text{“}ABORT\text{”})$;
9 **endfor**
10 **for** $q \in T$ **do**
11 $\quad \hat{q} \leftarrow hash(q)$, $M_T[q] \leftarrow \hat{q}$;
12 $\quad K_T[q] \leftarrow PRF_{S_U}(\hat{q})$;
13 $\quad C_{E_T}[q] \leftarrow Enc_{K_T[q]}(E_T)$;
14 $\quad AB_T[q] \leftarrow Enc_{K_T[q]}(\text{“}ABORT\text{”})$;
15 **endfor**

OblivSend does not address denial-of-service attacks.

Security Goals. OblivSend sets the following goals to address the above threats:

(a) **Expiration metadata privacy.** OblivSend ensures expiration metadata is totally at a data owner's control, and not visible in transit or at rest on either the server or the blockchain.
(b) **Server integrity auditing.** OblivSend uses the public audit-ability of a blockchain underpinned by its immutability feature to detect forged download state on a server before actual decryption takes place.
(c) **File confidentiality.** A client is not able to recover the encryption key and decrypt the file by guessing the current download state.
(d) **General metadata protection.** OblivSend does not reveal to the blockchain the following in plaintext: user IP, file URL, download limits, download state, upload and download timestamps.

OblivSend achieves the goals above based on common cryptographic assumptions and we provide extended discussion in Sect. 5.1.

5 Detailed Construction

In this section, we describe key components of OblivSend and present their algorithms. We also provide security analysis of OblivSend.

Upload.Generate. Run by the data owner at the beginning of the upload phase to generate a user secret S_U, a file encryption key FK that composed of two key elements (E_N, E_T), and two maps (M_N, M_T) of all members in the system allowed download number set N and time unit set T with their hashes. The data owner also generates a protection key from a pseudorandom function on S_U and a hash value of $n \in N$ or $t \in T$ (line 6, 12 in Algorithm 1) and ciphers the key

Algorithm 2: Upload.Encode

```
Input: N, l_N, m, k, λ, C_{E_N}, AB_N, H
Output: GBF_N
1 Initialise GBF_N;
2 for p ∈ N do
3   emptySlot ← −1;
    // under download limit
4   if p ≤ l_N;
5     final ← C_{E_N}[p];
6     for i = 0 to k − 1 do
        // get an index via hashing
7       j ← h_i(p);
8       if GBF_N[j] == NULL then
9         if emptySlot == -1 then
            // Reserve a location
10          emptySlot ← j;
11        else
            // generate a secret share
12          GBF_N[j] ←$ (0, 1)^λ;
13          final ← final ⊕ GBF_N[j];
14      else
          // reuse an existing share
15        final ← final ⊕ GBF_N[j];
16    endfor
      // store final in the reserved location
17    GBF_N[emptySlot] ← final;
    // over download limit
18  else
19    final ← AB_N[p];
20    for i = 0 to k − 1 do
21      j ← h_i(p);
22      if GBF_N[j] == NULL then
23        if emptySlot == -1 then
24          emptySlot ← j;
25        else
26          GBF_N[j] ←$ (0, 1)^λ;
27          final ← final ⊕ GBF_N[j];
28      else
29        final ← final ⊕ GBF_N[j];
30    endfor
31    GBF_N[emptySlot] ← final;
32 endfor
33 for i = 0 to m − 1 do
34   if GBF_N[i] == NULL then
       // store random strings
35     GBF_N[j] ←$ (0, 1)^λ;
36 endfor
```

elements using the protection keys (line 7, 13 in Algorithm 1). The data owner encrypts a file using FK, sends S_U to clients during the sharing phase, and sends M_N and M_T to a smart contract. The cipher elements (C_{E_N}, C_{E_T}) and payload messages (AB_N, AB_T) are to be added into GBFs in Upload.Encode.

Upload.Encode. Run by the data owner to construct two GBFs (GBF_N, GBF_T) encoding the cipher key elements (C_{E_N}, C_{E_T}). It has two purposes: 1) to encode the elements that can compose the file encryption key into GBFs (line 17 in Algorithm 2) to ensure E2EE; 2) to map the download limits into GBF locations (line 4, 7 in Algorithm 2) to preserve expiration metadata privacy meanwhile enforce expiration control. The data owner sends GBF_N and GBF_T to a server together with the encrypted file C and an upload timestamp. Algorithm 2 takes the number element and download number limit as an example. For download time limit, it takes inputs T, L_T, m, k, λ, C_{E_T}, AB_T, H, and outputs GBF_T.

Download.Compute. Run by the server on a download request from a client to compute GBF_N and GBF_T using the current download count c and elapse time unit e. If $c \in L_N$ and $e \in L_T$, shares of the cipher key elements will recover $C_{E_N}[c]$ and $C_{E_T}[e]$, otherwise cipher payload messages ($AB_N[c]$, $AB_T[e]$). The server returns the computation results R_N, R_T to the client.

Download.Validate. Run by the client to decipher the GBF results R_N and R_T using the hashes of current download state ($\hat{c^*}, \hat{e^*}$) fetched from the smart contract. If both elements are deciphered successfully (line 4, 5 in Algorithm 4), it proves that the current download state c and e used by the server are authentic, i.e. $c = c^*$ and $e = e^*$; otherwise, we must have $K_N[c^*] \neq K_N[c]$ and/or $K_T[e^*] \neq K_T[e]$ that are used to envelop the key elements in Upload.Generate (see

Algorithm 3: Download.Compute

```
Input: GBF_N, GBF_T, c, e, k, H
Output: R_N, R_T
Initialise R_N, R_T ← {0}^λ;
for i ∈ [k] do
    p ← h_i(c);
    R_N ← R_N ⊕ GBF_N[p];
    q ← h_i(e);
    R_T ← R_N ⊕ GBF_T[q];
endfor
return R_N, R_T;
```

Algorithm 4: Download.Validate

```
Input: S_U, R_N, R_T, ĉ*, ê*
Output: FK
Initialise E_N*, E_T* ← NULL;
  // element protection keys
K_N[c*] ← PRF_{S_U}(ĉ*);
K_T[e*] ← PRF_{S_U}(ê*);
  // fail on inconsistent download states
E_N* ← Dec_{K_N[c*]}(R_N);
E_T* ← Dec_{K_T[e*]}(R_T);
FK ← hash(E_N*||E_T*);
```

line 6, 12 in Algorithm 1). The unveiled secrets $(E_N{}^*, E_T{}^*)$ are either (E_N, E_T) or "ABORT" depending on whether the current download state satisfies the download limits. Only if $c \in L_N$ and $e \in L_T$, the secrets are the key elements and the client can reassemble FK and eventually decrypt the file.

5.1 Security Guarantee

We now present security guarantees of OblivSend w.r.t. the goals given in Sect. 4.3.

Expiration Metadata Privacy. OblivSend hides expiration metadata from a server yet is able to enforce the expiration control by using GBFs in Upload.Encode. The data owner maps each $n \in N$ and $t \in T$ to the GBF's locations and adds shares of cipher key elements only to the locations hashed from $n \leq l_N$ and $t \leq l_T$ (line 4–17 in Algorithm 2). All other locations are filled with cipher payload messages (line 18–31 in Algorithm 2) or random strings (line 35 in Algorithm 2). Although the server holds the GBFs, the standard secret sharing technique ensures the shares of the cipher key elements and payload messages are of the same λ-length hence indistinguishable, and each share reveals no information about the secret. OblivSend never discloses the expiration metadata to a smart contract either, and the only information exposed is the system download limit in M_N and M_T populated in Upload.Generate (line 5, 11 in Algorithm 1), which is visible to all OblivSend users hence not introducing extra security risks.

Further, OblivSend enforces the expiration control at the client side, hence neither the server nor the smart contract is aware of the decryption outcomes to deduce the download limits. If a server wants to learn the download limits, it needs to decrypt R_N and R_T (line 4, 5 in Algorithm 4): if the decryption succeeds, the download state c and e used are under the download limits; otherwise, over the limits. In order to decrypt R_N (or R_T), the server requires $K_N[c^*]$ (or $K_T[e^*]$) that is and output of PRF on S_U. A security parameter σ is used to generate S_U, and the probability of a server to find $K_N[c^*]$ is $2^{-\sigma}$, which is negligible for all sufficiently large σ. The smart contract does not have R_N or R_T, thus not able to decrypt them and infer the download limits.

Server Integrity Auditing. OblivSend makes use of the public audit-ability of a blockchain to precautionarily detect if a server has tampered its download state. Recall the immutability assumption of a standard blockchain in Sect. 4.3, the world download state store on a blockchain is immutable, which means that the hash state $(\hat{c^*}, \hat{e^*})$ fetched via the smart contract is authentic. If a server uses a forged download state, e.g. a replay attack, we must have $c \neq c^*$ and/or $e \neq e^*$. Note that the server computes R_N and R_T using its internal download state c and e, and the secret shares from mapped locations of c and e recover $C_{E_N}[c]$ (or $AB_N[c]$ if $c > l_N$) and $C_{E_T}[e]$ (or $AB_T[e]$ if $e > l_T$), which are encrypted using $K_N[c]$ and $K_T[e]$ respectively in Upload.Generate (line 7–8, 13–14 in Algorithm 1). The probability that a client can decrypt R_N using $K_N[c^*]$ is $Pr(c \neq c^* : K_N[c] = K_N[c^*])$. Since $K_N[i]$ is an output of a PRF on S_U and $\hat{c^*}$ (line 6 in Algorithm 1), the server's probability to trick the client into decrypting R_N computed from an illegitimate download number c is negligible if PRF is collision resistant.

Though OblivSend does not prevent a server from manipulating its state, it detects the inconsistency and prevents file decryption from happening. As long as one honest client reports the server's misbehaviour to the data owner after a decryption failure, the data owner can re-upload the file and share a new URL, hence such attack gains no information and little value.

File Confidentiality. OblivSend uses hash values rather than the original download numbers and time units to protect the two key elements E_N and E_T, so that a semi-honest client cannot recover the key elements and decrypt a file by guessing a download state that has not expired without non-trivial computation. In Download.Validate, the client already has R_N, R_T, S_U, and wants to get E_N and E_T not using $(\hat{c^*}, \hat{e^*})$ but trying a download state (u, v) that is as minimal as possible. In order to recover E_N and E_T, the client needs $K_N[c]$ and $K_T[e]$, hence $\hat{c}$ and $\hat{e}$ (line 2–5 in Algorithm 4). Therefore, the client needs to find a pair of u and v so that $\hat{u} = \hat{c}$ and $\hat{v} = \hat{e}$ and this event occurs with at most negligible probability if the hash function is collision resistant.

General Metadata Protection. OblivSend sends a hash file URL, uploads and downloads timestamps and the maps of system-allowed download numbers and time units to a smart contract, and the smart contract updates and keeps a world download state that includes a current count and elapse time unit corresponding to a file in a public ledger on a blockchain. However, OblivSend only publishes a digest of hashes to a ledger. Therefore, no extra trace will be visible to adversaries because of the preimage resistance property of hash functions. Since OblivSend assumes an anonymous network (in Sect. 4.3), users' IP addresses are garbled when communicating with a server or a smart contract, and OblivSend encrypts metadata such as file name, size, type in the same way as *Send* does [27]. Hence, OblivSend addresses general metadata privacy in file sharing.

6 Implementation and Evaluation

6.1 Implementation

We implement a command-line-based OblivSend prototype on Hyperledger Fabric programmed in Go. Since the purpose is not to measure the AES efficiency or network transmit throughput, we use a demo string instead of a real file in the prototype. We have the following settings: security parameters $\sigma = 128$, $l = 256$ (SH-256). The size of N (i.e. number of elements to be added to GBF_N) is 100 (maximum download number), and the size of T is 2016 (maximum 7 days with a minimum of 5 min), which follows *Send*'s setting. Security parameter $\lambda = 64$ that yields a negligible false positive probability 2^{-64}. The number of hash functions $k = 5$, and the length of GBF $m = \frac{kn}{ln2} \approx 1.44kn$ that is optimal [13], both of which can be passed dynamically during experiments. H is a family of 128-bit hash functions.

We present pseudo-codes of key functions performed by each party, and Pseudo-code 1 is an example that shows how a peer node executes a smart contract in response to a client's download request. Each peer in a blockchain network hosts a copy of the ledger, and OlibvSend can perform read and write operations against the ledger by invoking a smart contract which queries the most recent value of the ledger and returns it to OblivSend and/or updates the value of the ledger. In Pseudo-code 1, the smart contract takes a hash url and a download timestamp from the client's request, and queries the most recent value of the ledger. It first validates its local copy of the ledger and then returns the value, meanwhile increments the download count and synced an updated digest to the world state.

```
func smartContractDownload
input: Request
output: Response, nImg, tImg
  hashedUrl, dl = read hashedUrl from Request
  state = get world state from the ledger(hashedUrl)
  if error
    return error "Failed to get world state", NULL
  countDigest = state.countDigest
  if countDigest == NULL
    return error "Download count not found in world state", NULL
  hashCount = Hash(count) //download count stored in local memory
  if hashCount != countDigest
    return error "Inconsistent download count", NULL
  ulDigest = state.ulDigest
  if ulDigest == NULL
    return error "Upload timestamp not found in world state", NULL
  hashUl = Hash(ul) //upload timestamp stored in local memory
  if hashUl != ulDigest
    return error "Inconsistent upload timestamp", NULL
  etUnit = F(dl - ul)
  hashNMap = Hash(nMap) //number image array stored in local memory
  if hashNMap != state.nMapDigest
    return error "Inconsistent number image array", NULL
  hashTMap = Hash(tMap) //time image array stored in local memory
  if hashTMap != state.tMapDigest
    return error "Inconsistent time image array", NULL
  nImg = nMap[count] //get number image by download count
  count += 1
  countDigest = Hash(count)
  tImg = tMap[etUnit] //get time image by elapsed time unit
  digest = new DigestStruct(hashedUrl, countDigest, ulDigest, nMap_Digest, tMap_Digest)
  Put digest to the world state
    if error
          return error, NULL
  return success, nImg, tImg
```

Pseudo-code 1: Function smartContractDownload

Pseudo-codes of other main functions are enclosed in Appendix. Note that the blockchain architecture is out of scope hence the implementation of Hyperledger Fabric network, e.g. how to build the network, and how to install smart contract (aka chaincode) onto peers, are not detailed.

6.2 Evaluation

The prototype Hyperledger Fabric network is deployed on a single cloud instance. It consists of one orderer node and two peer nodes, and runs in a docker-local container environment. We created an instance in a Research Cloud on Ubuntu 18.04 LTS (Bionic) amd64 (with Docker) version, with 2 virtual CPUs and 8 GB RAM. We used a Dell Precision 5530 with Intel i7 2.6GHz CPU, 32 GB RAM to make a SSH connection to the cloud instance.

Running Time. During the experiments, we measured the total running time of the upload phase and download phase respectively. The upload phase starts when a data owner initiates the upload request and ends after sending data to a smart contract, which includes the time consumed to build the GBFs, generate keys, maps, a hash URL, and all underlying data processing. We also measured the total download time that starts from a client extracting the file URL and ends immediately after the client outputting the decrypted demo, which includes operation time at both the server side (computing the GBFs) and the smart contract side (looking up for hashes and communication overhead). The communication overhead when querying and syncing the world state in a ledger on a blockchain is recorded separately as latency time. We do not, however, include communication overhead at the smart contract end during the upload phase as it occurs after data owner successfully uploads the data hence that does not explicitly impact user experience. We set one client to request a download for each experiment and ran 1000 independent experiments with random download limits, and the calculated average time is recorded in Table 3.

Table 3. Average total running time (ms) (record size = 1000).

Phase	Operation	Latency	Running time
Upload	220.5283	NA	220.5283
Download	2.5385	1470.6911	1483.3837

We test the download number limit by fixing the time limit as the maximum of 7 days, and experiment download time limit separately by setting the download number limit as the default number 100. As can be seen in Fig. 4a and Fig. 4b, the total running times are consistent over different download limit settings due to the undifferentiated construction of GBFs. The average total running time that Data Owner takes to finish all upload operations is 220.53 ms, which is a satisfying performance. With regard to the download phase, the average total running time 1483.38 ms, of which the latency time constitutes over 99%. However, our proposed protocol is an privacy-enhanced extension of secure large file sharing system, and in a real scenario, downloading a 25-MB file over mobile can take 8 s and a 1-GB file takes 3 min on fixed broadband just for transit (according to [26], world-wide average download speed for fixed broadband and mobile are 74.64 and 30.47 Mbps as of March 2020), not considering all underlying data processing operations. Therefore, an average of 1.5-s delay does not have substantial impact from the perspective of user interaction and experience.

Scalability. OblivSend is a secure and impermanent file sharing system that is dedicated for confidential and intimate files, hence we refer to existing secure file sharing or messaging tools [37,45] to determine pragmatic maximum allowed download number and time, which are the size n (or t) of the GBFs. We consider the maximum set size $n = 5000$ and $t = 8640$ (i.e. expiration time from 5 mins to 30 days). According to [13], the running time of building a GBF increases almost linearly in the set size, and the estimated running time of building the GBFs on a 128-bit security parameter $\approx$1.3 s when uploading a file, which is not noticeable by an end user during the course of uploading a file.

Remark: The experiment demonstrates feasible application of GBF and smart contract in secure file sharing solutions, but a limitation of OblivSend is that it does not process download requests in a concurrent context. The order of a client raising a download request decides the current download count hence yields different decryption outcomes. An existing solution [21] is to have the server, not the client to publish data to a blockchain. However, this is not feasible in our protocol as OblivSend audits server's integrity using the immutable ledger on a

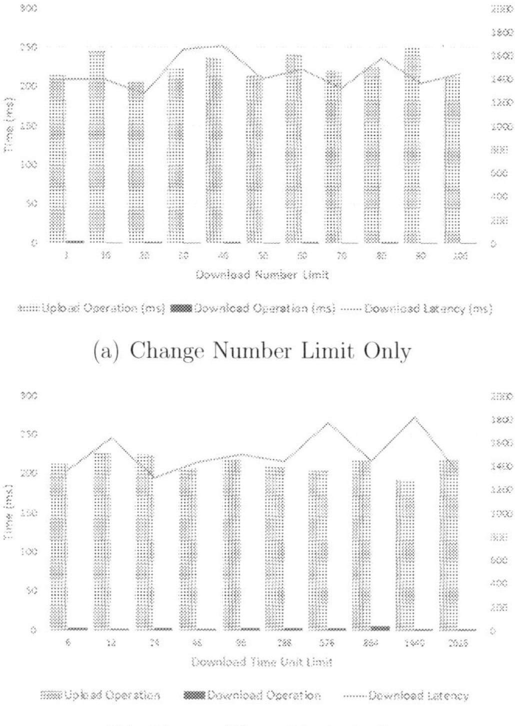

(a) Change Number Limit Only

(b) Change Time Limit Only

Fig. 4. Running time

blockchain as discussed in Sect. 5.1. The challenge related with concurrent access remains to be solved and future work for this topic.

7 Conclusion

We propose OblivSend, a lightweight privacy-preserving file sharing web service that for the first time protects expiration metadata from the server and meanwhile ensures E2EE by adopting cryptography protocols like garbled Bloom filter and novel Smart Contract technology. We have successfully implemented the design and built a prototype over a Hyperledger Fabric network. We also conducted experiments to evaluate its performance. The result is as expected and encouraging, demonstrating that OblivSend has stronger security without performance sacrifice. OblivSend precautionarily detects malicious mutations of a server's internal state, and we consider a simple scenario that one client requests download after another, both of which is open for further work.

References

1. Andoni, M., et al.: Blockchain technology in the energy sector: a systematic review of challenges and opportunities. Renew. Sustain. Energy Rev. **100**, 143–174 (2019)
2. Angel, S., Setty, S.: Unobservable communication over fully untrusted infrastructure. In: USENIX OSDI 2016 (2016)
3. Bloom, B.H.: Space/time trade-offs in hash coding with allowable errors. Commun. ACM **13**(7), 422–426 (1970)
4. Bonawitz, K., et al.: Practical secure aggregation for privacy-preserving machine learning. In: ACM CCS 2017 (2017)
5. Borisov, N., Danezis, G., Goldberg, I.: DP5: a private presence service. Proc. Priv. Enhancing Technol. **2015**(2), 4–24 (2015)
6. Chen, W., Popa, R.A.: Metal: a metadata-hiding file-sharing system. In: NDSS 2020 (2020)
7. Cheng, R., et al.: Ekiden: a platform for confidentiality-preserving, trustworthy, and performant smart contracts. In: IEEE EuroS&P 2019 (2019)
8. Christidis, K., Devetsikiotis, M.: Blockchains and smart contracts for the Internet of Things. IEEE Access **4**, 2292–2303 (2016)
9. European Union Commission: General data protection regulation (EU). Off. J. Eur. Union (OJ) **59**(1–88), 294 (2016)
10. Corrigan-Gibbs, H., Boneh, D., Mazières, D.: Riposte: an anonymous messaging system handling millions of users. In: IEEE S&P 2015 (2015)
11. Cui, H., et al.: PPSB: an open and flexible platform for privacy-preserving safe browsing. IEEE Trans. Dependable Secure Comput. **18**(4), 1762–1778 (2019)
12. Dingledine, R., Mathewson, N., Syverson, P.: Tor: the second-generation onion router. Technical report, Naval Research Lab, Washington DC (2004)
13. Dong, C., Chen, L., Wen, Z.: When private set intersection meets big data: an efficient and scalable protocol. In: ACM CCS 2013 (2013)
14. Dropbox: Dropbox Business Security: A Dropbox Whitepaper (2019). https://www.dropbox.com/static/business/resources/Security_Whitepaper.pdf
15. DropSecure: Enabling True File Transfer Security: How DropSecure Safeguards Your Confidential Data (2019). https://dropsecure.com/public/whitepaper/DropSecure_Whitepaper_web.pdf
16. Eskandarian, S., et al.: Fidelius: protecting user secrets from compromised browsers. In: IEEE S&P 2019 (2019)
17. Fitzpatrick, K.: Password Protect Files with Digify Passkey Encryption (2019). https://help.digify.com/en/articles/747136-password-protect-files-with-digify-passkey-encryption
18. Gmail: Send & Open Confidential Emails (2019). https://support.google.com/mail/answer/7674059
19. GnuPG: GnuPG - The Universal Crypto Engine (2017). https://gnupg.org/software/index.html
20. He, W., Akhawe, D., Jain, S., Shi, E., Song, D.: ShadowCrypt: encrypted web applications for everyone. In: ACM CCS 2014 (2014)
21. Hu, Y., Kumar, S., Popa, R.A.: Ghostor: toward a secure data-sharing system from decentralized trust. In: USENIX NSDI 2020 (2020)
22. Lazar, D., Zeldovich, N.: Alpenhorn: bootstrapping secure communication without leaking metadata. In: USENIX OSDI 2016 (2016)
23. Mayer, J., Mutchler, P., Mitchell, J.C.: Evaluating the privacy properties of telephone metadata. Proc. Natl. Acad. Sci. **113**(20), 5536–5541 (2016)

24. McMillan, R., Knutson, R.: Yahoo Triples Estimate of Breached Accounts to 3 Billion (2017). https://www.wsj.com/articles/yahoo-triples-estimate-of-breached-accounts-to-3-billion-1507062804
25. Min, H.: Blockchain technology for enhancing supply chain resilience. Bus. Horiz. **62**(1), 35–45 (2019)
26. Murnane, K.: Speedtest Global IndexHere's How Internet Speeds Fared for the World's Fastest and Largest Countries in 2018 (2018). https://www.speedtest.net/global-indexforbes.com/sites/kevinmurnane/2018/12/11/heres-how-internet-speeds-fared-for-the-worlds-fastest-and-largest-countries-in-2018/#3a2349984976
27. Nguyen, N.: Introducing Firefox Send, Providing Free File Transfers while Keeping your Personal Information Private (2019). https://blog.mozilla.org/blog/2019/03/12/introducing-firefox-send-providing-free-file-transfers-while-keeping-your-personal-information-private/
28. OpenPGP: Technical Standard (2016). https://www.openpgp.org/about/standard/
29. Primault, V., Lampos, V., Cox, I., De Cristofaro, E.: Privacy-preserving crowd-sourcing of web searches with private data donor. In: WWW 2019 (2019)
30. Proton AG Technologies: How Safe is Proton Mail? Security Features Explained (2019). https://proton.me/mail/security
31. Rösler, P., Mainka, C., Schwenk, J.: More is less: on the end-to-end security of group chats in signal, WhatsApp, and Threema. In: IEEE EuroS&P 2018 (2018)
32. Rusbridger, A.: The Snowden leaks and the public. The New York Review (2013)
33. Schneier, B.: Data and Goliath: The Hidden Battles to Collect Your Data and Control Your World. WW Norton & Company (2015)
34. SendSafely: Powerful Security That's Simple to Use (2019). https://www.sendsafely.com/howitworks/
35. Shamir, A.: How to share a secret. Commun. ACM **22**(11), 612–613 (1979)
36. Silverstein, J.: Hundreds of Millions of Facebook User Records Were Exposed on Amazon Cloud Server (2019). https://www.cbsnews.com/news/millions-facebook-user-records-exposed-amazon-cloud-server/
37. Snapchat: Snapchat Support (2019). https://support.snapchat.com/
38. SSH Communications Security Inc.: SFTP: A SSH Secure File Transfer Protocol (2019). https://www.ssh.com/ssh/sftp/
39. Szabo, N.: Formalizing and Securing Relationships on Public Networks (1997). https://ojphi.org/ojs/index.php/fm/article/view/548/469
40. Telegram: What is a Secret Chat in Telegram (2019). https://telegramguide.com/secret-chat-telegram/
41. de la Torre, L.: A Guide to the California Consumer Privacy Act of 2018. Available at SSRN 3275571 (2018)
42. Tutanota: Secure Emails at the Tip of Your Finger (2019). https://tutanota.com/security
43. Tyagi, N., Gilad, Y., Leung, D., Zaharia, M., Zeldovich, N.: Stadium: a distributed metadata-private messaging system. In: ACM SoSP 2017 (2017)
44. Van Den Hooff, J., Lazar, D., Zaharia, M., Zeldovich, N.: Vuvuzela: scalable private messaging resistant to traffic analysis. In: ACM SoSP 2015 (2015)
45. WhatsApp: WhatsApp encryption overview: technical white paper (2017)
46. Wolinsky, D.I., Corrigan-Gibbs, H., Ford, B., Johnson, A.: Dissent in numbers: making strong anonymity scale. In: USENIX OSDI 2012 (2012)
47. Zgraggen, R.R.: Smart insurance contracts based on virtual currency: legal sources and chosen issues. In: IECC 2019 (2019)

EarlyCrow: Detecting APT Malware Command and Control over HTTP(S) Using Contextual Summaries

Almuthanna Alageel[1,2](✉) and Sergio Maffeis[1]

[1] Department of Computing, Imperial College London, London, UK
{a.alageel18,sergio.maffeis}@imperial.ac.uk
[2] National Center for Cybersecurity, King Abdulaziz City for Science and Technology, Riyadh, Saudi Arabia

Abstract. Advanced Persistent Threats (APTs) are among the most sophisticated threats facing critical organizations worldwide. APTs employ specific tactics, techniques, and procedures (TTPs) which make them difficult to detect in comparison to frequent and aggressive attacks. In fact, current network intrusion detection systems struggle to detect APTs communications, allowing such threats to persist unnoticed on victims' machines for months or even years.

In this paper, we present EarlyCrow, an approach to detect APT malware command and control over HTTP(S) using *contextual summaries.* The design of EarlyCrow is informed by a novel threat model focused on TTPs present in traffic generated by tools recently used as part of APT campaigns. The threat model highlights the importance of the context around the malicious connections, and suggests traffic attributes which help APT detection. EarlyCrow defines a novel multipurpose network flow format called PairFlow, which is leveraged to build the contextual summary of a PCAP capture, representing key behavioral, statistical and protocol information relevant to APT TTPs. We evaluate the effectiveness of EarlyCrow on unseen APTs obtaining a headline macro average F1-score of 93.02% with FPR of 0.74%.

Keywords: Advanced persistent threats · Network intrusion detection · Command and control

1 Introduction

Advanced Persistent Threats (APTs) are known to be the most sophisticated long-term attack campaigns targeting highly protective organizations [2]. APTs are generally aware of internal defenses related to their target [42], and usually do not send spam, participate in DDoS attacks, or aggressively propagate to other hosts to spread infections at scale [22].

APT malware are those malicious tools known to be used by APT campaigns. The most common is the Remote Access Trojan (RAT), typically composed of a builder, stub, and controller. The builder initiates a new instance

W. Susilo et al. (Eds.): ISC 2022, LNCS 13640, pp. 290–316, 2022.
https://doi.org/10.1007/978-3-031-22390-7_18

stub upon the infection. The stub runs on the victim machine and contains a hard-coded Fully Qualified Domain Name (FQDN) or IP to communicate to the RAT controller, which resides on the Command and Control (C&C) server [41]. Rootkits, spyware, downloaders, and keyloggers may also be part of an APT campaign. APT malware such as DarkComet includes these functions in one ecosystem [22], which may capture the audio, explore files and drop malicious tools through visiting URLs [23]. Griffon, used by FIN 7, can gather information, load Meterpreter, and take screenshots [28]. Hutchins et al. [31] propose a kill chain to defend against APTs at various stages, including reconnaissance, weaponization, delivery, exploitation, installation, and C&C. These stages normally iterate over a long time [35]. In order to limit the damage inflicted by an APT, it is essential to detect them at an early stage, and in particular as they establish communication with the C&C. By inspecting honeypot data, we find that the communication to C&C starts immediately once the machine is infected. Several automated tasks are performed, including establishing *fallback channels* and downloading further payloads from the C&C server. These activities intentionally behave as legitimate web browser activities, attempting to evade Network Intrusion Detection Systems (NIDSs).

In Sect. 2, we introduce the first public measurement study of APT malware C&C communication to investigate the deployed TTPs. We leverage our measurements to identify the features necessary to recognize such TTPs at the network level, and compare them with existing features from the literature. We found that the use of evasive TTPs leads to significant overlap with legitimate behavior, confusing the decision boundaries based on some known features. Based on this analysis, we build EarlyCrow, a tool to detect APT activity in network traffic. EarlyCrow generates four sets of data focused on connections, hosts, destinations, and URLs. Features from these sets are grouped to form a ContextualSummary. The ContextualSummary has multidimensional features that help in building more informative random forest trees used for classification as described in Sect. 3. We evaluate EarlyCrow on traffic from APT malware excluded from the measurement study and training set in order to test generalization and mimic a real-world scenario (Sect. 4). Fresh malware samples are also investigated to confirm the feature importance identified by our measurement study on the training set. We also investigate how the performance of EarlyCrow is affected by different deployment scenarios, where it has visibility on HTTP traffic or where it can only observe opaque HTTPS traffic.

In summary, our main contributions are:

- We present an evidence-based analysis of various TTPs used by APTs. These TTPs are known to be used to evade NIDS [14]. We also introduce a measurement study on various APT malware over popular and novel features to capture TTPs usage.

- We implement EarlyCrow[1], a tool to detect evasive malicious communication over HTTP(S). EarlyCrow focuses primarily on APTs but is also effective against stealthy botnets.
- We evaluate the classification performance of new and existing features for malicious traffic detection under different scenarios distinguishing ATP, botnet, and legitimate traffic.

2 Threat Model

Defining a relevant threat model, and focusing on a narrow set of attacks are recommended best practices when proposing a novel NIDS [43]. There are several ways to approach threat modeling for APTs at the network level. We consider four popular cases of APT that involve HTTP(S) traffic, each of which deploys at least one C&C TTP. In Case I, the infected machine contains APT malware with a hard-coded FQDN. The malware issues a DNS query to resolve the FQDN to an IP address. The subsequent communication to the C&C server can be via HTTP or HTTPS. After that, the malware may initiate a *fallback channel*, another popular TTP used by APTs [19], using either of the strategies described in Cases I–IV, only this time no longer for the initial communication. In Case II, the APT malware connects to a URL whose domain component is a hard-coded IP address, in order to bypass malicious domain detectors, and its fallback channel can be established using the *DNS over HTTPS* (DoH) TTP [21], as in CobaltStrike [33], which is used by SUNBURST [24]. Case III is similar to Case I in using a hard-coded FQDN, but the subsequent communication uses raw TCP rather than HTTP during the malicious operation. Case IV is similar to Case II in using direct IP without DNS resolution, but then uses raw TCP communication as in Case III. Both Case III and IV may use fallback channel with various TTPs, although not including those related to HTTP(S).

Additional TTPs introduced by MITRE and relevant to APTs can be combined with the use of a fallback channel: *web protocol* [13] where an adversary may use HTTP to avoid network filtering and mimic legitimate and expected connections, *non-application protocols* [20] such as Raw TCP, UDP or ICMP, *encrypted channel* [18] to hide C&C malicious content, *fast flux* [17] is a sub-technique of *dynamic resolution* to obtain different IPs for the same FQDN, and *data obfuscation through protocol impersonation* [15] to impersonate legitimate use of HTTP or to mimic a trustworthy entity using a fake SSL/TLS certificate.

This paper focuses on Case I and II, where at least one malicious HTTP(S) connection exists between the infected host and C&C server. Other cases are challenging to detect with low False Positive Rate (FPR) at the network level only, and require additional host-level logs.

2.1 TTP Relevant Data

The TTPs considered here are a group of host and network-level techniques used by APTs to evade Host and Network IDSs. To track TTPs at the network level,

[1] EarlyCrow code, datasets, and experiments are publicly available at [1].

an investigator needs to collect "static" Indicators of Compromise (IoCs) for known APTs, or analyze sequences of network packets and assess the likelihood of specific TTPs manifested by the traffic behavior. Security vendors publish IoCs of discovered APTs. Novel attacks can be discovered when suspicious TTPs are being observed, as for instance in the HTTP request and response behavior.

IoC-Like Data. APT campaigns dedicate one or more *FQDN(s)* to locate C&C servers. They may mimic the targeted organization interests, or use *dynamic resolution*, which is another TTP [16] used to communicate back to C&C servers [3,22]. The resolved FQDN holds at least one A resource record. Some APTs provide several A resource records to provide fallback channels for follow-up connections. *URLs* are known to be used as IoCs, and used in HTTP-based malware detection [7,34,38,40]. Some APT malware download an executable file or pass other malicious FQDNs, IPs, or configuration commands in URL parameters of subsequent requests. A typical URL structure includes FQDN, nested folders (which we will refer to as *depth*), filename, parameters and values with a delimiter (&) to separate between them and (=) to assign value to the parameter, and encoded strings which typically contain %-encoding.

Traffic Data. Although multiple traffic-based TTPs were used by APTs in the past, it is challenging to capture them by configuring NIDS with straightforward rules. For this reason, we need to consider the context where malicious packets are sent. First, we need to cover the details of HTTP requests and responses, and then the traffic behavior of all protocols used for the same flow. *HTTP request and response context* involves consecutive HTTP transactions composed of several requests and responses. A request is mainly characterized by the URL, method type (e.g. GET, POST) and User-Agent (UA). Response headers specify among other properties, the content type and status codes. To detect APT malware, we need to efficiently store that information between two endpoints in one flow and enable the NIDS to extract valuable statistics at the packet level.

Due to the stealthiness and low-profile operation of APTs, we also need to provide a way to investigate *Traffic Behavior*. This can be achieved by storing packets arrival times, their lengths and other related information. Such a summary needs to cover the control and data planes of TCP, UDP and ICMP packets. With this summary on data points, NIDS designers can catch APTs TTPs such as *fallback channel* and using *non-application protocols*. For instance, a host contacting three different destinations after only one DNS query can be a sign of infection by the fallback channel technique. Another example is the *non-application protocol* TTP, when the APT malware opens a legitimate looking HTTP connection which is followed by a sequence of malicious raw TCP packets.

2.2 Measurements

We provide several measurements taken on the training set summarized in Table 2 and described in Sect. 4. Since our objective is to detect APTs at the early stage, all measurements are observed during the first 15 min of each connection. In Sect. 4.2, we will investigate these measurements and other proposed features, to see if they generalize to unseen malware.

Traffic Statistical Measurements. Statistical end-to-end observations may highlight the evasive behavior of APTs compared to legitimate actors. The presence of a slight deviation may reflect malicious use of three TTPs, including *non-application protocols*, *data obfuscation through protocol impersonation* and *web protocol*. Since this study focuses on malicious HTTP(S) usage, we measure the HTTP packets ratio across all classes. Other related protocols are also measured, including raw TCP and DNS ratios. Legitimate connections show a positive linear relationship between DNS and HTTP packets (Fig. 1). With every additional page requested by a user, such packets are exchanged with a remote web server in order to fetch additional resources. For APTs, we notice that DNS ratios are half or less than for legitimate or botnets, respectively. 95.2% of APTs do not exceed a 0.19 DNS ratio, compared to 0.38 for legitimate and 0.46 for botnets.

Next, we focus on DNS requests and conclude that almost no malicious behavior exceeds the legitimate, except for Conficker botnets, which use Domain Generation Algorithms (DGAs). 84% of APT or botnet traffic issues 2 or 6 requests at most, while legitimate traffic can generate up to 18. Once a domain is resolved to one or more IPs, a typical APT avoids requesting another DNS for the rest of HTTP communication unless they plan to establish another *fallback channel*. Another useful feature is the raw TCP ratio, which helps detect the *non-application protocols* TTP: a high ratio indicates the adversary uses HTTP as camouflage while still heavily relying on raw TCP. It is extremely rare for an APT to have a raw TCP ratio lower than 48.84%, whereas we observed minimum ratios of 2% of legitimate, and 0% of botnets.

Since we focus on the early stage of connections originating from the victim side, we found that around 70.58% of APTs receive 3.35 times more data than they send to the remote server, compared to 1.45 and 0.75 for legitimate and botnets, respectively. This is consistent with the threat model in [3], where an adversary uploads more tools on the victim's machine at the beginning of an APT campaign to continue other operations such as lateral movement, unlike botnets which may show more data exfiltration behavior. We also examine the number of resumed connections. Legitimate HTTP usage typically increases the number of resumed connections, since shortly after a web resource is downloaded, the TCP connection is terminated with FIN. Upon clicking another link, even for the same website, a new TCP three-way handshake is initiated. We count that as a resumed connection. With a web caching service, the scenario remains similar, although the server is contacted via a proxy or content delivery network (CDN). While legitimate and botnets connections may easily be resumed up to 21 times, APTs tend to terminate less (roughly 50% less). It seems plausible that APTs avoid frequent connection termination and resumption to increase stealthiness.

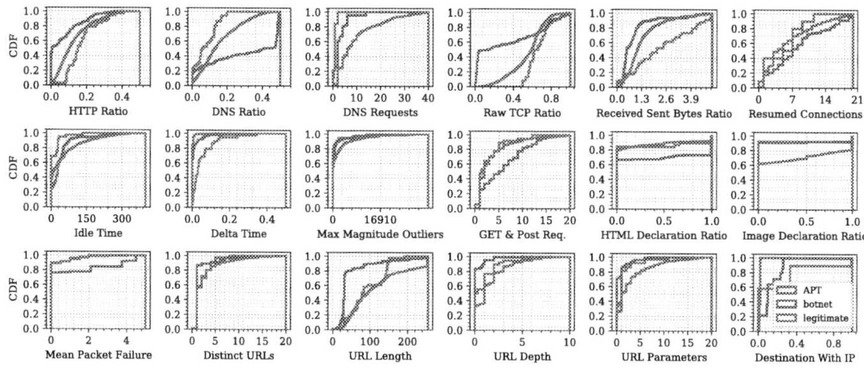

Fig. 1. Measurements for APT, botnets, and legitimate connections.

Time-Based Measurements. We measure *stealthiness and low profile* of APTs by monitoring time-based features. *Delta*, the packet inter-arrival time between a remote server and a host, is estimated based on the arrival time difference between packets, independently from their protocol. For 94.73% of cases, we found the mean delta time in seconds to be at most 23.5×10^{-2} for APTs, 6×10^{-2} for botnets and 0.5×10^{-2} for legitimate. Hence, APTs may act slower than botnets and legitimate by up to 4 and 47 times respectively.

A new metric, data packet exchange *idle time*, is proposed to measure the time difference between actual data packets. We found APTs idle time to be 3 and 6.57 times shorter than botnets and legitimate: 92% of cases have an idle time of at most 28, 84, and 184 s, respectively. Once APTs establish a communication channel, they send bursts of data packets (low idle time), then pause communications (high delta) until the next burst. We also measure the maximum magnitude of outliers which exceed the Simple Moving Average (SMA) with respect to the predefined bins described in Sect. 3.3. We found that for 84% of the cases, the maximum magnitude for APTs (0.338 KB) is half the one for botnets (0.676 KB), and 10% of the one for legitimate (3.33 KB). These three time-based features partially capture the *low and stealthy profile* of APTs compared to botnets or legitimate.

Remote Web Server. Analysis of contacted web servers may help identifying the *web protocol* and *fallback channel* TTPs. Typical web servers mostly adhere to best practices in setting up their HTTP configurations. APTs appear to be more professionally configured than botnets, but not as much as legitimate ones. For instance, the *packet failure* rate for legitimate servers and APTs (HTTP responses with status codes 4xx and 5xx) is relatively low. To be precise, 90% have at most one packet failure, while the botnets may receive as many as five. Total GET and POST requests are less similar. 92% of APTs and legitimates have 9 and 10 or less, respectively while the botnets have up to 14.

We also investigate the ratios of content types declarations. We focus on the ratios of HTML and images, since these are most frequently used in HTTP connections. 73% of APTs, legitimate and botnets declare HTML 2%, 2% and 98% of the time, so APT behavior in this case is similar to legitimate. However, due to the possible use of the *data obfuscation through protocol impersonation* TTP, we found that APTs and botnets are less likely to declare image type, which is not the case for web browsing activities. 70% of legitimate declare images 30% at most during a connection, while it is zero for both APTs and botnets.

Next, we measure the URL characteristics, due to their proven effectiveness for detecting malicious web servers. Measuring the distinct URLs accessed in a given network may highlight the rich number of web pages which is more likely to be legitimate [30,38]. We observe that APTs invest heavily in legitimate-looking pages, to evade NIDS that rely on URL-based features. For example, we find that 87% of botnets query only one URL, while legitimate and APTs query up to five and four, respectively. APTs have more resources than botnets in general. As depicted in Fig. 1, 90% of APTs have 3 nested folders (depth), close to legitimate, which is 4, while botnets have 1 at most. URL parameters differ even more: 87% of APTs and legitimate use 3 and 7, while botnets use only 1. Following that, URL length is determined by the length of FQDNs, depths, filenames, parameters, values, fragments, and strings. 90% of legitimate URL lengths are 249 or less, whereas APTs and botnets are up to 145 and 109. Finally, APTs deploy a fallback channel in several ways, as discussed in Sect. 2. We measure the number of HTTP(S) connections established to an IP without a previous domain resolution. 57.89% of APTs reached 32% of C&C with IP only, while it is 9% and 1% for botnets and legitimates. Therefore, it is unusual for legitimate to perform such behavior, while it is more common for APTs and occasional for botnets.

3 EarlyCrow

EarlyCrow detects malicious HTTP(S) connections, and in particular APT malware. In this section we discuss the architecture of EarlyCrow, and how the features used by EarlyCrow are extracted and updated.

3.1 Architecture Overview

EarlyCrow is composed of four main processes, as depicted in Fig. 2. First, it starts with buffering and dispatching using PairFlow (Fig. 2, ❶), which summarizes a PCAP into contextually relevant fields including packet behavior, domain and URL list, UA, status code, and content type for HTTP. After the PairFlow HTTP variant is generated, these flows are preprocessed for profile pivoting (Fig. 2, ❷) to generate three profiles: Host, Destination, and URL. Then, two types of feature extraction follow (PairFlow and profile features in Fig. 2, ❸) to form a ContextualSummary (Fig. 2, ❹) which is the input for a random forest classifier. When another PairFlow is received, it will follow the

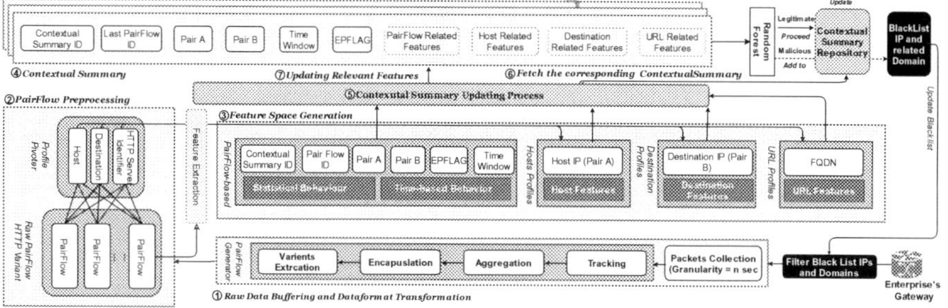

Fig. 2. Overview of the EarlyCrow architecture.

same workflow. A further step is required when the new PairFlow matches one of the previous ContextualSummary ID in the repository. The ContextualSummary updating process (Fig. 2, ❺) is responsible for updating the matched ContextualSummary to maintain the contextualization and reclassify again. The rest of this section discusses in detail the feature space generation and how the ContextualSummary is formed.

3.2 PairFlow

PairFlow is a proposed data format that allows the NIDS designer to quickly pivot flows into many profiles such as host, destination, and URL profiles. PairFlow data can also be used by detectors of malicious domains or IPs. Instead of detecting one flow according to the initiation and termination of TCP, protocol-based or time window, PairFlow digests all information to extract features later based on the whole context over time.

PairFlow receives raw PCAP data and stores these packets in a buffer until a time window of size t has passed. The buffer sends the current granular data with all the connections of a network during a time window, to the *Tracking* module to group unique pairs and label related packets. A unique pair refers to any (possibly bidirectional) connection observed between a host on the local network and a remote server. We take the *source* of the pair to be the local host, and the *destination* to be the remote server. Next, the *Aggregator* module adds a PairFlow ID and time window to the flow data. The Aggregator module is also responsible for marking packets according to their plane, extracting the domains and HTTP fields. Next, the *Encapsulation* module groups all these pieces of information contextually, so that all possible TTPs discussed in Sect. 2 can be analyzed later. Therefore, each pair of connections has a comprehensive description of their packets behavior (described in Sect. A.3), HTTP settings, accessed domains, and cipher suites setting. Finally, PairFlow outputs four additional JSON files which can be used by any external classifier. We only use the HTTP variant for EarlyCrow. The technical details for each component of PairFlow can be found in Appendix A.

3.3 PairFlow Features

EarlyCrow benefits from using the statistical features produced by PairFlow, which are presented in Appendix A and Table 5. It also extracts higher-level contextual features from the TCP and UDP planes.

Statistical Behavior. As we found in Sect. 2, where raw TCP ratio may reveal the *non-application protocols* TTP. We count the raw TCP ratio per PairFlow in addition to other protocols ratios such as DNS, which can also detect APTs malicious use of HTTP because it tends to request a domain resolution one time during a connection [3]. From Data Sub-Plane in Fig. 5, we calculate GET/POST requests and the fraction of status codes started with 1xx, 2xx, 3xx, 4xx, 5xx to identify the most salient behavior of such a connection. Using the control sub-plane, we count the termination of TCP connection FIN-ACK (0x11) during a PairFlow instead of the sequence of TCP handshaking, i.e., SYN, SYN-ACK, ACK (0x02, 0x12, 0x10) due to the lower computation cost. However, to exclude a typical HTTP flow (e.g., browsing sessions) and reduce false positives, we consider also the number of DNS requests during a given PairFlow, using the UDP plane. EarlyCrow calculates the number of declarations of content types and their ratios to the others in the data sub-plane. Examples of considered types include JavaScript, HTML, image, video, application, and text.

Time-Based Behavior. The challenge of time-based features is to identify APTs connections that operate at low-profile mode. First, we consider using a couple of time-based features from the PairFlow such as packet TTL, duration of the PairFlow, and delta packets inter-arrival time. We also measure the max/min/mean data packet exchange idle time using the data sub-plane, the difference between subsequent data packets' arrival time. During a typical web browsing session, there is little or no difference between delta packet inter-arrival time and data packet exchange idle time.

We propose additional time-based features that attempt to measure the stealthy behavior with time-series techniques. We present features based on the simple moving average (SMA). The purpose of the SMA is to average the data points over a time window of size t decided in advance, so that an analyst can identify when a data point is above or below such average. SMA_k can be described as follows: $\frac{1}{k}\sum_{i=n-k+1}^{n} p_i$, where p is the packet length, k is the number of previous data points in a time window, and n is the current data point. Since packets arrive asynchronously, in order to calculate an SMA we need to introduce a sampling rate such that packets arriving within two sampling events are combined together in a single point. For example, if the time window is one minute and we sample points every second then $k = 60$ and if we receive two packets of length respectively 128 and 32 between seconds 5 and 6, then $p_6 = 160$. After calculating the SMA, we can extract the number of outliers and their ratio and magnitude. Outliers are those points two times above the corresponding SMA_k. Therefore, we can capture the stealthy behavior of APTs, which has fewer outliers than legitimate and botnet traffic. However, it is also essential to find the number of packets below and above average. These features can capture the APTs that touch or slightly exceed the SMA, reflecting cautious operation.

3.4 Profiles Features

Profiles features are generated based on all PairFlows with longer time windows, for example lasting days, weeks, or even months. EarlyCrow queries the related information using a host IP, destination IP, and FQDN for the host, destination, and URL profiles, respectively. The purpose of the host profile is to identify whether that host has a sign of infection, such as discrepant information or a fallback channel. The destination profile may reflect those destinations that an enterprise can access and avoid some false positives. The URL profile helps identify the typical use of a given FQDN. FQDNs commonly accessed without parameters or values, especially with GET as method type, could signal the use of the *dynamic DNS* or *fast flux* technique to point to frequently changed IP addresses known to be used for APTs [3]. The URL profile helps pinpoint the malicious use of HTTP protocol from their past behavior. Nevertheless, APT cannot be easily detected based on such single features, so these will only contribute in part to the final classification.

Host Profile. The host profile aims to investigate the effect of infection on a machine behavior over $\hat{t}$ time, which should be longer than the selected granularity t time for PairFlow. Benign hosts should have specific characteristics in terms of resumed connections, DNS requests per flow, time difference of sequence connections, and type of UA used. When a host is infected with APT malware, its characteristics may move to another point further from the benign host centroid. For instance, it is suspicious for a host to initiate a connection by IP only, which is highly linked to a *fallback channel.* EarlyCrow investigates the number of resumed connections per flow for each host. Similarly, we extracted the DNS request per flow to identify a host with lower DNS requests than expected, which is also a sign of APTs using *dynamic resolution, DGA, and data obfuscation through protocol impersonation* TTPs.

In addition, we measure the Mean Time Difference of Sequenced Connections (MTDSC), which can help to identify *fallback channel.* MTDSC can be calculated as follows: $\frac{1}{n}\sum_{i=0}^{n} t_{i+1} - t_i$, where n is the number of new connections and t are their timestamps. The input timestamp should be the first packet sent or received from Control, UDP, or ICMP planes for any PairFlow, where the source is the same host. We also compute a ratio of connected destinations using IP only to those with FQDN. The feature can capture the APTs behavior of using DNS requests to locate the IP address of C&C; once the first channel is established, APT malware sends another IP as a fallback channel and starts another three-way handshake. It can also indicate the malicious use of *DoH.* As pointed out in Sect. 2, any client that uses HTTP will have an optional UA in a request packet, and it could be a (non-)browser, malicious string, or just an empty. Similar to [38], we extract several features for UA, including the distinct number of UAs and their popularity among an enterprise.

Destination Profile. The destination profile analyzes the servers contacted by internal hosts to find the characteristics of the provided services. We are interested in determining if it is normal for a destination to have fewer/more DNS requests, short/long data packet exchange idle times, high/low packet failure rates, sending/receiving dominant, and high/low resumed connections.

For instance, we measure the number of DNS requests per flow for a destination to investigate if such destination is using *dynamic resolution, DGA or data obfuscation through protocol impersonation* TTPs. An APT destination tends to have fewer DNS requests than usual. Once the domain is resolved and TCP establishment has been completed, it is rare to request more DNS packets. The legitimate use of HTTP(S) is to query the DNS packet every time they visit each page. Therefore, the number of DNS requests is directly proportional to HTTP packets. It is also essential to measure the destination data packet exchange idle time to identify legitimate web servers with a reasonable time to be idle for browsing. Again, the data packet exchange idle time here focuses only on the meantime of zero data exchange packets from a destination point of view without considering the control ones.

As pointed out in Sect. 2, some APTs use *protocol impersonation* such as HTTP as a camouflage to communicate with C&C. Thus, identifying the packet failure for each destination can explain if the failure comes from the destination itself or the PairFlow in Sect. 3.3. The objective is to find if a destination mimics web browsing activities while mainly communicating with the victims through raw TCP as *non-application protocol.* Another important aspect for each destination is calculating the number of resumed connections. Browsing behavior has frequently more resumed connections than the APT ones as we presented in our measurement study (Sect. 2.2). Finally, we observe the number of hosts connected to each destination. Popular web servers and botnets destinations are routinely contacted by a considerable number of hosts. In contrast, APTs typically infect as few as possible hosts, hence receiving few connections to their destinations.

URL Profile. We present URL-based features which are separated from those in the destination profile, as many FQDN-based URLs share the same IP or vice versa. The URL profile summarizes the standard behavior of resources and the traffic statistics for each FQDN or IP-based URL. We count here how many URLs are reached during a connection and how many are distinct. A malicious C&C server typically has fewer than a legitimate one (Sect. 1).

We also check if a URL has a query string, filename, and whether it has an executable extension, then calculate the fraction of the number of each field compared to the distinct number of URLs. A legitimate URL is likely to possess a filename with a variety of extensions. Other statistical features, i.e., Min/Max/Mean, are also calculated on URL length, depth, number of parameters, values, and fragments.

Table 1. EarlyCrow features. Note that features reused from the literature are computed from PairFlow data rather than from other data formats.

ID	Feature	New?	ID	Feature	New?
		I. PairFlow features			
1	Total bytes	[7,8,46]	28–31	Number and ratio below and above average	✓
2	Sent/received ratio	[7,8,38,46]	32–33	Number and ratio outliers	✓
3–9	Ratio of raw TCP, raw UDP, ICMP, DNS, HTTP, TLS and SSL packets	✓	34–37	Outliers magnitude Max/Min/ Mean/SD	✓
10–13	Ratio of HTTP response packets with 2xx, 3xx, 4xx, 5xx	[38]	38–40	Data packet exchange idle time Max/Min/Mean	✓
14–15	Ratio of frequent GET and POST	[38,40]	41	Active duration	✓
16–19	Content length total/Max/ Min/Median	✓	42–45	Packet TTL Max/Min/Mean/SD	✓
20–26	Ratio of content type Javascript, HTML, Image, Video, App, Text, and Empty	[38]	46–49	Delta packets interarrival time Max/ Min/Mean/SD	Similar to [7]
27	Number of resumed connections	✓	50	Number of DNS request	✓
		II. Host profile features			
51–53	Max/Min/Mean time difference of sequenced connections	✓	59	Distinct UAs per host	✓
54	Ratio of connected destination IP only to FQDN	✓	60	Inverse average of UA popularity	[39]
55–57	Max/Min/Mean of resumed connections per flow for a host	✓	61–62	Fraction of UA 1, and 5	[39]
58	Number of DNS request per flow for a host	✓	63	Ratio of UAs	[39]
		II. Destination profile features			
64	Number of hosts connected to destination	[39]	72	Number of distinct URLs associated to a destination	✓
65–67	Destination received/sent Max/ Min/Avg	✓	73–75	Destination Max/Min/Mean packets failure	✓
68–70	Destination data packet exchange idle time Max/Min/Mean	✓	76–81	Max/Min/Mean number and ratio of DNS request per flow for a destination	✓
71	Number of resumed connections per flow for a destination	✓			
		II. URL profile features			
82	Fraction of URLs filename	[38]	94–96	URLs values Max/Min/Mean	[7,38,40]
83	Fraction of URLs filename exe	✓	97–99	URLs fragments Max/Min/Mean	[38]
84	Number of distinct extensions	[38]	100	Fraction of query	[38]
85–87	URLs length Max/Min/Mean	[7,30,38,40]	101	Number of strings	✓
88–90	URLs depth Max/Min/Mean	[7,38,40]	102	Number of URLs and distinct ones	[32]
91–93	URLs parameters Max/Min/Mean	[7,30,38,40]			

3.5 ContextualSummary

When all features are extracted for a received PairFlow and profile-based features are prepared, the ContextualSummary module collects these features in one bundle to be dispatched to the classifier. When a new PairFlow is received, EarlyCrow checks the ContextualSummary repository to identify if the pair had been already processed in the past. If so, the PairFlow will be processed as described in the previous sections. Then, it will be dispatched to the updating process module to combine the new flow with the previous ones as described in the next section. The purpose is to track the same connection over time to catch malicious behavior. For example, if a malicious actor bypasses EarlyCrow for the first flow, it will be tracked over time until it gets blocked. Indicators associated to positive detections may stay in the ContextualSum-

MARY repository and the blacklists for training the classifier. In Table 1, we summarize all features included in CONTEXTUALSUMMARY.

3.6 CONTEXTUALSUMMARY Updating Process

While PAIRFLOWs are stored in a repository, the CONTEXTUALSUMMARY gets updated over time, using different rules for Host, Destination, and URL Profiles. If an incoming PAIRFLOW has no associated CONTEXTUALSUMMARY (Fig. 2, ❻), a new one is created. Otherwise the new PAIRFLOW is considered for feature extraction, causing an update of the corresponding features of the associated CONTEXTUALSUMMARY (Fig. 2, ❼). The time window is expanded with the new PAIRFLOW to describe the overall time window covered by the CONTEXTUALSUMMARY. However, updating profile-based features could cause higher time complexity because these profiles are to be updated for every different CONTEXTUALSUMMARY. Therefore, new profile-based features are recalculated every $\hat{t}$ time, such that $\hat{t} > t$, where t is the selected granularity for EARLYCROW. For instance, we can configure $\hat{t}$ at 15 min in our experimental settings, which is higher than t by 50% if t at 10 min.

EARLYCROW considers different methods to update features according to their data type. Numerical features are updated by using a weighted average. As shown in Fig. 2, each CONTEXTUALSUMMARY stores the last PAIRFLOW ID as a counter of previous ones to be used for the weighted average formula. EPFLAG-based features, Boolean data types, are updated with OR operation with an incoming one to summarize the overall protocol used during CONTEXTUALSUMMARY. For instance, APTs often have the DNS packets at the first PAIRFLOW, but not the subsequent one, as we discussed in Sect. 2. Therefore, updating the CONTEXTUALSUMMARY does not reset EPFLAG for the DNS. For Host-Profile features, strings of UA are stored to accurately extract other related UA, such as the number of distinct UAs which cannot be updated without having access to their strings.

4 Evaluation

This section evaluates EARLYCROW in a standard setting to investigate how our system performs against APTs and botnets. We evaluate EARLYCROW performance on the three datasets described below. The same experiments are performed on a baseline, inspired by MADE [38], which is a NIDS detecting C&C used by botnets, ransomware, and APTs. Since we assume EARLYCROW to run in parallel with a malicious-domain detector, we omit domain-related features, which would also not be relevant for the considerable portion of traffic conforming to the Case II pattern of Sect. 2.

4.1 Datasets

APT malware attacks a few targets in discontinued time-frames spanning months or years, unlike other malware and common attacks. Therefore, the chance of

Table 2. Dataset characteristics used for measurements (training set) and for unseen malware evaluation (testing set).

Label	Set	Malware families
Malicious (567,090 packets)	Training	Bitsadmin (0.09%), Carbank (0.05%), Conficker (27.56%), Mivast&Sakula (0.93%), NanoCore (0.13%), njRAT (28.45%), PlugX (0.11%), Remcos (0.87%), Sogou (3.65%), Virut (9.59%), Zebrocy (0.98%),
	Testing (unseen)	Ammyy (1.01%), ChChes (0.13%), CobaltStrike (0.39%), Dridex (0.23%), Emotet (0.02%), Empire (1.70%), FlawedAmmy (0.24%), ImminentMonitor (11.27%), MagicHound (0.40%), OnionDuke (0.14%), PoisonIvy (0.25%), Ramnit (0.21%), StrongPity (11.38%), Zeus (0.04%)
Legitimate (766,641 packets)		Training: 70%, Testing: 30%

finding a real network infected with various APT campaigns is unrealistic. We resort to raw PCAP captures from two different honeypot networks, each of which includes legitimate, APTs and botnets C&C connections (Table 2). These APTs are often temporarily inactive. Due to this, we run them during multiple time windows (April 2020–January 2021, October–November 2019) until each campaign's activities are resumed, and their command and control are activated.

APTraces. We run different active malware using Any.Run[2] sandbox machines to generate PCAP files. These malware families are known to be used by 48 APT campaigns, and they were active and tied to an APT campaign at the time of the capture. These include RATs (*njRAT, Imminent Monitor, Cross-RAT, Mivast & Sakula, NanoCore, PlugX, PoisonIvy*) and trojans (*Empire, OnionDuke, MiniDuke, Remcos, StrongPity, Zebrocy*). We also consider legitimate connections from the same sandbox to avoid data bias based on the victim machine, configuration settings, or temporal bias [5] against legitimate.

Malware Capture Facility Project (MCFP). The MCFP[3] includes malware used in APTs such as (*Magic Hound and Cobalt*), admin tools (*Ammyy*), and RATs (*njRAT*). We also add botnets captures that use HTTP(S) for C&C communication (*Conficker, Dridex, Emotet, Ramnit, Sogou, Virut, Zeus*) and normal traffic (CTU-Normal-12, 20–22). After PairFlow compiles the PCAPs and generates HTTP variant files, we build three combined datasets: APTs vs. Legitimate, botnets vs. Legitimate, and Malicious (APTs or botnets) vs. Legitimate.

4.2 Classification Performance

Classifiers are evaluated in two modes. First, HTTP-Mode, which assumes the administrator connects the NIDS to a web proxy to decrypt HTTPS and accesses features such as UA, HTTP response codes, content type, and URL. Second,

[2] https://any.run.
[3] https://www.stratosphereips.org/datasets-overview.

Table 3. Classification performance.

Classifier name	Known malware						Unseen malware					
	FPR	Prec.	Recall	Acc.	$F1$	$mF1$	FPR	Prec.	Recall	Acc.	$F1$	$mF1$
I. Dataset: APTs vs. Legitimate												
EarlyCrow	0.40	94.20	93.69	99.17	99.17	93.89	0.74	94.48	91.67	98.11	98.08	93.02
Baseline	0.49	92.4	89.09	98.75	98.73	90.45	0.00	98.04	75.00	96.22	95.63	82.33
EarlyCrow-HTTPS	0.51	92.85	93.18	99.03	99.03	92.79	0.74	94.68	92.81	98.28	98.26	93.72
Baseline-HTTPS	0.72	82.90	68.96	97.19	96.72	73.18	0.00	96.70	56.82	93.47	91.10	60.29
II. Dataset: Botnets vs. Legitimate												
EarlyCrow	0.48	96.49	95.40	98.92	98.91	95.90	0.19	96.77	92.01	99.26	99.24	94.25
Baseline	0.57	94.64	86.92	97.61	97.49	90.24	0.19	95.08	78.85	98.35	98.16	85.06
EarlyCrow-HTTPS	0.42	96.79	95.02	98.92	98.90	95.84	0.19	95.49	81.48	98.53	98.40	87.12
Baseline-HTTPS	0.96	90.73	80.76	96.39	96.14	84.79	0.00	48.25	50.00	96.51	94.79	49.11
III. Dataset: Malicious vs. Legitimate												
EarlyCrow	0.86	95.41	94.79	98.29	98.29	95.06	0.93	94.77	91.60	97.51	97.46	93.11
Baseline	0.93	93.76	88.20	96.97	96.86	90.68	0.19	95.89	76.10	94.85	94.15	82.62
EarlyCrow-HTTPS	0.93	95.07	94.76	98.23	98.23	94.89	0.93	94.27	89.22	97.01	96.92	91.54
Baseline-HTTPS	0.95	91.21	78.66	95.13	94.689	83.47	0.00	95.22	54.76	90.53	86.86	56.18

HTTPS-Mode, where the administrator places the NIDS at the network edge without deciphering HTTPS. Because of imbalanced classes of APT (3.9%) and botnet (8.3%) compared to legitimate, we focus on macro average F1-score ($mF1$) in Table 3.

Known Malware. We randomly split the training and testing sets ten times. Then, we take the average performance under two constraints. First, the malware should be presented in both sets. Second, the infected hosts and the destination C&C server should be unique and not leaked from training to testing. EarlyCrow obtains the best performance with $mF1$ of 93.89%, 95.9%, and 95.06% for the three datasets. Even in HTTPS mode, which cannot take advantage of plaintext HTTP features such as headers or URL details, EarlyCrow still outperforms the baseline on both three tasks, scoring 92.79%, 95.84%, and 94.89% respectively. Note that EarlyCrow can operate almost similar on both modes on known malware. However, we will investigate that on unseen malware.

Unseen Malware. We train our classifiers on the training set that used for our measurement study. Then we evaluate the performance against unseen malware described in Table 2. EarlyCrow obtains the best performance with $mF1$ of 93.02%, 94.25%, and 93.11% for the three datasets. On all three tasks in HTTPS mode, EarlyCrow surpasses the baseline, achieving 93.72%, 87.12%, and 91.54%. For EarlyCrow, the performance loss between known and unseen is marginally low (1.96% of $mF1$) in the third dataset, while the baseline suffers a loss of 8.04%.

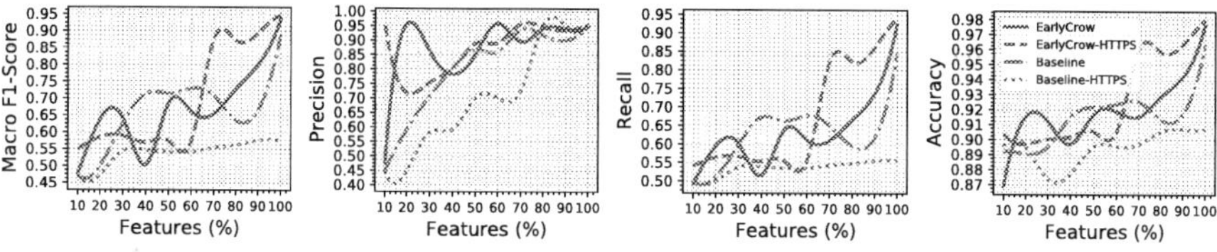

Fig. 3. Effect of using only the top % of features.

4.3 Discussion

We limit our discussion to the results of *unseen malware* on the third dataset presented in Table 2, which evaluates the generalization of EARLYCROW to mimic the real-world environment.

Features Diversity. The detection of APTs necessitates a spread of features, as presented in Sect. 2. In Fig. 3, we show the extent to which additional features affect the performance of the various classifiers. The first 10% of features for EARLYCROW show rapid improvements in terms of precision but with poor recall. Also, stronger features between 48% and 62% can improve the performance of *mF*1 up to 92.26% for EARLYCROW-HTTPS. Adding more features afterward increases the detection rate, enabling more unseen APTs to be detected. Furthermore, a system with diverse and strong features will require more time and resources to defeat as opposed to one that relies on a few particular features [47].

Top Features. We investigate the feature importance of the third dataset in HTTPS mode, which comprises APTs, botnets, and legitimate samples, because it is the one closest to a realistic scenario for APT hunting. Figure 4 illustrates the top features based on their information gain. MTDSC is an effective feature that reveals 82% of hosts infected with APTs and botnets spend up to 73.7 and 38.5 s, which are higher than 1.1 s of typical benign hosts, confirming the expected HTTP browsing. The longer time for APTs indicates using a *fallback channel*, which is generally established after a long time. Next, the average number of DNS requests for a host per connection is lower in APTs than botnets and legitimate, with 90% at most 2, 6, and 19, respectively. Interestingly, hosts infected with APTs have higher connections reaching further destinations by IP without *domain resolution* as *fallback channels*. This is consistent with our measurement study in Sect. 2.2. 70% of APTs use such an approach, with 88% or less for their connections, compared to only 1% for the legitimate.

While 60% of legitimate connections are repeated six times resumed or less, botnets are rarely disconnected, and APTs are weakly imitating legitimate *web protocol TTPs*, with two-thirds lower. Next, APTs and botnets are considerably slower than legitimate, with mean delta inter-arrival times at most 33.5×10^{-2}, 46×10^{-2}, and 0.5×10^{-2} seconds at 95% of their probability. We confirm that APTs tend to switch from HTTP to raw TCP for malicious operations representing *non-application protocols*. Within a PAIRFLOW, we find that 50%

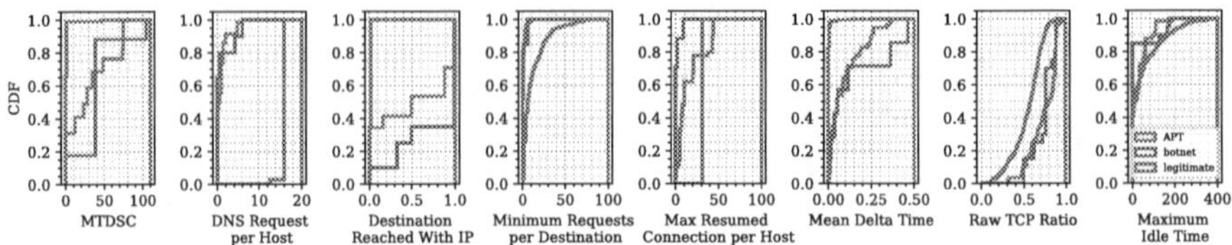

Fig. 4. Cumulative distribution of top features gains on the testing set for EarlyCrow-HTTPS.

of APTs rely on 81.09% (58.35% for legitimate) of the whole exchange packets on raw TCP, indicating the adversary use HTTP as camouflage while still relying on TCP for many tasks. Nonetheless, the APTs and botnets are faster regarding the difference between data packets. They tend to be shorter/faster than legitimate, where 90% of them take 104, 124, and 168 s, respectively.

Evasion Attacks. In Table 4, we break down the results of EarlyCrow-HTTPS on unseen malware. 92% of unseen malware are detected with at least one C&C communication, and 64% of different malware are fully detected. However, one server belonging to StrongPity is not detected in HTTPS. We found StrongPity is not using a fallback channel, and its measurement reflects a legitimate one. In HTTP mode, EarlyCrow managed to detect StrongPity because of its malicious URL characteristics, such as using `.exe` file extension, and lacks a rich web server (i.e., No. of URLs distinct) compared to the proportional data volume. Also, some C&C servers belonging to OnionDuke and Zeus managed to evade detection. These servers are established as fallback channels with minimum data transfers, which evade many features. Since the malware is detected on a specific machine, we recommend a SOC analysis to sanitize the victim machine from the malware to stop other possible C&C communications.

Table 4. Detection rate on unseen malware over HTTPS.

Malware	C&C servers	Detection (%)	Malware	C&C servers	Detection (%)
Ammyy	8	100	ImminentMonitor	4	75
ChChes	1	100	Magic-Hound	3	100
CobaltStrike	2	100	OnionDuke	6	33.34
Dridex	2	100	PoisonIvy	1	100
Emotet	13	53.84	Ramnit	2	100
Empire	5	100	StrongPity	1	0
FlawedAmmy	4	100	Zeus	3	33.34

4.4 Limitations

APT Campaigns. EarlyCrow is geared toward detecting the early stages of infection. Nevertheless, it is difficult to conclude which suspicious activities are due to advanced adversaries and which are due to mainstream malware variants. Hence, we recommend tracking APT campaigns and malware activities over a longer period of time on a live system. This could be done by deploying EarlyCrow on the network of several likely targets, such as a sovereign entity or large financial institution, over months and periodically reevaluating EarlyCrow reports against each APT campaign to drive further improvement. By maintaining our repository publicly accessible [1], we encourage collaboration with the open source and research communities to run EarlyCrow on their targeted networks and to share their findings for further improvements.

Adversarial Robustness. Previous work has studied adversarial attacks against deep learning based NIDS [12,26,27,36], and discussed robustness for traditional machine learning such as random forest [9,37,38]. Although EarlyCrow is motivated by the techniques used by APTs to evade NIDS, *Practical* and *Feature-space Attacks* [11,25] specifically targeting PairFlow fields and EarlyCrow features may still be possible. For instance, Random Interval-Time (RIT) [8,44] and Random Duplication (RD) [29] were used against botnets, and could be tested against APTs. The former generates adversarial samples by altering packets' arrival times, which APTs could easily do, although it may have less effect on lower volume traffic. The latter duplicates the number of packets randomly, and may be less useful to APTs, but still useful as a measure of robustness.

Practical and Feature-space Attacks [25] could also be considered. In a Practical Black-box Attack (PBA) the adversary knows what traffic features are selected by the classifiers, including in our case, the PairFlow fields from Table 5. Moreover, adversaries can access most features published in the past to adapt their traffic according to the targeted feature extraction to evade NIDS. We refer such assumption to Practical Gray-Box Attack (PGA) for those features used in the literature presented in Table 1. Another two attack configurations can be considered [11,25,48], including Feature-space Grey-box Attack (FGA), Feature-space Black-box Attack (FBA). FGA may attack all features produced by EarlyCrow, while the FBA is produced by the state of art baseline, i.e., reproducible Made and non-novel features in Table 1. However, there are several variations in finding the optimization of evasion attacks. We suggest to adopt variants of Euclidean norm [10,45] (l_p) for black-box configuration and free-range [49] for Gray-box.

Execution Time. EarlyCrow can speed up its execution by running its modules (of Fig. 2, ❸) in parallel using Hadoop, similar to [30], optimizing memory hierarchy, and pipelining the main processes (Fig. 2, ❶–❸). The current implementation aims to prove the concept and focuses on detection performance. Further investigations of how to improve and measure execution speed and memory footprint in a production environment are left for future work.

5 Related Work

There is very limited previous work on detecting APTs at the network level. Detecting C&C in general is the closest area. In our approach we test several features from the literature which can be relevant for APTs including URLs and UA features [32,38–40], traffic exchange bytes [7,8,38,46], HTTP content types [38,39], and GET and POST ratio [38,40]. Besides directly using such features, EarlyCrow pivots them into host, destination and URL profiles, and combines them in contextual summaries.

Some previous works focuses on detecting APTs in addition to other kinds of malicious communications [38,39]. Oprea et al. [39] propose a belief propagation (BP) algorithm to detect early-stage infection of APTs. They model enterprise communication using a bipartite graph with two vertices, hosts, and domains based on simulated attacks. Once the detector identifies a malicious remote host or domain based on several features, BP identifies communities of malicious domains with similar features that are part of the same attack campaign. Domain scores are calculated as a supervised linear regression weighted sum of features. As discussed in Sect. 4, APTs tend to infect a lower number of hosts than botnets. Therefore, EarlyCrow consider other features based on different TTPs discussed in Sect. 2.

EarlyCrow is closer to Made [38], which instead uses web proxy logs at the edge of an enterprise network to detect malicious C&C communications, including APTs. Made leverages features related to the communication, HTTP request, response and its content, URL, and UAs. These are used by a random forest classifier to assign a risk score for each connection. As discussed in Sect. 4, Made is not as effective on HTTPS traffic, which is nowadays harder to intercept and decrypt due to technical and legal requirements. In addition, EarlyCrow considers five other TTPs besides the *Web Application Protocol* TPP at the heart of Made.

ExeceScent [37] detects C&C domains by clustering incoming requests into five templates, including median URL path, URL query component, User-Agent, other headers, and destination network. These templates are used to estimate similarity scores to predefined Control Protocol Templates (CPT) centroids. However, this is open to evasion if an adversary copies the UA of the victim machine from the Windows Registry [9]. In addition, it is not possible to extract most HTTP header features when HTTPS is in use, which hinders the generalization process and may result in mixing APTs with legitimate ones in many clusters. A related approach [7] adopts similar features, only using histogram bins which also can be evaded using HTTPS.

BAYWATCH [30] is a filtering system to detect the beaconing of infected hosts. Universal and local whitelist are filtered, then beaconing can be detected using Fourier transform and Gaussian mixture model, awarding a high agglomerative hierarchical clustering score for strong periodicity. BAYWATCH filters URLs and domains that are likely to be legitimate. Unprocessed connections with all previous features are sent to a random forest for classification. BAYWATCH can be computationally expensive for only beaconing behavior, and many APTs also have non-beaconing connections. EarlyCrow detect malicious connections regardless of their pattern. Finally, Kitsune [36] adopts an ensemble of autoencoders, proving the efficiency of unsupervised deep learning to detect classic attacks such as ARP poisoning and SYN DoS, which are rarely used by APTs. As discussed in Sect. 1, we avoid using deep learning because of the scarce dataset representing various APTs TTPs, which is essential for deep learning models.

6 Conclusions

We presented a threat model for APTs which focuses on the TTPs used by adversaries to avoid existing NIDS. As part of our measurement study, we demonstrated the significant overlap between APT and legitimate behaviors, and clarified their characteristics. Taking this into account, we designed and implemented EarlyCrow, a tool which can detect APT malware network activities that are missed by current deployed defense mechanisms. Our results demonstrate the importance of using diverse features based on contextual fields to detect unseen APT malware. We recommend using EarlyCrow as an additional layer of defense, besides SIEM, Host Intrusion detectors (HIDS), and domain detectors. While EarlyCrow is motivated by the NIDS-avoiding behavior of APTs, adversarial attacks specifically targeting PairFlow fields and EarlyCrow features may still be possible. A study of adversarial defenses and their robustness, and deployment issues is left to future work.

A PairFlow

EarlyCrow defines a novel multipurpose network flow format called PairFlow, which is leveraged to build the contextual summary of a PCAP capture, representing key behavioral, statistical and protocol information relevant to APT TTPs. We discuss the details of each component in the following.

A.1 Tracking

Packets Retrieving. The tracking module identifies all unique pair connections on the network and filters out those using non-IP protocols (Fig. 5, ❶). For each unique pair connection, PairFlow tracks, bidirectionally, all packets related to a pair. These packets are designated with an initial Flow ID. The Flow ID holds unchanged for all packets during the same time window for a given pair connection. Each packet will maintain its individual index for the aggregation step later. Packets with the same Flow ID may also use different protocols. Therefore, each one has a one hot encoding flag called Encoding Protocol Flag (EPFLAG) used later for further filtering. These flags started with EPFLAG_Protocol, where a protocol is a subset of {TCP, UDP, DNS, ICMP, HTTP, SSL/TLS}.

DNS Requests and Responses. The tracked packets do not include DNS requests and responses, which are responsible for locating the IP address needed to establish a connection. That is due to the pair connection being between the host and the DNS server, which is different than the destination. Similar to [4], to track these DNS packets, a destination of the present pair will be used as a Local PTR to find all DNS response packets from the PCAP repository. Once found, the DNS response resource records will be used to find all related DNS requests. Now, any packets belonging to the pair connection are attached and sorted according to their arrival time. Those packets outside of time window are not included.

A.2 Aggregation

Header Generation. Besides the individual packet ID from the PCAP, every packet is also designated with a Flow ID composed of a ContextualSummary ID (CSID) and a PairFlow ID (PFID). The former is unique for the lifetime of a pair, while the latter is unique for a time window. Any packets from that PairFlow will always have the same Flow ID. To assign the PFID, the aggregation module will check the ContextualSummary repository to find if the pair has been processed in the past (Fig. 5, ❷). If so, the incoming PFID will be the last used PFID for the same pair and ContextualSummary ID, incremented by one. Otherwise, a new and unique ContextualSummary will be created, and the PFID will start with zero.

Packets Aggregation. The aggregator module creates a PairFlow to store PairFlow ID, sorted packet index, pair connection, time window, EPFlag, FQDNs, URL, UAs, SSL/TLS settings, and initial flow-based statistics. The initial flow-based statistics include the number of protocol-based packets (i.e., TCP, UDP, ICMP, HTTP, SSL/TLS, DNS packets), total (encrypted) bytes, total (encrypted) bytes sent/received. Time-based statistics include packet Time to Live (TTL) and delta packets interarrival time max/min/median and the flow duration at the same time window. Similar to [6], we separate TCP packets into data and control packets to be used later in the encapsulation process. Finally, preprocessed flows are dispatched to the encapsulation step for further processing.

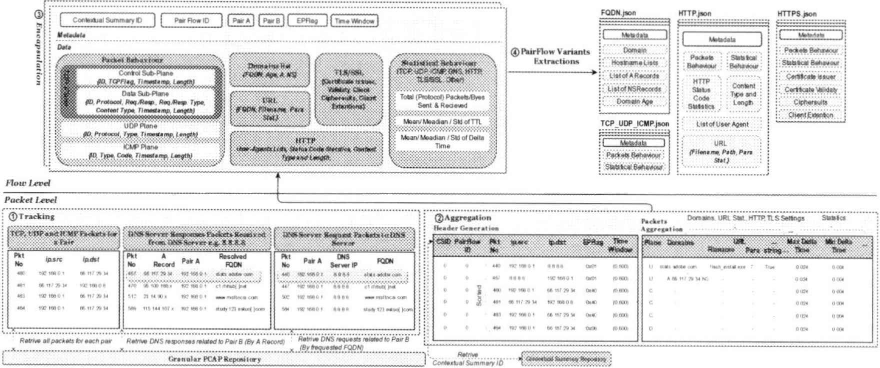

Fig. 5. Overview of the PAIRFLOW workflow.

A.3 Encapsulation

The encapsulation phase explicitly groups packet behavior, FQDN and URL, HTTP(S) and initial statistical behavior implicit in preprocessed flows in order to make contextual information readily available (Fig. 5, ❸). The data types involved include list of strings and tuples, Boolean and numeric fields, as shown in Table 5.

Packet Behavior. Packet Behavior encapsulates all packets according to their protocol type (TCP, UDP, and ICMP) in a list of tuples. The first element is the packet index for traceability of a given packet inside the original PCAP for further investigation.

The *TCP plane* involves the control and data sub-planes as shown in Fig. 5. Each packet in the data sub-plane holds protocol name, request/response and their types, content type, timestamp, and packet length for each packet. For example, an HTTP request packet can be described as (460854, 'HTTP', 'Request', 'GET', 'Empty Content', 1066.51, 383) and its response (460895, 'HTTP', 'Response', 200, 'text/javascript', 1066.86, 429). This helps the upper system work on time series traffic and monitor the anomaly for a given PAIRFLOW. Further packet-level statistical analysis such as counting GET/POST, HTTP response types, content analysis can be achieved as described in Sect. 3.3.

The control sub-plane provides the behavior of the initial connections before the data exchange begins, the TCP continuation, or the termination of the TCP connection. For example, when TCP establishes a connection with three-way handshaking, it will summarize SYN, SNYACK, ACK packets as follows (72095, '0x02', 215.73 s, 74), (72126, '0x12', 215.78 s, 70 B), (72127, '0x10', 215.78 s, 66 B). Then it will follow a stream of packets with TCP flag = 0x10 (ACK) until the connection is disconnected with flag FIN. This will be useful for analyzing any problem with time series or monitoring the discontinuity of such a PAIRFLOW as we can see in Sect. 3.4.

UDP plane records all UDP-based packets with protocol name, packet type, timestamp, and packet length. For example, if there are two packets for DNS which are request and response for a specific domain, they will be summarized as follows: (21160, 'DNS', 'DNS Request', 141.44 s, 75 B), (21219, 'DNS', 'DNS Response', 141.54, 547 B). *ICMP Plane* is similar to the *UDP plane* but for the ICMP only. However, the type and code are reporting ICMP settings for each packet. The plane can be helpful for any classifier detecting ICMP-based attacks.

FQDN and URL. As depicted in Fig. 5, *domain list* encapsulates all FQDNs related information in a list of tuples. Each tuple holds an FQDN, its A and NS resource records, and the domain age extracted from the WHOIS file. This helps malicious domain detectors, which often rely on FQDN strings, relative DNS zone, and WHOIS files. *URL* encapsulates each relevant element of URL during a connection in a tuple which includes FQDN, web page filename, the number of parameters, values and fragments, and whether it contains encoded strings or not.

HTTP(S). *HTTP* encapsulates HTTP-level information for a given connection, in particular, distinct HTTP server names, status codes, content types and UAs. *TLS Protocols* summarizes the security settings between a client and server. Cipher suites for both client and server are stored in a list. Cipher suites includes the key exchange/agreement (e.g. RSA, Elliptic-curve Diffie-Hellman (ECDH), Elliptic Curve Digital Signature Algorithm (ECDSA)), authentication (e.g. RSA), block/stream ciphers (e.g. AES, RC4) with their block cipher mode (e.g. CBC) and message authentication (e.g. MD5, SHA-x). Extension types are also listed for each connection which summarizes the cipher suite settings such as extended master secret, session tickets, and Elliptic Curve (EC) point formats. Supported Groups are also stored, known as the EC setting (e.g., secp256r1, secp521r1).

Initial Statistical Behavior. A few essential fields are important to be summarized statistically. We calculate max, min, mean packet TTL, delta packets interarrival time, and duration for a given PairFlow. We also calculate the total (encrypted) bytes and the ratio of sent/received (encrypted) bytes. Max, min, median of cipher suites bytes, and server and client extension bytes are also calculated. We also provide a statistical summary of individual protocol number of packets such as raw TCP, raw UDP, ICMP, DNS, HTTP, TLS, and SSL. We summarize statistical fields in Table 5.

Table 5. Summary of PairFlow data fields (B: Boolean, LS: List of Strings, LT: List of Tuples, N: Numerical).

ID	Field	Type	ID	Field	Type
I. Informative fields					
1	Flow ID	N	17	HTTP servers	LS
2–3	Source & destination	S	18	Status codes	LS
4	Packet data points	LT	19	Content type	LS
5	EPFLAG	S	20–21	Client and server ciphersuites	LS
6–12	EPFLAG raw TCP, raw UDP, ICMP, DNS, HTTP, TLS and SSL	B	22–23	Client and server extension types	LS
13	FQDN	LS	24–25	Client and server signature algorithms and hashes	LS
14	Resource records: type nameserver	LS	26–27	Client and server supported groups	LS
15	Resource records: type A	LS	28	ALPAN next protocol	LS
16	URL	LT	29	EC point format	LS
II. Statistics fields					
30	Total bytes	N	44–48	TTL Max/Min/Mean/SD	N
31–32	Total sent/received bytes	N	49–52	Delta packets interarrival time Max/Min/Mean/SD	N
33	Total encrypted bytes	N	53–56	Content length Total/Max/Min/Median	N
34–35	Total encrypted sent/received bytes	N	57–59	Client and server ciphersuites bytes Max/Min/Median	N
36–42	Number of raw TCP, raw UDP, ICMP, DNS, HTTP, TLS and SSL packets	N	60–62	Client and server extensions bytes Max/Min/Median	N
43	Duration	N			

A.4 Variants Extraction

PairFlow processing also exports four *variant* JSON files which can be used by any external classifier (Fig. 5, ❹). FQDN.json includes all domains and their hostname lists that have been accessed during a given PairFlow. In addition, resource records such as A, NS are also included and domain age extracted from WHOIS file, which appears to be useful for domain detection [3]. TCP-UDP-ICMP.json is dedicated for those classifiers use time-series for detection [6,30]. All three planes are presented here in addition to related statistical fields such as packet TTL and delta packets interarrival time. HTTP.json is employed for those interested to detect malicious HTTP connections [30,38]. Other classifiers may deploy HTTPS.json for detecting encrypted communications without deciphering the traffic [4]. A detailed study of the other variants is left for future work.

References

1. EarlyCrow github repository. https://github.com/ICL-ml4csec/EarlyCrowAPT
2. Ahmad, A., Webb, J., Desouza, K.C., Boorman, J.: Strategically-motivated advanced persistent threat: definition, process, tactics and a disinformation model of counterattack. Comput. Secur. **86**, 402–418 (2019)
3. Alageel, A., Maffeis, S.: Hawk-Eye: holistic detection of APT command and control domains. In: ACM SAC, pp. 1664–1673. ACM (2021)
4. Anderson, B., McGrew, D.: Identifying encrypted malware traffic with contextual flow data. In: ACM AISec, pp. 35–46 (2016)
5. Arp, D., et al.: Dos and don'ts of machine learning in computer security. In: USENIX Security (2022)
6. AsSadhan, B., Moura, J.M., Lapsley, D., Jones, C., Strayer, W.T.: Detecting botnets using command and control traffic. In: IEEE NCA, pp. 156–162. IEEE (2009)
7. Bartos, K., Sofka, M., Franc, V.: Optimized invariant representation of network traffic for detecting unseen malware variants. In: USENIX Security, pp. 807–822 (2016)
8. Bilge, L., Balzarotti, D., Robertson, W., Kirda, E., Kruegel, C.: Disclosure: detecting botnet command and control servers through large-scale netflow analysis. In: ACSAC, pp. 129–138 (2012)
9. Bortolameotti, R., et al.: DECANTeR: DEteCtion of anomalous outbouNd HTTP TRaffic by passive application fingerprinting. In: ACSAC, pp. 373–386 (2017)
10. Carlini, N., Wagner, D.: Towards evaluating the robustness of neural networks. In: IEEE S&P, pp. 39–57. IEEE (2017)
11. Clements, J., Yang, Y., Sharma, A., Hu, H., Lao, Y.: Rallying adversarial techniques against deep learning for network security. arXiv preprint arXiv:1903.11688 (2019)
12. Clements, J., Yang, Y., Sharma, A.A., Hu, H., Lao, Y.: Rallying adversarial techniques against deep learning for network security. In: IEEE SSCI, pp. 01–08. IEEE (2021)
13. The MITRE Corporation: Application layer protocol: web protocols. https://attack.mitre.org/techniques/T1071/001/. Accessed 18 Dec 2021
14. The MITRE Corporation: Command and control. https://attack.mitre.org/tactics/TA0011/. Accessed 18 Dec 2021
15. The MITRE Corporation: Data obfuscation: protocol impersonation. https://attack.mitre.org/techniques/T1001/003/. Accessed 18 Dec 2021
16. The MITRE Corporation: Dynamic DNS. https://attack.mitre.org/techniques/T1568/. Accessed 18 Dec 2021
17. The MITRE Corporation: Dynamic resolution: fast flux DNS. https://attack.mitre.org/techniques/T1568/001/. Accessed 18 Dec 2021
18. The MITRE Corporation: Encrypted channel. https://attack.mitre.org/techniques/T1573/. Accessed 18 Dec 2021
19. The MITRE Corporation: Fallback channel TTP. https://attack.mitre.org/techniques/T1008/. Accessed 18 Dec 2021
20. The MITRE Corporation: Non-application layer protocol. https://attack.mitre.org/techniques/T1095/. Accessed 18 Dec 2021
21. The MITRE Corporation: Protocol tunneling. https://attack.mitre.org/techniques/T1572/. Accessed 18 Dec 2021
22. Farinholt, B., Rezaeirad, M., McCoy, D., Levchenko, K.: Dark matter: uncovering the DarkComet RAT ecosystem. In: WWW, pp. 2109–2120 (2020)

23. Farinholt, B., et al.: To catch a ratter: monitoring the behavior of amateur DarkComet RAT operators in the wild. In: IEEE S&P, pp. 770–787. IEEE (2017)
24. FireEye: Highly evasive attacker leverages solarwinds supply chain to compromise multiple global victims with sunburst backdoor, 13 December 2020. https://www.mandiant.com/resources/evasive-attacker-leverages-solarwinds-supply-chain-compromises-with-sunburst-backdoor
25. Han, D., et al.: Evaluating and improving adversarial robustness of machine learning-based network intrusion detectors. IEEE J. Sel. Areas Commun. **39**(8), 2632–2647 (2021)
26. Hashemi, M.J., Cusack, G., Keller, E.: Towards evaluation of NIDSs in adversarial setting. In: ACM Big-DAMA, pp. 14–21 (2019)
27. Hashemi, M.J., Keller, E.: Enhancing robustness against adversarial examples in network intrusion detection systems. In: IEEE NFV-SDN, pp. 37–43. IEEE (2020)
28. Heinemeyer, M.: Fin7.5: the infamous cybercrime rig "FIN7" continues its activities. https://securelist.com/fin7-5-the-infamous-cybercrime-rig-fin7-continues-its-activities/90703//. Accessed 18 July 2021
29. Homoliak, I., Teknøs, M., Ochoa, M., Breitenbacher, D., Hosseini, S., Hanacek, P.: Improving network intrusion detection classifiers by non-payload-based exploit-independent obfuscations: an adversarial approach. EAI Endorsed Trans. Secur. Saf. **5**, 17 (2018)
30. Hu, X., et al.: BAYWATCH: robust beaconing detection to identify infected hosts in large-scale enterprise networks. In: IEEE/IFIP DSN, pp. 479–490. IEEE (2016)
31. Hutchins, E.M., Cloppert, M.J., Amin, R.M.: Intelligence-driven computer network defense informed by analysis of adversary campaigns and intrusion kill chains. In: Leading Issues in Information Warfare & Security Research, vol. 1, p. 80 (2011)
32. Invernizzi, L., et al.: Nazca: detecting malware distribution in large-scale networks. In: NDSS, vol. 14, pp. 23–26 (2014)
33. Jansen, W.: Abusing cloud services to fly under the radar. https://research.nccgroup.com/2021/01/12/abusing-cloud-services-to-fly-under-the-radar/. Accessed 18 Dec 2021
34. Ma, J., Saul, L.K., Savage, S., Voelker, G.M.: Beyond blacklists: learning to detect malicious web sites from suspicious URLs. In: KDD, pp. 1245–1254. ACM (2009)
35. Milajerdi, S.M., Gjomemo, R., Eshete, B., Sekar, R., Venkatakrishnan, V.: HOLMES: real-time APT detection through correlation of suspicious information flows. In: IEEE S&P, pp. 1137–1152. IEEE (2019)
36. Mirsky, Y., Doitshman, T., Elovici, Y., Shabtai, A.: Kitsune: an ensemble of autoencoders for online network intrusion detection. In: NDSS (2018)
37. Nelms, T., Perdisci, R., Ahamad, M.: ExecScent: mining for new C&C domains in live networks with adaptive control protocol templates. In: USENIX Security, pp. 589–604 (2013)
38. Oprea, A., Li, Z., Norris, R., Bowers, K.: MADE: security analytics for enterprise threat detection. In: ACSAC, pp. 124–136 (2018)
39. Oprea, A., Li, Z., Yen, T.F., Chin, S.H., Alrwais, S.: Detection of early-stage enterprise infection by mining large-scale log data. In: IEEE/IFIP DSN, pp. 45–56. IEEE (2015)
40. Perdisci, R., Lee, W., Feamster, N.: Behavioral clustering of HTTP-based malware and signature generation using malicious network traces. In: NSDI, vol. 10, p. 14 (2010)
41. Rezaeirad, M., Farinholt, B., Dharmdasani, H., Pearce, P., Levchenko, K., McCoy, D.: Schrödinger's RAT: profiling the stakeholders in the remote access trojan ecosystem. In: USENIX Security, pp. 1043–1060 (2018)

42. Schindler, T.: Anomaly detection in log data using graph databases and machine learning to defend advanced persistent threats. In: GI-Jahrestagung (2017)
43. Sommer, R., Paxson, V.: Outside the closed world: on using machine learning for network intrusion detection. In: IEEE S&P, pp. 305–316. IEEE (2010)
44. Stinson, E., Mitchell, J.C.: Towards systematic evaluation of the evadability of bot/botnet detection methods. In: WOOT, vol. 8, pp. 1–9 (2008)
45. Szegedy, C., et al.: Intriguing properties of neural networks. CoRR abs/1312.6199 (2014)
46. Tegeler, F., Fu, X., Vigna, G., Kruegel, C.: BotFinder: finding bots in network traffic without deep packet inspection. In: CoNEXT, pp. 349–360 (2012)
47. Wang, J., Qixu, L., Di, W., Dong, Y., Cui, X.: Crafting adversarial example to bypass flow-&ML-based botnet detector via RL. In: RAID, pp. 193–204 (2021)
48. Wang, Z.: Deep learning-based intrusion detection with adversaries. IEEE Access **6**, 38367–38384 (2018)
49. Zhou, Y., Kantarcioglu, M., Thuraisingham, B., Xi, B.: Adversarial support vector machine learning. In: KDD, pp. 1059–1067. ACM (2012)

Malware

ATLAS: A Practical Attack Detection and Live Malware Analysis System for IoT Threat Intelligence

Yan Lin Aung[1(✉)], Martín Ochoa[2], and Jianying Zhou[1]

[1] Singapore University of Technology and Design, Singapore, Singapore
{linaung_yan,jianying_zhou}@sutd.edu.sg
[2] Department of Computer Science, ETH Zürich, Zürich, Switzerland
martin.ochoa@inf.ethz.ch

Abstract. Recently, malware targeting IoT devices has become more prevalent. In this paper, we propose a practical **AT**tack detection and **L**ive malware **A**nalysis **S**ystem (ATLAS) that provides up-to-date threat intelligence for IoT. ATLAS consists of a hybrid IoT honeypot infrastructure, attack attribution, malware downloader and live malware analysis system. Since deployment, ATLAS received 859 distinct malware binaries targeting 17 real IoT devices. When compared with VirusTotal timestamps, 65% of these samples have been seen first by our infrastructure or are yet to be known to VirusTotal to date. Through static and dynamic analysis of 17 malware samples, we are able to identify not only the attack vectors, but also command & control (C&C) communication methods and other characteristics. We show that a novel adaptive clustering technique is capable of performing automated malware analysis to detect known malware families as well as 0-day malware. Evaluation with 204 ARM 32-bit malware results in detection of 44 clusters. Further in depth analysis on the selected samples that forms new clusters (potential 0-day malware) indicates that they are indeed novel variants of IoT malware using evolving attack vectors: 17 binaries formed new clusters and did not belong to any known cluster nor to VirusTotal.

Keywords: IoT Honeypot · Attack Detection · Live Malware Analysis · Threat Intelligence

1 Introduction

For the first time in 2020, the number of Internet of Things (IoT) connections from connected cars, smart homes, connected industrial equipment and machines, etc. surpassed the number of non-IoT connections from smartphones, laptops and computers. IoT is defined as a network of things that has physical or virtual representation in the digital world, sensing/actuation capability, a programmability feature and are uniquely identifiable [11]. By 2025, more than 30 billion devices will be connected to the Internet via sensors, processors and software in the home and workplace.

W. Susilo et al. (Eds.): ISC 2022, LNCS 13640, pp. 319–338, 2022.
https://doi.org/10.1007/978-3-031-22390-7_19

This demand for seamless connections of users and machines to the Internet has accelerated the deployment of 5G networks, which provide increased data rates, low-latency data communication for time-sensitive IoT applications and connectivity of massive numbers of IoT devices. On the other hand, the fourth industrial revolution, also known as Industry 4.0, refers to a range of new technologies that are fusing the physical, digital, and biological worlds together. This revolutionary shift has profound impacts on the way humans live, work and interact. Industry 4.0 solutions are highly dependent on IoT devices as the key source of data.

Rise of IoT Compromises: While the emergence of 5G, Industry 4.0 and IoT benefit users and stakeholders, it also opens opportunities to malicious actors to exploit vulnerabilities of these new technologies. Malware targeting IoT devices has become more prevalent in recent years, following the most notorious distributed denial-of-service (DDoS) attack by the Mirai malware in 2016. For just the past two years in retrospect, Nozomi Networks has reported an increase in threats to IoT and operational technology networks, especially by IoT botnets for the first six months of 2020. According to ReversingLabs, IoT malware samples increased by 7% in 2020 in comparison to 2019, while the number of attempted Telnet and Secure Shell (SSH) brute-force logins increased by 47%. For 2021, Kaspersky reported 1.51 billion breaches of IoT devices, up more than two fold increase from 639 million in 2020. Industry 4.0, 5G and widespread adoption of IoT increase attack campaigns and new forms of malware exploiting IoT vulnerabilities. Consequently, a detection system that provides up-to-date threat intelligence is imperative for early detection and mitigating risks thereby ensuring minimal impact on operational and business continuity [12,13].

Honeypot for IoT Threat Detection: Honeypots are security resources whose value lies in their ability to be probed, attacked and compromised. There are generally two types of honeypots: first, low-interaction honeypots, which present simulated or emulated environments to attackers, and second, high-interaction honeypots, which show real systems to attackers [18]. Honeypots are often used to survey the threat landscape. The characteristics of honeypots are that they are deceptive, discoverable, interactive, and monitored. In this work, we propose ATLAS, an attack detection and live malware analysis system for IoT threat intelligence. The ATLAS system implements a hybrid honeypot infrastructure and provides real-time threat intelligence for IoT security by detecting, attributing attacks and performing live malware analysis.

Our Contributions: (a) Design and implementation of a hybrid, lightweight and scalable IoT honeypot infrastructure that is capable of receiving attacks, attribution and downloading malware that targets IoT devices.

(b) A novel adaptive clustering technique that is capable of performing live malware analysis. The technique extracts the binary's call graph for each malware file downloaded to build clusters and detect novel malware.

(c) Analysis of 204 ARM 32-bit malware samples using the proposed technique, finding 17 0-day malware binaries since they form new clusters.

(d) Reverse engineering and analysis of 17 selected IoT malware downloaded by the honeypot. Using static and dynamic analysis techniques, in-depth understandings of the attack vectors, C&C methods, and additional characteristics specific to IoT malware are identified.

Organisation: The remainder of this paper is organised as follows. Section 2 describes design considerations and implementation of the proposed hybrid IoT honeypot infrastructure. Section 3 covers attribution of attacks received through IoT honeypots, malware downloading technique, reverse engineering of selected IoT malware and live malware analysis system. The evaluation results of downloaded malware binaries with VirusTotal (VT), in depth IoT malware analysis and adaptive clustering results are presented in Sect. 4. We summarize the related work in this field in Sect. 5 and conclude the paper in Sect. 6.

2 Hybrid IoT Honeypot Infrastructure

In this section, we describe the design and implementation of hybrid IoT honeypot infrastructure. Following an outline of attacker and system model, we discuss implementation details.

2.1 Attacker Model

We consider two types of attackers: (1) attackers in the initial phase of exploit creation and (2) attackers conducting large-scale attacks. An attacker in the former scenario explores Internet-connected devices and establishes a cyber kill chain, which consists of reconnaissance, weaponization, delivery, exploitation, installation, command-and-control, and action on intent phases. An attacker in the latter case aims to identify as many vulnerable devices as possible, exploit them, and gather them into a botnet to conduct large-scale attacks. For both scenarios, we assume the attacker is looking for real vulnerable devices to exploit and proliferate further.

2.2 Design

This section discusses various considerations taken into account when designing a honeypot infrastructure that exposes IoT devices to the Internet.

IoT Honeypot with Real and Emulated IoT Devices: We anticipate the proposed IoT honeypot infrastructure will include real IoT devices as well as low-interaction devices that emulate certain services (e.g. Telnet, SSH). Having real IoT devices as high-interaction honeypot maximizes the attack surface for the attackers allowing full access to the underlying system. We also note that recent IoT malware have exploited specific vulnerabilities present in certain manufacturers or types of IoT devices. Meanwhile, security researchers and industry experts use low-interaction honeypots to survey the threat landscape. Having low-interaction honeypot complements high-interaction counterparts and allows us to compare the efficacy of one or another.

Exposing IoT Honeypot on the Internet: It is imperative that our honeypot devices require public IP addresses to expose them on the Internet. Public IP addresses of Infrastructure as a Service (IaaS) or Virtual Private Server (VPS) belong to cloud service providers and they are identifiable via autonomous system (ASN). Alternatively, Virtual Private Network (VPN) service providers offer public IP addresses from servers located in various nations, allowing us to deploy our devices at different geolocations while they remain within the perimeter of our honeypot infrastructure. In contrast to Iaas and VPS, determining the true identity of VPN IP addresses requires a considerable amount of time and effort.

Network Traffic Collection and Malware Download: To detect the attacks targeting the devices in our honeypot, it is crucial to capture all network traffic coming into and exiting the honeypot infrastructure. Furthermore, we must detect outgoing connections made by devices as these may be attempts by malicious actors to establish network connections to C&C servers. Malware samples that correspond to the attacks provide further insight and enable in depth analysis of the threats.

Live Network Traffic Monitoring and Malware Analysis: As with typical security operations centers (SOCs), the honeypot infrastructure shall have the ability to detect and analyse activities on networks, IoT devices, and other systems and equipment (e.g. network switches, firewalls) hosting the infrastructure itself in real-time. Several monitoring and data analytics platforms exist, including ELK stack [5], Splunk [21], Security Onion [4], among others, which are widely used by industries and by security researchers alike.

Investigative measures are taken with the intent of discovering the scope and scale of attacks if anomalous activities are detected that are indicative of attacks being received and compromised. Such investigations include digital forensics, malware reverse engineering, and analysis. If the honeypot infrastructure will have a large number of devices, it is preferable to automate as much as possible and keep the time-consuming and resource-intensive work for last resort.

Orchestration of Honeypot Infrastructure: Ability to operate the honeypot infrastructure around the clock is crucial. As such, the design shall automate addition of new IoT devices, setting up of VPN connections to have public IP addresses, removal of existing devices. In addition, monitoring of the status of the entire infrastructure and orchestration of various components of the infrastructure in isolation are required.

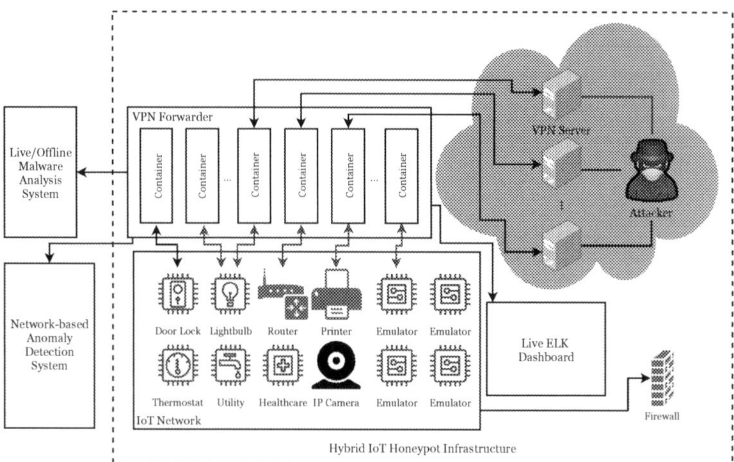

Fig. 1. Attack Detection and Live Analysis System for IoT (ATLAS)

Proposed Hybrid IoT Honeypot Infrastructure: Considering these design consideration aspects, we envision and propose a hybrid IoT honeypot infrastructure, as illustrated in Fig. 1. It consists of these main components: (1) VPN Forwarder, (2) IoT Network and (3) Live Dashboard. The following section provides details of each component.

2.3 Implementation

This section describes the implementation of the proposed hybrid IoT honeypot infrastructure based on the design considerations in the previous section.

Honeypot with Heterogeneous IoT Devices: The implementation phase begins with choosing which IoT devices will be exposed to the Internet. A basic query on Shodan search engine for IoT devices returns millions of results. IP cameras form majority of these results followed by home routers, printers, etc. We chose to include different kinds of IoT devices in our honeypot in order to provide a rich attack surface that can be used to detect recent threats and potential vulnerabilities in these devices. 17 real IoT devices, which include IP cameras, printer, smart plug, smart bulb, industrial control systems devices such as programmable logic controller (PLC), remote terminal unit (RTU), human-machine interface (HMI) as well as industrial control system (ICS) emulators based on *conpot* [19] are selected in our implementation. Table 1 shows the type, manufacturer, and model number of the IoT devices that have been selected and integrated into the honeypot.

VPN Forwarding with Docker Container: In order to scale the honeypot infrastructure as the number of devices increase, we adopted a lightweight approach to establish VPN tunnels to VPN servers and acquire public IP addresses.

Table 1. Details of Real and Emulated IoT Devices

Type	Manufacturer	Model	Location
IP Camera	D-Link	DCS-942L	Canada, US, UK
	D-Link	DCS-930L	US, UK, UK
	D-Link	DCS-5020L	UK
	Provision ISR	PT-838E	US, UK, Germany
	Vstarcam	C7837WIP (B)	Germany
IP Printer†	HP	Officejet Pro 6830	US, UK, Israel
Smart Plug	Belkin	WeMo F7C027uk (C75)	Czech
	Belkin	WeMo F7C063 (2B4)	Germany
	TP-Link	HS100 (8923)	Sweden
	TP-Link	HS100 (96DA)	Netherlands
Smart Bulb	TP-Link	LB130	Canada
Industrial Control System (ICS)	Schneider	Modicon Quantum 140	US
	Schneider	Modicon STBNIP 2212	US
	Schneider	Modicon STBNIP 2212	US
	Schneider	Magelis HMIGTO 6310	US
	Siemens	S7-1500	Netherlands, UK, US
Industrial Control System Emulator	Siemens	S7-200	UK
	Siemens	S7-200 (Variant)	US
	Siemens	S7-300 (IEC104, SNMP)	Israel
	Guardian	Tank Monitoring System	Germany
	Kamstrup	Smart Meter	Canada

† Two HP Officejet Pro 6830 IP Printers.

In particular, a customised docker container has been developed with the functionalities to establish VPN tunnels to servers in specified geolocations, to set up port forwarding to IoT devices on the IoT network (see Fig. 1) and automatic capturing of network traffic received on exposed public IP addresses.

We performed *nmap* port scan of IoT devices in their factory default state and the container exposes the same open ports as IoT device on the public facing network interface. Location column in Table 1 shows geolocations of IoT devices that have been exposed via corresponding IP addresses provided by VPN servers. Our implementation allows multiple containers to forward the network traffic to the same IoT device, thus increasing geographic presence given a limited number of actual IoT devices. For example, there are three containers which are forwarding the network traffic from the VPN servers located in Canada, US and UK for D-Link DCS-942L camera as shown in Table 1.

A set of shell scripts and a CSV file are used to automate the number of containers and their names, IP addresses, open ports, and forwarding IP addresses to the real IoT devices on the IoT Network. To expose an IoT device on the Internet, the user first connects the device to the IoT Network, then updates the CSV file with the necessary information and uses the script to establish end-to-end connectivity between VPN server and IoT device. With an aid of a shell script and also thanks to docker container, we could bring all containers or individual ones online or offline within seconds. There are a total of 17 real IoT devices and 5 ICS emulators (see Table 1) exposed to the Internet via 31 docker containers that forward network traffic from the VPN servers in various geolocations.

Live Network Traffic Monitoring with Elastic Stack: We have selected Elastic Search, Logstash and Kibana (ELK) stack for live monitoring and visualization of network traffic flowing to and from our honeypot infrastructure. Every docker container in *VPN Forwarder* captures the network traffic continuously. Using TShark, the PCAP files captured are converted into JavaScript Object Notation (JSON) format output. We created a customised template for Logstash, which is the log forwarding engine of ELK stack, to map selected attributes of JSON output and indexing in Elasticsearch subsequently. Further, we developed several custom scripts that query Elasticsearch to select the data that is most pertinent (e.g. the number of successful logins, HTTP URLs, etc). The results of these queries are then visualized with the Kibana dashboard.

Automation and Orchestration of Honeypot Infrastructure: When implementing the honeypot infrastructure, automation has been incorporated to the maximum extent possible. For the *VPN Forwarder*, the docker containers are orchestrated with *docker-compose*. Inside each docker container, VPN tunnelling, network traffic capturing and port forwarding are automated with shell scripts. Captured PCAP files are converted into JSON files with a Python script and ingested by Logstash component of ELK stack thus enabling visualization with various dashboards in Kibana almost instantly. Attack attribution implementation as described in the next section makes use of *inotifywait* to detect new PCAP files written to the file system and check any outbound connection attempts from any of IoT devices. Similarly, malware download and malware analysis implementation are automated. To realize the automation work to the maximum extent possible, we rely on native Linux functionalities such as *cron jobs*, *systemd services*, *rsync*, shell scripts and Python scripts.

3 Attack Detection and Live Malware Analysis

This section discusses attribution of attacks targeting IoT devices based on the hybrid honeypot infrastructure in Fig. 1 and the implementation of a malware downloader component. We also describe implementation of a machine learning-based live malware analysis technique and an offline reverse engineering environment for the analysis of IoT malware.

3.1 Attack Attribution

To detect network traffic originating from any of IoT devices on the *IoT Network*, we incorporated a network switch with span port functionality. All IoT devices are connected to the *IoT Network* via this network switch. The span port enables us to capture all network traffic at one place. For every PCAP file captured on the span port interface, we look for outbound connections, which are attempted connections to IP addresses outside of *IoT Network*. Outbound TCP connections are identified using TCP flags (*SYN* flag set and *ACK* reset) whereas outbound UDP traffic is identified as traffic originating from the devices in our honeypot and destined for outside of *IoT Network* VLAN.

We associate malicious outbound connection attempts (most likely to C&C server) are the effects of attack commands issued previously by an attacker. We, therefore, perform packet inspection of historical PCAPs, to attribute outbound connection attempt to its corresponding attack command. We start backtracking by identifying the outbound IP, IP of the device and the protocol over which the device communicates, and then filtering historical PCAPs accordingly. We inspect a maximum of 30 min of historical network traffic. Backtracking happens incrementally until we find the packet and hence the command that causes the outbound attempt. By this means, we are able to attribute an attack (exploit attempt) to an outbound connection.

3.2 Malware Download

Outbound connection attribution reveals the original attack command. The next step is to complete this connection with the malicious server and download attack payload. Allowing this operation on the devices in honeypot poses a risk of unknown malware taking control of devices, possibly the honeypot itself and unintentional proliferation of malware. The firewall in Fig. 1 blocks any outbound connections initiated from the *IoT Network*. We created an independent component, called *Malware Downloader*, to perform this downloading step independently and in isolation. We implemented a Python script for parsing of *WGET* and *TFTP* commands. It includes a listener that continuously listens for new messages indicating that new attack commands have been attributed to outbound connections. Every new message is then parsed to extract the command. Subsequently, the attack command is executed to establish a connection with the potential C&C server and download the malware.

3.3 Live Malware Analysis System

Many of the latest IoT malware are derived from the infamous Mirai malware and share many similarities. Because IoT devices use heterogeneous hardware and software, IoT devices vary greatly from each other. While many IoT devices run on ARM architecture, there are IoT devices that runs on PowerPC, SuperH SH-4, MIPS, etc. Once the IoT device is exploited, several binaries that target different CPU architectures are downloaded. Subsequently, the device is then infected with the binary that matches the underlying hardware. We have noted similar characteristics with the malware binaries downloaded by the *Malware Downloader* component as described in Sect. 3.2.

For the downloaded binaries, queries to the VT API are made to obtain the analysis report and establish the ground truth labels. VT provides detection results from the analysis of more than 60 security vendors for a given URL, IP address, domain name or file hash. However, each security vendor applies its own proprietary malware classification scheme independently resulting inconsistencies among labels from different vendors.

We have also evaluated AVClass2 [20], an automatic malware tagging tool that extracts clean tags and categorizes the malware sample based on the given labels (e.g. VT analysis report). AVClass2 aims to mitigate the inconsistent malware labelling issue and generates a generic tag for a given malware sample. AVClass2 is tested with the malware samples downloaded by our honeypot infrastructure and generate the corresponding tags. Since AVClass2 is designed to generate generic tags for malware that target a wide range of systems and software (e.g. Windows, Linux, etc.), specific labels for IoT malware are filtered out during the tag generation.

Our primary objective is to realize an automated system that analyzes the downloaded malware binaries and detect unknown (0-day) samples. Therefore, we decided to adopt an unsupervised machine learning based technique rather than establishing the ground truth labels for supervised classification.

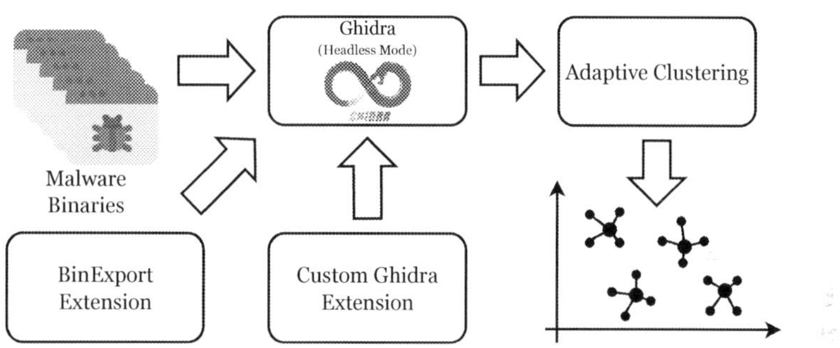

Fig. 2. Live Malware Analysis System

Figure 2 shows an automated live malware analysis system that has been implemented. The system comprises of (1) Ghidra, (2) BinExport, (3) Custom Ghidra Extension and (4) Adaptive Clustering components. Ghidra is the open-source reverse engineering tool developed by the National Security Agency (NSA). Ghidra headless analyser allows users to create projects, perform various binary analysis and run scripts without using the graphical user interface (GUI). BinExport is the extension for IDA Pro, Ghidra and Binary Ninja for exporting disassembly data into the protocol buffer format [9]. Custom Ghidra Extension is implemented by making use of BinExport and Ghidra headless analyser to generate the disassembly data for each malware binary. We rely on *inotifywait* to detect any new malware binary that has been downloaded. Subsequently, the headless analyser is run with the customised Ghidra extension to obtain the corresponding BinExport output file.

Adaptive Clustering in Fig. 2 mainly consists of (1) BinExport parser and (2) machine learning based adaptive clustering implementation. The BinExport parser takes in the BinExport file in protocol buffer format as generated by the custom Ghidra extension and parses it into JSON format. The BinExport file includes meta information such as executable name, id, architecture name, call graph and details of various read/write/executable sections, etc.

The adaptive clustering algorithm is implemented in Python and the pseudocode is listed in Algorithm 1. The Adaptive Clustering components is first initialised with the signature of a malware binary. The signature is composed with the function names (also known as mangled name) from the call graph. For each new malware binary, m, the Trend Micro locality sensitive hash (TLSH) distance between the signature of new malware binary and the signatures of malware binaries, which have been designated as the centroids of existing clusters, is computed (line 14 of Algorithm 1). TLSH is a locality sensitive hashing scheme developed by Trend Micro [15]. It is able to generate similar hash values for signatures which are closer to one and another. If TLSH distance between the new malware signature and all existing signatures is greater than $n \times \sigma$ (standard deviation), then a new cluster is formed (line 5 of Algorithm 1).

Otherwise, the new malware signature is added into the closest existing cluster. In such case, the new mean signature is re-computed using TF-IDF of all existing signatures in that cluster and the centroid signature, which is closest to the mean signature, is identified. The new standard deviation value is also re-computed. TF-IDF stands for term frequency (TF), which summarizes how frequently a given word (in our case, function name) appears within a document (call graph), and inverse document frequency (IDF), which downscales words that occur frequently in documents. By this means, the adaptive clustering component detects whether the newly download malware binary belongs to one of the existing clusters or differs significantly thus requiring further investigation and analysis.

3.4 Reverse Engineering of IoT Malware

Each time a new cluster is created by the automated malware analysis system, it indicates that the downloaded sample may be a 0-day malware and should be analyzed further. Hence, we have set up a reverse engineering environment with the following software and hardware components: (1) *IDA Pro 7.6 SP1* - A binary analysis tool commonly used by reverse engineers, malware analyst and cybersecurity professionals. It is also possible to use other open-source tool such as Ghidra [14] for binary analysis. (2) *Lumen* [1] - An open-source alternative Lumina server of IDA Pro for looking up of function signatures maintained in the database. (3) *Raspberry Pi (RPi) Kit* - Since most of IoT devices run on ARM architecture, RPi is a useful hacking kit to perform dynamic analysis of the downloaded malware binaries. (4) *ARM Linux Debug Server* - IDA Pro supports remote debugging. By running the debug server on the RPi target, the malware could be executed in a controlled manner and most of IDA Pro features (e.g. memory snapshot) are made available.

Reverse engineering begins with static analysis. In this step, the malware is first loaded into IDA Pro and searched for strings. For the malware with encrypted strings, decryption attempt is made with an aid of Python script. Then, Lumina plugin is run to resolve functions based on the signatures stored in

Algorithm 1. Adaptive Clustering Algorithm

```
procedure AdaptiveClustering(m)
    Get call graph g from malware m
    Get a list of call graph, G, of centroids of existing clusters
    d = GetMinimumDistance(G, g)
    if d > n * σ then                                          ▷ New Cluster
        Create a new cluster with m
        Update the existing cluster list
    else
        Add m into the closest cluster
        μ = GetNewMean(c)
        σ = sqrt(| (n*(σ^2+μ^2)+d^2)/(n+1) − μ^2) |)   ▷ n = # of malware in the closest cluster
    end if
end procedure

procedure GetMinimumDistance(G, g)
    Initialize TLSH distance list l
    tlsh_g = TLSH.HASH(g)
    for i ← 1, n do                                            ▷ n = # of clusters
        tlsh_i = TLSH.HASH(G_i)
        s = TLSH.DIFF(tlsh_g, tlsh_i)
        Append s to l
    end for
    Get Minimum TLSH distance d from l
    return d
end procedure

procedure GetNewMean(c)
    v = TfidfVectorizer                           ▷ Initialize TF-IDF vectorizer
    m = FIT_TRANSFORM(c)                          ▷ Return 2d document-term matrix m
    f = GET_FEATURE_NAMES                         ▷ Column names for matrix m
    Convert m into Pandas dataframe d
    Sum every element in each row of d            ▷ Each row is a malware in cluster c
    Compute average for each row
    return row r with absolute minimum difference as new mean μ
end procedure
```

the database. The functionality of the malware is analysed subsequently. Depending on the nature of IoT malware, certain samples may require dynamic analysis especially for packed binaries. In such cases, entry point to the malware execution is first identified via static analysis step. The malware is then copied over to the RPi target and ARM Linux Debug Server is run. A break point is set at the entry point in IDA Pro and the malware is executed. From the decryption stub, the original entry point is identified and the malware is unpacked. Then, memory snapshot of the malware is taken in IDA Pro and typical static analysis step proceeds as described earlier.

Putting it all together, **AT**tack detection and **L**ive Malware **A**nalysis **S**ystem (ATLAS) for IoT as depicted in Fig. 1 consists of the hybrid IoT honeypot infrastructure, attack attribution, malware downloader and live malware analysis system implementation.

4 Results

In this section, we describe experimental results obtained by analyzing malware downloaded by the ATLAS system and using adaptive clustering based on machine learning algorithm to detect both known and unknown (possibly 0-day) malware.

4.1 Evaluation of IoT Malware with VirusTotal

Whenever the *Downloader* component downloads malware, a timestamp is automatically prefixed to the file name of the binary. ATLAS-IoT downloaded 859 distinct malware (i.e. unique hashes) between August 2020 and October 2021. The malware targets x86, x86_64, PowerPC, SuperH SH-4, SPARC, MIPS, ARM and even NXP Coldfire CPU architectures. We perform evaluation with the analysis status and information available in VT. In particular, we compare our timestamp with that of the first submission recorded by VT. We have implemented a script that generates SHA256 hashes for the malware and makes API calls to VT to query the first submission and analysis status. The script populates the malware file name, SHA256 hash, our downloaded timestamp and API response from VirusTotal into a CSV file.

For 35% of the 859 distinct malware downloaded, VT has earlier timestamps compared to ours. On the other hand, we have earlier timestamps for 40% of the malware. For the remaining 25%, VT does not have these hashes and no first submission has been recorded yet as of 2 October 2021. These samples are potentially 0-day malware and worthy of in depth reverse engineering and analysis.

4.2 Analysis Results of Selected IoT Malware

From 859 distinct malware downloaded, 17 samples are selected for in depth analysis using the reverse engineering environment as described in Sect. 3.4. The selection consists of 14 ARM 32-bit, 2 x86 64-bit, 1 MIPS 32-bit malware. Malware samples were selected as follows: (1) 4 samples for which VT has earlier submission timestamp than ours, (2) 6 samples for which we detected earlier than VT and (3) 7 samples for which VT has no detection results yet. The details of the selected malware samples are provided in Table 2, which includes the MD5 hash, the ATLAS download timestamp, the VT first submission timestamp, and the VT malware family classification.

As described in Sect. 3, reverse engineering and analysis begin with the static analysis step. For each malware, we identify the attack vectors, information related to C&C server and other characteristics such as whether the malware has spreading and self-removing functionality, etc. Out of 17 malware samples, 16 of them are analysed statically whereas 1 malware requires dynamic analysis due to its advanced protection feature. Table 3 provides the analysis results. It is noted that majority of the selected malware includes TCP and UDP flooding attack vectors. Malware **4** features Lynx flooding attack. Malware **6**, **7**, **15** and **17** include Telnet scanner using default credentials to brute force the service with spreadable capability. Malware **3**, **9** and **11** feature GAME attack vector while malware **3**, **9**, **10**, **11** and **16** include OVH attack. Both GAME and OVH attack commands operates via UDP. The OVH attack may link to the attack on OVH DDoS protection service. Malware **7** and **15** have the functionality to download file from remote server.

Seven malware incorporate string obfuscation technique to bypass antivirus and intrusion detection system which use string-based signature detection. In this case, a decryptor script is developed for string de-obfuscation. There are five malware with C&C obfuscation mechanism with the intention to bypass intrusion detection system and intrusion prevention system, and also making the analysis harder. C&C obfuscation requires simulation of C&C server, perform dynamic analysis and debugging the malware to understand the C&C protocol.

Malware **15** uses Internet Relay Chat (IRC), a simple and low bandwidth communication method, for communication with C&C. The remaining malware used raw socket-based approach. Malware **2** and **16** have anti-debug functionality to slow down the reverse engineering and analysis. Malware **1**, **2** and **17** includes self-removal feature deleting the footprint on the file system once it is loaded and run in the memory.

Out of 17 malware analysed, malware **16** is the unique malware with advanced protection technique and attack vectors. Firstly, the malware itself is packed with a customised packer to slow down the reverse engineering process and to prevent antivirus from detecting using strings Indicators of Compromise. Therefore, the dynamic analysis approach as described in Sect. 3.4 is adopted for this malware. In contrast to other malware, this malware includes unique attack vectors such as LDAP flooding, TFTP flooding, CLOUDFLARE attack and possibly contains VPN tunnelling services.

Table 2. Details of Selected IoT Malware

Malware #	MD5 Digest	ATLAS	VirusTotal†	Malware Family
1	782b8dea8a9353b821fab883e6863b9d	**2020-08-12 20:18:00**	2021-03-18 07:29:10	Possible_GAFGYT.SMLBAT13
2	082105da330bcf138df65a651448a7fb	2020-08-30 14:46:54	**2020-08-20 04:02:06**	Backdoor.Linux.MIRAI.USELVGT
3	23c4dc508b448b5617edcde1394e51fa	**2020-10-15 20:43:03**	2020-10-16 06:18:52	Backdoor.Linux.BASHLITE.SMJC11
4	41f3c2b5447dca849c4d0d08394f4fb1	**2020-10-17 15:13:19**	—*	—*
5	7c73c7bcf51860ef189e737b8fc768fe	2020-10-28 20:43:18	**2020-10-28 20:27:45**	Backdoor.Linux.BASHLITE.SMJC11
6	e1c1a0c5921aaafa5a571d11d345de35	**2020-11-12 05:10:54**	—*	—*
7	3e69452a797839721c3a9a01859b5fb1	**2020-11-12 05:10:54**	—*	—*
8	ef71a2b29454dec5733603a2c06826d1	**2020-11-15 14:25:54**	—*	—*
9	19ce5594095d5afb79ee482289460bc1	2020-12-07 15:23:58	**2020-12-07 15:00:42**	Backdoor.Linux.BASHLITE.SMJC11
10	08b09cd034b0e49cc997ccffca9c1bee	**2020-12-07 22:53:50**	2020-12-08 07:58:24	Backdoor.Linux.GAFGYT.SMMR3
11	26a67ed287bb1e0bd9ac408183240ec6	**2020-12-08 00:23:58**	2021-03-19 08:43:33	Backdoor.Linux.MIRAI.USELVCJ21
12	cab62f356483f3aa9f599eee6dd20f6f	**2020-12-08 18:53:57**	2020-12-09 03:29:29	Backdoor.Linux.BASHLITE.SMJC3
13	db7a68a7634e5f8becb2901d4196e5d4	**2020-12-10 23:23:47**	2020-12-11 19:45:17	Backdoor.Linux.BASHLITE.SMJC3
14	38f6635f43fdb4824eb594e4378ec4b5	2021-01-19 15:23:34	**2021-01-17 20:51:40**	Backdoor.Linux.BASHLITE.SMJC2
15	99ac8799ac629f1e33afacc46738f2cb	**2021-01-20 15:38:43**	—*	—*
16	f8d56db7f48bae9f9ef46ec6e9c3a738	**2021-03-26 23:55:48**	—*	—*
17	6f2dcbb7f119391a15d09f337cedbd57	**2021-07-30 19:59:00**	—*	—*

† Queries to VirusTotal were made on 2 October 2021. * VirusTotal has not analyzed these malware yet. Hence, information is not available.

Detailed analysis of 17 malware and the corresponding VT analysis results shed light on detection of new or 0-day samples enabling us to evaluate formation of new clusters using the proposed adaptive clustering technique.

4.3 Adaptive Clustering Results

The adaptive clustering algorithm described in Sect. 3.3 determines whether the downloaded malware belongs to one of the existing clusters (i.e. a closely related variant of existing malware) or forms a new cluster (0-day malware).

We applied the adaptive clustering to 143 ARM 32-bit malware which have VT analysis results available. The algorithm performs clustering of the malware binaries within seconds. Figure 3 shows the adaptive clustering results. The black color node represents the centroid of a cluster whereas the red color nodes are members nodes in each cluster. Each cluster represents the malware binaries that are closely related to each other. The adaptive clustering results 29 clusters for 143 ARM 32-bit malware. We then analyzed the VT detection results from various security vendors. For 143 ARM 32-bit malware, Trend Micro detection engine reports 25 distinct classification labels. Malware Family column in Table 2 belongs to Trend Micro labels. Similarly, Kaspersky reports 15 labels with no detection results for 3 malware, 22 for Fortinet, 37 for Microsoft with no detection results for 8 malware and 19 for AVClass2. It is evident from the VT detection results that the classification scheme used by security vendors vary

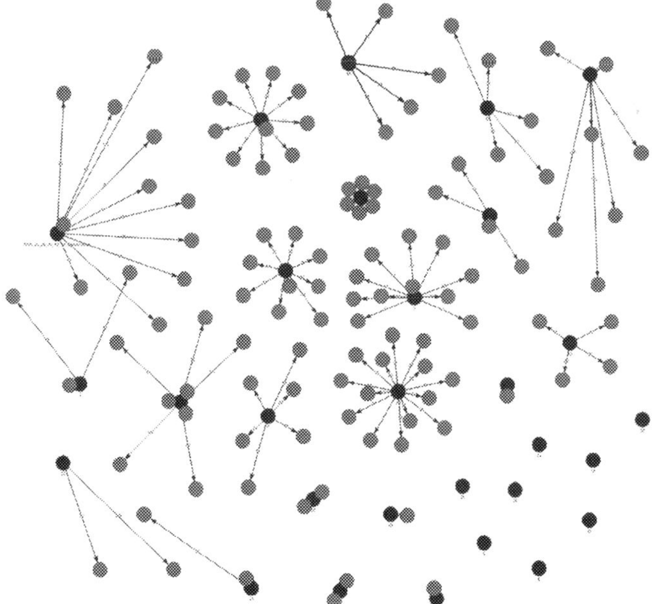

Fig. 3. Adaptive Clustering Results for 143 Malware

Table 3. Analysis Results for 17 IoT Malware

Malware #		1	2	3	4	5	6	7	8	9	10	11	12	13	14	15	16	17
Attack Vector	TCP	✓	✓	✓	✓	✓	✓	✓	✓	✓	✓	✓	✓	✓	✓	✓	✓	✓
	UDP	✓	✓	✓	✓	✓	✓	✓	✓	✓	✓	✓	✓	✓	✓	✓	✓	✓
	VSE	✗	✗	✗	✓	✗	✗	✗	✓	✓	✓	✓	✓	✓	✓	✗	✓	✗
	HTTP	✗	✓	✗	✓	✗	✓	✓	✓	✓	✓	✗	✓	✓	✓	✗	✓	✓
	HEX	✓	✗	✓	✗	✓	✓	✓	✓	✓	✓	✗	✓	✓	✓	✗	✓	✓
	LYNX	✗	✗	✗	✓	✗	✗	✗	✗	✗	✗	✗	✗	✗	✗	✗	✗	✗
	STD	✓	✗	✓	✓	✓	✓	✓	✓	✓	✓	✗	✓	✓	✗	✗	✓	✗
	TELNET	✗	✗	✗	✗	✗	✓	✓	✗	✗	✗	✗	✗	✗	✗	✓	✗	✓
	LDAP	✗	✗	✗	✗	✗	✗	✗	✗	✗	✗	✗	✗	✗	✗	✗	✓	✗
	GAME	✗	✗	✓	✗	✗	✗	✗	✗	✓	✗	✓	✗	✗	✗	✗	✗	✗
	VPN	✗	✗	✗	✗	✗	✗	✗	✗	✗	✗	✗	✗	✗	✗	✗	✓	✗
	TFTP	✗	✗	✗	✗	✗	✗	✗	✗	✗	✗	✗	✗	✗	✗	✗	✓	✗
	Cloudflare	✗	✗	✗	✗	✗	✗	✗	✗	✗	✗	✗	✗	✗	✗	✗	✓	✗
	OVH	✗	✗	✓	✗	✗	✗	✗	✗	✓	✓	✓	✗	✗	✗	✗	✓	✗
	ICMP	✗	✓	✗	✗	✗	✗	✓	✗	✗	✗	✓	✗	✗	✗	✗	✗	✗
	File Download	✗	✗	✗	✗	✗	✗	✓	✗	✗	✗	✗	✗	✗	✗	✓	✗	✗
	Spoofing	✗	✗	✗	✗	✗	✗	✗	✗	✗	✗	✗	✗	✗	✗	✓	✗	✗
	XMAS	✗	✗	✗	✓	✗	✗	✗	✓	✗	✓	✓	✓	✓	✗	✓	✓	✗
Packed		✗	✗	✗	✗	✗	✗	✗	✗	✗	✗	✗	✗	✗	✗	✗	✓	✗
String Obfuscation		✗	✓	✗	✗	✗	✗	✗	✓	✗	✗	✗	✓	✓	✗	✗	✓	✗
Anti-Debug		✗	✓	✗	✗	✗	✗	✗	✗	✗	✗	✗	✗	✗	✗	✗	✓	✗
Self-Removal		✓	✓	✗	✗	✗	✗	✗	✗	✗	✗	✗	✗	✗	✗	✗	✗	✓
Spreadable		✗	✗	✗	✗	✗	✓	✓	✗	✗	✗	✗	✗	✗	✗	✗	✗	✓
Command & Control	Obfuscation	✗	✓	✗	✗	✗	✗	✗	✓	✗	✗	✗	✓	✓	✗	✗	✓	✗
	Method	§	§	§	§	§	§	§	§	§	§	§	§	§	§	†	§	§
	IP:Port	#1: 142.11.xxx.xxx:277*																
		#2: —																
		#3: 78.141.xxx.xxx:111*																
		#4: 80.211.xxx.xxx:101*																
		#5: 107.173.xxx.xxx:666*																
		#6: 93.170.xxx.xxx:129*																
		#7: 93.170.xxx.xxx:129*																
		#8: 195.58.xxx.xxx:576*																
		#9: 85.204.xxx.xxx:717*																
		#10: 104.248.xxx.xxx:59372*																
		#11: 95.156.xxx.xxx:53071*																
		#12: 185.244.xxx.xxx:369*																
		#13: 104.248.xxx.xxx:48632*																
		#14: 95.214.xxx.xxx:666*																
		#15: 193.239.xxx.xxx:80*																
		#16: 107.172.xxx.xxx:839*																
		#17: 194.147.xxx.xxx:282*																

§ Raw socket for communication with C&C server. † IRC for communication with C&C server. * C&C IP addresses are anonymized.

significantly among each other and establishing a consistent ground truth has been challenging.

On the other hand, we have looked into the malware file names used with the exploits. As explained in Sect. 4.1, IoT exploits often download several binaries that target different CPU architectures. For example, one IoT exploit downloads four malware binaries for ARM CPU with ARMv4, ARMv5, ARMv6 and ARMv7 instruction set architectures. In such cases, the hashes of binaries are different though they share the same functionality since they are downloaded together one after another. Analyzing such patterns and malware file names for 143 samples results in 28 distinct groups (i.e. clusters) closely relating to 29 cluster produced by the adaptive clustering technique.

Next, we tested the adaptive clustering with 14 ARM 32-bit samples, which we performed in depth analysis in Sect. 4.2. In this case, 7 samples (**1**, **4**, **7**, **11**, **15**, **16**, **17**) highlighted with red color in Table 3 form new cluster and the remaining 7 samples are classified into the existing 29 clusters. Interestingly, VT does not have analysis results for 5 of the 7 samples. For other two samples, VT has the results because we were the first to submit them to VT. There is a strong correlation between the results of in depth analysis in Table 3 and the malware samples that form new clusters. These samples have relatively unique attack vectors and other characteristics such as packed status, anti-debug feature, self-removal and spreadable capability (cyan color in Table 3). Among the 7 samples, malware **16** has several unique characteristics (e.g. LDAP, VPN, TFTP, Cloudflare, OVH attack vectors) highlighting its significance for further investigation.

In addition, we have also applied the adaptive clustering to another 47 ARM 32-bit malware for which VT does not have analysis results. The adaptive clustering reports 10 new clusters in this case. Therefore, the analysis of 17 samples in Sect. 4.2, further evaluation with additional 47 samples and the results of adaptive clustering demonstrate that our proposed live malware analysis system is practical and capable of detecting 0-day malware. The detected 0-day samples are novel variants of IoT malware using evolving attack vectors and other unique characteristics as revealed by the in-depth analysis.

5 Related Work

This section reviews the existing work on design and implementation aspects of honeypots for IoT threat intelligence. Moreover, we examine techniques such as attack attribution, malware download, and malware analysis that have been integrated into the proposed honeypots for an end-to-end threat intelligence framework.

Pa Pa et al. [16] were the first to propose a honeypot exclusively for IoT. Using a honeypot called IoTPOT, they captured Telnet-based attacks on various IoT devices. IoTPOT consists of a low-interaction frontend responder cooperating with a high-interaction backend called IoTBOX. This work mainly focus on

Telnet-based attacks that target IoT devices and does not consider the exploitation via other network protocols (e.g. exploitation via HTTP targeting vulnerable web server in IoT devices). Captured malware samples were analyzed manually with an aid of IoTBOX to identify distinct malware families. Luo et al. [10] presented an automatic way to build an IoT honeypot called IoTCandyJar. It uses publicly available IoT devices on the Internet to gather responses to its own requests. They used heuristics and machine learning techniques to customize the scanning procedure for improving response logic.

Guarnizo et al. [6] proposed SIPHON, a high-interaction honeypot which incorporates real IoT devices. Authors used cloud service providers such as Amazon Web Services (AWS) to expose IoT devices through geographically distributed IP addresses on the Internet. The honeypot systems in [6] and [10] do not include attack attribution, malware download and analysis capabilities. Previous works by Amit et al. [22] and Aung et al. in [3] focus on the analysis of network traffic captured by the IoT honeypots, but do not incorporate automated live malware analysis for the detection of known malware families as well as 0-day malware.

Wang et al. [23] developed a hybrid IoT honeypot consisting of low-interactive components with Telnet/SSH services running in a virtual environment and vulnerable services in IoT devices, called IoTCMal. Their work primarily focuses on homology analysis of malicious samples by deploying IoTCMal on 36 VPS instances distributed in 13 cities of 6 countries.

Recently, Kato et al. [8] proposed X-POT, an adaptive honeypot framework that improves the observation capabilities of honeypots by utilizing the responses collected from the host through Internet-wide scanning. The authors deployed HTTP X-POT on the Internet and observed attacks targeting various IoT devices and captured several malware samples. The authors rely on VirusTotal and AVClass for malware analysis and labelling respectively. No automated live analysis was performed to detect variants of known malware families and 0-day malware.

Signature-based and behavorial-based methods are often employed for detection of IoT malware. Park et al. [17] proposed a method for constructing a behavioral graph representing the execution behavior for a family of malware instances in order to significantly improve detection rates. Wüchner et al. [24] proposed a malware detection approach that uses compression-based mining on quantitative data flow graphs to derive highly accurate detection models. As highlighted by Alrubayyi et al. in [2], both signature-based and behavorial-based methods are not suitable for detecting unknown (i.e. 0-day) malware. Therefore, the authors discussed recent advances in employing Artificial Immune Systems (AIS), which are intrusion detection algorithms inspired by human adaptive immune system techniques for better malware detection, especially for IoT. Recently, Jeon et al. [7] proposed a dynamic analysis for IoT malware detection scheme that uses convolution neural networks (CNN) in a cloud-based environment under a virtual embedded system to detect and classify IoT malware.

While honeypot systems have been proposed and implemented not only by research communities but also by security industries for IoT threat intelligence, our review revealed a need for an end-to-end framework that detects attacks, performs automated malware analysis, and classifies them into known and unknown families thereby providing the vital up-to-date threat intelligence for IoT.

6 Conclusion

In this paper, we proposed ATLAS, a practical attack detection and live malware analysis system for IoT threat intelligence. ATLAS exposed IoT devices on the Internet via a lightweight and scalable hybrid honeypot infrastructure. Using VPN tunnels, 17 real IoT devices and 5 ICS emulators are made accessible from 31 public IP addresses at different geographic locations. Despite having a smaller set of heterogeneous IoT devices, ATLAS received attacks and downloaded malware samples, of which 65% either have earlier timestamps or have unique hashes compared to VirusTotal. The adaptive clustering algorithm performs live analysis and classifies the malware samples into existing families or creates new clusters. Analysis of 204 ARM 32-bit malware samples using the proposed technique finds 17 0-day malware binaries that are indeed novel variants of IoT malware using evolving attack vectors.

Acknowledgements. This work is supported by the National Research Foundation of Singapore under its National Satellite of Excellence Programme entitled "Design Science and Technology for Secure Critical Infrastructure" (Award Number: NSoE_DeST-SCI2019-0002).

References

1. A., N.: Lumen - an alternative lumina compatible server for IDA Pro (2020). https://lumen.abda.nl
2. Alrubayyi, H., Goteng, G., Jaber, M., Kelly, J.: Challenges of malware detection in the IoT and a review of artificial immune system approaches. J. Sensor Actuator Netw. 10(4) (2021). https://www.mdpi.com/2224-2708/10/4/61
3. Aung, Y.L., Tiang, H.H., Wijaya, H., Ochoa, M., Zhou, J.: Scalable VPN-forwarded honeypots: Dataset and threat intelligence insights. In: Sixth Annual Industrial Control System Security (ICSS) Workshop. pp. 21–30. ACM, New York, NY, USA (2020)
4. Burks, D.: Security Onion - a free and open platform for threat hunting, network security monitoring, and log management (2021). https://securityonionsolutions.com
5. Elastic: Elasticsearch, Logstash and Kibana (ELK) stack (2021). https://www.elastic.co
6. Guarnizo, J.D., et al.: SIPHON: towards scalable high-interaction physical honeypots. In: Proceedings of the ACM Workshop on Cyber-Physical System Security, pp. 57–68. ACM (2017)
7. Jeon, J., Park, J.H., Jeong, Y.S.: Dynamic analysis for IoT malware detection with convolution neural network model. IEEE Access **8**, 96899–96911 (2020)

8. Kato, S., Tanabe, R., Yoshioka, K., Matsumoto, T.: Adaptive observation of emerging cyber attacks targeting various IoT devices. In: 2021 IFIP/IEEE International Symposium on Integrated Network Management (IM), pp. 143–151 (2021)
9. LLC, G.: BinExport - exporter component of BinDiff (2021). https://github.com/google/binexport
10. Luo, T., Xu, Z., Jin, X., Jia, Y., Ouyang, X.: IoTCandyJar: towards an intelligent-interaction honeypot for IoT devices. In: Proceedings of Blackhat (2017)
11. Minerva, R., Biru, A., Rotondi, D.: Towards a definition of the Internet of Things (IoT). IEEE Internet Initiative (2015). http://iot.ieee.org/images/files/pdf/IEEE_IoT_Towards_Definition_Internet_of_Things_Revision1_27MAY15.pdf
12. Neray, P.: Cloud-delivered IoT/OT threat intelligence (2021). https://techcommunity.microsoft.com/t5/microsoft-defender-for-iot-blog/cloud-delivered-iot-ot-threat-intelligence-now-available-for/ba-p/2335754
13. Nokia: Threat intelligence report 2020 (2021). https://www.nokia.com/networks/portfolio/cyber-security/threat-intelligence-report-2020
14. (NSA), N.S.A.: Ghidra - a software reverse engineering (SRE) suite of tools (2021). https://ghidra-sre.org
15. Oliver, J., Cheng, C., Chen, Y.: TLSH - a locality sensitive hash (2021). https://documents.trendmicro.com/assets/wp/wp-locality-sensitive-hash.pdf
16. Pa, Y.M.P., Suzuki, S., Yoshioka, K., Matsumoto, T., Kasama, T., Rossow, C.: IoTPOT: a novel honeypot for revealing current IoT threats. J. Inf. Process. **24**(3), 522–533 (2016)
17. Park, Y., Reeves, D.S., Stamp, M.: Deriving common malware behavior through graph clustering. Comput. Secur. 39, 419–430 (2013). https://www.sciencedirect.com/science/article/pii/S0167404813001351
18. Provos, N., et al.: A virtual honeypot framework. In: Proceedings of USENIX Security Symposium, vol. 173, pp. 1–14 (2004)
19. Rist, L.: Conpot - ICS/SCADA honeypot (2021). https://github.com/mushorg/conpot
20. Sebastián, S., Caballero, J.: AVClass2: Massive malware tag extraction from AV labels. In: Annual Computer Security Applications Conference, pp. 42–53. ACM, New York, NY, USA (2020)
21. Splunk: Splunk - data-driven security for the modern SOC (2021). https://www.splunk.com/en_us/cyber-security.html
22. Tambe, A., et al.: Detection of threats to IoT devices using scalable VPN-forwarded honeypots. In: Proceedings of the Ninth ACM Conference on Data and Application Security and Privacy, pp. 85–96. ACM, New York, NY, USA (2019)
23. Wang, B., Dou, Y., Sang, Y., Zhang, Y., Huang, J.: IoTCMal: towards a hybrid IoT honeypot for capturing and analyzing malware. In: ICC 2020–2020 IEEE International Conference on Communications (ICC), pp. 1–7 (2020)
24. Wüchner, T., Cisłak, A., Ochoa, M., Pretschner, A.: Leveraging compression-based graph mining for behavior-based malware detection. IEEE Trans. Depend. Secur. Comput. **16**(1), 99–112 (2019)

Dissecting Applications Uninstallers and Removers: Are They Effective?

Marcus Botacin[1,2](✉) and André Grégio[2]

[1] Texas A&M University, College Station, USA
[2] Federal University of Paraná (UFPR), Curitiba, Brazil
{mfbotacin,gregio}@inf.ufpr.br

Abstract. Developing a safe application is so important as to properly install it in a system, and not an application's tampered version. In a similar note, developers should properly care about applications' uninstall process to avoid leaving traces of sensitive data behind in the system or interfere with the remaining applications. Until now, the academic literature has paid little attention to uninstall procedures so far. Moreover, a whole ecosystem of application uninstallers has been created, making multiple uninstallers available in software repositories. A key point is to understand how these applications work so as to develop stronger systems. To this end, we present a landscape work evaluating the operation of the 11 most downloaded uninstaller applications from the three most popular Internet software repositories. We discovered that most of these applications are not very different from the native Windows uninstaller. Although evaluated uninstallers present a more organized User Interface, thus enhancing usability, they are only able to find the same installed application as the native Windows uninstaller, but not broken installations. Few uninstallers apply heuristics to find broken application installations. However, we show that those heuristics can be abused by attackers to remove third applications. Finally, we also show that none of the removers is resistant to malicious uninstallers that terminate the remover process.

Keywords: Uninstaller · Installer · Removal · Malicious code

1 Introduction

Safety and security are key aspects of any modern application. Thus, to cope with the safety and security requirements of a modern application, software engineers are often looking for ways of writing better code [11,19]. However, the challenge does not finish there. As important as developing a safe and secure application is to properly install this application in a system and not a tampered/vulnerable version of it [1]. Similarly, as important as properly installing an application is to uninstall it to not leave traces of sensitive data in the system [10] or interfere with the remaining applications.

W. Susilo et al. (Eds.): ISC 2022, LNCS 13640, pp. 339–359, 2022.
https://doi.org/10.1007/978-3-031-22390-7_20

Unfortunately, the academic literature has been giving little attention to uninstall procedures so far, and few to no works on the subject can be found in the major research paper databases. It causes us to have a poor understanding of an ongoing phenomenon: the popularity of application uninstallers, which can be found at hundreds in any popular Internet software repository and with a large number of downloads (e.g., 80K for `IoBit` and 400K for `Revo` in the Softonic repository). Application uninstallers (or removers) are often recommended by users in forums and/or websites [9] to be used in the cases where the native Windows uninstaller fails, but its consequences are not well understood.

To bridge this gap, we delve into the internals of Windows uninstallers to present a landscape of the operation of application uninstallers in this platform. We selected the 11 most popular apps from 3 popular software repositories (CNET [3], Softonic [22], and Softpedia [23]) and completely analyzed their operations regarding their removal capabilities, interactions with the user and with the operating system.

We discovered that, on the one hand, most of these applications are not very different from the native Windows uninstaller in operation, often displaying the same installed apps with no additional capability of searching for broken installations. On the other hand, the User Interfaces presented by these applications are clearly more detailed than the Windows' native one, presenting much more information, which might explain user's preference for them.

A few installers present advanced uninstall capabilities, such as the ability to perform system checkpoints or the application of heuristics to find files remaining from broken installations. We discovered that these capabilities and heuristics implicitly assume that the targeted uninstaller will be well-behaved. We demonstrate that multiple attacks are possible if a malicious uninstaller is the target of them, such as removing third-party files and even processes termination. In this scenario, the usage of the uninstallers would cause more harm than good.

In summary, our contributions are as follows: **(1)** We contextualize the usage of application uninstallers and the challenges associated with their use; **(2)** We present a summary of legitimate and malicious uninstaller's operations on Windows; **(3)** We discuss the limits of their application to the removal of protected applications.

This paper is organized as follows: In Sect. 2, we introduce related work and discuss the gap of understanding on the operation of uninstallers; In Sect. 3, we revisit the operation of uninstallers on the Windows system; In Sect. 4, we introduce the methodology we adopted to conduct our experiments and the research questions we aim to answer; In Sect. 5, we present experiments results regarding the actual operation of popular uninstallers; In Sect. 6, we discuss the implications of our findings; In Sect. 7, we draw our conclusions.

2 Related Work: Why Studying Uninstallers?

Before we explain how we evaluated uninstallers, it is key to understand why evaluating them is important. When a user is not satisfied with a software piece and wants to remove it, the straightforward option is to use the native Windows uninstall solution. However, it is not rare to find cases where the native uninstaller fails to remove an application. In these cases, it is common that users try to use standalone removal tools (Uninstallers and Removers), since it is also common to find websites recommending the use of this type of solution [9]. This ends up creating an entire ecosystem of application uninstallers, as can be found in any popular software repository (e.g., CNET [3]). This ecosystem must be studied and understood, as uninstalling software is as safety- and security-critical for a system as installing new ones.

Whereas the academic literature is full of good research on the software development topic (e.g., secure development and coding practices [11,19]), little attention has been given so far to the problem of uninstalling applications: We could find almost no research work in the main research paper databases (e.g., ACM, IEEE, Springer, and so on). Meanwhile, the largest part of the information users can find about uninstallers is delivered via grey literature [24] (i.e., websites, blog posts, and so on). Unfortunately, publications in this type of literature often do not present formal evaluations of uninstallers or a strong methodology to evaluate them, such that we understand that there is currently an understanding gap about the operation of these solutions.

We believe the subject has been given little attention so far because the uninstallation problem is often seen in the literature as a management problem [18] rather than also a technological problem. A few works in the literature address the uninstallation problem from a more technical point-of-view and, if so, they are very limited in scope (e.g., a forensic analysis of uninstalled steganography apps [28]). We believe that uninstallers must be studied more broadly to present a landscape, as recently done for applications installers [1].

The related work on application installers already pinpointed some limitations of the associated uninstallers, such as the improper definition of the uninstaller executable [1]. In this work, we aim to go further and analyze the behavior of the applications designed to uninstall these failure-prone applications. For instance, we aim to evaluate whether uninstallers can clean registry keys after the application removal. Previous research work has demonstrated that potentially sensitive information remained resident in the registry after the uninstall of some specific software [10].

Therefore, this work aims to shed light on the greater scenario of uninstallers operation. It is important to notice that application uninstallers are available to most platforms (e.g., Android [7]), but we focused our efforts in this paper on the Windows platform due to the popularity of uninstallers in this ecosystem.

3 Background: How Windows Supports Uninstallers?

Before understanding how third-party uninstallers operate, it is key to understand how Windows applications are installed and removed natively. On Windows, installers should register the installed applications with the Windows registry by creating an entry in the proper registry branch [13]. Applications installed for a single user must add their information to the key at `HKEY_CURRENT_USER\Software\Microsoft\Windows\CurrentVersion\App Paths`. Applications installed for all users in the machine should add their information to the key at `HKEY_LOCAL_MACHINE\Software\Microsoft\Windows\CurrentVersion\App Paths`.

The Windows' "Installed Apps" menu gathers information from these keys to display the installed apps and their removal/edit options. The first uninstallation problem is that nothing prevents an app from not registering with Windows (e.g., executable files directly extracted from compressed files–zips). In these cases, the application will be not found in the Windows' "Installed Apps" menu.

When the application registers itself with Windows, it must set some required registry keys, such as the application name, the provider, and the uninstaller path. Therefore, when a user requires an application to be uninstalled by the native Windows uninstaller, the uninstaller checks the path stored in this registry key and launches the registered removal process.

The problem with this approach is that nothing prevents an application to register a fake or a broken uninstall path, such that the uninstaller will not be able to create a process from it. In this case, the application is never really uninstalled. Although this is considered a bad practice according to the security policies of large software ecosystem providers (e.g., Google [8], Microsoft [17]), this strategy is often used by many applications available for user's download.

Another problem is that Windows completely trusts the invoked uninstaller to remove the application files and keys. However, if the application's native installer does not do a great job removing its own application, files and registry keys will remain in the system. Overall, there are many reasons why an application might be not properly removed, for instance:

- Installations without registering associated keys [12].
- Installers setting the `APPNOREMOVE` key [14], that prevents the native uninstall to launch the uninstall process.
- Implementation bugs, such as applications setting registry keys greater than 60 chars [15], which is unsupported by Windows.

When we consider the possibilities above discussed, we notice that the process of uninstalling an application is not straightforward. Therefore, we consider that understanding how uninstallers handle those conditions is essential for developing better applications.

The Role of the Third-Party Uninstallers. Face to this challenging removal scenario, third-party uninstallers promise to succeed in the cases where conventional removal fails. They promise not only to remove the applications listed by the Windows, but also to discover the ones that did not register with the Windows, remove files from previous, broken installation, and even defeat protections that prevent a software to be uninstalled. All these cases are evaluated in this paper.

4 Methodology: What Do We Aim to Discover? and How?

In this section, we present the questions we aimed to answer, the applications we considered in our analysis, and the approach for inspecting them.

Research Questions. We defined the following Research Questions (RQs) to help us to understand the uninstallers:

- **RQ1. What is the anatomy of the uninstallers?** This question aims to answer what are the modules and components of a typical uninstaller. It also aims to answer how uninstallers are structured.
  - **RQ1.1 Are there applications bundled in the uninstallers?** This derived question aims to answer whether additional components not essential to the uninstallers operations are added to them.
- **RQ2. How do uninstallers operate?** This question aims to answer how uninstallers interact with system components.
  - **RQ2.1 Do uninstallers include extra features?** This derived question aims to answer whether uninstallers provide non-traditional mechanisms to uninstall applications.
- **RQ3. What is the difference for the native uninstaller?** This question aims to answer whether there is any significant advantage on migrating to a standalone application.
- **RQ4. Do uninstallers handle drivers, services, and privileged components?** This question aims to answer what are the limits of uninstallers operations.
- **RQ5. Are there any performance gains in using an uninstaller?** This question aims to verify if claims of perceived performance gains made by some vendors and users are real.
- **RQ6. Do uninstallers leave files in the system?** This question aims to answer what is the potential of uninstallers for cleaning files.
  - **RQ6.1 Did uninstallers evolve?**. We repeated the experiments reported in the literature [10] to check whether the scenario changed over time.
- **RQ7. Are uninstallers able to remove protected applications?** This question aims to answer what are the capabilities of the uninstallers.
  - **RQ7.1 Are uninstallers resistant to tampering attempts?** This derived question aims to answer how resistant to malicious applications uninstallers are.
  - **RQ7.2 Are uninstallers able to remove malware?** This question aims to answer whether uninstallers can unlock resources from malicious processes, such as hypothesized by some users in forums [4–6].

Uninstallers Selection. To provide a landscape of the uninstallers, we followed the same strategy adopted in the reference study of application installers [1]: the

Table 1. Selected Uninstallers. We selected the most popular applications that were successfully downloaded and not part of a security solution. Columns represent, respectively, tool name, tool version, if they are embedded in security solutions (✓) or not (✗), if they were successfully downloaded (✓) or not (✗), if they run on VM (✓) or not (✗), and their ranking in the repositories. Empty fields mean that the data is not available and/or the criteria does not apply.

Uninstaller	Version	Security	Downloaded	VM	CNET	Softonic	Softpedia
Iobit	11.0.1.14	✗	✓	✓	1	2	
Revo	2.1.5.0	✗	✓	✓	2	1	2
Your	7.5.2014.3	✗	✓	✓	3		3
Advanced		✗	✗		4	6	8
Easy		✗	✗		5		
Wise	2.3.6.140	✗	✓	✓	6		
Ashampoo	10.10.00.13	✗	✓	✓	7	9	15
Zsoft	2.5	✗	✓	✓	8		12
Anvi	1.0	✗	✓	✓	9		
Smarty	4.9.6	✗	✓	✓	10		11
Puran	3.0	✗	✓	✓	11		
Handy	1.2	✗	✓	✓	12	12	
Absolute	5.3.1.26	✗	✓	✓	13		9
Ccleaner		✓			14		
Bazooka Adware		✓			15		
Uninstall Manager		✗	✗		16		
Total Uninstall	6.16.0	✗	✓	✗	17	10	5

search for applications in the most popular online software repositories. Our search in December/2021 revealed the existence of 275 uninstallers entries for the uninstaller keyword for CNET [3], 6 thousand for Softonic [22] (unfiltered), and 268 for Softpedia [23].

Unfortunately, we cannot handle these amounts via manual analysis, as required by the experiments we designed, such that we opted for selecting the applications ranked first in the repositories (the most downloaded ones), hypothesizing them to be more representative of the solutions most users install in their machines. We found a low agreement between the ranks of all repositories, such that we tried to maximize our coverage by considering the most popular apps in the higher rank positions in the majority of the repositories. We discovered that considering the CNET rank as a reference was the selection that maximize the rank position coverage.

From all possible uninstallers to be selected, we discarded those that were not successfully downloaded (e.g., server errors on the repository side and/or corrupted files), those that did not execute in Virtual Machines (VMs)–used for tests–,and also discarded those that were part of security solutions, since the analysis of security solutions is different from our goal of analyzing the uninstallers by themselves (specific analyses are reported in the academic literature [2]). Table 1 shows the 11 selected uninstallers and their respective rank positions for the multiple repositories. We also show the downloaded apps' versions for the sake of reproducibility.

Removed Apps Selection. The applications we targeted to remove using the uninstallers were the native applications installed with Windows, additional Microsoft products installed in typical user's machines (e.g., Office), and the top-10 most popular applications used by the users (e.g., browsers) according to the rankings of the same repositories that we downloaded the uninstallers. The number of applications used in each experiment varied according to their goals: a random one, when designing a malicious uninstaller; all of them simultaneously, when evaluating the presence of sensitive information.

Analysis Methodology: To inspect the uninstaller applications, we manually installed each of them into a fresh Virtual Machine (VM) and inspected the installed files (static analysis) and their interaction with system components while we interacted with the application's UI (interactive dynamic analysis). All monitoring was performed using either Microsoft native tools, such as `regedit`, for registry inspection, or Microsoft complements, such as SysInternals [16], for advanced system state inspection. The VMs were restored to the original state after each uninstaller was tested.

Copyright Information: During our experiments, no decompilation was performed so as to not violate the creator's copyright. All analyses were performed by statically examining the installed software files and/or the behavior of the applications during their normal execution.

5 Evaluation: What We Discovered?

In this section, we present our experiment's results and show how they contribute to understanding uninstaller's operations.

5.1 RQ1. the Anatomy

We started our investigation by analyzing the structure of the uninstallers, as summarized in Table 2. Our initial goal was to use the complexity of their constructions as a proxy for evaluating the complexity of their operations. Our initial hypothesis was that these installers would be complex pieces of software that integrate with multiple parts of the system to be able to perform the removal actions that the installers and the OS itself was not able to perform. Instead, we found that most applications were simpler than expected.

In fact, some uninstallers are even standalone applications, operating from a self-contained binary, which embeds all capabilities and presents all data hard-coded within it. Their simplicity associated with the great number of Windows libraries imported by them makes us to hypothesize then that they operate only like wrappers for invoking the proper Windows native functions designed to remove software.

Being a standalone application is not a problem, simplicity is desired, since the application is well-designed and follows the best practices. Interestingly, in the case of the `Anvi` installer, the standalone application does not register its own binary with the system, thus not appearing in the list of installed software. In some sense, the uninstaller application acts the same way that the software it is designed to remove acts.

Table 2. Uninstallers Anatomy. Files and Components. Columns represent, respectively, tool name, if they are registered with the Windows (✓) or not (✗), the number of executable files it is composed of, if it is composed of shared libraries (✓) or not (✗), the number of kernel drivers composing the tool, if the applications stores data in databases (✓) or not (✗), and if it relies on configuration files (✓) or not (✗).

Unnstaller	Register	EXE	DLL	Drv	DB	Config
Iobit	✓	21	✓	3	✓	✗
Revo	✓	1	✗	✗	✗	✗
Your	✓	6	✗	✗	✗	✓
Wise	✓	3	✗	✗	✓	✓
Ashampoo	✓	6	✓	✗	✓	✗
ZSoft	✓	2	✗	✗	✗	✓
Anvi	✗	1	✗	✗	✗	✗
Smarty	✓	2	✓	✗	✗	✗
Puran	✓	2	✗	✗	✗	✓
Handy	✓	1	✗	✗	✗	✗
Absolute	✓	4	✓	1	✗	✗

Even the uninstallers that are not standalone are not complex, with a minority presenting even libraries. We hypothesized initially that libraries would be used to implement custom removal algorithms, but we mostly found libraries used for compatibility (e.g., zlib for compression support). Similar reasoning can be applied for kernel drivers, which are found only in two uninstallers. Most uninstallers operate in the same privilege level as the software they aim to remove.

Even when they are not standalone binaries, most uninstallers do not keep usage sessions in the current system. We only found 3 uninstallers storing information about the system in databases (all cases in `sqlite` databases). In most cases, they simply use information hardcoded in the binaries or gathered from configuration (config) files (often stored in plain) to increase their removal capabilities and intelligence.

In the case of the `Wise` uninstaller, the configuration file stores a list of ratings for popular applications and also an application exclusion list (e.g., Firefox, Chrome, Opera), whose files will not be touched by the uninstaller, limiting the aggressiveness of the heuristics, but also the removal capabilities. Lists are also found in the Ashampoo uninstaller. In this case, a whitelist, protected against modifications only by filesystem permissions, is used by the application. It means that the applications present in the whitelist will not be removed from a system by the removal software and its heuristics. The approach used by the ZSoft uninstaller is of blocklisting applications. It means that the removal software looks for the presence of specific, known "bad" applications to be removed. We identified that the "bad" reputation of a given software is given by the StopBadware list [25], present in the configuration files of this application.

RQ1.1. Bundling. Most uninstaller applications are distributed in limited forms to incent a purchase, as shown in Table 3. As a limitation, a few of them will display ads to the user. The worst case, however, is when the uninstallers are delivered with additional packages bundled in the original file. In this case, whereas users are looking for an application to remove software from their system, the final result is that more software is installed, which is not reasonable.

Table 3. Application Bundling. Some uninstallers distribute other applications during their installation. Columns shows, respectively, the tool name, the type of contented bundled with it, if it displays ads (✓) or not (✗) and of which type (if available), and the license type.

Uninstaller	Bundled	Ads	Type
Iobit	Itop suite Itop screen recorder Itop vpn	Opera Driverbooster	Freemium
Revo	✗	✗	Freemium
Your	✗	✗	Shareware
Wise	✗	✗	Freeware
Ashampoo	✗	✗	Shareware
ZSoft	✗	✗	Freeware
Anvi	✗	✗	Shareware
Smarty	✗	✗	Shareware
Puran	✗	✗	Freeware
Handy	✗	Random Ads	Freeware
Absolute	Games	✗	Freeware

5.2 RQ2. Operation

The key goal of our investigation is to discover how uninstallers really remove the applications. For such, we requested the evaluated uninstallers to remove multiple applications under different settings. A summary of the uninstaller's capabilities is shown in Table 4.

Our first finding is that in an overall manner the uninstallers display the same installed application as Windows, which indicates that they search the same registry locations. Only two uninstallers performed a full registry search. On the one hand, broader searches are useful to find software not installed in standard locations. On the other hand, this strategy ends up generating false positive reports.

Table 4. Uninstallers Operation. Uninstallers first invoke the native uninstaller. Some apply heuristics after that. Columns show, respectively, tool name, if the list of installed apps is retrieved from the Windows subsystem or directly from the registry, if it invokes the native uninstaller (✓) or not (✗), if the removal process is automated (✓) or not (✗), and if it has custom removal heuristics (✓) or not (✗).

Uninstaller	List	Native	Auto	Custom
Iobit	Windows	✓	✓	✗
Revo	Windows	✓	✓	✗
Your	Windows	✓	✓	✗
Wise	Windows	✓	✓	✗
Ashampoo	Windows	✓	✗	✓
ZSoft	Registry	✓	✗	✗
Anvi	Windows	✓	✗	✓
Smarty	Windows	✓	✓	✗
Puran	Windows	✓	✗	✓
Handy	Registry	✓	✗	✗
Absolute	Windows	✓	✗	✗

We discovered that a universal uninstaller's strategy is to invoke the original uninstaller of the application to be removed before taking any other action to remove the software. This strategy is adopted by all evaluated applications. Whereas some applications seem limited to this functionality, acting only as another GUI for the removal process, some applications try to complement the removal procedure. In this sense, the uninstaller's philosophy seems more to try to clean residual entries than trying to remove applications by themselves.

The strategies used to perform additional cleanings are varied. Some uninstallers perform custom scans, asking the user if they want to remove a given file. It does not seem to be a significant advantage in comparison to manual removal procedures. The only clear benefit in it is to automatically locate files, but no decision is taken by the application. Other uninstallers try to add intelligence to the process by employing heuristics to automatically identify which files must be removed.

To evaluate the identified third-party uninstaller's capabilities in practice, we created a crafted application installation with an integrated custom uninstaller that purposely did not remove registry keys and installation files. We applied the third-party uninstallers to check their actions over the remaining installation artifacts. We summarize the results in Table 5.

Table 5. Removal Experiment. Heuristics might be tricked to remove the wrong files. Columns represent, respectively, tool name, if the tool was able to remove apps from the installed apps list (✓) or not (✗), if they were able to remove associated registry keys (✓) or not (✗), if they were able to remove associated files (✓) or not (✗), and if they are prone to remove wrong files (✓) or not (✗).

Uninstaller	List	Registry	Files	Wrong
Iobit	✓	✓	✓	✓
Revo	✓	✓	✓	✓
Your	✓	✓	✗	✗
Wise	✓	✓	✓	✓
Ashampoo	✓	✓	✓	✓
ZSoft	✓	✓	✗	✗
Anvi	✓	✗	✗	✗
Smarty	✓	✓	✓	✓
Puran	✓	✗	✗	✗
Handy	✓	✓	✗	✗
Absolute	✓	✗	✗	✗

All uninstallers were able to run the native uninstaller (our custom one) and thus remove the application from the list of installed apps. However, it does not mean that applications were fully uninstalled by all of them. Not all uninstallers were able to wipe the registry entries associated with the application that were intentionally left by our uninstaller. Similarly, not all of them were able to follow the paths stored in the registry keys and delete the files intentionally left in the filesystem. The only solutions able to perform this type of uninstallation were the ones using heuristics. The heuristic used by the uninstallers is to follow the path added to the `InstallLocation` key and suggest the removal of whatever is pointed by it.

A major drawback of using heuristics is that they provide no guarantee that they will remove correct files, and this characteristic might even be abused. To demonstrate that, we configured an application installation whose `InstallLocation` path points to another application's folders, unrelated to our targeted application. In all cases, the installers suggested removing the unrelated folders, even when we pointed them to native Windows folders, which might even break the system operation.

RQ2.1. Extra Features. In addition to their original function of uninstalling applications, many uninstallers also offer other facilities to the users. Table 6 summarizes the extra features we found on the evaluated uninstallers.

Table 6. Extra Features. Some uninstallers present additional monitoring and management resources. Columns show, respectively, tool name, if they filter installers by size (✓) or not (✗), by usage frequency (✓) or not (✗), if they handled installed updates (✓) or not (✗), if they have cleaning capabilities (✓) or not (✗), if they monitor new installations (✓) or not (✗), and if they create installation checkpoints (✓) or not (✗).

Uninstaller	Size	Freq.	Upd.	Clean.	Mon.	Checkpoint
Iobit	✓	✓	✗	✗	✓	✗
Revo	✗	✗	✗	✗	✗	✗
Your	✗	✗	✗	✓	✗	✗
Wise	✗	✗	✗	✗	✗	✗
Ashampoo	✗	✗	✓	✗	✓	✗
ZSoft	✗	✗	✗	✗	✗	✓
Anvi	✓	✗	✗	✗	✗	✗
Smarty	✗	✗	✗	✗	✗	✓
Puran	✗	✗	✗	✗	✗	✗
Handy	✗	✗	✓	✗	✗	✗
Absolute	✗	✓	✓	✗	✗	✗

Many features offered by the installers are focused on usability rather than on the removal process itself (e.g., identifying very large files, rarely used files, unattended update files left in the system, and so on). Some facilities are related to the removal but do not involve a specific process (e.g., cleaning the system), such that they were evaluated separately.

Two extra features are of our particular interest when evaluating uninstallers: (i) the ability to monitor new installations, and (ii) the ability of performing system checkpoints. These two functions are not natively provided by Windows and they would be useful to the users. We discovered, however, that these two functions are very limited in all uninstallers. We discovered, for instance, that the so-called monitors do not perform whole-system monitoring, as expected. Instead, they only search specific locations and registry keys, such that standalone installers are not identified (e.g., EXE files extracted from zip folders) and manual registry edits are also not reported.

The checkpoint mechanism works similarly on both evaluated uninstallers that offer this capability. The user takes a snapshot of the current system state (files and registry keys) before installing an application, installs it, and takes a new snapshot after it. The newly added files and registry keys are then reported. If the user asks for application removal, these files will be removed.

The snapshot mechanism is very fast, such that we hypothesized that the uninstallers do not look for file contents (not even a hash/digest). We evaluated this hypothesis by modifying an existing file and we discovered that this was also reported as a new file. We then hypothesized that the uninstaller was identifying it via the filesystem's modification time. We confirmed that by re-saving files, with no actual modification, during the snapshot, such that these files were reported as new. Whereas timing-efficient, this approach is problematic because it reports any modified file as belonging to the installed application and suggests its removal. When we modified a system file, this file was also suggested for removal, which might break the system operation.

5.3 RQ3. the Differences

One of the goals of this research work is to investigate the reasons why one would prefer a third-part uninstaller than the native solution. We did not discover many differences to support such migration, except the one here discussed.

Table 7. Applications with `NOREMOVE` option. Most uninstallers simply ignore the option. The set of columns show, respectively, tool name and if the tool was able to remove applications with the `NOREMOVE` option set (✓) or not (✗).

Uninstaller	Removed	Uninstaller	Removed
Windows	✗	ZSoft	✗
IoBit	✓	Anvi	✓
Revo	✓	Smarty	✓
Your	✓	Puran	✓
Wise	✓	Handy	✓
Ashampoo	✓	Absolute	✓

Applications might mark themselves to not be removed by setting the `APPNOREMOVE` key in the registry. In this case, the native Windows uninstaller will not display the uninstall button for that application, even though the application will still be displayed in the list of installed apps. We evaluated the behavior of the other uninstallers in this case. Table 7 shows that all uninstallers except for `ZSoft` simply ignore this registry key and invoke the registered uninstaller anyway. Whereas skilled users might perform manual registry editing to remove the key and allow the native Windows uninstaller to remove the application, we consider that in this scenario the third-part uninstallers perform better than the native one because even users with less knowledge about Windows internals can remove applications in this setting.

5.4 RQ4. Privileges

As important as to identify that a given resource must be removed is to have the ability to remove it. In practice, this might be challenging due to permission issues (e.g., a file might be locked, a process might still be running, the access to a key might require admin privileges). Therefore, we aimed to evaluate how uninstallers handle these conditions. We discovered that, since the uninstallers rely on the invocation of the original uninstaller, they have almost the same capabilities as them. In this sense, the uninstallers do not elevate themselves to admin, but they wait for the native uninstallers to do so to remove the files. If they do, the files are removed. If they do not remove a file that requires special permissions, the standalone uninstallers will not be able to remove them as well. Similarly, if the native uninstaller unloads kernel drivers and stops services, these will be removed. However, if the standalone uninstallers are required to remove them while running, any attempt will fail due to the lack of proper permissions. Whereas we understand that this scenario is somehow expected and thus acceptable, most uninstallers do not make it clear to the users. In our searches, we found that only the `Revo` uninstaller stated in its manual that drivers must be removed in safe mode [26].

5.5 RQ5. Performance

It is common to find users in Web forums recommending the use of uninstallers and/or cleaners to speed up system performance. The hypothesis behind it is that having fewer files and/or registry keys in the system would make searches faster, as the system would have to traverse smaller structures, which is a reasonable hypothesis at a first glance [20]. This "popular knowledge" become widespread to the point of that some solutions even advertise performance gains. Therefore, it is important to investigate to which extent these supposed performance gains are significant.

Two of the uninstallers solutions that we evaluated made explicit performance claims: `You Uninstaller` and `Ashampoo`. In the first case, the advertised cleaning function is, in fact, limited to a few pre-defined locations, such as browser's history, cookies, and so on. Even though this might have a (limited) impact on navigation, it is hard to consider these actions as a performance improvement to the system. In the second case, the uninstaller presents a solution to clean the registry tree as a whole. We evaluated its impact by taking a snapshot of the registry tree before and after the cleaning. We discovered that the solution is very conservative when removing keys. It only removes registry entries with no associated keys (empty), but it does not remove orphaned keys (e.g., keys that point to invalid paths). On the one hand, the solution works both for the current user (HKCU) as well as for the other uses (HKLM). On the other hand, it is very conservative and does not touch keys that affect the system (e.g., HKCR).

In the end, after an average of 10 repetitions, the solution removed 500 keys from an average of 318 thousand keys with 564 thousand associated values present in our fresh Windows installation. We consider that this result (less than 0.2% effect) is not significant to support claims of performance gains. To confirm this hypothesis, we executed 10 repetitions of a Windows registry benchmarking tool [21] and measured the depth of the traversed registry branches and the actual time spent traversing them. We noticed no statistical difference between the system state before and after the system cleanup.

5.6 RQ6. Remaining Files

A good uninstaller application should be able to remove all traces of an installed application from the registry and filesystem. Of course, this is the main task of the native application uninstaller, but since in this work we assume the user is using some other application because the native uninstaller already failed, we would like to verify whether the third-part uninstallers are able to bridge this gap. Unfortunately, they are not. Since most uninstallers only invoke the native uninstaller to remove the application, they end up failing in the same aspects as the original uninstaller. The uninstallers that perform additional heuristic checks indeed remove more files, but no uninstaller completely removed all files of any application we tested. This essentially happened because applications often install their files in two distinct locations: `Program Files`, for the binaries; and `AppData`, for the configuration files. Since only the first location is affected by the requirements to register the application with the Windows registry, the heuristics are only able to correlate this location with the installed application, always leaving the second folder untouched.

RQ6.1. Evolution. A major problem with files and registry keys left in the filesystem is that they can potentially reveal sensitive information about the users, as demonstrated by a previous work [10]. We repeated their experiment to verify if the situation improved with time and if the use of third-party uninstallers is a viable option for cleaning the system after an uninstall. To do so, we installed the same application considered in the original work (in updated versions) in a fresh Windows installation. We populated these applications with data from an entire day of use. For instance, for the mail client, we registered an account in it and sent and received emails. We inspected the filesystem and the registry after we uninstalled the applications using the native uninstaller and the third-part ones. We notice that no clear sensitive information is left by the native uninstaller (e.g., no key storing email addresses), which we might credit to enhancement to the native uninstaller itself over time. On the other hand, configuration and temporary files were still spread all over the filesystem after the installation. The files stored in the `AppData` folder were cleaned by the third-part uninstallers, but there were remaining files in other folders after the application of all solutions. Therefore, we conclude that whereas uninstallers might help removing some orphan files, they are not the solution for definitively eliminating all files, especially if one is concerned with privacy leaks.

5.7 RQ7. Protection

If uninstallers are supposed to remove badly-behaved applications, they should be protected at least against the basic types of interference attempts, such as termination. We inspected the uninstallers in search of signs of self-protection mechanisms to evaluate their protection level. We did not find, however, for all uninstallers, OS-independent protection mechanisms, which indicates that they assume that the software they will uninstall is well-behaved (i.e., they will operate following the best standards, ordinary methods, and not abusing interfaces).

For two uninstallers, we identified components that could be used to increase self-protection (e.g., kernel drivers that could be used to prevent access to the uninstaller files). We discovered, however, that these components are only part of the uninstaller engine and not part of self-protection modules (e.g., kernel drivers are used as callback mechanisms). In the case of the `Absolute` uninstaller, the driver could be terminated by any user/process having admin privileges (in the last instance, it could be even the application requested to be uninstalled). In the case of the `IoBit`, there were 3 drivers running in our test environment (responsible for the process, registry, and filesystem callbacks, respectively). Whereas the first two were resistant to termination due to the lack of proper permissions, the filesystem driver was easily terminated by the admin (which we interpreted as a bug, since the other 2 drivers were protected).

RQ7.1. Anti-tampering. To demonstrate uninstallers vulnerabilities due to the lack of self-protection mechanisms, we developed some attacks[1] that could be leveraged by a malicious application to not be removed by an uninstalling application.

Our first attack is based on the fact that the standalone uninstallers directly call from their main process the application registered in the registry as an uninstaller for the target application rather than calling them from a child/protected process. This allows the targeted uninstaller to identify the PID of their parent processes (the standalone uninstallers) and directly attempt to terminate this Process ID (PID). If no protection mechanism is employed, the attack will succeed and the targeted application remains installed in the system.

Table 8. Uninstaller Termination. Uninstallers can be terminated by the targeted uninstall application. The set of columns show, respectively, tool names, and if the installers were terminate (✓) or not (✗) by a malicious uninstaller.

Uninstaller	Terminated	Uninstaller	Terminated
Windows	Crashed	ZSoft	✓
IoBit	✓	Anvi	✓
Revo	✓	Smarty	✓
Your	✓	Puran	✓
Wise	✓	Handy	✓
Ashampoo	✓	Absolute	✓

[1] Attack demos available at: https://www.youtube.com/watch?v=Rkw6WbD-nMY, https://www.youtube.com/watch?v=mZPb7h4cy80, and https://www.youtube.com/watch?v=0AjFCZWUhfU.

We developed a Proof-of-Concept (PoC) uninstall application for this attack and registered it as the uninstall of an application to be removed by the standalone uninstallers. Table 8 shows this experiment's results. Whereas the Windows installer crashed, but did not terminate, all standalone uninstallers terminated before removing the targeted application.

The problem with the first attack is that terminating the application is noticeable for the user and might raise concerns. A more effective strategy would be to remove the application from the list of installed software without actually uninstalling it. We developed a second class of attacks with this goal by exploiting the facts that (i) installers have no self-protection mechanisms; and (ii) they rely on standard system interfaces for their operation.

Our second attack consisted of injecting a DLL into the uninstaller applications to hook the Windows APIs used by the uninstallers to remove our PoC application from the installed applications list. In other words, we developed a userland rootkit. Table 9 shows that we were able to inject the DLL and remove applications from the list of all standalone uninstallers when the processes were already launched with the injected DLL. It also shows that injection was possible in runtime into all but three uninstallers. The two failure cases are due to their process being protected against memory writes after the process setup phase, which is the only self-protection measure we found among all uninstallers we inspected.

Table 9. Uninstaller Tampering. External code might affect uninstaller's operations. Columns show, respectively, the tool name, if the tool is affected by code injection at startup (✓) or not (✗), at runtime (✓) or not (✗), and by external kernel drivers (✓) or not (✗).

Uninstaller	Userland		Kernel
	Startup	Runtime	
IoBit	✓	✗	✓
Revo	✓	✗	✓
Your	✓	✓	✓
Wise	✓	✓	✓
Ashampoo	✓	✓	✓
ZSoft	✓	✓	✓
Anvi	✓	✓	✓
Smarty	✓	✗	✓
Puran	✓	✓	✓
Handy	✓	✓	✓
Absolute	✓	✓	✓

We also developed a third attack that does not depend on code injection to demonstrate that the reliance on OS APIs is the weakest point of the uninstaller's security model. We developed a kernel driver that implements callbacks to prevent uninstallers from accessing registry keys associated with the targeted application, which could be performed by a malicious software that prevents uninstallations. In other words, we developed a kernel rootkit. Table 9 shows that this strategy succeeded against all uninstallers, removing the targeted application from the list of installed software without actually removing the application from the system.

RQ7.2. Anti-malware. Considering the self-protection limitations that we presented above, we understand that uninstallers are not suitable as a replacement for security solutions for the task of malware detection, as suggested in some Web forums, since an armored malware could terminate them or interfere with their operation. Moreover, we also did not find evidence of an actual capability of removing malware traces in any of the solutions. In our tests, we infected a system with multiple samples collected from VirusShare [27] (10 randomly-chosen samples tested against each uninstaller) that created `AutoRun` keys for persisting in the registry. Even after we manually removed the malicious binaries from the system and left the keys orphan, the uninstallers were still not able to detect it and remove these entries from the registry. In other words, the uninstallers were not able to identify that the malware samples were the original parents of the leftover AutoRun keys. This happens mostly because the removal heuristics used by the uninstallers rely on data that is often set by benign applications (paths in registry keys) that were not set by the malware samples.

6 Discussion: What Are the Implications of Our Findings?

Based on our findings, we here present a brief discussion about some implications of our findings.

The Need for Better Uninstallers Using Current Technology. Whereas most of the investigated uninstallers did not present significantly greater removal capabilities than the native Windows one, all of them present a better user interface (UI)/user experience (UX), in the sense that applications are categorized, ranked, locations are displayed, and so on (see RQ 2.1). These information pieces are not available in the standard Windows tool. We believe that this might be one of the reasons why users adopt this kind of solution rather than using the native installer. Therefore, OS developers (e.g., Microsoft/Windows) should investigate refactoring and enhancement possibilities of their native solutions. We believe that incorporating the features from the third-part solutions to a native system is an immediately applicable action that does not depend on the development of new technologies.

The Need for Better Uninstallers Using Next-gen Technology. Whereas enhancing the UI/UX is an immediately applicable action, enhancing the removal capabilities depends on the development of new technologies. When we analyze the removal procedure, we observe that uninstallers fail to remove files remaining from broken installation because no system component keeps track of processes' interactions all the time. Therefore, for the development of an efficient uninstallation procedure, systems would have either to (i) monitor the system constantly to identify which files/registry keys/so on were accessed by each process; or (ii) tag the touched files so one could identify to which applications a file/registry key belongs. If we develop a tagging mechanism, one could remove files associated with a process by looking at the registry keys tags or, otherwise, remove registry keys associated with a process by looking for the tags assigned to a file belonging to that process. Efficiently tagging resources consists of a significant open research problem that must be addressed by the research community.

Study Limitations. Whereas this study presented a comprehensive analysis of the most popular uninstallers, thus covering a significant user base, it is important to highlight that this study is noth exhaustive. The manual approach required to inspect the uninstallers limited the number of uninstallers that our research team was able to analyze. We understand that our current findings are a first step to shed light on the uninstallers landscape. For the future, more research is warranted to cover a greater number of uninstallers, of distinct nature, and covering distinct platforms.

7 Conclusion

In this work, we investigated the operation of the 11 most downloaded application uninstallers from the 3 most popular Internet software repositories. We analyzed their operation against well-behaved and malformed uninstallers to characterize their weak and strong aspects. Based on our experiments, we concluded the following about their operation: **(1)** Most installers are similar to the native Windows uninstaller, finding the same installed applications and not locating broken installations; **(2)** Some installers provide interesting additional features, such as creating a system checkpoint, but this feature might corrupt files if not applied immediately after the broken application installation; **(3)** The heuristics employed by a few installers to clean broken installation files might be abused by a malicious uninstaller to force the removal of third-party's files; **(4)** The installers are not resistant against a malicious uninstaller designed to terminate the uninstaller application.

We recommend the OS vendors to: **(1)** Redesign their uninstallation systems. The third-part uninstallers all present better application organization than the native uninstaller (e.g., categorizing them), such that this might work as an incentive for users adopting this type of solution rather than the native one.

We recommend for users: **(1)** Do not confuse removing an application from the installed apps list with actually removing the application files. Sensitive files might still be resident in the filesystem after an application removal; **(2)**

Application uninstallers are not secure robust enough to remove malware, thus they should not be used as a replacement for Antiviruses and security solutions.

Reproducibility. All code developed for our experiments are available at https://github.com/marcusbotacin/Uninstallers.

Acknowledgments. The authors would like to thank the Brazilian Ministry of Education for supporting this work (Research Project "Plataforma MEC de Recursos Educacionais Digitais", Funding Agency: Fundo Nacional de Desenvolvimento da Educação - FNDE, TED n. 10.959).

References

1. Botacin, M., Bertão, G., de Geus, P., Grégio, A., Kruegel, C., Vigna, G.: On the security of application installers and online software repositories. In: Maurice, C., Bilge, L., Stringhini, G., Neves, N. (eds.) DIMVA 2020. LNCS, vol. 12223, pp. 192–214. Springer, Cham (2020). https://doi.org/10.1007/978-3-030-52683-2_10
2. Botacin, M., et al.: Antiviruses under the microscope: a hands-on perspective. Comput. Secur. **112** , 102500 (2022)
3. CNET: Uninstall - search (2021). https://download.cnet.com/s/uninstall/?platform=linux
4. Forum, A.: When does one use REVO uninstaller? (2013). https://forum.avast.com/index.php?topic=127051.0
5. Forum, I.: CBS/CNET recommended i use an uninstaller to remove their malware (2014). https://forums.iobit.com/topic/12814-cbscnet-recommended-i-use-an-uninstaller-to-remove-their-malware/
6. Forum, V.: My opinion of revo uninstaller pro (2003). https://forum.videohelp.com/threads/351573-My-opinion-of-Revo-Uninstaller-Pro
7. Google: Uninstallers - google play. https://play.google.com/store/search?q=uninstaller (2021)
8. Google: Unwanted software policy (2021). https://www.google.com/about/unwanted-software-policy.html
9. Hoffman, C.: Should you use a third-party uninstaller? (2015). https://www.howtogeek.com/172050/htg-explains-should-you-use-a-third-party-uninstaller/
10. Kim, Y., Lee, S., Hong, D.: Suspects' data hiding at remaining registry values of uninstalled programs. In: e-Forensics. ICST (Institute for Computer Sciences, Social-Informatics and Telecommunications Engineering) (2008)
11. Liou, J.-C., Duclervil, S.R.: A survey on the effectiveness of the secure software development life cycle models. In: Daimi, K., Francia III, G. (eds.) Innovations in Cybersecurity Education, pp. 213–229. Springer, Cham (2020). https://doi.org/10.1007/978-3-030-50244-7_11
12. Microsoft: Adding and removing an application and leaving no trace in the registry (2018). https://docs.microsoft.com/en-us/windows/win32/msi/adding-and-removing-an-application-and-leaving-no-trace-in-the-registry
13. Microsoft: Application registration (2018). https://docs.microsoft.com/en-us/windows/win32/shell/app-registration#registering-verbs-and-other-file-association-information
14. Microsoft: Configuring add/remove programs with windows installer (2018). https://docs.microsoft.com/en-us/windows/win32/msi/configuring-add-remove-programs-with-windows-installer

15. Microsoft: Program is not listed in add/remove programs after installation (2018). https://support.microsoft.com/en-us/topic/program-is-not-listed-in-add-remove-programs-after-installation-0866db2a-f8d9-fb0f-16d2-850f5072e536
16. Microsoft: Windows sysinternals (2021). https://docs.microsoft.com/en-us/sysinternals/
17. Microsoft: Software download products & services, freeware & shareware (2022). https://about.ads.microsoft.com/en-us/policies/restricted-categories/software-freeware-shareware#uninstall-functionality
18. Primiero, G., Boender, J.: Managing software uninstall with negative trust. In: Steghöfer, J.-P., Esfandiari, B. (eds.) IFIPTM 2017. IAICT, vol. 505, pp. 79–93. Springer, Cham (2017). https://doi.org/10.1007/978-3-319-59171-1_7
19. Ramirez, A., Aiello, A., Lincke, S.J.: A survey and comparison of secure software development standards. In: 2020 13th CMI Conference on Cybersecurity and Privacy (CMI) (2020)
20. Raymond: The performance cost of reading a registry key (2005). https://devblogs.microsoft.com/oldnewthing/20060222-11/?p=32193
21. RegBench: Regbench, windows registry benchmark utility (2017). https://bitsum.com/regbench.php
22. Softonic: Uninstallers - search (2021). https://www.softonic.com.br/s/uninstallers
23. Softpedia: Uninstallers - search (2021). https://www.softpedia.com/dyn-search.php?search_term=uninstallers
24. Soldani, J.: Grey literature: a safe bridge between academy and industry? SIGSOFT Softw. Eng. Notes **44**(3), 11–12 (2019). https://doi.org/10.1145/3356773.3356776, https://doi.org/10.1145/3356773.3356776
25. StopBadware: Zango. https://www.stopbadware.org/tags/zango?__cf_chl_jschl_tk__=pmd_a220ec1f116838d84c8791496582d0446d9606f7-1632851755-0-gqNtZGzNAc2jcnBszQjO (2009)
26. Uninstaller, R.: How to force uninstall a program that won't uninstall (2021). https://www.revouninstaller.com/blog/how-to-force-uninstall-a-program-that-wont-uninstall/
27. VirusShare: Virusshare (2021). https://virusshare.com/
28. Zax, R., Adelstein, F.: Faust: Forensic artifacts of uninstalled steganography tools. Digit. Invest. **6**(1), 25–38 (2009). https://doi.org/10.1016/j.diin.2009.02.002, https://www.sciencedirect.com/science/article/pii/S1742287609000267

Representing LLVM-IR in a Code Property Graph

Alexander Küchler(✉) and Christian Banse

Fraunhofer AISEC, Garching, Germany
{alexander.kuechler,christian.banse}@aisec.fraunhofer.de

Abstract. In the past years, a number of static application security testing tools have been proposed which use so-called code property graphs (CPGs), a graph model which keeps rich information about the source code while enabling its user to write language-agnostic analyses. However, they suffer from several shortcomings. They work mostly on source code and exclude the analysis of third-party dependencies if they are only available as compiled binaries. Furthermore, they are limited in their analysis to whether an individual programming language is supported or not. While often support for well-established languages such as C/C++ or Java is included, languages that are still heavily evolving, such as Rust, are not considered because of the constant changes in the language design. To overcome these limitations, we extend an open source implementation of a code property graph to support LLVM-IR which can be used as output by many compilers and binary lifters. In this paper, we discuss how we address challenges that arise when mapping concepts of an intermediate representation to a CPG. At the same time, we optimize the resulting graph to be minimal and close to the representation of equivalent source code. Our case-study on detecting cryptographic misuse indicates that existing analyses can be reused and that the analysis time is comparable to operating on source code. This makes the approach suitable for a security analysis of large-scale projects.

1 Introduction

Despite huge efforts of researchers and industry put into identifying vulnerable software, many software systems still suffer from various security weaknesses. The concept of code property graphs (CPG) [1] has been introduced to simplify identifying vulnerabilities and bugs in the source code of programs. A CPG covers properties of abstract syntax trees (AST), control flow graphs and data flow graphs, among others, thus containing all information relevant for a security analysis. The CPG enables its user to identify vulnerabilities or bugs by performing reusable graph queries. This perk led to a widespread adaption and several implementations [1–7]. Even if the graphs mimic the source code with a minimal loss of information, the graph provides an abstraction of the actual code. This abstraction is suitable to support a language-agnostic analysis of software.

W. Susilo et al. (Eds.): ISC 2022, LNCS 13640, pp. 360–380, 2022.
https://doi.org/10.1007/978-3-031-22390-7_21

Unfortunately, the implementations are limited with respect to the supported programming languages since each language requires a separate translation.

As compilers suffer from a similar problem, the use of intermediate representations (IR) has become popular. The IR abstracts from the programming language but, in many cases, still contains a significant amount of high-level information such as the types of variables which is lost in the compiled binary and can barely be recovered [8]. The lack of such information can worsen the analysis results. The Low Level Virtual Machine (LLVM) project proposes LLVM-IR [9], a very popular IR. Numerous compiler frontends exist to translate source code to LLVM-IR. E.g., clang[1] translates the languages C, C++ and Objective-C to LLVM-IR and has been extended by Apple to support Swift[2]. Other frontends exist to support a wide range of programming languages (e.g., Rust).

While LLVM-IR was designed for compilers, it is also frequently used as output format of binary lifters [10–13]. This way, a lifter supporting multiple architectures and types of binary files can avoid the need to implement the translation for different flavors of assembly code or application binary interfaces. As binary lifting has meanwhile become a stable technique [14], its output can be used to perform a security analysis of the binary without requiring the sources.

If source code is available, analyzing the differences between the code and the binary can identify the security implications of compiler optimizations [15]. E.g., side channel vulnerabilities introduced by compilers are still a major concern of developers of cryptographic libraries [16]. As LLVM-IR can be emitted at all stages of the compilation, it can already contain such vulnerabilities.

In this paper, we show how we overcome shortcomings of existing CPG tools by enabling the analysis of LLVM-IR in such a graph. This bridges the gap between the analysis of source code written in higher-level programming languages and the analysis of programs (or dependencies) that may exist only in binary form. When including support for LLVM-IR in a CPG, several challenges arise from the static single assignment (SSA) form, the exception handling routine, instructions missing in high-level programming languages and significantly different syntactic representations of some concepts in LLVM-IR and other languages.

Contrary to prior work, we do not require to run any LLVM passes beforehand, helping us to keep the graph smaller. At the same time, we aim to retrieve as much high-level information as possible and map the code to high-level concepts whenever possible. Rather than handling LLVM-IR-specific instructions, e.g., *cmpxchg*[3], only as a generic function call, we translate the concepts into existing CPG node types that represent the behavior of a higher-level programming language. This allows us to re-use existing concepts in queries, such as if-statements or pointer referencing. Our case-study shows that our integration

[1] https://clang.llvm.org/.

[2] https://github.com/apple/llvm-project.

[3] The *cmpxchg* instruction compares a given argument against a value stored in a memory address. If they are equal, a new value, specified in a second argument is stored in memory. This is similar to `if(*addr == arg0) *addr = arg1;` in C/C++.

of LLVM-IR into a CPG enables us to identify misuses of cryptographic APIs, a common security weakness. It further shows that we support not only the analysis of programs whose source code is available, but also of lifted binaries, enabling us to identify weaknesses and vulnerabilities regardless of the source code's availability. In summary, our contributions are as follows:

- We present the first mapping of all LLVM-IR instructions to existing CPG nodes with full compatibility to the existing structure. This ensures that existing analyses are fully compatible with the representation.
- We show how we can keep the size of the CPG minimal.
- We are the first to include LLVM-IR's exception handling routines in a CPG.
- We extended the open source project *cpg*[4] to support our concepts.

2 Background

2.1 The Code Property Graph

The *cpg* project [7] enables a graph-based representation of source code of different programming languages. To date, the focus lies in Java and C/C++ but experimental support for Python, Go and TypeScript is also available. The goal of the project is to provide a language-agnostic representation of the source code. This enables a security expert to identify vulnerabilities or bugs. Furthermore, the *cpg* library comprises a way to store the graph in neo4j[5], and makes the graph accessible via a command line interface. For some cases, the library can also evaluate the value which can be held by a node. All this allows a security expert to write custom queries either to the graph database or the in-memory representation of the CPG. The *cpg* library is designed in a way to allow reusing these queries among all supported programming languages. To fulfill this goal, the *cpg* library implements a thorough class hierarchy which accounts for various types of statements and expressions. The CPG encodes information such as the class hierarchy of the code under analysis, the control flow graph, and the call graph in a single graph. The current design mainly targets object-oriented programming languages. To deal with a possible lack of some code fragments or errors in the code, the library is resilient to incomplete, non-compilable and to a certain extent even incorrect code.

2.2 The LLVM Intermediate Representation

The Instructions. The LLVM-IR is used as IR of the LLVM project. Its main purpose lies in providing an abstraction of code to ease the optimization and analysis of the program in a language- and architecture-independent way. The LLVM-IR holds values in global variables (prefixed with `@`) and local variables (prefixed with `%`) both of which can be named or unnamed. The LLVM-IR follows

[4] https://github.com/Fraunhofer-AISEC/cpg.

[5] https://neo4j.com/.

the static single assignment (SSA) form. Hence, every variable can be written to exactly once. This limitation does not affect global variables as they are represented as memory locations and are accessed via store or load operations.

Overall, the LLVM-IR differentiates between 65 instructions. Of these, 13 are arithmetic operations, 6 are bitwise operations, and 13 instructions cast types. The remaining instructions call functions, handle exceptions, load from or store to memory, manipulate aggregated types or jump to other program locations. The instructions can be enhanced with metadata to note the calling convention, optimizations or desired properties of functions and parameters, among others.

Besides the basic instructions, LLVM-IR contains numerous so-called "intrinsics". Those are functions which model certain standard library functionality, or model frequent actions which have to be represented differently on different architectures. Some intrinsics repeat or refine basic instructions, others insert functionality such as the automated memory management in Objective-C.

The LLVM-IR supports a simple type system and differentiates between a set of primitive types and aggregated types such as structs, arrays and vectors. Additionally, LLVM-IR has a type for labels (i.e., jump targets), metadata and a so-called token which is used by certain instructions to transport information. Overall, the type system resembles C rather than object-oriented programming languages. In fact, object-oriented concepts are handled by the respective language frontend in LLVM. The frontend translates the object-oriented properties to concepts such as VTables for overriding methods, and method name mangling to support overloaded functions. In the case of Objective-C, it uses the dynamic dispatching strategy. Other languages make use of similar concepts.

Accessing LLVM-IR. The LLVM project offers a C++ and a C API to parse LLVM-IR and LLVm bitcode files. As the CPG project is mainly implemented in Java, access to the API has to be provided via the Java Native Interface (JNI). We use the open source project javacpp-presets[6] which provides access to the C API via JNI. Unfortunately, the C API has a flat type hierarchy in its functions to access the LLVM-IR's AST, thus making the parsing of instructions and the extraction of their elements more error-prone if not parsed correctly[7]. However, as our evaluation in Sect. 6 shows, our implementation works in a stable way.

3 Related Work

Code Property Graphs. Researchers and industry proposed multiple use cases and implementations of CPGs and analysis tools [1–7,17,18]. All of these tools differ in their support for programming languages.

Closest to our work is the tool `llvm2cpg` [19] which uses Joern [5] as graph representation. The respective CPG represents most instructions as function calls and does not try to infer any of the high-level information. Furthermore, it uses the *reg2mem* LLVM pass to address the φ instruction of LLVM-IR, which significantly increases the code base. This results in additional instructions present in the graph and thus slows down the analysis and makes it more error-prone.

[6] https://github.com/bytedeco/javacpp-presets/tree/master/llvm.

[7] Typically, an incorrect API call leads to a segfault.

liOS [18] constructs a CPG holding assembly instructions and the function bodies lifted to LLVM-IR to analyze iOS apps. The graph model cannot be used to represent source code. Furthermore, liOS does not specifically address LLVM-IR instructions since the analyses mainly operate on assembly code.

Plume [4] and Graft [3,20] only support Java bytecode, a different low-level language. Plume builds the graph incrementally to analyze data flows and has been merged into Joern in a revised version. Graft follows a similar goal. Other tools [1,5,7,17] analyze source code and differ in their level of abstractions and supported languages. Some tools extend CPGs for specific use cases, e.g., analyzing cloud apps [6] or finding vulnerabilities with deep learning [2].

Graph-Based Security Analysis. Various other works investigated in the usage of other graph-based representations of the source code to identify bugs or vulnerabilities [21–23] or similar code fragments [24,25], traverse the graph [26] or improve the analysis [27]. These works aim to provide a rich basis for analyzing the graphs. Many of the proposed techniques operate on other graph structures (e.g. the AST). However, the CPG combines a multitude of information and includes the respective relations, thus making the required information available for the analysis. Hence, these approaches can still be applied to the CPG.

Static Analysis of Multiple Programming Languages. Other works target the analysis of multiple programming languages [28–33]. Some of the frameworks rely on language-agnostic ASTs [34,35] or aim to provide a common pattern for the AST of multiple languages [36,37]. However, ASTs are cannot be used to find all kinds of bugs as they do not contain the required information [1]. Teixeira et al. [38] even propose to translate source code to a custom language.

Furthermore, various intermediate representations (IRs) have been proposed either for compilers (e.g., LLVM [39], GIMPLE [40], HIR [41], or CIL [42]), or specifically targeting code analysis (e.g. VEX IR [43], jimple [44], BIL [45], REIL [46], ESIL [47], DBA [48,49] or RASCAL [50]). Since the IRs are often tailored to a specific use case or language, they differ in the information available in the instructions and their abstractions. Many of the IRs are integrated in analysis toolchains whose analyses are often specific to a use case and cannot easily be ported to other tools. Therefore, integrating such IRs in an abstract analysis platform like the CPG can enable further generalized security analysis.

Numerous tools [51–63] can analyze multiple programming languages. However, they can often barely share the analyses between the languages. The CPG representation allows reusing analyses across languages.

4 Enabling the Analysis of LLVM-IR with Code Property Graphs

Existing graph-based approaches to security analysis mostly focus on the analysis of programs with available source code. In this section, we present our approach which also enables static security analysis of lifted binaries using CPGs. E.g., this allows us to detect the misuse of cryptographic functions, as shown in our evaluation (Sect. 6.1). In detail, we describe how we map different LLVM-IR instructions to CPG nodes while reusing only existing node types. We show how to represent LLVM-specific constructs similar to their equivalents in already supported programming languages. We show how to model 1) arithmetic and logical instructions, 2) access to aggregate types, 3) the φ instruction and 4) LLVM-IR's exception handling routine with a minimal increase of nodes.

4.1 Basic Instructions

Many instructions are known from other programming languages. We can coarsely differentiate between arithmetic and logical operations, operations which enforce specific interpretations of types, and operations which are composed of numerous steps but are often performed atomically on the CPU. In this section, we explain how we include those respective instructions in the CPG.

Almost all programming languages have a common subset of instructions or operations. This includes arithmetic, bitwise and logic operations, or comparisons which we map to their representation in high-level languages (`+`, `-`, `*`, `/`, `%`, `^`, `&`, `|`,`«`, `»`, `<`, `<=`, etc.). Other instructions like jumps, calls, return instructions are modeled with their representation in C code. For if- and switch/case-statements, the branches or cases contain a simple goto statement. Later, a CPG pass removes such indirections whenever possible to reduce the size of the graph.

For some instructions, LLVM-IR can enforce a specific interpretation of the types of the arguments. E.g., the instructions `udiv`, `sdiv` and `fdiv` represent a division and are mapped to the binary operator `/`. Yet, they interpret the values as unsigned (`udiv`), signed (`sdiv`) or floating point value (`fdiv`). In the CPG, we add typecasts to the arguments to enforce the correct interpretation. In the context of a security analysis, such information helps to determine the type and signedness of values for detecting numerical errors (e.g., integer overflows).

In addition, some comparators of floating point values check if a number is ordered or not (i.e., if it is `NAN`). We split these comparisons into a check if the number is ordered and the actual comparison. E.g., the comparators `ult` and `olt` compare two floating point values and are mapped to the `<` operator. However, the `ult` comparison checks if a value `a` is unordered or less than value `b` and thus is modeled as the statement `std::isunordered(a)||a<b`. Similarly, we model the `olt` comparison with `!std::isunordered(a)&&!std::isunordered(b)&&a<b`.

Some of LLVM's instructions like `atomicrmw` and `cmpxchg` are known from assembly code rather than high-level languages and perform multiple operations atomically. The `cmpxchg` instruction loads a value from memory and replaces it with an operand if the value equals another operand. In the CPG, we model this by a block of statements holding the comparison, an if statement and the assignment in the then-branch. We annotate the block to keep the information that all this is performed atomically. Similarly, we model `atomicrmw` as a block of statements performing a load, an optional comparison and if-statement and an assignment to a variable. By modeling these instructions with a representation similar to source code, we simplify subsequent analyses. In contrast, prior work [19] models these instructions as a call to custom functions.

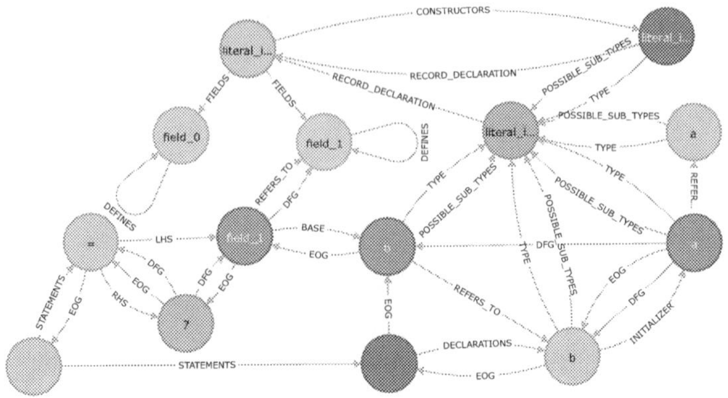

Fig. 1. The graph representing the insertvalue instruction. We can see the literal struct which is generated as well as the access to the field.

4.2 Handling Aggregate Types

High-level languages provide syntactic means to access elements of complex types like arrays, structs or objects. In LLVM-IR, arrays and structs are still available and their values can be accessed by special instructions. Since operations on such types offer a frequent attack surface (e.g., for memory corruptions), an accurate modeling of aggregated types and handling the access to their elements is relevant for a security analysis.

For arrays which are represented as a vector, the instructions `extractelement` and `insertelement` provide access to the elements. Both instructions are represented as an `ArraySubscriptionExpression` in the CPG, one being the left-hand side of the assignment and one the right-hand side. For all other aggregate types, the instructions `getelementptr`, `extractvalue`, and `insertvalue` model the access to the element either by the index inside an array or by the position of a field inside a structure. The code `%b = insertvalue i32, i8 %a, i8 7, 1` shows how the second element of the variable `a` is set to 7. We model the instruction as a copy of `a` to the variable `b` and an assignment of the value `7` to the accessed `field_1`. Figure 1 shows the resulting graph with the initialization of `b` on the bottom right, and the access to the field on the left.

The example uses an interesting concept of LLVM-IR: a so-called literal structure, a struct whose layout is defined in the instruction. For such structs, we generate a type which is identified by the types of its fields. Hence, all literal structs with the same list of fields are regarded as the same type. In our example, the struct is named `literal_i32_i8` and has the fields `field_0` of type `i32` and `field_1` of type `i8`. The top left of Fig. 1 shows the declaration of the type. While the instructions `insertvalue` or `extractvalue` read or write values from memory, it is sometimes desirable to retrieve a pointer to an element of a structure. For this case, the instruction `getelementptr` computes a memory address without accessing memory. Listing 1.1 illustrates the usage of this instruction on a named struct. Listing 1.2, in turn, shows the same code written as C. Figure 2a shows the definition of the named struct and the connections between the fields for the graph retrieved from LLVM-IR. The result is remarkably similar to the graph in Fig. 2b which represents the C code. This similarity lets us reuse existing analyses for the graphs retrieved from LLVM-IR and shows that the graphs are structurally identical. In fact, the relations between variables and fields could be better resolved which can lead to improved analysis results.

Listing 1.1. The instruction getelementptr for a named struct

```
%RT = type { i8, [10 x [20 x i32]], i8 }
%ST = type { i32, double, %RT }
define i32* @foo(%ST* %s) {
  %arrayidx = getelementptr inbounds %ST, %ST* %s,
    i64 1, i32 2, i32 1, i64 5, i64 13
  ret i32* %arrayidx
}
```

Listing 1.2. The C code for the example in Listing 1.1

```
struct RT { char A; int B[10][20]; char C; };
struct ST { int X; double Y; struct RT Z; };
int *foo(struct ST *s) {return &s[1].Z.B[5][13];}
```

4.3 The φ-Instruction

The SSA form enforces that each variable is assigned exactly once in LLVM-IR. However, in some cases, it is required to assign a value multiple times. A frequent example is a loop counter which is set before executing the loop and is updated on each iteration. To allow such behavior without duplicating code and without storing the values in memory, the φ-instruction is used. It assigns the target variable one of the inputs based on the previously executed basic block (BB).

As most programming languages do not have such an instruction, there is no fitting node to represent this in the CPG. To address this issue, prior work [19] relied on the LLVM reg2mem pass[8] which translates the instruction to multiple load and store operations. However, this pass also transforms the access to other variables and thus significantly increases the size of the resulting CPG. As this reduces the scalability of subsequent analyses, we avoid this LLVM pass. We collect all φ-instructions during the translation. Finally, we parse the instructions to identify the predecessor BBs and add an assignment to the target variable at the end of the BB. To keep the CPG clean, we further insert a declaration of the variable at the beginning of the function containing the φ-instruction and all BBs[9]. This, however, breaks the SSA form. The snippet in Listing 1.3 contains the φ-instruction while Listing 1.4 shows the function's model in the CPG.

[8] https://llvm.org/doxygen/Reg2Mem_8cpp_source.html.

[9] For all other variables, the statement of the assignment performs the declaration.

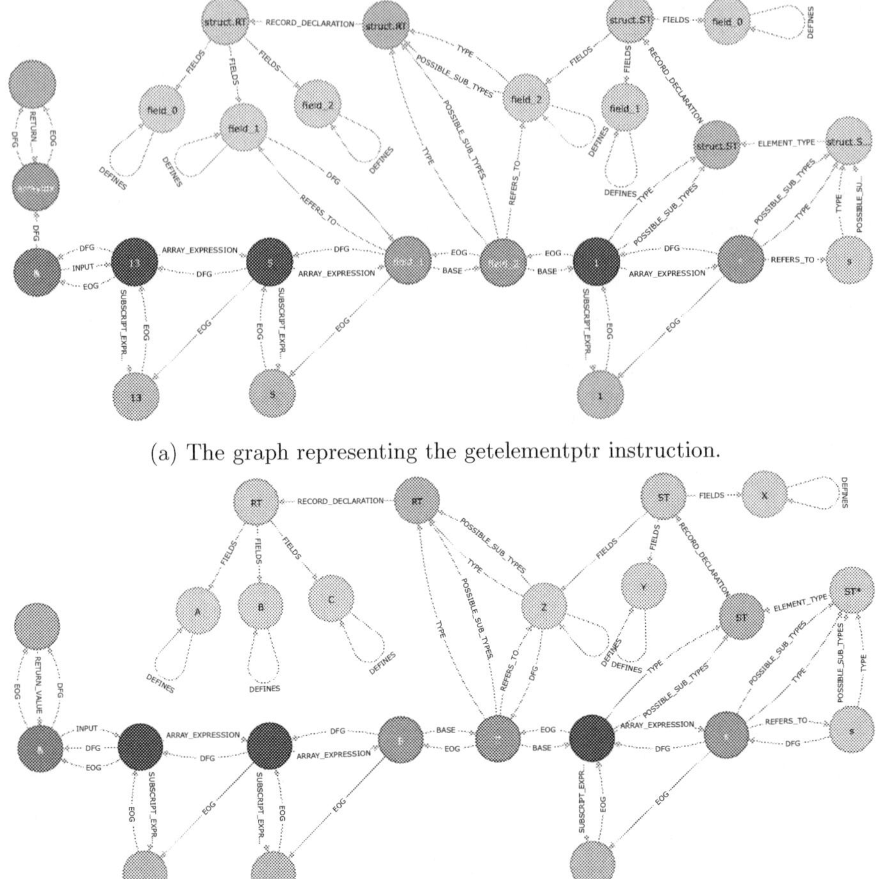

(a) The graph representing the getelementptr instruction.

(b) The graph representing the C code.

Fig. 2. LLVM-IR using getelementptr and equivalent C code result in structurally nearly identical CPGs. The CPG contains structs (light pink) and their fields (beige), constants (green), the method argument (yellow) and return statement (purple). The elements in arrays (brown) and fields are accessed (dark pink). (Color figure online)

4.4 Exception Handling

For a security analysis, a suitable representation of the exception handling is necessary to identify weaknesses which originate from a missing or incorrect handling of errors. Since LLVM-IR offers a rich system for exception handling, this information should also be included in the CPG. The CPG represents exception handling routines with try-catch statements. To make the LLVM-IR fit into this pattern, we need to identify which instructions form a try-block and which ones form a catch-block. Concerning the try-block, we represent the `invoke` instruction as a try-block surrounding a function call and a goto-statement.

Listing 1.3. Code snippet using the φ-instruction.

```
define i32 @main(i32 %x) {
  %cond = icmp eq i32 %x,
      10
  br i1 %cond, label %BB1,
    label %BB2
BB1:
  %a = mul i32 %x, 32768
  br label %BB3
BB2:
  %b = add i32 %x, 7
  br label %BB3
BB3:
  %y = phi i32 [ %a, %BB1
      ],
    [ %b, %BB2 ]
  ret i32 %y
}
```

Listing 1.4. Snippet using the φ-instruction as modeled in the CPG.

```
define i32 @main(i32 %x) {
  ; VariableDeclaration of
      %y
  %cond = icmp eq i32 %x,
      10
  br i1 %cond, label %BB1,
    label %BB2
BB1:
  %a = mul i32 %x, 32768
  %y = %a
  br label %BB3
BB2:
  %b = add i32 %x, 7
  %y = %b
  br label %BB3
BB3:
  ret i32 %y
}
```

For the catch-blocks, however, such a straightforward model is not possible. In LLVM, the `catchswitch` instruction selects a matching `catchpad` based on the signature of the catchpad-instruction of a basic block. The catchpad contains the code of the catch-block and is ended by a `catchret` instruction. However, the matching and signature cannot easily be transferred to a high-level name. Therefore, we model this construct as a catch-block which catches all exceptions and contains if-statements representing the signature matching. If none of them matches, the exception is thrown again. The remaining constructs such as the `cleanuppad` and its `cleanupret` instruction are not modeled specifically.

Another way to mark a catch-block is the `landingpad`-instruction which, again, filters for the right object to catch. Once more, the matching is specific to the programming language and thus, modelling this is left to future work. If we cannot translate the instructions to concepts supported by the CPG, we model them as special functions similar to the LLVM intrinsics.

5 LLVM-Specific CPG Passes

The frontend parses and translates the code linearly with the exception of handling the φ statement. This, however, leads to a state where some of the nodes generated by the frontend serve as intermediate steps and can therefore be optimized after having processed the whole code base. In particular, as we will show, we inline unconditional jump targets and improve the generated catch-blocks. This clean-up phase takes place in a pass over the CPG nodes and serves to increase the stability and scalability of subsequent security analyses.

First, none of the conditional jumps (if-statements) and switch/case-statements incorporates a meaningful body of statements. Instead, they are modeled as goto statements to other basic blocks (BB). E.g., after the translation, an if-statement looks as follows: `if(cond){goto BB1;}else{goto BB2;}`. The pass identifies all BBs which have only a single predecessor and replaces the respective goto-statement with the BB. Note that we do not perform this transformation if multiple predecessors exist because it would increase the number of nodes.

Second, the pass removes the instructions which serve as intermediate steps during the generation of catch-blocks. Recall that a catch-block is initially modeled by catching all types of exceptions or objects, since, e.g. when translating the `invoke` instruction, we do not yet know which exceptions are handled inside the block. However, in the case of a `landingpad` instruction, we have a single object which is caught and the respective instruction is at the beginning of the generic catch-block. Therefore, we can refine the object which is caught and remove the intermediate step. For other exception handling techniques, in turn, we have empty throw statements which should propagate the exception caught by the generic catch block if none of the switch/case-statements match the actual object. Since we can now flatten the graph by removing unnecessary indirections (e.g., unconditional jumps as above, or simply wrappers around statements which had been introduced by the line-by-line translation), we can easily propagate the object caught by the generic catch-block to the throw statements.

As we explicitly aim to handle lifted or decompiled code, a second pass can remove method stubs, i.e., methods whose only purpose is to call a library method. The main purpose of this pass is to simplify subsequent analyses.

6 Experimental Evaluation

To reuse the same analyses for the graphs constructed from source code as well as the ones containing LLVM-IR, we carefully designed the translation in a way to mimic the concepts used in source code as closely as possible. In this section, we first show a case study which advocates that we can reuse queries that aim to identify security concerns in source code to query LLVM-IR. Second, we test the implementation against the Rust standard library to show the applicability of the approach to large-scale projects. All measurements were performed on a Ubuntu 20.04 running on an Intel i5-6200U CPU and 20 GB of RAM.

6.1 Case Study: Cryptographic Misuse

This case study is driven by the anticipated usages of the CPG on LLVM-IR. First, it should enable a security analysis of the LLVM-IR without the need to rewrite existing analyses. Second, it should be scalable by introducing a minimal number of nodes. The toolchain should be able to operate on LLVM-IR emitted during the compilation of a program (subsequently, we call this "compiled LLVM-IR") or when lifting a binary (we call this "lifted LLVM-IR"). To show that these properties are fulfilled, we 1) compare the sizes of graphs retrieved from compilers

Table 1. Results for detecting misuse of cryptographic libraries.

	Analysis time [ms]	# Nodes	# Functions	Problem found
Source Code				
Original file	171	328	38	Yes
macOS M1 using XCode				
Compiled ll	1091	5279	151	Yes
Lifted ll	256	1743	76	Yes
Decompiled	179	971	149	No
Ubuntu x86-64 clang				
Compiled ll	163	1371	57	Yes
Lifted ll	127	911	48	Yes
Decompiled	80	594	101	Yes
Ubuntu x86-64 g++				
Lifted ll	242	1702	89	Yes
Decompiled	148	1137	200	Yes
Linux AArch64 (cross compiled)				
Lifted ll	250	1891	93	Yes
Decompiled	158	1176	209	Yes
Linux arm 32 bit (cross compiled)				
Lifted ll	132	1123	51	Yes
Decompiled	71	626	102	Yes

and lifters, 2) compare the runtime of the analysis, and 3) show that the weakness can be identified with the same analysis in all samples.

We implemented a TLS-client in C++ which uses the `openssl` library. It accepts the insecure hashing algorithm MD5 as one of the options. First, we tested the toolchain against the original cpp file, which identified the respective issue. Next, we used XCode on macOS with the M1 chip and clang on Ubuntu running on a x64 CPU to emit the LLVM-IR which can be retrieved during compilation. As LLVM-IR also serves as target LLVM-IR for many lifters, we lifted binaries of the test file which had been compiled on the Mac and on Ubuntu with various compilers. We use RetDec [10] to lift the binaries to LLVM-IR and also decompiled them to a C-style file[10]. Table 1 summarizes the analysis time, how many nodes and functions are included in the graph and if the problem could be found successfully. We discuss the observations in the following paragraphs.

Size of the Graphs. One of our goals is to keep the sizes of the graph small. Therefore, we compare the size of the graphs retrieved from compiled and lifted LLVM-IR and when decompiling a binary file.

[10] We compiled a custom version of RetDec to update the disassembler and support the `endbr64` instruction which had not been supported at the time of the experiments.

One observation is the significant increase in functions contained in the LLVM-IR compared to the original C file. This can be explained by stubs introduced by the compiler. Note, however, that RetDec seems to remove some of the functions which have been introduced during compilation. This reduction facilitates and speeds up a subsequent security analysis on the resulting graph.

Not only does RetDec reduce the number of functions contained in the binary but it also reduces the number of nodes compared to compiled LLVM-IR. This observation is in-line with recent research which found that some lifters, including RetDec, can reduce the complexity of the code represented by LLVM-IR as well as the number of elements it contains [14] while keeping the main functionality of the code available. The authors further observed that RetDec's output is not suitable for recompiling in most cases. However, as the CPG library aims to handle incomplete, non-compilable and to a certain extent even incorrect code, this limitation should not affect the representation and further analysis.

Compared to the lifted LLVM-IR, the decompiled C files contain more functions but less nodes. This is explained by the possibility to summarize multiple LLVM-IR instructions in a single C statement. Overall, the reduction of nodes can be explained by RetDec's passes which aim to eliminate unnecessary code.

Runtime of the Analysis. We ran the translation to the CPG and the bug detection query 100 times for each of the files and report the average runtimes in Table 1. First, it is interesting to note that the analysis time of the decompiled files is comparable to the one of the original cpp-file. The reduced number of nodes explains the speedup in some cases. The overall analysis time for the LLVM-IR files is ranging between 0.74 to 11.1 times the time of the original file. It is notable that the graphs retrieved from the LLVM-IR files contain 2.8 to 16.1 times the amount of nodes of the original file and still the runtime improved.

Identification of Weaknesses. To detect the misconfiguration in the test file, we implemented a query to identify the arguments of calls to the function `SSL_CTX_set_cipher_list`. To implement this analysis, we use the constant propagation implemented in the analysis module included in the CPG library[11].

With the query, we are able to identify the flaw in the original C file and in the compiled and lifted LLVM-IR files. However, when decompiling the binary compiled on macOS using the M1 chip, we failed to identify the misuse. We manually investigated the case and found that the CDT library[12] which the CPG library uses for parsing the C file fails to identify the name of a field. Therefore, the data flow between the field and the method call is not resolved.

Stability of the Translation. All samples could be represented in the CPG without crashes. However, the LLVM-IR retrieved during compilation of a program contains a much richer semantics and uses various different instructions. This results in warnings, some of which show that nested instructions are not yet handled. The other ones indicate that a different scoping for variables in a try-catch block is expected because LLVM-IR's scoping differs to other languages.

[11] https://github.com/Fraunhofer-AISEC/cpg/tree/master/cpg-analysis.

[12] https://www.eclipse.org/cdt/.

Table 2. Performance when analyzing Rust libraries.

#	Filename	LoC	# Nodes	# Functions	# Errors	Analysis time [ms]
1	addr2line	879	2327	29	9	3641
2	adler	488	1707	25	2	507
3	alloc	4925	13482	253	91	6505
4	cfg_if	9	1	0	0	23
5	compiler_builtins	9990	34304	338	0	23670
6	core	80193	263729	3608	1879	2872096
7	gimli	23702	72845	411	43	112269
8	hashbrown	276	529	26	0	193
9	libc	1477	3619	130	0	646
10	memchr	11063	40602	257	108	32639
11	miniz_oxide	15760	54868	294	166	79863
12	object	14174	50060	277	5	47806
13	panic_abort	71	87	9	0	124
14	panic_unwind	927	2619	67	25	610
15	proc_macro	92115	244010	5488	2570	15260350
16	rustc_demangle	14669	44069	437	309	43281
17	rustc_std_workspace_alloc	9	1	0	0	107
18	rustc_std_workspace_core	9	1	0	0	102
19	std	157377	468223	5923	2629	9303378
20	std_detect	558	1921	15	0	659
21	unwind	106	230	2	0	273

6.2 Application to the Rust Runtime

To assess the applicability to real-world programs, we retrieved the LLVM-IR from the standard and core libraries of Rust. We chose Rust since it is not yet supported by the CPG implementation and provides the option to compile to LLVM-IR. Overall, the test set includes 21 distinct LLVM files which are listed in Table 2 together with their size and the results. We report the time it took to translate the file (including various CPG passes) as well as the number of nodes which could not be parsed accurately. For the latter, we need to extend the LLVM-specific translation to include more cases of "nested" LLVM expressions.
Stability. We want to assess the maturity level of the translation step against a large and unknown codebase consisting of a total of 428,777 lines of LLVM-IR. To measure this, the graph includes specific nodes, called `ProblemNode`, for each expression which could not be parsed correctly. While we handle all types of instructions, some arguments of the instructions can be computed in line by type casts, or simple arithmetic operations, among others. Overall, we could observe 7,836 of such `ProblemNodes`, which accounts for 0.60% of all 1,299,234 nodes. This result is encouraging and indicates that the current implementation is already capable of handling the vast majority of all combinations of statements[13].

[13] We will manually investigate the ProblemNodes to parse the statements in the future.

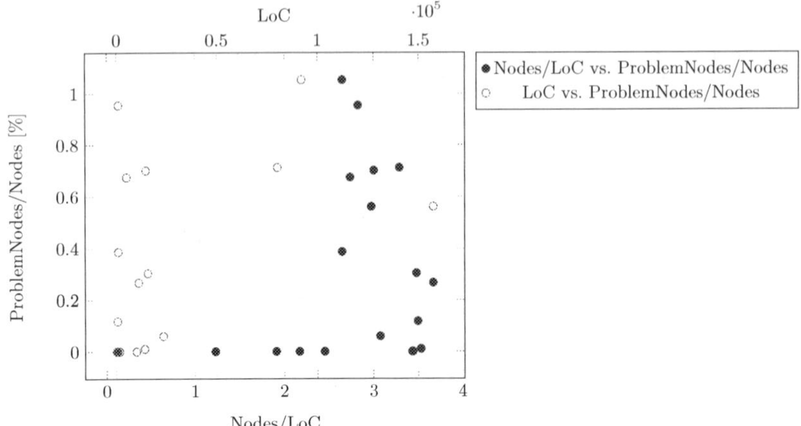

Fig. 3. Relation between lines of code, nodes in the CPG and the fraction of ProblemNodes. For non-trivial samples, the error-rates are randomly distributed.

The fraction of nodes which cannot be handled differs significantly among the samples and ranges between 0% to 1.05%. Larger files are more likely to lead to an error during the translation. In addition, it is possible that the varying amount of complexity of the code could trigger more errors. To validate this, we set the average number of CPG nodes per line of code as complexity of the LLVM instructions. Among the samples, this ratio ranges between 1.22 and 3.67.

We plot this relation in Fig. 3. Neither of the graphs gives a strong indication for this idea since the error rates seem to be randomly distributed for all non-trivial samples. Neither the size nor the complexity of the samples lead to a conceptual limitation. Instead, some samples use unsoppurted expressions more frequently which can easily be addressed in the implementation.

Scalability. Another goal is to assess the scalability of the implementation on real-world software with many lines of code. Two factors can impact the analysis time: The lines of code and the number of nodes in the graph. According to Table 2, an increase of LoC leads to more nodes in the graph in most cases. Figure 4 plots the time of the analysis (i.e., the translation to the CPG and all CPG passes but the `ControlFlowSensitiveDFGPass`) for the number of nodes. With the exception of one sample, the analysis time seems to grow linearly depending on the number of nodes in the graph. Interestingly, when we only consider the analysis time of the LLVM-specific translation and pass of the CPG, the outlier is no longer present. This shows that the LLVM-related translation and CPG pass do scale well even for larger samples but that some of the other CPG passes seem to perform poorly in the presence of a specific combination of nodes.

Comparison to Prior Work. To compare our approach to prior work which relied on LLVM's reg2mem pass to remove φ nodes, we ran our toolchain but

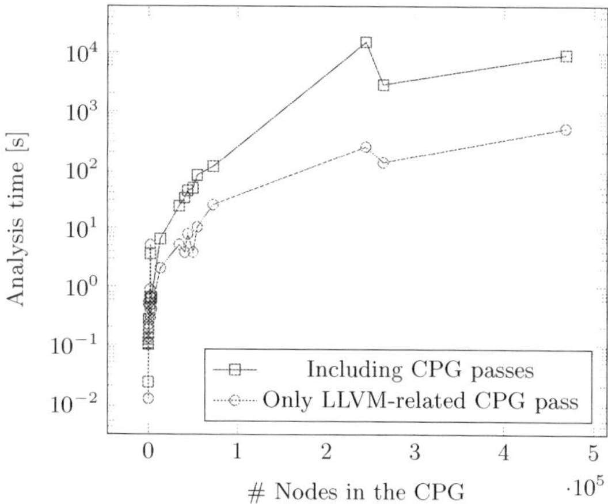

Fig. 4. Analysis time vs. # Nodes. Note the logarithmic y scale.

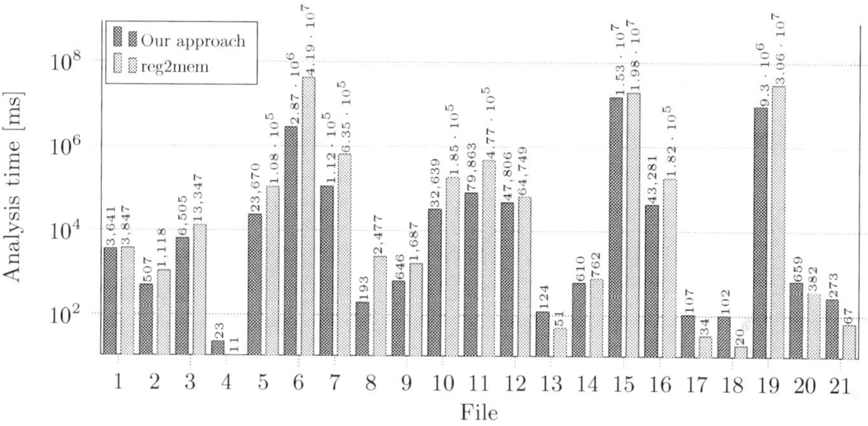

Fig. 5. Comparison of the analysis time of our approach and prior work for each file of Table 2. Our analysis typically finishes much faster.

first executed the respective pass. As Figs. 5 and 6 show, our approach leads to a significant reduction of nodes and time required to generate the graph.

7 Discussion

Our evaluation suggests that our translation and CPG model can unify source code and low-level representations such as LLVM-IR in a single graph representation. This increases the reusability of analyses and queries on the graph.

We found that the LLVM-IR retrieved from binary lifters is significantly easier to handle by the graph. This is due to the fact that most lifters tend to

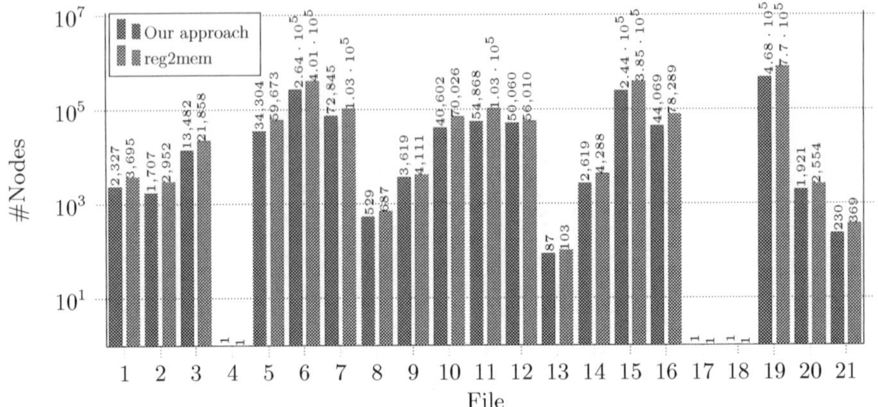

Fig. 6. Comparison of the number of nodes of our approach and prior work for each file of Table 2. Our CPG contains fewer nodes.

use rather conservative steps for their translation. This results in the LLVM-IR being closer to assembly code with comparably simple types of instructions. The LLVM-IR retrieved during the compilation, in contrast, features numerous highly specialized instructions which typically make the translation more difficult. Furthermore, the graphs retrieved from lifted binaries are typically smaller than the ones which can be retrieved when the LLVM-IR is retrieved during the compilation. This makes it an interesting application since it simplifies and speeds up the analysis. Last, we found that the graph of the decompiled binary is only marginally smaller than the one holding the lifted LLVM-IR instructions. This small advantage will, however, not outweigh the error-prone and time-consuming decompliation step in most scenarios which is required to retrieve the code.

Validity of the Results. The main threat to the validity of the findings is the set of test samples. In particular, as we could see in Sect. 6.1, the compiler has a significant impact on the generated LLVM-IR and the resulting complexity which needs to be handled by our toolchain. Hence, testing the toolchain against different compilers and configurations might lead to different results. To address this potential issue, we used XCode on macOS and clang on Ubuntu, and we also generated the LLVM-IR with Rust's crates build system. Furthermore, we used a binary lifter to showcase a possible application to such a scenario.

Limitations. As our evaluation against the Rust standard library showed, a small amount of instructions could not be parsed correctly. This is explained by the possibility of LLVM-IR to hold sub-statements for the arguments. While we do handle the concepts and operators (e.g., casts), their potential usage in a specific sub-statement needs to be added to the translation step. To identify all possible combinations, a more extensive testing is required.

Future Work and Research Directions. The resulting graph can be used as an entry point for further research to better include specifics of certain platforms. One example is the analysis of the LLVM-IR emitted by XCode for apps written in Apple's programming languages Swift or Objective-C. Their calling conventions differ significantly from other programming languages. As an example, Objective-C makes use of a dynamic dispatching routine which requires extensive tracing of a method's arguments to recover type information and the method name as a string [18,64]. This information is present in the CPG but has to be combined to identify the calls. Similarly, it is necessary to model Swift's calling conventions and memory model since it differs significantly from the one of C++ [65,66]. However, to date, the differences are not fully explored. Future work should identify differences and integrate this knowledge into the CPG.

Furthermore, software written in C or C++ can rely on macros which are used similar to function calls in the source code and represented as such but are replaced with their specific implementation in LLVM-IR. This discrepancy needs to be addressed appropriately to better analyze such programs. In the current stage, addressing such inconsistencies between source code and the binary is left to manual efforts of the user of the cpg library. Additional efforts are necessary to reduce these manual efforts and ease the usability of the analysis toolchain.

Last, adapting the solution to the analysis of closed-source software is promising. Once such scenario is the analysis of cloud functions while auditing a configuration of the cloud deployment. In such scenarios, the source code might not be available to the auditor but an image (e.g., of a container) together with the compiled binary of the function can be accessed and analyzed. Hence, lifting those functions to LLVM-IR and finally using this representation for an analysis is promising to improve the analysis of cloud setups.

Recent research [14] showed that lifting is a stable technique for many applications. However, lifted or decompiled binaries still suffer from a lack of information which are crucial for a security analysis [8]. Hence, further research should study which gaps still exist to apply existing tools to lifted binaries.

Generalizability. Since the SSA form is also used by other IRs (e.g. Shimple [67], WALA [63], SIL [68]), some of the challenges generalize to those IRs. Hence, the concepts presented in this paper can be reused to add further code representations using the SSA form to the CPG. Furthermore, some parts of our concept could be ported to other projects which suffer from similar issues. However, the applicability and impact depend on the projects' data models.

8 Conclusion

We showed how we extended an open source CPG implementation to handle LLVM-IR. While the majority of instructions can easily be mapped to the high-level equivalents, the φ instruction and the LLVM exception handling instructions impose challenges to the translation. However, we could transform the program to the CPG representation with a reasonable increase in nodes while prior work suffered from huge performance penalties. The similarity between the resulting graph and the one of the code fractions in high-level languages allows to reuse existing analyses detecting security weaknesses or bugs. Our evaluation suggests that the approach scales to larger projects. Future work is necessary to include characteristics of some programming languages (e.g. Swift), to add analyses for further use cases, such as analyzing closed-source cloud functions, binaries and side-channel vulnerabilities, and to study the gaps of binary lifting.

Acknowledgement. This work was partially funded by the Horizon 2020 project MEDINA, grant agreement ID 952633. We thank the reviewers and our shepherd Jianchang Lai for their suggestions improving this paper.

References

1. Yamaguchi, F., Golde, N., Arp, D., Rieck, K.: Modeling and discovering vulnerabilities with code property graphs. In: IEEE Symposium on Security and Privacy (2014)
2. Xiaomeng, W., Tao, Z., Runpu, W., Wei, X., Changyu, H.: Cpgva: code property graph based vulnerability analysis by deep learning. In: International Conference on Advanced Infocomm Technology (2018)
3. Keirsgieter, W.: Graft. https://github.com/wimkeir/graft
4. Effendi, D.B., et al.: Plume. https://github.com/plume-oss/plume
5. Joern - the bug hunter's workbench. https://github.com/joernio/joern
6. Banse, C., Kunz, I., Schneider, A., Weiss, K.: Cloud property graph: connecting cloud security assessments with static code analysis. In: IEEE International Conference on Cloud Computing (2021)
7. Weiss, K., Banse, C.: A language-independent analysis platform for source code. (2022)
8. Mantovani, A., Compagna, L., Shoshitaishvili, Y., Balzarotti, D.: The convergence of source code and binary vulnerability discovery - a case study. In: ASIA Conference on Computer and Communications Security (2022)
9. Llvm language reference manual. https://llvm.org/docs/LangRef.html
10. RetDec: a retargetable machine-code decompiler. https://retdec.com/
11. Dinaburg, A., Ruef, A.: Mcsema: static translation of x86 instructions to LLVM. In: ReCon Conference (2014)
12. Yadavalli, S.B., Smith, A.: Raising binaries to LLVM IR with McToll (Wip paper). In: 20th ACM SIGPLAN/SIGBED International Conference on Languages, Compilers, and Tools for Embedded Systems (2019)
13. Galois Inc.: reopt. https://github.com/GaloisInc/reopt
14. Liu, Z., Yuan, Y., Wang, S., Bao, Y.: Sok: demystifying binary lifters through the lens of downstream applications. In: Symposium on Security and Privacy (2022)
15. Balakrishnan, G., Reps, T.: Wysinwyx: what you see is not what you execute. ACM Trans. Program. Lang. Syst. **32**(6), 202–213 (2010)
16. Jancar, J., et al.: "they're not that hard to mitigate": what cryptographic library developers think about timing attacks. In: IEEE Symposium on Security and Privacy (2022)
17. Click, C., Paleczny, M.: A simple graph-based intermediate representation. In: ACM SIGPLAN Workshop on Intermediate Representations (1995)
18. Schütte, J., Titze, D.: LIOS: Lifting IOS apps for fun and profit. In: International Workshop on Secure Internet of Things (2019)
19. Denisov, A., Yamaguchi, F.: LLVM meets code property graphs. https://blog.llvm.org/posts/2021-02-23-llvm-meets-code-property-graphs/

20. Keirsgieter, W., Visser, W.: Graft: Static analysis of java bytecode with graph databases. In: Conference of the South African Institute of Computer Scientists and Information Technologists (2020)
21. Urma, R.G., Mycroft, A.: Source-code queries with graph databases-with application to programming language usage and evolution. Sci. Comput. Program **97**, 127–134 (2015)
22. Yamaguchi, F., Lottmann, M., Rieck, K.: Generalized vulnerability extrapolation using abstract syntax trees. In: Annual Computer Security Applications Conference (2012)
23. Yamaguchi, F., Maier, A., Gascon, H., Rieck, K.: Automatic inference of search patterns for taint-style vulnerabilities. In: IEEE Symposium on Security and Privacy (2015)
24. Gascon, H., Yamaguchi, F., Arp, D., Rieck, K.: Structural detection of android malware using embedded call graphs. In: ACM Workshop on Artificial Intelligence and Security (2013)
25. Baxter, I., Yahin, A., Moura, L., Sant'Anna, M., Bier, L.: Clone detection using abstract syntax trees. In: International Conference on Software Maintenance (1998)
26. Rodriguez, M.A.: The gremlin graph traversal machine and language (invited talk). In: Symposium on Database Programming Languages (2015)
27. Lam, M.S., et al.: Context-sensitive program analysis as database queries. In: ACM SIGMOD-SIGACT-SIGART Symposium on Principles of Database Systems (2005)
28. Caracciolo, A., Chis, A., Spasojevic, B., Lungu, M.: Pangea: a workbench for statically analyzing multi-language software corpora. In: Working Conference on Source Code Analysis and Manipulation (2014)
29. Flores, E., Barrón-Cedeño, A., Moreno, L., Rosso, P.: Cross-language source code re-use detection using latent semantic analysis. J. Univers. Comput. Sci. **21**, 1708–1725 (2015)
30. Flores, E., Barrón-Cedeño, A., Rosso, P., Moreno, L.: Towards the detection of cross-language source code reuse. In: International Conference on Application of Natural Language to Information Systems (2011)
31. Angerer, F.: Variability-aware change impact analysis of multi-language product lines. In: International Conference on Automated Software Engineering (2014)
32. Mushtaq, Z., Rasool, G., Shehzad, B.: Multilingual source code analysis: a systematic literature review. IEEE Access **5**, 11307–11336 (2017)
33. Mayer, P., Schroeder, A.: Cross-language code analysis and refactoring. In: Working Conference on Source Code Analysis and Manipulation (2012)
34. Schiewe, M., Curtis, J., Bushong, V., Cerny, T.: Advancing static code analysis with language-agnostic component identification. IEEE Access **10** (2022)
35. Zügner, D., Kirschstein, T., Catasta, M., Leskovec, J., Günnemann, S.: Language-agnostic representation learning of source code from structure and context. In: ICLR (2021)
36. Rakić, G., Budimac, Z., Savić, M.: Language independent framework for static code analysis. In: Balkan Conference in Informatics (2013)
37. Strein, D., Kratz, H., Lowe, W.: Cross-language program analysis and refactoring. In: International Workshop on Source Code Analysis and Manipulation (2006)
38. Teixeira, G., Bispo, J.a., Correia, F.F.: Multi-language static code analysis on the lara framework. In: ACM SIGPLAN International Workshop on the State Of the Art in Program Analysis (2021)
39. Lattner, C., Adve, V.: Llvm: A compilation framework for lifelong program analysis & transformation. In: Symposium on Code Generation and Optimization (2004)

40. Gimple. https://gcc.gnu.org/onlinedocs/gccint/GIMPLE.html
41. The hir. https://rustc-dev-guide.rust-lang.org/hir.html
42. ECMA, S.: Ecma-335 common language infrastructure (CLI), December 2002
43. Nethercote, N., Seward, J.: Valgrind: a framework for heavyweight dynamic binary instrumentation. In: ACM SIGPLAN Conference on Programming Language Design and Implementation (2007)
44. Vallee-Rai, R., Hendren, L.J.: Simple: simplifying java bytecode for analyses and transformations (1998)
45. Brumley, D., Jager, I., Avgerinos, T., Schwartz, E.J.: Bap: a binary analysis platform. In: Computer Aided Verification (2011)
46. Dullien, T., Porst, S.: Reil: A platform-independent intermediate representation of disassembled code for static code analysis. In: CanSecWest (2009)
47. ESIL. https://book.rada.re/disassembling/esil.html
48. Bardin, S., Herrmann, P., Leroux, J., Ly, O., Tabary, R., Vincent, A.: The BINCOA framework for binary code analysis. In: Gopalakrishnan, G., Qadeer, S. (eds.) CAV 2011. LNCS, vol. 6806, pp. 165–170. Springer, Heidelberg (2011). https://doi.org/10.1007/978-3-642-22110-1_13
49. David, R., et al.: BINSEC/SE: a dynamic symbolic execution toolkit for binary-level analysis. In: Conference on Software Analysis, Evolution, and Reengineering (2016)
50. Klint, P., van der Storm, T., Vinju, J.: Rascal: a domain specific language for source code analysis and manipulation. In: International Working Conference on Source Code Analysis and Manipulation (2009)
51. Facebook: Infer static analyzer. https://fbinfer.com/
52. Sonarqube – code quality and code security. https://www.sonarqube.org/
53. Checkmarx. https://checkmarx.com/product/cxsast-source-code-scanning/
54. Solar appscreener. https://solarappscreener.com/
55. Codacy. https://www.codacy.com/
56. Codeql. https://codeql.github.com/
57. Avgustinov, P., De Moor, O., Jones, M.P., Schäfer, M.: QL: Object-oriented queries on relational data. In: European Conference on Object-Oriented Programming (2016)
58. De Moor, O., et al.: Keynote address: ql for source code analysis. In: Working Conference on Source Code Analysis and Manipulation (2007)
59. Codechecker. https://codechecker.readthedocs.io/en/latest/
60. Coverity scan static analysis. https://scan.coverity.com/
61. Deepsource – fast and reliable static analysis platform. https://deepsource.io/
62. Lgtm.com. https://lgtm.com/
63. Wala. https://github.com/wala/WALA
64. Egele, M., Kruegel, C., Kirda, E., Vigna, G.: Pios detecting privacy leaks in IoS applications. In: Network and Distributed System Security Symposium (2011)
65. Tiganov, D., Cho, J., Ali, K., Dolby, J.: Swan: a static analysis framework for swift. In: ACM Joint Meeting on European Software Engineering Conference and Symposium on the Foundations of Software Engineering (2020)
66. Kraus, M., Haupert, V.: The swift language from a reverse engineering perspective. In: Reversing and Offensive-Oriented Trends Symposium (2018)
67. Umanee, N.: Shimple: an investigation of static single assignment form. Master's thesis, McGill University (2006)
68. Groff, J., Lattner, C.: Swift intermediate language - a high level IR to complement LLVM (2015). https://llvm.org/devmtg/2015-10/#talk7

Why We Need a Theory of Maliciousness: Hardware Performance Counters in Security

Marcus Botacin[1,2](✉) and André Grégio[2]

[1] Texas A&M University, College Station, USA
[2] Federal University of Paraná (UFPR), Curitiba, Brazil
{mfbotacin,gregio}@inf.ufpr.br

Abstract. Hardware Performance Counters (HPCs) are at the center of a research discussion: Is their use effective for malware detection? In this paper, we try to clarify the discussion by evaluating prior work presenting HPC criticism and highlighting their implicit assumptions and the potential research opportunities created by them. We discovered that HPCs are particularly good at detecting malware that exploits architectural side-effects, but not as good as traditional detection approaches at detecting pure-software malware, such that detection approaches must be combined. We also identified that most of the controversy about HPCs originates from researchers not clearly stating which type of malware they were considering. Thus, we claim the need for a theory of maliciousness to better state malware threats and evaluate proposed defenses.

Keywords: Performance counter · Malware · Science of security

1 Introduction

Modern processors [11] are equipped with special registers (counters) that automatically count the occurrence of some CPU events (e.g., cache hits, branch predictions) during code execution. Researchers have recently pointed HPCs as a promising way to detect malware [1,5,6], via the identification of (ab)normal execution profiles. However, no technique presents only benefits and some HPC researchers started to present criticism to HPCs for malware detection. The most significant one is that HPC metadata might not be informative about the execution content. An implicit assumption of most work in the HPC field is that a misbehavior at the software level corresponds to a misbehavior at the hardware level. Whereas this is a plausible hypothesis, it has been revealed not true in many cases. A significant work on HPC criticism (presented in [21] and extended in [22]) demonstrated the case of a ransomware sample that is malicious at the software level but indistinguishable at the hardware level, which led to the authors of these papers claiming HPCs' infeasibility for malware detection.

W. Susilo et al. (Eds.): ISC 2022, LNCS 13640, pp. 381–389, 2022.
https://doi.org/10.1007/978-3-031-22390-7_22

At the same time that the presented criticism emerged, new publications about HPC kept appearing, and even Intel decided to adopt a HPC-based approach in its security products [12], exactly to tackle the problem of ransomware. This controversy immediately leads to the question: Is there anyone right and/or wrong in this controversy? To answer this broad question, we (i) revisited the problem of detecting malware using HPCs by analyzing the findings of some representative works published in the academic literature; and (ii) We investigated the root cause of the contradictory results. We discovered that the distinct works adopt different definitions of malware: some involving only software effects, and others involving hardware effects. We present experiments to demonstrate that HPCs are much more effective in identifying hardware than software side effects. Therefore, in our view, the controversy can be solved (or mitigated) if an integrated view is employed in the analyses.

Further, we understand that the differences on the understanding of what is malware and the effectiveness of the proposed detection solutions come from the lack of a widely accepted theory of maliciousness, which should clearly establish which effects are or not considered malicious and thus help judge which defenses are suitable for these cases. In other words, we believe that answering the question of whether malware is well-defined or not via a theory of maliciousness also answers the question of whether HPCs are suitable for malware detection or not by delimiting their scope and goals.

While this theory is not fully elaborated by the security community, we present ideas to help driving this development. More specifically, we propose the concept of attack space reduction, which involves the reduction of the possibilities of action of a given sample, a goal that is clearly accomplished by HPCs, since arbitrary malicious constructions designed to trigger architectural side-effects are blocked by HPC models that enforce standard executions in terms of metadata.

2 Results on HPC for Malware Detection: Is It Effective?

What is reported about HPCs for malware detection? To understand whether the discussion about HPC applications for malware detection is justified or not, we surveyed the literature and found examples that demonstrate the origin of the controversy. Our goal in this work is not to present an exhaustive survey of all published work in the field (which is presented in [1,22]), but to highlight the distinct conclusions about the same aspect. Therefore, we searched papers in the most popular research repositories for computer science (ACM, IEEE, and Springer) and screened the papers with the HPC keyword in the title and/or abstract that was cited at least once. We noticed that each paper represents its result using a different metric, and that they reached distinct conclusions. To illustrate the extreme cases (greatest variation): (i) The work of Botacin et al. [1] presented accuracy rates ranging from 36% to 97% and concluded that using HPCs for malware detection was feasible; (ii) Demme et al. [5] presented FPRs ranging from 35.7% to 83.1% and also concluded that HPCs for malware detection was feasible; (iii) whereas Zhou et al. [22] presented F1-scores ranging from 14.32% to 78.75% and concluded HPC for malware detection was unfeasible. Face that huge variation, a better evaluation of the reasoning made by the distinct authors is required to understand the discussion involving HPCs.

What Is Behind the Conclusions? On the negative side, Zhou et al [22] clarify to us what motivates their uncertainty: "*The underlying assumption for previous HPC-based malware detectors are that malicious behavior affects measured HPC values differently than benign behavior. However, it is questionable, and in fact counter-intuitive, why the semantically high-level distinction between benign and malicious behavior would manifest itself in the micro-architectural events that are measured by HPCs.*" In fact, only a few studies so far investigated the side effects of malware execution at the architectural level, which makes this a reasonable argument until further research is developed. On the positive side, the authors that concluded that HPCs are effective also have a good argument. They indeed presented scenarios in which HPC-based detection was possible. If HPC-based detection is possible in many scenarios, nobody would care if one has already identified the correlation between detection and HPC values or not. It would be simply used. Thus, the discussion turns also into a matter of if the obtained results are robust enough for allowing conclusions about HPCs applicability.

Are These Datasets Enough? Once the discussion turned into an experimental robustness discussion, it is important to investigate how experiments were performed. Zhou et al [22] again explain their criticism of the studies with positive conclusions: "*the correlations and resulting detection capabilities reported by previous works frequently result from small sample sets and experimental setups that put the detection mechanism at an unrealistic advantage.*". This indeed demonstrates an experimental fragility. The problem with this criticism is that most of the criticizing studies also suffer from the same problem that they point out. Once again to show extreme cases, the works with a positive conclusion for HPC applications used only 4K [1] and 503 [5] samples, whereas the works with a negative conclusion for HPC application used only 2.3K [22] and 313 [4] samples. We notice that the considered datasets are all limited, especially in comparison to studies using other techniques for malware detection, such as typical ML classifiers. Thus, greater conclusions can only be taken if more studies are performed. Therefore, we conclude that the discussion about HPC is worth to be addressed and that further research is warranted. The next step is to understand how to contribute to this discussion.

3 A View on Debunking: Is Malware Well Defined?

Is a Single Counter-Example Enough? Zhou et al [22] developed a ransomware sample not detected by the HPC-based approach to claim its infeasibility. In their own words "*We also demonstrate the infeasibility in HPC-based malware detection with Notepad++ infused with a ransomware, which cannot be* *detected in our HPC-based malware detection system*". The authors are right in their feeling that some events cannot be differentiated and logically this single counter-example debunks the feasibility of HPCs. So, is the discussion finished? To answer this question, we must take a closer look and try to understand: Why did researchers care about proving it? Cohen's work [3] already proved in the '80s that a perfect malware detector does not exist. Isn't this work just an extension of this conclusion? It happens that security is by nature a practical subject and researchers and companies are always trying to find ways to detect malware in practice, in the average case, regardless of their limitations for specific cases. In this sense, if we accept that single counter-examples discard entire techniques, such as HPCs, we should have also to discard signatures, since they have already been proven evadable [18], even though they are still used by AVs [20]. Similarly, we should have to stop using ML, since adversarial attacks have been demonstrated [15], even though the ML use has increased over time for ML drawbacks mitigation). Therefore, the discussion about HPC should not be whether mechanisms can be bypassed or not, but in which cases. The HPCs' use would make sense if it is good at detecting some type of malware or in some specific scenario.

When HPC Are Suitable? When HPC are suitable? In the argumentation against HPCs, Zhou el al [22] state that: "*we believe that there is no causation between low-level micro-architectural events and high-level software behavior.*". Whereas this argument makes sense for malware samples that act maliciously by invoking high-level APIs, this statement misses an entire class of attacks: those that act maliciously by exploiting architectural side-effects. We are currently aware of many attacks that exploit side effects and that can be detected via the architectural anomalies that they cause, such as (i) RowHammer [7], that can be detected via the excessive number of cache flushes [14]; (ii) ROP attacks [9], that can be detected due to the excessive number of instruction misses [19]; and (iii) DirtyCoW [8], that can be detected due to excessive paging activity.

The architectural nature of these attacks suggests that HPCs might be particularly good at detecting samples targeting it. To evaluate this hypothesis, we repeated previous work's strategies and developed two classifiers: The first is based on typical dynamic features used in ML detectors, such as tuples of invoked functions over time [10]; and the second using the performance counters supposed to detect the aforementioned events [1]. We performed all tests in a Linux environment, using the `perf` tool for HPC data collection, and considered the 10-folded evaluation of a set of 1K malware samples (we identified 50 to target the architecture) and 1K goodware collected from the system directories.

To create the test dataset, we relied on a collection of all 5K unique Linux malware samples available in the Virusshare (`virusshare.com`) and Malshare (`malshare.com`) repositories between 2012–2020, thus constituting a representative set of the existing Linux malware threats. At each test run, we randomly sampled a subset of this greater dataset to build a test dataset with an equal number of x86 samples for each year. The random sampling respects the family distribution observed in the original collection: 24% of Exploits, 22% of Virus, 20% of Backdoors, 10% of Rootkits, and 4% of Generic labels. All samples that cause side-effect were labeled as Exploits, according to the application of AVClass [17] over Virustotal (`virustotal.com`) labels.

This distribution between samples that cause and do not cause side-effects was selected to reflect the proportion of samples that we found in the wild during our research, limited by the current number of samples causing side-effects available in the online malware repositories. We fine-tuned hyper-parameters for all tested classifiers and we are reporting the results for the best combination (RandomForest classifier in both models).

Comparing the accuracy results for the tested classifiers (remember that the dataset is balanced), we notice that the traditional (non-HPC) ML approach outperforms the HPC one in the overall scenario (93.4% vs. 85.55%), which is compatible with Zhou et al's. However, if we isolate the evaluation of the "ordinary" samples from those that cause side-effects, we notice that the whole detection capability of typical ML systems is due to the classification of "ordinary" samples (98% vs. 85%). The HPC approach significantly outperformed it when classifying the samples that cause side effects (6% vs 96%). The impact of these two datasets in the final result is proportional to their relative presence on the dataset. We expect architectural malware to become more popular over time.

4 Towards a Definition of Malware Detection Effectiveness

The Need for Better Positioning. The presented experimental results show that one cannot simply claim HPC is not good for malware detection. While this result is somehow expected, why haven't other researchers framed the problem *as such*? In our view, the controversy originated because there is not a consensus in the research community as a whole about what is **objectively** considered malware and therefore how to handle it. We do not find consensus Even if we look to the NIST standards [16]. All definitions are broad and do not characterize samples regarding their form or precise target, even though they all state that malware is something undesired. Whereas most people, including researchers, might have developed a generic feeling about malware as something undesired and that the solution for it is to get rid of malicious files, the few attempts towards formally defining malware have been often revealed as problematic in the detection context due to the multiple corner-cases about the subject. The hardness in defining malware is made clear when we consider the "tricky" cases. Following are some of the multiple examples: (i) can software be considered malicious for some users and not for others?; (ii) can a performed action be considered malicious in the context of one software piece but legitimate for another?; and finally, (vi) in the specific context of this work, if the malware target is the system architecture and not another application or data, is it still malware? And how to handle this case? While these questions are not formally answered, researchers have been working with **operational definitions** of malware, which might suffice for most research work, but sometimes might lead to controversies as the one here presented.

When Zhou et al [22] criticize HPC, their implicit assumption (operational definition) is that malware is the "ordinary" samples employing high-level constructs, as it is clear in "*both ransomware and benignware use cryptographic APIs, but the ransomware maliciously encrypt user files, while the benignware safeguards user information.*", thus discarding the samples that intentionally cause side effects. However, it is hard to not consider these sample's activities as malicious, especially because both types of attacks might be associated: A sample might cause side-effects to escalate privileges and further cause more impacting harm via high-level actions. This highlights the need for better positioning attacks and defenses in a context. So, how to advance toward a definition? And, how to advance towards more defenses against whatever malware can be?

Towards better positioning. In our view, we need a theory of maliciousness to measure malware attacks and defenses. In science, concepts do not exist without a theory [2] (one possible view of science). Thus, one could not measure malware attacks and defenses without a theory of maliciousness–composed **not only** by the definition of what is considered malware, but **it also** brings multiple implicit and explicit consequences, such as how to measure the malware problem. Therefore, the point of this paper is not that we need only an extended taxonomy to include malware samples that cause side effects, but we need a theory of malware that explains why this type of sample is considered malicious and how we detect them (eventually using HPCs). Thus, a good theory of maliciousness should shape our understanding of the problem and provide tools/methods to let us know if we succeeded in controlling it.

Whereas we would like to be able to provide a complete theory of maliciousness, we acknowledge that this can only be achieved in the future by integrated community work. Meanwhile, we can give some hints about how it might look like using HPCs as a good example. We understand that a key contribution to a theory of maliciousness is the concept of attack space, i.e., the possibilities of actions that an attacker has over a resource to be protected. For HPCs, the attack space is defined in two dimensions: software and hardware, as shown in Fig. 1. There, an application can be positioned somewhere in the plane defined by the software interactions it performs and the hardware effects it causes to perform these interactions. As defenders, we are interested in blocking both undesired software behaviors as well as their architectural roots and consequences.

Figure 1a illustrates the current scenario, in which we have an unbounded attack space, with malware and goodware samples mixed all over the space, as any malware implementation is allowed. Figure 1b illustrates what happens when HPCs are applied: the space is partially bounded in the performance direction, clearly positioning the (performance anomalous) samples out of the boundaries as malware. Though, there are still some remaining malware and goodware samples mixed in the (non-anomalous performance) bounded space, which explains why additional classifiers (such as typical ML ones) are still required for complete malware detection. When these are applied, the attack space is constrained in the software direction, as shown in Fig. 1c. More formally, we can start hypothesizing

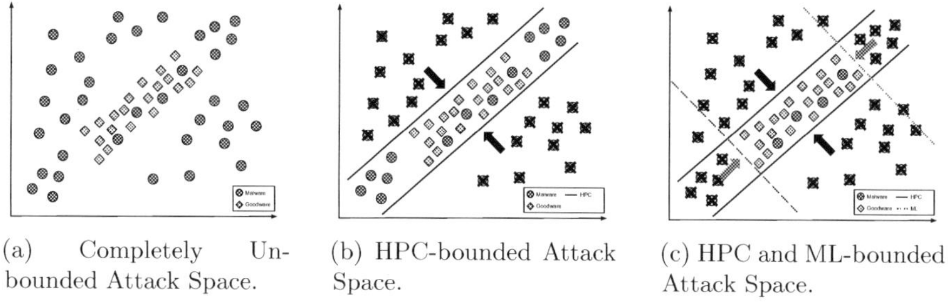

(a) Completely Unbounded Attack Space.

(b) HPC-bounded Attack Space.

(c) HPC and ML-bounded Attack Space.

Fig. 1. The role of HPCs in security. Reducing the attack space.

the definition of the security provided by a solution as to how much it bounds the attack space, even though reducing it from a "greater" infinite. The key insight behind that is that it inverts the incentives. In an unbounded space (e.g., no performance restrictions), malware authors are free to place their samples anywhere, which requires defenders to counteract the attacks. In a more bounded space, such as the ones provided by HPCs, attackers are forced to conform their payloads to the behavior and/or form of the benign/desired applications, which is supposedly harder and more costly.

Attack Surface vs. Attack Space. The attack space concept resembles the attack surface concept [13]. Whereas they have similar goals, they have a significant difference: the attack surface concept aims to limit the number of objects susceptible to being attacked, but it does not say anything about the nature of the possible attacks, which might be potentially infinite; the attack space concept does not say anything about the number of susceptible objects, but it limits the characteristics of the attacks to be performed against them. Thus, we understand them as complementary aspects to be evaluated in conjunction.

Making HPC Practical. A way to evaluate if a technology contributes to making systems more secure is to verify if its addition to a set of existing techniques reduces the attack space. We intentionally refer to a set of techniques because it is naive to imagine that a standalone technology will reduce the attack space in all dimensions. In light of this definition and of the previous experiments, we believe that HPCs increase security. When HPCs are combined with typical ML detectors, the detection rate is increased to a value (97.9%) that is not reached by any solution individually for both sample datasets. Thus, HPCs should be seen as part of a pipeline of malware detectors that contribute to security by establishing borders in specific dimensions (e.g., architectural).

5 Conclusion

We revisited the problem of malware detection using HPCs to clarify the existing controversy about its feasibility. We discussed the current attempts to support and debunk HPCs and concluded that (i) although the discussion is justified, since research works present contradictory verdicts about the HPCs' feasibility for malware detection based on a wide range of metrics, (ii) we cannot discard HPCs as useful, since they present particularly good results for malware samples that cause side effects. We identified that most of the controversy comes from distinct interpretations of the malware concept, which sometimes considers only software effects and sometimes also includes hardware side effects. In summary, we recommend HPCs application as part of a pipeline of security solutions.

References

1. Botacin, M., et al.: The AV says: your hardware definitions were updated! In: 2019 14th International Symposium on Reconfigurable Communication-centric Systems-on-Chip (ReCoSoC), pp. 27–34 (2019). https://doi.org/10.1109/ReCoSoC48741.2019.9034972
2. Chalmers, A.: What Is This Thing Called Science? University of Queensland Press, Chicago (2013)
3. Cohen, F.: Computer viruses: Theory and experiments. Comput. Seurec. **6**, 22–35 (1987)
4. Das, S., Werner, J., Antonakakis, M., Polychronakis, M., Monrose, F.: Sok: the challenges, pitfalls, and perils of using hardware performance counters for security. In: 2019 IEEE Symposium on. Security and Privacy (SP) (2019)
5. Demme, J., et al.: On the feasibility of online malware detection with performance counters. In: ISCA. ACM (2013)
6. DeRose, L.A.: The hardware performance monitor toolkit. In: Sakellariou, R., Gurd, J., Freeman, L., Keane, J. (eds.) Euro-Par 2001. LNCS, vol. 2150, pp. 122–132. Springer, Heidelberg (2001). https://doi.org/10.1007/3-540-44681-8_19
7. ExploitDB: Rowhammer (2015). https://www.exploit-db.com/exploits/36310
8. ExploitDB: Linux kernel 2.6.22 < 3.9 - 'dirty cow' 'ptrace_pokedata' race condition privilege escalation (/etc/passwd method) (2016). https://www.exploit-db.com/exploits/40839
9. ExploitDB: Pms 0.42 - local stack-based overflow (rop) (2017). https://www.exploit-db.com/exploits/44426
10. Galante, L., Botacin, M., Grégio, A., de Geus, P.: Machine learning for malware detection: Beyond accuracy rates. In: Brazilian Security Symposium (SBSeg). SBC (2019)
11. Intel: Intel® 64 and IA-32 Architectures Software Developer's Manual. Intel (2013)
12. Intel: a new tool for cybersecurity - intel threat detection technology (2021). https://www.intel.com/content/www/us/en/architecture-and-technology/vpro/idc-security-report.html
13. Kurmus, A., Sorniotti, A., Kapitza, R.: Attack surface reduction for commodity OS kernels: trimmed garden plants may attract less bugs. In: Proceedings of the Fourth European Workshop on System Security. EUROSEC 2011, ACM (2011)
14. Li, C., Gaudiot, J.L.: Detecting malicious attacks exploiting hardware vulnerabilities using performance counters. In: IEEE COMPSAC (2019)
15. Martins, N., Cruz, J.M., Cruz, T., Henriques Abreu, P.: Adversarial machine learning applied to intrusion and malware scenarios: a systematic review. IEEE Access **8**, 35403–35419 (2020). https://doi.org/10.1109/ACCESS.2020.2974752

16. NIST: Glossary (2021). https://csrc.nist.gov/glossary/term/malware
17. Sebastián, M., Rivera, R., Kotzias, P., Caballero, J.: AVCLASS: a tool for massive malware labeling. In: Monrose, F., Dacier, M., Blanc, G., Garcia-Alfaro, J. (eds.) RAID 2016. LNCS, vol. 9854, pp. 230–253. Springer, Cham (2016). https://doi.org/10.1007/978-3-319-45719-2_11
18. Tasiopoulos, V.G., Katsikas, S.K.: Bypassing antivirus detection with encryption. In: 18th Panhellenic Conference on Informatics, PCI 2014, pp. 1–2. ACM (2014)
19. Wang, X., Backer, J.: SIGDROP: Signature-based ROP detection using hardware performance counters (2016)
20. Wressnegger, C., Freeman, K., Yamaguchi, F., Rieck, K.: Automatically inferring malware signatures for anti-virus assisted attacks. In: AsiaCCS. ACM (2017)
21. Zhou, B., Gupta, A., Jahanshahi, R., Egele, M., Joshi, A.: Hardware performance counters can detect malware: myth or fact? In: AsiaCCS. ACM (2018)
22. Zhou, B., Gupta, A., Jahanshahi, R., Egele, M., Joshi, A.: A cautionary tale about detecting malware using hardware performance counters and machine learning (2021). https://seclab.bu.edu/papers/perf_cnt_dtsi_2021.pdf

Anatomist: Enhanced Firmware Vulnerability Discovery Based on Program State Abnormality Determination with Whole-System Replay

Runhao Liu, Bo Yu(✉), Baosheng Wang, and Jianbin Ye

College of Computer, National University of Defense Technology, Changsha, China
{runhaoliu,yubo0615,bswang,jb_ye20}@nudt.edu.cn

Abstract. With the widespread deployment of Internet of Things (IoT) devices, firmware vulnerabilities can result in considerable damage. However, existing firmware fuzzing methods, which rely on program exception signals, can only find memory corruption vulnerabilities that lead to program crashes. Fuzzing also misses vulnerabilities that exist in the execution path but are not triggered. To solve this problem, we propose Anatomist, the first enhanced firmware vulnerability discovery method based on program state abnormality determination with whole-system replay. The Anatomist first identifies the dangerous operation candidates during whole-system replay. Using single-path symbolic tracing, Anatomist determines whether the program states of dangerous operation candidates are abnormal. Also, Anatomist identifies vulnerabilities on the execution path based on program state abnormality determination. We implemented Anatomist and compared the results of Anatomist with those of FirmAFL, the most advanced firmware vulnerability discovery method, on the FirmAFL dataset. The experimental results showed that Anatomist increased the vulnerability discovery speed by 741.64% on average. Additionally, Anatomist successfully found 3 0-day vulnerabilities in 3 firmware, including 2 memory corruption vulnerabilities and 1 logic vulnerability. The experimental results demonstrated that Anatomist augments firmware vulnerability discovery in two aspects. Anatomist can detect untriggered vulnerabilities on the execution path that are missed by fuzzing. In addition, Anatomist can also identify logic vulnerabilities that cannot be detected by fuzzing.

Keywords: Firmware vulnerability · Augmented vulnerability discovery · Whole-system

1 Introduction

There are many firmware vulnerabilities and they are either introduced by upstream supply chains or caused by flawed implementation of firmware. As

W. Susilo et al. (Eds.): ISC 2022, LNCS 13640, pp. 390–407, 2022.
https://doi.org/10.1007/978-3-031-22390-7_23

many embedded devices are deployed in production and life, firmware vulnerabilities can cause significant damage to the real world, such as AMNESIA:33 vulnerabilities [1], NAME:WRECK vulnerabilities [2], and attacks on Smart-UPS devices [3]. However, the discovery of firmware vulnerabilities is challenging for three reasons. First, firmware is widely deployed on various platforms with nonstandard underlying operating systems, using diverse instruction sets such as ARM and MIPS [4–6]. Second, firmware vulnerabilities are complex and difficult to detect. Different interactions can trigger firmware vulnerabilities, such as network messages, file streams and standard input and output streams. Additionally, the phenomenon of logic vulnerability [7], such as information leakage, command injection, and authentication bypass vulnerabilities, is unnoticeable and will not cause abnormal program behaviors. Therefore, detecting these vulnerabilities is difficult. Third, firmware runs in embedded environments with limited resources, and some program analysis methods [8] do not work well in these environments. Thus, an effective vulnerability discovery method for multi-type firmware vulnerabilities is urgently needed.

Currently, the most advanced firmware vulnerability discovery method is FirmAFL [9], the high-throughput greybox fuzzer of IoT firmware. By combining system-mode emulation and user-mode emulation in a novel way, FirmAFL exhibits high compatibility (system-mode emulation) and provides high throughput (user-mode emulation). However, fuzzing has two main shortcomings. First, fuzzing relies on program exception signals to find memory corruption vulnerabilities [10], and cannot detect logic vulnerabilities [7] that do not cause programs to crash, such as command injection, information leakage, and authentication bypass vulnerabilities. Second, fuzzing refers to a process of repeatedly running a program with generated inputs that may be syntactically or semantically malformed [11]. The vulnerability is only triggered when the program execution path passes the vulnerability and the generated inputs satisfy the vulnerability conditions. There are cases where the program execution path passes through the vulnerability but the inputs do not meet the vulnerability conditions. Fuzzing cannot find these untriggered vulnerabilities that are present in the execution path.

Program states cover the memory, registers, and program semantics when running. Program states always remain normal during execution, but abnormal program states will cause vulnerabilities. Memory state abnormalities lead to memory corruption vulnerabilities [10], and logic semantic state abnormalities lead to logic vulnerabilities [7]. For example, the memory state is abnormal if the memory writing operation oversteps the bounded memory object, which leads to a memory overflow vulnerability. The semantic state will be abnormal if the arguments of command execution function can be controlled by users, which leads to a command injection vulnerability. The root causes of every type of vulnerability are different. Program state abnormalities are closer to the root causes of the vulnerability than the program exception signal. Determining program state abnormalities caused by different vulnerabilities requires custom rules based on expert knowledge.

Rather than relying on program exception signals, some vulnerability discovery methods based on program states, such as Bunkerbuster [12] and Timeplayer [13], have been proposed. These methods identify vulnerabilities by checking whether the program state is abnormal according to custom vulnerability rules. However, due to the limited resources of embedded platforms, capturing execution traces using hardware processor tracing functions [14] prevents Bunkerbuster from being used in firmware. Timeplayer is designed to find only uninitialized variable vulnerabilities and cannot discover other multi-type vulnerabilities that are widespread in firmware. How to effectively discover multi-type firmware vulnerabilities, including memory corruption and logic vulnerabilities remains an open question.

Based on our observations, we identified the following two challenges: **C1:** How do we obtain accurate semantics required by constructing program states while the target program in firmware is running? IoT devices always remove their debug interfaces. The source codes of firmware are also unavailable. Additionally, due to the limited resources and the nonstandard underlying systems of embedded platforms, some existing program analysis methods cannot be applied with firmware. **C2:** Although program states can convey more information about vulnerabilities than program exception signals, how do we effectively discover multi-type firmware vulnerabilities based on the program state? After obtaining the firmware runtime semantics, it is also necessary to determine where and with which criteria the program state needs to be checked.

Thus, to develop a better solution, we propose Anatomist, the first enhanced firmware vulnerability discovery method based on program state abnormality determination with whole-system replay. The augmentation is twofold. First, Anatomist can detect untriggered vulnerabilities as long as the execution path passes through them. Second, Anatomist can identify both memory corruption vulnerabilities and logic vulnerabilities. To overcome **C1**, we choose the whole-system deterministic record and replay [15] to extract runtime semantics of firmware. To overcome **C2**, we first identify dangerous operation candidates during deterministic replay and then determine whether the symbolic program states of these candidates are abnormal during single path symbolic tracing.

Anatomist records the execution of firmware in whole-system mode, saves the snapshot and the execution record, and finally replays the whole system execution process. During this replay, Anatomist automatically taints network message inputs and records the execution path of the target program. To demonstrate the effectiveness of our approach, Anatomist defines two types of dangerous operations, corresponding to the memory corruption class overflow vulnerability and the logic class command injection vulnerability. During the replay, if Anatomist finds that the target program is performing a dangerous operation that is affected by the tainted inputs, Anatomist extracts information regarding the operation, such as the taint label of the inputs affecting the operation, the PC value of the operation, and other information relevant to program state abnormality determination.

After obtaining information about dangerous operation candidates, Anatomist performs single-path symbolic tracing [16] based on the recorded program execution path of the target software. Single-path symbolic tracing performs symbolic execution [17] along the recorded execution path. Anatomist partially symbolizes network messages based on all recorded taint labels that affect the dangerous operations instead of symbolizing all network messages. When symbolic execution reaches the recorded dangerous operation, Anatomist extracts the constraints of the corresponding symbolic inputs and determines whether the dangerous operation satisfies the program state abnormality condition based on the symbolic constraints and the recorded dangerous operation information. Finally, Anatomist locates the vulnerable code if any program state is determined to be abnormal.

We implemented Anatomist and performed experiments to evaluate its effectiveness. We directly compared the performance of Anatomist with that of the state-of-the-art firmware vulnerability discovery method, FirmAFL, on the FirmAFL dataset. The experimental results showed that Anatomist increased the vulnerability discovery efficiency by 741.64% on average. In addition, Anatomist found 3 0-day vulnerabilities in 3 firmware. In summary, we make the following contributions:

- We developed the first enhanced firmware vulnerability discovery technique based on program state abnormality determination with whole-system replay. It identifies dangerous operation candidates during whole-system replay, determines whether the program states of dangerous operation candidates are abnormal during single-path symbolic path tracing, and finally identifies the vulnerabilities.
- We designed and implemented a novel method, Anatomist. By defining dangerous operations, Anatomist can not only detect memory corruption vulnerabilities and logic vulnerabilities, but can also identify untriggered vulnerabilities on the execution path.
- We compared Anatomist with the state-of-the-art firmware vulnerability discovery method, FirmAFL, and the experimental results showed that Anatomist increased the vulnerability discovery efficiency by 741.64% on average. Anatomist also found 3 0-day vulnerabilities in 3 firmware.

The remainder of the paper is organized as follows: We introduce the background and provide an example that motivates our research in Sect. 2. In Sect. 3, we provide an overview of our Anatomist approach, specify the detailed design and describe the implementation. Then, we demonstrate the evaluation results on experimental subjects in Sect. 4. The discussion is in Sect. 5 and we conclude the paper in Sect. 6.

2 Background and Motivation

2.1 IoT Fuzzing

Fuzzing has been proven to be one of the most effective ways of discovering unknown bugs and has been widely used in both industry and academia. For IoT firmware, there are some wellknown fuzzing methods.

IOTFUZZER [18] is an automatic blackbox fuzzing framework designed specifically for detecting memory-corruption flaws in IoT firmware. Most IoT devices are controlled through their official mobile apps. These apps often contain rich information about the protocol they use to communicate with devices, such as command (seed) messages, URLs, and encryption/decryption schemes. Based on these observations, IOTFUZZER runs a protocol-guided fuzz without a priori knowledge of the protocol. Without heavyweight protocol analysis, IOTFUZZER is lightweight, reliable, and capable of generating effective test payloads.

Avatar [19] is a framework that enables complex dynamic analysis of embedded devices by orchestrating the execution of an emulator together with the real hardware. By forwarding I/O accesses from the emulator to the embedded device and dynamically optimizing the distribution of code and data between the two environments, Avatar constructs a hybrid execution environment consisting of both a processor emulator (QEMU) and real hardware, where *Avatar* acts as a software proxy between the emulator and the real hardware. *Avatar* also applies a whitebox fuzzing tool to this hybrid execution environment. Based on *Avatar*, *Avatar*^{2} [20] is further upgraded to a dynamic multi-target orchestration framework to enable interoperability between different dynamic binary analysis frameworks, debuggers, emulators, and real physical devices.

Firmadyne [21] is the first automated dynamic analysis system to specifically target Linux-based firmware on network-connected COTS devices in a scalable manner. Using an instrumented kernel, Firmadyne realizes software-based full system emulation to analyze thousands of firmware binaries automatically. Based on the observation that simple heuristics can often avoid widespread emulation failure cases, FirmAE [6] developed several arbitration techniques to address these failures and achieve a far greater emulation success rate.

FirmAFL [9], built on top of AFL and Firmadyne, is the first high-throughput greybox fuzzer for IoT firmware. By augmenting process emulation with full system emulation, FirmAFL addresses the performance bottleneck caused by system-mode emulation and achieve high-throughput greybox fuzzing for IoT firmware.

However, the abovementioned fuzzing methods detect vulnerabilities according to program exception signals. Therefore, these methods cannot discover logic vulnerabilities that do not cause the program to crash. Additionally, vulnerability triggering requires program inputs to meet certain conditions. Therefore, vulnerabilities that exist in the execution path but are not triggered cannot be detected by fuzzing methods. In essence, existing fuzzing methods identify vulnerabilities based on vulnerability symptoms (e.g., crashes) rather than program state abnormalities (e.g., memory state corruption).

2.2 Program State Based Vulnerability Discovery

In recent years, some bug hunting approaches based on program state abnormality determination have been proposed, such as Bunkerbuster [12] and Timeplayer [13]. Bunkerbuster is designed for terminal programs that run on a regular Linux system. First, Bunkerbuster collects end-host data using hardware processor tracing, cleverly inferring input structures and segmenting traces. Then, Bunkerbuster reconstructs symbol states based on execution traces to achieve better vulnerability detection and root cause analysis. Bunkerbuster can effectively detect and localize 4 types of vulnerabilities: overflow, use-after-free, double free, and format string bugs. However, gathering data using hardware processor tracing [14] prevents Bunkerbuster from being used in firmware due to the restricted resources of embedded platforms.

Timeplayer is designed for effectively detecting the use of uninitialized variables and contains two key techniques: differential replay and symbolic taint analysis. Timeplayer records a program execution in multiple instances, replays two different instances with vanilla and poisoned values of memory, and finally compares differences of program states to find the event of using an uninitialized variable. After that, Timeplayer determines the exact location where the variable was allocated using a symbolic taint analysis. However, Timeplayer is designed specifically to find the uninitialized variable vulnerability and cannot be used to detect multi-type vulnerabilities of the firmware.

2.3 Motivating Example

Listing 1.1 shows an example, CVE-2017-3193, a stack overflow vulnerability, and the 0-day vulnerability discovered by Anatomist, a command injection vulnerability. For the convenience of presentation, some unimportant codes have been omitted. Program *cgibin* reads the environment variable $HTTP\_SOCAACTION$ (line 6) and directly copies it to the stack variable buf (line 10) without any length check, which causes the stack overflow vulnerability. The buf variable is finally passed as an argument to the *system* function (line 14) after being checked and processed (line 13). The buf string is not strictly limited, which ultimately leads to a command injection vulnerability. Notably, the command injection vulnerability is a new 0-day vulnerability discovered by Anatomist but missed by FirmAFL in our experiments.

In practice, the fuzzing method mutates $HTTP\_SOCAACTION$ to find vulnerabilities. The overflow vulnerability will be discovered only if $HTTP\_SOCAACTION$ exceeds buf and causes *cgibin* to crash. However, when $HTTP\_SOCAACTION$ does not exceed buf, the vulnerability is not triggered and cannot be discovered, even if the execution path passes this vulnerability. Additionally, since this logic class command injection vulnerability

```
int hnap_main(int a1, int a2,int *a3)
{
    char* env, process_env;
    char buf[256];
    /* Read from environment variable*/
    env = getenv("HTTP_SOAPACTION");
    /* Simple process*/
    process_env = strrchr(v5, '/')+1;
    /* Copy to stack without length check*/
    strcpy(buf,process_env); //Overflow

    /* Check and process the buf.*/
    check_and_process(buf);
    system(buf); //Command injection

    /* Omitting unimportant codes */
    ...
    return 0;
}
```

Listing 1.1. CVE-2017-3193 and the 0-day vulnerability discovered by Anatomist.

does not crash *cgibin*, the fuzzing method cannot detect it. Two important questions remain: How do we find vulnerabilities that exist in the execution path but have not been triggered? How do we find multi-type firmware vulnerabilities, including memory corruption and logic vulnerabilities?

3 Method

Motivated by the considerations discussed above, we propose Anatomist, the first enhanced firmware vulnerability discovery method based on program state abnormality determination with whole-system replay. An overview of our approach is shown in Fig. 1. Anatomist makes improvements in two key areas. First, Anatomist is capable of discovering untriggered vulnerabilities present on the execution path. Second, Anatomist can find both memory corruption vulnerabilities and logic vulnerabilities. Beginning with a virtual machine containing the firmware, Anatomist records the execution process and generates snapshot and execution records. Then, Anatomist performs a whole-system deterministic replay to replay the execution process. During this replay, Anatomist identifies dangerous operation candidates (Subsect. 3.1). Then, Anatomist determines whether the dangerous operation causes the program state abnormality during the single-path symbolic tracing (Subsect. 3.2). If the program state is abnormal, the dangerous operation leads to a vulnerability. We use an example to explain the workflow of Anatomist (Subsect. 3.3), and the implementation details are presented in Subsect. 3.4.

3.1 Dangerous Operation Candidates

Programs perform some dangerous operations, such as memory writing and command execution, and these operations can often cause program state abnormali-

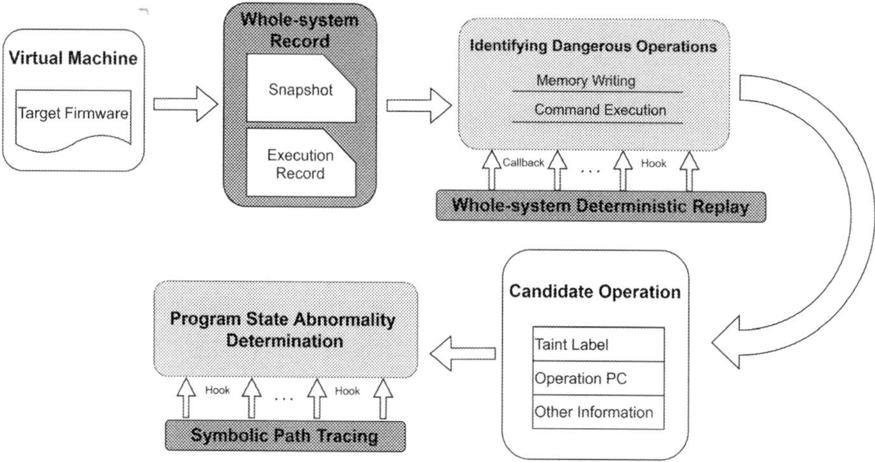

Fig. 1. An overview of Anatomist.

ties if not performed correctly. Specifically, memory overflow vulnerabilities only occur during memory operations. Taking the command injection vulnerability as an example of logic vulnerabilities, command injection vulnerabilities only occur during command execution. Therefore, program dangerous operations are prerequisites for vulnerability triggering. Based on our observations, we found that if the program performs a dangerous operation that can be influenced by network message input, this dangerous operation has the potential to cause the program state to be abnormal. Therefore, we identify these operations as candidates for further verification by the program state abnormality determination.

Because of the limited resources of embedded platforms, some program analysis methods do not work well [8]. We use the whole-system record and replay [15] to extract the runtime semantics of firmware. Whole-system deterministic record and replay is a technology that records the whole system execution of a running virtual machine for replay later. This technique can access all codes and all data, enabling iterative, deep, whole-system analysis, and can be flexibly applied to embedded scenarios, overcoming the challenge **C1**. We make a virtual machine image of the firmware, then record the execution process of the virtual machine, and finally save the snapshot and execution records. We replay the execution process to identify dangerous operation candidates and save the execution path. To demonstrate the effectiveness of our method, we defined two types of dangerous operations, memory writing and command execution, corresponding to memory corruption class overflow vulnerabilities and logic class command injection vulnerabilities. Program logic flaws in the implementation result in logic vulnerabilities. Logic vulnerabilities allow attackers to perform malicious operations by utilizing the program normal functions without violating the program memory states. Common logic vulnerabilities include command injection, authentication bypass and information leakage vulnerabilities. In this paper, we choose the command injection vulnerability as the target of logic vulnerability mining.

During the whole-system replay, Anatomist automatically taints the network message inputs. If any of the two previously defined dangerous operations are affected by the inputs, Anatomist records related information for the program state abnormality determination later. Specifically, a writing operation is considered to be affected by the inputs if the memory that stores the length of the writing operation is tainted; a command execution operation is considered to be affected by the inputs if any parameter of the command execution functions is tainted. The information recorded for the memory writing operation includes the PC of the operation, the input tainted labels that influence the operation, and the size of the destination memory space being written. For the command execution operation, related information is recorded, including the PC of the operation and the input tainted labels that influence command execution.

3.2 Program State Abnormality Determination

After obtaining the dangerous operation candidates, single-path symbolic tracing is performed to determine whether the program states of dangerous operation candidates are abnormal according to the recorded execution path. Single-path symbolic tracing can avoid the most significant shortcoming of symbolic execution: state explosion. Keeping the execution path of the target program the same, this technique treats data as symbolic (multiple possible values) data, places constraints on the symbolic data, and tracks the possible data values that can reach a program state [16]. Additionally, based on previously recorded input taint labels affecting dangerous operation candidates, Anatomist only symbolizes these influential inputs, rather than all inputs, reducing the overhead of symbolic execution and further improves execution efficiency.

When the PC of a candidate memory writing operation is hit by the single-path symbolic tracing, Anatomist extracts the symbolic constraints corresponding to the taint labels, which represent the length of the writing operation. It determines whether the constraint can be larger than the size of the memory space being written. If it can be satisfied, the dangerous operation will lead to a memory state abnormality and further cause a memory overflow vulnerability.

When symbolic execution performs a candidate command execution operation, Anatomist extracts the symbolic constraints corresponding to the taint labels, which represent the command execution string. Suppose this constraint is not strictly limited and can be interspersed with malicious commands. In that case, this dangerous operation can cause a semantic state abnormality, which can lead to a command injection vulnerability.

As mentioned above, to overcome the challenge **C2**, Anatomist first identifies two types of dangerous operation candidates and records related information during the whole-system replay. Then, Anatomist performs single-path symbolic tracing to determine further whether the operations cause the program states to be abnormal. Using this technique, Anatomist augments two aspects of firmware vulnerability discovery: 1) the ability to discover untriggered vulnerabilities on

```
1  int main(){
2      char *recv_buf = malloc(10);
3      SOCKET servSock;
4      sockaddr_in sockAddr;
5      SOCKADDR clntAddr;
6      /*Omitting unimportant codes*/
7      ...
8
9      /*Establishing socket communication*/
10     bind(servSock, (SOCKADDR*)&sockAddr, sizeof(SOCKADDR));
11     listen(servSock, 20);
12     int nSize = sizeof(SOCKADDR);
13     SOCKET clntSock = \
14         accept(servSock, (SOCKADDR*)&clntAddr, &nSize);
15     /*Receiving network message inputs*/
16     int strLen = recv(clntSock, recv_buf, 10, 0);
17
18     /*Doing dangerous operations*/
19     int length = (int)recv_buf[0];
20     char dst[256] = "";
21     memcpy(dst,recv_buf+1,length); //Dangerous operation
22     system(recv_buf+5);            //Dangerous operation
23
24     /*Omitting unimportant codes*/
25     ...
26     return 0
27 }
```

Listing 1.2. An example code that explains the Anatomist's workflow.

the execution path; and 2) the ability to find both memory corruption vulnerabilities and logic vulnerabilities.

3.3 Workflow

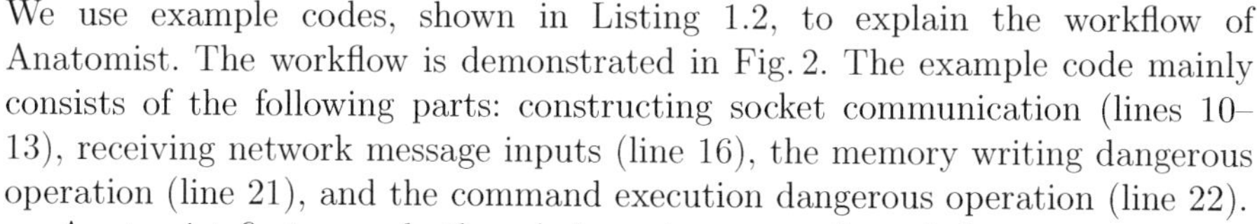

We use example codes, shown in Listing 1.2, to explain the workflow of Anatomist. The workflow is demonstrated in Fig. 2. The example code mainly consists of the following parts: constructing socket communication (lines 10–13), receiving network message inputs (line 16), the memory writing dangerous operation (line 21), and the command execution dangerous operation (line 22).

Anatomist first records the whole system execution of the target program and then deterministically replays this process in whole-system mode. During this replay, Anatomist identifies the dangerous operation candidates and saves the execution path of the target program. When the replay performs the message receiving (line 16), Anatomist automatically taints the received messages, and the tainted label is $0 - 9$. When the replay performs the memory writing dangerous operation (line 21), Anatomist finds that the length of this writing operation is tainted, and this operation is affected by the tainted memory, so Anatomist records information regarding this candidate operation: the tainted label [0] which influences this operation, the address PC_{memcpy} and the length of dst. When the replay performs the command execution operation (line 22),

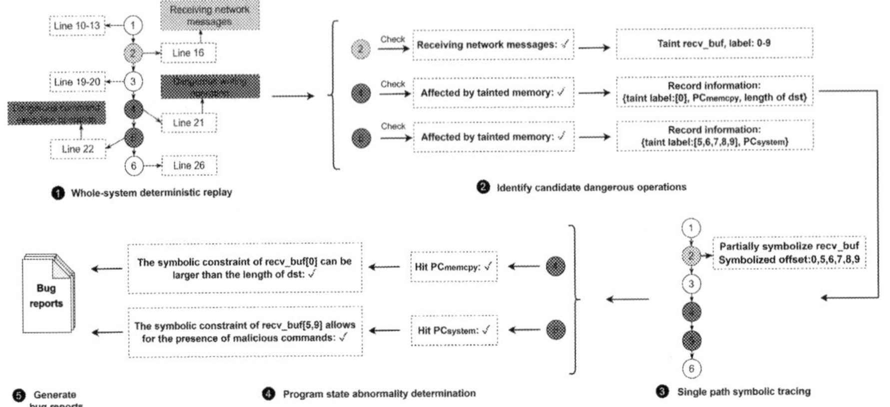

Fig. 2. The workflow of Anatomist while discovering vulnerabilities in Listing 2.

Anatomist finds that the argument of *system* is tainted and this operation is affected by the tainted memory, so Anatomist records information regarding this candidate operation: the tainted labels $[5, 6, 7, 8, 9]$ which influence this operation and the address PC_{system}.

After obtaining the dangerous operation candidates, Anatomist performs single-path symbolic tracing according to the recorded path. When symbolic execution performs message receiving, Anatomist partially symbolizes the received messages based on recorded taint labels $[0, 5, 6, 7, 8, 9]$. During single-path symbolic tracing, Anatomist determines whether the program states of candidate operations are abnormal. When symbolic execution hits PC_{memcpy}, Anatomist extracts the constraint of $recv\_buf[0]$ according to recorded tainted labels. After inspection, Anatomist finds that the constraint can be larger than the length of dst, which causes the memory state to be abnormal and leads to a memory overflow vulnerability. When symbolic execution hits PC_{system}, Anatomist extracts the constraint of $recv\_buf[5, 9]$. After the check, Anatomist finds that the constraint allows the presence of malicious commands, which causes the semantic state to be abnormal and leads to command injection vulnerability. After the program state abnormality determination, Anatomist generates the bug reports.

3.4 Implementation

In this paper, we use the whole-system deterministic record and replay [15] to extract the required runtime semantics. Whole-system deterministic record and replay records the execution scenario and allow users to develop multiple plugins based on the replay to conveniently extract semantics. We implement Anatomist based on PyPanda [22] with rich interfaces and make the virtual machine images of the firmware with the firmware emulation tool FirmAE [6].

We use PyPanda to start the prepared virtual machine image, interact with the virtual machine using sending packet scripts, record the whole system execution of the virtual machine, and save the initial snapshot and the execution records. During the whole-system replay, we extract our needed runtime semantics and identify dangerous operation candidates. PyPanda provides multiple callback and hook mechanisms, which allow users to monitor various events. We use the *cb_before_block_exec* callback to obtain the execution path of the target program. Hooking functions used to receive messages, such as *read* and *recv*, we obtain the address and the length of network inputs. Utilizing the *taint_label_ram* function, we taint these inputs. For command execution dangerous operation candidates, we hook related functions, such as *system* and *execve*. When the hook is triggered, we use the *taint_check_ram* function to determine if any function parameter is tainted. If any of them is tainted, we use the *taint_get_ram* function to obtain taint labels. For memory writing dangerous operation candidates, we hook functions related to memory copy, such as *strcpy* and *memcpy*. To obtain the length of the memory being written, we need to determine whether the memory belongs to stack or heap. For the stack, we use the distance between the memory address and the stack bottom as the memory length; for the heap, we hook functions related to heap allocation and release, such as *malloc* and *free*, dynamically maintain the heap list and record the size of each heap according to the function parameters.

We implement part of the program state abnormality determination based on angr [23]. After obtaining the dangerous operation candidates and the target program execution path, by customizing the *explore* technique, we make the symbolic execution explore along the recorded path to determine whether the program states of dangerous operation candidates are abnormal. When the symbolic execution hits the PC of the dangerous operation candidate, we extract the symbolic constraint corresponding to the taint labels. Then, we use the Z3 solver [24] to determine if there is a solution to the expression that makes the program state abnormal, e.g., the length of the write operation is greater than the legal space of the memory being written. If there is a solution, the dangerous operation can make the program state abnormal and lead to a vulnerability.

4 Evaluation

The experiments were performed on Ubuntu 16.04 with 16 GB of RAM and an Intel Core i9 CPU with 4 cores (i9-9880H, 2.30 GHzx4). In this section, we address the following questions in our evaluation:

- Is Anatomist effective compared to existing techniques and is it able to detect untriggered vulnerabilities? We compared the results of Anatomist to those of FirmAFL, the state-of-the-art firmware vulnerability discovery method, on the FirmAFL dataset. Our experiments showed that Anatomist increased the vulnerability discovery efficiency by 741.64% on average and identified untriggered vulnerabilities (Subsect. 4.1).
- Is Anatomist able to detect unknown firmware vulnerabilities, including memory corruption and logic vulnerabilities? We selected 3 firmware. By analyzing regular messages captured on the network, Anatomist found 3 new 0-day

Table 1. Experimental comparison of Anatomist and FirmAFL on the FirmAFL dataset.

ID	Type	Vendor	Device	FirmAFL	Anatomist	Improvement
CVE-2017-3193	Memory overflow	Dlink	DIR-850L	2 h 43 m 3 s	6 m 6 s	2672.95%
CVE-2016-1558	Memory overflow	Dlink	DAP-2695	2 h 59 m 4 s	3 m 48 s	4712.28%
EDB-ID-38720	Memory overflow	Dlink	DIR-817LW	19 m 11 s	6 m 59 s	274.70%
EDB-ID-24926	Memory overflow	Dlink	DIR-815	1 h 31 m 58 s	44 m 14 s	207.91%
			Average:	1 h 53 m 19 s	15 m 17 s	741.64%

vulnerabilities, 2 buffer overflow vulnerabilities and 1 command injection vulnerability. Two CNVD IDs were issued (Subsect. 4.2).

Dataset and Selection Criteria. We chose FirmAFL, the most advanced firmware vulnerability discovery method, to compare with our method and conducted experiments on its dataset. However, we could only reproduce 4 of the test cases in the dataset using its open source code. The remaining cases crashed and quit during reproduction. Therefore, we performed a comparison experiment on these four test cases. Additionally, we selected three types of target devices, DIR-850L, DCS-930L, and Tenda AC15, which are easily accessed firmware, as targets for vulnerability mining and captured some regular network messages of these devices, which were used as inputs to Anatomist.

4.1 Comparison with FirmAFL

We successfully reproduced four test cases of FirmAFL's dataset using its open source code, but the rest of the test cases crashed and exited during the reproduced process. Therefore, we compared Anatomist with FirmAFL using these four test cases. In our experiments, we first used FirmAFL to perform a fuzzing process on the target firmware. During this process, we sent the mutated inputs generated by FirmAFL to Anatomist synchronously. Anatomist deeply analyzed this execution path based on program state abnormality determination and identified vulnerabilities that were present in the path but had not been triggered.

The experimental results are shown in Table 1. Using the CVE-2017-3193 on DIR-850L as an example, FirmAFL fuzzed out the crash at 2 h 43 m 3 s, but Anatomist found this vulnerability at 6 m 6 s. This means that FirmAFL generated a mutated input at 6 m 6 s, and the execution path corresponding to this input passed through the vulnerability, though the program did not crash. Therefore, FirmAFL missed this untriggered vulnerability. FirmAFL continued to mutate the input until 2 h 43 m 3 s, when the vulnerability was triggered and the program crashed. However, when Anatomist analyzed the mutated input generated by FirmAFL, Anatomist accurately identified the untriggered vulnerability based on program abnormality determination as soon as the execution path passed the vulnerability, avoiding wasting resources.

Anatomist detects vulnerabilities on average 741.64% more efficiently than FirmAFL and can significantly improve the efficiency of existing fuzz-based

Table 2. Newly discovered 0-day vulnerabilities.

ID	Type	Vendor	Device	Version	Time(s)
CNVD-2021-34233	Memory overflow	Dlink	DSC-930L	1.05	41.5
CNVD-2021-37577	Memory overflow	Tenda	Tenda AC15	15.03	51.3
Reported	Command injection	Dlink	Dir-850L	1.03	49.6

firmware vulnerability mining methods. Anatomist can find untriggered vulnerabilities based on program state abnormality determination when the program execution path passes through a vulnerability, instead of waiting until a mutated input signals a program exception. Anatomist also avoids the waste of resources associated with fuzzing, which misses untriggered vulnerabilities on the execution path and continues mutating the input until the program crashes.

4.2 Discovering New Vulnerabilities

For convenient access to firmware, we selected three types of target devices, namely, DSC-930L, Tenda AC15, and Dir-850L. We implemented Anatomist to perform vulnerability mining on three firmware. The vulnerability discovery results are shown in Table 2. The "Time(s)" column represents the time spent by Anatomist to analyze the network packet which passed the vulnerability codes. Anatomist successfully discovered 3 0-day vulnerabilities, including 2 memory corruption class overflow vulnerabilities and 1 logic class command injection vulnerability. Two vulnerabilities were issued 2 CNVD IDs and one vulnerability has been reported.

The two memory corruption class 0-day vulnerabilities were discovered by analyzing regular messages captured on the network, which did not cause the program to crash. However, based on program state abnormality determination, Anatomist found vulnerabilities in the execution path that could lead to an abnormal program memory state. In addition, by analyzing the mutated inputs generated by FirmAFL, Anatomist found the command injection 0-day vulnerability in the execution path. Even if this vulnerability was not triggered and was missed by FirmAFL, Anatomist found the abnormal program semantic state where the user could control the command string parameter.

Compared to fuzzing, which can only find memory corruption vulnerabilities that lead to program crashes, Anatomist can successfully identify memory corruption and logic vulnerabilities. Based on program state abnormality determination, Anatomist can locate the abnormal program state, identify the vulnerability and further discover the vulnerabilities missed by fuzzing, significantly improving the effectiveness of vulnerability mining.

5 Discussion

5.1 Vulnerability Class

In this paper, we defined two types of dangerous operations corresponding to memory corruption overflow vulnerability and logical command injection vulnerability. Anatomist discovers vulnerabilities by determining whether the program state of these two types of dangerous operations is abnormal. In this paper, the two types of dangerous operations were sufficient to illustrate Anatomist's ability to uncover both types of vulnerabilities and their effectiveness and clearly detail the workflow. However, this can be expanded further by adding more types of dangerous operations to identify more types of vulnerabilities, such as memory corruption heap vulnerabilities [25] and logical information leakage vulnerabilities [26]. This can be accomplished with engineering efforts, and we will implement them in the next step. In addition, we tested Anatomist on 4 test cases in the FirmAFL dataset, and Anatomist successfully located all vulnerabilities. We will use Anatomist to analyze more vulnerability datasets to evaluate the false positives and false negatives of the vulnerability detection results.

5.2 Obtaining Input

In contrast to fuzzing, which automates the process of mutating input to find program vulnerabilities, Anatomist requires program input to determine if the program state on the execution path is abnormal. However, this is not a disadvantage of Anatomist. Unlike fuzzing's lightweight, high-frequency program testing, Anatomist deeply analyzes the known execution path to identify potential untriggered vulnerabilities based on program state abnormality determination. Anatomist complements the fuzzing technique; mutated inputs generated by fuzzing can be sent to Anatomist for more thorough state abnormality determination, which can find vulnerabilities that are missed by fuzzing, avoiding wasting resources. In addition, regular network messages can be used as input to Anatomist. Our experiments showed that untriggered vulnerabilities may be present in the normal execution path of a program, and Anatomist can identify new vulnerabilities in this way.

5.3 Path Exploration

Anatomist is currently only able to determine the program state abnormal for a single path, and we will develop it for multi-path exploration. Existing methods for path exploration include Bunkerbuster [12], Directed Greybox Fuzzing [27], and VulFuzz [28].

Based on vulnerability root causes, Bunkerbuster uses bug class-specific search strategies, including use after free, double free, overflow and format string vulnerabilities, to expand the set of reconstructed states and to find vulnerable codes. Results have shown that Bunkerbuster's exploration heuristics are more effective than breadth-first and depth-first searches.

VulFuzz, a vulnerability-oriented fuzz framework, employs security vulnerability metrics to direct and prioritize fuzz testing toward the most vulnerable components. This approach assigns weights to thoroughly test the most vulnerable components. VulFuzz assigns a weight to each identified vulnerable function. Seeds able to pass vulnerable functions are given higher priority. Based on the coverage table and weighted function count, VulFuzz determines whether a seed input should be added to the high-priority queue, low-priority queue, or disregarded.

Directed Greybox Fuzzing (DGF) is a technique that explores program paths in a directed manner, aiming to generate inputs to efficiently reach a given set of target program locations. On a high level, DGF treats reachability as an optimization problem and utilizes a specific meta-heuristic to minimize the distance of the generated seeds to the targets. DGF employs a simulated annealing-based power schedule that gradually assigns more energy to seeds closer to the target locations and less energy to seeds farther away.

We will investigate path state space exploration techniques based on previous work. The mechanism of path state space composition, the representation of path state spaces, and path state exploration techniques need to be carefully considered. The aim is to eventually explore multiple path state spaces, efficiently explore program paths that are more prone to vulnerabilities, and perform program state abnormality determination on top of these paths to discover unknown vulnerabilities.

6 Conclusions

In this paper, we present Anatomist, the first enhanced firmware vulnerability discovery method based on program state abnormality determination with whole-system replay. Based on the whole-system record and replay, Anatomist identifies two types of dangerous operation candidates. Then, using single-path symbolic tracing, Anatomist further determines whether any program state of the dangerous operation candidate is abnormal. Finally, Anatomist detects the vulnerability if any program state is abnormal.

We compared Anatomist with FirmAFL, and the experimental results showed that Anatomist increased the vulnerability discovery efficiency by 741.64% on average. Additionally, Anatomist discovered 3 0-day vulnerabilities on 3 firmware. Anatomist can find memory corruption and logic vulnerabilities in firmware. Additionally, Anatomist can identify untriggered vulnerabilities missed by fuzzing, avoid the waste of resources typical of fuzzing, and greatly improve the efficiency of vulnerability discovery.

Acknowledgements. This work was supported by the Natural Science Foundation of China (61902416, 61902412) and the Natural Science Foundation of Hunan Province in China (2019JJ50729).

References

1. The 33 vulnerabilities impacting millions of IoT, OT and it devices that present an immediate risk for organizations worldwide. https://www.forescout.com/resources/amnesia33-research-report-executive-summary/
2. The name:wreck vulnerability impacts nearly 100 million IoT devices. https://www.forescout.com/resources/namewreck-breaking-and-fixing-dns-implementations/
3. The attach on smart-ups devices. https://www.theregister.com/2022/03/09/tlstorm_apc_ups_critical_zero_days/
4. Sivakumaran, P., Blasco, J.: argXtract: Deriving IoT security configurations via automated static analysis of stripped arm cortex-m binaries. In: Annual Computer Security Applications Conference, pp. 861–876 (2021)
5. Feng, X., et al.: Snipuzz: Black-box fuzzing of IoT firmware via message snippet inference. In: Proceedings of the 2021 ACM SIGSAC Conference on Computer and Communications Security, pp. 337–350 (2021)
6. Kim, M., Kim, D., Kim, E., Kim, S., Jang, Y., Kim, Y.: FirmAE: towards large-scale emulation of IoT firmware for dynamic analysis. In: Annual Computer Security Applications Conference, pp. 733–745 (2020)
7. Shoshitaishvili, Y., Wang, R., Hauser, C., Kruegel, C., Vigna, G.: Firmalice-automatic detection of authentication bypass vulnerabilities in binary firmware. In: NDSS, vol. 1, p. 1 (2015)
8. Kim, Y., Kim, Y., Kim, T., Lee, G., Jang, Y., Kim, M.: Automated unit testing of large industrial embedded software using concolic testing. In: 2013 28th IEEE/ACM International Conference on Automated Software Engineering (ASE), pp. 519–528 (2013). https://doi.org/10.1109/ASE.2013.6693109
9. Zheng, Y., Davanian, A., Yin, H., Song, C., Zhu, H., Sun, L.: {FIRM-AFL}:{High-Throughput} greybox fuzzing of {IoT} firmware via augmented process emulation. In: 28th USENIX Security Symposium (USENIX Security 19), pp. 1099–1114 (2019)
10. Feng, H., Li, H., Pan, X., Zhao, Z., Cactilab, T.: A formal analysis of the FIDO UAF protocol. In: Proceedings of 28th Network And Distributed System Security Symposium (NDSS) (2021)
11. Manès, V.J., et al.: The art, science, and engineering of fuzzing: a survey. IEEE Trans. Softw. Eng. **47**(11), 2312–2331 (2019)
12. Yagemann, C., Chung, S.P., Saltaformaggio, B., Lee, W.: Automated bug hunting with data-driven symbolic root cause analysis. In: Proceedings of the 2021 ACM SIGSAC Conference on Computer and Communications Security, pp. 320–336 (2021)
13. Cao, M., et al.: Different is good: detecting the use of uninitialized variables through differential replay. In: Proceedings of the 2019 ACM SIGSAC Conference on Computer and Communications Security, pp. 1883–1897 (2019)
14. Thalheim, J., Bhatotia, P., Fetzer, C.: Inspector: data provenance using intel processor trace (PT). In: 2016 IEEE 36th International Conference on Distributed Computing Systems (ICDCS), pp. 25–34. IEEE (2016)
15. Dovgalyuk, P.: Deterministic replay of system's execution with multi-target QEMU simulator for dynamic analysis and reverse debugging. In: CSMR, pp. 553–556 (2012)
16. Yagemann, C., Pruett, M., Chung, S.P., Bittick, K., Saltaformaggio, B., Lee, W.: {ARCUS}: symbolic root cause analysis of exploits in production systems. In: 30th {USENIX} Security Symposium ({USENIX} Security 21) (2021)

17. Baldoni, R., Coppa, E., D'elia, D.C., Demetrescu, C., Finocchi, I.: A survey of symbolic execution techniques. ACM Comput. Surv. (CSUR) **51**(3), 1–39 (2018)
18. Chen, J., et al.: Iotfuzzer: Discovering memory corruptions in IoT through app-based fuzzing. In: NDSS (2018)
19. Zaddach, J., Bruno, L., Francillon, A., Balzarotti, D., et al.: Avatar: a framework to support dynamic security analysis of embedded systems' firmwares. In: NDSS, vol. 14, pp. 1–16 (2014)
20. Muench, M., Nisi, D., Francillon, A., Balzarotti, D.: Avatar 2: a multi-target orchestration platform. In: Proceedings of the Workshop Binary Anal. Res. (Colocated NDSS Symp.), vol. 18, pp. 1–11 (2018)
21. Chen, D.D., Woo, M., Brumley, D., Egele, M.: Towards automated dynamic analysis for linux-based embedded firmware. In: NDSS, vol. 1, p. 1 (2016)
22. Craig, L., Fasano, A., Ballo, T., Leek, T., Dolan-Gavitt, B., Robertson, W.: PyPANDA: taming the pandamonium of whole system dynamic analysis. In: Workshop on Binary Analysis Research (BAR), vol. 2021, p. 21 (2021)
23. Shoshitaishvili, Y., et al.: Sok:(state of) the art of war: offensive techniques in binary analysis. In: 2016 IEEE Symposium on Security and Privacy (SP), pp. 138–157. IEEE (2016)
24. Moura, L.D., Bjørner, N.: Z3: An efficient SMT solver. In: International conference on Tools and Algorithms for the Construction and Analysis of Systems, pp. 337–340. Springer (2008). https://doi.org/10.1007/978-3-540-78800-3_24
25. Wang, H., et al.: Typestate-guided fuzzer for discovering use-after-free vulnerabilities. In: 2020 IEEE/ACM 42nd International Conference on Software Engineering (ICSE), pp. 999–1010. IEEE (2020)
26. CVE-2014-0160, a memory leakage vulnerability in OpenSSL. https://www.cvedetails.com/cve/CVE-2014-0160
27. Böhme, M., Pham, V.T., Nguyen, M.D., Roychoudhury, A.: Directed greybox fuzzing. In: Proceedings of the 2017 ACM SIGSAC Conference on Computer and Communications Security, pp. 2329–2344 (2017)
28. Moukahal, L.J., Zulkernine, M., Soukup, M.: Vulnerability-oriented fuzz testing for connected autonomous vehicle systems. IEEE Trans. Reliabil. **70**(4), 1422–1437 (2021)

AI Security

AspIOC: Aspect-Enhanced Deep Neural Network for Actionable Indicator of Compromise Recognition

Shaofeng Wang, Bo Lang(✉), Nan Xiao, and Yikai Chen

School of Computer Science and Technology, Beihang University, Beijing, China
{zy2006158,langbo,cecilexiao9780,yk_chen}@buaa.edu.cn

Abstract. A crucial component of unstructured threat information is the Indicator of Compromise (IOC), which includes malicious IP addresses and domain names. Because non-malicious IP addresses and domain names exist in the threat intelligence texts, the extracted IOCs are often blended with benign entities. Therefore, the current IOC extraction methods are limited in accuracy when determining whether an entity is malicious. In this paper, the problem of IOC recognition is defined as the issue of aspect-level text polarity classification and an aspect-enhanced deep network model for IOC recognition (AspIOC) is presented. While proposing a pre-training model, the network combines IOC contextual characteristics with IOC character features. We collect about 100,000 samples and construct a dataset using an open-source web platform. The experimental results demonstrate that the accuracy and F1 of the proposed IOC discovery method are 99.92%. Our model is better than the most advanced methods currently in use and satisfies industry standards for IOC recognition.

Keywords: Indicator of compromise · Deep neural network · Aspect-level text polarity classification

1 Introduction

The format of the indicators such as IP addresses and domain names are comparatively uniform. However, non-malicious IPs and domain names frequently appear in threat intelligence materials. Using regular expressions makes it hard to determine whether the extracted results are malicious. With the addition of artificial features and the designation of non-malicious entities as O (Other) entities, Dionísio [3] and Long [11] adopted the concept of named entity recognition. Nevertheless, the predictive power of this method is limited because it is challenging to provide the appropriate initial IOC embeddings for the classic BiLSTM network. Liao [9] and Zhu [19] attempted to represent contextual information by adopting the text classification approach and developing syntactic dependency. But the syntactic dependency mechanism relies on an external language model

W. Susilo et al. (Eds.): ISC 2022, LNCS 13640, pp. 411–421, 2022.
https://doi.org/10.1007/978-3-031-22390-7_24

and can easily inject wrong clues, also the text classification model does not consider the characteristics of threat intelligence text, and therefore the accuracy is low.

In view of the above problems, this paper proposes a neural network integration model called AspIOC. The model is based on aspect feature improvement to extract IOCs in threat intelligence reports. For the first time, we regard the issue of identifying malicious IPs and domain names as aspect-level text polarity classification, where the aspect word is the IP or the domain name in a sentence. The AspIOC consists of three parts: the character-level feature extraction from the aspect terms, the contextual feature extraction by the pre-training model, and the interactive feature extraction from the aspect terms and the context. Experimental results show that the model can detect malicious IP addresses and domain names more effectively. To sum up, the main contributions of this paper are as follows:

- For the first time, we model the IOC recognition problem as an aspect-level sentiment analysis problem. The importance of IOCs in the threat intelligence texts is just like the aspect phrases in the regular texts, hence the notion of aspect-level sentiment analysis methods is appropriate to this issue.
- The multi-model fusion technique is adopted, which significantly improves the performance of our method. The fused models involve the DistillBERT pre-training model, the interactive fusion model of aspect words and context, and the aspect word character-level feature extraction model.
- We construct a sentence-level dataset with 100,420 IP addresses and domain names. The accuracy and F1 of our model are both 99.92%, which outperform the state-of-the-art models.

2 Related Work

There are two paradigms to extract IOC objects. The first is named entity recognition, and the other is the filtering technique. Dionísio [3] automatically extracted character-level and word-level features using BiLSTM and CRF models. Long [11] was inspired by the attention mechanism model such as Transformer. His work incorporated the self-attention mechanism into BiLSTM and also combined some artificial rules. Zhao [18] improved the extraction accuracy by using a multi-granularity feature set and n-gram character composition. By creating the syntactic dependency graph, Liao [9] and Zhu [19] divided the IOCs into several attack phases. The former specifically developed a set of contextual feature words and described the relationship between the extracted object and the feature words. Kazato [6] used the GCN model to compute IOC malice levels, while Kuyama [7] used the attribute characteristics of domain names as input to develop an SVM classification model.

The aspect-level sentiment analysis model has attracted much attention in the problem of text polarity classification. Tang [13] presented the TD-LSTM and TC-LSTM models. Wang [15] emphasized the function of aspect terms based on TC-LSTM. With the advent of the attention mechanism, Chen [1] reconstructed the BiLSTM and GRU structures based on the memory network. Liu [10] used GRU networks to learn the weight of each memory unit. Huang [5] created several interactions between aspect terms and contextual words. The crucial component of Fan's work [4] was the more nuanced interaction between the context and the aspect term in the representation calculation. Emotion analysis began to use the pre-training model Bert [2] in 2018. After giving the Bert model both a complete sentence and a contextual section close to the aspect word, Zeng [17] used attention and pooling approaches to integrate the two outputs.

In our method proposed in this paper, we first pre-extract IOCs using regular expressions, and then innovatively establish a deep neural network based on the idea of aspect-level sentiment classification, and also combine the context and character features of aspect words to improve the model's performance.

3 Model

The structure of AspIOC is shown in Fig. 1. In AspIOC, the embedding layers convert the sentence and aspect terms to embedded vectors. We then feed word embeddings and the char embeddings of the aspect term into the interactive feature extraction model and the contextual feature extraction model to generate two vectors, i.e., the interactive feature output and the contextual feature output, which are rich in semantic information. We also feed char embeddings into the character-level feature extraction model, which outputs three character-composition feature vectors based on different attention mechanisms, i.e., Bilinear, Dot-product, and MLP. The five vectors in the output layer are then combined and spliced into one vector which is used to get the classification result of the model. We will further describe these three feature extraction models in the following parts.

3.1 IOC Character-Level Feature Extraction Based on Attention Mechanisms

Due to the two characteristics of IPs and domain names in threat intelligence, i.e., invalidation handling and the randomness of character composition, we propose an IOC character-level feature extraction model based on attention mechanisms.

To prevent users from clicking on links and accessing malicious websites by mistake, writers invalidate the harmful IPs and domain names in the threat intelligence texts by changing their original forms to forms containing special symbols as shown in Table 1. However, the scope for such processing is limited. As to the security-related corpus we obtain, invalidation handling is absent in 32% of malicious IP samples and 75% of domain names. Hence, invalidation handling can not be regarded as an essential feature.

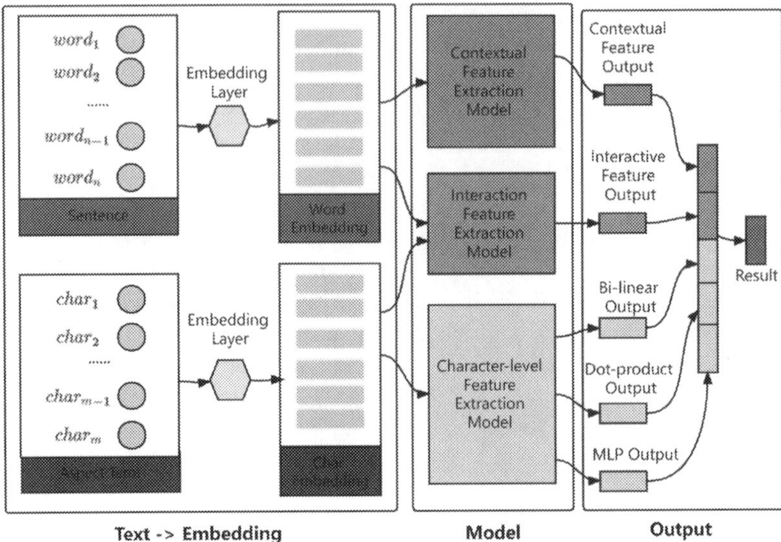

Fig. 1. The AspIOC's fundamental architecture

Table 1. Conversion examples in invalidation handling

Original forms	IOC special symbols
.	[.] or (.) or (DOT) or [dot] or [d0t]
@	[at] or (AT)
http	hxxp
https	hxxps

In addition, a significant number of malicious domain names are generated by using random algorithms, and the character composition of these malicious domains differs from that of non-malicious domain names [16]. The attention mechanism is proposed for identifying crucial details quickly. For example, we want the model to focus on the specific blocks of IPs and domain names, such as invalid processing replacement components.

Furthermore, the attention weight matrix [12] in this study is calculated in three ways: Dot-product, Bi-linear, and MLP. Each method involves calculating the weight value of each character of an aspect word, then weighting the character vector according to the weight value and fusing it to create a feature vector.

(1)Dot-product

Key matrix K^{N*M} and Query matrix Q^{1*M}. $Weight\_Score = Q * K^{\top}$.

(2)Bi-linear

Key matrix K^{N*M}, Query matrix Q^{1*M}, and parameter matrix W^{M*M}. $Weight\_Score = Q * W^{\top} * K^{\top}$.

(3)MLP

Key matrix K^{N*M}, Query matrix Q^{1*M}, and parameter matrix W^{2M}.After increasing the dimension and replication operations, the K and Q matrix change into $K^{'1*N*M}$ and $Q^{'1*N*M}$, $Weight\_Score = tanh([K^{'}, Q^{'}] * W)$.

These three mechanisms have different numbers of trainable parameters and are increasingly complex, and they can extract different level features of IOCs, i.e., shallow, middle, and deep level features. The output of the aspect word character-level feature extraction model is then generated by connecting the vectors produced by the three attention algorithms.

3.2 Contextual Feature Extraction of IOCs Based on DistillBERT

Our contextual feature extraction model is built using DistillBERT[1] from the HuggingFace[2] open source community, as shown in Fig. 2.

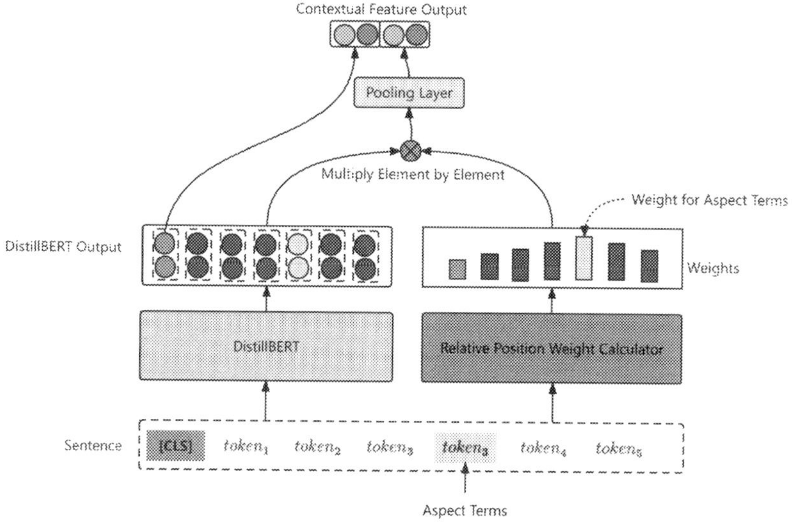

Fig. 2. The IOC contextual feature extraction model based on DistillBERT

The *Contextual Feature Output* in Fig. 2 consists of two separate pieces. The DistillBERT output generates the left half of the vector, corresponding to the position of the "[CLS]" [2]. The output vector on the right half combines the position of the aspect term with the feature extraction result of DistillBERT. We calculate the relative position weight of each word based on its distance from the aspect term. Formula 1 calculates the value α in the weight matrix: L is

[1] https://huggingface.co/distilbert-base-uncased.
[2] https://huggingface.co/.

the distance between the word and the aspect term's edge, and a is a distance threshold that determines whether to decay amount α [17].

$$\alpha = \begin{cases} 1 - \frac{L-a}{sentence\_length}, & L > a \\ 1 & , else \end{cases} \tag{1}$$

3.3 Interactive Feature Extraction of IOC Aspect Words and Context

The interactive feature extraction model of aspect terms and context is built, as shown in Fig. 3. Aspect word vectors and IOC context vectors are two independent inputs in the model which interact deeply through attention mechanisms. Unlike the model in Sect. 3.3, which treats complete sentences as input, the model in this section focuses more on vectors of aspect words.

The fundamental structure of the model is constructed by eight-fold stacking one basic unit, and the residual network idea is introduced to prevent the gradient from disappearing in the deep network. The basic unit is shown in the dotted box in Fig. 3.

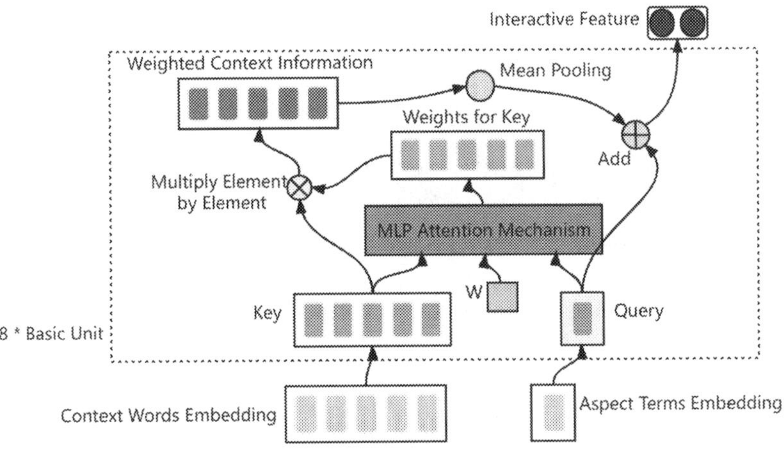

Fig. 3. The architecture of an interactive feature extraction model for context and aspect terms

As shown in Fig. 3, the $Query$ matrix represents the aspect word, the Key matrix represents the context, and the feature interaction between the aspect word and the context contains two parts: (1) When calculating $Weights\ for\ Key$, $Query$ and Key complete the feature interaction through the parameter W. The matrix $Weights\ for\ Key$ is calculated using the MLP attention mechanism in Sect. 3.2. (2) The matrix $Weighted\ Context\ Information$, as the intermediate result of the basic unit, is added to the $Query$ matrix of the current unit, and the final result is the $Interactive\ Feature$.

4 Experiment

4.1 Dataset Construction

We collect the data for constructing our dataset through an open web platform. We have developed a threat data collector to automatically collect network threat data from a variety of sources, including international security blogs (e.g., Dark Reading[3], Threatpost[4]), hacker forum posts (e.g., Blackhat[5], Hack5[6]) and security announcements (e.g., Microsoft[7], Cisco[8]). Some open-source English short text datasets (e.g., Yelp Dataset[9], sentiment140 Dataset[10]) form part of the data. The following are two examples. "The device sent the spear-phish from the VPN IP 193.180.255[.]2" is a malicious sample and "Qianxin Threat Intelligence File In-depth Analysis Platform (https://sandbox.ti.qianxin.com/sandbox/page)" is a non-malicious one.

After manual download and automatic crawler gathering, we use regular matching to see if it contains IPs, domain names, or invalidated handling structures to complete sentence-level filtering. In Table 2, the variables *IP* and *Domain* represent the regular expressions to extract IPs and domain names, and the other two are intermediate variables. Then we use VirusTotal[11] to further filter the obtained IPs and domain names and finally get 50,235 malicious samples and 50,185 non-malicious samples. There are about an equal amount of samples in each category.

Table 2. The regular expression

<table>
<tr><th>Variable</th><th>Pattern</th></tr>
<tr><td>invalid_handle_dot</td><td>'(?:\.|\[\.\]|\(\.\)|\(dot\)|\(d0t\)|\[dot\]|\[d0t\]){1}'</td></tr>
<tr><td>IP</td><td>'(?i)(\ d{1,3}'+invalid_handle_dot+'){3}\ d{1,3}'</td></tr>
<tr><td>exp_domain</td><td>'([a-zA-Z0-9][-a-zA-Z0-9]{0,61}'+invalid_handle_dot+')+
(?:com|edu|gov|int|mil|net|org|biz|info|
pro|name|museum|network|coop|aero|xxx|xyz|
idv|cn|eu|uk|us|fr|de|gs)'</td></tr>
<tr><td>Domain</td><td>'(?i)(?<![-a-z0-9_\\./])'+exp_domain+'(?![-a-z0-9_\\./])'</td></tr>
</table>

[3] https://www.darkreading.com/.
[4] https://threatpost.com/.
[5] https://www.blackhat.com/.
[6] https://forums.hak5.org/.
[7] https://docs.microsoft.com/zh-cn/security-updates/securitybulletins/securitybulletins.
[8] https://www.cisco.com/c/zh_cn/support/security/security-manager/products/security-advisories-list.html.
[9] https://www.yelp.com/dataset.
[10] https://www.kaggle.com/datasets/kazanova/sentiment140.
[11] https://www.virustotal.com/gui/.

4.2 Comparative Experiment and Result Evaluation

The proposed IOC recognition algorithm AspIOC is compared to state-of-the-art models on the aspect-level text classification task in Table 3, including TNET_LF [8], AOA [5], and MGAN [4] with attention mechanism, Bert-SPC [2], Roberta-SPC [20] with pre-training model, and ASA-WD [14] with both pre-training model and graph neural network.

The experiment employs identical super-parameter settings to ensure a fair comparison. The optimizer is Adam. The rate of learning is 2e-5. There are 16 batches, 40 epochs, and an 85-word sentence limit. Table 3 presents the results of the experiment.

Table 3. Results of the experiment

Model	Accuracy	Macro F1	The number of trainable parameters
TNET_LF	99.07%	99.07%	3700352
AOA	98.59%	98.59%	2890802
MGAN	98.71%	98.71%	3616202
Bert-SPC	99.74%	99.74%	109483778
Roberta-SPC	99.86%	99.86%	124647170
ASA-WD	99.38%	99.38%	122068226
AspIOC(ours)	**99.92%**	**99.92%**	68454710

4.3 Ablation Experiments

Ablation experiments are performed on the three parts of AspIOC using a step-by-step superposition model structure. In Table 4, Attention represents the attention-based character-level feature extraction model, Interactive-Feature represents the interaction feature extraction model, Dbert represents the Distill-BERT contextual feature extraction model, and Bert represents the replacement of the DistillBERT with Bert-base.

Table 4. Ablation experiment results of AspIOC

Model	Accuracy	Macro F1	The number of trainable parameters
Attention	99.23%	99.23%	996302
Interactive-Feature	99.32%	99.32%	362402
Attention+Interactive-Feature	99.81%	99.81%	1268402
Attention+Interactive-Feature+Bert	99.89%	99.89%	111574070
Attention+Interactive-Feature+Dbert	**99.92%**	**99.92%**	68454710

In Table 5, we ablate three attention mechanisms (i.e., Bi-linear, Dot-product, and MLP) in the character-level feature extraction model to verify their effectiveness. The Dot-product works best when the mechanisms perform alone. The experimental results of the two combinations are relatively the same, and the combination of the three mechanisms achieves the best result.

Table 5. Ablation experiment results of three attention mechanisms

Model	Accuracy	Macro F1	The number of trainable parameters
MLP	98.04%	98.04%	272101
Bi-linear	98.17%	98.17%	361501
Dot-product	98.23%	98.23%	271501
MLP+Bi-linear	99.03%	99.03%	633601
MLP+Dot-product	99.05%	99.05%	544401
Bi-linear+Dot-product	99.08%	99.08%	633001
MLP+Bi-linear+Dot-product	**99.23%**	**99.23%**	996302

5 Conclusion

In this paper, in order to accurately identify meaningful IOC in unstructured threat intelligence texts, an aspect-enhanced IOC recognition model AspIOC is proposed. For the first time, we introduce aspect-level sentiment analysis into the investigation of IOC recognition, inspired by the compositional characteristics of IOC characters and the crucial role of IOCs in the semantics representation of the threat intelligence texts. AspIOC uses DistillBERT to obtain the IOC contextual semantic features, integrates three attention mechanisms to extract IOC character-level features, and also obtains interaction features from these two kinds of features. We collect about 100,000 samples using an open-source web platform. Experimental results show that the recognition performance of AspIOC is better than that of the state-of-the-art IOC recognition and text classification models. Future research on the IOC recognition systems will focus on more complex scenarios, such as IOC detection in unstructured threat information like images.

References

1. Chen, P., Sun, Z., Bing, L., Yang, W.: Recurrent attention network on memory for aspect sentiment analysis. In: Proceedings of the 2017 Conference on Empirical Methods in Natural Language Processing, pp. 452–461 (2017)
2. Devlin, J., Chang, M.W., Lee, K., Toutanova, K.: BERT: pre-training of deep bidirectional transformers for language understanding. arXiv preprint arXiv:1810.04805 (2018)

3. Dionísio, N., Alves, F., Ferreira, P.M., Bessani, A.: Cyberthreat detection from twitter using deep neural networks. In: 2019 International Joint Conference on Neural Networks (IJCNN), pp. 1–8. IEEE (2019)
4. Fan, F., Feng, Y., Zhao, D.: Multi-grained attention network for aspect-level sentiment classification. In: Proceedings of the 2018 Conference on Empirical Methods in Natural Language Processing, pp. 3433–3442 (2018)
5. Huang, B., Ou, Y., Carley, K.M.: Aspect level sentiment classification with attention-over-attention neural networks. In: International Conference on Social Computing, Behavioral-Cultural Modeling and Prediction and Behavior Representation in Modeling and Simulation, pp. 197–206. Springer (2018). https://doi.org/10.1007/978-3-319-93372-6_22
6. Kazato, Y., Nakagawa, Y., Nakatani, Y.: Improving maliciousness estimation of indicator of compromise using graph convolutional networks. In: 2020 IEEE 17th Annual Consumer Communications & Networking Conference (CCNC), pp. 1–7. IEEE (2020)
7. Kuyama, M., Kakizaki, Y., Sasaki, R.: Method for detecting a malicious domain by using only well-known information. Int. J. Cyber-Secur. Digital Forens. **5**(4), 166–175 (2016)
8. Li, X., Bing, L., Lam, W., Shi, B.: Transformation networks for target-oriented sentiment classification. In: Proceedings of the 56th Annual Meeting of the Association for Computational Linguistics (Volume 1: Long Papers), pp. 946–956 (2018)
9. Liao, X., Yuan, K., Wang, X., Li, Z., Xing, L., Beyah, R.: Acing the IOC game: toward automatic discovery and analysis of open-source cyber threat intelligence. In: Proceedings of the 2016 ACM SIGSAC Conference on Computer and Communications Security, pp. 755–766 (2016)
10. Liu, Q., Zhang, H., Zeng, Y., Huang, Z., Wu, Z.: Content attention model for aspect based sentiment analysis. In: Proceedings of the 2018 World Wide Web Conference, pp. 1023–1032 (2018)
11. Long, Z., Tan, L., Zhou, S., He, C., Liu, X.: Collecting indicators of compromise from unstructured text of cybersecurity articles using neural-based sequence labelling. In: 2019 International Joint Conference on Neural Networks (IJCNN), pp. 1–8. IEEE (2019)
12. Luong, M.T., Pham, H., Manning, C.D.: Effective approaches to attention-based neural machine translation. arXiv preprint arXiv:1508.04025 (2015)
13. Tang, D., Qin, B., Feng, X., Liu, T.: Effective LSTMs for target-dependent sentiment classification. arXiv preprint arXiv:1512.01100 (2015)
14. Tian, Y., Chen, G., Song, Y.: Enhancing aspect-level sentiment analysis with word dependencies. In: Proceedings of the 16th Conference of the European Chapter of the Association for Computational Linguistics: Main Volume, pp. 3726–3739 (2021)
15. Wang, Y., Huang, M., Zhu, X., Zhao, L.: Attention-based LSTM for aspect-level sentiment classification. In: Proceedings of the 2016 Conference on Empirical Methods in Natural Language Processing, pp. 606–615 (2016)
16. Yu, B., Pan, J., Hu, J., Nascimento, A., De Cock, M.: Character level based detection of DGA domain names. In: 2018 International Joint Conference on Neural Networks (IJCNN), pp. 1–8. IEEE (2018)
17. Zeng, B., Yang, H., Xu, R., Zhou, W., Han, X.: LCF: a local context focus mechanism for aspect-based sentiment classification. Appl. Sci. **9**(16), 3389 (2019)
18. Zhao, J., Yan, Q., Liu, X., Li, B., Zuo, G.: Cyber threat intelligence modeling based on heterogeneous graph convolutional network. In: 23rd International Symposium on Research in Attacks, Intrusions and Defenses (RAID 2020), pp. 241–256 (2020)

19. Zhu, Z., Dumitras, T.: ChainSmith: automatically learning the semantics of malicious campaigns by mining threat intelligence reports. In: 2018 IEEE European Symposium on Security and Privacy (EuroS&P), pp. 458–472. IEEE (2018)
20. Zhuang, L., Wayne, L., Ya, S., Jun, Z.: A robustly optimized BERT pre-training approach with post-training. In: Proceedings of the 20th Chinese National Conference on Computational Linguistics, pp. 1218–1227 (2021)

HeHe: Balancing the Privacy and Efficiency in Training CNNs over the Semi-honest Cloud

Longlong Sun(✉), Hui Li, Shiwen Yu, Xindi Ma, Yanguo Peng, and Jiangtao Cui

Xidian University, Xi'an 710126, China
{llsun,swyu}@stu.xidian.edu.cn, {hli,xdma,ygpeng,cuijt}@xidian.edu.cn

Abstract. Convolutional Neural Networks (CNNs) have been widely used in various areas. As the training of CNNs requires powerful computing resources, data owners are now employing clouds to accomplish the task. However, this inevitably introduces serious privacy issues against the data owners, as the training images are now outsourced to the clouds, who may illegally spy on the content of the images for potential benefit. In this work, we propose HeHe, a CNN training framework over encrypted images with practical efficiency via additively homomorphic encryption and a delicate interaction scheme in CryptoHeader, which are shallow layers of the network. To evaluate whether the image content is preserved through a processing system, we propose (α, β)-*recoverable*, a novel image privacy model, and theoretically prove HeHe is robust against it. We test HeHe on several datasets in the aspects of accuracy, efficiency, and privacy. The empirical study justifies that HeHe is practical for the CNN training over encrypted images while preserving the accuracy with acceptable training cost and content leakage.

Keywords: Convolutional neural networks · Privacy preservation · Homomorphic encryption

1 Introduction

Thanks for the convenience brought by cloud computing, a large number of convolutional neural network (CNN) applications are gradually outsourced to public clouds, which we refer to as cloud service providers (CSP). As a result, the data owner (DO) can now accomplish the computation-intensive CNN training task at a very low cost by outsourcing the training work to a particular CSP, without buying and implementing a powerful and expensive GPU platform or large storage devices themselves. In this regard, a new paradigm emerged alongside, Deep Learning as a Service (DLaaS). However, DLaaS inevitably introduces privacy issues against the DO, as the CSP may spy on the data of the DO for training.

For instance, a medical institution collects many medical images and wants to train a disease diagnosis model, with which the workload of doctors can be

W. Susilo et al. (Eds.): ISC 2022, LNCS 13640, pp. 422–442, 2022.
https://doi.org/10.1007/978-3-031-22390-7_25

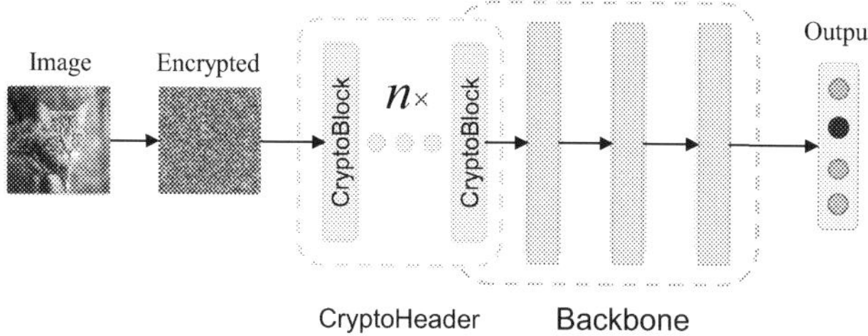

Fig. 1. HeHe: Using encrypted images to train convolutional neural networks.

significantly reduced. Obviously, DLaaS makes a great sense in this scenario, where a CSP will be employed to store the dataset and train a CNN. Small hospitals or doctors can use the trained model to analyze and make diagnoses by merely uploading their medical images. However, both the training and inference require uploading patients' medical images to the cloud, which inevitably brings in privacy issues. In another case, suppose that a CSP proposes a new model and provides training and inference services to users who want to apply the model over their own dataset. Meanwhile, the CSP may want to kept the model secret against potential competitors, thus the model training can only be completed in the cloud and the users have to outsource their data to the CSP.

In all these scenarios, the sensitive data uploaded to the CSP suffer from significant privacy issues as follows, even if the CSP strictly follows the CNN training procedure. First, the CSP (or some internal employees) may spy on the private images or use them for benefit; Second, the CSP may be attacked by an outsider adversary, who will probably obtain all these sensitive images.

As a promising cryptographic primitive, homomorphic encryption (HE) provides opportunities to perform a series of operations over ciphertext, which is adopted in privacy computing recently [4,7,9,15]. However, these schemes mainly focus on *inference*, but not *training*, which is more complex. Existing HE schemes suffer from three limitations to be applied in practical training tasks: *1)* The noise amount of a ciphertext grows with the increase in the number of operations, too much noise will cause incorrect decryption. Training involves backpropagation and the computation chain is longer, which limits the depth of networks. *2)* Some specific operations during network training, *e.g.,* comparison (in max-pooling and ReLU), division and logarithm (in the cross entropy), are not supported by HE schemes. *3)* The computational cost of HE (especially ciphertexts multiplication) is expensive, orders of magnitude larger than plaintexts. The training of deep networks is a kind of computation-intensive task. We advocate that it is impractical to carry out all operations solely over ciphertext.

In this regard, we propose **HeHe** (**He**ader **H**omomorphic **e**ncrypted) to enable training CNNs over encrypted images with satisfactory efficiency. First, driven by the limitation 3), we propose to encrypt only the first few shallow layers of the network, instead of all layers. The layers trained over ciphertexts are referred to as CryptoHeader, as shown in Fig. 1. Such an idea is originated from the following observation. Sensitive personal identifier information is leaked more in detailed visual features (*i.e.*, shallow layers) than semantic features (*i.e.*, deep layers). For instance, when training a car classifier, sensitive information like license plate numbers is only observable from visual features, and when training the character recognizer, sensitive information such as personal handwriting characteristics can be easily detected from visual features [31]. The introduction of CryptoHeader avoids the computation of cross-entropy under ciphertext (with aspect to limitation 2)), which cannot be realized in HE schemes, and reduces the amount of the ciphertexts computation significantly.

Second, we design an interactive training protocol under the cooperation of the DO and the CSP, where the length of ciphertexts computation chain is kept limited, and the computation over ciphertext on the CSP is restricted to additions instead of ciphertext-wise multiplication (with aspect to limitations 1)&2)). In this way, HeHe avoids the usage of fully homomorphic encryption (FHE), which is far from practical [26], and employs only additively homomorphic encryption (AHE), which is widely adopted in cloud privacy [2,29,39]. Third, through encrypted gradient computation in batch-based update, we reduce the information leakage of a single input image to the CSP.

Another problem needs to consider is how to determine the number of CryptoBlocks. To this end, we propose (α, β)-*recoverable*, a pixel-level privacy model, to estimate the leakage of visual information for images. Given predefined privacy requirements (*i.e.*, α and β) and backbone networks for training tasks, we present a strategy to estimate the minimum number of CryptoBlocks to meet the privacy requirements. Our contributions are summarized as follows.

- We proposing a CNN training framework over encrypted images. The shallow layers are trained over ciphertext, while the deep layers are not. In this way, the sensitive identifier information involved in the images can be effectively protected while the overall training cost is kept in an acceptable volume.
- For training CryptoBlocks over ciphertext, we design an interactive training scheme. Through the scheme, the CSP no need to implement FHE to perform non-linear activations, such that the cost and training errors can be reduced.
- We design an index structure to enable the CSP to perform the backpropagation independently, thus reducing the number of interactions. Besides, we propose to decrypt and update the gradients of parameters based on the sum of a mini-batch, such that the gradients for a single sample are not leaked.
- We propose a novel privacy model in terms of visual recovery rate and prove that HeHe is secure under it. We evaluate different datasets and networks in experiments and justify the effectiveness and efficiency of our framework.

2 Related Work and Preliminaries

Privacy-Preserving Machine Learning. There are many schemes for private inference [6,7,9,17,21,24,30]. Compared with inference, training is much more complex, which introduces a series of challenges. Although some schemes are proposed for training shallow models [12,13,34]. Training deep networks privately is far from practical usage due to the overhead or rigorous settings.

GELU-Net [39] is a secure two-party computing protocol to complete the training over the encrypted data samples. The scheme is based on homomorphic encryption and the noise injection mechanism. Similarly, some researchers designed secure multi-party computation protocols [25,35,36] to complete the training of machine learning models. Compared with the homomorphic encryption methods, the training speed had been greatly improved. However, they require more than two CSPs to collaborate and also assume that there is no collusion between CSPs, which is hard to guarantee in practice.

Convolutional Neural Network. Convolutional Neural Networks is a stack of different layers, such as the convolution, pooling, activation, BatchNorm, and fully connected layers. Some recent studies have proposed models that reach hundreds of layers [14,16]. The convolutional, max-pooling, and ReLU layers are three basic layers in CNNs. The convolution can be represented as: $\mathbf{y} = \sum_{w,h} \mathbf{x}(j+w, k+h)\mathbf{K}(w,h) + \mathbf{b}$, where $\mathbf{K}$ is a $w \times h$ filter and $\mathbf{b}$ is the bias. The max-pooling layer is: $\mathbf{y} = \max(\sum_{w,h} \mathbf{x}(j+w, k+h))$, it's parameter-free and used to compress feature maps. The most commonly used activation function is ReLU: $\mathbf{y} = \max(\mathbf{0}, \mathbf{x})$. It mainly provides non-linearity to improve the fitting ability of the model. For a more detailed introduction, we recommend to read [11].

Additively Homomorphic Encryption. Additively homomorphic encryption is a public-key cryptosystem that supports the addition on encrypted values and obtains the encrypted sum. Compared with FHE, the construction of AHE is simpler and more efficient in computation [1]. Our scheme will use Paillier [28], and its homomorphic addition and scalar multiplication are:

$$\begin{aligned} Enc(x_1 + x_2\,(mod\ n)) &= Enc(x_1) \cdot Enc(x_2)\left(mod\ n^2\right), \\ Enc(k \cdot x_1\,(mod\ n)) &= Enc(x_1)^k \left(mod\ n^2\right), \end{aligned} \tag{1}$$

where n is a parameter of the public key.

3 Problem Statement

3.1 System Model

In DLaaS, users offer data to the cloud, and the cloud provides computing services. We follow this paradigm. Model training is completed with the joint participation of the data owner (*i.e.*, client) and cloud service provider (*i.e.*, server). There are two basic entities in our framework:

- *Client.* The client manages private and public keys and owns the training images. The client has limited computational resources to train a CNN itself.
- *Server.* A server is employed to perform the CNN training task. It holds the client's public keys and supports CNNs' computations over ciphertext that are encrypted using Paillier. In addition, we assume the server has extensive computing capability and never suffers from computational resources.

Notably, in this work, we focus on model training. Thus, how the trained model is further used is beyond the scope of this paper.

3.2 Privacy Model

Our goal is to protect the client's training images against potential adversaries, *i.e.,* defending input inference attack. In our setting, the server is *honest-but-curious*, which is a common assumption widely adopted in related works [17,21, 25,35,39]. That means, the server interacts with the client following the protocol strictly to ensure correct training, but curiously makes additional attempts to illegally access and spy on training data for benefit. In our training system, only one cloud is employed, which is different from the schemes that are based on secure multi-party computation [25,35].

In our problem setting, an adversary $\mathcal{A}$ will try various methods to grab the original image content. Unfortunately, to the best of our knowledge, there is no measure to estimate whether and how much the visual content within an arbitrary image is leaked. In this regard, hereby we propose a novel criterion, namely (α, β)*-recoverable*, to evaluate the content leakage for a given image, the definition of (α, β)*-recoverable* is as follows.

Definition 1. ((α, β)-recoverable). *For a RGB image M, which is processed by a system Σ, an adversary $\mathcal{A}$ towards Σ can observe it as M'. First, transform $M(M')$ to a uniform color space [5,22] $M_{ucs} = (J, a, b)$ $(M'_{ucs} = (J', a', b'))$. For each pixel $x_i \in M$, let x'_i denotes the observed pixel in M', compute perceptual distance:*

$$\Delta E_i^* = \sqrt{(J_i - J_i')^2 + (a_i - a_i')^2 + (b_i - b_i')^2}.$$

Then we call M is (α, β)-recoverable if

$$\frac{\sum_{i=1}^{m}\left(\frac{\Delta E_i^*}{\max(\Delta E^*)} \le \beta\right)}{m} \le \alpha, (0 \le \alpha, \beta \le 1),$$

where $\max(\Delta E^*)$ is the domain size of perceptual distance, and m is the number of pixels in M.

Herein β describes the similarity threshold of pixel level, and α describes the similarity threshold w.r.t. the whole image. Generally, the larger α and smaller β refers to a weaker privacy requirement for a system Σ, which correspondingly demands a stronger ability of the adversary $\mathcal{A}$. For instance, $(1, 0)$*-recoverable* requires the adversary to get the original image content pixel-by-pixel exactly. In particular, let $\Pr_\Sigma(\alpha, \beta)$ be the probability that a system Σ to be (α, β)-*recoverable*, then we consider Σ to be secure under (α, β)-*recoverable* when $\Pr_\Sigma(\alpha, \beta)$ is small enough. Experiments to verify the effectiveness of the (α, β)-*recoverable* are presented in Appendix A.

4 Proposed Framework

CNNs are generally composed of multiple stacking structures, we design a protocol, namely CryptoBlock, for implementing several stack structure of CNN

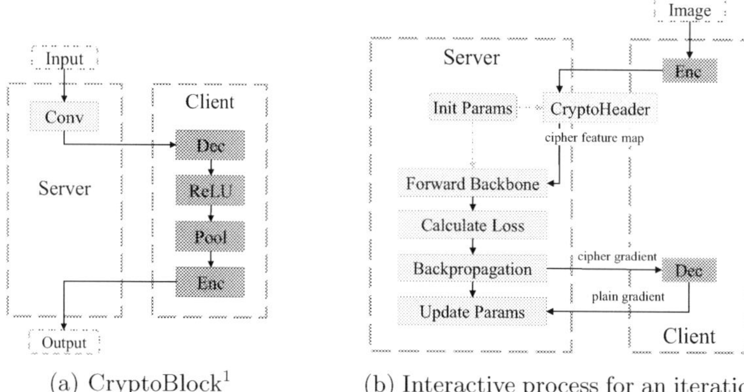

(a) CryptoBlock[1] (b) Interactive process for an iteration

Fig. 2. The training process of HeHe framework. (No need to encrypt the output of the last CryptoBlock (Line 17 of Algorithm 1).)

Algorithm 1. HeHe Forward Propagation

Input: A batch $\mathcal{B}$ contains b images, $\mathcal{B} = (\mathbf{x}_1, \mathbf{x}_2, \cdots, \mathbf{x}_b)$
Output: The category-probability vectors $\mathcal{Y}$
1: ***Client***:
2: Shuffle and encrypt $\mathcal{B}$ as $[\mathcal{B}]$, send $[\mathcal{B}]$ to server
3: Assign $[\mathcal{F}_0] \leftarrow [\mathcal{B}]$, $[\mathcal{F}_0] = ([\mathbf{f}_1], [\mathbf{f}_2], \cdots, [\mathbf{f}_b])$
4: **for** k in $1 : n$ **do**
5: ***Server***:
6: **for** i in $1 : b$ **do**
7: Get feature map $[\mathbf{f}_i^c] \leftarrow Conv_{HE}([\mathbf{f}_i], \theta_k)$
8: Pack feature maps $[\mathcal{F}_k^c] = ([\mathbf{f}_1^c], [\mathbf{f}_2^c], \cdots, [\mathbf{f}_b^c])$
9: Send $[\mathcal{F}_k^c]$ to client and store $[\mathcal{F}_k^c]$
10: ***Client***:
11: Decrypt $[\mathcal{F}_k^c]$ as $\mathcal{F}_k^c$
12: $\mathcal{F}_k \leftarrow MaxPool(ReLU(\mathcal{F}_k^c))$
13: **if** $k < n$ **then**
14: Encrypt $\mathcal{F}_k$ as $[\mathcal{F}_k]$
15: Send $[\mathcal{F}_k]$ to server
16: **else**
17: Send $\mathcal{F}_k$ to server
18: ***Server***:
19: Forward propagation rest CNN layers $\mathcal{Y} \leftarrow Forward(\mathcal{F}_n)$

---

over ciphertext. As shown in Fig. 2a, we assign the server to perform the computation of encrypted convolutional layers and the client to complete ReLU and max-pooling layers. During the forward propagation, each CryptoBlock requires one interaction with the client. CryptoHeader is adaptively composed of n CryptoBlocks, where n is a hyperparameter to balance the trade-off between efficiency and privacy leakage. Figure 2b illustrates the overall interactions between client and server for a single training iteration of HeHe.

In this section, we first introduce the forward and backward propagations of HeHe in Sects. 4.1 and 4.2. Next, we introduce how to use the index to accelerate backpropagation in Sect. 4.3. Finally, we give the privacy analysis of HeHe in Sect. 4.4.

Algorithm 2. HeHe Backpropagation

Input: The output $\mathcal{Y}$, the target of batch $\mathcal{T}$, and server stored $(\theta, [\mathcal{F}^c])$
Output: The updated CNN

Server:
  Backward the rest CNN layers $\mathcal{G}^f_n \leftarrow \mathit{Backward}(\mathcal{Y}, \mathcal{T})$
for k in $n : 1$ **do**
  Client:
    Get $\mathcal{G}^f_k$ from server
    $\mathcal{G}^p \leftarrow \mathit{BackMaxPooling}\left(\mathcal{G}^f_k\right)$
    $\mathcal{G}^r \leftarrow \mathit{BackReLU}\ (\mathcal{G}^p_k)$
    Send $\mathcal{G}^r$ to server
  Server:
    $[\mathcal{G}^w_k] \leftarrow \mathit{BackConvWeight}_{HE}\ (\mathcal{G}^r_k, [\mathcal{F}^c_{k-1}])$
    $\mathcal{G}^f_{k-1} \leftarrow \mathit{BackConvInput}\,(\mathcal{G}^r_k, \theta_k)$
Server:
  Assign $[\mathbf{g}_i] \leftarrow \left(\left[\mathcal{G}^w_{1,i}\right], \left[\mathcal{G}^w_{2,i}\right], \cdots, \left[\mathcal{G}^w_{n,i}\right]\right)$
  Sum all gradients $[\Delta] \leftarrow \sum_{i=1}^{b} [\mathbf{g}_i]$
  Send $[\Delta]$ to client
Client:
  Decrypt $[\Delta]$ as Δ, send Δ to server
Server:
  Update $\theta_i \leftarrow \theta_i - \frac{1}{b}\gamma\Delta_i$ in CryptoHeader

4.1 Forward Propagation

Given the proposed schemes of CryptoHeader as well as CryptoBlock, Algorithm 1 outlines the forward propagation in HeHe. For each CryptoBlock, the server takes charge of convolution over ciphertext and outputs the results, which are kept encrypted to the client (Lines 5–9). Upon receiving the convolution results, the client decrypts them with the private key. Then it performs ReLU and max-pooling sequentially over the plaintext like the classical forward propagation. Afterward, it encrypts the results with the public key and sends the ciphertext to the server (Lines 10–17), which will continue to perform the convolution iteratively then. When n CryptoBlocks have been accomplished, the server continues with the forward propagation over the rest layers in plaintext without the help of the client anymore (Lines 18–19).

During the whole procedure, ciphertext-based operations are restricted to only the convolution, where the parameters of the model are all learned on the server and can be directly used. Therefore, the homomorphic convolution operation $Conv_{HE}$ can be regarded as the dot product of encrypted input $[\mathcal{F}]$ and plain kernel parameters θ, based on Eqs. (1). As there is no multiplication of ciphertexts, the forward propagation can be implemented based on AHE.

4.2 Backpropagation

During backpropagation, the server computes the rest plaintext layers of the backbone network in the same way as traditional CNN training to get the gradient $\mathcal{G}^f_n$ corresponding to the nth CryptoBlock's output, then computes the gradients of each CryptoBlock in reverse order.

Algorithm 3. Construct Index $\mathcal{I}$.

Input: The input feature map $\mathcal{F}^c$
Output: The output feature map $\mathcal{F}$ and the index $\mathcal{I}$

$\mathcal{F}^r \leftarrow ReLU(\mathcal{F}^c)$
$\mathcal{F}, \mathcal{I} \leftarrow MaxPool(\mathcal{F}^r)$
for each entry $\mathcal{F}_i$ in $\mathcal{F}$ **do**
    if $\mathcal{F}_i = 0$ **then**
        $\mathcal{I}_i \leftarrow -1$

Algorithm 4. Use Index $\mathcal{I}$.

Input: The $\mathcal{I}$ and input gradient $\mathcal{G}^f$
Output: The output gradient $\mathcal{G}^r$

Initialize the gradient $\mathcal{G}^r \leftarrow \{0\}$
for each entry $\mathcal{I}_i$ in $\mathcal{I}$ **do**
    if $\mathcal{I}_i \neq$ -1 **then**
        $\mathcal{G}^r[\mathcal{I}_i] \leftarrow \mathcal{G}^f[\mathcal{I}_i]$

For each CryptoBlock, since the computation of max-pooling and ReLU layers are completed in the client, the server sends the feature map $\mathcal{G}^f$ to the client. Then the client completes the backpropagation of the max-pooling and ReLU layers and sends output $\mathcal{G}^r$ to the server. Next, the server back propagates the convolutional layer and gets the gradients of the convolutional kernel. According to the backpropagation of CNNs, the gradients $[\mathcal{G}^w]$ of convolutional kernels can be obtained by the homomorphic convolution $BackConvWeight_{HE}$ from input $[\mathcal{F}^c]$ and output $\mathcal{G}^r$, based on Eqs. (1). Then, the server computes the gradients $\mathcal{G}^f_{k-1}$ of the input, which can be obtained by performing the convolution over $\mathcal{G}^r_k$ and the convolutional kernel θ. Since both $\mathcal{G}^r_k$ and θ are plaintext, the obtained gradients $\mathcal{G}^f_{k-1}$ are also plaintext, thus the plaintext $\mathcal{G}^f_{k-1}$ can be fed into the next CryptoBlock to compute the next layer's gradients. The procedure is summarized in Algorithm 2.

The above description indicates that the computation of backpropagation does not require any multiplication over ciphertexts, either. After computing the gradients of CryptoHeader, the server gets the encrypted gradients $[\Delta]$. Different from the scheme in [39], we take mini-batch as the unit during the training phase. Hence, before sending the gradients to the client, we sum up the encrypted gradients of all images following the homomorphic addition mechanism. This method protects every single image's gradients. Finally, when the client decrypts and returns the plaintext gradients Δ to the server, the server can update the model parameters, where b is the batch size and γ is the learning rate.

4.3 Index $\mathcal{I}$

During the forward propagation, for the max-pooling layer, the traditional CNN training implementation employs an index table to mark the correct positions for gradients, which are to be computed within the backpropagation phase. In our scheme, as the client executes ReLU and max-pooling within CryptoBlock during forward propagation and we do not wish the server to query the client again for such index during backpropagation, we redesign the index table so that the gradient propagation of ReLU and max-pooling layers can be completed simultaneously no matter the feature map is encrypted or not.

To realize that, we additionally attach a label over the original index table to indicate whether the corresponding neuron is activated by ReLU or not. Algorithms 3 and 4 illustrate the detailed process for building the index structure during forward propagation and how it can be used during backpropagation. We can use Algorithm 3 to compute $\mathcal{I}$ and send it to the server (Line 12 of

Algorithm 1), and use Algorithm 4 to replace lines 4–8 of Algorithm 2. Notably, $\mathcal{G}^r[i]$ refers to the ith entry of matrix $\mathcal{G}^r$ according to Z-Order.

Therefore, with the index $\mathcal{I}$, during the backpropagation, there is only one interaction with the client after all gradients of CryptoBlocks are computed. Assuming that the CryptoHeader consists of n CryptoBlock, the training of a batch requires $n+1$ interactions.

4.4 Privacy Analysis

First, to ease the understanding, we consider the probability for an image to be (α, β)-*recoverable* against an adversary without knowledge from Σ.

Lemma 1. ((α, β)-*recoverable* probability of random guess). *For an image M containing m pixels, and an processing system Σ that leaks no information about M, then the probability for Σ to be* (α, β)-recoverable *over M is*

$$\Pr_{\Sigma}(\alpha, \beta) = \sum_{i=\alpha m}^{m} \binom{m}{i} \beta^i (1-\beta)^{m-i}.$$

Proof. For a single pixel x, from Definition 1, we have $\frac{\Delta E_x^*}{\max(\Delta E^*)} \leq \beta$, assume the color distribution in nature is uniform, then whether x is recoverable is a Bernoulli trial with $p=\beta$. For all m pixels, it's a binomial distribution $\mathcal{B}(m, \beta)$, thus $\Pr_{\Sigma}(\alpha, \beta) = 1 - \mathrm{CDF}_{\mathcal{B}}(\alpha m)$.

In our framework, the deep layers of the network are not encrypted and computed by the server, which inevitably introduces some information leakage during the training. This information can be used by some adversaries to infer the original content of the input image.

In the forward propagation, an adversary from the server-side can access the following. *1)* The plain feature map $\mathcal{Z}_n$ of the CryptoHeader's output. *2)* The index $\mathcal{I}$ of each CryptoBlock. On the other hand, in the backpropagation, an adversary from the server-side can access: *1)* The plain gradients $\mathcal{G}_f$ of each feature map in CryptoHeader. *2)* The plain summed gradients Δ of each batch. Given the above information leakage, we shall discuss the probability for HeHe to be (α, β)-*recoverable* under the semi-honest model in the following.

Proposition 1 (The (α, β)-*recoverable* probability in forward propagation of HeHe). *In forward propagation of HeHe, for an image M with m pixels, the probability of HeHe to be* (α, β)-recoverable *is*

$$\Pr_{\Sigma}(\alpha, \beta) = \begin{cases} 1 & \text{if } \alpha \leq \frac{m_r}{m} \\ \sum_{i=\alpha m - m_r}^{m-m_r} \binom{m-m_r}{i} \beta^i (1-\beta)^{m-m_r-i} & \text{if } \alpha > \frac{m_r}{m} \end{cases}$$

and $m_r = \lambda^n m \prod_{i=1}^{n} k_i^{-2}$, where n denotes the number of CryptoBlocks, λ denotes the averaged activate rate of ReLU, and k_i is the kernel size of ith max-pooling layer.

Proof. The adversary gets plain $\mathcal{F}_n$, to recover the input data $\mathcal{X}$. As described in Algorithm 1, let $f(\cdot)$ denote the forward propagation of CryptoHeader, then $\mathcal{F}_n = f(\mathcal{X})$. If the CryptoHeader is invertible and the adversary gets inverse function $f'(\cdot)$, it could recover plain input $\mathcal{X}$ through $\mathcal{X} = f'(\mathcal{F}_n)$. Therefore, we need to analyze the invertibility of CryptoHeader.

CryptoHeader consists of convolutional, ReLU, and max-pooling layers. First, we study the invertibility of those layers. Afterward, the invertibility of CryptoHeader is discussed.

(a) The invertibility of three layers.
Convoluational layer performs linear operations. Let the weights of the convolutional be $\boldsymbol{w}$, and n_i (*resp.*, n_o) denote the size of input (*resp.*, output) feature map $\boldsymbol{f}_i$ (*resp.*, $\boldsymbol{f}_o$). For each convolutional patch $\boldsymbol{x}_k$, there is $f_k = \boldsymbol{w} \cdot \boldsymbol{x}_k, 1 \leq k \leq n_o$. Therefore, using $\boldsymbol{f}_o$ to derive $\boldsymbol{f}_i$ can be formalized as solving the following linear system of n_o equations with respect to n_i variables: $\boldsymbol{W}\boldsymbol{X} = \boldsymbol{f}_o$, where $\boldsymbol{W}$ is an $n_o \times n_i$ matrix, $\boldsymbol{X}$ is a column vector with n_i entries, and $\boldsymbol{f}_o$ is a column vector with f_o entries. The convolution is a sliding window operation and every patch is different, therefore, the row vectors of $\boldsymbol{W}$ are linearly independent and the rank of the augmented matrix $\boldsymbol{A}$ is $r(\boldsymbol{A}) = \min(n_i, n_o)$. If $n_i > n_o$, then $r(\boldsymbol{A}) = n_o < n_i$, so the system has infinite solutions and convolutional layer is non-invertible. Otherwise (*i.e.*, $n_i \leq n_o$), then $r(\boldsymbol{A}) = n_i > n_o$, so the system has a single solution and the convolutional layer is invertible.

ReLU layer executes $f(\boldsymbol{x}) = \max(\boldsymbol{0}, \boldsymbol{x})$ for each value of feature map $\boldsymbol{f}$. Thus the negative value is mapped to 0, which is non-invertible; and the positive value remains unchanged, which is invertible. Let λ denote the averaged activate rate, where $\lambda = \Pr(x > 0)$, so λm values of input can be recovered.[1]

Max-pooling layer performs: $f(\boldsymbol{x}) = \max(\boldsymbol{x})$ for each pooling patch $\boldsymbol{x}_k$ of input feature map $\boldsymbol{f}$, thus only the maximum value is reserved. With the help of the index $\mathcal{I}$, which is built in Algorithm 3, the adversary can map the maximum value to the original input. Let k denote the pooling size such that the size of pooling patch is k^2, therefore, $k^{-2}n$ elements of input can be recovered.

(b) The invertibility of CryptoHeader.
Summarize the above analysis, the invertibility of CryptoHeader can be divided into two cases:

case 1) There exists a convolutional layer in CryptoHeader such that $n_i > n_o$. Then this convolutional layer is non-invertible, which makes the CryptoHeader non-invertible. Therefore, in this case, the probability of (α, β)-*recoverable* directly follows Lemma 1.

case 2) All convolutional layers in CryptoHeader satisfy $n_i \leq n_o$, thus all convolutional layers are invertible. We first compute the number of recovered elements m_r, to achieve it, we compute the recovery rate of each layer and multiply them to get the total number of recovered elements.

---

[1] Although λ cannot be estimated accurately in CNNs, it has been empirically studied and justified to be bounded by 0.25 [10].

Assume the number of CryptoBlocks in CryptoHeader is n. For the ith CryptoBlock, let k_i denote the kernel size of the max-pooling layer, and λ denotes the averaged activate rate of ReLU, then $m_r = \lambda^n m \prod_{i=1}^{n} k_i^{-2}$. Therefore, if $\alpha \le \frac{m_r}{m} = \lambda^n \prod_{i=1}^{n} k_i^{-2}$, the recovery probability is 1, and for $\alpha > \frac{m_r}{m}$, as the adversary has no information about other elements, applying Lemma 1, the probability can be obtained.

Proposition 2 (The (α, β)-*recoverable* probability in backpropagation of HeHe). *In backpropagation, for an image M with m pixels, the probability of HeHe to be* (α, β)-recoverable *is equivalent to random guess in Lemma 1.*

Proof. From Line 10 of Algorithm 2, for the first convolutional layer, the adversary wants to get the plaintext input image $\mathcal{F}_0$. Consider the worst case that *BackConvWeight* is invertible, the adversary already has the plaintext gradient of feature map $\mathcal{G}_1^f$, so it can use the inverse function of *BackConvWeight* to recover input if he can obtain the convolutional kernel's plaintext gradient of M. However, it's infeasible in HeHe.

In our framework, only the summed gradients over a batch of convolutional kernels, namely Δ, are decrypted and sent to the server, this ensures that the server cannot access the convolutional kernel's plaintext gradient of a single image $\mathcal{G}^w$, thus the adversary cannot recover the input data through the inverse function of *BackConvWeight*. Therefore, the adversary can not infer any information of the original image during the backpropagation.

In a word, the privacy guarantee of our framework comes from: *1)* The invertibility of the neural network. *2)* Encrypt key information in the training, such as CryptoHeader and gradient $\mathbf{g}_i$ in backpropagation.

Notably, the probability for the HeHe framework to be (α, β)-*recoverable* is determined by the parameters of the CryptHeader, regardless of the selection of the backbone network. The client could adjust the parameters $\{n, k\}$ according to the required privacy level to adapt the appropriate CryptoHeader.

5 Experiments

We empirically demonstrate the performance of HeHe on benchmark datasets and study the results in terms of accuracy, efficiency, and privacy, respectively.

5.1 Experiments Setup

Datasets and Networks. MNIST is a 28×28 pixels gray handwritten digit dataset [20], containing 60,000/10,000 images to train/test. We use the LeNet-5 [20] as the backbone network and replace the first n convolutional layers with CryptoHeader. Due to the pixel redundancy of MNIST, we adopt the same preprocessing method as [12] to perform 2× subsampling of original images. The SVHN is a 32×32 RGB digit dataset [27], containing 73,257/26,032 images to train/test. We adopt the DenseNet-40 [16] as the backbone network while

Table 1. Model architectures for different datasets

Dataset	CryptoHeader						Network
	CryptoBlock 1	α	CryptoBlock 2	α	CryptoBlock 3	α	
MNSIT	$\begin{bmatrix} \text{conv } 3\times 3 \\ \text{out}_{ch}=6 \\ \text{ReLU} \\ \text{pool } 2\times 2 \end{bmatrix}$	1/16	$\begin{bmatrix} \text{conv } 3\times 3 \\ \text{out}_{ch}=16 \\ \text{ReLU} \\ \text{pool } 1\times 1 \end{bmatrix}$	1/4	N/A	N/A	LeNet-5
SVHN	$\begin{bmatrix} \text{conv } 3\times 3 \\ \text{out}_{ch}=12 \\ \text{ReLU} \\ \text{pool } 2\times 2 \end{bmatrix}$	1/16	$\begin{bmatrix} \text{conv } 3\times 3 \\ \text{out}_{ch}=18 \\ \text{ReLU} \\ \text{pool } 1\times 1 \end{bmatrix}$	1/4	$\begin{bmatrix} \text{conv } 3\times 3 \\ \text{out}_{ch}=18 \\ \text{ReLU} \\ \text{pool } 1\times 1 \end{bmatrix}$	1/4	DenseNet-40
CIFAR-10	$\begin{bmatrix} \text{conv } 3\times 3 \\ \text{out}_{ch}=12 \\ \text{ReLU} \\ \text{pool } 2\times 2 \end{bmatrix}$	1/16	$\begin{bmatrix} \text{conv } 3\times 3 \\ \text{out}_{ch}=18 \\ \text{ReLU} \\ \text{pool } 1\times 1 \end{bmatrix}$	1/4	$\begin{bmatrix} \text{conv } 3\times 3 \\ \text{out}_{ch}=18 \\ \text{ReLU} \\ \text{pool } 1\times 1 \end{bmatrix}$	1/4	DenseNet-100

the first convolutional layer is replaced by CryptoHeader. Also, we preprocess images using 2× subsampling similar to MNIST. The CIFAR-10 dataset [19] contains 32×32 RGB images of 10 common objects, containing 50,000/10,000 to train/test. We select the DenseNet-100 [16] as the backbone network. These datasets are widely used by researchers [14,16,20,39].

CryptoHeader. In our framework, the CryptoHeader is composed of n CryptoBlocks, and the different settings of n will directly affect the training performance. Therefore, for the models used in different datasets, we vary the settings of n to evaluate the performance of different CryptoHeader structures. In particular, we vary $n = \{1, 2, 3\}$ except for LeNet-5 in MNIST, which is only applicable for $n = \{1, 2\}$, as LeNet-5 only has two convolutional layers. Table 1 shows the CryptoHeader and backbone networks that are used in different datasets, as well as the recovery rate α of each CryptoBlock. We configure all convolutional layers with kernel size 3 and max-pooling layers with kernel size 2 or 1 (equivalent to no pooling), the out_{ch} denotes the output channel size of convolutional layer. These configurations are similar to the mainstream CNNs study [14,16].

Furthermore, we could customize the parameters and the number of CryptoBlocks according to different training requirements to get better performance.

Implementation Details. We conduct our experiments on Alibaba Cloud ECS c6.8xlarge instances with Intel Xeon(Cascade Lake) Platinum 8269 @ 2.5 GHz. The client and server are in the WAN setting and the peak bandwidth is 100 Mbps. We implement HeHe scheme in python based on the Paillier library *python-paillier*[2] and the popular deep learning framework *PyTorch*. For a fair comparison, we train MNIST and SVHN without any data augmentation; we

[2] python-paillier, https://github.com/n1analytics/python-paillier.

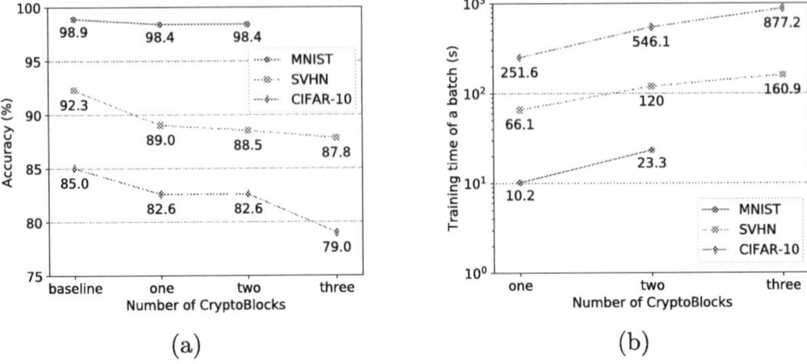

Fig. 3. The accuracy and overhead of varying the number of CryptoBlocks.

follow the popular data augmentation setting that is widely used for CIFAR-10 [14,16]. We choose Adam [18] as the optimizer and use the default learning rate 0.001. The models for MNIST and SVHN are trained in 10 epochs, and CIFAR-10 is trained in 20 epochs with a batch size of 256.

5.2 Comparison of Different CryptoBlocks

We evaluate the effect of the numbers of CryptoBlocks employed in HeHe, in all three perspectives, including accuracy, efficiency, and privacy.

For each dataset, we use the original backbone network in plaintext (*i.e.*, LeNet-5 for MNIST, DenseNet-40 for SVHN, and DenseNet-100 for CIFAR-10) as baseline approaches for training comparison and adopt the same hyperparameters in our HeHe. Figure 3a shows the prediction accuracy for the trained models for each dataset by varying the value of n. Obviously, as n increases, the prediction accuracy of MNIST remains almost the same. However, for SVHN and CIFAR-10, there exist some gap between the baseline and HeHe. By profoundly investigating the models and implementations, we find the following reasons for this phenomenon. *1)* To reduce the computational overhead, we set up a smaller number of kernels for the first convolutional layer than the original model (from 24 to 12); *2)* The image size of both SVHN and CIFAR-10 datasets are 32×32 pixels, which are small. When dealing with small images, the baseline DenseNet model does not use pooling operations to avoid information loss [16]. However, there are pooling layers in our CryptoHeader, which will introduce the loss of accuracy. When trained on large-size images, the state-of-the-art CNNs [14,16] adopt max-pooling layers, so we shall have the same model structure as the baselines. Therefore, the loss of accuracy introduced by the above difference, whether max-pooling is employed or not, will be eliminated in the scenario[3].

The computational overhead of HeHe mainly comes from the homomorphic evaluation of ciphertexts, which is inefficient compared with the computations

[3] We do not show the results in large-size datasets due to the limited computing resources we have currently.

Table 2. Accuracy comparison

Scheme	MNIST	SVHN	CIFAR-10
Square [9]	98.3%	19.6%	25.2%
Polynomial [7]	98.7%	25.9%	35.0%
GELU-Net [39]	96.9%	N/A	N/A
HeHe	98.4%	88.5%	82.6%
Plaintext baselines	98.9%	92.3%	85.0%

in plaintext. Figure 3b shows the training time of one batch with batch size 256, and the training time increases almost linearly with the number of CryptoBlocks for all the datasets and corresponding models.

According to Sect. 4.4, for the non-invertible elements of input, HeHe does not disclose any information about them and thus approximate recover is avoided. Therefore, our framework could satisfy any setting of β. Next, we compute the minimum value of α_{min} that different CryptoHeaders can satisfy, as shown in Table 1. α_{min} can be computed as: $\alpha_{min} = p_{sub}^{-2} \times \prod_{i=1}^{n} \alpha_i$, where p_{sub} is the stride of subsampling used in input preprocess. In our experiment, we set $p_{sub} = 2$ for MNIST and SVHN; and set $p_{sub} = 1$ for CIFAR-10. α_i is the recovery rate of the ith CryptoBlock. For MNIST, obtain $\alpha_{min} = \{1/64,\ 1/256\}$ for two CryptoHeader configurations; in SVHN, $\alpha_{min} = \{1/64,\ 1/256,\ 1/1024\}$ for three CryptoHeader configurations; in CIFAR-10, $\alpha_{min} = \{1/16,\ 1/64,\ 1/256\}$. Finally, we compute the probability of HeHe to be (α, β)-*recoverable* using Proposition 1, for a recommend setting $(\alpha = 0.5, \beta = 1/3)$ in Appendix A. It can be easily proved that we can achieve $\Pr_{\Sigma}(0.5, 1/3) < 10^{-15}$ for all models under the aforementioned settings. It is small enough to satisfy the proposed privacy criterion in the end of Sect. 3.2.

Generally, increasing the number of CryptoBlocks will enhance privacy, but will bring more computational overhead. In the following, we fix the number of CryptoBlocks to 2 to compare accuracy and overhead against baseline methods.

5.3 Predication Accuracy

In this part, we test the prediction accuracy using the trained model of HeHe and the baseline plaintext approach. Besides, for this group of tests, we also compare HeHe with a group of privacy-preserving *inference* schemes of CNNs.

For the inference over encrypted images, many schemes use the FHE [6,9,14, 15]. However, due to the limitation of FHE, some structures in CNNs need to be approximated. On the one hand, the max-pooling widely adopted in state-of-the-art CNNs is robust to extract salient features [3]. As the homomorphic encryption doesn't support numerical comparison between ciphertexts, the network for inference over encrypted images cannot use the max-pooling layer. Existing schemes adopt average-pooling instead [9,39]. Furthermore, since the homomorphic encryption is unable to support division directly, the sum function $\sum x_i$ is

Table 3. Training time of one batch

Scheme		MNIST	SVHN	CIFAR-10
HeHe	Forward	16.7 s	87.5 s	388.2 s
	Back	6.6 s	32.5 s	157.9 s
	Total	23.3 s	120 s	546.1 s
GELU-Net (forward) [39]		85.5 s	N/A	N/A
Plaintext baselines		0.1 s	0.2 s	4.3 s

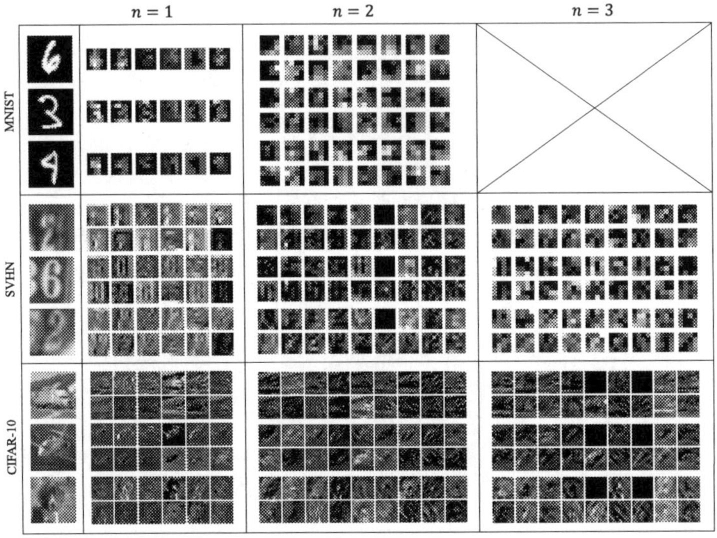

Fig. 4. The feature maps generated by CryptoHeaders in different models.

used to approximate the average pooling [9]. On the other hand, the activation function is an important structure in CNNs that significantly affects the non-linear mapping and the convergence of the training. Unfortunately, homomorphic encryption cannot address this operation either, so CryptoNets [9] adopts the square function instead, while some other schemes use higher-order polynomial functions [7,15]. Although polynomial can bring better approximation, repeated multiplications will cause decryption failure and huge time overhead, so it's far from practical. As a comparison, we additionally test the prediction accuracy for both square and polynomial approximations for the activation function in this group of experiments. In particular, we adopt the square approximation in CryptoNets [9] and the second-order polynomial $y = 0.125x^2 + 0.5x + 0.25$ approximation that are recently proposed in [7], respectively.

Different from inference, training a CNN has to update the model parameters iteratively, so the accuracy loss in the above approximations will be enlarged across iterations. For deep network and large image classification tasks, the accuracy loss is more significant. As shown in Table 2, for the MNIST dataset, the approximation does not cause significant accuracy loss because a shallow network, LeNet-5, is adopted as the backbone. However, for both SVHN and CIFAR-10, as deep networks are adopted (*i.e.*, 40 and 100 convolutional layers respectively), the training will not converge due to the approximation.

To overcome this problem, one related effort, namely GELU-Net [39], selects to compute the activation function on the client, such that there is no accuracy loss as approximation is never used. However, since GELU-Net needs to repeatedly add and remove noise during the training to achieve privacy protection, it will reduce the training accuracy. Furthermore, because GELU-Net does not provide any mechanism for implementing the BatchNorm layer, it cannot be applied to deep networks.

Our HeHe framework does not encrypt BatchNorm layers so that it can be applied to the training of deep CNNs. Compared with the existing schemes, we achieve the best accuracy for deep CNNs.

5.4 Training Time

In this part, we show the training time compared with baselines in the tested datasets. For reference, we also showcase the cost of the state-of-the-art privacy-preserving CNN training scheme, GELU-Net [39][4]. Table 3 lists the training time of one batch, including the forward and backward propagation. Compared with GELU-Net, we achieve 5× speed-up for the forward propagation.

Although HeHe has introduced significant costs compared with plaintext baselines, to the best of our knowledge, it is the most practical solution for the CNN training over encrypted images that preserves the accuracy with acceptable training cost. HeHe is especially appealing in many scenarios when the training images are sensitive. Besides, as an early effort in the privacy-preserving CNN training, we suggest an effective way that future works can follow and make improvements. Notably, due to the limitation of computing power, HeHe on our experimental platform is time-consuming. In fact, for practical applications, the model training can rely on much powerful computing resources in a cloud, and the network except CryptoHeader can also be significantly accelerated by a powerful GPU cluster, so the training time of HeHe can be greatly reduced.

5.5 Visual Effect Study

In Sect. 4.4, we have given the probability of an image processing system to be (α, β)-*recoverable*, To justify our proposed privacy model as well as HeHe empirically, we perform a group of visual study over the images M' that can be observed by an honest-but-curious adversary from the server-side.

[4] As [39] does not provide enough details for reproduction, we can only list the cost reported in their paper for reference. Besides, they only reported the cost of inference, which is equivalent to the forward propagation.

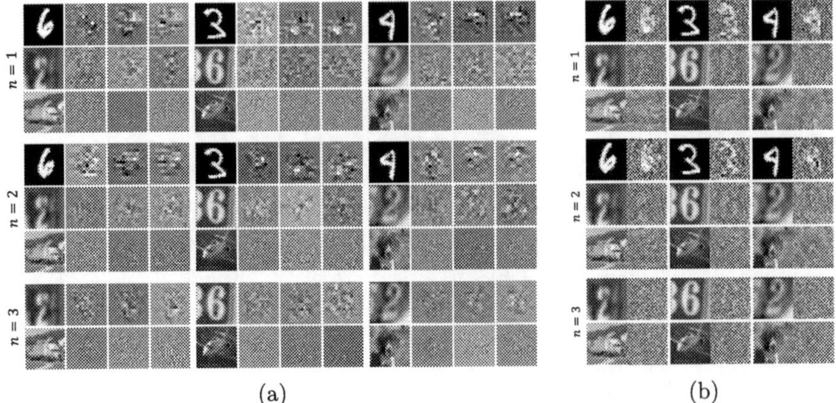

Fig. 5. Visual effects of two potential attacks. (a) The gradients of images in different models, (b) recovered images from the CryptoHeader's output.

Firstly, we visually examine the feature maps generated from CryptoHeader by varying the number of CryptoBlocks as $n = \{1, 2, 3\}$ in different datasets. The results of the plaintext feature maps that can be observed by the server are shown in Fig. 4. After the computation of several CryptoBlocks, the information related to image recognition has been transformed from visual features to high-level abstracts, so these feature maps are visually indistinguishable.

Secondly, some works propose to visualize the feature maps based on gradients [37,38], so we additionally visually present the gradients. As shown in Fig. 5a, we extract the gradients in different stages during training, including the beginning, the middle, and the end, respectively. For the MNIST dataset, the training network is relatively simple. Thus the gradient propagates to the input image, which can reflect a tiny amount of contour information but is enough to blur the specific digits. The other two datasets can be completely confused.

Notably, although there exist some methods [32,33] that are claimed to be able to recover the original images more clearly, they have to modify the propagation of activation layers in the network. However, as the activation layers of CryptoHeader in our framework are completely performed by the client, the server cannot maliciously tamper with the activation layers, HeHe is robust against these approaches.

Besides, recently there exist some efforts that aim to recover the original image based on feature maps [8,23]. Following these efforts, we adopt their method to recover the images through the plaintext feature maps observed by the server within HeHe. Figure 5b shows the original images and the recovered ones side-by-side. In line with [23], the recovering model works as follows, we fix the training model and inject random noise into the input images and optimize the input under the supervision of CryptoHeader's output of the original image. For the MNSIT, as it is the gray image and the context (*i.e.*, digit) is extremely simple, this method can get a very blurred contour. For the other two datasets, it is difficult to optimize the noise according to the original image. Notably, ordinary image classification tasks can never be so simple as MNIST. Therefore, we advocate that HeHe is robust enough in ordinary image classification tasks even in face of the latest learning-aware image recovery models.

6 Conclusion

We elaborately drew the HE into the CNNs' training and proposed HeHe, a new encrypted training framework over the semi-honest CSP. We construct the CryptHeader, which consisted of n CryptBlocks, to realize the training over encrypted images with practical efficiency while preserving the content of images. Further, we designed interactive forward propagation and backpropagation to avoid using the expensive FHE. All these efforts achieve a better trade-off between utility and privacy. We proposed (α, β)-*recoverable* to evaluate how the image content is preserved through an processing system and theoretically prove that HeHe is robust against it. Although HeHe has introduced high costs compared with plaintext baselines, to the best of our knowledge, it is the most practical solution for deep CNNs training over encrypted images that preserves the accuracy with acceptable training cost.

Acknowledgements. This work is supported by National Natural Science Foundation of China (No. 61972309 and No. 62272369) and the Key Technology Innovation Project of Hangzhou (2022AIZD0132).

A Adaptability of (α, β)-*Recoverable*

The (α, β)-*recoverable* attempts to bridge the pixel recoverable and image privacy. To feel the recovery rate of different leakage intuitively, we generate different noisy images and compute the recovery rate *i.e.*, α under different β settings (we adapt CAM02UCS [22] as color space), some results are shown in Fig. 6. After compare the different β, we empirically choose $\beta = 1/3$ as a suitable threshold, because it makes the change of α perceptually uniform.

Note that both α and β are preset by users based on their privacy requirement. After many empirical estimates, we give recommend values $\alpha = 0.5, \beta = 1/3$, and we adapt them in HeHe experiments.

One drawback of (α, β)-*recoverable* is it could not measure the similarity for some posteriori transformations *e.g.*, rotation and translation. But these only happen when the adversary gets the outsourced images used by users. Fortunately, it cannot happen in HeHe, because the images are encrypted by users. Thus, under the application scenario of HeHe, (α, β)-*recoverable* can measure the recovery rate of the image soundly.

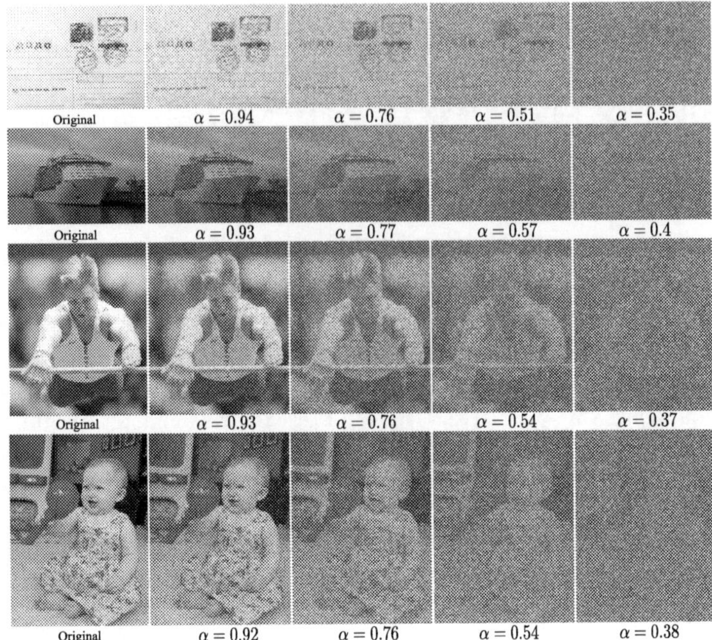

Fig. 6. The recovery rate of different leakages ($\beta = 1/3$).

References

1. Acar, A., Aksu, H., Uluagac, A.S., Conti, M.: A survey on homomorphic encryption schemes: theory and implementation. ACM Comput. Surv. **51**(4), 79:1–79:35 (2018)
2. Bost, R., Popa, R.A., Tu, S., Goldwasser, S.: Machine learning classification over encrypted data. In: Proceedings of 22nd Annual Network and Distributed System Security Symposium (2015)
3. Boureau, Y., Bach, F.R., LeCun, Y., Ponce, J.: Learning mid-level features for recognition. In: Proceedings of the IEEE Conference on Computer Vision and Pattern Recognition, pp. 2559–2566 (2010)
4. Bourse, F., Minelli, M., Minihold, M., Paillier, P.: Fast homomorphic evaluation of deep discretized neural networks. In: Proceedings of 38th Annual International Cryptology Conference on Advances in Cryptology, pp. 483–512 (2018)
5. Central Bureau of the Commission Internationale de l'Éclairage (Vienna, Austria): Cie (1978) recommendations on uniform color spaces, color-difference equations, and metric color terms. Supplement 2 to CIE publication 15 (E1.3.1) 1971/(TC1.3) (1978)
6. Chabanne, H., de Wargny, A., Milgram, J., Morel, C., Prouff, E.: Privacy-preserving classification on deep neural network. IACR Cryptology ePrint Archive **2017**, 35 (2017)
7. Chou, E., Beal, J., Levy, D., Yeung, S., Haque, A., Fei-Fei, L.: Faster cryptonets: leveraging sparsity for real-world encrypted inference. arXiv:1811.09953 (2018)

8. Dosovitskiy, A., Brox, T.: Inverting visual representations with convolutional networks. In: Proceedings of IEEE Conference on Computer Vision and Pattern Recognition, pp. 4829–4837 (2016)
9. Gilad-Bachrach, R., Dowlin, N., Laine, K., Lauter, K.E., Naehrig, M., Wernsing, J.: CryptoNets: applying neural networks to encrypted data with high throughput and accuracy. In: Proceedings 33rd International Conference on Machine Learning, pp. 201–210 (2016)
10. Glorot, X., Bordes, A., Bengio, Y.: Deep sparse rectifier neural networks. In: Proceedings of the 14th International Conference on Artificial Intelligence and Statistics, pp. 315–323 (2011)
11. Goodfellow, I., Bengio, Y., Courville, A.: Deep Learning. MIT Press, Cambridge, MA (2016). https://www.deeplearningbook.org
12. Han, K., Hong, S., Cheon, J.H., Park, D.: Logistic regression on homomorphic encrypted data at scale. In: Proceedings of the 33rd AAAI Conference on Artificial Intelligence, pp. 9466–9471 (2019)
13. Hartmann, V., Modi, K., Pujol, J.M., West, R.: Privacy-preserving classification with secret vector machines. In: CIKM, pp. 475–484 (2020)
14. He, K., Zhang, X., Ren, S., Sun, J.: Deep residual learning for image recognition. In: Proceedings of the IEEE Conference on Computer Vision and Pattern Recognition, pp. 770–778 (2016)
15. Hesamifard, E., Takabi, H., Ghasemi, M.: Deep neural networks classification over encrypted data. In: Proceedings 9th ACM Conference on Data and Application Security Privacy, pp. 97–108 (2019)
16. Huang, G., Liu, Z., van der Maaten, L., Weinberger, K.Q.: Densely connected convolutional networks. In: Proceedings of the IEEE Conference on Computer Vision and Pattern Recognition, pp. 2261–2269 (2017)
17. Juvekar, C., Vaikuntanathan, V., Chandrakasan, A.: GAZELLE: a low latency framework for secure neural network inference. In: Proceedings of the 27th USENIX Security Symposium, pp. 1651–1669 (2018)
18. Kingma, D.P., Ba, J.: Adam: a method for stochastic optimization. In: Proceedings of the 3rd International Conference on Learning Representations (2015)
19. Krizhevsky, A., Hinton, G., et al.: Learning multiple layers of features from tiny images. Technical report, University of Toronto (2009)
20. LeCun, Y., Bottou, L., Bengio, Y., Haffner, P., et al.: Gradient-based learning applied to document recognition. Proc. IEEE **86**(11), 2278–2324 (1998)
21. Liu, J., Juuti, M., Lu, Y., Asokan, N.: Oblivious neural network predictions via MiniONN transformations. In: Proceedings of the 24th ACM SIGSAC Conference on Computer and Communication Security, pp. 619–631 (2017)
22. Luo, M.R., Cui, G., Li, C.: Uniform colour spaces based on ciecam02 colour appearance model. Color Res. Appl. **31**(4), 320–330 (2006)
23. Mahendran, A., Vedaldi, A.: Understanding deep image representations by inverting them. In: Proceedings of the IEEE Conference on Computer Vision and Pattern Recognition, pp. 5188–5196 (2015)
24. Mishra, P., Lehmkuhl, R., Srinivasan, A., Zheng, W., Popa, R.A.: DELPHI: a cryptographic inference service for neural networks. In: Proceedings of 29th USENIX Security Symposium, pp. 2505–2522 (2020)
25. Mohassel, P., Zhang, Y.: SecureML: a system for scalable privacy-preserving machine learning. In: Proceedings of 38th IEEE Symposium on Security Privacy, pp. 19–38 (2017)

26. Naehrig, M., Lauter, K.E., Vaikuntanathan, V.: Can homomorphic encryption be practical? In: Proceedings of the 3rd ACM Cloud Computing Security Workshop, pp. 113–124 (2011)
27. Netzer, Y., Wang, T., Coates, A., Bissacco, A., Wu, B., Ng, A.Y.: Reading digits in natural images with unsupervised feature learning. In: Proceedings of the Workshop Deep Learning Unsupervised Feature Learning Neural Information Processing System (2011)
28. Paillier, P.: Public-key cryptosystems based on composite degree residuosity classes. In: Proceedings of the 17th Annual International Conference on Theory Application Cryptographic Techniques, pp. 223–238 (1999)
29. Popa, R.A., Redfield, C.M.S., Zeldovich, N., Balakrishnan, H.: CryptDB: protecting confidentiality with encrypted query processing. In: Proceedings of the 23rd ACM Symposium on Operating System Principles, pp. 85–100 (2011)
30. Rathee, D., et al.: CrypTFlow2: practical 2-party secure inference. In: Proceedings of the 27th ACM SIGSAC Conference on Computer and Communications Security, pp. 325–342 (2020)
31. Ryffel, T., Pointcheval, D., Bach, F., Dufour-Sans, E., Gay, R.: Partially encrypted deep learning using functional encryption. In: Proceedings of the 33rd Annual Conference on Neural Information Processing System, pp. 4519–4530 (2019)
32. Selvaraju, R.R., Cogswell, M., Das, A., Vedantam, R., Parikh, D., Batra, D.: Grad-CAM: visual explanations from deep networks via gradient-based localization. Int. J. Comput. Vis. **128**(2), 336–359 (2020)
33. Springenberg, J.T., Dosovitskiy, A., Brox, T., Riedmiller, M.A.: Striving for simplicity: the all convolutional net. In: Proceedings of the Workshop 3rd International Conference on Learning Representations (2015)
34. Tsikhanovich, M., Magdon-Ismail, M., Ishaq, M., Zikas, V.: PD-ML-Lite: private distributed machine learning from lightweight cryptography. In: Proceedings of the 22nd Information Security Conference, vol. 11723, pp. 149–167. Springer (2019). https://doi.org/10.1007/978-3-030-30215-3_8
35. Wagh, S., Gupta, D., Chandran, N.: Securenn: Efficient and private neural network training. IACR Cryptology ePrint Archive **2018**, 442 (2018)
36. Wagh, S., Tople, S., Benhamouda, F., Kushilevitz, E., Mittal, P., Rabin, T.: FALCON: honest-majority maliciously secure framework for private deep learning. Proc. Priv. Enhanc. Technol. **2021**(1), 188–208 (2021)
37. Yosinski, J., Clune, J., Nguyen, A.M., Fuchs, T.J., Lipson, H.: Understanding neural networks through deep visualization. arXiv:1506.06579 (2015)
38. Zeiler, M.D., Fergus, R.: Visualizing and understanding convolutional networks. In: Proceedings of the European Conference on Computer Vision, pp. 818–833 (2014)
39. Zhang, Q., Wang, C., Wu, H., Xin, C., Phuong, T.V.: GELU-NET: a globally encrypted, locally unencrypted deep neural network for privacy-preserved learning. In: Proceedings of the 27th International Joint Conference on Artificial Intelligence, pp. 3933–3939 (2018)

Deep Learning Assisted Key Recovery Attack for Round-Reduced Simeck32/64

Lijun Lyu[1,2], Yi Tu[3(✉)], and Yingjie Zhang[4,5]

[1] State Key Laboratory of Information Security, Institute of Information Engineering, Chinese Academy of Sciences, Beijing, China

[2] School of Cyber Security, University of Chinese Academy of Sciences, Beijing, China

[3] Division of Mathematical Sciences, School of Physical and Mathematical Sciences, Nanyang Technological University, Singapore, Singapore

tuyi0002@e.ntu.edu.sg

[4] Beijing Institute of Mathematical Sciences and Applications, Beijing, China

[5] Yau Mathematical Sciences Center, Tsinghua University, Beijing, China

Abstract. In CRYPTO'2019, Gohr firstly introduced deep learning into differential cryptanalysis. He successfully found 5/6/7/8-round neural differential distinguishers of Speck32/64 and mounted key recovery attacks against 11/12-round Speck32/64 with a variant of Bayesian optimization. In this paper, we make some improvements to Gohr's framework and apply it to Simeck32/64. We also present some parameter tuning experience for running deep learning assisted key recovery attacks. As proof, we obtain 8/9/10-round neural differential distinguishers for Simeck32/64 and successfully recover the penultimate round and last round subkeys for 13/14/15-round Simeck32/64 with low data complexity and time complexity.

Keywords: Deep learning · Neural distinguisher · Key recovery attack · Block cipher · Simeck

1 Introduction

Deep learning [1], as an important branch of machine learning, is a rapidly evolving pattern analysis method. It has been widely used in various fields, such as machine translation [2,3] and autonomous driving [4]. In the field of cryptography, Rivest [5] first pointed out in ASIACRYPT'1991 various connections between cryptography and machine learning and suggested some possible research directions for the cryptanalytic applications of machine learning. Since then, some scholars have begun to study the application of machine learning methods in cryptography with little success, and it was not until deep learning tools were proposed that the field began to develop rapidly and attract the attention of the community. At present, deep learning has been applied to cryptographic implementations [6–8], side-channel attacks [9–11] and cryptanalysis.

W. Susilo et al. (Eds.): ISC 2022, LNCS 13640, pp. 443–463, 2022.
https://doi.org/10.1007/978-3-031-22390-7_26

Differential cryptanalysis [12] is one of the mainstream analysis techniques for modern block ciphers. It was proposed by Biham and Shamir to break the Data Encryption Standard (DES) block cipher, and today it has been developed into many variants [13–16] and applied to various block ciphers. The first step in differential cryptanalysis is to construct differential distinguishers of the cryptographic primitives. Then an attacker can carry out the key recovery attacks based on the differential distinguishers. To reduce the manual workload, some automatic tools, such as Mixed Integer Linear Programming (MILP) [17,18], Constraint Programming (CP) [19,20] and Boolean Satisfiability Problem or Satisfiability Modulo Theories (SAT/SMT) [21,22] are used to improve differential cryptanalysis. In addition, machine learning, especially deep learning, is also used as an auxiliary tool to participate in differential cryptanalysis.

Gohr's work [23] in CRYPTO'2019 is groundbreaking in combining deep learning and differential cryptanalysis. He firstly obtained some powerful cryptographic distinguishers by training deep residual neural networks and then mounted a key recovery attack by utilizing the obtained neural distinguishers with a variant of Bayesian optimization. As a result, Gohr found 5/6/7/8-round neural differential distinguishers of Speck32/64 and performed successful key recovery attacks against 11/12-round Speck32/64.

Gohr's work has attracted a lot of attention. Some related work [24,25] try to study the interpretability of Gohr's framework, and some [26–35] attempt to make some improvements to Gohr's framework and better apply it to block ciphers such as Speck, Simon and Simeck. Most improvements focus on the part of neural distinguishers. They investigated the data format of training the neural distinguishers, the network structure of building the neural distinguisher, and even the selection of the fixed plaintext difference, with the aim of obtaining neural distinguishers with higher accuracy or covering more rounds. Only a few explored key recovery attacks on top of neural distinguishers. Fu et al. [26] first promoted the accuracies of neural distinguishers by proposing the polytope differential neural distinguishers with the concept of $(d+1)-$polytope ($d-$difference). Then they compared three different ways of performing key recovery attacks using different types of neural distinguishers and concluded that when using a mix of a single differential neural distinguisher and a polytope differential neural distinguisher for the key recovery attack, the key recovery success rate and data/time complexity were well balanced. As a result, Fu et al. implemented 13-round actual key recovery attacks based on deep learning against Simeck32/64 with a low data and time complexity. Bao et al. [31] introduced the generalized neutral bits techniques and the framework of conditional differential neural cryptanalysis. They sought to improve the success rate of deep learning assisted key recovery attacks, considering not only the accuracies and the number of rounds of neural distinguishers, but also the classical differential paths spliced in front of neural distinguishers. They also explored deep learning assisted key recovery attacks from the perspective of data complexity. As proof, they carried out successful key recovery attacks on 13-round Speck32/64 and 16-round Simon32/64. Even so, this field is still worthy of further exploration.

Fu et al. and Bao et al. both selected neural distinguishers with high accuracies, without considering the actual features of deep learning-based key recovery attacks. Can we further improve deep learning assisted key recovery attacks if we choose the neural distinguishers considering the intrinsic nature of deep learning assisted key recovery attacks instead of only considering the accuracies?

In this paper, we choose appropriate neural distinguishers from the viewpoint of key recovery attacks and discuss parameter tuning in deep learning assisted key recovery attacks. To prove the effectiveness of our work, we take Simeck32/64 as an example. We firstly train 8/9/10-round neural distinguishers of Simeck32/64, where the fixed plaintext difference of training/validation/test datasets are chosen from literature [36] or found by the MILP model. Then we plot the wrong key response profiles of all the neural distinguishers we got and choose the distinguishers with the same input plaintext difference and with the wrong key response profiles of obvious statistical patterns, as well as those splicing after one relatively long classical differential path with high probability and sufficient neutral bits. In the stage of key recovery attacks, we summarize some experience with parameter tuning that can get successful results as quickly as possible. As a result, we mount 13/14/15-round deep learning assisted key recovery attacks against Simeck32/64 successfully. A brief summary of our results and previous results is presented in Table 1. As shown in Table 1, our deep learning assisted key recovery attack on Simeck32/64 takes two more rounds than previous work that also leverages deep learning. Whether the traditional method or the deep learning method recovers the same number of key bits under the same number of attack rounds, our method has obvious advantages in time complexity and data complexity than the previous methods.

The organization of this paper is as follows. Section 2 briefly describes the lightweight block cipher Simeck and introduces Gohr's deep learning assisted key recovery attack framework. In Sect. 3, we introduce our improved deep learning assisted key recovery attack framework in details. In Sect. 4, we apply the improved framework to Simeck32/64 and mount 13/14/15-round deep learning assisted key recovery attacks for Simeck32/64 successfully. Finally, we conclude this paper in Sect. 5.

2 Preliminaries

2.1 Description of Simeck

Simeck [40] is a family of iterated lightweight block ciphers proposed by Yang, Zhu, Suder, Aagaard, and Gong in CHES'2015. The design of Simeck combines the Simon and Speck block ciphers proposed by NSA, which leads to a more compact and efficient implementation in hardware.

The round function of Simeck is composed of three operations: bit-wise XOR ($\oplus$), bit-wise AND ($\&$), and left circular shift ($\lll$). Let (L_{i-1}, R_{i-1}) and K_i be the input state and subkey of the i-th round of Simeck, respectively. Then the output state of the i-th round is (L_i, R_i), which can be computed as follows:

Table 1. Summary of key recovery attacks on Simeck32/64

Rounds	Data complexity	Time complexity	Success rate	Number of recover key bits	Reference
13	2^{22}	2^{56}	86.7%	64	[37,38] ♯
	2^{30}	2^{36}	99.7%	64	[39] ♮
	$2^{17.7}$	$2^{32.8}$	98%	64	[26] ♭
	2^{16}	$2^{27.95}$	88%	64	This paper ♭
14	2^{24}	2^{56}	86.7%	64	[37,38] ♯
	2^{32}	2^{38}	84.1%	64	[39] ♮
	2^{23}	$2^{32.99}$	88%	64	This paper ♭
15	2^{32}	2^{56}	86.7%	64	[37,38] ♯
	2^{24}	$2^{33.90}$	88%	64	This paper ♭

Data complexity $= 2^k \times n_c \times 2$. Where k is the number of neutral bits, n_c is the number of structures, and 2 corresponds to two ciphertexts in a pair of ciphertexts. Time complexity is calculated based on that one-second equals to $2^{23.304}$ full-round encryptions of Simeck32/64 on the device we use for the key recovery attacks.
♯: The success rate is calculated according to [38]. The time/data complexity under the fixed success rate is calculated with the method in [37].
♮: The time complexity given in [39] is that of recovering one bit key, which is scaled here.
The token ♭ use deep learning for key recovery attacks, while the tokens ♯, ♮ use traditional methods.

$$\begin{aligned} L_i &= F(L_{i-1}) \oplus R_{i-1} \oplus K_i, \\ R_i &= L_{i-1}, \end{aligned} \tag{1}$$

where

$$F(x) = (x\&(x \lll 5)) \oplus (x \lll 1). \tag{2}$$

Generally, Simeck$2n/mn$ denotes Simeck with $2n$ bits block size and mn bits key size, where n is the word size, and n is required to be 16, 24, or 32. In this paper, we mainly focus on Simeck32/64. For Simeck32/64, let (L_0, R_0) be the plaintext, then the ciphertext can be denoted as (L_{32}, R_{32}). The subkeys for each round are generated from a master key by a key schedule. For the concrete key schedule algorithm, the reader can refer to [40].

2.2 Introduction to Deep Learning Assisted Key Recovery Attack Framework

In [23], Gohr first presented neural distinguishers trained by deep residual neural networks (ResNet) [41], then developed a highly selective key search policy on top of neural distinguishers based on a variant of Bayesian optimization. In this paper, we call Gohr's framework the deep learning assisted key recovery attack. The overall framework of deep learning assisted key recovery attack is shown in Fig. 1 and will be introduced in details in this subsection.

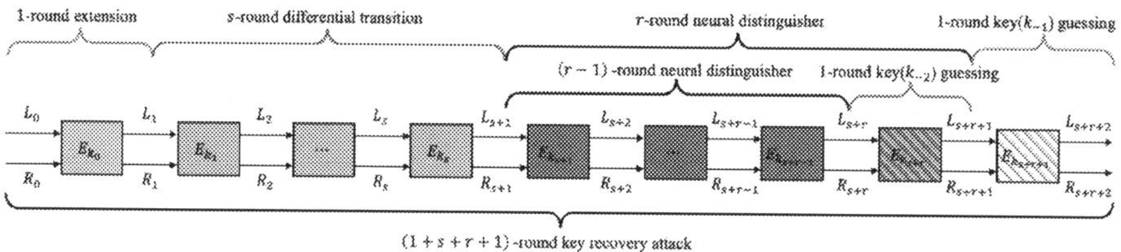

Fig. 1. The framework of deep learning assisted key recovery attack

Neural Distinguisher Based on Differential Cryptanalysis. Obtaining a valid cryptographic distinguisher is the first and crucial step in performing a key recovery attack. In general, the purpose of a cryptographic distinguisher is to distinguish between CIPHER and RANDOM. Due to the difference in the statistics used for distinguishing, there are differential distinguishers, linear distinguishers and integral distinguishers. Gohr's neural distinguishers are essentially "all-in-one" differential distinguishers [42]. The neural networks can be trained as neural distinguishers to distinguish between the ciphertext pairs encrypted by plaintext pairs with a fixed difference and the ciphertext pairs encrypted by random plaintext pairs.

In this part, we will elaborate on how to obtain the r-round neural distinguisher against a specific cipher. The steps are as follows:

1. Build the neural network to be trained.
2. Generate the corresponding datasets against the r-round target cipher, including the training dataset, validation dataset, and test dataset.
3. Train the neural network with the corresponding datasets to become the neural distinguisher.

Firstly, we discuss the type of neural network that can be trained as a neural distinguisher. In Gohr's work, he chose ResNet. The core component of ResNet is the residual block, also known as skip connection. ResNet can alleviate the gradient disappearance problem in deep neural network training, and deeper networks can be trained. Thus, it is a good choice to train the neural network with residual blocks such as ResNet as a neural distinguisher. As for the specific structure of ResNet, it should be designed according to the objective cipher to be distinguished.

For training the neural network we had built, we need to generate the training dataset, validation dataset and test dataset. These datasets are generated in the same way but differ in quantity. The generation of datasets is based on the fixed plaintext difference and describe as follows:

1. Generate n uniformly distributed plaintext pairs $(P_i, P_i^{'})$ and n uniformly distributed keys K_i according to the block size and key size of the objective cipher. Then generate n uniformly distributed binary-valued real/random labels Y_i. All the above are generated by using the Linux random number generator.

2. If $Y_i = 1$, replace $(P_i, P_i^{'})$ with $(P_i, P_i \oplus \Delta)$, where Δ denotes the plaintext difference chosen in advance. Moreover, $(P_i, P_i \oplus \Delta)$ are called the real plaintext pairs, while the others are called the random plaintext pairs.
3. Encrypt the real/random plaintext pairs by the r-round objective cipher to obtain the corresponding ciphertext pairs. Furthermore, the ciphertext pairs with the real labels $Y_i = 1$ are called the real samples, while the others are called the random samples.

Obviously, the goal of neural network training is to distinguish between CIPHER and RANDOM, which can be regarded as a binary classification task. Therefore, we take accuracy as the performance metric. Theoretically, as long as the accuracy of the trained neural network is steadily greater than 0.5, we think it is a valid neural distinguisher. Furthermore, the higher the accuracy, the stronger the discrimination ability of the neural distinguisher.

Key Recovery Attack on Top of Neural Distinguishers. To demonstrate the utility of the neural distinguishers as research tools, Gohr constructed a partial-key recovery attack based on Bayesian Search on top of the $(r-1)$-round and r-round neural distinguishers. The overall framework is shown in Fig. 1.

Firstly, the r-round neural distinguisher is extended to a $(s+r)$-round distinguisher by prepending a s-round differential transition $\Delta' \longrightarrow \Delta$ with a probability of p_{dt}, where Δ is the fixed plaintext difference used in the $(r-1)$-round and r-round neural distinguishers.

Then the $(s+r)$-round distinguisher is extended by one round by encrypting the initial plaintext pairs to the desired difference Δ'. This step is at no additional cost for ciphers where the subkey addition occurs after the non-linear operation in the round function.

The last and most important step is the partial-key recovery attack, that is recovering k_{-1} and k_{-2} in the Fig. 1. To rank candidate subkeys, the following equation is used to compute the score of the candidate subkey k by combining scores $Z_{i,k}$ returned from individual ciphertext pairs:

$$v_k := \sum_{i=1}^{n} log_2(Z_{i,k}/(1 - Z_{i,k})). \tag{3}$$

where n is the number of ciphertext pairs used for grading the subkey once, and $Z_{i,k}$ denotes the response value of the neural distinguisher for the partially decrypted ciphertext pairs $(C_{i,k}, C'_{i,k})$. $(C_{i,k}, C'_{i,k})$ is decrypted by one round under the subkey k from the ciphertext pairs (C_i, C'_i).

In one trial decryption, Eq. 3 is firstly computed for subkey candidates k_{-1} using the r-round neural distinguisher. If the score for some k_{-1} exceeds the threshold c_1, decrypt the ciphertext pairs $(C_{i,k_{-1}}, C'_{i,k_{-1}})$ by one more round under the subkey k_{-2} to the ciphertext pairs $(C_{i,k_{-2}}, C'_{i,k_{-2}})$, and grade k_{-2} by Eq. 3 using the $(r-1)$-round neural distinguisher. If the score for k_{-2} exceeds the threshold c_2, return the current subkeys guess (k_{-2}, k_{-1}).

During the process of a deep learning assisted key recovery attack, there are some key points to pay attention to, which are elaborated as follows.

- The neutral bits [43] are introduced to enhance the signal of the extended $(s + r)-$round distinguisher. Suppose that there are k neutral bits in the s-round differential transition $\Delta' \longrightarrow \Delta$, and one plaintext pair conforms the differential $\Delta' \longrightarrow \Delta$, then by flipping the neutral bits of the plaintext pair, a plaintext structure consisting of 2^k conforming plaintext pairs is generated. By doing this, the samples fed to the neural distinguisher are more likely to be of the desired distribution.
- A standard exploitation-exploration technique, namely Upper Confidence Bounds, is used to focus the key search on the most promising ciphertext structures. During the process of key recovery, we generate n_c plaintext pairs at random that satisfy the difference after one round of encryption is Δ' and construct the corresponding $(1 + s + r + 1)$-round ciphertext structure for each plaintext pair. Considering how the ciphertext structures are generated, it is inefficient to spend the same amount of computation on every ciphertext structure. In general, we execute $m(m > n_c)$ iterations to guess the subkeys. In each iteration, we pick one ciphertext structure and try to search the subkeys. After one trial decryption is made on each ciphertext structure, calculate a priority score for each ciphertext structure by Eq. 4 and determine the order of the ciphertext structures to be tested according to the scores. In Eq. 4, w^i_{max} is denoted as the highest distinguisher score of the i-th ciphertext structure obtained so far. n_i is the number of previous iterations in which the i-th ciphertext structure has been selected and j is the number of the current iteration. α is set to $\sqrt{n_c}$, where n_c is the number of ciphertext structure available. Each time the test of the ciphertext structure is finished, the scores of all the ciphertext structures are updated.
- Bayesian optimization is used to construct an effective key search algorithm, which is presented in Algorithm 1. An important observation is that the wrong key randomization hypothesis does not always hold for one-round decryption. More specifically, the expected response of the neural distinguisher upon wrong-key decryption will depend on the bitwise difference between the trial subkey and the real subkey. By precomputing the wrong-key response profile of the neural distinguisher, which is illustrated in Algorithm 2, one can attempt to decrypt on a small set of subkey candidates after another rather than on all possible subkey candidates. This can significantly reduce the search space of subkey candidates, thus saving a lot of computational budgets. In addition, in each iteration, the Bayesian Key Search Algorithm is first applied to recover k_{-1}, and then used to recover k_{-2}.

$$s_i := w^i_{max} + \alpha\sqrt{log_2(j)/n_i}. \tag{4}$$

For more details on deep learning assisted key recovery attacks, please refer to [23, 44].

Algorithm 1: Bayesian Key Search Algorithm [23,31]

Input:
$C = \{C_0, C_1, \cdots, C_{m-1}\}$: a ciphertext structure;
$\mathcal{ND}$: a neural distinguisher;
μ, σ: the wrong key response profile of $\mathcal{ND}$;
n: the number of subkey candidates to be generated within each iteration;
l: the number of iterations.

Output:
L: the list of tuples of recommended subkeys and their scores.

$S := \{k_0, k_1, \cdots, k_{n-1}\} \leftarrow$ choose n values at random without replacement from the set of all subkey candidates.
$L \leftarrow \{\}$
for $t = 1$ *to* l **do**
  for $\forall k_i \in S$ **do**
    for $j = 0$ *to* $m - 1$ **do**
      $C'_{j,k_i} = F^{-1}_{k_i}(C_j)$
      $v_{j,k_i} = \mathcal{ND}(C'_{j,k_i})$
      $s_{j,k_i} = log_2(v_{j,k_i}/(1 - v_{j,k_i}))$
    end
    $s_{k_i} = \sum_{j=0}^{m-1} s_{j,k_i}$; `/* the combined score of` k_i `*/`
    $L \leftarrow L||(k_i, s_{k_i})$
    $m_{k_i} = \sum_{j=0}^{m-1} v_{j,k_i}/m$
  end
  for $k \in \{0, 1, \cdots, 2^{16} - 1\}$ **do**
    $\lambda_k = \sum_{i=0}^{n-1}(m_{k_i} - \mu_{k_i \oplus k})^2/\sigma^2_{k_i \oplus k}$
  end
  $S \leftarrow \text{argsort}_k(\lambda)[0 : n - 1]$; `/* Pick` n `subkeys with the` n `smallest score to form the new set of candidate subkeys` S `*/`
end
return L

3 Our Deep Learning Assisted Key Recovery Attack Framework

In the previous section, we introduced the general framework of deep learning assisted key recovery attacks, which usually can be seen as a two-step process. The first step is to train long-round neural distinguishers with high accuracies, where accuracy is the performance metric of the neural distinguisher. The second step is to perform a partial key recovery attack using Bayesian optimization after prepending a classical differential transition in front of the neural distinguisher.

In traditional differential cryptanalysis, the first step is to search for the differential distinguisher with high probability, where probability is the performance metric of traditional differential distinguisher. A high-probability differential distinguisher is also an advantageous prerequisite when recovering partial keys in the second step. Inspired by this, the researchers of neural differential

Algorithm 2: Wrong-key Response Profile Precomputation

Input:
$\mathcal{ND}$: a r-round neural distinguisher;
n: the number of real subkeys k used for averaging.
Output:
μ_δ: the mean of the response of $\mathcal{ND}$ for the trial subkey $k \oplus \delta$;
σ_δ: the standard deviation of the response of $\mathcal{ND}$ for the trial subkey $k \oplus \delta$.

for $\delta \in \{0, 1, \cdots, 2^{16} - 1\}$ **do**
  for $i = 1$ *to* n **do**
    $C'_{k_i \oplus \delta} = F^{-1}_{k_i \oplus \delta}(C_i)$;   /* C_i is a $(r+1)$-round ciphertext pair, F^{-1} is the decryption round function of the target cipher, and k_i is the last-round real subkey of C_i */
    $R_{i,\delta} = \mathcal{ND}(C'_{k_i \oplus \delta})$
  end
  $\mu_\delta = \sum_{i=1}^{n} R_{i,\delta}/n$
  $\sigma_\delta = \sqrt{\sum_{i=1}^{n} (R_{i,\delta} - \mu_\delta)^2}/\sqrt{n}$
end
return μ_δ,σ_δ

distinguisher also naturally take the acquisition of high-accuracy neural distinguisher as the research goal, and believe that this is beneficial to the subsequent key recovery attacks based on Bayesian optimization. However, deep learning assisted key recovery attacks based on Bayesian optimization differ from traditional key recovery attacks. In the traditional key recovery attack, probability is not only the performance metric of the differential distinguisher, but also plays a key role in the key recovery attack, that is, it affects the success rate and the data complexity of the key recovery attack. However, in deep learning assisted key recovery attacks, accuracy is the performance metric for judging neural distinguisher. While in the Bayesian key search algorithm, it is the wrong key response profile of the neural distinguisher that plays an important role. The classical differential transition before the neural distinguisher also affects the data complexity of the deep learning assisted key recovery attack.

Based on the above discussion, in this paper, we shift the focus from the neural distinguisher with high accuracy to the neural distinguisher suitable for Bayesian key search, that is, neural distinguisher with the following properties: (1) The wrong key response profile of the neural distinguisher is as regular as possible; (2) The probability of the classical differential transition is high enough and the number of neutral bits searched for the classical differential transition is more enough. The complete deep learning assisted key recovery attack procedure including our improvement is summarized as follows.

1. Train the $(r-1)/r$-round valid neural distinguishers with the fixed input difference $\Delta_1, \Delta_2, \cdots, \Delta_p$ for the target cipher, respectively.
2. Precompute the wrong key response profile for each of the $(r-1)/r$-round neural distinguishers.

3. Pick the neural distinguishers with regular wrong key response profiles and denote the input difference as $\Delta_1, \Delta_2, \cdots, \Delta_s$, respectively.
4. Search for the s-round classical differential transition $\Delta' \longrightarrow \Delta_i (i = 1, \cdots, q)$ with high probability using the MILP model for each fixed input difference we denoted in the previous step.
5. Search for neutral bits for each $\Delta' \longrightarrow \Delta_i (i = 1, \cdots, q)$.
6. Pick the neural distinguishers if the prepended classical differential transition has high enough probability and more enough neutral bits.
7. Perform the $(1 + s + r + 1)$-round deep learning assisted key recovery attack with careful parameter tuning.

3.1 The Choice of Input Difference of Neural Distinguishers

During training a neural distinguisher, the plaintext difference corresponding to the real sample is required to be chosen in advance, which is called the input difference of the neural distinguisher for convenience. A large number of experiments have proved that the input difference of the neural distinguisher affects the number of rounds and accuracy of the neural distinguisher. In this part, we present two methods to select the input difference of the neural distinguisher.

Method 1: Select the input difference of the classical differential path from the existing literature as the input difference of the neural distinguisher. The choice of input difference of the neural distinguisher determines the distribution of the real samples. The goal is to make the distribution of real and random samples as different as possible. This goal is consistent with the goal of traditional differential distinguisher. Therefore, it is reasonable and efficient to choose the input difference of the classical differential path as the input difference of the neural distinguisher.

Method 2: Firstly, the input differences of the classical differential transition with high probabilities were searched out with the MILP model, and then the neural distinguishers with these input differences were trained with short epochs, and finally the input differences of the neural distinguishers with higher accuracy were selected to further train long epochs. This method is essentially an extension of previous method. At the same time, considering that the deep learning experiment is time-consuming, this method performs a preliminary screening of a large number of input differences with fewer epochs before moving to formal training the neural distinguisher, saving a significant amount of time.

The above two methods are both practical and, to some extent, ensure the effectiveness of the neural distinguishers obtained while avoiding a large number of invalid attempts.

3.2 The Experience of Tuning Parameters in Deep Learning Assisted Key Recovery Attack

In the deep learning assisted key recovery attack, the choice of parameters plays a decisive role in the success rate and complexity of the attack. In this part, we list some of our experience in parameter tuning for reference by other peers.

- **Number of Structures**: The number of ciphertext structures to be generated. The higher the value is set, the more plaintext pairs are generated randomly, the more likely it is to find conforming pairs and then generate ciphertext structures composed of conforming pairs, and the more likely it is to successfully recover the subkeys. While the data complexity will be increased. In order to trade off data complexity and success rate of the attack, if the probability of classical differential transition is p_{dt}, the number of structures is best set to a value greater than $1/p_{dt}$, like $2/p_{dt}$.
- **Number of Iterations**: The number of iterations of Bayesian optimization. The larger the value is set, the more likely it is to select the more optimal ciphertext structure for key recovery. Meanwhile, it is possible to run all the iterations because the guess key is not returned in advance, increasing the running time. The number of iterations should be set considering both the success rate and time complexity of the attack. It is recommended to set it to twice the number of structures.
- c_1/c_2: The thresholds for guessing the last and penultimate rounds subkeys. The smaller the value of c_1 is set, the more combinations of (k_{-2}, k_{-1}) will verified in the next step, and vice versa. The smaller the value of c_2 is set, the larger the bitwise difference between the guess subkeys and the real ones. If c_2 is set too large, it is possible to fail to guess the subkeys due to too strict requirements. The choice of c_1/c_2 affects the success rate and time complexity of the attack. We have not found a clear direction of adjustment for c_1/c_2. In practice, we adjust them based on the specific results of the experiment.
- **Neutral Bits**: The neutral bits used in the deep learning assisted key recovery attack. Obviously, the more neutral bits used in the attack, the more data complexity and the higher success rate of the attack. Therefore, we can reduce the data complexity of the attack by using as few neutral bits as possible while ensuring the success rate of the key recovery attack.

4 Applications to Simeck32/64

In this section, we present our experimental results on Simeck32/64 to demonstrate the effectiveness of our work[1]. Our best attack is the 15-round deep learning assisted key recovery attack against Simeck32/64, which is expected to succeed with a data complexity of 2^{24} and a time complexity of $2^{33.90}$, and its success rate is roughly 88%. Our attacks have a lower data/time complexity compared with previous work. The comparison can be seen in Table 1.

4.1 Neural Distinguishers of Simeck32/64

To carry out deep learning assisted key recovery attacks against Simeck32/64, the first step is to obtain valid neural distinguishers of round-reduced Simeck32/64.

[1] The experiments of training neural distinguishers reported in this paper are performed on a workstation with an NVIDIA GeForce RTX 2080 Ti GPU, while the experiments of key recovery attacks reported in this paper are executed on a workstation with an NVIDIA Tesla V100 GPU.

In this subsection, we will describe the details on how to train the neural distinguishers for Simeck32/64 and precompute the corresponding wrong key response profiles for these neural distinguishers.

As shown in Subsect. 2.2, the steps of training a neural distinguisher can be divided into three steps. We explain the specific process step by step as follows.

The first step is to build the network to be trained. Because the block size and key size of Simeck32/64 and Speck32/64 are the same, we adopt the same neural network structure as that of Gohr, which has been shown to be a good choice by Gohr.

The second step is to generate the training/validation/test dataset to train the neural distinguisher. Firstly, for training a neural distinguisher, we generate a training dataset of size 10^7 and a validation/test dataset of size 10^6, that is, $n = 10^7$ for the training dataset and $n = 10^6$ for the validation/test dataset. The number of real and random samples in both datasets are balanced. Secondly, for the real samples, we use two methods described in Subsect. 3.1 to choose the plaintext difference Δ, also called the input difference of the neural distinguisher. Using the first method, we try $\Delta = (0x8000, 0x4011)$, $(0x0001, 0x8022)$, $(0x0008, 0x0114)$, $(0x0010, 0x0228)$, which are input difference of classical differential distinguisher chosen from [36]. Using the second method, we try $\Delta = (0x8000, 0x0001)$, $(0x0001, 0x0003)$, $(0x0002, 0x0046)$, $(0x0040, 0x08c0)$. Thirdly, for training an r-round neural distinguisher, the real/random samples are generated by encrypting an r-round Simeck32/64. Here, we try $r = 8, 9, 10$.

The third step is to train the neural network to become the neural distinguisher. Each training covers 50 epochs; and for each epoch i, the learning rate l_i is set to $l_i := \alpha + \frac{(n-1)-i \ mod \ n}{n-1} \times (\beta - \alpha)$, with $\alpha = 10^{-5}, \beta = 2 \times 10^{-3}$, where n is the number of training epochs (here $n = 50$). In practical, to ensure the accuracy of neural distinguisher is greater than 0.5 strictly, we claim that the neural distinguisher with an accuracy higher than 0.51 is a valid distinguisher.

The results on the neural distinguishers of Simeck32/64 can be found in Table 2. Furthermore, the wrong key response profiles of these neural distinguishers can be precomputed with the Algorithm 2 and the results can be found in Fig. 2 and Fig. 3. In each subplot, the abscissa represents the bitwise difference in decimal between the trial subkey and the real subkey and the ordinate represents the mean of the response of the r-round neural distinguisher for the trial subkey. In the title of each subplot, the first term denotes the number of rounds of the neural distinguisher, and the second term denotes the input difference of the neural distinguisher. As can be seen from Table 2, if the input differences of the neural distinguishers are different, the accuracies of the neural distinguishers are also different. This is because the distributions of real samples corresponding to different input differences are actually different. The abilities to distinguish between real and random samples are naturally different. Combining Table 2 with Fig. 2 and Fig. 3, it is clear that a higher-accuracy neural distinguisher does not necessarily have a more regular wrong key response profile. Thus the accuracy and the wrong key response profile are actually two different metrics for the neural distinguisher.

Table 2. Neural distinguishers of Simeck32/64

Input difference (Δ)	Rounds (s)	Test accuracy
(0x8000,0x4011)	8	0.6503
	9	0.5519
	10	0.5213
(0x0001,0x8022)	8	0.6310
	9	0.5534
	10	0.5201
(0x0008,0x0114)	8	0.6488
	9	0.5563
	10	0.5204
(0x0010,0x0228)	8	0.6498
	9	0.5565
	10	0.5219
(0x8000,0x0001)	8	0.7531
	9	0.6323
	10	0.5423
(0x0001,0x0003)	8	0.7510
	9	0.6316
	10	0.5302
(0x0002,0x0046)	8	0.7529
	9	0.6271
	10	0.5438
(0x0040,0x08c0)	8	0.7498
	9	0.6334
	10	0.5421

4.2 Search Neutral Bits for Classical Differential Transition of Simeck32/64

Splicing a s-round classical differential transition in front of the $(r-1)/r$-round neural distinguishers is the second step in performing a deep learning assisted key recovery attack. The connection requirement is that the output difference of the classical differential transition and the input difference of both neural distinguishers are the same. To make the distinguisher longer, the classical differential transition prepended to the neural distinguisher is desired to be as long as possible. Meanwhile, in order to amplify the distinguisher's signal in the process of the key recovery attack, the probability of the classical differential transition is desired to be as high as possible and the number of neutral bits searched for the classical differential transition is desired to be as large as possible.

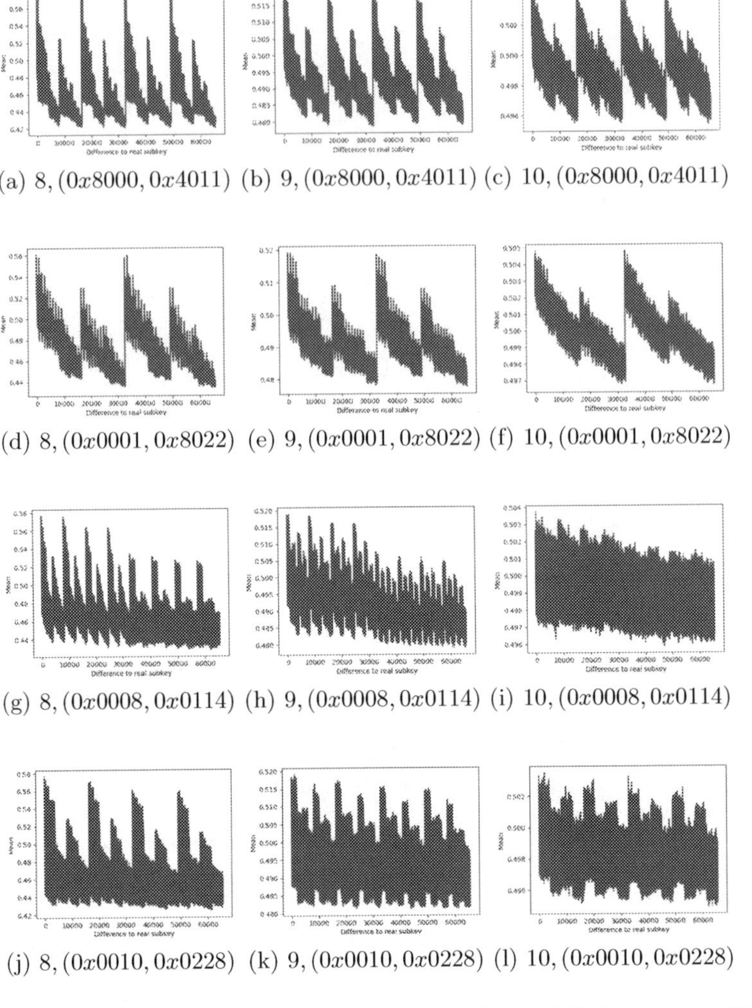

(a) 8, $(0x8000, 0x4011)$ (b) 9, $(0x8000, 0x4011)$ (c) 10, $(0x8000, 0x4011)$

(d) 8, $(0x0001, 0x8022)$ (e) 9, $(0x0001, 0x8022)$ (f) 10, $(0x0001, 0x8022)$

(g) 8, $(0x0008, 0x0114)$ (h) 9, $(0x0008, 0x0114)$ (i) 10, $(0x0008, 0x0114)$

(j) 8, $(0x0010, 0x0228)$ (k) 9, $(0x0010, 0x0228)$ (l) 10, $(0x0010, 0x0228)$

Fig. 2. The wrong key response profile of 8/9/10-round neural distinguishers with input difference $(0x8000, 0x4011)$, $(0x0001, 0x8022)$, $(0x0008, 0x0114)$, $(0x0010, 0x0228)$ for Simeck32/64.

In the previous subsection, we obtained 8 sets of neural distinguishers with different input differences and plotted the corresponding wrong key response profiles. As can be seen from Fig. 2 and Fig. 3, the wrong key response profiles of the neural distinguishers with some input differences are more regular than the wrong key response profiles of the neural distinguishers with other input differences. Furthermore, the wrong key response profile is critical to the optimization step of the Bayesian key search algorithm. That is, in the process of key recovery attacks, the neural distinguishers with more regular wrong key response profiles can better optimize the process of Bayesian key search. As a result, we pick the

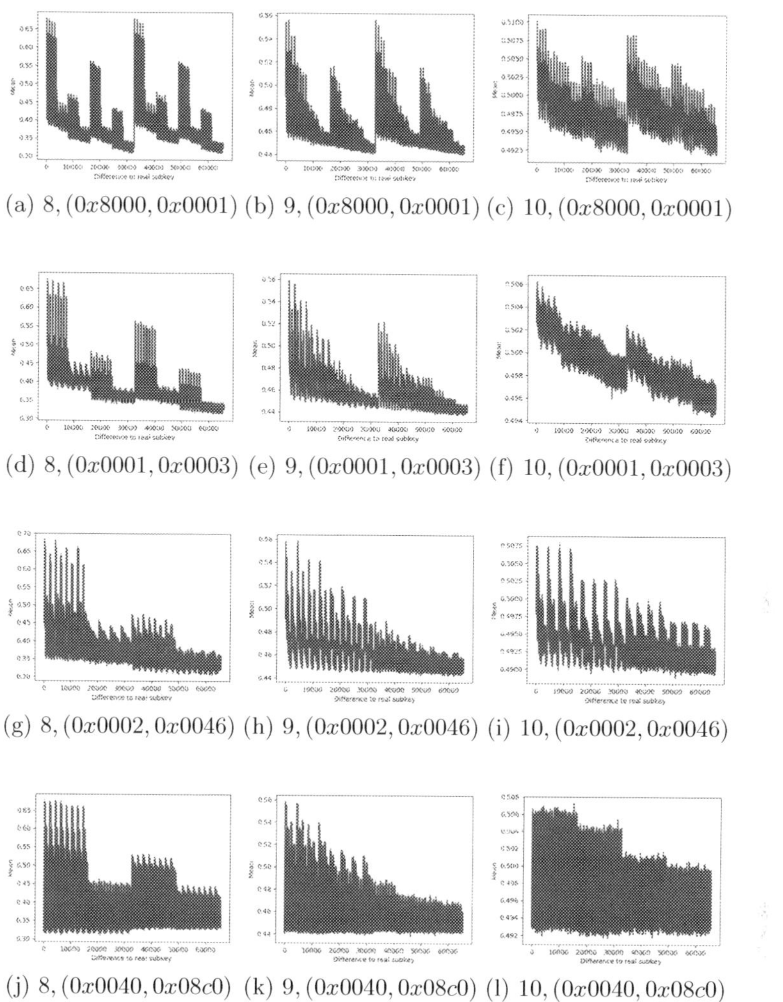

(a) 8, $(0x8000, 0x0001)$ (b) 9, $(0x8000, 0x0001)$ (c) 10, $(0x8000, 0x0001)$

(d) 8, $(0x0001, 0x0003)$ (e) 9, $(0x0001, 0x0003)$ (f) 10, $(0x0001, 0x0003)$

(g) 8, $(0x0002, 0x0046)$ (h) 9, $(0x0002, 0x0046)$ (i) 10, $(0x0002, 0x0046)$

(j) 8, $(0x0040, 0x08c0)$ (k) 9, $(0x0040, 0x08c0)$ (l) 10, $(0x0040, 0x08c0)$

Fig. 3. The wrong key response profile of 8/9/10-round neural distinguishers with input difference $(0x8000, 0x0001)$, $(0x0001, 0x0003)$, $(0x0002, 0x0046)$, $(0x0040, 0x08c0)$ for Simeck32/64.

neural distinguishers with input difference $(0x8000, 0x4011)$, $(0x0001, 0x8022)$, $(0x8000, 0x0001)$, $(0x0001, 0x0003)$ and consider splicing the classical differential transition in front of them.

We use the traditional MILP method to search for the classical differential transitions with high probability. In the MILP model, a constraint is added to ensure that the output difference of the differential transition is equal to the input difference of the neural distinguishers we choose in advance. The optimization solver used to solve the MILP model is Gurobi [45]. After the classical differential transition is obtained, the neutral bits can be found by a simple exhaustive search. The experimental results are listed in the Table 3. From Table 3, we can easily see that when the input difference of the neural distinguisher is $(0x8000, 0x0001)$, the prepended classical differential transitions have higher probabilities and more numbers of neutral bits. Therefore, we finally choose the neural distinguishers with the input difference $(0x8000, 0x0001)$ to perform deep learning assisted key recovery attack in the sequel. All of the above are precomputed before the actual attack, which are not included in the complexity of the key recovery attack.

Table 3. Classical differential transition of Simeck32/64

Round(s)	Input(Δ')	Output(Δ)	Prob.(p_{dt})	Neutral bits
2	(0x0002, 0x4015)	(0x8000,0x4011)	2^{-8}	[0, 27, 23, 17, 14, 29, 12, 13, 8, 7, 6, 4, 2, 1, 10]
3	(0x4015, 0x8028)		2^{-16}	[1, 7, 13, 28]
4	(0x8000, 0x4014)		2^{-18}	[12]
2	(0x0004, 0x802a)	(0x0001,0x8022)	2^{-8}	[1, 24, 18, 15, 28, 13, 11, 14, 8, 7, 5, 3, 2, 9, 30]
3	(0x802a, 0x0051)		2^{-16}	[2, 8, 14, 29]
4	(0x0001, 0x8028)		2^{-18}	[13]
2	(0x8002, 0x0004)	(0x8000,0x0001)	2^{-6}	[0, 29, 27, 25, 24, 23, 19, 18, 17, 15, 30, 14, 12, 10, 9, 8, 7, 6, 4, 3, 2, 1, 13, 31]
3	(0x0004, 0x800a)		2^{-8}	[11, 24, 18, 15, 14, 13, 28, 30, 8, 7, 3, 2, 1, 9]
4	(0x8008, 0x0017)		2^{-14}	[1, 2, 8, 14, 29]
5	(0x0001, 0x8008)		2^{-16}	[13]
2	(0x0004, 0x000b)	(0x0001,0x0003)	2^{-6}	[0, 28, 25, 24, 19, 18, 15, 30, 13, 14, 9, 8, 7, 4, 3, 2, 1, 10, 31]
3	(0x0008, 0x0015)		2^{-10}	[0, 2, 3, 8, 9, 12, 14, 15, 29]
4	(0x0010, 0x002b)		2^{-14}	[13]

4.3 Deep Learning Assisted Key Recovery Attacks of Simeck32/64

In this part, we will show the experimental results of our 13/14/15-round deep learning assisted key recovery attack for Simeck32/64. For each experiment with different parameters, we executed 100 tests. For each test, we claimed it is successful when the hamming weight of the difference between the real and guessed subkeys is no more than 2.

Table 4. Parameters used in the 13/14/15-round deep learning assisted key recovery attack of Simeck32/64

Rounds	Number of structures	Number of iterations	c_1	c_2
13	2^7	2^8	10.0	10.0
14	2^9	2^{10}	10.0	10.0
15	2^9	2^{10}	10.0	10.0

Table 5. 13-round deep learning assisted key recovery attack of Simeck32/64

Neutral bits	Data complexity	Time complexity	Success rate
[0, 29, 27, 25, 24, 23, 19, 18]	2^{16}	$2^{27.95}$	88%
[0, 29, 27, 25, 24, 23, 19]	2^{15}	$2^{27.76}$	84%
[0, 29, 27, 25, 24, 23]	2^{14}	$2^{27.30}$	72%
[0, 29, 27, 25, 24]	2^{13}	$2^{27.30}$	38%
[0, 29, 27, 25]	2^{12}	$2^{26.63}$	15%

For deep learning assisted key recovery attack against 13-round Simeck32/64, we prepended the 2-round classical differential transition $(0x8002, 0x0004) \rightarrow (0x8000, 0x0001)$ with the probability 2^{-6} in front of the 8/9-round neural distinguishers to recover the 12/13-round subkeys. For 14-round Simeck32/64, we prepended the 3-round classical differential transition $(0x0004, 0x800a) \rightarrow (0x8000, 0x0001)$ with the probability 2^{-8} in front of the 8/9-round neural distinguishers to recover the penultimate and last subkeys. For 15-round Simeck32/64, we spliced the same 3-round classical differential transition as that in the 14-round attack in front of the 9/10-round neural distinguishers to recover the 14/15-round subkeys. After our careful adjustment, other parameters except the neutral bits used in the experiments are shown in Table 4. We change the data complexity by controlling the number of neutral bits used in the experiments. The results of the 13/14/15-round attacks are shown in Table 5, Table 6, and Table 7, respectively. Generally, the more neutral bits used in an attack, the higher the data/time complexity of the attack, and the higher the success rate of the attack. However, since the plaintexts used for the attack are randomly generated and the number of tests is limited, the time complexity and success rate of the attacks are only experimental results rather than theoretical results. Therefore, there are some experimental results with higher data complexity but lower time complexity or success rate.

Table 6. 14-round deep learning assisted key recovery attack of Simeck32/64

Neutral bits	Data complexity	Time complexity	Success rate
$[11, 24, 18, 15, 14, 13, 28, 30, 8, 7, 3, 2, 1, 9]$	2^{24}	$2^{34.06}$	85%
$[11, 24, 18, 15, 14, 13, 28, 30, 8, 7, 3, 2, 1]$	2^{23}	$2^{32.99}$	88%
$[11, 24, 18, 15, 14, 13, 28, 30, 8, 7, 3, 2]$	2^{22}	$2^{31.93}$	85%
$[11, 24, 18, 15, 14, 13, 28, 30, 8, 7, 3]$	2^{21}	$2^{31.12}$	86%
$[11, 24, 18, 15, 14, 13, 28, 30, 8, 7]$	2^{20}	$2^{30.29}$	87%
$[11, 24, 18, 15, 14, 13, 28, 30, 8]$	2^{19}	$2^{29.51}$	83%
$[11, 24, 18, 15, 14, 13, 28, 30]$	2^{18}	$2^{28.98}$	79%
$[11, 24, 18, 15, 14, 13, 28]$	2^{17}	$2^{28.73}$	81%
$[11, 24, 18, 15, 14, 13]$	2^{16}	$2^{28.55}$	57%
$[11, 24, 18, 15, 14]$	2^{15}	$2^{29.03}$	30%
$[11, 24, 18, 15]$	2^{14}	$2^{27.39}$	4%

Table 7. 15-round deep learning assisted key recovery attack of Simeck32/64

Neutral bits	Data complexity	Time complexity	Success rate
$[11, 24, 18, 15, 14, 13, 28, 30, 8, 7, 3, 2, 1, 9]$	2^{24}	$2^{33.90}$	88%
$[11, 24, 18, 15, 14, 13, 28, 30, 8, 7, 3, 2, 1]$	2^{23}	$2^{33.07}$	79%
$[11, 24, 18, 15, 14, 13, 28, 30, 8, 7, 3, 2]$	2^{22}	$2^{32.12}$	82%
$[11, 24, 18, 15, 14, 13, 28, 30, 8, 7, 3]$	2^{21}	$2^{31.32}$	82%
$[11, 24, 18, 15, 14, 13, 28, 30, 8, 7]$	2^{20}	$2^{30.24}$	81%
$[11, 24, 18, 15, 14, 13, 28, 30, 8]$	2^{19}	$2^{30.00}$	68%
$[11, 24, 18, 15, 14, 13, 28, 30]$	2^{18}	$2^{30.05}$	51%
$[11, 24, 18, 15, 14, 13, 28]$	2^{17}	$2^{29.21}$	23%
$[11, 24, 18, 15, 14, 13]$	2^{16}	$2^{28.89}$	13%

5 Conclusion

In this paper, we shift our focus from increasing the accuracy of neural distinguishers to selecting the neural distinguishers that are appropriate for Bayesian key search algorithm. Then, we performed the deep learning assisted key recovery attack against round-reduced Simeck32/64. As a result, we were able to attack the 13/14/15-round Simeck32/64 successfully with a lower data/time complexity than traditional wisdom. As far as we know, this is currently the optimal deep learning assisted key recovery attack against Simeck32/64. In addition, we summarize two methods for picking the input difference of the neural distinguisher and the experience of parameter tuning for the deep learning assisted key recovery attack. Furthermore, we explore the relationship between the success rate and the data complexity of deep learning assisted key recovery attack in the experiment.

Acknowledgement. We would like to thank the anonymous reviewers for their valuable comments and suggestions. The first author is supported by the National Natural Science Foundation of China (Grant No. 62202460 and Grant No. 62172410) and the National Key Research and Development Project (Grant No. 2018YFA0704704 and Grant No. 2018YFB0803801). The second author is supported by the Start-up Grant from Nanyang Technological University in Singapore (Grant 04INS000397C230), and grants from Ministry of Education in Singapore (Grants RG91/20 and MOE2019-T2-1-060). The last author is sponsored by the Beijing Postdoctoral Research Foundation (Grant No. 2022-ZZ-070).

References

1. Goodfellow, I., Bengio, Y., Courville, A.: Deep Learning. MIT Press, Cambridge (2016)
2. Bahdanau, D., Cho, K., Bengio, Y.: Neural machine translation by jointly learning to align and translate. arXiv preprint arXiv:1409.0473 (2014)
3. Wu, Y., et al.: Google's neural machine translation system: bridging the gap between human and machine translation. arXiv preprint arXiv:1609.08144 (2016)
4. Chen, C., Seff, A., Kornhauser, A., Xiao, J.: Deepdriving: learning affordance for direct perception in autonomous driving. In: Proceedings of the IEEE International Conference on Computer Vision, pp. 2722–2730 (2015)
5. Rivest, R.L.: Cryptography and machine learning. In: Imai, H., Rivest, R.L., Matsumoto, T. (eds.) ASIACRYPT 1991. LNCS, vol. 739, pp. 427–439. Springer, Heidelberg (1993). https://doi.org/10.1007/3-540-57332-1_36
6. Baryalai, M., Jang-Jaccard, J., Liu, D.: Towards privacy-preserving classification in neural networks. In: 2016 14th Annual Conference on Privacy, Security and Trust (PST), pp. 392–399. IEEE (2016)
7. Carbone, M., et al.: Deep learning to evaluate secure RSA implementations. IACR Trans. Cryptogr. Hardw. Embed. Syst. 132–161 (2019)
8. Ling, X., et al.: Deepsec: a uniform platform for security analysis of deep learning model. In: 2019 IEEE Symposium on Security and Privacy (SP), pp. 673–690. IEEE (2019)
9. Maghrebi, H., Portigliatti, T., Prouff, E.: Breaking cryptographic implementations using deep learning techniques. In: Carlet, C., Hasan, M.A., Saraswat, V. (eds.) SPACE 2016. LNCS, vol. 10076, pp. 3–26. Springer, Cham (2016). https://doi.org/10.1007/978-3-319-49445-6_1
10. Picek, S., Samiotis, I.P., Kim, J., Heuser, A., Bhasin, S., Legay, A.: On the performance of convolutional neural networks for side-channel analysis. In: Chattopadhyay, A., Rebeiro, C., Yarom, Y. (eds.) SPACE 2018. LNCS, vol. 11348, pp. 157–176. Springer, Cham (2018). https://doi.org/10.1007/978-3-030-05072-6_10
11. Timon, B.: Non-profiled deep learning-based side-channel attacks with sensitivity analysis. IACR Trans. Cryptogr. Hardw. Embed. Syst. 107–131 (2019)
12. Biham, E., Shamir, A.: Differential cryptanalysis of des-like cryptosystems. J. Cryptol. **4**(1), 3–72 (1991)

13. Blondeau, C., Gérard, B.: Multiple differential cryptanalysis: theory and practice. In: Joux, A. (ed.) FSE 2011. LNCS, vol. 6733, pp. 35–54. Springer, Heidelberg (2011). https://doi.org/10.1007/978-3-642-21702-9_3
14. Knudsen, L.R.: Truncated and higher order differentials. In: Preneel, B. (ed.) FSE 1994. LNCS, vol. 1008, pp. 196–211. Springer, Heidelberg (1995). https://doi.org/10.1007/3-540-60590-8_16
15. Knudsen, L.: Deal-a 128-bit block cipher. Complexity **258**(2), 216 (1998)
16. Biham, E., Biryukov, A., Shamir, A.: Cryptanalysis of skipjack reduced to 31 rounds using impossible differentials. In: Stern, J. (ed.) EUROCRYPT 1999. LNCS, vol. 1592, pp. 12–23. Springer, Heidelberg (1999). https://doi.org/10.1007/3-540-48910-X_2
17. Sun, S., Hu, L., Wang, P., Qiao, K., Ma, X., Song, L.: Automatic security evaluation and (related-key) differential characteristic search: application to SIMON, PRESENT, LBlock, DES(L) and other bit-oriented block ciphers. In: Sarkar, P., Iwata, T. (eds.) ASIACRYPT 2014. LNCS, vol. 8873, pp. 158–178. Springer, Heidelberg (2014). https://doi.org/10.1007/978-3-662-45611-8_9
18. Zhou, C., Zhang, W., Ding, T., Xiang, Z.: Improving the MILP-based security evaluation algorithm against differential/linear cryptanalysis using a divide-and-conquer approach. IACR Trans. Symmetric Cryptol. 438–469 (2019)
19. Gerault, D., Minier, M., Solnon, C.: Constraint programming models for chosen key differential cryptanalysis. In: Rueher, M. (ed.) CP 2016. LNCS, vol. 9892, pp. 584–601. Springer, Cham (2016). https://doi.org/10.1007/978-3-319-44953-1_37
20. Sun, S., et al.: Analysis of AES, SKINNY, and others with constraint programming. IACR Trans. Symmetric Cryptol. 281–306 (2017)
21. Sun, L., Wang, W., Wang, M.: Automatic search of bit-based division property for ARX ciphers and word-based division property. In: Takagi, T., Peyrin, T. (eds.) ASIACRYPT 2017. LNCS, vol. 10624, pp. 128–157. Springer, Cham (2017). https://doi.org/10.1007/978-3-319-70694-8_5
22. Liu, Y., De Witte, G., Ranea, A., Ashur, T.: Rotational-XOR cryptanalysis of reduced-round speck. IACR Trans. Symmetric Cryptol. 24–36 (2017)
23. Gohr, A.: Improving attacks on round-reduced Speck32/64 using deep learning. In: Boldyreva, A., Micciancio, D. (eds.) CRYPTO 2019. LNCS, vol. 11693, pp. 150–179. Springer, Cham (2019). https://doi.org/10.1007/978-3-030-26951-7_6
24. Benamira, A., Gerault, D., Peyrin, T., Tan, Q.Q.: A deeper look at machine learning-based cryptanalysis. In: Canteaut, A., Standaert, F.-X. (eds.) EUROCRYPT 2021. LNCS, vol. 12696, pp. 805–835. Springer, Cham (2021). https://doi.org/10.1007/978-3-030-77870-5_28
25. Chen, Y., Yu, H.: Bridging machine learning and cryptanalysis via EDLCT. Cryptology ePrint Archive (2021)
26. Chaohui, F., Duan, M., Wei, Q., Qianqiong, W., Zhou, R., Hengchuan, S.: Polytopic differential attack based on deep learning and its application. J. Cryptol. Res. **8**(4), 591–600 (2020)
27. Su, H.-C., Zhu, X.-Y., Ming, D.: Polytopic attack on round-reduced Simon32/64 using deep learning. In: Wu, Y., Yung, M. (eds.) Inscrypt 2020. LNCS, vol. 12612, pp. 3–20. Springer, Cham (2021). https://doi.org/10.1007/978-3-030-71852-7_1
28. Chen, Y., Hongbo, Yu.: Neural aided statistical attack for cryptanalysis. IACR Cryptology ePrint Archive 2020/1620 (2020)
29. Chen, Y., Hongbo, Yu.: Improved neural aided statistical attack for cryptanalysis. IACR Cryptology ePrint Archive 2021/311 (2021)
30. Chen, Y., Shen, Y., Yu, H., Yuan, S.: A new neural distinguisher considering features derived from multiple ciphertext pairs. Cryptology ePrint Archive (2021)

31. Bao, Z., Guo, J., Liu, M., Ma, L., Yi, T.: Conditional differential-neural cryptanalysis. IACR Cryptology ePrint Archive 2021/719 (2021)
32. Tian, W., Bin, H.: Deep learning assisted differential cryptanalysis for the lightweight cipher simon. KSII Trans. Internet Inf. Syst. **15**(2), 600–616 (2021)
33. Hou, Z., Ren, J., Chen, S.: Cryptanalysis of round-reduced simon32 based on deep learning. IACR Cryptology ePrint Archive 2021/362 (2021)
34. Hou, Z., Ren, J., Chen, S.: Sat-based method to improve neural distinguisher and applications to simon. IACR Cryptology ePrint Archive 2021/452 (2021)
35. Hou, Z., Ren, J., Chen, S.: Improve neural distinguisher for cryptanalysis. Cryptology ePrint Archive (2021)
36. Kölbl, S., Roy, A.: A brief comparison of Simon and Simeck. In: Bogdanov, A. (ed.) LightSec 2016. LNCS, vol. 10098, pp. 69–88. Springer, Cham (2017). https://doi.org/10.1007/978-3-319-55714-4_6
37. Zhang, Y., Lyu, L., Qiao, K., Zhang, Z., Sun, S., Hu, L.: Automatic key recovery of feistel ciphers: application to SIMON and SIMECK. In: Deng, R., et al. (eds.) ISPEC 2021. LNCS, vol. 13107, pp. 147–167. Springer, Cham (2021). https://doi.org/10.1007/978-3-030-93206-0_10
38. Selçuk, A.A.: On probability of success in linear and differential cryptanalysis. J. Cryptol. **21**(1), 131–147 (2008)
39. Bagheri, N.: Linear cryptanalysis of reduced-round SIMECK variants. In: Biryukov, A., Goyal, V. (eds.) INDOCRYPT 2015. LNCS, vol. 9462, pp. 140–152. Springer, Cham (2015). https://doi.org/10.1007/978-3-319-26617-6_8
40. Yang, G., Zhu, B., Suder, V., Aagaard, M.D., Gong, G.: The Simeck family of lightweight block ciphers. In: Güneysu, T., Handschuh, H. (eds.) CHES 2015. LNCS, vol. 9293, pp. 307–329. Springer, Heidelberg (2015). https://doi.org/10.1007/978-3-662-48324-4_16
41. He, K., Zhang, X., Ren, S., Sun, J.: Deep residual learning for image recognition. In: Proceedings of the IEEE Conference on Computer Vision and Pattern Recognition, pp. 770–778 (2016)
42. Albrecht, M.R., Leander, G.: An all-in-one approach to differential cryptanalysis for small block ciphers. In: Knudsen, L.R., Wu, H. (eds.) SAC 2012. LNCS, vol. 7707, pp. 1–15. Springer, Heidelberg (2013). https://doi.org/10.1007/978-3-642-35999-6_1
43. Biham, E., Chen, R.: Near-collisions of SHA-0. In: Franklin, M. (ed.) CRYPTO 2004. LNCS, vol. 3152, pp. 290–305. Springer, Heidelberg (2004). https://doi.org/10.1007/978-3-540-28628-8_18
44. Gohr, A.: Improving attacks on round-reduced Speck32/64 using deep learning. In: Boldyreva, A., Micciancio, D. (eds.) CRYPTO 2019. LNCS, vol. 11693, pp. 150–179. Springer, Cham (2019). https://doi.org/10.1007/978-3-030-26951-7_6
45. Gurobi Optimization. Gurobi optimizer (2008)

CFL: Cluster Federated Learning in Large-Scale Peer-to-Peer Networks

Qian Chen[1], Zilong Wang[1(✉)], Yilin Zhou[1], Jiawei Chen[1], Dan Xiao[1], and Xiaodong Lin[2]

[1] State Key Laboratory of Integrated Service Networks, School of Cyber Engineering, Xidian University, Xi'an 710071, China
{qchen_4,jiaweichen98}@stu.xidian.edu.cn, zlwang@xidian.edu.cn
[2] School of Computer Science, University of Guelph, Guelph, Canada
xlin08@uoguelph.ca

Abstract. High bandwidth, data privacy issues, and single point of failure require the development of Federated learning (FL) in large-scale peer-to-peer (P2P) networks. In this paper, we propose the first fine-grained global model training protocol, dubbed CFL, which is efficient and privacy-preserving. Rigorous analyses show that CFL guarantees the privacy and data integrity and authenticity of local model update parameters under two widespread threat models. Ingenious experiments on the Trec06p and Trec07 datasets show that the global model trained by CFL has good classification accuracy, rapid convergence rate, and dropout-robustness. Compared to the first global model training protocol for FL in P2P networks, CFL improves communication efficiency and computational efficiency.

Keywords: Federated learning · Peer-to-peer network · Communication efficiency · Privacy-preserving

1 Introduction

Federated learning (FL) [12] relies too much on the central server. However, the central server gives rise to several drawbacks: (1) untrustworthy [6]; (2) high computational costs and high bandwidth requirements [10]; (3) single point of failure [5,7]. As a result, how to deploy FL without the central server deserves deep research, which is referred to as the *decentralized FL* [7] or *FL in peer-to-peer (P2P) networks* [2].

Consequently, some *decentralized FL* involving algorithms [1,5,15], and frameworks [3,7,9,13] have been proposed successively. Also, decentralized vertical FL has been studied [6,11,16]. However, all existing decentralized FL works are coarse-grained, which cannot guide the global model training in practice. Recently, Chen *et al.* [2] proposed a fine-grained PPT protocol for *FL in P2P*

This work was supported by NSFC (No. 62172319, U19B200073).

W. Susilo et al. (Eds.): ISC 2022, LNCS 13640, pp. 464–472, 2022.
https://doi.org/10.1007/978-3-031-22390-7_27

networks. However, PPT has several shortcomings. **First**, PPT is inefficient for *FL in large-scale P2P networks* where massive clients are involved. **Second**, PPT is vulnerable to hijacking attacks [8], which leaves a potential privacy leakage risk to the system. **Third**, the signature scheme in PPT requires extra storage space and heavy computational power. Therefore, an intuitive question is *How to efficiently and securely achieve FL in large-scale P2P networks.*

Our response to this question is a Cluster Federated Learning (CFL) global model training protocol. Specifically, we expand the system model of PPT [2] by involving large amounts of clients. To improve the communication efficiency of the system, CFL aggregates local model update parameters hierarchically. Instead of leveraging the digital signature scheme, CFL guarantees security and computation efficiency through the authenticated encryption scheme, whose key is established by a random pairwise keys scheme enhanced by a proposed key revocation mechanism which improves the security against hijacking attacks [8]. To the best of our knowledge, CFL is the first fine-grained model training protocol for *FL in large-scale P2P networks*, which is efficient and privacy-preserving.

The main contributions are as follows:

A Global Model Training Protocol for FL in Large-Scale P2P Networks. We propose a fine-grained global model training protocol for FL in large-scale P2P networks. Compared to the PPT protocol, larger amounts of clients could train the global model in a higher communication and computation efficient manner with the deployment of the proposed CFL protocol.

A Secure and Privacy-Preserving Protocol. The proposed CFL protocol can protect the privacy of the client's individual local contributions by a random noise, which is generated initially and eliminated ultimately. Besides, CFL guarantees the data integrity and authenticity of local contributions by leveraging the authenticated encryption scheme. Particularly, CFL can guarantee the confidentiality of the communication key against hijacking attacks [8].

Experimental Evaluation. We conduct experiments on the Trec06p and Trec07 datasets, which demonstrate that the proposed CFL protocol can ensure the classification accuracy and the rapid convergence rate of the global model. Also, the dropout-robustness of the system is achieved by CFL. More importantly, CFL improves communication efficiency by 43.25% and computational efficiency by 0.87% compared to PPT [2].

2 Background

2.1 System Model

In the context of *FL in large-scale P2P networks*, potential clients $\mathbb{U}=\{u_i|i=1,\cdots,Z\}$ have constant wireless communication ranges. The clients in $\mathbb{U}$ truly participate in the global model training process are target clients, denoted by $\mathbb{C}=\{c_i|i=1,\cdots,N\}$, $\mathbb{C}\subseteq\mathbb{U}$. Each target client c_i has a local dataset $\mathcal{D}_i$ of size $|\mathcal{D}_i|$ containing private training data. Besides, a server loosely connected with a few potential clients is responsible for coordinating FL tasks, which means the server cannot aggregate clients' local contributions directly. The goal of target clients is to collaboratively train a global ML model W.

Communication Model. All data is transmitted through public communication channels. In addition, all target clients can only communicate with their single-hop neighbor clients within their constant wireless communication ranges, and only a few clients could communicate with the server directly.

2.2 Threat Model

In the context of *FL in large-scale P2P networks*, security and privacy are the most important concerns. Thus, we consider the internal semi-honest participants threat model and the external malicious adversaries threat model [2,12]. We further consider hijacking attacks [8] from external malicious adversaries when establishing communication keys, which is thoughtless in PPT [2].

In the internal semi-honest participants threat model, the server and target clients perform prescribed operations honestly but are curious about others' local model update parameters, which means they could infer private information from others' local model update parameters by model inversion attacks [4].

In the external malicious adversaries threat model, a malicious adversary $\mathcal{A}$ could execute tampering attacks [14] and impersonation attacks [14] to threaten the data integrity and the authenticity of aggregated local contributions. More seriously, $\mathcal{A}$ could execute hijacking attacks, where $\mathcal{A}$ hijacks honest participants to obtain the communication keys, and hence tampers with the aggregated model update parameters when aggregating local contributions.

3 System Design

CFL first divides all potential clients into several clusters $\mathbb{L}=\{L_h|h=1,2,\cdots\lambda\}$ based on their constant wireless communication ranges. Thus, the local contributions can be aggregated hierarchically, i.e., aggregation within a single cluster and aggregation across clusters subsequently. For gravity, we regularize the symbols in a specific cluster $L_h \in \mathbb{L}$. The potential clients in L_h are denoted by $\boldsymbol{U}_h=\{u_{h,i}|i=1,2,\cdots,z_h\}$, and all $\boldsymbol{U}_h$ $(h=1,2,\cdots,\lambda)$ make up $\mathbb{U}$, i.e., $\mathbb{U}=\bigcup_{h=1}^{\lambda}\boldsymbol{U}_h$. The clients that actually participate in a specific round of global model training are target clients, denoted by $\boldsymbol{C}_h=\{c_{h,i}|i=1,2,\cdots,n_h\}$, $\boldsymbol{C}_h\subseteq\boldsymbol{U}_h$, and all $\boldsymbol{C}_h$ $(h=1,2,\cdots,\lambda)$ make up $\mathbb{C}$, i.e., $\mathbb{C}=\bigcup_{h=1}^{\lambda}\boldsymbol{C}_h$.

Then, CFL establishes communication keys for potential clients within a single cluster through a proposed **Secure Communication Key Establishment Protocol** in Fig. 1.

After establishing communication keys, all potential clients collaboratively train the global model. Taking the t-th round as an example, the server first distributes a global model W^t to the potential clients directly connected to it. These potential clients subsequently pass W^t to other potential clients within

Secure Communication Key Establishment Protocol

- **Communication key establishment:**
  - Each potential client $u_{h,i}$ generates its identity $ID_{h,i}$.
  - Each identity is matched with m_h other randomly selected identities.
  - Each client pair associated with two identities obtains a pairwise key from a key pool $\mathcal{K}$.
  - $u_{h,i}$ generates a key ring $\boldsymbol{R}_{h,i} = \{(ID_{h,i\alpha}, k_{h,i\alpha}) | \alpha = 1, \cdots, m_h\}$.
  - $u_{h,i}$ broadcasts a plaintext $a_{h,i}$ and m_h encrypted messages $A_{h,i\alpha}$ using $k_{h,i\alpha}$ in $\boldsymbol{R}_{h,i}$, shown as $A_{h,i\alpha} \leftarrow \boldsymbol{CK.Enc}(k_{h,i\alpha}, a_{h,i})$.
  - $u_{h,j}$ tries to decrypt $A_{h,i\alpha}$ using $k_{h,j\alpha}$ in $\boldsymbol{R}_{h,j}$, shown as $a'_{h,i} \leftarrow \boldsymbol{CK.Dec}(k_{h,j\alpha}, A_{h,i\alpha})$.
  - $u_{h,j}$ compares $a'_{h,i}$ with the plaintext $a_{h,i}$, seeking for shared keys.
  - $u_{h,i}$ and $u_{h,j}$ establish the communication key $K_{hi,hj}$ by XOR.
- **Key revocation:**
  - $u_{h,i}$ is assigned m_h voting keys $\{v_{h,i\alpha} | \alpha = 1, \cdots, m_h\}$ and the hash values of the voting keys of $m_h - 1$ other voting members $\mathcal{H}(v_{h,i\beta})$, where $\mathcal{H}(\cdot)$ is the hash function, and $1 \leqslant \beta \leqslant m_h$.
  - When $u_{h,\mathcal{A}'\alpha}$ votes against $\mathcal{A}'$, it broadcasts $v_{h,\mathcal{A}'\alpha}$ in forms of plaintext.
  - $m_h - 1$ other voting members verify $\{0, 1\} \leftarrow \boldsymbol{Verify}\left(\mathcal{H}\left(v_{h,\mathcal{A}'\alpha}\right), \mathcal{H}'\left(v_{h,\mathcal{A}'\alpha}\right)\right)$.
  - Once validated, the vote is marked, shown as $\mathcal{H}\left(v_{h,\mathcal{A}'\alpha}\right) \leftarrow \left(v_{h,\mathcal{A}'\alpha}, \nu\right)$, where ν is a mark.
  - If the number of marked votes is not less than l_h, $\mathcal{A}'$ will be revoked.
- **Re-keying:**
  - The affected clients restart the **Communication key establishment** part to build new communication keys.

Fig. 1. Secure communication key establishment protocol.

the same cluster. Afterwards, $c_{h,i}$ initializes the local model as W^t, and trains it on its local dataset $\mathcal{D}_{h,i}$, shown as:

$$w_{h,i}^t \leftarrow \boldsymbol{Train}(W^t, \mathcal{D}_{h,i}). \tag{1}$$

Then, $c_{h,i}$ calculates the local model update parameters, shown as:

$$x_{h,i}^t = w_{h,i}^t - W^t. \tag{2}$$

Subsequently, $c_{h,i}$ calculates its weighted local model update parameters $X_{h,i}^t = p_{h,i} x_{h,i}^t$, where $p_{h,i} = \frac{|\mathcal{D}_{h,i}|}{\sum_{i=1}^{n_h} |\mathcal{D}_{h,i}|}$.

Next, all target clients aggregate their local model update parameters within their clusters. We illustrate the aggregation process within a single cluster as the **Inner-Cluster Model Aggregation Protocol** in Fig. 2.

Subsequently, each leader client uploads sum_h^t directly to the server, and the server aggregates all $sum_h^t, h = 1, \cdots, \lambda$, shown as:

$$SUM^t = \sum_{h=1}^{\lambda} q_h sum_h^t, \tag{3}$$

where $q_h = \frac{\sum_{D_i \in L_h} |\mathcal{D}_i|}{\sum_{i=1}^{N} |\mathcal{D}_i|}$ is the aggregation weight of the cluster L_h. Consequently, the server updates the global model, shown as:

$$W^{t+1} = W^t + SUM^t. \tag{4}$$

Finally, the server distributes W^{t+1} to all potential clients, and the target clients iteratively train and aggregate until the global model converges to the optimal result W^*. By integrating the above processes, wo obtain the proposed CFL protocol, illustrated in Fig. 3.

Inner-Cluster Model Aggregation Protocol

- **Local Model Training:**
  - $c_{h,i}$ performs local model training and holds $X^t_{h,i}$ to be uploaded.
  - $c_{h,i}$ broadcasts that it would participate in the global model update.
- **Model Disturbance:**
  - The server randomly chooses a leader client $c_{h,1}$.
  - $c_{h,1}$ generates a random noise s^t_h to disturb $X^t_{h,1}$, shown as $\hat{X}^t_{h,1} = X^t_{h,1} + s^t_h$.
- **Transmission and Aggregation:**
  - $c_{h,1}$ chooses a neighbor $c_{h,2}$ and broadcasts the choice.
  - $c_{h,1}$ encrypts $\hat{X}^t_{h,1}$, shown as $(Y^t_{h,1}||\sigma^t_{h,1}) \leftarrow$ ***AE.Enc*** $\left((\hat{X}^t_{h,1}||\tau^t_{h,1}), K_{h1,h2}\right)$.
  - $c_{h,1}$ sends $Y^t_{h,1}||\sigma^t_{h,1}$ to $c_{h,2}$.
  - $c_{h,2}$ decrypts $Y^t_{h,1}||\sigma^t_{h,1}$, shown as $(\hat{X}^t_{h,1}||\tau^t_{h,1}) \leftarrow$ ***AE.Dec*** $\left((Y^t_{h,1}||\sigma^t_{h,1}), K_{h1,h2}\right)$.
  - $c_{h,2}$ calculates $\hat{X}^t_{h,2} = \hat{X}^t_{h,1} + X^t_{h,2}$.
  - $c_{h,2}$ performs the broadcast, encryption, and send operations as $c_{h,1}$ does.
  - The remaining target clients successively perform the same operations as $c_{h,2}$ does until c_{h,n_h} receives the aggregated result.
  - c_{h,n_h} aggregates its local contributions, shown as $\hat{X}^t_{h,n_h} = \sum_{i=1}^{n_h} X^t_{h,i} + s^t_h$.
- **Cluster model Aggregation:**
  - c_{h,n_h} sends $\hat{X}^t_{h,n_h}$ back to $c_{h,1}$.
  - $c_{h,1}$ subtracts s^t_h and calculates $sum^t_h = \sum_{i=1}^{n_h} X^t_{h,i}$.

Fig. 2. Inner-cluster model aggregation protocol.

CFL for FL in Large-Scale P2P Networks (high-level view)

Step 1. All potential clients distributed in the P2P network are divided into several clusters according to their wireless communication range.
Step 2. The potential clients in each cluster establish communication keys according to the *Secure Communication Key Establishment Protocol.*
Step 3. All target clients in every cluster perform local model training.
Step 4. All target clients within each single cluster perform aggregation according to the *Inner-Cluster Model Aggregation Protocol.*
Step 5. All target clients perform aggregation across clusters to obtain the global model update parameters.
Step 6. The server updates the global model.
Step 7. The server distributes the updated global model to all potential clients.
Step 8. The server determines whether the global model converges:
If so, stop training; Otherwise, go back to step 3.

Note:
① The *neighborhood broadcast* mechanism is adopted to record the behaviors of all clients.
② A newly joined client u_{new} will perform step 2-8.

Fig. 3. High-level view of the CFL protocol.

4 Security Analysis

CFL is Privacy-Preserving Facing an Honest-but-Curious Server. To defend against model inversion attacks [4] from the server, CFL aggregates local contributions in a privacy-preserving manner, where the server can only obtain the aggregation result rather than the individual local model update parameters.

CFL is Privacy-Preserving Facing Honest-but-Curious Target Clients. To resist model inversion attacks [4] from target clients, a random noise is introduced to disturb the aggregated model update parameters. Therefore, all target clients can only obtain disturbed local contributions or the intermediate aggregation results, rather than the precise local model update parameters.

CFL is Privacy-Preserving Facing Honest-but-Curious Potential Clients. CFL adopts the authenticated encryption to protect aggregated model update parameters. Therefore, an honest-but-curious potential client cannot eavesdrop the plaintext of other's local model update parameters.

CFL Guarantees the Data Integrity and Authenticity of the Aggregated Model Update Parameters. To defend against tampering attacks [14] and impersonation attacks [14], CFL adopts authenticated encryption, where the authentication tag can effectively resist unauthorized tampering of messages and verify whether the sender is a trusted source.

CFL Guarantees the Confidentiality of the Communication Keys. The **Secure Communication Key Establishment Protocol** is enhanced by a voting-based *key revocation* mechanism to remove the contaminated keys, thereby eliminating the possibility of malicious adversaries stealing communication keys. Therefore, the confidentiality of the communication key is ensured.

5 Experiments and Evaluation

In this section, we conduct the experiments in a spam classification scenario. All experiments are implemented on the same computing environment (Linux Ubuntu 16.04, Intel i7-6950X CPU, 64 GB RAM and 5TB SSD) with Tensorflow, Keras and PyCryptodome.

5.1 Experimental Setting

Dataset. The datasets used in our experiments consist of Trec06p and Trec07, which are two English e-mail datasets from the real world. The Trec06p dataset contains 12910 hams and 24912 spams in the main corpus with messages, and Trec07 contains 25220 hams and 50199 spams.

Parameter Tuning. We first divide Trec06p into a training set and a testing set, and the training set is adopted to train the original global model. In addition, the Trec07 dataset is divided into two parts. One part is further divided into 100 local datasets for target clients. The other part serves as the Trec07 testing set to evaluate the global model performance. The ML model is Convolutional Neural Network (CNN). The gradient descent algorithm is set as SGD. Besides, we use the *AES-GCM-128bit* algorithm for authenticated encryption.

5.2 Experimental Results and Evaluation

To validate the model performance, we evaluate the accuracy and loss value of the global model in Fig. 4. After 14 rounds of global model training, the global model converges, and the accuracy and loss value of the final global model are 99.32% and 0.0356 on the Trec07 testing set. The results show that CFL guarantees the convergence of the global model with high classification accuracy. Besides, to validate the dropout-robustness of CFL, we randomly set 15% dropout clients. In this case, the global model converges at 16 rounds, and the accuracy and loss value of the global model are 99.26% and 0.0343, which are close to the values without dropout clients. That is, CFL is dropout-robust.

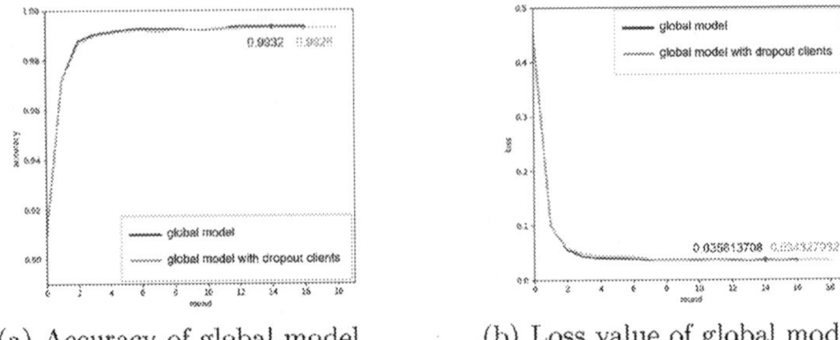

(a) Accuracy of global model. (b) Loss value of global model.

Fig. 4. Global model performance on the Trec07 testing set.

More importantly, we record the averaging communication times achieving a round of aggregation in Table 1. Compared to PPT [2], CFL improves the communication efficiency by about 43.25%. Such an improvement benefits from the cluster-based division.

Table 1. Communication times

Percentage of dropout clients (%)	0	1	2	5	10	15
CFL's communication times	105	106	104	105	102	92
PPT's communication times	191	186	185	184	172	164

In addition, we record the time of each operation in Table 2, where the authenticated encryption (decryption) in our protocol consumes less time than the encryption (decryption) and signature (verification) in the PPT protocol [2], which achieves a 0.87% improvement in terms of computational efficiency.

Table 2. Computational performance

Index	Operations	Time(ms/1000 byte)
1	Encryption(AES-128 bit)	170.8248
2	Decryption(AES-128 bit)	0.0282
3	Signature(Elgamal-2048 bit)	0.0003
4	Verification(Elgamal-2048 bit)	0.0071
5	Encryption (AES-GCM-128 bit)	169.3596
6	Decryption(AES-GCM-128 bit)	0.0163

6 Conclusion

Aiming to solve the problems of a single point of failure and high communication costs in FL, we propose a CFL protocol for *FL in large-scale P2P networks*, focusing on efficient and privacy-preserving model training. Some interesting researches could further improve CFL in the future. On the one hand, an effective design for FL in dynamic P2P networks could flourish the development of decentralized FL in practice. On the other hand, along with the hardware development of clients, a computation-friendly homomorphic encryption algorithm could improve the communication efficiency of the system more.

References

1. Assran, M., Loizou, N., Ballas, N., Rabbat, M.: Stochastic gradient push for distributed deep learning. In: Proceedings of the 36th ICML, 9–15 June 2019, Long Beach, CA, USA, pp. 344–353 (2019)
2. Chen, Q., Wang, Z., Zhang, W., Lin, X.: PPT: a privacy-preserving global model training protocol for federated learning in P2P networks. arXiv preprint arXiv:2105.14408 (2021)
3. Dubey, A., Pentland, A.: Differentially-private federated linear bandits. In: Proceedings of the 33rd NeurIPS, 6–12 December 2020, virtual, pp. 6003–6014 (2020)
4. Fredrikson, M., Jha, S., Ristenpart, T.: Model inversion attacks that exploit confidence information and basic countermeasures. In: Proceedings of the 22nd ACM SIGSAC CCS, 12–16 October 2015, Denver, CO, USA, pp. 1322–1333 (2015)
5. Gibiansky, A.: Bringing HPC techniques to deep learning. Technical report, Baidu Research (2017)
6. He, C., Tan, C., Tang, H., Qiu, S., Liu, J.: Central server free federated learning over single-sided trust social networks. arXiv preprint arXiv:1910.04956 (2019)
7. Hu, C., Jiang, J., Wang, Z.: Decentralized federated learning: a segmented gossip approach. arXiv preprint arXiv:1908.07782 (2019)
8. Hu, Q., Du, B., Markantonakis, K., Hancke, G.P.: A session hijacking attack against a device-assisted physical-layer key agreement. IEEE Trans. Industr. Inf. **16**(1), 691–702 (2019)
9. Li, Q., Wen, Z., He, B.: Practical federated gradient boosting decision trees. In: The 34th AAAI, 7–12 February 2020, New York, NY, USA, vol. 34, pp. 4642–4649 (2020)
10. Lian, X., Zhang, C., Zhang, H., Hsieh, C., Zhang, W., Liu, J.: Can decentralized algorithms outperform centralized algorithms? A case study for decentralized parallel stochastic gradient descent. In: Proceedings of the 31st NeurIPS, 4–9 December 2017, Long Beach, CA, USA, pp. 5330–5340 (2017)
11. Marfoq, O., Xu, C., Neglia, G., Vidal, R.: Throughput-optimal topology design for cross-silo federated learning. In: Proceedings of the 33rd NeurIPS, 6–12 December 2020, virtual, vol. 33, pp. 19478–19487 (2020)
12. McMahan, B., Moore, E., Ramage, D., Hampson, S., Arcas, B.A.: Communication-efficient learning of deep networks from decentralized data. In: Proceedings of the 20th AISTATS, 20–22 April 2017, Fort Lauderdale, FL, USA, vol. 54, pp. 1273–1282 (2017)

13. Ramanan, P., Nakayama, K.: Baffle: blockchain based aggregator free federated learning. In: IEEE International Conference on Blockchain, 2–6 November 2020, Rhodes, Greece, pp. 72–81 (2020)
14. Stallings, W.: Cryptography and Network Security. Pearson Education India, Noida (2006)
15. Yang, K., Jiang, T., Shi, Y., Ding, Z.: Federated learning based on over-the-air computation. In: 2019 IEEE ICC, 20–24 May 2019, Shanghai, China, pp. 1–6 (2019)
16. Yang, S., Ren, B., Zhou, X., Liu, L.: Parallel distributed logistic regression for vertical federated learning without third-party coordinator. arXiv preprint arXiv:1911.09824 (2019)

Bilateral Privacy-Preserving Task Assignment with Personalized Participant Selection for Mobile Crowdsensing

Shijin Chen[1], Mingwu Zhang[1(✉)], and Bo Yang[2]

[1] School of Computer Science, Hubei University of Technology, Wuhan, China
csmwzhang@gmail.com
[2] School of Computer Science, Shaanxi Normal University, Xi'an, China
byang@snnu.edu.cn

Abstract. Mobile crowdsensing (MCS) as an emerging data collection paradigm allows people to collect data for more effective decision-making. Task assignment as an integral part of MCS plays an important role in the working of the system. However, the balance between system efficiency and result accuracy is still a challenge to be solved, while the privacy of requesters and task participants are needed to be considered during assigning tasks. This paper proposes a bilateral privacy-preserving task assignment scheme with personalized participant selection for MCS. With the design of a privacy-preserving top-k selection sub-protocol, the proposed scheme supports the task requester to personalize the selection of participants for task assignment. The balance between efficiency and accuracy is entirely determined by the preference of the task requester. The proposed scheme provides the protections of the privacy of both the task content and personalized parameters of the requester and the status and identity of the participants. Simulation experiments are performed on smart devices with a real-world dataset, and the results demonstrate the effectiveness of the proposed task assignment scheme compared to the previous work.

Keywords: Task assignment · Participant selection · Privacy · Mobile crowdsensing

1 Introduction

With the rapid development of the Internet of Things, numerous existing smart devices have a wide variety of sensors embedded (e.g., GPS, camera and thermometer), which establishes the basis for the implementation of mobile crowdsensing (MCS) [4,6]. MCS as an emerging data collection paradigm allows people to collect data for better decision making through a crowd of smart devices, and it has been used in various fields such as traffic violation [8], environmental monitoring [10] and health application [2,9].

W. Susilo et al. (Eds.): ISC 2022, LNCS 13640, pp. 473–490, 2022.
https://doi.org/10.1007/978-3-031-22390-7_28

Task assignment, as an integral part of MCS, allows a task requester (TR) relying on the crowdsensing service provider (CSP) to select task participants with matching task requirements [5,18]. During the task assignment process, each task participant (TP_i) does not want private data (e.g., computational capacity, network bandwidth, data size, and address location) to be leaked. Arguably, these status data expose the privacy of task participants, such as data privacy, identity privacy and location privacy [14,26]. In addition, there are privacy concerns regarding the personalized parameters and the task content of the TR. These privacy issues hinder their willingness to participate in the system [17,25,28].

In general, task assignment in MCS considers three main aspects: efficiency, accuracy and privacy [20]. However, balancing efficiency and accuracy is challenging while preserving privacy. For example, the server has to wait for all participants to submit their model updates before aggregation in federated learning (FL), which will decrease the system efficiency of model aggregation in resource-constrained devices in MCS [24]. Some existing works consider the adoption of participant selection to improve the efficiency [12,23,27] for MCS. However, these works cannot support personalized privacy-preserving task assignment and maintain an ideal accuracy. Some studies support personalized privacy-preserving task assignment, however, they either take insufficient consideration on the privacy of task content, favor individualized choices of participants or ignore the preferences of requester for the task [7,19,21]. Besides that, how to maximize the protection of privacy data of the TR and participants while supporting personalized participant selection is also a challenge [11].

To address the challenges mentioned above, we propose a bilateral privacy-preserving task assignment with personalized participant selection for MCS. We consider a combination of efficiency, accuracy and privacy issues. Particularly, we present a secure top-k selection protocol based on the weighted Euclidean algorithm. The TR can choose the suitable participants according to different preferences. The choice between efficiency and accuracy is left entirely to the TR. In terms of privacy, a secure top-k selection protocol protects the personalized parameters for TR and the status for participants. Moreover, we protect the task content with broadcast encryption and hide the identity of the participants from the TR. Our contributions in this work are summarized as follows.

- We present a secure top-k selection protocol that allows a requester to personalize the selection of participants for the task based on the requirements of the task, which can balance efficiency and accuracy.
- In our scheme, it achieves the protection of the privacy of personalized parameters and task content of the TR, as well as the status data of the participants. At the same time, the identities of the selected participants are kept private from the TR.
- We give the concrete scheme and provide the security analysis. We also provide the experiential results of FL task assignment on multiple smart devices with a real-world dataset. The experiments demonstrate the effectiveness of our scheme.

Roadmap. The remainder of this paper is organized as follows. Some essential preliminaries are given in Sect. 2. In Sect. 3, we give a detailed description of the problem, including the system model, security model, and design goals. Next, we present the concrete construction in Sect. 4. We provide the security analysis in Sect. 5. Finally, we give the experimental results in Sect. 6 and summarize our work in Sect. 7.

2 Preliminaries

In this section, we review some preliminaries in our scheme.

2.1 Weighted Euclidean Distance

The weighted Euclidean distance (WED) [22,29] is considered an effective method for computing the distance of two vectors, which can be expressed as Eq. (1), where $\overrightarrow{X} = (x_1, x_2, ..., x_l)$, $\overrightarrow{Y} = (y_1, y_2, ..., y_l)$ are two l-dimensional vectors, and $d(\overrightarrow{X}, \overrightarrow{Y})$ denotes the WED between vectors $\overrightarrow{X}$ and $\overrightarrow{Y}$. $\overrightarrow{U} = (u_1, u_2, ..., u_l)$ is a weight vector to balance the influence of different dimensions on distance and $\overrightarrow{X}$ can be defined as a reference point.

$$d(\overrightarrow{X}, \overrightarrow{Y}) = \sqrt{\sum_{i=1}^{l} u_i (x_i - y_i)^2} \tag{1}$$

Furthermore, to facilitate the adaptation to homomorphic cryptosystem, we can transform Eq. (1) as follows.

$$\left[d(\overrightarrow{X}, \overrightarrow{Y})\right]^2 = \sum_{i=1}^{l} u_i x_i^2 - 2u_i x_i y_i + u_i y_i^2 \tag{2}$$

2.2 Homomorphic Encryption

Rivest et al. proposed the concept of homomorphic encryption [15], in which the proposal of homomorphism allows us to perform operations on ciphertexts without decryption. To facilitate the design of scheme, we introduce an additively homomorphic cryptosystem, i.e., Paillier encryption scheme [13], and it consists of three algorithms: *HE.KeyGen*, *HE.Enc* and *HE.Dec*, which are described as follows.

- *HE.KeyGen*: The key generation algorithm takes as input a security parameter κ. Let p and q be two randomly selected large prime numbers, and $|p| = |q| = \kappa$. Compute $N = pq$ and $\lambda = lcm(p-1, q-1)$. Define function $L(u) = (u-1)/N$ where $\mu = (L((1+N)^\lambda \bmod N^2))^{-1}$. Finally set public key $pk = (N, 1+N)$ and private key $sk = (\lambda, \mu)$.

- *HE.Enc*: The encryption algorithm takes as input a message $m \in \mathbb{Z}_N$ and public key pk. Then the plaintext m can be encrypted as Eq. (3), where $r \in \mathbb{Z}_N^*$ is a random number.

$$c = HE.Enc(m, pk) = (1 + N)^m \cdot r^N \bmod N^2 \tag{3}$$

- *HE.Dec*: The decryption algorithm takes as input a ciphertext c and a private key $sk = (\lambda, \mu)$, and compute

$$m = HE.Dec(c, sk) = L(c^\lambda \bmod N^2) \cdot \mu \bmod N \tag{4}$$

Let m_1 and m_2 be two plaintexts. We denote $[\![m]\!]_{pk}$ as the ciphertext of m under pk. The homomorphic properties can described as follows.

- *Additive homomorphism*:

$$[\![m_1 + m_2]\!]_{pk} = [\![m_1]\!]_{pk} * [\![m_2]\!]_{pk} \tag{5}$$

- *Scalar-multiplication homomorphism*:

$$[\![m_1 \cdot m_2]\!]_{pk} = ([\![m_1]\!]_{pk})^{m_2} \tag{6}$$

2.3 Broadcast Encryption

The idea of broadcast encryption is based on the Identity-based encryption (IBE) system and is come up with to reduce computational and communication overhead when sharing data to multiple users [3].

- *BE.KeyGen*: Let $\mathbb{G}$ as a bilinear map group with prime order p, the algorithm first sets a random number $\alpha \in \mathbb{Z}_p$ and a generator g. Then it computes $g_i = g^{(\alpha^i)} \in \mathbb{G}$, where $i \in \{1, 2, ..., K, K+2, ..., 2K\}$. With a random number $\gamma \in \mathbb{Z}_p$ is picked, it can compute $v = g^\gamma \in \mathbb{G}$. Besides, the public key is computed as Eq. (7).

$$PK = (g, g_1, ..., g_K, g_{K+2}, ..., g_{2K}, v) \in \mathbb{G}^{2K+1} \tag{7}$$

  Then the private key for each participant TP_i is computed as Eq. (8).

$$SK_i = g_i^\gamma \in \mathbb{G} \tag{8}$$

- *BE.Enc*: Given a set of privileged users $\mathcal{P}_k$, the algorithm picks a random number $r \in \mathbb{Z}_p$. The session key can be computed as Eq. (9).

$$KEY = e(g_{K+1}, g)^r \in \mathbb{G}_T \tag{9}$$

  The header Hdr is computed as Eq. (10).

$$Hdr = \left(g^r, (v \cdot \prod_{j \in \mathcal{P}_k} g_{K+1-j})^r \right) \in \mathbb{G}^2 \tag{10}$$

  With the session key KEY, a message can be encrypted by other available cryptosystems (e.g., AES).

– *BE.Dec*: For simplicity, the algorithm defines $Hdr = (C_0, C_1)$. Any participant $TP_i \in \mathcal{P}_k$ can use the known information $(Hdr, PK, i, SK_i, \mathcal{P}_k)$ to derive the session key as in Eq. (11).

$$KEY = \frac{e(g_i, C_1)}{e(SK_i \cdot \prod_{j \in \mathcal{P}_k, j \neq i} g_{K+1-j+i}, C_0)} \tag{11}$$

Next, the ciphertext can be decrypted by the session key KEY and the corresponding decryption algorithm.

3 Problem Formulation

This section is dedicated to the presentation of system model, threat model and design goals.

3.1 System Model

There exist four types of entities in the system: **Key Generation Center** (KGC), **Task Requester** (TR), **Crowdsensing Service Provider** (CSP) and **Task Participant** (TP_i), which is shown in Fig. 1.

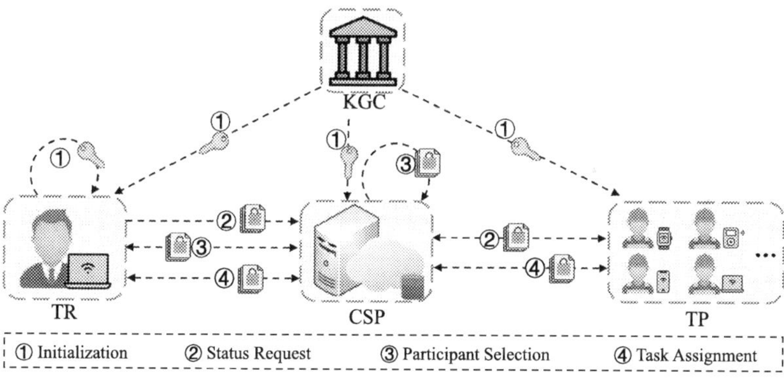

Fig. 1. System model

– **Key Generation Center** (KGC): KGC is a trusted third party responsible for generating the private key for each participant. When the key generation process is finished, KGC can go offline without participating in the task assignment process.
– **Task Requester** (TR): Each TR can request status data from the participants via CSP and select the best k participants to participate in the task by the weighted Euclidean distance algorithm. But TR does not want the reference point and weight vector it employs in the weight Euclidean algorithm to

be leaked to anyone. Also, the content of the task can only be decrypted by the selected participants, and no entity without permission should decrypt the content of the task (including CSP).

- **Crowdsensing Service Provider** (CSP): The CSP is responsible for forwarding status data and aggregating the information of k participants when they are selected. Specifically, the CSP is required to receive personalized participant selection requests from TR. Then, the CSP broadcasts the request to all participants and receives response ciphertexts from those willing to participate in the task. CSP sends the disordered ciphertext to TR and negotiates with TR to compute a task ciphertext that can only be decrypted by the selected k participants. Finally, the CSP broadcasts the processed task cipher to all participants.
- **Task Participant** ($\mathrm{TP_i}$): Suppose there are K participants in MCS. Each participant $\mathrm{TP_i}$ periodically collects its status data (e.g. CPU, memory, bandwidth, battery and data size), then reports them to CSP. After a participant $\mathrm{TP_i}$ is selected, $\mathrm{TP_i}$ can decrypt the task content. However, participants do not expect the privacy of status data to be revealed.

3.2 Threat Model

All entities except KGC in the MCS system are assumed to be *semi-honest*, namely *honest-but-curious*, meaning they will follow the agreed-upon protocol but will try to learn as much as the data during the protocol performing, while KGC is a trusted entity. Based on the capabilities of the above entities, we can define the list of private data as follows.

- **Input**: The reference point $\overrightarrow{X}$ as well as the weight vector $\overrightarrow{U}$ of the TR and the status vector of each participant $\mathrm{TP_i}$ are required to be kept secret from others. Furthermore, the identity of the selected participants should be kept private from the TR.
- **Output**: The task content T encrypted by the TR can be correctly decrypted only by the selected k participants and should be kept secret from others.

In addition, we assume that all external polynomial time adversaries have the ability to eavesdrop on the communication channel between TR, CSP and $\mathrm{TP_i}$. But external adversaries will have no access to any useful information other than the ciphertext. However, the external adversaries should not have access to any useful information except ciphertexts.

3.3 Design Goals

We give a formal description of the goals that our scheme needs to be achieved.

- **Personalized Participant Selection**: TR can select participants with different status by customizing the reference point and the weight vector. For example, TR can reduce the time required to perform a task by prioritizing participants with higher computational performance and lower network latency. Also, TR can get better results by prioritizing participants with more sensing data.

- **Bilateral Privacy Preservation**: The proposed scheme provides the protection of the privacy data defined in Sect. 3.2. For example, the status data and identity of all participants are private. Also, all parameters adopted by the TR to select participants also need to be preserved.
- **Practicality**: The task assignment scheme should be efficient, specifically, the proposed scheme should be validated in experiments and have a better practicality than the previous work.

4 Our Scheme

In this section, at first we give an overview of the proposed scheme and the building blocks, and then we provide the concrete construction of our scheme.

4.1 Overview

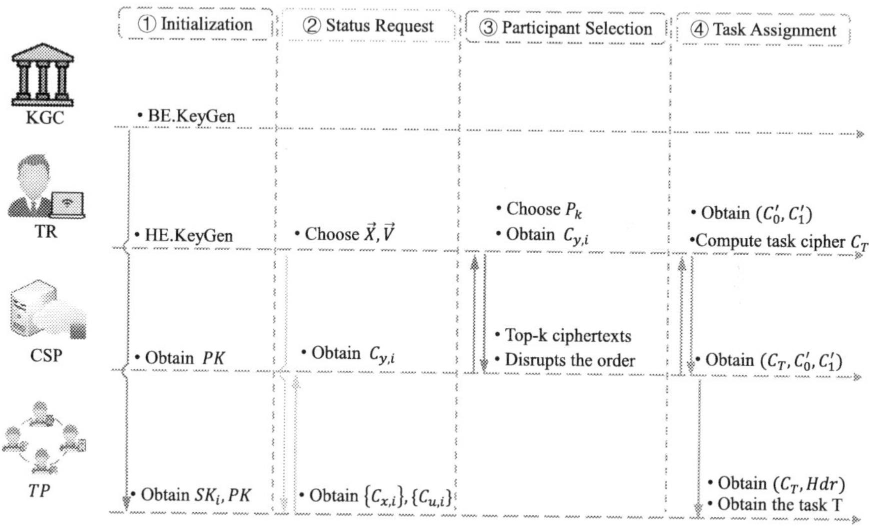

Fig. 2. Overview of the scheme

As shown in Fig. 2, the workflow of our scheme consists of four phases as follows.

1. **Initialization**: In this phase, KGC runs the *BE.KeyGen* algorithm to assign the corresponding private key to each participant $\mathrm{TP_i}$ and exposes the public key. Similarly, TR performs the *HE.KeyGen* algorithm to obtain the key pair and publishes the public key.

2. **Status Request**: In order to collect status data for participant selection, TR selects an optimal vector $\overrightarrow{X}$ and a weight vector $\overrightarrow{U}$, and then encrypts them. Next, TR distributes it to each participant TP_i via CSP. Each TP_i needs to collect its status data(e.g., network bandwidth, computing power, and the number of samples in the smart device) periodically, encrypts them and sends the cipher messages to CSP.
3. **Participant Selection**: The CSP rearranges all ciphertexts and sends them to the TR. TR can decrypt these ciphertexts, sort them to get the top-k indexes, and send them to CSP. After that, a collection of k selected participants $\mathcal{P}_k$ can be generated by CSP.
4. **Task Assignment**: To securely and efficiently assign tasks to participants, CSP aggregates the information of k participants and sends it to TR. A temporary session key KEY is selected by TR to encrypt the task content. Then, TR delivers the encrypted task content and broadcast the header to the CSP. Once the broadcast header is processed by the CSP, it will be broadcast to all participants along with the task cipher. Eventually, the selected k participants can decrypt and obtain the content of the task.

4.2 SKS-WED Protocol

We provide a secure top-k participant selection in MCS, namely, SKS-WED protocol, described in Algorithm 1. Particularly, TR chooses a vector $\overrightarrow{X} = (x_1, x_2, ..., x_l)$ as a reference point and a weight vector $\overrightarrow{U} = (u_1, u_2, ..., u_l)$, where $l(l \geq 2)$ is the dimension of the vector. Next, TR can encrypt the status data as Eq. (12) by using the Paillier encryption algorithm *HE.Enc*. Note that, the selection method of two vectors is based on previous experience, which is beyond the scope of this paper. We will give a example in the experiment.

$$\begin{cases} C_{x,i} = [\![-2u_i x_i]\!]_{pk_c} \\ C_{u,i} = [\![u_i]\!]_{pk_c} \end{cases} \tag{12}$$

Then TR broadcasts $(\{C_{x,i}\}_{i\in\{1,...,l\}}, \{C_{u,i}\}_{i\in\{1,...,l\}})$ to TP_i. TP_i collects the status data $\overrightarrow{Y}_i = (y_{1,i}, y_{2,i}, ..., y_{l,i})$ periodically and then aggregates them as Eq. (13) and sends the aggregated ciphertext to TR.

$$C_{y,i} = \prod_{j=1}^{l} (C_{x,j})^{y_{j,i}} \cdot (C_{u,j})^{y_{j,i}^2} \tag{13}$$

Eventually, TR decrypts $C_{y,i}$ to compute Eq. (14) and selects the k participants with the smallest d_i after sorting.

$$\begin{cases} d_i' = HE.Dec(C_{y,i}, sk_c) \\ d_i = d_i' + \sum_{j=1}^{l} u_j x_j^2 \end{cases} \tag{14}$$

Algorithm 1. SKS-WED protocol

Input: TR holds reference point $\overrightarrow{X}$ and weight vector $\overrightarrow{U}$ and key pair (pk_c, sk_c), a set of all K participants $\mathcal{P}$.
Input: $\mathrm{TP_i}$ holds the status data $\overrightarrow{Y}_i$.
Output: Optimal k participants $\mathcal{P}_k = \{TP_1, TP_2, ..., TP_k\}$.

TR do:
for $i \leftarrow 1$ **to** l **do**
  $C_{x,i} \leftarrow$ ***HE.Enc***$(-2u_i x_i, pk_c)$
  $C_{u,i} \leftarrow$ ***HE.Enc***(u_i, pk_c)
end for
Send $\{C_{x,i}\}_{i\in\{1,...,l\}}, \{C_{u,i}\}_{i\in\{1,...,l\}}$ to $\mathrm{TP_i} \in \mathcal{P}$.

$\mathrm{TP_i}$ do:
for $i \leftarrow 1$ **to** l **do**
  $C_{y,i} \leftarrow \prod_{j=1}^{l} (C_{x,j})^{y_{j,i}} \cdot (C_{u,j})^{y_{j,i}^2}$
end for
Send $C_{y,i}$ tp TR.

TR do:
for $i \leftarrow 1$ **to** K **do**
  $d_i' \leftarrow$ ***HE.Dec***$(C_{y,i}, sk_c)$
  $d_i \leftarrow d_i' + \sum_{j=1}^{l} u_j x_j^2$
end for
Sorts $\{d_i\}$.
Chooses $\mathcal{P}_k = \{TP_1, TP_2, ..., TP_k\}$ with the smallest $\{d_i\}$.
return $\mathcal{P}_k$.

4.3 Concrete Construction of Our Scheme

In this section, we present the detailed construction of bilateral privacy-preserving task assignment with personalized participant selection. As in Fig. 2, it consists of four steps such as ***Initialization***, ***Status Request***, ***Participant Selection*** and ***Task Assignment***.

4.3.1 Initialization

1. KGC runs the *BE.KeyGen* algorithm with the number of participants K to generate $PK = (g, g_1, ..., g_K, g_{K+2}, ..., g_{2K}, v), SK_i = g_i^{\gamma}$. Next, KGC publishes PK and sends SK_i to each participant TP_i separately over a temporary secure channel.
2. TR chooses a security parameter κ and runs the *HE.KeyGen*(κ) algorithm of homomorphic cryptosystem to get $pk_c = (N, 1 + N)$ and $sk_c = (\lambda, \mu)$, TR then publishes pk_c.

4.3.2 Status Request

1. TR chooses two vectors $\overrightarrow{X} = (x_1, x_2, ..., x_l)$ and $\overrightarrow{U} = (u_1, u_2, ..., u_l)$ based on specific scenario requirements. Next, TR encrypts $\overrightarrow{X}$ and $\overrightarrow{U}$ by Eq. (12).

2. TR broadcasts $\left(\{C_{x,i}\}_{i\in\{1,...,l\}}, \{C_{u,i}\}_{i\in\{1,...,l\}}\right)$ to all participants via CSP.
3. $\mathrm{TP_i}$ collects its status data $\overrightarrow{Y}_i$, encrypts the status data $\overrightarrow{Y}_i$ by Eq. (13) and reports $C_{y,i}$ to CSP.

4.3.3 Participant Selection

1. CSP disrupts the order of the received ciphertext, and forwards cipher messages to the TR.
2. Upon TR receives $C_{y,i}$ from all K participants in $\mathcal{P}$, TR selects the $k(k \geq 2)$ participants with the smallest d_i as $\mathcal{P}_k = \{TP_1, TP_2, ..., TP_k\}$. For more detailed computations, please refer to SKS-WED protocol in Sect. 4.2.
3. Next, TR sends the index of the top-k ciphertexts to CSP so that the CSP can rearrange the top-k indexes to generate the set of participants $\mathcal{P}_k = \{TP_1, TP_2, ..., TP_k\}$.

4.3.4 Task Assignment

1. With the set of participants $\mathcal{P}_k$ and a random number r', CSP computes Eq. (15) and sends (C'_0, C'_1) to TR.

$$\begin{cases} C'_0 &= g^{r'} \\ C'_1 &= (v \cdot \prod_{j\in\mathcal{P}_k} g_{K+1-j})^{r'} \end{cases} \tag{15}$$

2. TR sets a random number r, computes (C^*_0, C^*_1) as Eq. (16).

$$\begin{cases} C^*_0 &= (C'_0)^r \\ C^*_1 &= (C'_1)^r \end{cases} \tag{16}$$

   Besides, TR can compute the session key KEY as in Eq. (9). With a symmetric encryption algorithm $SE.Enc$, TR encrypts the task content T following Eq. (17). Then, TR sends (C_T, C^*_0, C^*_1) to CSP.

$$C_T = SE.Enc(KEY, T) \tag{17}$$

3. CSP computes Hdr as in Eq. (18) and broadcasts (C_T, Hdr) to all participants.

$$Hdr = \left((C^*_0)^{\frac{1}{r'}}, (C^*_1)^{\frac{1}{r'}}\right) \tag{18}$$

4. A selected participant $\mathrm{TP_i}$ can derive the session key KEY according to Eq. (11), and then employs the decryption algorithm $SE.Dec$ to obtain the task content T as in Eq. (19).

$$T = SE.Dec(KEY, C_T) \tag{19}$$

5 Security Analysis

Theorem 1. *The status data of participants is computationally indistinguishable.*

Proof: Given the leakage function $\mathcal{L}= \{pk_c, sk_c, \{x_i\}_{i\in[1,\dots,l]}, l, d\}$, where $d = \sum_{i=1}^{l} x_i y_i$. Besides, two probability models $Real(\kappa)$ and $Ideal(\kappa)$ defined as follows.

$Real(\kappa)$: A challenger $\mathcal{C}$ runs the $HE.KeyGen(\kappa)$ algorithm to get (pk_c, sk_c), publishes pk_c and sends sk_c to $\mathcal{A}$. Then, chosen by $\mathcal{A}$. So $\mathcal{A}$ can sends $\{C_i\}_{i\in[1,\dots,l]}$ to $\mathcal{C}$, where $C_i = [\![x_i]\!]_{pk_c}$. Next, $\mathcal{C}$ chooses $\{y_i\}_{i\in[1,\dots,l]}, y_i \in \mathbb{Z}_N$, to computes $C_y = \sum_{i=1}^{l} C_i^{y_i}$ and sends C_y to $\mathcal{A}$. So $\mathcal{A}$ can decrypts C_y to obtain $l = \sum_{i=1}^{l} x_i y_i$.

$Ideal(\kappa)$: Similarly, a simulator $\mathcal{S}$ has pk_c and (pk_c, sk_c) owned by $\mathcal{A}$. Next, $\mathcal{A}$ chooses $\{x_i\}_{i\in[1,\dots,l]}, x_i \in \mathbb{Z}_N, l > 1$ and sends $\{C_i\}_{i\in[1,\dots,l]}$ to $\mathcal{C}$. $\mathcal{C}$ randomly chooses $\{y_i'\}_{i\in[1,\dots,l-1]}, y_i \in \mathbb{Z}_N, y_l' = \frac{d-\sum_{i=1}^{l-1} x_i y_i'}{x_l}$, to computes $C_y' = \sum_{i=1}^{l} C_i^{y_i'}$ and sends C_y' to $\mathcal{A}$. So $\mathcal{A}$ can decrypts C_y' to obtain $d' = \sum_{i=1}^{l} x_i y_i'$.

As d and d' have the same value, $\mathcal{A}$ does not have a negligible advantage to distinguish $\{y_i\}$ and $\{y_i'\}$ in $Real(\kappa)$ or $Ideal(\kappa)$. Therefore, the status data of participants is protected.

Theorem 2. *The privacy data $\overrightarrow{X}$ and $\overrightarrow{U}$ is semantically secure against chosen plaintext attack if the Decision Composite Residuosity (DCR) assumption holds.*

Proof: The Paillier cryptosystem has been proven to be semantically secure under the indistinguishable against chosen plaintext attack (IND-CPA) model under the DCR assumption [13]. As the ciphertext of $\overrightarrow{X}$ and $\overrightarrow{U}$ fully obeys the Paillier cryptosystem, the privacy data is secure under the IND-CPA model. Thus, the privacy data of CSP does not reveal to a PPT adversary $\mathcal{A}$.

Lemma 1. *If the K-Bilinear Diffie-Hellman Exponent (K-BDHE) assumption holds, then the broadcast encryption cryptosystem is computationally indistinguishable against the chosen ciphertext attack (IND-CCA) [3].*

Theorem 3. *The task content of the requester is privacy-protected against the chosen ciphertext attack if and only if the broadcast encryption system is chosen-ciphertext secure and the symmetric encryption system is also secure.*

Proof: As stated in Lemma 1, the broadcast encryption employed in the proposed scheme is secure under the IND-CCA model. The key adopted in the proposed scheme to encrypt the task content T is derived from broadcast encryption, and the algorithm employed to encrypt T is the encryption algorithm in the symmetric cryptosystem. If a PPT adversary $\mathcal{A}$ can break our scheme, then it can use our scheme to break the above cryptosystem. Since the above schemes have been proven to be secure, our scheme is also secure.

Theorem 4. *The identities of the participants are privacy-protected against TR if and only if the discrete logarithm problem (DLP) is difficult.*

The CSP in the proposed scheme incorporates a random number r' as an exponent when aggregating participant information. If a PPT adversary $\mathcal{A}$ can identify the participants, then he can use our scheme to attack the DLP problem. This is contrary to the fact that the DLP is difficult and therefore the identity of the participants is privacy-protected.

6 Experiments

We have implemented our scheme in a series of simulation environments and describe it detailed in this section. To demonstrate that the proposed task assignment scheme is effective, we simulated the scheme in a scenario where a FL training task for handwritten digit recognition.

6.1 Experimental Setting

We conduct a series of experiments on a cloud server as the CSP and several smart devices as TP_i with different performances as shown in Table 1 to verify our scheme. The configuration of the cloud server is given below.

- CPU: Intel Xeon Gold 6240R @ 16x 2.394 GHz
- RAM: 16 GB
- OS: Ubuntu 20.04.3 LTS x86_64

Table 1. Hardware configuration for participants

Properties	Honor8-Lite	Raspberry-Pi-4B	Redmi-K30-Pro
CPU	Kirin 655	BCM 2835	Snapdragon 865
RAM	4 GB	4 GB	8 GB
OS	EMUI 5.0	Raspberry Pi	MIUI 13
Kernel	Linux 5.4.0	Linux 5.4.0	Linux 5.4.0

Also, we employ the Charm-crypto [1] based Python 3.7 as the cryptographic library. Then, some conditions were constructed following the experimental steps of Zhang et al. [27] and Wang et al. [16]. Specifically, we simulate 1000 TP_i in MCS. Their computational power and the number of samples fit a Gaussian distribution with a mean of 60 and a standard deviation of 10. Unless otherwise specified, the security parameter used is $\kappa = |p| = |q| = 512$ and the model accuracy testing experiments with a fixed seed. The two vectors adopted by CSP for participant selection are $\overrightarrow{X} = (100, 100)$ and $\overrightarrow{U} = (1, 1)$.

The CSP and TP_i need to collaborate together in the built experiments to perform a crowdsensing task (e.g., recognizing the written words of people in a region). As a result, we deploy a convolutional neural network (CNN) for the FL classification task by using the MNIST dataset with PyTorch framework. Specially, the CNN model consists of three 5×5 convolution layers with ReLU activation function, and the first two of which follow a 2×2 max pooling. Then, there are two fully connected layers activated by the ReLU function and the softmax function, respectively. Moreover, the hyperparameters of the model can be described as follows. The epoch of the global model is 100, which means that CSP needs to perform 100 rounds of aggregation operations. Local epoch for each TP_i is 10 and batch size is 8. Learning rate for all entities is 0.01 with SGD momentum is 0.9. Besides, we will give other detailed parameters in the experimental results.

6.2 Performance Evaluation

Based on the above experimental condition configuration, we present a series of results separately.

Figure 3 shows a comparison of the computational overhead of reporting status data with different smart devices as TP_i. Further, the comparison of different numbers of status data encrypted by the TP_i during the status data reporting phase is depicted in Fig. 3a, where the number of encrypted status data is set from 2 to 50. Fig. 3b illustrates the comparison of the encryption TP_i's status data for different security parameters. Obviously, with the security parameter set to $\kappa = 512$, even if TP_i needs to report about 50 pieces of status data, its computation cost will not exceed 0.2 s. Similarly, TP_i takes less than 0.2 s to report two encrypted status data with parameter $\kappa = 1024$. Compared to the time consumption of model training, our computational overhead in the participant selection method is almost negligible while preserving the privacy of TP_i.

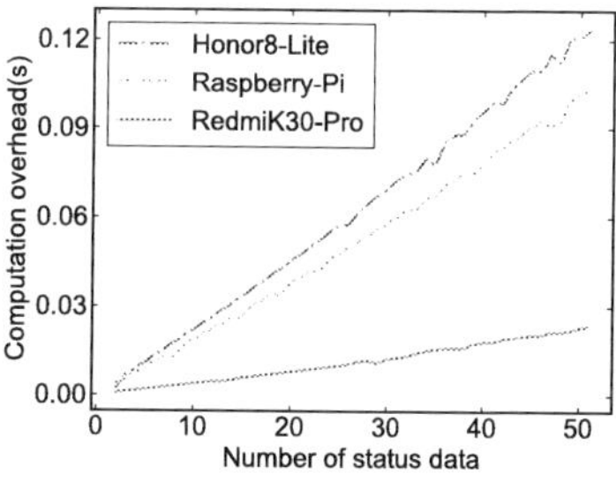

(a) Computational overhead for encrypting 2 to 50 status data on smart devices.

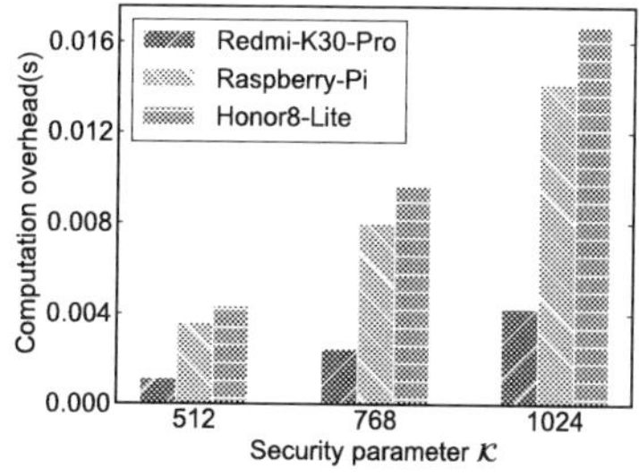

(b) Computational overhead for reporting two status data under different κ.

Fig. 3. Comparison of the participant's status data reporting

Next, we will analyze the computational overhead of our overall scheme compared with FedSky in two different cases. We configure some key parameters as follows. Each TP_i reports its local sample size and computational power as $\overrightarrow{Y}_i$, and these data all conform to a Gaussian distribution with mean as 60 and standard deviation as 10. In particular, computational power is the average size of training dataset processed in a minute by TP_i and the number of training rounds is 100. The participant selection constraints for FedSky are set to [10, 1000]. As shown in Fig. 4a and Fig. 4c, we simulate two cases where 100 participants are selected from 1000 participants. All the status data in Case 1 follow an ideal Gaussian distribution, while Case 2 includes an artificially added point. The existence of the special point is justified by the fact that a participant may have a lot of sample data but has a limited computational power. It is worth noting that the training time of FL in MCS is affected by the slowest TP_i processing the local samples among all selected participants. Thus, the efficiency of FedSky will be greatly affected when there is a TP_i as the special red point wrapped by a circle in the system. In Fig. 4b and Fig. 4d, the computational overheads of the above two cases for one-round training are presented and additional cases of selecting 10 and 50 participants are considered. Our scheme has a high com-

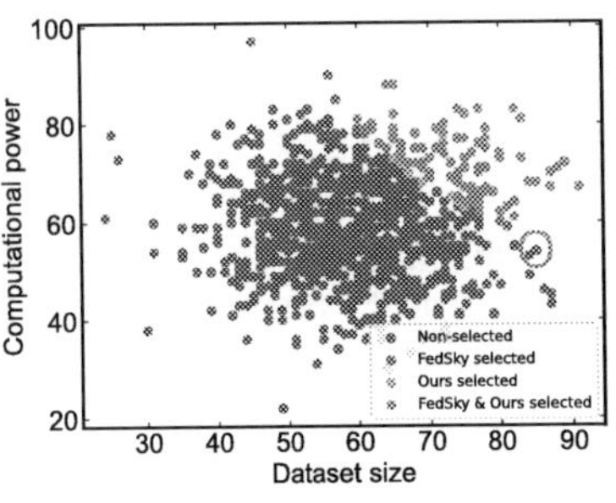

(a) Distribution of $\overrightarrow{Y}_i$ in Case 1.

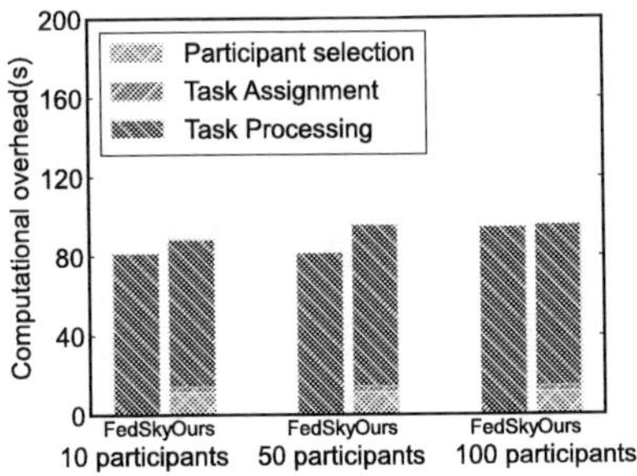

(b) Computational overhead comparison in an ideal case.

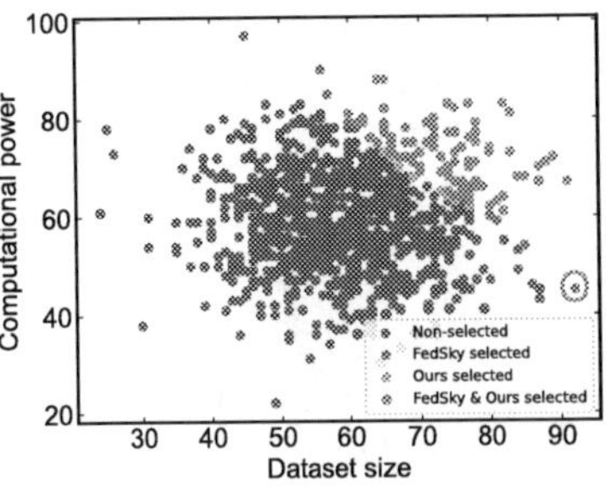

(c) Distribution of $\overrightarrow{Y}_i$ in Case 2.

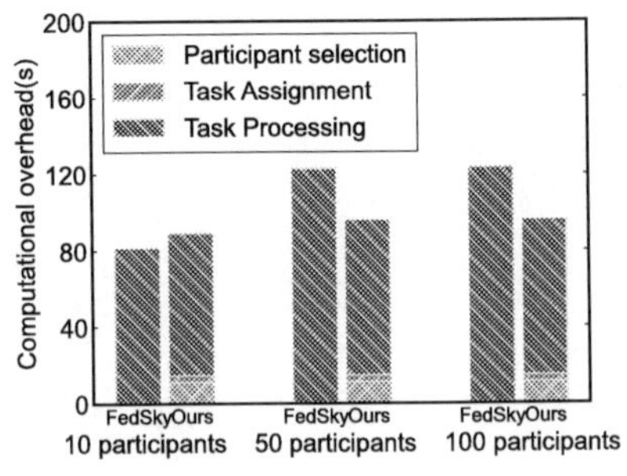

(d) Computational overhead comparison in a special case.

Fig. 4. Two cases, the computational power and the number of samples conform to a Gaussian distribution with mean as 60 and standard deviation as 10.

putational overhead in the participant selection process because of the use of single-threaded homomorphic encryption to protect the status data of the participants. However, our scheme avoids these issues to improve training efficiency with personalized participant selection.

We also compare the accuracy of our model with FedSky in Fig. 5 for different numbers of TP_i selected. In particular, we set TP_i to provide its computational power and local sample size, and the upper and lower bound constraints in FedSky are set to 10 and 100 respectively. Similarly, the computing power and the number of local samples in TP_i fit a Gaussian distribution with standard deviation is 10 and mean is 60, and the number of training rounds shown is from 6 to 100. It can be seen that the accuracy of our scheme with a larger number of participants selected is almost comparable to that of FedSky.

Meanwhile, as shown in Fig. 6, we also compare the FL task accuracy under two different data distributions, independent identical distribution(IID) and non-independent identical distribution(Non-IID). Concretely, different participants are randomly assigned with different samples in the IID setting, where the main classification samples in the Non-IID setting accounts for 70%, and the remaining samples are randomly obtained from others. Moreover, we collect accuracy data

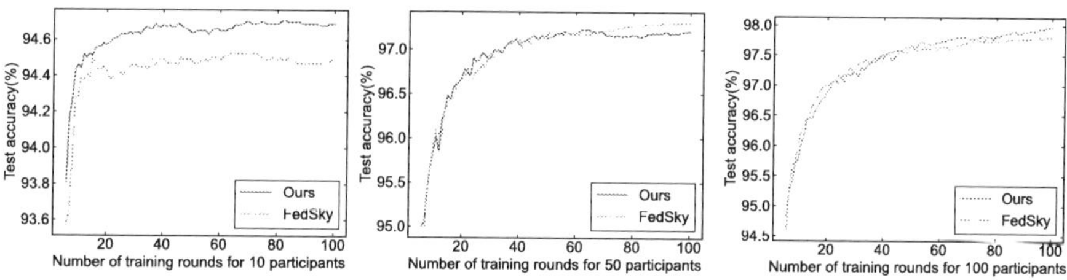

(a) Testing accuracy for 10 participants. (b) Testing accuracy for 50 participants. (c) Testing accuracy for 100 participants.

Fig. 5. Comparison of model testing accuracy for the case of choosing different number of TP_i.

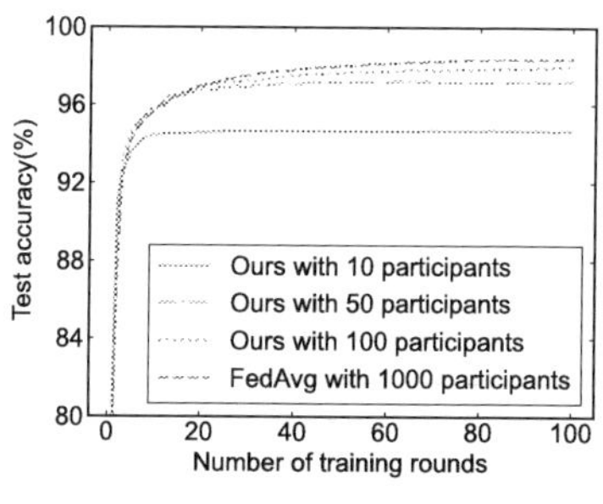

(a) Comparison of different number of TP_i under IID dataset.

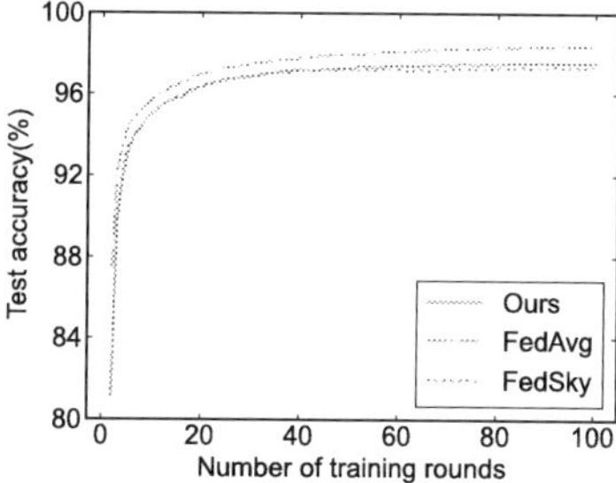

(b) Comparison of the accuracy under Non-IID dataset.

Fig. 6. Comparison of the accuracy under different distributions.

from 2 to 100 rounds. Fig. 6a shows that our scheme can obtain an accuracy close to that of FedAvg even if only 100 participants are selected to participate in the training task. Furthermore, our accuracy comparison with FedSky is shown in Fig. 6b. Overall, our scheme can guarantee security and training efficiency while obtaining a relatively close accuracy.

7 Conclusion

In this work, we propose a bilateral privacy-preserving task assignment with personalized participant selection for mobile crowdsensing system. Specifically, we provide the SKS-WED protocol as a top-k selection sub-protocol to perform the selection of participants in relatively excellent conditions to decrease the impact of resource-constrained devices. In addition, the TR can personalize the reference point and weight parameters to adjust the participant selection, i.e., select participants with more data to improve the accuracy of the results. Moreover, the privacy of both the selection parameters, the task content for TR and the status data, the identity for participants also be protected. Finally, we demonstrate the feasibility of our scheme through some necessary analyses, comparisons with previous work, and a series of experiments. In the future, we will consider the issue of matching participants under multi-tasking and further improving system efficiency.

Acknowledgements. This work is supported by the National Natural Science Foundation of China under grants 62072134 and U2001205, and the Key projects of Guangxi Natural Science Foundation under grant 2019JJD170020, and the Key Research and Development Program of Hubei Province under Grant 2021BEA163.

References

1. Akinyele, J.A., et al.: Charm: a framework for rapidly prototyping cryptosystems. J. Cryptogr. Eng. **3**(2), 111–128 (2013)
2. Amrullah, A., Al Rasyid, M.U.H., Winarno, I.: Implementation and analysis of IoT communication protocols for crowdsensing and crowdsourcing in health application. In: 2021 International Electronics Symposium (IES), pp. 209–214. IEEE (2021)
3. Boneh, D., Gentry, C., Waters, B.: Collusion resistant broadcast encryption with short ciphertexts and private keys. In: Shoup, V. (ed.) CRYPTO 2005. LNCS, vol. 3621, pp. 258–275. Springer, Heidelberg (2005). https://doi.org/10.1007/11535218_16
4. Capponi, A., Fiandrino, C., Kantarci, B., Foschini, L., Kliazovich, D., Bouvry, P.: A survey on mobile crowdsensing systems: challenges, solutions, and opportunities. IEEE Commun. Surv. Tutor. **21**(3), 2419–2465 (2019)
5. Chen, Y.Y., Lv, P., Guo, D.K., Zhou, T.Q., Xu, M.: A survey on task and participant matching in mobile crowd sensing. J. Comput. Sci. Technol. **33**(4), 768–791 (2018)
6. Ganti, R.K., Ye, F., Lei, H.: Mobile crowdsensing: current state and future challenges. IEEE Commun. Mag. **49**(11), 32–39 (2011)

7. Gao, H., Zhao, H.: A personalized task allocation strategy in mobile crowdsensing for minimizing total cost. Sensors **22**(7), 2751 (2022)
8. Jiang, Z., et al.: Crowdpatrol: a mobile crowdsensing framework for traffic violation hotspot patrolling. IEEE Trans. Mob. Comput. (2021). https://doi.org/10.1109/TMC.2021.3110592
9. Ku, H., Susilo, W., Zhang, Y., Liu, W., Zhang, M.: Privacy-preserving federated learning in medical diagnosis with homomorphic re-encryption. Comput. Stand. Interfaces **80**, 103583 (2022)
10. Liu, J., Shen, H., Narman, H.S., Chung, W., Lin, Z.: A survey of mobile crowdsensing techniques: a critical component for the internet of things. ACM Trans. Cyber-Phys. Syst. **2**(3), 1–26 (2018)
11. Liu, Y., Kong, L., Chen, G.: Data-oriented mobile crowdsensing: a comprehensive survey. IEEE Commun. Surv. Tutor. **21**(3), 2849–2885 (2019)
12. Nishio, T., Yonetani, R.: Client selection for federated learning with heterogeneous resources in mobile edge. In: ICC 2019-2019 IEEE International Conference on Communications (ICC), pp. 1–7 (2019)
13. Paillier, P.: Public-key cryptosystems based on composite degree residuosity classes. In: Stern, J. (ed.) EUROCRYPT 1999. LNCS, vol. 1592, pp. 223–238. Springer, Heidelberg (1999). https://doi.org/10.1007/3-540-48910-X_16
14. Perez, A.J., Zeadally, S.: Secure and privacy-preserving crowdsensing using smart contracts: issues and solutions. Comput. Sci. Rev. **43**, 100450 (2022)
15. Rivest, R.L., Adleman, L., Dertouzos, M.L., et al.: On data banks and privacy homomorphisms. Found. Secure Comput. **4**(11), 169–180 (1978)
16. Wang, H., Kaplan, Z., Niu, D., Li, B.: Optimizing federated learning on non-IID data with reinforcement learning. In: IEEE INFOCOM 2020-IEEE Conference on Computer Communications, pp. 1698–1707. IEEE (2020)
17. Wang, H., Yang, Y., Wang, E., Liu, X., Wei, J., Wu, J.: Bilateral privacy-preserving worker selection in spatial crowdsourcing. IEEE Trans. Dependable Secure Comput. 1–14 (2022). https://doi.org/10.1109/TDSC.2022.3186023
18. Wang, J., Wang, L., Wang, Y., Zhang, D., Kong, L.: Task allocation in mobile crowd sensing: state-of-the-art and future opportunities. IEEE Internet Things J. **5**(5), 3747–3757 (2018)
19. Wang, Z., et al.: Personalized privacy-preserving task allocation for mobile crowdsensing. IEEE Trans. Mob. Comput. **18**(6), 1330–1341 (2018)
20. Wang, Z., et al.: When mobile crowdsensing meets privacy. IEEE Commun. Mag. **57**(9), 72–78 (2019)
21. Wang, Z., et al.: Towards personalized task-oriented worker recruitment in mobile crowdsensing. IEEE Trans. Mob. Comput. **20**(5), 2080–2093 (2020)
22. Xu, C., Wang, N., Zhu, L., Zhang, C., Sharif, K., Wu, H.: Reliable and privacy-preserving top-k disease matching schemes for e-healthcare systems. IEEE Internet Things J. **9**(7), 5537–5547 (2022)
23. Xu, G., Li, H., Zhang, Y., Xu, S., Ning, J., Deng, R.H.: Privacy-preserving federated deep learning with irregular users. IEEE Trans. Dependable Secure Comput. **19**(2), 1364–1381 (2022)
24. Yu, Z., Ma, H., Guo, B., Yang, Z.: Crowdsensing 2.0. Commun. ACM **64**(11), 76–80 (2021)
25. Zeng, B., Yan, X., Zhang, X., Zhao, B.: BRAKE: bilateral privacy-preserving and accurate task assignment in fog-assisted mobile crowdsensing. IEEE Syst. J. **15**(3), 4480–4491 (2020)
26. Zhang, M., Song, W., Zhang, J.: A secure clinical diagnosis with privacy-preserving multiclass support vector machine in clouds. IEEE Syst. J. **16**(1), 67–78 (2022)

27. Zhang, X., Lu, R., Shao, J., Wang, F., Zhu, H., Ghorbani, A.A.: Fedsky: an efficient and privacy-preserving scheme for federated mobile crowdsensing. IEEE Internet Things J. **9**(7), 5344–5356 (2022)
28. Zhao, B., Tang, S., Liu, X., Zhang, X., Chen, W.N.: iTAM: bilateral privacy-preserving task assignment for mobile crowdsensing. IEEE Trans. Mob. Comput. **20**(12), 3351–3366 (2020)
29. Zhu, H., Gao, L., Li, H.: Secure and privacy-preserving body sensor data collection and query scheme. Sensors **16**(2), 179 (2016)

Communication-Efficient and Secure Federated Learning Based on Adaptive One-Bit Compressed Sensing

Di Xiao(✉), Xue Tan, and Min Li

College of Computer Science, Chongqing University, Chongqing 400030, China
xiaodi_cqu@hotmail.com

Abstract. Federated learning (FL) enables multiple clients to jointly train a global model without exposing local private datasets. The main challenges for FL include communication efficiency, privacy and robustness. In order to reduce the transmission cost of FL, there are currently some attempts to apply compressed sensing (CS) and quantization strategies as well as a combination of both. Insufficiently, they ignore privacy and robustness. Differential privacy (DP) can guarantee privacy by adding noise to gradient updates, but the convergence or performance of the model will be reduced. In order to overcome the shortcomings of existing methods, we propose the CS-DP-SignSGD algorithm to address the above challenges. Specifically, the model updates are compressed and quantized, which greatly reduces the transmission cost. The one-bit quantization strategy SignSGD based on the majority voting mechanism, which has natural Byzantine robustness, is used. Since CS reduces the model size, CS-DP-SignSGD adds Gaussian noise to the compressed model, which can reduce the amount of added noise and improve model quality without losing privacy. More notably, we propose an adaptive threshold selection scheme to sparsely represent gradients in the CS process, which achieves a certain degree of protection for the sparse representation strategy. Finally, we carry out privacy and convergence analyses of the algorithm. Experiments on the MNIST and Fashion-MNIST datasets demonstrate the effectiveness of our proposed method.

Keywords: Federated learning · Compressed sensing · SignSGD · Efficiency · Privacy · Byzantine robustness

1 Introduction

The challenges faced by traditional centralized machine learning include the high transmission cost of centralized data, the exposure of sensitive data to the server, and data privacy without guarantee. A kind of distributed machine learning algorithm-Federated learning (FL) is proposed in [1], where clients can jointly train a global model without sharing private data. The FL model in this paper

W. Susilo et al. (Eds.): ISC 2022, LNCS 13640, pp. 491–508, 2022.
https://doi.org/10.1007/978-3-031-22390-7_29

consists of a server and several clients, and is trained according to the following steps: Step 1: The server sends the initial global model to the selected clients in this round of training. Step 2: Each client trains the model with local data and transmits gradient updates back to the server. Step 3: The server aggregates the gradients from clients, and then sends the aggregated gradients to clients to update the local model and perform the next round of training.

The advantages of FL include: First, it provides confidentiality for each participant's training data by sharing only model updates rather than raw data. Second, in order to reduce communication cost, the client can perform multiple rounds of local SGD iterations, and then send model updates to the server. Third, in each round of training, only some clients can be selected to update and train the global model, which will further reduce the communication overhead and make this method more favorable for situations involving a large number of clients. It is pointed out in [1] that the communication cost in FL is still much larger than the computational cost. Even though the FL system has reduced a large amount of transmitted data by transmitting model updates, such models like neural networks still contain a large number of parameters. For example, the convolutional neural network in [1] contains 1,663,370 parameters. In order to reduce the transmission cost, gradient quantization is proposed in [2] and [3] to achieve data compression in both upstream and downstream communications. In [2], SignSGD with majority voting is proposed, in which only the signs of the gradients are transmitted to the server, thereby greatly saving the communication overhead. However, quantization only reduces the bits of a single gradient and does not contribute to the total number of gradients. Compressed sensing (CS) enables sampling below the Nyquist rate and near optimal reconstructed signal, thereby reducing computational overhead and the number of measurements. Currently, CS has also been applied to reduce the number of gradients transmitted in FL [4].

In [5], the one bit-CS algorithm that only retains the sign of the measurements is applied to FL, but privacy protection is not considered in the algorithm. Besides, its sparse representation strategy for gradients is to remove most of the gradients with small values, i.e., keep the gradients of Top-K. This sparse representation uses a fixed threshold to filter gradients, but the training process of the model varies between different clients and different iteration rounds, so this is not reasonable. Furthermore, when the attacker knows the positions of the K largest gradients retained in each round, he can easily infer that the rest of the gradients are set to 0.

FL guarantees the privacy of training data by transmitting gradients. However, if the gradients are leaked, the attacker can use the gradients to infer whether a certain piece of data [6] or group attribute [7] is included in the data set of a client, or even recover all the training data [8]. Fortunately, differential privacy (DP), a widely used privacy model [9], can provide privacy protection for each participant. It provides DP guarantee by adding noise to the shared gradients. However, the amount of noise added is proportional to the model size (number of model parameters or weights). The more noise is added, the lower of the convergence or the weaker of the model performance. It is proposed in [4] to compress gradients before adding noise, which can reduce the scale of adding noise and improve the convergence of the model.

There may be also malicious clients in FL systems. Malicious clients can compromise the global model by modifying local training data or model updates sent to the server. This eventually results in the global model exhibiting low accuracy on normal datasets or datasets specifically chosen by the attacker. A number of Byzantine robust FL methods are proposed in [10,11], which are resistant to malicious clients. The main idea of these methods is to mitigate the influence of statistical outliers among the clients' model updates, but requires additional computational cost in the detection of outliers. It has been shown in [2] that SignSGD based on the majority voting mechanism has Byzantine robustness in the aggregation of quantized gradients, and can still show better performance in systems with more than half of malicious clients.

To the best of our knowledge, there is no related research that can overcome all the above-mentioned problems and obtain a FL algorithm that combines high communication efficiency, privacy protection and robustness. Our proposed CS-DP-SignSGD algorithm combines CS and SignSGD to greatly reduce the communication cost in both upstream and downstream communications, and introduces an adaptive threshold selection method to sparsely represent gradients. At the same time, in order to prevent the privacy and security risks brought by gradient leakage, Gaussian noise is added to the compressed gradients to provide DP protection for all gradients, and the Byzantine robustness of SignSGD is used to make the model resistant to malicious client attacks.

In summary, our contributions are as follows:

(1) For the first time, CS, one-bit quantization and DP are introduced into FL, and an efficient, secure and Byzantine robust CS-DP-SignSGD algorithm is proposed. By using CS, the amount of noise that needs to be added is reduced, and the model performance is improved while reducing the transmission cost in both upstream and downstream communications.
(2) An adaptive threshold selection scheme is proposed when the gradient is sparsely represented. Based on the absolute value of the gradient, the K-th largest absolute value of the gradient is adaptively selected as the threshold to filter out the unimportant gradients.
(3) The proposed algorithm is used to perform image classification tasks on two commonly used datasets. Compared with the FedAvg and SignSGD baseline algorithms, the model accuracy is improved by about 6% and 3%, respectively. The sparse representation proposed makes the model converge faster, and the model performance remains optimal in the end compared to Top-K.

2 Preliminary

2.1 Compressed Sensing

Compressed sensing (CS) [12] is a breakthrough signal acquisition and manipulation paradigm that performs simultaneous sensing and compression, leading reducing computational overhead and number of measurements. A signal $x \in \mathbb{R}^n$ working under CS is assumed to have a sparse representation $s \in \mathbb{R}^n$ in some basis or dictionary $\Psi \in \mathbb{R}^{n \times n}$, that is,

$$x = \Psi s, \tag{1}$$

Here, s is K-sparse if $\|s\|_0 = K$. Ψ denotes Discrete Fourier/Cosine or Wavelet Transform. If x is already sparse, then Ψ can be the identity matrix which corresponds to the canonical sparsity basis. With the assumption on the sparsity, CS performs the linear sensing step with the sensing operator $\Phi \in \mathbb{R}^{m \times n}$, acquiring a small number of measurements $y \in \mathbb{R}^m$, with $m < n$ and $m = \gamma \times n$, where γ is the compression ratio:

$$y = \Phi x. \tag{2}$$

(2) represents both the sensing and compression step that can be realized at the sensor level. Hence, we obtain a limited number of measurement y for other processing steps from CS sensors. Combining (1) and (2), the CS model can be written as

$$y = \Phi \Psi s. \tag{3}$$

In some applications, we need to reconstruct x from the measurement y. The reconstruction of x is often considered to find the sparsest solution for an underdetermined linear system.

$$\min_s \|s\|_0 \quad \text{s.t.} \ \|y - \Phi \Psi s\|_2 \leq \epsilon, \tag{4}$$

where ϵ is the amount of residual error allowed in the approximation. Numerous algorithms have been proposed to solve the problem in (4) over the years, which could be roughly categorized into linear programming algorithms [12] and greedy algorithms [13]. Among these algorithms, iterative hard thresholding (IHT) algorithm has been widely studied. This reconstruction method is robust to observation noise and can guarantee near-optimal reconstruction.

2.2 Local Differential Privacy (LDP)

Many companies including Google, Apple, and Microsoft employ local differential privacy (LDP) to combat inference attacks against shared data values [9]. The users in an LDP system will upload perturbed data values instead of the raw data values. A formal definition of LDP is provided in Definition 1. The privacy loss consumption of the algorithm output is captured by the privacy budget ϵ. $\epsilon = 0$ means that the input and output are unrelated, achieving perfect privacy protection; $\epsilon \longrightarrow \infty$ means that there is no privacy guarantee.

Definition 1. Let $\mathrm{A} : 2^{\mathcal{X}} \to \mathcal{Y}$ be a randomized algorithm. The algorithm A is (ϵ, δ) –local differentially private, where $\epsilon, \delta > 0$, if and only if for all data entries $D_1, D_2 \in \mathcal{X}$ and all outputs $Y \in \mathcal{Y}$, we have:

$$Pr\left[\mathrm{A}\left(D\right)_1 \in Y\right] \leq exp\left(\epsilon\right) Pr\left[\mathrm{A}\left(D\right)_2 \in Y\right] + \delta. \tag{5}$$

If $\delta = 0$, A is $\epsilon-$local differentially private. For two adjacent inputs D_1 and D_2, which differ by at most one piece of data, the purpose of LDP is to make the distributions of $\mathrm{A}(D_1)$ and $\mathrm{A}(D_2)$ are as close as possible, and the degree of similarity is measured by ϵ and δ.

3 The Proposed Algorithms

3.1 CS-DP-SignSGD

The proposed CS-DP-SignSGD scheme is presented in Algorithm 1, all the clients are initialized with the same model structure and parameters w_0. Since aggregation servers are often limited in bandwidth or computing power, such as base stations in wireless communication, only a part of clients can be selected by the server to participate in aggregation. This paper uses the randomization method to choose the clients, which is proposed in [1]. Before the t-th round of iteration training ($t \geq 0$), a set I_t containing k_t clients is randomly selected to participate in this round of iteration.

Each client uses the data set and the current model w_t to train locally for k rounds, and obtains the updated model $w_t^i \leftarrow SGD(w_t, D_i), i \in I_t$. Then the update of each local model is obtained as $d_t^i \leftarrow w_t^i - w_t, i \in I_t$. Because it requires high cost to directly transmit d_t^i to the server, CS-DP-SignSGD performs gradient compression and quantization firstly, and then transmits the one-bit measurements to the server. To be more specific, the sparse representation of local updates d_t^i is realized using Algorithm 2. The sparse vector $g_t^i \in \mathbb{R}^N$ is given as $g_t^i \leftarrow$ **Algorithm 2** (d_t^i).

According to CS theory, the aggregation operation on all measurements is equivalent to the same operation on original gradients. By analyzing the Byzantine Robustness of SignSGD, we propose to preserve signs of all gradients before compression, which can ensure the aggregating of the measurements is equivalent to aggregating the signs of all gradients. The operation of taking the signs of gradients can be expressed as $c_t^i \leftarrow sign(g_t^i)$, where $c_t^i \in \mathbb{R}^N$. Then, c_t^i is compressed with a random measurement matrix $A_t \in \mathbb{R}^{M \times N}$ $(M < N)$, which gets the compressed measurements $y_t^i \leftarrow A_t c_t^i$.

DP protection is achieved by adding noise to the gradients. The scale of the added noise is positively related to the sensitivity S, which in turn is often proportional to the model size N. The more noise you add, the larger the perturbation error will be, and the worse the model convergence or performance will be. In the proposed algorithm, the perturbation error is less since noise is added to the compressed measurements with the size $M < N$. Specifically, we employ Analytic Gaussian Mechanism to add noise on gradients. Each client uses the one-bit compressor $dpsign(\cdot)$ with DP proposed in [14] to quantize the measurements, and then transmits $dpsign(y_t^i)$ to the server. The $dpsign(\cdot)$ is defined as (6).

Definition 2. For any given gradient y_t^i, the compressor outputs $dpsign(y_t^i, \epsilon, \delta)$, the j-th entry is given by

$$dpsign(y_t^i, \epsilon, \delta)_j = \begin{cases} 1, & with\ probability\ \Phi\left(\frac{\left(y_t^i\right)_j}{\sigma}\right) \\ -1, & with\ probability\ 1 - \Phi\left(\frac{\left(y_t^i\right)_j}{\sigma}\right), \end{cases} \tag{6}$$

where δ is the noise scale satisfying $\Phi\left(\frac{\triangle}{2\sigma} - \frac{\varepsilon\sigma}{\triangle}\right) - e^{\varepsilon}\Phi\left(-\frac{\triangle}{2\sigma} - \frac{\varepsilon\sigma}{\triangle}\right) \leq \delta$ (Analytic Gaussian Mechanism [15]).

Algorithm 1: CS-DP-SignSGD

Input: initial parameters w_0, global round T, learning rate η, compressor dpsign$(\cdot)$, measurement matrix A_t, current residual error vector e_t, error decay rate λ.
Output: optimized parameters w_{T+1}.
Initialization: All clients are initialized with the same global model with parameters w_0.

for $t = 0, ..., T$ **do**
  A set I_t of clients are randomly chosen.
  for $i \in I_t$ in parallel do
    $w_t^i \leftarrow SGD\left(w_t, D_i\right)$
    $d_t^i \leftarrow w_t^i - w_t$
    $g_t^i \leftarrow$ **Algorithm 2** $\left(d_t^i\right)$
    $c_t^i \leftarrow sign\left(g_t^i\right)$
    $y_t^i \leftarrow A_t c_t^i$
    Send dpsign$(y_t^i)$to server.
  end
  The server does:
    push $y_t^{glo} \leftarrow sign\left(\frac{1}{k_t}\sum_{i \in I_t} dpsign\left(y_t^i\right) + e^t\right)$ to the clients.
  update residual error:
    $e^{t+1} = \lambda * e^t + (1 - \lambda) * \left(\frac{1}{k_t}\sum_{i \in I_t} dpsign\left(y_t^i\right) - \frac{1}{k_t} y_t^{glo}\right)$
  for $i \in \{1, 2, ..., I_t\}$ **in parallel do:**
    $r_t \leftarrow BIHT\left(A_t, g_t^{glo}\right)$
    $w_{t+1} \leftarrow w_t - \eta r_t$
  end
end
Return w_{T+1}.

When the server receives one-bit measurements from multiple clients, it will use a majority-based voting strategy to fuse the measurements and compensate for the error caused by quantization, which can be expressed as

$$y_t^{glo} \leftarrow sign\left(\frac{1}{k_t}\sum_{i\in I_t} dpsign\left(y_t^i\right)+e^t\right), \tag{7}$$

where e^t represents the quantization error, and the update of this error is

$$e^{t+1}=\lambda * e^t+(1-\lambda) * \left(\frac{1}{k_t}\sum_{i\in I_t} dpsign\left(y_t^i\right)-\frac{1}{k_t}y_t^{glo}\right), \tag{8}$$

where λ is the decay rate of the error. Then, the fusion result $y_t^{glo} \in \{-1,1\}^M$ is transmitted back to all clients. Each client reconstructs the global model update r_t based on the received y_t^{glo} by means of the BIHT algorithm [16], i.e., $r_t \leftarrow BIHT\left(A_t, g_t^{glo}\right)$. Each client updates the global model $w_{t+1} \leftarrow w_t - \eta r_t$, where η is the learning rate.

3.2 Sparse Representation of Gradients with Adaptive Threshold

In our approach, CS is used to compress gradients. According to the CS theory, the sparse signal model can ensure a high compression rate. As long as the target signal has a sparse representation in a known basis or frame in advance, the original signal can be reconstructed without distortion. However, the gradients of the model often cannot meet the requirement of sparse representation, that is, most of the gradients are not 0. At the same time, according to the previous works [17], most gradients updated by clients are insignificant with values close to 0. The gradient is negligible for model aggregation operation if the gradient is close to 0. Therefore, the client can achieve sparse representation of gradients by reserving only the Top-K most important values (with gradient values much larger than 0), and set the rest of gradients to 0. However, in the face of a powerful attacker, this sparse method has certain vulnerability. Once the attacker obtains the positions of the Top-K gradients, it can be inferred that the rest of the gradients are set as 0.

In this paper, we compare $\left|d_t^i[j]\right|+\rho$ with $\theta+\nu$ to evaluate whether $d_t^i[j]$ is significant, where θ is the threshold, ρ and ν are Gaussian noises used to distort the original gradient and the threshold for comparison. Note that if a gradient is larger, the probability that it can pass the evaluation is higher, which means it is more significant. Inspired by the Top-K algorithm, which is widely used to select significant gradients for compression in FL model compression algorithm, we adaptively set θ by considering the K-th most significant gradient. Different from the Top-K sparse algorithm, which is always fixed to reserve the Top-K gradients, the adaptive threshold method can only guarantee that larger gradients have a greater probability of being reserved. DP noises will be added to distort both gradients and the threshold in our method. This makes the Top-K gradients no longer be reserved every time. Assuming that the attacker knows the positions of the Top-K gradients, he cannot directly infer that the gradients in the rest of the positions are set to 0. Sparse representation of gradients with adaptive threshold is provided in Algorithm 2. All gradients are judged: if

$\left|d_t^i\left[j\right]\right| + \rho > \theta + \nu$, then $d_t^i\left[j\right]$ will be put into set β_t. Therefore, only the Top-P gradients in the set are retained and the others are set to 0. Finally the sparse representation g_t^i of all gradients can be obtained.

Algorithm 2: Sparse Representation of Gradients with Adaptive Threshold

---

Input: the gradients of the t-th round d_t^i, the number of preserved gradients P
Output: the sparse representation of gradients g_t^i.
Sort $d_t^i\left[j\right]$ in decreasing order and θ is equal to the K-th largest absolute value.
for j=0,...,d **do**
  Generate Gaussian noise $\rho = N\left(0, \sigma^2\right)$, $\nu = N\left(0, \sigma'^2\right)$
  If $\left|d_t^i\left[j\right]\right| + \rho > \theta + \nu$, $d_t^i\left[j\right]$ then
    Put $d_t^i\left[j\right]$ into set β_t
  end
end
Sort β_t and only reserve the Top-P values.
for j=0,...,d **do** // The d represents the number of gradients in d_t^i
  if $d_t^i\left[j\right]$ in β_t then
    $g_t^i\left[j\right] = d_t^i\left[j\right]$
  end
  else
    $g_t^i\left[j\right] = 0$
  end
end
Return g_t^i.

---

4 Theoretical Analysis

4.1 Privacy Analysis

The server can only access the noisy measurements from multiple clients which is sufficiently perturbed to ensure DP. It is emphasized that the sparse representation process is ultimately to obtain P preserved gradients. Therefore, the privacy protection of sparsified gradients is discussed in this subsection.

Theorem 1. (Privacy of CS-DP-SignSGD). CS-DP-SignSGD is $(\epsilon, \delta)-$differentially private for any $\varepsilon > 0$ and $\delta \in (0, 1)$.

Proof. In order to prove the CS-DP-SignSGD is $(\epsilon, \delta)-$differentially private, we just need to prove $dpsign(\cdot, \varepsilon, \delta)$ is $(\epsilon, \delta)-$differentially private [18]. We start from the one-dimension scenario and consider any two items a, b that satisfy $\parallel a - b \parallel_2 \leq \triangle_2$. Without loss of generality, assume that $dpsign(a, \varepsilon, \delta) = dpsign(b, \varepsilon, \delta) = z$. Then we get

$$P\left(dpsign(a, \varepsilon, \delta) = z\right) = \Phi\left(\frac{a}{\sigma}\right) = \int_{-\infty}^{a} \frac{1}{\sqrt{2\pi}\sigma} e^{-\frac{x^2}{2\sigma^2}} dx. \quad (9)$$

$$P\left(dpsign(b, \varepsilon, \delta) = z\right) = \Phi\left(\frac{b}{\sigma}\right) = \int_{-\infty}^{b} \frac{1}{\sqrt{2\pi}\sigma} e^{-\frac{x^2}{2\sigma^2}} dx. \tag{10}$$

and

$$\frac{P\left(dpsign(a, \varepsilon, \delta) = z\right)}{P\left(dpsign(b, \varepsilon, \delta) = z\right)} = \frac{\int_{-\infty}^{a} e^{-\frac{x^2}{2\sigma^2}} dx}{\int_{-\infty}^{b} e^{-\frac{x^2}{2\sigma^2}} dx} = \frac{\int_{0}^{\infty} e^{-\frac{(x-a)^2}{2\sigma^2}} dx}{\int_{0}^{\infty} e^{-\frac{(x-b)^2}{2\sigma^2}} dx} \tag{11}$$

According to Analytic Gaussian Mechanism [15], we can derive that $e^{-\varepsilon} \leq \left|\frac{P(dpsign(a,\varepsilon,\delta)=z)}{P(dpsign(b,\varepsilon,\delta)=z)}\right| \leq e^{\varepsilon}$ with probability at least $1 - \delta$.

For the multi-dimension scenario and considering any two items a, b that satisfy $\parallel a - b \parallel_2 \leq \triangle_2$ and $v \in \{-z, z\}^d$, we have

$$\frac{P\left(dpsign(a, \varepsilon, \delta) = v\right)}{P\left(dpsign(b, \varepsilon, \delta) = v\right)} = \frac{\int_{D} e^{-\frac{\|x-a\|_2^2}{2\sigma^2}} dx}{\int_{D} e^{-\frac{\|x-b\|_2^2}{2\sigma^2}} dx}, \tag{12}$$

where D is some integral area depending on v. Similarly, we get that $e^{-\varepsilon} \leq \left|\frac{P(dpsign(a,\varepsilon,\delta)=v)}{P(dpsign(b,\varepsilon,\delta)=v)}\right| \leq e^{\varepsilon}$ with probability at least $1 - \delta$.

We have proved $dpsign(\cdot, \varepsilon, \delta)$ is (ϵ, δ) −differentially private. Therefore, what the server gets is the noisy measurements. Our emphasis on security is also derived from this, and subsequent $sign(\cdot)$ and $BIHT(\cdot)$ will not affect the security of the process.

4.2 Convergence Analysis

In order to facilitate the convergence analysis, the following commonly adopted assumptions are made.

Assumption 1. (lower Bound). For all w and an optional result F^*, we have objective value $F(w) \geq F^*$.

Assumption 2. (Smoothness). For any w_i and w_j, we require for the non-negative constant L.

$$F(w_i) \leq F(w_j) + \langle \bigtriangledown F(w_j), w_i - w_j \rangle + \frac{L}{2} \left\| w_i - w_j \right\|_2^2 \tag{13}$$

where $\langle \cdot, \cdot \rangle$ is the standard inner product.

Assumption 3. The total number of clients (i.e., k_t) is odd. Assumption 1 and 2 are standard for non-convex optimization [19] and Assumption 3 is to ensure there always exists a winner in the majority vote [16], which can be relaxed.

In this paper, a typical federated optimization problem with k_t normal workers in CS-DP-SignSGD is considered to minimize the finite-sum objective of the form

$$\min_{w \in \mathbb{R}^d} \; F(w), \qquad s.t \;\; F(w) \triangleq \frac{1}{k_t} \sum_{i=1}^{k_t} f_i(w), \tag{14}$$

where $f_i(w)$ is the loss function defined by the private dataset of client i and the current global model w.

Theorem 2. (Convergence of CS-DP-SignSGD). When Assumption 1, 2 and 3 are satisfied, by running Algorithm 1 T rounds with the learning rate $\eta = \frac{1}{k_t \sqrt{Tn}}$, we have

$$\frac{1}{T} \sum_{t=1}^{T} \frac{\|\nabla F(w^t)\|_2^2}{\alpha} \leq \frac{\left[F(w^{(1)}) - F^* + (C^2 + LC^2 + L^2\beta\gamma)\right]\sqrt{n}}{\sqrt{T}}, \tag{15}$$

where $\alpha \geq \alpha_0$ is a constant, $\gamma \in (0, 1]$ is the compression ratio, β and C are two positive constants, L is a non-negative constant and the dimension of compressed gradients is $\mathbb{R}^{\gamma n}$.

The proof of Theorem 2 follows the strategy of taking $q^t = w^t - \eta k_t \mathcal{B}(e^t)$ such that q^t is updated in a similar way as w^t in the non error-feedback scenario, where $B(\cdot)$ is the simplification version of algorithm $BIHT(\cdot)$. For brevity, the decay rate λ in Algorithm 1 is omitted, so $e^{t+1} = e^t + \frac{1}{k_t}\sum_{i=1}^{k_t} \hat{y}_t^i - \frac{1}{k_t} y_t^{glo}$, where $\hat{y}_t^i = dpsign(y_t^i)$.

Lemma 1. Let $q^t = w^t - \eta k_t \mathcal{B}(e^t)$, we have

$$q^{(t+1)} = q^{(t)} - \eta \mathcal{B}(\textstyle\sum_{i=1}^{k_t} \hat{y}_t^i). \tag{16}$$

Proof.

$$\begin{aligned} q^{t+1} &= w^{t+1} - \eta k_t \mathcal{B}(e^{t+1}) \\ &= w^t - \eta r_t - \eta k_t \mathcal{B}(e^{t+1}) \\ &= w^t - \eta r_t - \eta k_t \mathcal{B}(e^t + \frac{1}{k_t}\textstyle\sum_{i=1}^{k_t} \hat{y}_t^i - \frac{1}{k_t} y_t^{glo}) \\ &= w^t - \eta k_t \mathcal{B}(e^t) - \eta \mathcal{B}(\textstyle\sum_{i=1}^{k_t} \hat{y}_t^i) \\ &= q^{(t)} - \eta \mathcal{B}(\textstyle\sum_{i=1}^{k_t} \hat{y}_t^i). \end{aligned} \tag{17}$$

According to [18], there exists a positive constant $\beta > 0$ such that $\mathbb{E}\left[\|e^{(t)}\|_2^2\right] \leq \beta\gamma n, \forall t$. Therefore, we have

$$\begin{aligned}
&\mathbb{E}\left[F(q^{(t+1)}) - F(q^{(t)})\right] \\
&\leq -\eta k_t \mathbb{E}\left[\left\langle \triangledown F(q^{(t)}), \frac{1}{k_t}\mathcal{B}(\textstyle\sum_{i=1}^{k_t}\hat{y}_t^i)\right\rangle\right] + \frac{L}{2}\mathbb{E}\left[\left\|-\eta\mathcal{B}(\textstyle\sum_{i=1}^{k_t}\hat{y}_t^i)\right\|_2^2\right] \\
&= \eta k_t \mathbb{E}\left[\left\langle \triangledown F(w^{(t)}) - \triangledown F(q^{(t)}), \frac{1}{k_t}\mathcal{B}(\textstyle\sum_{i=1}^{k_t}\hat{y}_t^i)\right\rangle\right] \\
&\quad + \frac{L\eta^2}{2}\mathbb{E}\left[\left\|\mathcal{B}(\textstyle\sum_{i=1}^{k_t}\hat{y}_t^i)\right\|_2^2\right] - \eta k_t \mathbb{E}\left[\left\langle \triangledown F(w^{(t)}), \frac{1}{k_t}\mathcal{B}(\textstyle\sum_{i=1}^{k_t}\hat{y}_t^i)\right\rangle\right]
\end{aligned} \tag{18}$$

We bound the first term as

$$\begin{aligned}
&\eta k_t \mathbb{E}\left[\left\langle \triangledown F(w^{(t)}) - \triangledown F(q^{(t)}), \frac{1}{k_t}\mathcal{B}(\textstyle\sum_{i=1}^{k_t}\hat{y}_t^i)\right\rangle\right] \\
&\leq \frac{\eta^2 k_t^2}{2}\mathbb{E}\left[\left\|\frac{1}{k_t}\mathcal{B}(\textstyle\sum_{i=1}^{k_t}\hat{y}_t^i)\right\|_2^2\right] + \frac{1}{2}\mathbb{E}\left[\left\|q^t - w^t\right\|_2^2\right] \\
&= \frac{\eta^2 k_t^2}{2}\mathbb{E}\left[\left\|\frac{1}{k_t}\mathcal{B}(\textstyle\sum_{i=1}^{k_t}\hat{y}_t^i)\right\|_2^2\right] + \frac{L^2\eta^2 k_t^2}{2}\mathbb{E}\left[\left\|e^{(t)}\right\|_2^2\right] \\
&\leq \frac{\eta^2 k_t^2}{2}\mathbb{E}\left[\left\|\frac{1}{k_t}\mathcal{B}(\textstyle\sum_{i=1}^{k_t}\hat{y}_t^i)\right\|_2^2\right] + \frac{L^2\eta^2 k_t^2\beta\eta n}{2}
\end{aligned} \tag{19}$$

We can know there exists $C > 0$ such that $\mathbb{E}\left[|\mathcal{B}(dpsign(\cdot)|\right] \leq C$ based on [16]. Then, the last term can be bounded as

$$\begin{aligned}
&-\eta k_t \mathbb{E}\left[\left\langle \triangledown F(w^{(t)}), \frac{1}{k_t}\mathcal{B}(\textstyle\sum_{i=1}^{k_t}\hat{y}_t^i)\right\rangle\right] \\
&= -\eta k_t \mathbb{E}\left[\sum_{j=1}^{n} \triangledown F(w^{(t)})_j \frac{1}{k_t}\mathcal{B}(\sum_{i=1}^{k_t} dpsign((y_t^i)_j))\right] \\
&\leq -\eta k_t \textstyle\sum_{j=1}^{n} \left|\triangledown F(w^{(t)})_j\right| \dfrac{C\left|\triangledown F(w^{(t)})_j\right|}{\alpha} = -\eta k_t \dfrac{C\left\|\triangledown F(w^{(t)})_j\right\|_2^2}{\alpha}
\end{aligned} \tag{20}$$

Plugging (19) and (20) into (18) yields

$$\begin{aligned}
&\mathbb{E}\left[F(q^{(t+1)}) - F(q^{(t)})\right] \\
&\leq \frac{\eta^2 k_t^2}{2}\mathbb{E}\left[\left\|\frac{1}{k_t}\mathcal{B}(\textstyle\sum_{i=1}^{k_t}\hat{y}_t^i)\right\|_2^2\right] + \frac{L^2\eta^2 k_t^2\beta\eta n}{2} \\
&\quad + \frac{L\eta^2 k_t^2}{2}\mathbb{E}\left[\left\|\frac{1}{k_t}\mathcal{B}(\textstyle\sum_{i=1}^{k_t}\hat{y}_t^i)\right\|_2^2\right] - \eta k_t \frac{C\left\|\triangledown F(w^{(t)})_j\right\|_2^2}{\alpha} \\
&\leq \frac{(\eta^2 k_t^2 C^2 + L\eta^2 k_t^2 C^2 + L^2\eta^2 k_t^2\beta\gamma)n}{2} - \eta k_t \frac{C\left\|\triangledown F(w^{(t)})_j\right\|_2^2}{\alpha}
\end{aligned} \tag{21}$$

Rewriting (21) and taking average over $t = 1, 2, 3, ..., T$ on both sides, we have

$$\begin{aligned} \frac{1}{T}\sum_{t=1}^{T}\frac{\|\nabla F(w^t)\|_2^2}{\alpha} \leq & \frac{(\eta k_t C^2 + L\eta k_t C^2 + L^2\eta k_t C^2 \beta\gamma)n}{2} \\ & + \sum_{t=1}^{T}\frac{\mathbb{E}\left[F(q^{(t)}) - F(q^{(t+1)})\right]}{\eta k_t T} \end{aligned} \tag{22}$$

Taking $\eta = \frac{1}{k_t\sqrt{Tn}}$ and $w^{(1)} = q^{(1)}$ yields (15).

5 Performance Evaluation

5.1 Datasets and Experimental Setup

Datasets and models: The model used by the local client is a simple feed-forward neural network with 64 hidden units. It is important to emphasize that our main goal is not to achieve state-of-the-art accuracy, but to verify the effectiveness of our proposed method. The datasets are MNIST dataset and Fashion-MNIST dataset. MNIST dataset contains 60000 training images and 10000 test images of handwritten digits from 0 to 9. Fashion-MNIST dataset contains 60000 training images and 10000 test images of ten different classes of fashion items. The experiments are conducted on a Windows platform with an AMD Ryzen 7 5800H CPU and 32 GB RAM.

Implementation details: The FL system contains a central server and I_t clients. In the following experiments, I_t is fixed at 30, which means 30 clients will be randomly selected to participate in the training in each round. The number of labels c is fixed at 10, which is assigned to each client and can be used as a metric to measure the data heterogeneity. For fair comparison, we set the same hyper-parameters (batch size as 256, local epoch as 2, and learning rate as 0.01) for all algorithms on both datasets. We set L_2 norm bound as 1, privacy budget $\epsilon = 1$, error decay rate $\lambda = 0.5$, the level of sparsity to be 0.001, and the compression ratio is fixed at $\gamma = M/N = 0.5$.

5.2 Comparison Between the Proposed Algorithm and the Baseline Algorithms

We compare the performances of the proposed algorithm and the baseline methods including FedAvg [1], SignSGD [2], and DP-SignSGD [14] on the MNIST and Fashion-MNIST datasets. It can be easily observed from Fig. 1 that, on the MNIST dataset, CS-DP-SignSGD significantly outperforms SignSGD and FedAvg and slightly outperforms DP-SignSGD. Similar results can also be seen from Fig. 2 for Fashion-MNIST.

The reason is that the injected noises in DP-SignSGD and CS-DP-SignSGD act as regularization technique. Meanwhile, much noise added will result in the negative impact on model performance. The application of CS reduces the amount of data in the early stage, which reduces the amount of Gaussian noise added later, and the model performance can be further improved. But at the same time, CS will also bring a certain gradient reconstruction error. When communication rounds is less than 30, performance of the proposed method is lower than DP-SignSGD due to the reconstruction error. As the number of communication rounds increases, compared with DP-SignSGD, the proposed method reduces the amount of added noise and the performance increases roughly 2%–3% finally. In addition, we notice that FedAvg does not outperform all other baselines under the same hyper-parameter setting and communication rounds between the server and clients. Because FedAvg converges slowly, it can perform better by increasing the local training time, reducing the local mini-batch size and assigning a much larger initial learning rate that decays exponentially [20]. In addition, we notice that the model accuracy obtained when training with Fashion-MNIST dataset is lower than MNIST. After analysis, we believe the reason is that the model used in this paper is only for the verification of the scheme, which is relatively simple and is not suitable for more complex classification tasks.

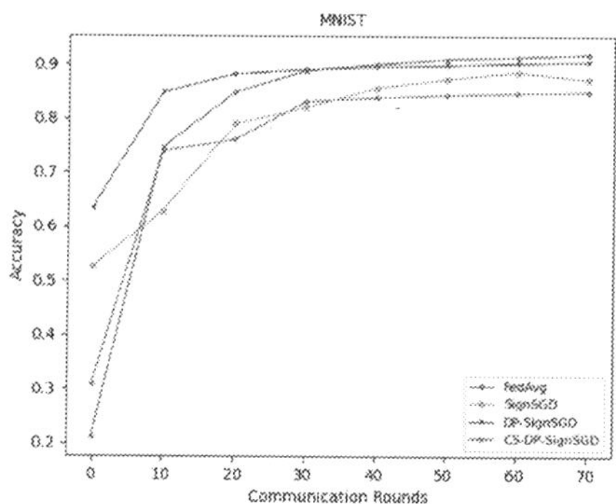

Fig. 1. MNIST test accuracy

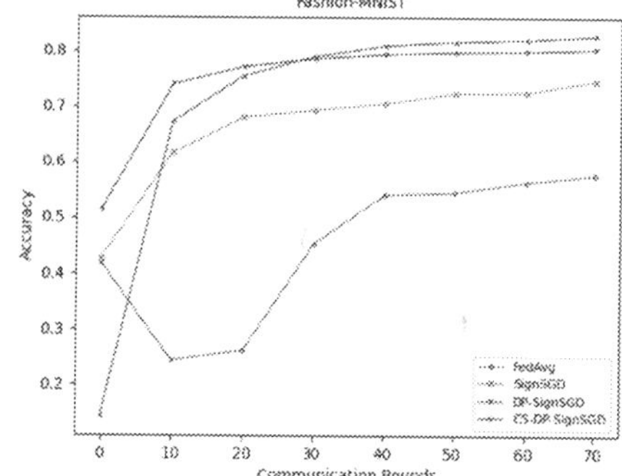

Fig. 2. Fashion-MNIST test accuracy

In terms of communication efficiency, all the SignSGD based methods reduce the communication overhead each round by 32 times compared with FedAvg using full-precision gradients. CS-DP-SignSGD uses CS on the basis of SignSGD. In the experiments, the compression ratio is set to 0.5, which further reduces the communication overhead to 1/64 of FedAvg. As shown in Fig. 3, in the case of the same communication overhead, CS-DP-SignSGD performs more iteration rounds, and the corresponding accuracy is higher, followed by SignSGD. In addition, it needs to be emphasized that the communication cost of DP-SignSGD is the same as that of SingSGD, so it is not shown here.

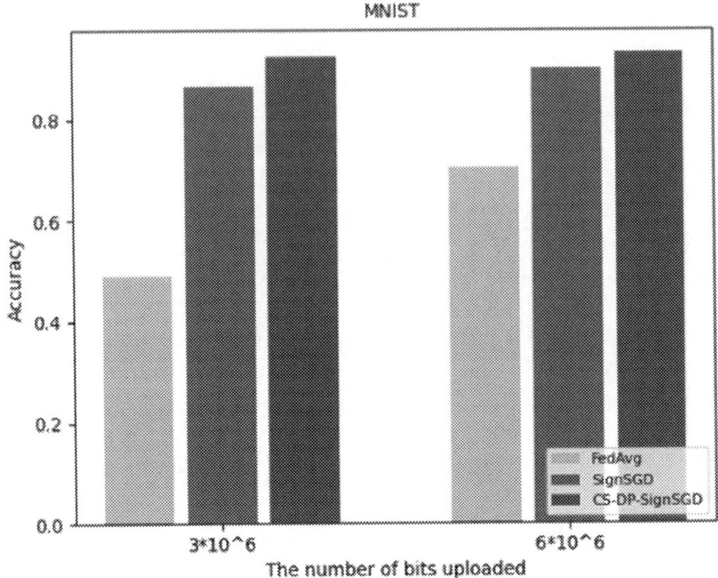

Fig. 3. Test accuracy attained by FedAvg, SignSGD and CS-DP-SignSGD after uploading a certain amount of data to the central server.

5.3 Sparsifying Methods

In order to verify the superiority of our proposed sparse representation algorithm, as shown in Fig. 4, we obtain different model performances on the MNIST dataset by using three sparse representation methods for CS-DP-SignSGD, that is, random gradient preservation, Top-K gradient preservation, and the adaptive threshold sparsifying. As can be seen from the figure, the proposed sparsifying in this paper is significantly better than random gradient preservation and slightly better than Top-K sparse method [21]. On the one hand, it shows that the larger the gradient, the greater the impact on the model performance, and with only some of the largest gradients, we can achieve the same model performance as using all the gradients. On the other hand, compared to Top-K gradient preservation, the adaptive threshold sparsifying proposed in this paper performs slightly better because of the more flexible preservation of gradients. By performing the same experiment on the Fashion-MINIST dataset, we obtain similar experimental results as the MNIST dataset from Fig. 4.

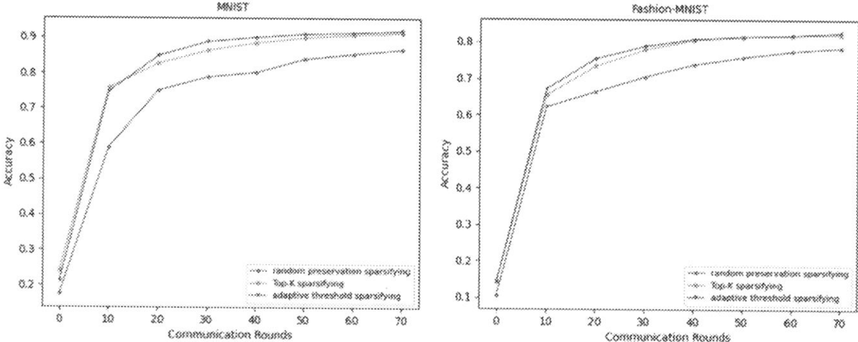

Fig. 4. The accuracy of CS-DP-SignSGD with random preservation sparsifying, Top-K sparsifying and adaptive threshold sparsifying in MNIST and Fashion-MNIST.

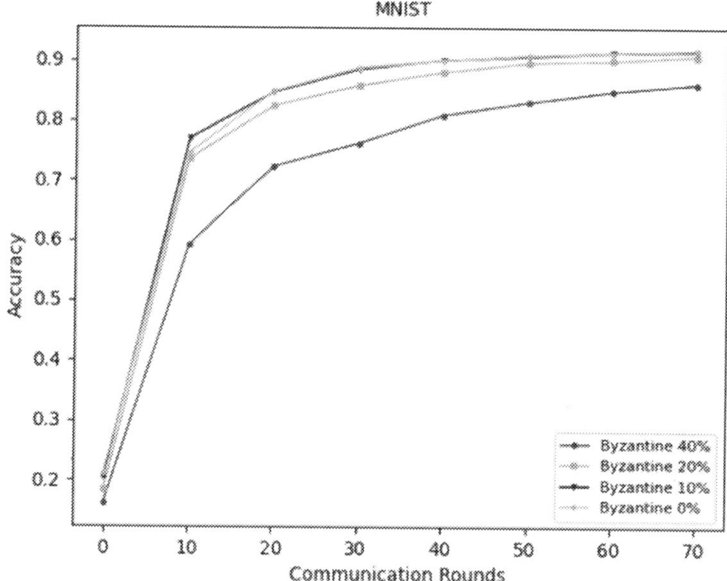

Fig. 5. The performance of CS-DP-SignSGD with different percentage of Byzantine parties in MNIST.

5.4 Byzantine Robustness

In addition to normal participants in FL, there may be Byzantine attackers who destruct the global model by modifying the local dataset or the model uploaded to the server. Ultimately, the corrupted model shows poor performance on common datasets or specific datasets. In this paper, we mainly consider the attacker who destroys the model, and assume that the attacker uses a stronger attack than randomly changing the gradient sign, that is, reversing the signs of all uploaded gradients, i.e., byzantine:$sign\left(y_t^i\right) = -sign\left(y_t^i\right)$. In the meantime, we ignore the attack method of rescaling the gradients, because SignSGD just aggregates all the signs of gradients, which is naturally robust to the attack of changing the value of the gradients.

Figure 5 shows the model accuracy of the CS-DP-SignSGD algorithm against different numbers of Byzantine attackers on the MNIST dataset. It can be found that when 40% of the participants are Byzantine attackers, the performance of the algorithm CS-DP-SignSGD proposed in this paper can still remain stable. Furthermore, we compare the robustness of the proposed algorithm with other algorithms. As shown in Fig. 6, when 20% of the participants are Byzantine attackers, in the early stage of training, the accuracy of CS-DP-SignSGD is low due to the reconstruction errors. But when the number of iterations reaches a certain number, the proposed algorithm approaches and finally slightly outperforms DP-SignSGD. This shows that CS-DP-SignSGD also has a good performance in Byzantine robustness under the requirement of communication efficiency and security. The robustness of CS itself can enhance the Byzantine attack resistance capability of CS-DP-SignSGD to a certain extent.

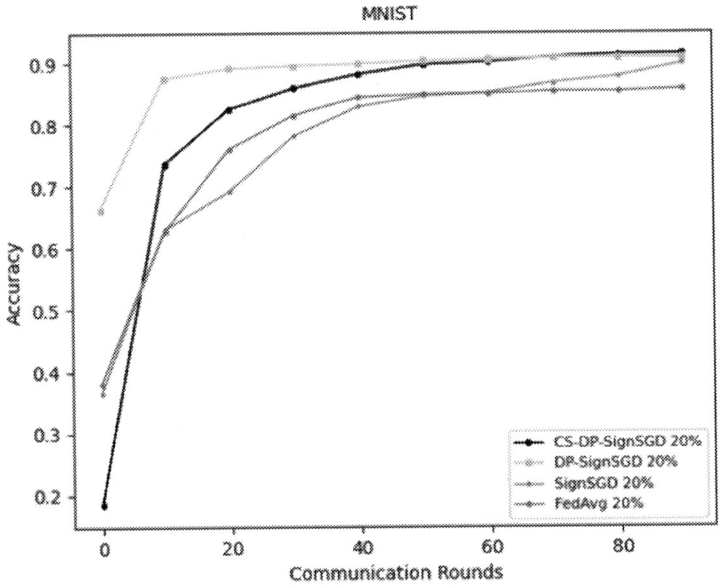

Fig. 6. Test accuracy with Byzantine attackers in MNIST.

6 Conclusion

Based on SignSGD, CS and DP, we propose an efficient and secure FL algorithm CS-DP-SignSGD. In the proposed algorithm, the compressed and quantized one-bit measurements are aggregated by the server, and then the aggregated gradients are sent to the clients for reconstruction to obtain the currently updated model. The proposed scheme realizes data compression in both upstream and downstream communications, which greatly improves the communication efficiency and the privacy protection of gradients. Different from the traditional Top-K sparse representation method, the adaptive threshold sparsifying is innovatively proposed to sparsely represent gradients, which protects the sparsifying rules and enhances the security of the sparsifying process. Theoretical analyses prove the privacy and convergence of the proposed scheme. Through the experiments on the datasets MNIST and Fashion-MNIST, it is proved that the proposed algorithm is superior to both the FedAvg and SignSGD algorithms in terms of model performance and communication efficiency. Some future research avenues include exploring how to further enhance the robustness of FL systems under various Byzantine attack scenarios and applying CS tools to more complex FL scenarios, such as decentralized FL and vertical FL.

Acknowledgment. The work was supported by the National Key R&D Program of China (Grant No. 2020YFB1805400), the National Natural Science Foundation of China (Grant No. 62072063) and the Project Supported by Graduate Student Research and Innovation Foundation of Chongqing, China (Grant No. CYB22063).

References

1. McMahan, B., Moore, E., Ramage, D., Hampson, S., Arcas, B.A.: Communication-efficient learning of deep networks from decentralized data. In: Artificial Intelligence and Statistics, pp. 1273–1282. PMLR (2017)
2. Bernstein, J., Zhao, J., Azizzadenesheli, K., Anandkumar, A.: signSGD with majority vote is communication efficient and byzantine fault tolerant. arXiv preprint arXiv:1810.05291 (2018)
3. Alistarh, D., Grubic, D., Li, J., Tomioka, R., Vojnovic, M.: QSGD: communication-efficient SGD via gradient quantization and encoding. In: Advances in Neural Information Processing Systems, vol. 30, pp. 1707–1718 (2017)
4. Kerkouche, R., Ács, G., Castelluccia, C., Genevès, P.: Compression boosts differentially private federated learning. In: 2021 IEEE European Symposium on Security and Privacy (EuroS&P), pp. 304–318. IEEE (2021)
5. Li, C., Li, G., Varshney, P.K.: Communication-efficient federated learning based on compressed sensing. IEEE Internet Things J. **8**(20), 15531–15541 (2021)
6. Nasr, M., Shokri, R., Houmansadr, A.: Comprehensive privacy analysis of deep learning: passive and active white-box inference attacks against centralized and federated learning. In: 2019 IEEE Symposium on Security and Privacy (SP), pp. 739–753. IEEE (2019)
7. Melis, L., Song, C., De Cristofaro, E., Shmatikov, V.: Inference attacks against collaborative learning. arXiv preprint arXiv:1805.04049 (2018)
8. Zhu, L., Liu, Z., Han, S.: Deep leakage from gradients. In: Advances in Neural Information Processing Systems, vol. 32, pp. 14774–14784 (2019)
9. Dwork, C., Roth, A., et al.: The algorithmic foundations of differential privacy. Found. Trends Theor. Comput. Sci. **9**(3–4), 211–407 (2014)
10. Ghosh, A., Hong, J., Yin, D., Ramchandran, K.: Robust federated learning in a heterogeneous environment. arXiv preprint arXiv:1906.06629 (2019)

11. Muñoz-González, L., Co, K.T., Lupu, E.C.: Byzantine-robust federated machine learning through adaptive model averaging. arXiv preprint arXiv:1909.05125 (2019)
12. Donoho, D.L.: Compressed sensing. IEEE Trans. Inf. Theory **52**(4), 1289–1306 (2006)
13. Blumensath, T., Davies, M.E.: Iterative hard thresholding for compressed sensing. Appl. Comput. Harmon. Anal. **27**(3), 265–274 (2009)
14. Lyu, L.: DP-SIGNSGD: when efficiency meets privacy and robustness. In: ICASSP 2021-2021 IEEE International Conference on Acoustics, Speech and Signal Processing (ICASSP), pp. 3070–3074. IEEE (2021)
15. Balle, B., Wang, Y.-X.: Improving the gaussian mechanism for differential privacy: analytical calibration and optimal denoising. In: Proceedings of the 35th International Conference on Machine Learning, pp. 394–403. PMLR (2018)
16. Jacques, L., Laska, J.N., Boufounos, P.T., Baraniuk, R.G.: Robust 1-bit compressive sensing via binary stable embeddings of sparse vectors. IEEE Trans. Inf. Theory **59**(4), 2082–2102 (2013)
17. Lin, Y., Han, S., Mao, H., Wang, Y., Dally, W.J.: Deep gradient compression: reducing the communication bandwidth for distributed training, arXiv preprint arXiv:1712.01887 (2017)
18. Jin, R., Huang, Y., He, X., Dai, H., Wu, T.: Stochastic-sign SGD for federated learning with theoretical guarantees, arXiv preprint arXiv:2002.10940 (2020)
19. Wei, K., et al.: Federated learning with differential privacy: algorithms and performance analysis. IEEE Trans. Inf. Forensics Secur. **15**, 3454–3469 (2020)
20. Xu, X., Lyu, L.: Towards building a robust and fair federated learning system, arXiv e-prints, pp. arXiv-2011 (2020)
21. Stich, S.U., Cordonnier, J.-B., Jaggi, M.: Sparsified sgd with memory. In: Adv. Neural. Inf. Process. Syst. **31**, 4452–4463 (2018)

Author Index

Alageel, Almuthanna 290
Asano, Kyoichi 75
Aung, Yan Lin 319

Banse, Christian 360
Botacin, Marcus 339, 381

Chandramouli, Pranav 84
Chang, Sang-Yoon 84
Chen, Biwen 250
Chen, Jianzhang 194
Chen, Jiawei 464
Chen, Qian 464
Chen, Shijin 473
Chen, Yikai 411
Chen, Zhao 110
Cui, Jiangtao 422

Emura, Keita 75

Gao, Ying 20
Gatlin, Jacob 40
Graves, Lynne 40
Grégio, André 339, 381
Gu, Dawu 133
Guo, Shangwei 250

Jia, Dingding 110
Jiang, Yuting 92

Küchler, Alexander 360

Lai, Shangqi 269
Lang, Bo 411
Li, Bao 110
Li, Hanyu 20
Li, Hui 422
Li, Min 491
Li, Xiuxiu 162
Li, Yingying 153
Lin, Xiaodong 464
Liu, Joseph K. 269
Liu, Runhao 390
Lu, Xianhui 110
Lyu, Lijun 443

Ma, Xindi 422
Maffeis, Sergio 290
Malluhi, Qutaibah M. 3
McDonald, J. Todd 40
Mirzaei, Arash 229

Nepal, Surya 269

Ochoa, Martín 319

Peng, Yanguo 422

Raavi, Manohar 84

Sakzad, Amin 229
Shen, Yanjun 269
Shi, Gongyu 133
Steinfeld, Ron 229
Sun, Longlong 422
Sun, Shi-Feng 269

Takayasu, Atsushi 75
Tan, Xue 491
Tang, Bo 250
Tian, Haibo 194
Tu, Binbin 175
Tu, Yi 443

Wang, Baosheng 390
Wang, Geng 133
Wang, Kunpeng 162
Wang, Qichun 153
Wang, Shaofeng 411
Wang, Yongge 3
Wang, Yuzhu 53
Wang, Zilong 464
Wei, Jianghong 92
Wuthier, Simeon 84

Xiang, Tao 250
Xiao, Dan 464

Xiao, Di 491
Xiao, Nan 411
Xu, Yongqing 214

Yampolskiy, Mark 40
Yang, Bo 473
Yang, Jiyun 250
Ye, Jianbin 390
Yu, Bin 269
Yu, Bo 390
Yu, Chen 175
Yu, Jiangshan 229
Yu, Shiwen 422
Yu, Wei 162
Yu, Yu 214
Yuan, Xingliang 269
Yung, Moti 40

Zhang, Fangguo 194
Zhang, Kaiyi 214
Zhang, Min 175
Zhang, Mingwu 53, 473
Zhang, Yingjie 443
Zhou, Jianying 319
Zhou, Xiaobo 84
Zhou, Yilin 464

Printed in the United States
by Baker & Taylor Publisher Services